年

〰〰

◎ this book is dedicated ◎

<u>*to those who stay still*</u>

"The man standing in his own kitchen-garden
with the fairyland opening at the gate, is the man with large ideas.
His mind creates distance; the motor-car stupidly destroys it."

"On Rudyard Kipling and Making the World Small"
G. K. Chesterton (*Heretics* 1905) ↑ & ↓

〰〰
月 月 月 月 月 月 月 月 月 月 月 月
〰〰

<u>*and the poetry in all*</u>

"The sense that everything is poetical is a thing solid
and absolute; it is not a mere matter of phraseology or persuasion.
It is not merely true, it is ascertainable. . . . I remember a long time ago
a sensible editor coming up to me with a book in his hand, called *Mr. Smith*
or *The Smith Family,* or some such thing. He said, "Well, you won't get any of
your damned mysticism out of this," or words to that effect. I am happy to say
that I undeceived him; but the victory was too obvious and easy. In most cases
the name is unpoetical, although the fact is poetical. In the case of Smith
the name is so poetical that it must be an arduous and heroic matter
for the man to live up to it. The name of Smith is the name
of one trade that even kings respected, it could claim
half the glory of that *arma virumque* which all
epics acclaimed. The spirit of the smithy
is so close to the spirit of song that
it has mixed in a million poems
and every blacksmith is a
harmonious black-
smith"

〰〰
日 日
〰〰

☆

子規
shiki
明治廿九
meiji yr.29

俳句の盛運を祝す
toasting the future of haiku
宝飾に俳句の神を祭らんか
hôshoku ni haiku no kami o matsuran ka

shall we not celebrate
the gods of haiku
on our hôrai

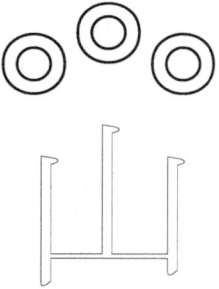

The *hôrai* is a *m*ountain of youth
(see chapter 8) set up for every New Year.
Shiki is known for promoting realism, but his haiku
show what he really sought: *enchantment*. If the ancient
Gods of Japan were associated with the mighty Mount Fuji,
the spirit of haiku is found within our hearts and all they encompass.
What expresses that more than this miniature of the magical mountain isle
Chinese now call Feng-lai! Hunters once feted the gods of the mountain where they
sought game. Shiki, with tuberculosis, could not climb the mountain, but he could bring it to him.

注　Poet, editor and essayist **Masaoka Shiki** (1867 - 1902) was the first to clearly use the term "haiku" for what had been called many things (*haikai, hokku*) and is, with Kyoshi (1874 - 1959), considered the co-parent of modern haiku. "Celebrate" in the original *ku* is joyous, as in English, but includes connotations of "pray to" and "make offerings to."
蛇足：「祭」は「山」を連想、「宝飾」（188頁を参照）に「蓬莱」あり。　Snake-legs = Meiji Era (1868-1912). M29 is 1896.

All translations, *unless otherwise indicated*, are from the original Japanese by the author.
本書中他者に翻訳クレジットを明記したもの
以外の英訳は、すべて筆者によるものですよ.

古句礼賛といふ
佳句駄句問わず
無責任きわまる
全く私的歳時記

の

新年部

四冊の内の二冊
健康と金しだい
次の二冊は後日

This is an old color painting of the mountain-island of Hôrai. I smoothed out the edges on the top and bottom and raised the contrast to improve the black and white. We see a crane of a thousand years and an odd-looking turtle of ten-thousand years with lucky brine dripping from what should be a mossy back kept clean to show the plates. Feet rather than flippers turn the sea turtle into a tortoise; then again, is it not *walking* upon the water? (Seriously, most lucky-brine-trail turtles painted are the type once found in ponds!) The model Hôrai found in homes for the New Year are hardly so fantastic. Most are humble representations as minimalistic as the featureless Japanese wooden doll. The trumpet shell (also *triton* or *conch*) in Japanese is a *horagai* or "tall-tale shell." Associated with mountain wizards, they could conjure things out of, or into, the air. Far from head-footed nautilae, these belly-footed shellfish no more belong on the surface of the sea than a tortoise.

The 5th Season

in praise of olde haiku
<u>a saijiki</u> *of delightful density*

// \\

volume
I

new year ku
< books 1 & 2 of 4 >

<u>selected, translated and essayed by</u>
robin d. gill

道可道
非常道

paraverse press

This is the 7th book published by paraverse press,
home of truly creative nonfiction, which is to say,
nonfiction that is neither journalism, nor history,
nor how-I-overcame-this-or-that. We are afraid
our books will not help you get rich, healthy
or up-to-date. Whatever their subject,
they offer one thing, always the same
yet different; and *that* is ideas,
*"food for thought,
all you can eat!"*

©
2007
paraverse press
all rights reserved

but, please quote freely, so long as you
cite this book and take care to check the *Errata*
at <u>http://www.paraverse.org</u>

We invite the Library of Congress to help us catalog for,
as you can see below, this book has many faces! Meanwhile
please enjoy our Publisher's Cataloging-in-Publication:

The Fifth Season
Poems for the Re-creation of the World,
or, the Japanese New Year, Books I & II of four
comprising Volume I of the delightfully dense and awfully
eccentric saijiki *In Praise of Olde Haiku* (I.P.O.O.H.) introduced,
selected, translated and essayed by robin d. gill.
**Includes the original of all Japanese poems,
a bibliography, poet and poem indexes.**

ISBN # 0-9742618-9-0 (pbk)
13-digit: 978-0-9742618-9-8

1. Haiku – Translations into English
2. English poetry – Translations from Japanese
3. Japan – Culture – Edo Era, Meiji (17-20c)
4. New Year's Celebration – Japan
5. Nonfiction – Literature – essay
6. *saijiki – shinnenbu*

I. Gill, Robin D. II. Series: IPOOH

1st edition, 2007, on the date of the Luni-solar New Year!
The reading copy may or may not be identical.
◎
Printed by Lightning Source
in the United States and United Kingdom;
distributed by Ingram, Baker & Taylor, etc.;
available from Amazon , B&N, etc..
◎
For more information, please visit our web site, www.paraverse.org.
If you have further questions, write us at <u>info@paraverse.org</u> or whatever e-mail
address is given at the site. *Forget snail-mail!* Your author-publisher *is* a snail.

Poetry *in the* Far East *and* Far West

> A Far Oriental *thinks* poetry, which may possibly account for the fact that in mind-pictures the relative importance of man and mountain stands reversed... Nor is it to woman that turn his thoughts [sic]. Mother Earth is fairer, in his eyes, than are any of his daughters. To her is given the heart that should be theirs.... With us, unfortunately, the love of Nature is apt to be considered a mental extravagance peculiar to poets.... For an ordinary mortal to feel a fondness for Mother Earth is a kind of folly, to be carefully concealed from his fellows.
>
> – Percival Lowell   THE SOUL OF THE FAR EAST (1888) [1]

Over a hundred years later, this gap – the Sinosphere, with its largely nature-oriented art, and the West with its idolization of muscular men and adoration of fleshy women (anorexia being the flip-side) – between civilizations has narrowed. The convergence has come from both sides. Much modern Far Eastern poetry resembles that of the West: personal complaint, boring to all but the poet and a few fellow sufferers. 19c and 20c North Americans created a rich literature of nature-essay, and haiku has made great inroads in some parts of Europe and the Americas. Yet, for all of that, the culture of the Occident is still fixated on the human. Notwithstanding the fine sensibilities of many Usanian poets, who tend to live in closer touch with raw nature than most of their more urban/e Japanese counterparts, haiku might as well be limerick for the *vast majority* of my compatriots, for, 5-7-5 format or not, nature is absent. And, reading Spanish-language haiku, one finds that even the literati tend to dwell on romantic phenomena such as the moon and ocean at the expense of the rest of the world. It is not that love between humans or longing for the eternal feminine (who, as Lafcadio Hearn noted, is absent in Japan) has *no* place in haiku. It is that it is not central to it, and deserves only a minor part in the larger play of the seasons, be they four, or five.

I hope the poetry found in this IPOOH *saijiki* (haiku almanac) will help elucidate the nature of that "fondness for mother earth" which surprised Lowell and hint at how we, too, may develop and express it in poetry; for, as we find and link ourselves to this greater reality, fresh air fills the mind, chasing out petty worries before they can grow into opera. Writing haiku is medicine for the soul. If you would live happy, *haiku*. If you would die happy, *haiku*. I dedicate this book to all who stay still, & to the memory of Richard Wright who wrote 4,000 haiku. His deathday is my birthday. - rdg

---

1) Lowell's Thesis やれやれ ! *The Soul of the East* contrasts a totally impersonal East with a totally personal West, carrying the thesis to the point of absurdity in the style later adopted (with proper qualification) by Barthes in *Empire of Signs*. Although Lowell's examples are selective and often misguided, it is pleasant to find a book boldly applying New England style metaphysics to Japan!

くる年のものしり皃や暦売　収月 万句合
kuru toshi no monoshirigao ya koyomiuri shûgetsu (early 18c)
(coming year's thing-knowing-face/s calendar-seller/s)

a know-it-all face
about the year to come
the calendar man

~~~~~~

Picture from *Edo Shôbai-zue*『江戸商売図絵』by Mitani Kazuma 三谷一馬,Chuokoron-sha 1995. Reproduced from a print by Nisei Utagawa Kunisada (1823-80)『童謡妙々車』安政二年　二世歌川国定画. Mitani (1912-), an artist and student of folk-history, who took painstaking care to preserve and bring out all relevant detail found in old prints of the vendors, performers and other street people of old Edo, explains further that *no one could just make and sell calendars*. In late-17c Edo, the government gave permission to 11 shops in Edo who would dispatch their salesmen, many of whom were elderly gentlemen, rather than movie-actor-like characters such as this salesman. Mitani thinks the 19c picture is a reproduction of a mid-18c picture because the calendars are wedged between split-bamboo. I would like a close-up with details on how it was done, but am thankful for this!

Table of Contents 目次

IPOOH series *preface* 11
Foreword for Volume I, *The Fifth Season*, The Place of the New Year 35

Book 1 (of 4)
年の内の佐保姫 *toshi-no-uchi-no-haru*	I	When Spring Jumps the Gun. 45
去年今年もよき空論 *kozo-kotoshi*	II	Last Year, too, Starts This Year. 59
十二支尽しと牛の涎 *jûni-shi*	III	Looking for the Animal of the Year. 77
初日出と寝正月 *hatsu-hinode*	IV	Witnessing the Sun, or, *Up and Adam!* 91
粗も新玉も魂の春 *aratama-no-haru*	V	The New Spring as a Gem or Soul. 115
元日の昔は今は昔 *ganjitsu*	VI	This Day Beyond Time, the Original. 131
御慶、年礼、年賀 *gyokei, nenrei, nenga*	VII	Greetings by Mouth and Mail. 153
蓬莱山と不老の心 *hôrai*	VIII	Mountain of Youth in the Parlor. 179
初霞の喩え学 *hatsu-gasumi*	IX	On Both Sides of the First Mist. 207
年玉の秀句主は子供 *toshi-dama*	X	Presents without Santa Claus. 219

Book 2 (of 4)
花の春 *hana-no-haru*	XI	Everyone's Birthday. 241
福寿草って微々たる花 *fukuju-sô*	XII	A Little Golden flower. 275
宝船に乗って初夢を *hatsu-yume*	XIII	First Dream Cargo Cult? 291
借着でも著衣始 *kiso-hajime*	XIV	First Dress-up. 319
初水にわが代者を *hatsu-mizu*	XV	Beauty/health from Young Water. 331
鏡餅が時間旅機 *kagami-mochi*	XVI	Rice Rock of Ages as the Sun and Moon. 351
餅花盛りは冬になるが *mochi-bana*	XVII	Artificial Sweet/sticky-rice Flowers. 367
油嘗める嫁さん *yome-ga-kimi*	XVIII	A Bride with Whiskers and a Tail. 377
若菜摘めば *wakana-tsumi*	XIX	Picking Young Green Things. 387
叩き、そして舌打ち鬼 *nana-kusa-tataki*	XX	Beating and Eating them. 417

出典、句引、句主引 <u>Bibliography</u> 445. *Index* of *Poets* 451 & *Poems* 456 & *People* 461 & *Oddities* 462

↓ <u>Tentative</u> themes for the second part (㊦)of the New Year Volume (**Book 3** and **Book 4**), to be completed *if/when* 1000 copies of the first (㊤) have sold, or the IPOOH project receives substantial support ($/¥).

Book 3 (of 4) 門松・年神・初烏鶏雀・初詣・年酒・万歳やら・若恵比寿・年+屠蘇酒・猿回し・書初め・初暦
1) *kadomatsu* (♂&♀ "gate-pine," my favorite NY theme), 2) *Toshi-gami* (the year as a god), 3) *hatsu-garasu, hatsu-tori* (first crow & first crowing) & *hatsu-suzume* (first sparrows) = ny sounds. 4) *hatsu-môde* (the new year shrine visit), 5) *manzai* (humor & trick-or-treat?), *shishimai* (lion dance) & *hatsu-shibai* (drama), 6) *waka-ebisu* (master prosperity, young as ever), 7) *toso+toshi-zake* (toasting our health & the new year's), 8) *saru-mawashi* (monkey visit), 9) *kaki-zome* (first writing/poetry), 10) *hatsu-goyomi* (new-calendar);

Book 4 注連飾り・宿の春・お雑煮・小松引=ネの日・小正月・歯固・藪入・幟・独楽、鞠・初あれこれ
11) *shimekazari* (hanging decoration, including fern), 12) *Yado-no haru* (spring on the road), 13) *ozôni* (new year stew) 14) *komatsu-biki* (pulling up small-pine) & *ne-no-hi* (root-day), 15) *ko-shôgatsu* (small/woman's new-year) `16) *ha-gatame* (tooth-hardening), 17) *yabu-iri* (servants' holiday), 18) *nobori* (kites in a new sky), 19) *koma, mari, haneko* (ny games: tops, balls, shuttle-cocks), 20) *hatsu arekore* (first this and that!)

(mostly the same in all volumes)

1
haiku in japanese & english

A Japanese haiku is a short – some say, one-breath[1] – poem touching upon seasonal phenomena, including things human. There is no end-rhyme *per se*, but there is *much more* internal rhyme than generally recognized, and good poems often have a snap to them, or failing that, a sound suitable to the subject. Most are 17 *syllabets* (my term for uniformly short syllables that can be written with a single letter of a phonetic syllabary). Japanese feel that *syllabets* clumped in fives and sevens sound poetic. While 5-7-5 is the most common pattern, it is found in less than half of the old *ku*.[2] Those that read better parsed 12-5, 7-5-5, 5-5-7, 5-12 etc. , taken together, comprise a majority. Haiku written with a brush, especially when the paper is square, are usually split into two or three lines, but most penned or printed in Japanese are single line; so it is common to find *dozens per page*. Aseasonal haiku exist, *but only as exceptions included with a body of properly seasoned work*.[3]

It is *wrong* to count syllables in English. Our first failure at numbers – when we tried to mimic our own Classic (romance language) poetry – should have taught us better centuries ago. English syllables are hopelessly irregular and, on average, half-again longer than the Japanese *syllabet*. If we would strive for some uniformity in *our* haiku, we must utilize something we have: *a good beat*. Japanese beat is so weak that some say the syllabets are always equally stressed and/or identical in length (both things patently absurd). Our *beat*, if we would only teach it (or, *them*), can even be recognized by children. I noticed, independently of Blyth – who discovered it long before me (unfortunately, after he had finished one of his two major haiku series) – that Japanese haiku, even when the syllabet count exceeds the ideal (in old haiku, 6 and 8-count clumps of syllabets are fairly common) – usually have 7-8 beats; and, so, I think, should *ours*.

1. **One-Breath Poem?** Flemish haiyû Geert writes: "I have a big mouth, so my haiku are rather short."(*Jokerman*). Seriously, a strong *caesura* may cause a pause which will necessitate a second breath for the unfit majority of us.
2. ***Ku* as in *Coo*.** Japanese use *ku* more than *haiku* when discussing individual *ku* or types of *ku*. It is short and avoids the need to call *hokku* or *haikai* by the modern term "haiku," though I may sometimes do that, too.
3. **Aseasonal Haiku** Returning to the semi-tropics=South Florida, land of my birth, I found the seasonal requirement difficult. It is not so much that there are less seasonal changes, but that even when they can be found they are often too unfamiliar to share with others in a form as brief as haiku, where many of the best *ku* exist in a symbiotic or parasitic relationship with other *ku* on the same theme. I find that including something about the time of *day* makes a poem *seem* more haiku, even if it wouldn't help placement in a haiku almanac. Without the connection to *some kind of* time, or *flow, outside of the writer*, haiku risks becoming narcissistic and if the *ku* in question treats a subject too obscure to evoke a response in the intended readership, it is best embedded in an essay (*haibun*).

2
what exactly is *olde* haiku?

Most of the haiku in IPOOH are not merely pre-modern, but wear the patina of centuries and may even reflect the lyrical and romantic traditions of ancient Japanese poetry though many are not of the elegant ilk (*shûku* or *kaku*) generally associated with "classic haiku" (*kotenteki-haiku*) in Japan, and some are downright vulgar. But, why the archaic, if not obsolete, *olde?* I use the old spelling not *despite* but *because* it is odd and reflects the unsettled nature of the transcription and content of the poetry. In respect to the *writing,* if you pretend you are doing acrostics and patiently compare the Romanization and the originals in this book, you may also get a feel for the variety of *transcription* even if you do not actually read Japanese. As Shakespeare spelled his own name in many ways, Japanese poets rarely wrote their own poems the same way twice and the editors of anthologies took more liberty yet, for the promiscuous mix of two syllabaries and synonymous Chinese characters offer Japanese far greater freedom than found in the English of any era (And were my damn Ms-Word not so limited, the variety would have been greater yet. I had to jettison many old characters). As for the oddity of the *content* – which I choose to affirm in the manner of G. K. Chesterton, when he wrote that *we enjoy expecting the unexpected* – it will become apparent as you read.

My use of the word "haiku" is a more serious matter. Some people reserve it for modern haiku and feel it wrong to apply it to poems written before the word came into common use (late-19c) and others insist it be limited to a certain style of haiku that I would call Bashônian (more in part 5, below). In *this* book, it refers to all poems that might, by the loosest of standards, be called haiku *today*, even if they might have been called *hokku, jiku,* or something else when they were written within the proto-haiku traditions of *renga* (linked-verse) or *haikai*.[1] Be that as it may, for the sake of economy = elegance, I seldom use the word. Instead, I follow the Japanese practice of referring to a poem already assumed to be a haiku as a *ku*.

My *Praise* includes a minority of *ku* which are not old, much less *olde.* Many are by Shiki, who, together with Kyoshi, is regarded as the father of modern haiku. Whatever Shiki may have argued about haiku, I feel his *work* makes him as much a fine tail on the old as head of the new. There is also a smattering of contemporary haiku, Japanese and, more rarely, English, by adults and children, who, to paraphrase an ancient claim made about a longer form of Japanese poetry with respect to people of different classes) are *equal in haiku,* when I judge they complement the older material. There are also a few themes developed primarily or entirely by modern haiku. I include some of these to put the olde haiku and their themes into broader perspective and because I will not let consistency deprive us of any particularly interesting material.

---

1. Haiku & Haikai & Hokku. In *Haiku World*, William J. Higginson boldly sorts out poems written in non-Japanese languages into *haiku, hokku* (for *renga*) and *senryû*. I do not try to sort out the first two, for my "olde haiku" include both, and because I find that many if not most of the poems in the anthologized *hokku* of the 15-16c *renga* tradition (such as found in the *Hokkuchô* of Sôgi *et al*) were not really *meant* for opening a sequence (*i.e.,* for *hokku*) as most Japanese now assume, but were as good stand-apart poems as anything called *haiku* today. Shiki was right to include them in his *Categorical*. I am also far less quick to call a *ku* a *senryû*, because *haikai* existed prior to *senryû* proper, when poets felt comfortable with *ku* that today would be tossed out as *senryû* (or *zappai*). What I call a *senryû,* then, is a *ku* that was published in a collection of *senryû*. So, what *is* senryû? We shall see.

3
why translation *needs* explanation

Haiku is minimal poetry. Most of the meaning must be found between the phrases, or *words* – with haiku generally one line when written in Japanese (if parsed, it is for calligraphic, individual presentation) we cannot read between *lines* – to comprehend them. The presumption, or rather prejudice, that haiku are supposed to be read *sunao ni*, i.e. without much thought, in a pure if not utterly naive frame of mind disregarding allusion, pun and circumstance, is common in Japanese haiku circles, yet one can find many books explaining almost all of the poems of Bashô and Buson, and some *ku* by other famous haiku poets, and these books are accepted by the same people whose common reaction to a question about the content of a haiku is "Just read the poem *sunao ni* (as it is)."

This apparent contradiction is understandable. On the one hand, there is much that most of us do not know, that we must be informed of in order to appreciate many of the best haiku. On the other hand, allowing explanation is thought to hurt the progress of a neophyte, for a good *ku* is supposed to contain all that is needed to appreciate it. Do we want people writing poems that must be explained by their authors for us to appreciate them? Unfortunately, the *no-explanations* school fails to distinguish between the boring explanations that deprive us of a chance to make up our minds, the bad explanations (sometimes embedded within the *ku*) used to prop up an otherwise failed poem, and those *necessary* to help readers lacking language skills or familiarity with the larger body of haiku and/or the subject matter (shared by the poet and his contemporaries who were fine without explanation), and those intended from the start to be read in conjunction with the *ku,* eg., with the dance of prose+*ku* called *haibun*.

With translation, especially of old *ku,* which even modern Japanese often cannot crack, explanation should be *the rule*, not the exception. It is needed, for the meaning of a haiku is often so obscure in translation that even a specialist must return to the Japanese (all too often not provided) to find it. In some cases, not a tenth of the information in the original reaches the non-Japanese reader. Yet, we find book after book of translations with spare notes, if any. Less than fluent author/translators and ignorance on the part of editors, publishers and readers with respect to the difficulty, if not impossibility of translation between exotic tongues may play a role in this, but I suspect the main culprits are 1) the unstated presumption that poems ought to float within a broad expanse of nothing, 2) a visual silence unsullied by notes (which are super- stitiously believed to scare off readers), and 3) a lack of awareness of the density (*i.e.*, multiple layers of meaning and multiple readings[1]) of olde *ku* – are they presumed to be simple because they are so short? With the publication of Makoto Ueda's *Bashô and His Interpreters* (1992), there is no longer any excuse for the latter.

---

1. *Finnegans Wake* **and Haiku** Joyce's punning – eg., "thuarpeatrick" (thou art peter / tu es petrus / thwart / peatricks / pea tricks / etc) – does, with the help of a handful of languages, what Japanese does with its ample native homophones (aided by Chinese characters) alone. The *thuarpeatrick* example comes from R. A. Wilson's discussion of Joyce's "context-dependent language" in *"The Illuminati Papers"* (And/Or Press Inc. 1980). The very title of Joyce's book, which, believe it or not, has been carried over to the Land of the Rising Pun, is a treat for the Jung at heart. Note: *such dense punning is far easier to digest in haiku-size tidbits.*

4
the *sea slug*, for example

Most haiku translation amounts to fraud. This is not so much because of the information lost in translation as because the readers are not told about it. I apologize to the translators of the *ku* I will use to prove my point because, other than the omission of notes, their only crime was to have caught my eye with their beautiful translation of a *ku* on the theme addressed by my first book in English, *Rise, Ye Sea Slugs!*

ukigoto o kurage ni kataru namako kana   by shôha (-1771)

Sad stories
whispered to the jellyfish
by the seaslug

Who could complain of Addiss and Yamamoto's translation (aside from center-formatting, I have not changed it), which, *taken by itself,* is excellent? The well-chosen sibilants create a slishy water-world and the length, about 8 beats, matches the original. But, there is so much *more* to the original than one might guess from the translation alone!

First, we need to be told what the "sea slug" *is*. All Japanese know the *namako* is a sea cucumber. In haiku, it is generally translated as a *sea slug* (to biologists and many others, a different creature) for the best of poetic reasons (brevity and metaphorical suitability). *Second,* we are unsure of "sad." The Japanese *"uki,"* suggests the suffering of an unsatisfied lover or personal suffering of the sort we might call "troubles" *and* is a homophone for *"floating,"* itself identified with our world of woe (or *maya*) in general and an unsettled or low-life in particular (The sphere of prostitutes and gamblers is called *"ukiyo,"* or "floating world."). *Third,* our "jellyfish" is not theirs, which, written with the Chinese characters 海=SEA+MOON=月, elicits the image of a sea cucumber on the seabed confiding in the "moon" floating above. *Fourth,* if the moon is not enough, the pronunciation of "jellyfish," *kurage,* also means "dark," a coincidence that the older tradition of *waka* developed into wonderful punning metaphor of melancholy. *Fifth,* the sea slug/cucumber, not the stories, is the subject in the original syntax. This matters because the creature was trope in the process of development. Some haiku and haibun made it out to be a wandering hermit, while others turned it into a lover. A *ku* by Shôha's friend Buson even described *a man* squirming with pent-up longing as a *namako*. *Sixth,* the *namako* was tied to melancholy as its mouth was lacerated by a goddess for remaining mum in the face of the request by the gods to speak up and pledge allegiance (as other animals did) according to the *Record of Ancient Matters*.

I will not give *my* reading of the poem here, but I think you can see that even a *ku* which seems childish may have much more to it, and can not be naively or naturally comprehended. Perhaps I should point out that the past is a foreign country wherever you live: many Japanese, too, need to be made aware, or more aware of this.

A HAIKU MENAGERIE: **Living Creatures in Poems and Prints** by Stephen Addiss with Fumiko and Akira Yamamoto (Weatherhill: 92/98). Despite the sin of omission, this square, coffee-table book is a gem. It has an excellent selection of poems and *paintings*, and provides something very rare: well-written short bios of the poets and artists.

5
the *bashôism* problem

There is a general consensus in and out of Japan on what a good haiku is and is not. True, there are "haiku" printed in the Occident few in Japan would recognize as such, but most of what is published by conscientious English language haiku journals and sites [1] would, I think, please Japanese haiku-lovers. As a corollary, the old Japanese haiku lucky enough to be reprinted (often time and time again) in Japan and the West, and those left to feed silverfish in old books are generally the same, too. This correspondence is natural, for most people who gather haiku in English are either not fluent enough readers of Japanese to seek out their own favorites, or gentle souls who follow the judgment of the authorities in Japan or their representatives in the West.

My idea of what is a good haiku, of what makes a *ku* worth reprinting is far from conventional. The haiku establishment in Japan, for all its nods toward new themes and acceptance of human emotion, generally favors something that has come to be called objective realism and tends to be associated with Shiki (-1902) and Kyoshi (-1959), though the idea was long the very heart of what I would call *Bashôism, i.e.*, the belief that the discipline Bashô brought to haiku is an unmitigated good [2] and the last word. *Theoretically*, I concur. Obstacles make poets jump higher, formal containment builds up creative pressure. There is no question that Bashô stimulated the poets of his day, beginning with his "disciples," to reach new levels of excellence. But that is only half the story. Carried to an extreme, rigor ends up stifling creativity when poets, vying to be the most sincere, call one another to task for petty reasons while humbly professing to be *more Bashô than thou*. Take this example from Issa's *Saigoku-kikô*:

初時雨風もぬれずに通りけり

first cold shower:
the wind, too, passes through
without getting wet

是を無理理屈ト云り。

This is what is called forced [impossible] logic [rationalization].

朝顔につるべとられてもらひ水

the morning glory
takes over the well-bucket
i borrow water

是等華を惜たるは珍重なれど、もらひ水といへるに、我と云持ものあり。もの念入過る也。又理屈に落。問云、何として理を逃ん。

This regret for a morning glory is overdone, and to speak of borrowing water [from another's well] is to bring in the personal baggage called the self (*ware to iu mochimono*). The poem is too precious (*neniri-sugiru*). And, it falls into [the trap/sin of] rationalization (*rikutsu ni ochi*). (西国紀行＝全集５).

The poems are by Chiyo (1701-75), the greatest female haiku poet (also, Chiyo-jo, Chiyo-ni). By using terms like "logic/rationalization" and "forced," Issa denigrates the cold-rain poem as shallow=Chinese, as opposed to genuine=Japanese. As a matter of fact, the first cold rain (IPOOH vol 5 = winter bk I) came at a dry time of year and Chiyo's only fault, if you choose to call it so, was to describe reality in a hyperbolic, *i.e.*, poetic manner. If such criticism raises my hackles, Issa's *poetically*-correct criticism of the morning-glory *ku* infuriates me.[3] It is all well and fine for Issa to laugh at the elegant haiku world's affection for an element he professed to hate and want nothing to do with, such as snow. Such an attitude (for which Issa is well-known) is recognizably part of his hayseed *persona*. But, there is nothing false or "precious" in Chiyo's feelings for the flowering plant. We *can* naturally fall for the colors of certain morning glories. I, a leaf-lover with no particular interest in flowers, can still recall the beautiful brown-purple flower of *a particular morning glory* I wanted to preserve – and, color aside, Chiyo may well have found the extent to which the plant took over the bucket in a single night remarkable enough to want to *share with someone else* – actually show it to them – before wresting away her bucket. *What is unnatural about that?*

Issa wrote this criticism at a time when he was remarkable unproductive. A spunky guy, he eventually got over his misguided purism and wrote some of the most emotive haiku ever written, as well as not a few very clever (and enjoyable) ones. Many haiku poets never manage to escape their training. True, their poems are seldom bad, but, unfortunately, they are equally seldom really interesting. Does this not hold as true for today as it was in Issa's time?

---

1. English Haiku I am not just trying to be nice. There may well be as many good haiku produced in the West as in Japan today. The sensitivity, creativity, and exuberance found in print and on the web is heart- warming (Susumu Takiguchi of the World Haiku Club describes and examples what makes it good far better than I can. See "In Praise of Non-Japanese Haiku). When it comes to children's haiku, however, the work I have seen on the Japanese side is, on the whole, better. Perhaps, our children need *more* discipline and Japanese adults, *less*.

2. Objective Realism? In his influential book *The Japanese Haiku*, Kenneth Yasuda wrote that a poet with a proper "haiku attitude" would not even be aware "of how beautiful the object is or of how he is affected by it." In the 1950's, when he was first published, strict Bashôism, the Zen teaching of unattached spontaneity, German romanticism of becoming a thing, itself, and the North American positivist fiction of absolute objectivity came together with a vengeance, making an insane idea like this seem like something not only possible but desirable (If objectivity is so damn important, why not just turn over haiku to the computer?). As a matter of fact, even in his later years, Bashô, himself, wrote subjective and emotionally expressive poems. Eg., respectively, *"As fall nears / our hearts draw close: / a small room"* (*aki chikaki kokoro no yoru ya yojôhan*); *"Plaintive / the lingering love-cry / of deer at night"* (*bii to naku shirigoe kanashi yoru no shika*). Rightly understood, Bashô's statement that "the quality of charm is not to speak of charm" (Yasuda trans) is less an injunction against directly stating feelings as it is a *common-sense of good style*, as applicable to Western prose as to Japanese poetry. As my mother puts it: Don't *say* something is interesting, *show* it. *My* rule is that subjectivity (explicitly stated emotions, ideas and taste) in haiku is fine, provided it interests readers who do not know the poet. *Do whatever you want so long as you do not bore us.* Note that since English cannot show emotional intensity by slight changes (one or two syllabet) in conjugations (*zo, yo*), or by articles (*ya, kana*), as Japanese can, live poems may require not only exclamation points, but the addition of emotionally charged words, especially interjections.

3. Morning Glory Nonsense. Kyoshi, perhaps unwittingly, repeated part of Issa's misguided criticism in a 1950's radio broadcast. As summarized by Donegan and Ishibashi in their lengthy treatment of the broadcast and its aftermath: *". . . he said that Chiyo-ni, in the morning-glory haiku, should have observed nature and not have personified it. He felt she was conceited, showing off her kindness and phony fûga, or elegance. It was ridiculous, he declared, to ask a neighbor for water just because she didn't want to break the flower's vine."* (CHIYO-NI, *Woman Haiku Master:* 1998) However, I also feel that defending Chiyo as *enlightened* or *acting from unselfish motives* (the usual explanation) is almost as wrong as Kyoshi's attack. The *ku* has long been popular with ordinary Japanese, who find it as perfectly understandable as I do, without resorting to religion (See more at book's end).

6
more *kinds* of haiku

I hold there are *many* kinds of good haiku. It is as wrong to confine one's appreciation to *shûku*, the subtle "excellent" or "superior *ku*," or the slightly less exceptional *kaku*, "good *ku*" usually anthologized by the Japanese, as it is to demand all haiku be Zen.

There are *ku* far from fine that merit appreciation for being particularly *warm*, *playful*, *metaphysical*, *impassioned*, *mysterious*, *bluesy*, *artless*, *mimetic*, *ethnological*, *observant*, etc. [1] A *ku* can be no more than a hint, an unfinished sketch the reader must finish, or as complete as an aphorism. They can be interesting in and of themselves or only *in retrospect*, purely for their historical significance. I will not substantiate these claims in the preface; you will find examples enough of these hitherto ignored types of haiku in this book and in all my books of and on haiku.

Please do not misunderstand me. I have no quarrel with superior *ku*. It is simply that they, alone, do not satisfy me. Do I lack the strict attention of the serious student of haiku? Or, am I a low-brow who seeks all sorts of poetry for the same reason I listen to blues, bluegrass, Cajun and country as well as Indian raga and classical music? The larger problem, however, is that I am not alone. *That* is why the best *ku* are not necessarily the best introduction to haiku. Some sensitive souls may benefit from encountering Bashô's *"On a mountain trail, something dear and delicate, a violet"* (*yamaji kite naniyara yukashi sumirekusa*) in primary school, but I fear more Japanese were *bored* if not immunized against haiku by that experience. Would it not be better to first introduce *ku* more interesting to children and adults unfamiliar with haiku?

But, content aside, there is one way all good haiku are alike: *Every word counts.* For translators, that is a problem, for the closest equivalent syntax and vocabulary may be no-counts in the target language. Because *my* intent is to depict *themes* as fully as possible, I confess to introducing more than a few *ku* of shallow content and wretched style. These are usually easy to translate, for I feel no compunction to do them justice. Unlike the elegant *shûku* that usually lose something in translation, these *gain!* Often they gain so much they may even seem better *ku* than the good ones.[2] I feel so badly about failing to express in translation what makes the better *ku* better that I am tempted to translate bad ones poorly. I rarely do so. It might be fair to the poets, but not to the readers, for that gain helps offset the loss on the best *ku* and keep the average up.

---

1. Types of Haiku in Japanese Besides the *shûku*, or "superior-verse," and *kaku*, or "good-verse," making up the bulk of anthologies, there are a few recognized types of haiku with more explanatory names: *karumi-no-ku* (light-verse) is a term of approbation, for Bashô in his last days put in a good word for lightening up, *byôsha-teki* (pictorial) is good, especially when it describes *ku* by Buson, who was an artist, *kochô-teki-na* (hyperbolic~) and *jichô no ku* (self-scorn~) – more commonly called *issa-chô* (issa- style) – are neutral terms, while *richi-teki-na* (intellectual~), *gikô-teki-na* (technical/artificial~) and *shûkan-teki-na* (subjective ~) are critical – mudslinging Japanese-style – terms. But the emphasis on *shûku* to the exclusion of others has prevented the development of names for types of haiku I would see recognized. I am creating a vocabulary for this in Japanese: *onku* (warm-verse), *yûku* (playful-verse), *jôku* (emotive-verse), *tekku* (philosophical-verse), *guku* (foolish-verse: a word used by Sôgi (1420-1502), *myôku* (sublime-verse) *etc. Haiku-Taipu*, a selection of Shiki's *ku*, arranged by type is in progress.

2. Good & Bad Poetry. Robert Frost's observation that *"poetry is what is lost in translation"* can be qualified: *good* poetry is lost in translation. *Bad* poetry is a different matter altogether. Frost might respond: *"Bad poetry is not poetry."* Perhaps. But, *in translation, Robert, it can be.*

7
the idea of a *saijiki*

As Lafcadio Hearn (1850 - 1904) pointed out at length, English poems lack "a system of arrangement enabling the student to discover quickly all that has been written about a particular subject – such as roses, for example, or pine trees, or doves, or the beauties of the autumn season. There is nobody to tell you where to find such things . . ." (*On Poetry,* ed. by Tanabe, Ochiai, Nishizaki: The Hokuseidô Press 1934/8).

The arrangement of poems by seasons antedates haiku. It is found in some volumes of Japan's oldest anthology of poetry, *Manyôshû* (c760), though the seasons are more a backdrop for poems of congratulation, longing, bereavement, etc. than the subject. With *Kokinshû* (905), we get more nature but still, in Blyth's words, "the real subjects are not those of the insects, grasses and flowers, but the feelings of the poets." In *Shinko- kinshû* (1205), we finally find not only seasonal sections but poems that really are about nature. [1] *Renga* (linked- verse) poets in the 14c continued this trend and in the late-15c, we find guides suggesting natural subjects appropriate to each month. The *Hokkuchô* (発句帳) anthology of 8000+ *hokku* and *hiraku*[2] by Sôgi (1421-1502),[3] his teachers, students and their students, compiled retrospectively in the early-17c was completely seasonalized, as were most of the 16c and 17c *haikai* anthologies. Some 17c anthologies included lists of seasonal themes and some explanations as well as selections of *ku*, forming the prototypes for what we now call *saijiki*.[4]

A *saijiki* is sometimes called a "haiku almanac." They *are* almanacs because they cover seasonal phenomena from constellations to sea-slug-dragging (anti-mole charm), but are *not* almanacs in that most do not cover phenomena specific to that year. Perhaps, *saijiki* should be called perennial almanacs. Typically, a short definition and history of a seasonal theme is followed by a sampling of *ku*. My favorite *saijiki* is the five-volume *Haikai Saijiki* published by Kaizôsha (mine is pieced together from several printings spanning the first-half of the 20c). It has about 16,000 terms, gathered under a tenth that many general themes, entertaining natural history and a fine selection of 75,000 haiku. Kôdansha's 1675-page modern single-volume *Nihondaisaijiki*, the only large illustrated *saijiki* within my limited budget, has an index of almost 17,000 terms, many synonymous for only (!) 5,000 themes,[5] of which the editors have 500 marked as basic. I'd estimate it contains 30,000 or 40,000 haiku, 90% of which are modern.

The translated *ku* in Blyth's *Haiku* (Spring, Summer, Autumn & Winter vols.) provide a hint of the riches found in a *saijiki*, but Blyth, for better or worse, was too much the Zen aesthete to fully introduce *phenomena*, cultural or natural. A partial French translation of a Japanese *saijiki* (a review claims it does more justice to the *fauna* than the *flora*) has been published, but the only English *saijiki* translations so far are the unfinished "Japanese Haiku Topical Dictionary" at the U VA library's e.text site and a smaller selection of "The Five Hundred Essential Season Words" at a renku (linked verse) home site.[6] In so far that a *saijiki* is largely *a tool for the poet*, and, like any almanac, locally oriented, this is understandable. There are, however, innovative *saijiki* in English. *Haiku World – An International Poetry Almanac* (1996) by William J. Higginson and Gabi Greve's on-line World Kigo Database are my favorites. [7] Though not quite *saijiki*, David G. Lanoue's Haiku-guy website offers thousands of Issa's *ku* arranged by seasonal theme.

1. **Seasons in Old Poetry.** A more nuanced but all-too-short discussion can be found in chapter 2 of William J. Higginson's *The Haiku Seasons* (1996).

2. **Hokku, Hiraku and . . .** The *hiraku* 平句 is an ordinary "peon" *ku* in renga, i.e., not the lead-off, second *ku* or moon/flower *ku*. Collections were supposed to be all *hokku*, for they were synonymous with good *ku*. But, the fact is that many *ku* clearly not intended to be *hokku* were often included. The word I prefer for miscellaneous *ku* (what came to be *haiku* with Shiki) is not *hiraku* but the less prejudicial term *tada-ku* 只句 or "simply/just [a] *ku*." It was first used in the *Tsukuba Mondô* about 1370. At that time, a *hai-ku* meant a comical-*ku*, if anything.

3. **Sôgi and Haiku** While contemporary *saijiki* I have seen do not include *ku* by Sôgi, he wrote hundreds if not thousands that clearly qualify as haiku. I demonstrate this by including scores of them in an IPOOH spin-off, *Cherry Blossom Epiphany.* I became aware of Sôgi's import to haiku thanks to Shiki's huge categorical anthology, which includes hundreds if not thousands of his *ku*. (Shiki's 12-volume *Categorical* divides *ku* into more sub-themes than a *saijiki*, but includes no explanation.).

4. ***Saijiki*** **Development** Kebukisô (hair-blowing grass) in 1645 had lists of season-words and *ku* but not together. *Yamanoi* (mountain well) in 1647 achieved the mix of terms/definitions+examples found in modern *saijiki*. The seasonal scheme (*kiyose*) of these and other working books of *haikai* was referenced by the first major Japanese almanac, *Nihon Saijiki* (1688) and the natural and local history approach of this and other almanacs influenced *haikai* in turn. The first *Haikai-saijiki* (with 2,600+ season-words) was published by Bakin in 1803. Seikan 青藍 expanded it to 3,400 *kigo* added more description of natural items (Bakin's was more attentive to festivals) and republished it as *Shiorisô* (Bookmark-grass) in 1851.

5. **5000 Themes** The editor of a *saijiki* is free to include whatever seasonal theme he or she (or the contributing editors, for it is usually a collective task) wishes to have, *though it may not yet have a single poem*, or none considered good enough to print. The intention, I suppose, is to tempt poets to write haiku on that theme for the next edition. Thus, some of the 5000 themes in the Kodansha *saijiki* have not even one example *ku*.

6. **On-line Japanese Saijiki Translations.** The University of Virginia's Japanese text initiative "Haiku Dictionary" is a more-or-less full translation of a Japanese *saijiki* for beginners (*Nyûmon Saijiki*) published under the aegis of the largest Haiku Poets Association in Japan, the Haijin Kyôkai. The 500 season words are those selected by Yamamoto Kenkichi, my favorite haiku editor. Both projects are headed by W.J. Higginson, whose fine eye for biological and taxonomic detail are the perfect complement for Blyth (and equally irresponsible me?).

7. **Favorite International Saijiki** Higginson's book has "680 seasonal and nonseasonal topics," with examples from a score of languages. If world haiku exists, it is this book. Among other things, it taught me that East Europe was a haiku hothouse. ◎ Gabi Greve's warm and open World Kigo site not only provides the informal cultural context for Japanese seasonal topics but links to local *saijiki* for places as different as Alaska, Chesapeake Bay, Germany, India, Kenya and Romania, *and* provides in-depth information on Japanese religious ceremonies (being seasonal, important for haiku) found nowhere else. ◎ For a demonstration of what *the saijiki spirit* offers poetry (enlightenment?), browse Jane Reichhold's *A Dictionary of Haiku, Classified by Season Words with Traditional and Modern Methods*, kindly available on-line. It is far more beautiful than its title might suggest. (FBG!)

8

why IPOOH is *barely* a saijiki

Though divided into 5 parts – the standard 4 seasons and, following Japanese poetic tradition, the holiday season as well [1] – with 4 books per season (published two at a time at first, but later to be expanded for separate publication) – IPOOH is too limited to be called a proper *saijiki*, because only 200 themes (40 per season) would be insufficient to fully flesh-out the year even if they were chosen for their importance, which they are not. Some of my themes are minor items reflecting my eclectic *taste* more than anything else: there is no logical way to justify the inclusion of *princess-bride[mouse]* (New Year), *Tsukuba [pot-carrying] festival* – one for each man a woman slept with that year (Spring), *bamboo[dutch]-wives* (Summer), *clackers* [devices used to guard fields] (Fall), sea cucumbers (Winter), and so forth,[2] other than to say that *shôki* (early-phase) *haikai,* or proto-haiku itself was *partial to the strange.*

Yet, I will not expand the number of themes. There are already too many to develop sufficiently to give the reader who does not know Japanese the background to really get into the haiku. Had I not found early on that I could write *separate*, full-length books on interesting themes for others who share my desire for further exploration, I might have cut down the number of themes yet further to 5 or 10 per season and illustrated them with hundreds of *ku* each. Readers already familiar with my spin-offs, where each theme gets a large book with up to 3,000 haiku, know that, as odd as it may seem in this field of literature where *ku* are doled out as parsimoniously as are syllabets, there is something to be said for an exhaustive approach. One reviewer, editor of an online magazine of poetry, warned her readers that "If you read it (my 1,000 *ku* book, *Rise, Ye Sea Slugs!*), I can guarantee you will not be the same when you finish it." The author believes her, for *he* was not the same after he *wrote* it! Monomania, the intense pursuit of single things, whether it be a line of *experiments*, a poetic *theme* or a foreign *language*, brings unexpected benefit more sober (?), i.e., *general,* studies do not.

Moreover, I do two things unsuitable for a proper *saijiki* in this book. *First,* I do not follow the established order of the *saijiki* season's internal divisions: 1) a temporal sense of season 時候; 2) sky-oriented phenomena 天文; 3) earth-bound phenomena 地理; 4) everyday human-life (food, drink, clothing, work, etc.) 人事 or 生活; 5) religious and cultural events & observances 行事; 6) animals 動物; 7) plants 植物; 8) sundry 雑. And, *second,* the themes in the four books allotted to each season do not follow one another from one book to the next. Each book starts afresh, with a theme close to the season's start, rather than making a single calendrical sequence, where the end of Book II would take us half-way through the season, at which point Book III would begin. In other words, IPOOH gives four alternative takes on each of the five seasons. I have no quarrel with how a standard *saijiki* orders themes within each season and invite readers to learn more about it; and, I realize that, poetic or not, an "almanac" should not keep starting over and over. But, my *saijiki,* if it can be so called, is intended for *reading* rather than *reference*. For whatever reason, it reads better this way.

While I *do* mean to challenge the way *translated* haiku has been introduced, it is not my intention to criticize work done in English on *saijiki*. My only complaint would be an indirect one: it seems to me that more attention might be given to *the Journals of Henry Thoreau*, for unknown to him, he was slowly and surely groping toward an American (New England, anyway) *saijiki*. Had he only lived longer . . . *Mostly, I am grateful for everything that has been done.* Thanks to the hard work of others in and out of Japan to do up *saijiki* properly – i.e., to create working haiku almanacs in Japanese, English and other languages – I am free to be a rascal and improvise.

9

egalitarian vs. *representative* selection

This is not to say standard *saijiki* are perfect. They cannot be, for there are many inherent trade-offs. *Global* vs. *local* → Ideally, each town would have its own *saijiki*

1. Five Seasons. The NY season, born when New Year and Spring were divorced by the Westernization of the calendar – comprises *a fifth season* in haiku. My arrangement is modern in its five-part division, but old because New Year *ku* come *before* Spring, rather than tailing Winter (More in the introduction to this *IPOOH* Vol. 1, *The Fifth Season*).

2. Major & Minor Themes. Checking Kôdansha's *saijiki*, I see one of my minor themes among the top-500 (though no stretch of imagination would put it into the top-200). Can you guess which one it is? (A: The *sea slug!*). Anyone interested in the clearly minor Bamboo wife, may find 9 *ku* after the "Homes & Gardens" ch. in *Topsy-Turvy 1585*.

to reflect its unique culture and nature; but one *hates* to break off with greater poetic tradition. People down in Kyûshû (South Japan) do not want to lose Bashô, Buson and Issa, snow and all. *More background* vs. *more poems* → The best poems are not always the best to illustrate the theme and readers will differ in their desire for more natural history or more *ku*. *Old* vs. *new poems* → Good poetry is timeless and dead poets cannot push their work, so it behooves us to keep it alive, but if contemporary poets are not published their poems will be lost before they are found. *Major* vs. *minor themes* → This trade-off is the least recognized of all, but perhaps the most important, for it touches upon both the purpose and efficacy of haiku.

Before the mid-20c, *saijiki* usually gave *much* more space to major themes such as *plum* and *cherry blossoms*, the (fall) *moon*, *heat*, *cold*, and *snow* than to minor ones. That is to say, the number of haiku per theme was roughly representative of the number actually written. There was a 100 or 1000-fold difference in the number between the most and least popular ones. Today, the difference is but 10-fold, if that. Thematically speaking, the *saijiki* has grown increasingly egalitarian. Because of this, the great majority of good *ku* on these popular subjects – which I would guess include the majority of *all* good haiku! – no longer appear in even the largest *saijiki*.[1] Perhaps, editors wish to steer haiku away from hackneyed themes and encourage poets to take up more of nature. This, by itself, is a laudable aim; but I think it is mistaken, for working a well-developed theme is the hardest challenge a poet faces, and reading poems on a familiar theme is usually more satisfying than reading about something one may not have personally encountered. There is also a built-in contradiction in the modern attitude, for even as explanation is discouraged, the greater number of themes unfamiliar to most readers begs for more of it than ever!

I repeat myself, but let me explain why I champion *explanation* one last time. Haiku have been compared to snapshots, but words are *not* pictures. The image (if the *ku* is one which has an image, which is not always the case) is not really in the *ku*. Something in the words triggers the reader's mind to call up or create an image. One can see an unfamiliar landscape or plant in a photo for the first time with delight, but the same cannot be said about reading a *ku* about the same. Because I happened to walk by a galaxy of *kosumosu* (cosmos) every day on my way to work, I came to write dozens of *ku* about this flowery firmament on weed-thin stalks floating in the lingering heat of Fall. But, for all my delight in experiencing the lightness of being through these flowers – *Was this, I asked myself, the gravity of the moon?* – and my joy to be a pioneer of the Cosmos (or, so I thought: but the 1977 anthology of the largest haiku association in Japan included a phenomenal 80 Cosmos *ku* (See: 『季題別現代俳句選集』: 平成九)!), I soon learned my *ku* meant little or nothing to those unfamiliar with the plant. Unless I were to add pictures and explanations to my "snapshots," the cosmos could not be shared in any meaningful way. So, I did not stop writing haiku about plum (which some insist upon translating as "apricot" because they are) and cherry-blossoms, which *everyone*, in Japan, at least, had ample first-hand experience with.

The main body of IPOOH is modern in that it gives almost as much attention to minor themes as major ones. That is wrong for, as I have already lamented, it means that many good *ku* written on major themes must be left out. But I can make up the loss with single theme spin-off volumes, and treating unequal themes equally is less a problem in translation, for when almost *any* theme is equally foreign to most readers, the number of examples and amount of explanation required to familiarize them with minor or major themes is about the same.

Popular Themes. Older *saijiki* were content with page after page with hundreds of poems on single themes, but today things must be chopped smaller to the measure of modern man. Two or three dozen haiku is usually the limit. The exception is the occasional publication of the haiku by the members of Japan's largest association of haiku poets 季題別現代俳句選集(俳人協会編), which gives space for hundreds of *ku* by members on major themes, but it is a seasonally arranged anthology with no explanations rather than a *saijiki* proper.

10
novel thematic development

As the reader will come to understand while reading this book, it is not enough to know Japanese nature or even the culture. To really comprehend an olde haiku, one must know *other* olde haiku on the same subject, and in some cases, the sequence of poems within which it appeared,[1] and even the older *waka*, or other types of literature the poet was familiar with. Only rarely can *one* haiku be properly appreciated.[2]

So, how does one introduce many *ku* about a single seasonal theme? To my mind, this is *the* central problem for editors of haiku. With tiny themes, it may be possible to simply introduce all the decent *ku* on the subject in chronological order. But, with larger themes, it just does not work. It is hard to read more than a couple dozen such *ku*. Granted, we have positive reasons (avoiding hackneyed themes and encouraging novelty) for the reduced presence of major theme haiku in modern *saijiki*, but there is a negative reason, too. Blyth writes that

> in Shiki's monumental Complete Classified Collection of Haiku (『分類俳句全集』 – I call it Shiki's *Categorical*), there is such an excess of system that the poetry is swamped with it. For example, there are no less than fifty classes of fans alone." (Note to preface of *Haiku in Four Seasons: Spring*)

I disagree about the nature of the problem. The *Categorical* does not have an *excess* of system but one largely *useless* for subdividing its 120,000 haiku: the sub-themes are almost entirely *nominal*, which is to say, classed in accord with the presence or absence of a word, phrase or thing most of which might be called *phenomenological* (Is/isn't there a *human, tool, plant, animal* or some type of *weather*, etc. in the *ku*). In the case of a minor theme, such as *sea slugs* (63 *ku*), such divisions are irksome, for a single chronology would be far more useful than the 8 classes used. But, when facing *hundreds of pages* of cherry-blossom-viewing, the largely worthless categories infuriated me, not simply because they exist (they can simply be ignored), but because I feel that their existence prevented the invention of better alternatives.[3]

How, then, *should* sub-themes be arranged? I wish *I* knew. Each theme in this *saijiki* and my spin-offs is a fresh experiment. *Rise, Ye Sea Slugs!* (2003) suggested that metaphorical classes (*cold* sea slugs, *meek* sea slugs, *sleepy* sea slugs . . .) were ideal, but with *Fly-ku!* (2004), I ended up relying more on behavior-based classes (*swatting* flies, *missing* flies, *living with* flies, etc.), and my latest effort, *Cherry Blossom Epiphany*, uses both of these, as well as *chronological* classes (blossoms: from *first-bloom* to *full-bloom*, *fall* and blossom-viewing: from *wait* to *hunt* to *viewing* to *return*), phenomenological classes (*haze, rain, wind*), nominal classes (types of cherry trees: *dog-cherry, elephant-cherry, granny-cherry, late-cherry*), and conceptual classes (blossoms and *death*, *Buddhism*, *nationalism*). A useful yet universal scheme of classification for all haiku themes seems unlikely. I am afraid that even Leibniz might have thrown in the towel before the human experience of sea slugs *and* cherry blossoms (*In other words, different classes will need to be devised for different themes*).

The classes by which the *ku* are arranged within each of the 200 chapters = seasonal themes (*kigô*) in IPOOH proper are not so well developed as with the spin-offs. This is both because one must work intensively with huge numbers of *ku* to make out the classes, and because such categorizing is not as important for a short presentation. It does not take great organization to keep a theme on track for twenty or thirty pages and if it wanders, well, isn't that the nature of an essay? Be that as it may, I do not just toss all the *ku* on a given theme into a chapter. I make a preliminary effort to group them in classes that may or may not hold up to book-length expansion. Readers familiar with the most ambitious thematic presentation to date, Blyth's *Haiku* – which gives ten, twenty or thirty fine *ku* for some themes – will find IPOOH goes much further. I am far from content with the result, but confident that all the themes introduced are treated more thoroughly than they have been by anyone else to my knowledge, and hope that it suffices to allow both first-time readers of haiku and the haiku enthusiast to enjoy the *ku* far more than they could otherwise, though, perhaps, not quite as much as the people who composed them and their contemporaries did.

1. Sequences. Many olde *ku* appear first in a linked-verse (*renga*) sequence. Unfortunately, most I find, being in collections, are out of context and I can only cross my fingers and hope to catch some of the wit.

2. Single Haiku. Where I argue the impossibility of appreciating semiologically dense haiku by themselves, Lu Ji (261-303) makes a far broader complaint: there is something intrinsically unsatisfying about short poems. Poem #12, "A One-String Harp," as translated by Tony Barnstone and Chou Ping: *"When an author composes too short a poem, / it trails off with a lonely feeling / like looking down at solitude with no friends / or peering into the vast sky, disconnected. / One string on a harp is crisp and sweet / but sings without resonance and harmony."* (*The Art of Writing* Shambala: 1996) The rarity of haiku-length poems in the world supports him; but millions of people enjoy haiku in Japan and, increasingly, throughout the world. *Why?* Though these hyper-short poems first worked in the tightly networked world of linked-verse, they bloomed with the spread of *written* collections of 5-7-5 *ku* because, I think, once we know many poems of similar format and theme, individual ones come to be appreciated *in a manner similar to that of any collectable.* Of course, some *ku* can satisfy us *as is*. And, there is great pleasure in writing a good *ku*. This suggests that "short" is not always "too short." But, I will grant it is *possible* Lu Ji is correct, and haiku delight us only because we have other literature (in my case, non-fiction essays) and diverse media to enjoy.

3. Haiku Sub-themes. The editors of Shiki's *Categorized* haiku anthology (it was posthumously published) subconsciously knew the worthlessness of their sub-themes, for they are written so small that only the main theme (repeated in large type on each page) catches the eye! But, I am forever grateful so many *ku* were gathered and find some of the classes occasionally useful.

11
three types of *translation?*

1) A verbatim rendition [1] is provided in parenthesis directly under the romanization *(phonetic reading) of the original. It looks ridiculous because word-for-word translation between languages as discognate as English and Japanese is ridiculous. Post*positions rather than *pre*positions, *suf*fixes rather than *pre*fixes, articles that *follow* rather than *lead*, indirect verbal indications of attribution rather than quotation marks or obvious phrases, such as "he said," emphatic or emotive particles pegged on verbs where English requires the unvocalized exclamatory mark or whole words, usually connected with religion or excreta, lack of number and sex, grammatical devices with no English equivalent such as verb+*ni-keri* for finality or the *o*+noun/gerund expressing either respect or simply that something pertains to another, the so-called *kireji,* or cut-off word *kana* (or *ya*), that may mean almost anything or nothing (I write 'tis/!/? for it), countless homophonic puns: and, worst of all, *active verbs followed not by the object but by their subjects, which they also modify* (Many poems are *no more than modified nouns*!) [2] are rarely carried intact across the exotic divide. I use symbols: "=" for homophones, *e.g.,* "within = house" (both *uchi*); "/ " for multiple possibilities *e.g.,* mouse/mice or connotations, gem/ball/precious (all *tama*); and "[ ]" for additional information suggested but not specified by the original: *eg.* "[I] went," or, together with "+" to supply information verbal in the original but not translatable.

Because it looks like hell, I keep the font small and readers are warned to keep telling themselves that *English directly Japanesed would look equally odd*. But this weirdness, together with my explanation, shows the interested reader something other books of translated poetry generally do not: *what is going on,* and, at the same time, gives me more liberty to play with the sense-translation – the real translation – secure in knowing I am not misleading the reader, nor opening myself up to criticism by a specialist who might otherwise think my divergence from the original a mistranslation.

2) *My sense translation* [3] is, *as a rule* – which is to say, not always – *7-beat (2-3-2), and divided into 3 centered lines with no capitalization, sparse punctuation, and a smattering of rhyme. Perhaps half of the haiku are provided with a title.*

Taking up these elements one by one:

7-beat in English, as noted earlier, matches the length of the Japanese better than 17 syllables, while 6-beat and 8-beat sometimes do well enough.

Centering is a matter of aesthetics. Unlike English, where a single *horizontal* line has little or no thingness,[4] a single line haiku written *vertically* in Japanese, looks good. It forms an objéct, a work of art suitable for hanging. This enjoyable visual experience is what I would reproduce here, and thank goodness for computers which make it easy!

---

1. Verbatim Rendition. In Japanese, this is called *chikugoyaku*. I first called it "transliteration" but found it puzzled some readers. "Word-for-word translation" is more a description than a term. It bears a resemblance to *parsing* in so far as it is a strange-looking aid to understanding, but I would reserve that term for chopping up lines of poetry. *Gloss* was suggested, but many people do not know the word.
2. There are 4 ways to translate such a *ku*. 1) To switch the noun-subject from the tail to the head of the sentence, in which case, the entire sentence, or action, becomes the subject (*change in emphasis*). 2) Leave it in place at the end, which requires the verb become passive, and peg it and the rest of the words to the subject as a modifying phrase (*weakened style*). Or, 3), we can make the whole poem into a hyphenated chain of modifiers coming to a head in the subject (*syntax-wise correct, but ugly as sin*). Finally, there is 4) the creative alternative. The first two are common in translation. The third is never done. The last is best, but hard to pull off, for it requires both skill and good luck (the existence of the right *whatever* to find).
3. Sense Translation English lacks a clear vocabulary for translation. "Literal translation" is a good term for what Japanese call "direct-translation" (*chokuyaku*). But, its supposed antonyms, "figurative translation," or "loose translation," wrongly suggest that what is not literal is rather inexact and sloppy. This may hold *some* truth for translation between cognate tongues, but when exotic tongues are involved, the direct/literal is often, if not usually, misleading (See *ORIENTALISM & OCCIDENTALISM*). English needs a commonly accepted term for what Japanese call an *iyaku*, or "meaning-translation," signifying a translation that does not get hung up on reproducing words and/or syntax, but goes for the heart or spirit of the original. I debated between the obvious but long "meaningful translation" and the more confusing but short "sense-translation." The poet in me chose the latter.
4. Single-Line Haiku While haiku on small paintings are

often parsed into two, three or more lines, the *printed* Japanese haiku is almost without exception a single line, with no parsing whatsoever. The only successful example of a single-line *ku* I recall seeing in English was Ginzberg's mosquitoes blown over the swamp: the subjects' horizontal movement fit the form so well it saved it.

I usually avoid capitalization and punctuation for two reasons. First, they hurt the *visual* symmetry of my presentation. True, lack of punctuation will slow you down, as you wonder if a pause, exclamation or interrogative is called for. But, note, Japanese often chew a haiku, they read it over again before swallowing. There is no need to race. Granted, reading *aloud* is synonymous with poetry in the Occident at the dawn of the 21c. To gain a readership, even poems better to eye than ear must be sprayed from the mouth in public performance. (Should we all, then, become blind like Homer? I say *we are primates* and should not be ashamed to use our *eyes*.) [1] Second, grammatical signs kill the ambiguity preserved in the unpunctuated original. This ambiguity often helps a word or phrase *pivot,* which is to say mean one thing when read in conjunction with what comes *before* and something else when read with what *follows*.

Japanese haiku rhyme and alliterate more than most people (in Japan, or out) realize. Written in a single line, such rhyme that exists is hard to spot, but the sound sequences repeat far more than chance (more so in some poets than others). I rhyme less often than not, for traditional haiku is itself not consistent, and favor an AAB rhyme scheme, with imperfect vowel rhymes rather than full rhymes, as this is closest to Japanese internal rhyme and a good last line should be strong enough to trounce rhyme, but I am not adverse to an occasional ABA in the tradition of Brazilian haiku (or Kenneth Yasuda in English) or even an ABB. Strict avoidance of rhyme, noticeable in some modern schools of poetry, is unnatural. The point is not whether we rhyme or do not rhyme but whether the poem has the appropriate sound-sense. This varies according to its subject and mood.

Like Harold Stewart, who insists on couplets for the best of reasons (though I am not convinced), I add titles to supply information that squeezed into the poem would ruin it, or to bring out wit that might otherwise be lost. Yet, I must confess to playing with many of them in a totally frivolous manner – which the italics are supposed to convey – when my wit so wills.

3) *Many poems have extra translations.* Like supplementary titles, multiple readings are often the only way to re-create all the facets of a complex poem, when trying to squeeze too much information into a single translation would kill it, and not including that information – regretfully, standard practice with haiku translation – would constitute negligence with respect to the intent of the original. Since a reading that expresses part of a poem is not quite the same thing as the poem itself, I hesitate to call it *the* translation. Instead, I call one of a number of possible alternative and/or complementary readings, nonetheless beholden to the original, a *paraverse*. While writing *Rise, Ye Sea Slugs!* I discovered that by printing these paraverses in multiple column *clusters*, one can experience them as a single object, a *composite translation,* simultaneously faithful to the original and original, if not poetic, in its own right.

---

1. Visual Experience of Poetry Because of the beauty of their hand-writing and the large number of double readings dependent on visual discrimination, Japanese poetry is not so oppressively aural as ours. But, please do not think my appreciation for poems as visual objects extends to Occidental "pattern-poems," which I find akin to the childish titillation of topiary art. So saying, I admit my centered translation may seem the same to some.

So far, so good. But I must confess to questionable uses of *paraversing* at times.

Sometimes I feel I have failed to create what should be the definitive translation of a poem and *want to* leave matters hanging. Readers blessed with poetic grace, who spot weak paraverses (or single translations) are invited to suggest improvements to, or replacements for, these failures due to my imperfect understanding of the original, limited vocabulary and word-craft skills, and lack of time=money to redo my work until it works. The next edition can be partly yours.

I also take extraordinary poetic license, creating poems that not only bring out facets of the original but *add new angles*. When I do this, it is generally when I am on a roll and the fun I have is readily picked up by the attentive reader. In some cases, I use my pen name 敬愚= *keigu,* "respectful fool" or "respectfolly" (a pun on "respectful tool" = 敬具, a standard term for closing letters), and separate the poem from the multi-translation cluster, but usually I just leave it in. I confess but feel no need to apologize for this. Contemporary Japanese poets who have seen me do it to their poems in translation enjoy it very much, and I trust that the poets of olde would not have complained. So long as it is obvious and entertaining to others, why not play around? So saying, I will try not to overdo this in the IPOOH *saijiki*; it is more suited to the eccentric spin-offs.

DILEMMA FACED BY TRANSLATORS WHO WOULD PLEASE READERS

Months after William J. Higginson lauded *Rise, Ye Sea Slugs!* and my "raising the bar in terms of a translator's responsibility" in *Modern Haiku* (Winter-Spring 2004), he thoughtfully e-mailed to say that, on further thought, he did have reservations about *some* of my translations. First, he discovered a number of multiple translations questionable for the reasons given above. On that, I pleaded *guilty as charged.* In an ideal world, I would have delayed publication until I had all the translations just right, but poverty demanded I put the book to bed, *ready or not.* Second, he discovered a genuine dilemma, something no amount of leisure can solve. I tended to take excessive liberty with the syntax of the original. Sometimes, the word order *must* be turned around for reasons I have already given, but Higginson noted, again correctly, that I not infrequently did so *gratuitously* (i.e., in a situation where a passive verb was not my only alternative). As a conscientious translator, that bothered him. Here, however, I was not ready to plead guilty. Or rather, I *was* guilty, *but only for the best of reasons*. While this may seem a bit too much to slip into a foreword, I will try to explain why wrong may be right, for, even as this unsolvable problem troubles me, it delights me as *a new instance of relativity* I have never seen noted, much less addressed.

Rise, Ye Sea Slugs! is a one-theme book. I knew readers would quickly come to realize that each *ku* (and there are 900+) was bound to include a sea slug. The *ku* where I juggled the syntax were usually ones where the slug was last, of which there are many because *sea slug* in Japanese is 3 syllabets, ナマコ *na-ma-ko,* and Edo era poets were not shy about ending *ku* with the 2-syllabet *kana* ('tis/!/?), generally called a *kireji,* or break-making word, but so common it amounted to little more than a standardized filler (one reason it was to fall out of fashion). Together, they made 5 syllabets, so *Rise* had virtually *hundreds* of poems ending in ~ *namako kana.* Were the sea slug 4-syllabets in Japanese, instead, most of the poets would have added a 1-syllabet *kireji,* particle, postposition or emphatic (*ya, o, ni, wa, ga, yo, zo,* etc.), and placed it at the head of the *ku,* where I would have been perfectly happy to let it stay in translation. As it was, my choice was to substitute another element of the *ku* for the sea slug in the punch-line position or deprive my reader of the element of surprise. Since my first aim was to entertain, how could I *not* play fast and loose with the syntax?

But, Higginson fired back: *What about your responsibility to the poet?* He had a point. All I can say is this: *Sorry, poet! I choose to favor my readers and can only hope you understand.*

But, what if someone reprints one of your translations? This is trickier. If the text within which the *ku* appears is *not* purely sea slug, one would hope that the quoting writer, having read my word-for-word rendition, might switch the sea slug back to the last line. Unfortunately, such would be highly unlikely; people are not used to quoting with slight changes and I failed to clearly point out the problem and suggest the solution, as I should have. As, indeed, I am doing here.

That is to say, if you quote a poem I translate, you are free to rearrange it when the word-for-word suggests it is appropriate and the surprise will not be lost as a result.

Additionally, after reading hundreds of translated haiku paying close attention to the word order, I have come to the conclusion that keeping the first part first and last part last is not always best, *even for poems read alone*. Often, the most natural English translations demand the part of a sentence/poem that comes *before* and *after* a colon, dash or dots (I seldom use the latter two because they destroy the visual symmetry) reverse the order of the Japanese word or clause. I do not know *why* this is so. It just *is*. Changing the order of a flow of experience may be wrong, but sacrificing the quality of the translation *as poetry* to maintain that order is worse. Fortunately, the fact that language itself does not perfectly follow the sequence of real experience suggests we are all quite capable of reordering things ourselves.

12

easy romanization

Japanese has the same 5 vowel sounds as the Latin tongues. Learn to pronounce all the vowels in *Buenos Aires* and you have mastered 90% of Japanese pronunciation. When meeting a double consonant, pause for a second just before it, then pop out the consonant explosively. Now you have 95% down. When a "y" follows a consonant (eg Kyôto), keep it tight against that consonant. 97% (It is *not* "kiyoto"). Soften "f" halfway to "h" and "g" halfway to "n." When the "n" comes at the end of a word, close your lips and palatalize it for a while. If you have to, hold your nose to pronounce it. Pronounce the Japanese "r" halfway like an "l." 98%. Forget about the "o" *vs*. "ô" and "u" *vs*. "û." These differentiate double vowel sounds, which count as two syllabets, from short ones. Most of us can do no better with such long and short vowels than Japanese can do with "l" and "r." I include the marks for the convenience of people who read Japanese and, in some cases, need them to help identify the romanized word.

13
apologia

In respect to previous books, I have been warned by more than one person not to destroy my authority by indicating what I have failed to do or confessing all I am uncertain of. If it were only a matter of style, I would be the first to agree that qualifications are poison (*You may rest assured that the body of this book will not plod for lack of bold generalization*); but I *hate* pretentiousness, and that includes *passive pretension,* such as failing to admit doubt. In this book, as in all my books to date, I shall openly record my uncertainty so the reader will not make the mistake of trusting me where I do not trust myself. If that lessens my authority, fine. I have never claimed to be an authority. It is enough to know what I know and what I do not know. There will, however, be one change: my direct appeals for assistance with this or that unsolved puzzle shall, from this book on, be made in Japanese alone, for I can understand how such *asides to the knowing* might irritate the reader to whom they are *not* addressed. (しかも、日本語の読めない人に助けを求めても無理でしょう、ね！).

I question Japanese about *ku* in which I have little confidence – I even have a bulletin board just for that purpose – but have not yet succeeded in rounding up enough expert help to keep pace with my endless questioning. And, much help is needed, for even an expert may fail to agree on how to flesh-out the paltry bones of meaning in a given *ku*.[1] Second and third opinions are needed. My uncertainty is one reason I try to give the reader enough information about questionable *ku* to judge the strictness/looseness of any interpretation *for him or herself.* The other reason for so much information – particularly the ugly word-for-word rendition – is my unusual style of translation. Details will be provided below, but, here, let me just confess once and for all that it is more than likely that *in my zeal to discover the wit* (as a translator, my faith is that every poem, properly understood, is interesting) *in the original and recreate it or something equivalent in translation, I come up with many readings the poet never intended, deluding myself and misleading my readers.*[2] Of course, I could avoid this by playing safe,[3] but that would betray the playful spirit of the poets. If Blyth sometimes erred on the side of Zen, I would err on the side of wit. Hopefully, most of my inventions are apt enough to be called *ben trovado* – good as true – something the poet would have been happy to own up to as his or her own. And, finally, where my play goes beyond reasonable bounds – most commonly in translated haiku's least developed area, *titles* – I trust the patent absurdity of my invention absolves me of responsibility. Yes, I *will* fool around; but I will not fool *you.*

---

1. Expert Disagreement. See Makoto Ueda's *Bashô and His Interpreters: Selected Hokku with Commentary* (1991) for many fine examples of experts disagreeing about both the intent and worth of a poem.

2. Inventions. I am hardly the first to sin in this way. A *senryû* jokes about writers filling in Bashô's famous old pond *ku* with commentary that would have been new to the poet himself (*furu-ike e okina no shiranu chû o ire*).

3. Safe? *I joke.* As demonstrated in *Orientalism & Occidentalism: Is the Mistranslation of Culture Inevitable?* when exotic tongues are involved, accurate direct translation, *i.e.,* playing it safe, is literally impossible.

A New Year Sampling

人間も神の心よけさの春　治長 反故集
ningen mo kami no kokoro yo kesa no haru   jichô 1783
(people-too/even, god's/s' mind/heart/s [+emphatic] morning's spring=ny)

<blockquote>
people, too
are the mind of god
new year's day
</blockquote>

<blockquote>
new year dawns
even men now share
the mind of god
</blockquote>

<blockquote>
we have the heart
and mind of our gods
new year's day
</blockquote>

<blockquote>
yes, men, too
have divine hearts
on new year's
</blockquote>

Kami is untranslatable, for it has no specific number and its attributes are unlike those of our "God" or, for that matter, the G/gods of the Ancient West. Long articles (perhaps books!) have been written on the unsuitability of Occidental language for grasping Japanese concepts of deity. Some go so far as to claim that using Occidental vocabulary guarantees confusion and would have us adopt the Japanese term *kami* when writing in English to reduce the bias inherent to a language developed under monotheism. Here, I believe that *kami* evokes a state of being pure-of-heart, yet *also* conjures up vague images of the anthropomorphic gods at the creation. The original has no verb whatsoever and only implies a sort of identity or equivalence of human/s and god/s; but, would English scan without "are," "share" or "have?" And *kokoro*, the Japanese pronunciation of the Chinese character 心 that has long been the favorite of all characters (it wins popular character surveys every year) is almost as tricky. How we translators *hate* to choose between "mind" and "heart" when it means *both* and *this*:

<blockquote>
people sharing
the spirit of their gods:
it's new year's
</blockquote>

It also means *spirit* and, here, *that* seems more natural. The meaning of the *ku*, itself, will become apparent only in so far that we come to know the Japanese New Year.

喰ふて寝て起て見たれば初日哉　也有
kuute nete okitemitareba hatsuhi kana   yayû 1701-83
(eating sleeping waking looking/looked-if/when, first-day/sun=ny!/'tis)

<blockquote>
eating, sleeping
and waking up does it
new year's here
</blockquote>

<blockquote>
i ate, i slept
i woke and i beheld
the first day
</blockquote>

<blockquote>
i eat, i sleep
i wake and find it
the new year
</blockquote>

世の中は食ふてはこして花の春　重厚　句双紙 天明六年
yononaka wa kuute hakoshite hananoharu jûkô 1786 加藤郁乎＝俳林随筆
(world-among-as-for, eating, shit-doing/done, blossom/flowery-spring[new year's])

<table>
<tr><td>

life is *this:*
you eat, take a shit
and it's spring

</td><td>

what is life?
you eat, take a shit &
the flowers

</td></tr>
</table>

"Flower/y spring" means *the New Year*. "Flowery" is too literal in English, so I killed it for separate readings of "spring" and "flowers." The common Japanese connotations are *precious, beautiful, flourishing* and *festive*. More important, it is the standard adjective for the Spring-as-New-Year (as "Merry" goes with Christmas and "Happy" with New Year). However, it *also* implies flowers. If you would imagine them, take care not to place them in the fields, for the flower of the New Year is a *tree* flower, the *ume*, traditionally translated as "plum", but properly rendered "apricot" by the garden translator. Yâyu's *ku* may be a no-frill *haiku* just recording the fact that he has retired and as a wealthy man can leave all chores and ceremonial duties to others and enjoy a particularly simple (this, we will later see, is an ideal) New Year. Yet, it seems as *philosophical* in its materialism as the previous *ku* was in its spiritualism. Jûkô's opening more directly evokes the philosophy of the wild Zen abbot Ikkyû, which is barely visible in Yayû's *ku*. It is why I chose the proverbial "you" rather than the "I" used in two of the three readings of Yayû's *ku*. Some might censure thinking haiku like these, but the New Year is the natural season for reflection, is it not?

都哉蒔砂匂ふ花の春　心成　大三物
miyako kana makizuna niou hana no haru shinsei 1697
(capital/kyoto!/'tis!: scatter-sand smells/glows flower/y-spring)

the old capital
spring redolent with
scattered sand

I added the "old" because *miyako* means Kyôto, at that time the old capital, for Edo was the *de facto* seat of power and prosperity. White beach sand (or something like it) may have served instead of good-luck salt (tossed and/or clumped up by gates). It was scattered on the road before important processions and in front of many gates on festive occasions of which the New Year was the greatest. This was particularly the case in Kyôto, the Imperial seat at the time. Kyôto was far from the sea, but traditionally received tributes from the coast, including skewered sea cucumber and, perhaps, sand (砂も貢物の中かどうか専門家にお訊ねしたいところです). These ritual uses of salt and sand bespeak the ancient maritime roots of the Japanese.

<table>
<tr><td>

this is the capital
fresh sand illuminates
our new year

</td><td>

capital *indeed*
flowery spring's aglow
with new sand

</td></tr>
</table>

The "illuminates" and "aglow" reflect the problematic verb *niou*, which first means "smell/s," but in classical literature means to *glow* in a beautiful way! The italicized "this" and "indeed" capture what I take to be the significance of the *kana* at the end of the first 5-syllabets, which is not a mere "cutting-word," or a hyphen of sorts, as some might think of it, but clearly *emphatic*, or even exclamatory here. Drop lightly colored beach sand into a still dreary winter set, add an exclamation or think "ah!" as you read the first line of the first translation and you may grasp the mood of the original, which is impossible to convey in one translation without notes.

元日や大樹のもとの人ごころ 白雄
ganjitsu ya taiju no moto no hitogokoro   shirao -1792
(original-day[new-years]:/! large-tree's base's people's/s'heart/s/mind/s)

it's new year's
we feel at rest below
a huge tree

the first day   it's day one
all our spirits under   our spirits ring
a mighty tree   the world tree

all men sit
at the foot of the world-tree:
it's day one

This *ku* provides ample example of why perfect translation between Japanese and English is, in a sense, impossible. **First**, note that the Japanese 元日 *ganjitsu.* 元= *gan* is the first character of "wellness" (元気) and means the original state of things; 日 = *jitsu* is day. Together, they signify "New Year's Day;" but Japanese boasts several *other* proper names or terms for that day, which in English has but one, or two, if you include the ellipsis used to save the beat for the first reading, above. We might also say that, in Japanese, there is, strictly speaking, no "*New* Year's *Day*," for "new" is applied to the *year* and/or *season* – *shinnen* (新年) is literally "new-year" and *shinshun* (新春) "new-spring" – but "new" is not found in any Japanese terms for that day, which seems more a day out of time than in it: You might think of the *traumzeit* (Why does German seem better than English here?), or *dream-time* of the Aborigine. **Second**, the *ya,* a "cutting-letter," which shares elements of a colon, exclamation point (i.e., *emphatic*) and declaration, demanded that "Day" be cut to fit in the "It's" before "New Year's." In respect to the second reading, the original does not say "the *first* day." Japanese has a different word for that, 初日, *shonichi* or *hatsuhi*. I used "*first*-day" because it suggests "*original*-day" – both serving for *that* day in Japanese – and, marked with "the," has a subtly emphatic nuance appropriate to convey the untranslatable *ya*. The reader might wish to add an exclamation. I do not usually do so when translating into a symmetrical format for reasons explained in the Preface. **Third**, *kokoro,* or "heart/mind/spirit/feelings," here, in combination with *hito* (human), pronounced *gokoro* is a word that requires dozens if not scores of translations. We will run into it hundreds of times in the course of this book. Here, I used the verb "feel" for the first reading, "spirit/s" for the second and third, and let "sitting at the foot of" *imply* the whereabouts of the same in the last reading. **Fourth**, we must consider the identity of that tree. When tree and *moto,* meaning "base" or "origin" come together, Japanese tend to think of people of all classes sitting under a cherry tree partying together, hence, the last reading where all men "sit." But "large/huge" *also* suggests the hoary/holy cypress found around most large shrines, which we are more likely to hug, hence, the "ring," a conceit common to trees in English, in the the third reading. I also wondered whether Shirao was thinking of the Chinese idea of a World Tree from which the sun rose and set, but googling the *ku,* discovered that an anthology written in Shirao's own hand prefaced the *ku* with four characters, 東都鶏旦 , meaning it was *New Year's Day, Year of the Cock, in the Eastern Capital,* i.e. Edo = Tokyo. The Cock was the Year Animal of the Shôgun who unified and brought peace to Japan and, by extension, his house, which continued to rule from the new capital (no longer Kyôto). This suggests the large tree alluded to the Shôgun, or his realm, as he was actually called "big-tree-shôgun," an expression deriving from China, where a certain behind-the-scenes general who was a heroic fighter in battle had the custom of letting others run about boasting of the exploits they did or did not do, while retiring to the shade of a large tree where he would sit and humbly listen while others talked. In other words, the *ku,* which may, **Fifth**, also evoke the proverb that one should "seek the shade of a big tree to gather" together (寄らば大樹の陰), is a celebration of the House of Tokugawa and the peaceful times. So explained, the poetry seems cheapened; but, on second thought, what is wrong with honest appreciation for rulers who deserve it?

天地のはしめもけさの霞哉　昌叱
ametsuchi no hajime mo kesa no kasumi kana   shôshitsu -1603
(heaven-earth's beginning too, this-morning[new year's] mist!/'tis)

in the beginning
of heaven and earth this
morning mist!

立帰る年も環や神代より　絢堂 元除春遊
tachikaeru toshi mo tamaki ya kamiyo yori   kendô 1799
(stand-return/bound/ing year-even ring/bracelet/necklace god-era-from)

from the *godera*　　　　　　　　　　　　the year, too, this:
the year's a ring: rising　　　　　　　　a circle unbroken from
only to return　　　　　　　　　　　　the age of the gods

富士ばかり残して見せる霞かな　文雞 元除春遊
fuji bakari nokoshite miseru kasumi kana   bunkei 1797
(fuji only leaving/left-shows mist[subject]!/?/'tis)

does it leave　　　　　　　　　　　　the spring mist
just fuji for our view?　　　　　　　　leaves for our eyes
the spring mist　　　　　　　　　　　mt. fuji alone

The relationship of the mist and Mount Fuji to the New Year will be explored later. Here, we'll look at the second *ku* in the cluster, which is representative of the semiological complexity of some old New Year's *ku*. *Tamaki* derives from *ta(te) =hand+maki=wrap* and refers to bracelets, arm-bands and other wrap-around adornment as well as *a gem in the shape of a large ring,* i.e. circle. The latter includes life-saver shaped large stone (jade) icons (?) standing for the yin-yang (rising and falling dragon), or endless force/s of creation, and is the main connotation intended. The compound verb *tachi-kaeru* evokes standard New Year's metaphor, *the re-bounding wave* (Japan has more rocky shores than sandy beaches). Literally, it means "stand/rise+return." We imagine a wave rising up as well as rebounding. The same "rise" is idiomatic for the arrival of something.

*it loops back
from dreamtime, our new
year is a ring!*

Forgive my adoption of Aborigine metaphor, with *dreamtime*. As a ring looks like a wave rising up and spilling over when seen directly from the side, *i.e.*, a cross-section of a tubeline. The author's respectfool alter, 敬愚 (*keigu*) is bolder yet:

*the new year
rears up: pipeline from
the godera*

*new year wave
we shoot the gem tube
to our origin*

Keigu has not heard of any ancient Japanese surfers but he has seen Hokusai's wave mighty wave with Fuji under its curl and knows one thing: once upon a time, the Japanese did string noodle-like gems on their *tamaki*. The "gem" in his "gem tube" is not entirely fictitious either. While *tamaki* is etymologically *ta-maki,* or "hand-wrap," as mentioned already, the *tama* part of the word cannot help but be noticed differently in a New Year's poem because *tama,* written 玉*,* means "gem," which used as a modifier means "beautiful" or "valuable," and is conventionally applied to the most "precious" gift we can receive, time to live, a New Year. Indeed, this *tama,* which, as a homophone, enjoys a punning relationship or identity with the soul (魂) – traditional trope strung up gem=souls to create what we might call "heartstrings" – is so closely bound to the New Year that it will get an entire chapter of this book. Since these strings of gems break, while the collective string of years does not, the words of a familiar song come to mind. *When the circle . . .*

~~~~~~

the も *of it*

I often come across haiku glosses which miss the poet's wittiest observation for lack of attention to the *mo,* or, "even." It marks *a riddle,* meaning that must be drawn from *without*, as it does not lie between the lines. Because *mo* also functions as an emphatic, even good Japanese readers often overlook it; but my experience with the poet I have read most closely, Issa, suggests *mo* usually alludes to *something* specific. In the case of the *ku* we have been discussing, the question is this: Why is the "year" given a *mo?* I do not have the answer. Is it because the year, as a unit of time which everyone knew flew "like an arrow" (linear time was not only a Judeo-Christian concept as often claimed), was expected to be straight? Or, is it because someone who comes back from a sentence of banishment for life (the most severe punishment in ancient times), called a *tachikaeri-mono,* had to wear a *tamaki* bracelet/necklace or something for life, and this is being facetiously equated with the circularity of the miraculously resurrected year? The stylist in me would have ended above, with *"When the circle . . . ,"* but my exacting side wants to know exactly what the poet and his best readers knew. It is why I sometimes write to myself, where I would prefer (and invite) expert *glosses.* (専門家諸君の、御＜欄外注＞を、求めております。絢堂の句の「も」の言わんとする所など、教えて下されば、感謝します！載せます。)

◎ ◎ ◎ ◎ ◎ ◎ ◎ ◎ ◎ ◎ ◎
Maybe New Year, Maybe Not.

I do not know when this young woman made what is apparently her very first waraji. It may not be for the New Year. But, for me, these simple straw sandals, tied on the feet, reify, which is to say, express in material form, the spirit of the Japanese New Year and what is most precious about Japanese culture.
◎ ◎ ◎ ◎ ◎ ◎ ◎ ◎ ◎ ◎ ◎

IPOOH
volume
I
foreword

The 5th Season

the place of the new year

歳時記を世に問ふ年の改る　稲畑汀子
saijiki o yo ni tou toshi no aratamaru inahata teiko
(haiku-almanac[obj] world-to/by question/challenge year's renew)

with the saijiki
questioning the world
the year is renewed

trans. W.J. Higginson
Haiku World (my centering)

During the Tokugawa (1603-1867) and Meiji (1868-1912) eras when most of the poems in this book were written, the New Year was celebrated in, or, more precisely *brought in* the Spring with second new moon after the Winter solstice.

When Japan adopted the Gregorian solar calendar, winter was split in two. This complicated things for haiku poets. Personal journals, faithfully reflecting day-to-day reality, had to add a "Winter after the New Year" or "Winter, second part" after the New Year, where Spring was supposed to be, or else leave a blank space between the winter and the New Year to return to and fill in after the holiday season ended. But the first of the five seasons, the one I call the "5th Season" *because we take the other four for granted*, still fell between Winter and Spring in the five-part calendrical scheme used by *saijiki* (haiku almanacs), so editors who dealt with extant *ku* could simply re-shuffle them, *i.e.,* take the post-New Year pre-Spring work and drop it into the correct season, *Winter*, as if nothing had happened.

Still, the editors were not home free. Since books are not circular or global – though it is easy to imagine an electronic essay or novel with no end that begins wherever we happen to start it – the New Year could not, practically speaking, rest *between* Winter and Spring unless the book started with Winter, an idea that does not appeal to Japanese. So, the New Year Season had to either *start* the *saijiki* or *end* it.[1] At the outset of the 20c, the New Year was generally placed at the head of the year=book, in memory of where it had been, and where, perhaps, the editors hoped it might eventually return once Japan made its way into the world and could dare to stop conforming with the West. But Japan lost the War and, being in no position to push its own calendrical agenda, pretty much gave up on the old New Year.[2] The New Year section moved to where it remains today, after Winter, bringing up the tail of the year it once headed. I think this may be one reason for so many 5-volume *saijiki* in the 20c. So long as each volume bears the *name* of the season rather than a number, they do not impose an order on the reader. But, today, most Japanese are perfectly content with the New Year's position at the end of a one-volume *saijiki;* and the only person I know who is infuriated by it is . . . *me.*

Since the New Year today is clearly in the winter, I grant that it makes sense to have it pegged on to that season. Moreover, I realize there is something to be said for relegating the part of the year that concerns largely human affairs to the back of the almanac. Nature's spring does, after all, antedate ours. One might argue that it is more progressive in an ecological sense to minimize humankind. Still, there is a counter-argument to be made – see what you think by the time you finish this book – and I would think that anyone familiar with the old Japanese New Year cannot help but feel a little sad about what came to pass to what the leading season, now forced to sit in the back of the *saijiki* and feel sorry for its turn of fortune. Or, at least *I do.*

---

1. New Year Placement Today Thanks to the computer, text can be endless and start wherever we choose to alight. The New Year may rest *between* Winter and Spring without being forced to choose between tailing the former or heading the latter. Then, again, it need not be between anything anymore.

---

the neglected new year season

何事もなくて春たつあした哉 士郎
nanigoto mo nakute haru tatsu ashita kana shirô -1813
(whatever things-not, spring stands=comes morning!/'tis)

without fanfare
the new year stands up
this morning

nothing at all
the new year comes
this morning

nothing to it
at dawn, here comes
the spring

In all 5-volume *saijiki* I have seen, the *New Year Volume*, despite the shortness of the period – primarily the first 3 days, but also the first week, or "within-the-pine" period, and, less intensely, the first 15 days (with the *Small*, or *Woman's New Year* on the 15th = *full-moon*), and, nominally, though overlapping Spring, the entire month – was as large, or almost as large as the other four. I point this out because such is not the case for old haiku *in translation*. Blyth, in his multi-volume *Haiku,* offers less than 20 pages to the New Year, while he gives well over 200 pages each to the other seasons. His beautiful paragraph-long introduction, opening with the exact words I should have used to begin this Foreword – *"The New Year is a season by itself"* – proves he knew what was what; but Blyth never comes out and tells us *why* he made the editorial decision to short-change the *season*. One can only guess. Is it because Blyth, Zen enthusiast, was not enamored with ritual? Or, is it because the New Year section (*shin-nenbu*) of the *saijiki* includes abundant cultural idiosyncrasies, many common to the Sinosphere but not the West that must be explained? If a touch of *Nature* makes all men kin, *Culture* divides us. (What, for example, is that "nothing" doing in the above *ku* by Shirô?) Yet, Blyth seemed to enjoy explaining things in his splendid books of Edo era *senryû*. Was he, perhaps, reluctant to sully the higher art of haiku with the same?

Despite the difficulty, the rewards gained by reading and translating New Year haiku may well be larger than that for the natural seasons. I did not *know* this until I got well into my translation of New Year poems. It surprised me, for, truth told, I am partial to nature writing, and was myself unfamiliar with most of the New Year themes when I began this book. I had no confidence I could make them interesting to *myself*, much less entertain readers; but I think I have succeeded. In order to do so, I had to devise new words and/or retain Japanese words. My methods owe more to *Clockwork Orange* than any haiku translations I know of, and for that reason, I cannot just show you an example. I can only bear witness to my experience. When I reread my translations of haiku on *Hôrai,* The Mountain of Youth, I become enchanted and, if I am not mistaken, the same will happen to you, after reading enough to transport yourself into the supernatural landscape of the 5th season, once the *first* for all humans.

The "spring" that "stands" – *meaning* the New Year that *comes* – in the above *ku*, does so upon *nothing,* for in Japanese (as in Russian, with its *nichyevo*), a common idiomatic meaning of *nothing* is that *everything is fine.* So, we have the poet surviving to gain another year, the New Year being the communal birthday, while simultaneously evoking the image, or rather lack of image, of a blank slate or a vacuum. This, starting from nothing, represents the natural fertility of the cosmos where life germinates from *within* (as opposed to the *created* one of the Jew, Christian or Muslim). *Nothing*, then, bears the New Year, which, in the form of Spring, "stands up" on its own and instantly becomes *something.* As *nothing*, the New Year is pure portent; as *something,* it is primal abundance; as both, it is the origin.

Think of the typical sequence in a sleight-of-hand performance. First, we have an object, say the Old Year and everything old, which is to say, *every thing.* Next, this is veiled, and lest we do not believe it is gone, we are shown there is nothing. Finally, we are pleasantly surprised to find something new, something bright and beautiful, with breasts or flowers or wings or long ears materialize before our eyes. The Japanese New Year is something like that. What we ultimately witness is magic that refreshes us and re-enchants the world in which we are both the magician and the audience.

Blyth and others who wrote on traditional haiku can be faulted for neglecting the New Year. Contemporary haiku almanacers serving the practical needs of the haiku-writing community cannot. Still, *The 5th Season* may offer ideas for how non-Japanese culture/s might better develop their own holiday season haiku. Note that in Europe, too, the holiday was originally not a *day* but a *season* of 12 days, and sometimes more.

the benefit of people-centered haiku

花の春人の世界となりにけり 義量 大三物
hana no haru hito no sekai to narinikeri   giryô 1697
(flower/y-spring man's world becomes[+finality])

    the new spring   posh new year
of the flowers so soon   on day seven, humans
     man's world   take it over

                  flower spring
              it really is the world
                  of humanity

Haiku has long been regarded as pure nature poetry and anything human relegated to *senryû*. Contrary to what is generally assumed, the main mark of *senryû* was not the human *per se*, but human *types*. Like most black humor, it played with categories rather than individuals, unless they were famous. Modern *senryû* in Japan or the West tends to record individuals rather than types and, to my mind, is far closer to haiku than traditional *senryû*. I hope this book will make it clear, once and for all, that haiku can bear far more human presence than people not familiar with olde *ku* might realize.

This is not to say that the human is overlooked in modern haiku. There are two major sections for human affairs in each season of the standard haiku almanacs today, *jinji/seikatsu* (what we eat, wear and do in daily life [1]) and *gyôji* (celebrations and observances, religious and personal, i.e., death-days [2]). Moreover, contemporary haiku has far more self than its spokespersons might admit. I do not mean this as criticism, for the haiku self is rarely self-absorbed in the manner of modern poetry. In haiku, even the personal helps us remember rather than forget the greater world. But, to the extent that the New Year loses ground, and it *is* losing ground in Japan, as its allotted space with respect to the other seasons shrinks with each new *saijiki*, the human element diminishes, for the New Year is the only season *primarily* about culture.

This makes the *historical* value of New Year's haiku greater than that of *ku* from the other four seasons. True, some of the plants and animals in old haiku are no longer with us; but, quantitatively speaking, the loss of wildlife is *nothing* compared to the loss of human culture over the last century. If Japan has kept much tradition alive, more yet has passed away, or is in danger of doing so today. Like Living Cultural Treasures, olde haiku help preserve these vanishing cultural memes. Compressed to 17 syllabets, most contemporary readers need help to unzip (computerese for decoding+ expanding) them, but the information is all there. A Japanese editor called my book with 1000 *ku* about sea cucumbers an *exhibit*, for it presents a variety of haiku and not only the *shûku*, or masterful *ku*, usually anthologized. This volume, if I may be so bold as to characterize my own work, might rather be called a *museum of haiku* dedicated to the conservation of the heart of traditional Japanese culture.

We might also ask what role New Year *ku* play within the greater haiku culture. First, there is the first this and that: the *first ku of the year*, the first water, first sex and first god-knows-what, . . . – anything is game. This sensitivity to annual firsts would seem to have primed the pump for other firsts, such as the first-butterfly of spring, first bonito of summer, first buckwheat of fall, and first snow of winter. Then, there was a tradition antedating the independent *ku*, of starting a chain of linked-verse with a New Year's *ku*. So the New Year *ku* set the mood for what followed. But, I am thinking of something else, something larger yet. New Year *ku* benefit the whole body of haiku in a fundamental if less obvious way. Though a poetry of *culture* may not inform us about the country or the wild, it does help us to concentrate on certain aspects of nature we might otherwise take for granted (such as the sunrise or certain herbs ritually eaten) and bond us, thus providing the connection needed to compose *con sentimento*. The poetry of culture also keeps that of nature from becoming monotonous. I wonder if the modern haiku world realizes how important this different note is to holding our interest as poets and our attention as readers. (I realize this is terribly abstract. See if it makes more sense after you read this book!).

The *ku* by Giryô leading off this section is tricky. The seventh day of the New Year is "people's day," *hito-no-hi* or *jinjitsu* 人日). I think the *ku* refers to this, but also mourns the passing of the "flower-spring," the enchanted period synonymous with the first week of the New Year, as it is humanized, which is to say, turned into the humdrum everyday world. The verb *nari,* or "become" suffixed with ~*nikeri* suggests something emphatically final, or done for good. My "so soon" is a substitute for "has become" that saves a syllable and restores the emotion in ~ *nikeri* not found in "has." My third reading is unlikely, but I cannot rule out the possibility that this is a philosophical *ku* recognizing the fact that the beautiful paradise of the beginning re-enacted every year is, in the final event, a human invention, our own re-creation.

1. Human Life. The Japanese have many words where English has but one "life." With haiku, it mostly means *seikatsu,* literally "bio+kine," or "life-activity"→ "a living" or "life-style." With a plethora of "life/lives" to choose from, there was no way to "just translate" *Life* for the title of the Japanese version of said magazine. So they adopted it and gained yet another near-synonym: *raifu!*

2. Deathday The word in Japanese is the name of the poet + one character meaning *the anniversary of a death.* Celebrated where we celebrate *birth*days, "deathdays" (cf OED) seems appropriate. The deathdays of famous *haijin* are kept by many who participate in haiku. The only problem is that the dates are not really the same with the new calendar. *Year of death* is, likewise, valued over birth.

philosophical and supernatural

立ちにけり世を思ふ故にけさの春　惟中
tachinikeri yo o omou yue ni kesa-no-haru   ichû   1638 -1711
(stands/begins[+fin./regret?] world-about think/care/love ergo this-morning's spring)

spring dawn

yes, it's here!
because i love this world
another year!

yes, it's here!
because of their concern
another year!

This *ku* includes a phrase (*yo o omou yue ni*) rare enough to point to *waka* #99 from the famous *Hundred Poet Collection,* in which the retired 13c Emperor Go-toba confesses *"How I love men / and how I hate them – / Silly isn't it // a man this worried from / worrying about the world!"* i.e., the wretched condition of the country, his reign. (ひともをしひともうらめしあぢけなく世を思ふゆゑに物思ふ身は　後鳥羽院).[1]↓

1. Go-toba-in's Waka. At first glance, the Emperor's *waka* only coughs up Buddhist catechism – all suffering comes from desire growing out of attachment to the world based on the mistaken assumption it is real – but, read slowly, we find a pinch of paradox in the melancholy *waka*. First, *mono omou* was standard trope for worrying about love or other personal problems, which were set against the larger world=society, while, here, concern for said world is what causes the *mono omou*. I am also touched by his mixed feelings about humans expressed so baldly. I, who once had so severe a case of *save-the-world-itis* that a family friend replied to my earnest appeal for help with this or that project as follows "The world will not save us, so why should we save *it!*" feel I understand Go-toba perfectly. Perhaps, I would be happier had I listened to that cynical advice, but it is hard to retire from caring.

Ichû's *ku* may joke about the smaller sphere of *his* worldy concerns in contrast to the larger ones of the Emperor. As he does not describe his feelings for the world in negative terms, Ichû may also be confessing his desire for a long life, something considered the mark of an unenlightened, if not small or even cowardly character. Finally, it is possible he feels thankful for the way the Descendents of the Gods – *i.e.* good Emperors such as Gotoba, who commissioned the third great anthology of classical Japanese poetry, the *Shin-kokinshû* – cared for the world they ruled over the ages, resulting in an unbroken chain of *Japanese* New Years to celebrate.

a naïve and almost surely mistaken reading of ichû's ku
coming from the author's love for certain solar rites
& kept because of the commentary that follows

because i love
the world, the sun rises
this spring dawn

here for good
because i love the world
new year dawns

because we
think about the world
another year

another year
has come because
we care

The New Year is a question. Who hasn't heard the story of the child, who, asked by a parent what he (or she) was doing, said "Drawing God." When the parent kindly points out that no one can tell what God looks like, the child pipes up, "Well, they *will* when I am done!" As with God, all of us are both parent and child to the Year.

With the annual restart occurring at what seems an arbitrary date – the metaphysically inclined cannot help but question the coming of the Year itself. If it must be in mid-winter, why not on the shortest day of the year, when the Sun=day turns the corner and starts gaining strength? Or, why not go back further to Fall, when the buds for the flowers of Spring start to form? The Celts did. Or, conversely, wait to celebrate a given flower's first-bloom in the Spring? But, as they say, *one flower, does not make the Spring*. Who says the cold-loving plum's (*ume*) blossom alone suffices? For confidence sake, why not hold off until Easter, when Spring is in full bloom in all but the far North? Then, every lily can trumpet the rebirth of time!

In Japan's case, with a millennium-old poetic tradition of playing off lunar and solar calendars (see ch.1), and the present day New Year being a recent import to boot, the degree and intensity of this awareness of the arbitrary nature of the date is far greater than in the Occident (At least, in the English-speaking world. The French and Rus-

-sians had some relatively recent calendrical adventures and *must* wonder sometimes.) For these reasons, even when no philosophy is explicit, there is always a high level of awareness informing New Year haiku, old or new. Japanese, or at least those with a poetic sensibility, did not and still do not take the calendar for granted.

But none of my explanation does justice to the *magnificence* of the Japanese New Year, a celebration combining the explosive energy of our New Year's Eve with the joy of Christmas, personal connectedness of birthdays, patriotic identification of the Fourth of July, sacred renewal of faith that is Easter and natural rebirth called Spring. The Japanese New Year is so overwhelming, so sublime, that comparison to the New Year of the West seems specious. Japanese are, on the whole, not religious in the Western sense of believing the tenets of an ancient faith and being absolutely certain about the existence of imaginary beings and places. Yet, I would guess that thanks to the traditional New Year, as many if not more Japanese have *experienced* something I would call "sacred" as have people in the more obviously religious United States.

I have emphasized the greater proportion of human and cultural elements in New Year haiku, but if I had to sum it all up in a word, I would call the 5th season *supernatural*.

---

world=saijiki=haiku

The *saijiki* is not only printed on paper but written large in the poet's heart. Considering how people of faith test the world, i.e., whatever happens, against their Books, I am tempted to capitalize *saijiki* despite the fact the Sinosphere does not have capital letters and there is no *bona fide* catholic *saijiki* (Then again, is there *any* book suited to all times and places? Only to people who close their eyes. *Haijin* (haiku-people) who follow the *Way of the Saijiki* are faithful to local truths as well as their book.). I love William J. Higginson's translation of Inahata Teiko's haiku (*with the saijiki / questioning the world / the year is renewed*), quoted at the head of this foreword, for making me imagine the poet, eyes peeled, ears pricked and nostrils flared (so to speak) *witnessing* the New Year. But, by accident or artifice (probably the former, for Higginson is not so wild – a positive word for *irresponsible* – as Yours Truly), his reading is almost certainly what I call a *paraverse*, a new poem reflecting or derived from the original, rather than a translation. The same could be said of *my* first try:

new year's

again we ask
the world about
our haiku

That is to say, each year, the world challenges our models of it, makes us rethink the basis for our art. (from *The Fifth Season*, first draft)

The verb (問ふ) *tou* can confuse those of us who are not native-speakers of Japanese. It means anything from *call out to, initiate a dialogue with,* i.e., *question,* to *predict* (e.g. fortune-telling), *investigate* (a crime), *suspect, accuse,* or *charge*. In the original, it is grammatically awkward to have the world questioned *with* the *saijiki,* except in the sense that the world is asked *about* it. My reading gets that right, but reverses the syntax and takes great liberty in replacing the "*saijiki*" with "haiku," "world renews" with a title, and adding "again." Perhaps I could have translated the *ku* more accurately, but all my attempts committed Wildes's only unpardonable sin, *they were boring*. Be that as it may, I felt both Higginson's and my readings failed to address a question implied by the original: Why mention the relationship of the world and the saijiki *this* year? A good traditional *ku* (*traditional* because the use of ふ rather than う after the verb's character is old-fashioned for a contemporary (her full name is given) poet) should incorporate circumstances that make the content *particularly* fitting, rather than merely express a generality, however poetic or true it might be. So, I questioned my friends-in-haiku as to whether the poet might not have just finished editing or publishing a *saijiki* and was concerned about how it might fare in the literary world.

> this the year
> the world will test
> our *saijiki*

The first reply came from *haiyû* ∀Q (in a (^∀^) mood), who thought my guess was probably correct. I googled Inahata Teiko and sure enough, she was not only a poet, but, among other things (grand-daughter of Kyoshi, president of the Japan Traditional Haiku Association and director of the Kyoshi Memorial Museum), the editor of a major *saijiki*. The *ku* in question was made on/for New Year's 1986 and concerned the long-awaited publication of the *Hototogisu New Saijiki* (『ホトトギス新歳時記』), the first major sequel to her grandfather Kyoshi's 1934 "Revised and Corrected New Saijiki" (『改訂新歳時記』), in May of that year. The plans for the *saijiki* were finalized to commemorate the 1,000[th] edition of the magazine *Hototogisu* in 1980. As such editing is a collective endeavor, I use "our" rather than "my" and, bearing in mind the fact that the readers of *Hototogisu* were fellow poets, can now add one last reading:

> with the fate of
> our *saijiki* in your hands
> the year renews

Likewise, for *The Fifth Season*. I am sure the coming New Year will not feel the same for me and, after reading this book, I hope you will recall it on your next New Year. The mixed luni-solar New Year of the Chinese, *who still celebrate it* (中華文明万歳！), for what Christians call 2007, is the *Year of the Boar* and falls on 18 February. The Japanese date [1] may be a day (sometimes, a month) off that of the Chinese, but we shall ignore it, for the Japanese now celebrate the New Year on 1 January, exclusively.

---

1. Additional Hard Facts: 1) According to 江戸博学芸課資料・図書係長(the head of the library at the Edo Studies and Art Archives?), 近松 鴻二 (Chikamatsu Isoji?), the earliest date for a Japanese traditional New Year was 21 January by the Gregorian calendar, the latest 22 February, or 52 days after the GC New Year, while the mean fell on 6 February, 37 days after. 2) A less important but more entertaining detail: According to Kai Michiko (『季語の底力』 = the latent power of seasonal words, 2003), when the Japanese government mandated the change to the Gregorian calendar, they gave less than a month's advance notice. On 11/9 of the Japanese calendar in Meiji 5 (1872), they announced that 12/3 would be January 1st Meiji 6 (1873) of the new calendar. Needless to say, so sudden a change was inconvenient. *Why so sudden?* Civil servants, traditionally paid an annuity, had recently switched to a monthly salary, and the government was in the red. Because the next year required an intercalary 13th month (the reason the calendars were less than a month apart was that the year was lagging, as luni-solar calendars are wont to do), it so happened that, not one, but *two* months' salary could be economized!

三句
about the moon

春もはや立ぞ一ヒ二フ三ケの月　一茶
haru mo haya tatsuzo hi fu mika no tsuki　　issa　1818
(spring-already stands/arrives one, two, three-day (crescent) moon)

spring is about
to gain its feet, *one, two,*
three-day-moon

I would guess the solar spring, or *risshun* (stand-spring) this year barely lagged the official coming of the New Year with the new moon. Issa plays with the idiom to give us the image of little Spring learning how to stand up. In five months, his daughter Sato will be born and the next year he will echo this with a *ku* (*hae warae*...) for her. As you will see later, she becomes *two* with the New Year. What is remarkable about Issa's "one, two, three" *ku* is the ease with which he skips over what might be called *the moon problem* – the lack of a lunar presence on New Year's – to connect it to the Spring, itself synonymous with that New Year, despite the slight chronological discrepancies we have already noted.

正月はみんなが足袋はく月夜哉　　道彦
shôgatsu wa minna ga tabi haku tsukiyo kana　michihiko -1819
(right-month[new year's day]-as-for, everyone tabi wears moon-night 'tis)

the new year　　　　　　　　　　the new year
is a fall full-moon　　　　　　the full-moon with *tabi*
with all in *tabi*　　　　　　　　on all of us

This *must* be metaphor. The new moon of the New Year is no more visible than a just fertilized human egg. White formal *tabi* (sock/slippers) would be worn by all proper moon-viewers, but only a minority went moon-viewing – it was especially favored by monks and poets – while all the world dressed up to celebrate the New Year, with many, if not most, up all night to view the rising sun. The solemn yet quietly joyful atmosphere is also similar, but the *tabi* would show the moonshine in the fall and lamp/torch/candle-light and the dawn's first light on New Year's, that is *Correct-Moon/th Day*.

一夜あけて月のはるたつ夕かな　宗祇
hitoyo akete tsuki no haru tatsu yûbe kana sôgi 1420-1502
(one night open/skipped moon's spring appears evening 'tis/!)

skipping a night　　　　　　　　a night later
this evening is spring　　　　luna gets her spring
for the moon!　　　　　　　　　　this evening

Sôgi, not Bashô, is the poet to whom I am most indebted for what *I* like in haiku (See *Cherry Blossom Epiphany,* which is full of his *ku*). Here, he has noted that the moon, theoretically lined up between the Hour, Day=Sun and Year at the First dawn, is not actually visible until the evening of the second night of the New Year. By emphasizing *that* evening with the *kana=!,* he seems, to me, to make a novel appeal for special attention to be granted to the same. Why only celebrate the first *sun*rise? Why not the first appearance of the moon? I am afraid his appeal did not work. The only seasonal "first-moon" (*hatsuzuki*) I can find in the *saijiki* refers to the early phase of the mid-fall moon, the favored one, called simply "[the] *moon,*" "*famous* moon," or "*bright* moon" in haiku.

年の内
toshi-no-uchi

1

WHEN SPRING JUMPS THE GUN

年の内に春たちける心を
toshinouchi ni haru tachikeru kokoro o
(year-within-in, spring comes [+emphatic] idea[+obj])
ふゆの春卵をのぞくひかりかな 成美
fuyunoharu tamago o nozoku hikari kana　　seibi - 1816
(year-within-spring-comes mind-re: winter's spring: egg-at/in peek light!/?/'tis)

conceptus

spring in winter
a ray of light strikes
a clutch of eggs

A literal translation of the seasonal theme *toshi-no-uchi* is "year's-inside," or "within the year." In olde haiku, it means *the arrival of Spring in the winter*. Strictly speaking, this occurs once every two or three years, when *solar* spring (midway between the winter solstice and spring equinox) falls ahead of *lunar* spring, *i.e.,* The New Year, which starts with the new moon and varies year to year. Since the speed of Nature's Pageant also varies, in a less predictable manner to be sure, we find *toshi-no-uchi* [1] occasionally used in a loose manner to refer to unseasonable warmth, or blossoms, or cats making love within the winter=old-year. If this is not confusing enough, modern *saijiki* sometimes include another *toshi-no-uchi* heading signifying *things that must be taken care of before New Year*, when one is not so pressed for time as at the very last part of the year (called *shiwasu,* another seasonal term), but still need to get a move on. *This* "year- within" has nothing to do with *ours,* and we will hear no more of it.

Despite the fact that almost all *saijiki* place *toshi-no-uchi* in the Winter alone, I put it at the head of this book because, by anticipating the New Year, the *ku* on that theme *seem to me* psychologically part of the New Year, and because doing so helps throw light upon the nature of this first/fifth Japanese Season. In classical poetry (*waka*) collections, the *toshi-no-uchi* (or *nennai risshun* 年内立春) was put at the head of the year, but it was placed in the Winter as early as the late-15c by *renga,* the linked-verse that bore the first poems we might now call "haiku." This scheme was then followed by Teitoku and other 16 and 17c *haikai* masters we credit with making wit and vernacular language a mark of short-form Japanese poetry. So I am *not* following convention here. Shiki's *Categorical*, compiled in the early 20c, but comprised entirely of olde *ku*, splits *toshi-no-uchi* (spring-in-winter) *ku* into two sections, putting 54 in the Winter (and they are not the contemporary usage as *things that must be done before New Year's*) and 22 in the New Year. This is rare. I first thought it reflected post-Westernization (i.e. Gregorian) calendar angst, but later learned that Shiki was very conscious of the intrinsically unsettled relationship of the New Year and Spring that, I believe, is reflected in many of the best haiku of the season.

spring in winter	the spring light	a ray of light
a light that spies	peeks into new year's	illuminates the egg
within an egg	quickening egg	spring in winter

I have not solved the lead *ku*. It could not be *purely* metaphor and still be haiku, so I understand why my Japanese friends favor the concrete egg/s struck by sunshine and are not interested in divining whether the egg *belongs* to Winter or *embodies* its house, or checking whether or not eggs were ever held up to the sunlight to see within, in which case, "peek" (*nozoku*) might actually mean "peek," rather than, or *as well as,* "strike." An older *ku, not* about premature Spring, but *the first sunrise* of the year hints at light passing through an egg: *"Egg Country – / shining through it, how pure / the first sun!"* (玉子の國すかすに清し日の始 幽山 江戸ベンケイ *tamago no kuni sukasu ni kiyoshi hi no hajime* - yûzan 1680). Here, egg may allude to the "origin-country" (though I prefer to imagine a chicken coop or collection of dolls made from eggs), a sort of national boast, but, regardless of the details, the metaphor of *egg-striking/spying light* is too salient to be ignored. Nor is it born *ex nihilo*. There is a Chinese saying that *Eggs stand up on the Solar Spring* (「立春の日には卵が立つ」). Whether they stand on end by themselves or with some human help it does not say, but we can easily imagine such a saying gave rise to many *ku*. One, bearing a similar prescript (*nennai-risshun no kokoro o*) specifying the subject is the Spring's premature arrival, pun-metaphors the "new-gem-year" as a freshly hatched egg before giving the clincher: It was "The Year of the Chicken" (あら玉にかへりて立や酉の年 慶友 *aratama ni kaerite tatsu ya torinotoshi* – keiyû 1651?). I will not translate that *ku* here, for the concepts of *the gem/ball* and *year-animal* (and how they dovetail with the primarily observation-based poetry) are subjects requiring chapters of their own.

今年とも去年とも見ゆる柳哉　蓼太
kotoshi to mo kozo to mo miyuru yanagi kana   ryôta 1707-87
(this year and last year, too, seen-can [be] willow/s 'tis/!/?)

premature spring

it can be seen	like a willow
as this year or that	in the wind, blowing from
a willow tree	year to year!

The usual way to translate a haiku like this one would be to stop with the first reading. But what does it *mean?* If we would *really understand* the original, it is necessary to *guess*. And guessing implies more than one possible answer. My second translation assumes a well-known *ku* about a willow that belongs to a different house/owner depending upon which way the wind blows, underlies Ryôta's metaphor. In Shiki's *Categorical,* this *ku* follows one by Shifû: *"Within the year / spring is set to go / look, buds!"* (年の内にそろりと春は木の芽哉 紙風 失出典、年付 *toshinouchi ni sorori to haru wa konome kana*). The question of whether the year's age should begin with conception (in the Fall), when the embryo becomes a fetus (in mid-Winter), quickens (late Winter), or birth (Spring) may be asked for all of nature and not just man. This makes me wonder if the correct reading for Ryôta's *ku* might not be –

spring signs

what counts:
the willow's new leaves
or its catkins?

Or, have the catkins caught the poet's eye? Probably not. My *haikai* instinct says he is joking about the character of the editor of an ancient anthology – the first poem of which wavered back and forth on this matter, calling him a willow. We will discuss that poem, a *waka*, in a moment, but first, it bears noting that the earliest *ku* definitely by the patron saint of haiku, Matsuo Bashô, addressed that very same calendrical anomaly:

春や来し年や行きけん小晦日　芭蕉
haru ya koshi toshi ya ikiken kotsugomori   bashô 1644-94
(spring!/?/&/: came year!/?/ went-not? penultimate day)

the warmth of splitting hairs

two days early!
has spring, then, come?
or the year gone?

before year's end

this undue warmth!
did spring just come in?
or did winter go?

The *structure* of nineteen year-old Bashô's haiku is requisitioned from the 69th story of the early-10c *Tales of Ise,* where a waking lover is unsure of whether something happened in a dream or reality. *"Did you come / or did I go?"* (*kimi ya koshi ware ya ikiken ~*) and, I believe, cleverly reverses *toshikoshi*, a term transliterating as *year-pass*, and meaning New Year's Eve. The *concept* behind Bashô's poem comes from the very first poem in the second major anthology of ancient Japanese poetry, the *Kokinshû,* or "old-recent-collection" (905). Here is what Shiki (poet, editor and critic considered the father (or, with Kyoshi, co-father) of modern haiku) had to say about the poem and the *Kokinshû* editor, Ki no Tsurayuki:

> Tsuruyuki is a bad poet, and the *Kokinshu* a worthless collection . . . . Take down the *Kokinshu* and open it to the first page. The first thing you will come across is this really disgustingly insipid poem:
>
> *Toshi no uchi ni / Haru wa kinikeri / Hitotose o / Kozo to ya iwamu / Kotoshi to ya iwamu*
>
> (Spring has come within the old year: shall we call the year "this year,"
> or shall we call it "last year"?)
>
> The poem is so silly that it fails to rise even to the level of vulgar wit, as if one were to say, "This child of mixed blood, born between a Japanese and a foreigner – are we to call it 'Japanese,' or should we call it a 'foreigner'?" . . . (from Brower transl., cited by McCullough and further abbreviated and unparsed by me.)

It is always refreshing to hear someone attack a man and a book revered for a thousand years, but Shiki is unfair. "Silly" or not, the poem, by Ariwara no Motokata, embodies one of the best aspects of the Japanese poetic tradition: it is a *meta-verse* reflecting upon a poetic convention. Tsurayuki chose and placed the poem where he did because it reminds us how arbitrary a calendar is.[1] This arbitrariness is not bad. The contradictions, or rather *play* between the lunar, solar and local (or climatic) years make us more aware, make life more interesting. If the natural calendar jumped the gun, not just the Spring, but the New Year itself was called into question. Motokata was playing with convention and the original poem has the snap one expects for an expression of wit. To be correctly felt – as opposed to merely rationalized, the translation *must* be equally witty:

calendar conundrum

spring is in the air today
so tell me if i may
call *this* year *last* year
before new year's day!

↑ **1. *The Calendar Question.*** If young Bashô followed Motokata, Motokata doubtless knew poem #4492 of the *Manyôshû* (8c), Japan's oldest collection of poetry. The *Manyôshû* poem, in a straightforward manner, simply points out the discrepancy between a moon-count by which it was still winter and some mist that indicated spring had arrived. I mention this (to me) boring poem only because critics who love the *Manyôshû* but come down hard on the first song of the *Kokinshû* (10c) never do. I might add that the third poem in the Kokinshû, by anonymous, proves Tsurayuki's fascination for seasonal contradictions: *"It came you say? / Where, then, is the spring haze / On Mt. Yoshino / Capital of flowers / Snow keeps falling"* (*harugasumi tateru ya izuko miyoshino no yoshino yama ni yuki wa furitsutsu* anon. 春霞たてるやいづこみよしののよしの山に雪はふりつつ よみひとしらず Note: I add more explanation to this *waka* than I do with most haiku.) The "it" (not in Japanese where the subject need not be specified) would be *the solar spring*. This *waka* is followed by others about spring coming in the snow.

~~~~~~

The original is no AABA verse; but I submit that my reading is, nonetheless, closer to the spirit of the original than the usual boring translation (I have seen several; none were interesting enough to add anything to the plain translation by Bower included in the above quote of Shiki's opinion). And one might argue that rhyme is just compensation for the boringly descriptive English terms "last year," "this year" and "New Year's Day," which lack the punch of their Japanese counterparts, specific words that have the ring of *proper names*.

> *Coming spring: a time when last year is chased away* – Shigeyori 1631
> 来る春は去年を追出し時分哉　重頼　えのこ *kuru haru wa kozo o oidashi jibun kana*

> *New Year's day: this is the start for real coming & going* – Ikkô 1759
> 花の春真の行来のはしめ哉　一耕 *hana no haru shin no yukiki no hajime kana*   (☆ch.note)

If Motokata and Tsurayuki drew our attention to *names*, *i.e.*, the nominal identification of time, young Bashô, by contrasting *verbs*, makes us think of the dynamics of temporal change such as those in the two *ku* given above in single-line translation. Do New Years *come* (like new growth overlaying old)? Or do the Old Years *go* (like peeling pages off a calendar)? Or does one come and one go? How does the New Year relate to the world? Is it a stage that one Year mounts while another leaves? Or, do they pass by like floats in a parade? Shoot by like arrows? Or, is there just one real year, *the* Year, which is handed-off from Season to Season like a baton? Or do they, rather, play tug-of-war with it? Worse yet, could the Years fight it out and kill or exile one another? Be that as it may, we can bet that the "enlightened" Bashô did not think much of his clever juvenilia. Still, I think it a good start. What better first poem than a question with a good pedigree that sets one to pondering? And, what is wrong with the occasional *ku* that takes us beyond objectivity to places only accessible by metaphor?

連歌師の去年とやいはん冬の春　許六
rengashi no kozo to ya iwan fuyu no haru kyoroku -1715
(link-verse-teacher's last year-as-for, say-not winter's spring)

> should i call you
> the renga master's *kozo*?
> spring in winter

Using "last year" rather than the Japanese *kozo* with its name-like quality (a near-homophone, *kozô*, means "boy" or young monk, but the quality mostly comes from its being a noun rather than a description), would ruin the *ku*. Once the renga masters, which is to say, the link-verse establishment, made the premature spring a winter phenomenon, it belonged to *that* year and could not possibly pertain to the next. The puzzle posed by the first song of the *Kokinshû* was moot. But this did not spoil all the fun. The meta-poetic logical tradition exemplified by Ariwara no Motokata's *waka* and Bashô's *ku* continued for hundreds of years, but no poem I know of succeeded in tying the premature Spring to real emotion, until this:

年の内に春は来にけりいらぬ世話 一茶 文化十三
toshinouchi ni haru wa kinikeri iranu sewa   issa 1764-1829
(year-inside=house, spring's done come: unneeded help)

thanks but no thanks

spring, go home!
old man winter doesn't
need your help

early spring

hold your horses!
the winter and i do not
need your help

there is a season

do-goody spring,
must you barge right into
winter's house!

Bolder than Bashô in his requisition, Issa took the first 13 syllabets[1] of his haiku *directly* from Motokata's in/famous *waka*.[2] His last 5, *iranu sewa,* a rude colloquialism for "unneeded help," brings to life the puns on the "inside" (*uchi*) of the year as "house" and the year (*toshi*) as an elder. Issa was not the first to develop the "house" pun. Here are a couple *ku* by Teimon (Teikoku school) poets in the *"year-within- stands-spring"* (年内立春) section of a playful old anthology, the *Konzanshû*:

年の内へふみこむ春の日脚哉 季吟 崑山集
toshinouchi e fumikomu haru no hiashi kana   kigin 1651
(year-within=house-into tramping-enter spring's sun-leg/feet=rays!/'tis)

forcing the new year

those rays of sun!
spring already has a foot
in winter's door

Rays of sun, like rain hanging from distant clouds, are called *ashi* (legs/feet) in Japanese. Cf.: an even older forced entry *ku*: "It forced its way / into the wintery year / a spring day [=the spring sun]" (年の内へをし入りしたる春日哉 利清 えのこ集 *toshinouchi e oshiiri shitaru harubi kana*   risei 1633).

立春の隣へ来るや門たがへ 宗房 崑山集
risshun no tonari e kuru ya kado tagae   sôbo 1651
(stands-spring's neighbor's-to comes: gate mistake)

How the Old Year got New Year's visitor

oops, wrong house!
spring knocks up the door
of his neighbor

---

1. Syllabet? In case you skipped the introduction, I repeat this once. Japanese syllables are written with single phonetic letters, called a "syllabary" by linguists. I coined *syllabet* because "syllable" misleads us. Most 17-*syllable*-long haiku in English are *much* longer than Japanese haiku. The Greek *mora* is similar enough to the Japanese syllabet, but the term is opaque (as are the Japanese terms sometimes introduced) to the English speaker, whereas mine transparently combines "syllable" and "alphabet." I hope it will catch on and encourage you to use it.

2. Borrowing. Playing with older poems was common in olde haiku. Shirô (-1813), a poet whose work Issa sometimes borrowed, or, rather, improved upon, also incorporated the identical first 13 syllabets from Motokata's *waka*, and ended "~ a fresh=green mat" (*ao-mushiro*), while yet another contemporary, Gako, wrote the same, ending with a more conventional *ame-no-oto,* or "the sound of rain." We will see both in a few pages.

The *Konzanshû* (1651) poets took the crude forced entry of the *Enokoshû* (1633) and turned it into a variety of metaphors. But so did others. From a 1645 collection:

来る春は年のうちへやとまりがけ 元弘 毛吹草
kuru haru wa toshi no uchi e ya tomarigake genkô 1645
(coming spring-as-for, [old]year-in=house-to: stay-over)

here to stay

spring visits
old man winter's house
and moves in

Tomarigake (stay over) is the perfect verb. Spring becomes a relative or maid who moves in to stay. Indeed, another *ku*, content-wise what later came to be called a *senryû*, published about this time takes advantage of "Spring" (*Oharu*: the "O" is honorific) being a common name for a maid-servant to joke that sure enough such a maid is "year-within," which is to say best enjoyed (by the male employer) while still young, or before she is replaced at the end of the year, as was standard in Japan, where servants generally had yearly contracts (下女の名かおはるは年の内のもの 保友 夢見草 *gejo no na ga oharu wa toshinouchi no mono* hoyû 1656).

ゑいやっと越えぬる年や二またげ 重方 毛吹草
eiya'tto koenuru toshi ya futamatage shigekata 1645
(eiya [exclamation] cross year:/! two-crotch=straddling)

precocious primavera

she lets slip	grunting aloud
an *eiya!* straddling	spring hangs a split
two years	o'er two years

I fear my "grunting" and "crotch strain" are uglier than the original verbal exclamation, *eiya to,* made by Japanese exerting themselves. English speakers may grunt or groan at such a time, but lack words to improve these guttural noises.[1] Shiki's *Categorical* places this poem in the New Year *nennai-risshun* (year-within-comes-spring) section, right after this *ku* from the same anthology: *"New Year past / Spring comes again / after a break* (年こえて又立つ春や中やすみ 望一 毛吹草*toshi koete mata tatsu haru ya nakayasumi* môichi 1645). This *ku*, including the same "crossing" (*koete*) and a homophone for "crotch" (*mata* = again/crotch), suggests the subject is the unmentioned Spring. When this Spring was not only personified but named, she was Sao-hime, Princess Sao, a goddess more Chinese than Japanese, today almost extinct (while the *femme fatál* Yuki-onna = Snow-woman is as popular as ever). I was tempted to give her a whole chapter, but decided to save her cameo appearance for Spring proper. Some more:

Beautiful Grunts Frois, in the 16c, noted that Europeans were silent when rowing or sculling whereas Japanese *always* vocalized (see TOPSY-TURVY 1585). English has chanties with "heave- ho" in the refrains, but these were sung in more limited circumstances, and generally by groups. Japanese even today, improve their grunts much as we unconsciously make our sneezes come out "achoo!" And, it is, likewise, an individual matter. In the 20c, "yosshokkoi!" was more common than "eiyatto." The sounds in question are clean and bely our word *grunt*.

佐保姫の荷は届たり年の内　乙由
saohime no ni wa todoitari toshinouchi　otsuyû -1739
(sao-princess's luggage=trousseau arrived etc. year-within=house)

ready to move in

princess sao's
trousseau arrives before
the new year

so the trousseau
of princess sao has made it
to the yearhouse

The *year-within=house* pun in the original does not translate. The first reading avoids the problem and the second creates a "year-house." This view of the irrepressible Princess rushing to move in her personal effects is much better than a slightly later claim she arrived early because she was quick to get hitched – literally, in a "man-hurry" (佐保姫の男いそぎや年の内　淡々 *saohime no otokoisogi ya toshinouchi* tantan - 1761) or witty haiku which put her in less reputable company: *"Princess Sao / opens a stall for spring / in the old year"* (佐保姫も春の出店や年の内　鐵冠 *saohime mo haru no demise ya toshinouchi* tekkan 1731). In this last, context says that *toshi-no-uchi* does not make the usual "house" pun but suggests a near homophone: *toshi-no-ichi*, or "year-end market," while the fact that "selling-spring" means *prostitution* in Japanese adds a risqué element to the poem. Poems about a natural phenomenon with a personal name tend to be outlandish. The more elegant poems about the premature spring do not mention Princess Sao by name.

早春　春もやゝ禮儀和らく女かな　春来 アルス
sôshun　haru mo yaya reigi yawaragu onna kana　shunrai 18c
(early spring // spring-even slightly etiquette softens woman!/'tis/?)

an early one

so spring, too
will bend her etiquette:
that's a woman!

softening rules
a wee bit: spring must
be a woman!

Different cultures in different times attribute the strict upholding of social mores to the natural characteristics of one or the other gender. In Japan, at this time, were men the moralists (which is to say, more likely to conflate etiquette and morals and therefore insist upon traditional behavior)?

白足袋を踏おろしけり冬の春　成美
shirotabi o fumioroshikeri fuyu no haru　seibi -1816
(white-tabi/s [+obj.?] tread-down[+emph/:] winter's spring)

snow-white

spring descends
into the world of winter
white *tabi*

This poem by Seibi, whose name, "becomes-beauty" reflects his aesthetic focus very well, does not actually mention a woman. The white bifurcated socks (that serve for slippers inside) called *tabi* are beautiful, but, I fear, easily soiled. Seibi captures the coincidence of premature spring of the solar calendar and snowfall. It is an elegant *ku*, but Issa's "unneeded help" poem trumps it, and, needless to say, the comical older poems, *because it has feeling*. One does not always want the winter to be quickly over with any more than one always wants to jump up out of bed. Hibernating can be good when you are deeply troubled, for spring thaws out things better left frozen.[1] As an old (1205) *waka* puts it *"When spring comes / my iced-up sleeves / melt down / and serve only / to lodge the moon."* (haru kureba sode no kôri mo tokenikeri morikuru tsuki no yadori bakari ni Shinkokinshû #1439). The wet sleeves typically come from crying for a lover one cannot meet. But, to return to my argument, Issa's "unneeded help" *ku* (pg.49) *should be* the best known of all *toshi-no-uchi* haiku and it is regrettable that is not written out in full even in the anthology of Issa's complete work (一茶全集１：信濃毎日新聞社). The editors err when they give only the last five syllabets (*iranu-sewa*: "unneeded help"), treating it as a mere *variant* of another of Issa's *toshi-no-uchi* poems written four years earlier, which, likewise, took its first 13 syllabets from Ariwara no Motokata, but ended with "~ the loves of cats" (~ *neko-no-koi*)![1]

perversity

spring arrives
in the winter of the year
cats in heat!

Thanks to the English colloquialism for cats in rut/oestrus, the translation, for once, beats the original. Still, this *ku* is a mere parody of the ancient *waka*, worth a chuckle, and certainly not as good as his complaint to the early spring. It is *wrong* to treat the one *ku* as a variant of the other, when, as shown earlier, there are many haiku (not only by Issa) that start the very same way.

千代の早春

After centuries where *toshi-no-uchi* was always placed in the Winter section of seasonal anthologies and *saijiki,* it came to lose the appeal it enjoyed as an anomaly. Perhaps, that is why Issa wrote only four *ku* on it. The poet who owns the subject belongs to the previous century: Chiyojo (-1775). She wrote *at least a dozen, most good;* and 5 of the 11 *ku* listed in the *nennai-risshun* heading of the Kaizôsha haiku almanac [2] on this theme are hers. We shall see most (seven) of her *ku* in the following pages.

1. Issa Brooding. The year Issa wrote "unneeded help," (*iranu sewa*), his wife Kiku lost a lot of money in a lottery, their first son was born and quickly died, Kiku's father was seriously burned, cucumber plants were stolen right from their yard when they were out moon-viewing, etc. A lot of bad karma was going around. So the idea that maybe Issa wanted more time to brood makes sense. But, he was a tough character and may have just noticed an old poet can get a lot of work done cooped up with nothing to do but poke his young wife. (He often recorded coitus 交合 in his journal). Or, to take an opposite tack, Issa may be making a dig at Kiku for warming up his – Old Man Winter's – house, making it hard to be melancholy as a poet ought to be (For the melancholy tradition, see the "*kankodori,* or nothing-doing bird" in IPOOH's summer vol. if/when it is published). &, do you know the country number by Kinky Friedman about how his woman ruined his career by making him too happy to write good weepers?

2. The Loves of Cats Issa has scores of *ku* about cats in heat. Why so many? Because it is noticed in both town and country and is easily haiku'ed, as it is a *bona-fide* Spring theme: *"It's New Year's! / From within the (moonless) dark / cats in heat*= 元日や闇（くら）いうちから猫の恋 *ganjitsu ya kurai uchi kara neko no koi* issa)!

3. Kaizôsha Saijiki. This *saijiki* is noteworthy for boldly giving many poems by a single poet when that poet clearly "owns" a theme. Most *saijiki* editors lack the guts to include more than 2 or 3 *ku* by a single poet for any theme. In the Kaizôsha *saijiki,* Buson gets plenty for "peony" and Issa for "dew," especially the "white dew" (white being a homophone for *not knowing*) about which he waxed metaphysical. Both Chiyo and Issa are horribly underrepresented in Shiki's *Categorical,* so this attentiveness to giving credit where it is due on the part of the editors doubly delights me. We need such editors today.

年のうちの春やしらずに行もあり　千代女
toshinouchi no haru ya shirazu ni yuku mo ari　chiyojo -1775
(year=aged-within's spring: not-knowing, [someone/thing] go/es, too, are)

unsung

spring in winter sometimes the year ends before i know it		an early spring or can it sometimes be that winter sneaks off?
	spring comes within the year: some quietly leave, too	
spring snuck in this winter: sometimes they sneak off too		there is spring in old age, though some never know her

The center reading, where I make explicit the "come" which the "go/leave" implies by contrast, is my favorite. But *who* or *what* leaves? ∀Q favors someone who dies, despite the fact the character for "departed," as in died, is usually written with the character 逝, not 行. Or could it be the Old Year in the winter of it/his life? *Some* Springs? Because the connotation of *toshi* includes "aged" as well as "year/s," the poem might also be read allegorically to mean the year is senile and doesn't even notice the visitor, or that some old men or women enjoy a spring of sorts, while others quietly fade away, i.e. die. Or could Chiyo mean she doesn't always notice the solar spring falling within the winter = last year until it is too late, for the year is over?

十のもの幾つぞ年の内　千代女
jūnomono ikutsu zo toshinouchi　chiyojo -1775
(ten-thing-how many?![+vernacular emphatic] year-within)

ten and how
many years this spring
in the winter

A hundred years earlier, Teitoku (-1653) allegorized a New Year's Day where the solar spring lagged: *"This year: / a child raised by winter / and spring"* ([年明けて立春の有ける元日] 冬と春の中にてそだつことし哉　長頭丸[*toshi akete risshun no arikeru ganjitsu*] *fuyu to haru no naka nite sodatsu kotoshi kana*). Chiyo's *ku* is barely better. It plays upon the comparison of the age of the *moon* to the age of a young woman in folk-song and implies that Spring, coming early is precocious. Yet, it helps set the mood for the next, a far better *ku* that Englishes worse because of the lack of a term for *dirtying something by wearing it*.

着よこしたなりに春とやとしの内　千代女
kiyogoshita nari ni haru to ya toshinouchi　chiyojo -1775
(wear-soiled becomes spring=swollen!/?/: year-within)

new clothing worn out before new year early spring	a spring like fine dress soiled by wear within the year

People wore new clothing, or newly washed and resewn clothing, for the New Year. One wouldn't want to wear it early and risk getting it soiled. "Worn out" is a bit too much, but good if "out" is read two ways. "Soiled" is good for being short, but has an undesireable connotation in English. The *ku* is a bit risqué because wearing clothing is traditional trope for sexual acquaintance: long-time partners were called "old clothes" and *cheating* (I prefer the country music term to the legalistic "adultery") was justified in the *Manyôshû* as "borrowing clothes." Spring who comes early is no virgin and possibly pregnant. A *ku* by a poet whose name transliterates as "heart-paper" actually uses the imperative Chiyo only suggested: *"Don't dirty it / on the rump of the old year! / the bloom of spring"* (よこすなよ師走の中の花の春　心祇 (古今？) 句鑑 (？) *yogosuna yo shiwasu no naka no hana no haru*　shingi 1777). Forgive my "rump!" No body parts are even hinted at in the original. The term for "year-end" (*shiwasu*) cannot be properly translated. It is a very busy time with everyone running around paying and collecting debts before the deadline. We do not imagine *rumps* so much as dust or mud, thrown up by millions of heels and, more important, a desperate mood and action completely at odds with that of the New Year which we will come to know soon.

春めかぬ言葉（詞）つかひや年の内　千代
haru meganu kotoba tsukai ya toshinouchi　chiyo -1775
(spring-like-not word-usage!/?/: year-within)

the language
fits not the spring
already here

The people running about furiously trying to get their year's business done so they can make a clean start have little time to be polite, much less exchange the formal and informal pleasantries associated with the arrival of the Spring-as-New-Year. The translation *works,* though background was needed.

見出さばや何かの春をとしの内　　千代女
midasabaya nani ka no haru o toshinouchi　　chiyojo -1775
(see-out[spy/find]-would: something-or-other of spring, year/age-within)

could i but find something of the spring within the year	could i but find something of spring in my winter

This seems both *more* modern for being less anthropomorphic, yet *less* modern for using a strongly emotional classic phrase of longing "~*baya.*" Chiyojo's *ku* fuses the phenomenological and astronomical springs. "Year" can also mean "years" and, hence, "old age." I imagine Chiyo wrote this when she considered herself over the hill. But note that she also wrote: *"Only the plum / is the real thing / spring in winter"* (梅ばかり誠の事やとしの内　千代 *ume bakari makoto no koto ya toshinouchi*).

年のうちの春やたしかに水の音　千代女
toshinouchi no haru ya tashika ni mizu no oto　chiyojo 1764
(year-within's s spring?/!/: certainly water's sound)

music to the ears

spring before new year: sure enough the sound of water	i hear water! so spring really *is* before the new year!

The sound of water made from melting snow heard trickling underfoot, is a classical sign of spring. Here is the *ku* by Gakô mentioned earlier in connection with Issa's complaint against early spring.

年の内に春は来にけり雨の音　雅郊 再現
toshinouchi ni haru wa kinikeri ame no oto　gakô 1777
(year-within, spring comes[+finality]: rain's sound)

hark!

spring has come
within the year: hear
the sound of rain!

Look and you shall see. Listen and you shall hear. Gakô's poem is good but lacks the subjective appeal of Chiyo's, with her *tashika ni*, an adverb evoking slight doubt, or puzzlement while ostensibly "sure."

梅ばかりまことのことや年の内　千代女 再現
ume bakari makoto no koto ya toshinouchi　chiyojo -1775
(plum [tree blossoms] only the real thing: year's within)

timely blossoms

only the plum
is the real thing: spring
before new year

Chiyojo implies that the solar spring by itself rings hollow. There is a slight possibilty of a B-side reading (an allusion to motherhood, perhaps, but I am not familiar enough with Chiyo to know). But even without it, Chiyo's *ku* is good for having an opinion rather than simply stating a fact, as does this earlier *ku*:

.年の内に春いち早し梅の花　宗因
toshinouchi ni haru ichi hayashi ume no hana sôin -1682
(year-within-in spring first /early/fast plum-blossom/s/tree)

the first to spring
within the old year:
plum blossoms!

Another pre-Chiyo early-spring plum poem:

年の内の春や夜市の鉢の梅　桃隣
toshinouchi no haru ya yoichi no hachi no ume tôrin -1719
(year-within's spring: night-market's potted plum/s[flowering apricots])

early bloom

potted plums
in the night-market: spring
before new year

Potted plums are kept in warm places to speed their blossoming for sale to people who take them home for the luni-solar New Year. Because some are already in bloom, they happen to be appropriate for the early solar spring. Objective, yet significant, Tôrin's *ku* is a classic fine poem, a *shûku*.

としの内に春は来にけり青筵 士郎
toshinouchi ni haru wa konikeri aomushiro shirô -1813
(year-within-to spring comes[+finality]: green/new mat)

in the winter
i have found my spring
this new mat

The scent of a new green rice-straw mat is more Spring than flowers. Is this is a *Thank you* poem for such? This older *ku*: *"It's New Year's! / First, something fresh / a crude mat"* (正月や先つ清きもの粗筵 朱廸=迪? じゃく 宇院の法師 *shôgatsu ya mazu kiyoki mono aramushiro* shuteki -1706) is not so clever, but gets to the core of the traditional New Year. The *kiyoki* translated as "fresh," also means *pure* and *clean*. Something I'll repeat: Japanese did not assign value only to precious metals and shiny finish as "we" did. They had a second, deeper appreciation for freshly formed, *obviously crude* creation.

としのうちに春をハルヲと抜参り 巴人 -1742
toshinouchi ni haru o haru o to nukemairi hajin 『巴人の全句を読む』
(year-within, "[because it's / give us] spring!" [x2] [so saying] escape-[shrine-]visit)

the natural excuse

so spring is here
before the year: we're off
to play the pilgrim!

sin permiso

spring! spring!
calling on the gods
before new year

pre-spring shrine visit

why wait
for the old year to die?
let's go!

off to the shrine!

give us spring!
they shout, flying out of
winter's house

nuke-mairi

give me spring!
spring! the old man
flees his home

time to play

the old year
says "no", but spring! oh, spring
calls us out!

The *nuke-mairi*, was a shrine visit generally made in the early spring, after the New Year, when a subordinate could take off on a pilgrimage to a major Shrine without obtaining his or her employer's or master's or parent's permission (*nuke* means "pull-out/escape") because proof-of-visit gave the returning pilgrim immunity from punishment. Here, the question is to whom the early solar spring gives an excuse to take off early. Maruyama *et al* ↓ believe it to be hot-headed young people. Maybe. I prefer to imagine an elderly person, a retiree living in the home he has already turned over to his son.

1. This ↑, the most dynamic, human-centered haiku on *Spring-within-the-year* I know, only found me because Hajin taught Buson, so a Buson study group under the guidance of Maruyama Kazuhiko anthologized and explained his poems, and a friend who knew I appreciated round-table style (many people giving their interpretation of the same poem) books happened to see it and send it to me. We must put more old haiku in-type or on-line. Hajin's *ku* is far better than many included in Shiki's *Categorical* such as, say, *"This Spring / has no days for play: / Within the Year"* (遊ふ日の分らぬ春や年の内　蜘柳 *asobu hi no wakaranu haru ya toshinouchi* chiryû? 1777). *I.e.*, Solar Spring or not, everyone is so busy pursuing year's end activities that they have no leisure.   There may be a "B" side reading: *"The Age Gap // Young Spring / has no chance to sport / in Winter's house!"*

A Final Peek

年の内に春を覗くや遠眼鏡　澗龍
toshinouchi ni haru o nozoku ya tômegane   kanryû 1761?
(year-within[=house]-in, spring spy on! long-glasses [telescope])

<table>
<tr><td>spying on spring
within winter's house!
my telescope</td><td>peeping at spring
from winter's house
my spy-glass</td></tr>
</table>

We began the chapter peering into the egg of winter. We end on a more outward-looking note, celebrating an object that came to be associated with the mist of spring. Needless to say, the telescope can, in fact, search out pockets of early green, and this habit of looking for first signs is one mark of the haiku mind and, for that matter, the mind of the man I most wish could have known haiku, Henry Thoreau. A *kibyôshi* cartoon book published in 1796 was to take the idea of spying to the limit by depicting telescopes capable of viewing within the human heart (人心鏡写絵 *hitogokoro kagami no utsushie* 山東京伝: I got this on the web, but see Adam Kern's work, if you are curious about this genre).   This reminds me that yet another reading of the above *ku* is possible, though not probable:

spying out spring
within the heart of winter
our telescopes

~~~~~~

☆ **Chapter note.**   Do you recall the name of the poet who wrote that that *Blossom-spring = the new year was the start of real going to and fro*, Ikkô? In Japanese, it is 一耕, literally, *One-tilling*. The name is not in my only book listing haiku poets (『俳句人名辞典』), but I did find 22 *other* poets out of about 1,350 listed had names beginning with "one" (一) and that turned out to be the most common first character used. It was followed by 18 starting with "white/blank" 白 (*haku*), 17 with "simple/element" 素 (*so*), 16 with "religion/founder[& after Sôgi's name]" 宗 (*sô*), 15 with "plum" 梅 (*bai*), "moon" 月 (*getsu*) and "spring" 春 (*shun*). *Why* do I note this? Because, there is much of the back-to-the-beginning, keep it elemental, celebrate the fresh, *i.e.*,   New Year's spirit in those *noma de plume!*

Making Early Spring Lyrical

I was delighted to finish up the chapter and leave a single blank page here for readers who tire of print or prefer buying books with plenty of *nothing* rather than *something,* for the waste is more luxurious. But, I was presented with Kato Ikuya's book 『市井風流』 (city well cool) after the second rewrite and, even though I read and marked it quickly, lost track of two *ku* I wanted to include in this book because of my having to move and only found it when searching for something else (a date, which, as it turned out, was never found) *after* I already paginated the book and did half the index. So, they must go here, or nowhere. In retrospect, these *ku* fill a gap between the merely nominal early spring *ku* of the Teimon (Teitoku) school and the emotional *ku* of Issa's that I praised because I *knew* it from the heart yet forgot not to chuckle. Here, we have a touch of the nominal and something we might call lyrical observation:

年の内に春来て漏るや雪の屋根　石牙
toshi no uchi ni haru kite moru ya yuki no yane sekiga -1797
(year's within spring comes/came/ing leaks!/?/: snowy roof/s)

    within the year   snowy roofs
spring comes and how it leaks   spring already leaking into
    the snowy roof   the old year

籠の内に春は来にけり鶯菜　勝安　境海草
kago no uchi ni haru wa kinikeri uguisu-na shôan 1660
(basket-within spring-as-for comes[+fin.+emph.] bushwarbler-greens/rape)

within my basket
spring has come for good
warbler greens!

Unless Sekiga, a physician and benevolent man, found joy in the music of drops leaking into pots of water, the first *ku* seems a subtle complaint of the type Issa made when he noted he was not happy with Spring's early arrival. The "within" does, of course, pun as "house," but the roof covers that well enough that the *ku* translates decently enough. The second *ku* does not mention the "year" at all, but the parallels imply it and the implication is confirmed by the name of the variety of early *na,* or "rape" (rapina, canolla, etc.), *uguisu,* the bird associated with the blossom of the New Year, the flowering apricot usually translated as "plum." The bird is usually translated as "nightingale" though sticklers prefer "Japanese bush warbler." Here, I dropped "rape" for "greens" because modern English has ruined the word and took the "warbler" to save a syllabet (and, *more important*, a beat). Now the greater part of the blank page has been lost, we might as well see two more from Katô's sampling of cool *ku:*

いかに寝てけふも春なりあすも春　丈石　　　　年の内に春はキリスト祭哉　月庵 1930
ika ni nete kyô mo haru nari asu mo haru jôseki -1779　　*toshinouchi ni haru wa kirisuto matsuri kana* gessan?
(how sleep today too spring becomes tomorrow too spring)　　(year-within-in/on spring-as-for christian festival/fest/carnival)

  how can i sleep   within the year
with today being spring &   spring is a veritable
  tomorrow, too   christian rite

The first is clear even without its prescript: *"Spring on New Year's Eve"* (大晦日立春). By now, we know Spring means its Coming. The second, modern *ku,* is probably a take on *Xmas falling before Year's End,* though we could think of Christ's birth and later rebirth from death as a double Spring.

去年今年
kozo-kotoshi

一 ── 2

LAST YEAR STARTS TODAY!

歳旦や年々けふの初むかし　了輔 霞袋
saitan ya toshidoshi kyo wa hatsumukashi   ryôho 1829
(new year's day! year-year today-as-for, first-olden[days]=last-year)

new year's day
year after year today
bears the past

year after year
today starts the past
it's new year's

Japanese has many terms for "old." The one translated as "the past" in this *ku, mukashi,* means what is long past, the olden days. "Once upon a time" is *mukashi* repeated twice, or *ima wa mukashi,* "Now [it's] the past." My "bears" and "starts" replaces *first,* as "first-olden times" (*hatsu-mukashi*) is awkward. Strictly speaking, "olden times" means the old year created by the new. It was also the name of a tea.

高砂や去年を捨つゝ初昔　鬼貫
takasago ya kozo o sutetsutsu hatsu mukashi onitsura -1738
(high-sand:/! last-year[obj] throw-away-as/while first-past)

happy dunes　　　　　dune village peace　　　　what dunes!
as we dump last year　we sweep out last year　last year leaves the pine
our first past　　　　renewing our past　　　　our new past

The poet may be on a dune watching the sun rise from the sea, or he may just be feeling good, for Takasago (high-sand) was shorthand for Takasago-no-miya, a place with felicitous associations famous from a Noh play where the protagonist meets a happy aged couple who suddenly appear to sweep below a pair of pines (not *twin* as in my dict.), likewise in perfect harmony. Here, I kept the phrase "first-past" in one reading. We shall run into scores of *ku* about *"first-"* (*hatsu*) *this* or *that,* yet none will sound as good in English as in the original. Ears are more conservative than eyes and seldom appreciate novelty. An "our" instead of the default *the* pegged onto "first" seems to help. Note that neither of the above *ku* contains the exact seasonal theme of the chapter, *kozo-kotoshi,* literally, "last-year-this-year." But the *idea* is the same. Indeed, Kodansha's large *saijiki* lists *kozo-kotoshi* and *hatsu-mukashi,* or "first-past," under the same large *kozo* (last-year) heading. Yamamoto Kenkichi explains that, until the mid-20c, *kozo-kotoshi* was pretty much a word restricted to haiku. Even the pedagogically inclined NHK, the public radio that has a larger share of ears in Japan than the BBC in England, always referred to *yuku toshi* (the leaving year) and *kuru toshi,* the coming year, when ringing out the old and ringing in the new with 108 tolls of the bell in its midnight broadcast, and avoided the expression, which was fast becoming obsolete, when, in 1950, the novelist Kawabata Yasunari (later to win a Nobel) found the following *ku* posted large at the Kamakura railroad station and wrote an essay bringing it national attention:

去年今年貫く棒の如きもの　虚子
kozokotoshi tsuranuku bô no gotoki mono　kyoshi 1874-1959
(last-year-this-year: piercing/running-through pole-like thing)

this-year-last
something like a pole
runs through

While "Spring within the Old Year" did not survive the Westernized calendar for obvious reasons, I doubt that *kozo-kotoshi* would have become obsolete even without this famous poem by Kyoshi. So long as we have *new* years, we must have *old*. Every year bears twins, and the expression is attractive. But, so saying, how does Kyoshi's *pole* (*bô*) relate to the years? Apparently, they are identical:

> Last year, which has just gone,
> And this year, which has just arrived;
> The two are but like
> A single, continuous wooden bar.　　　　trans. Susumu Takiguchi

Takiguchi's reading (from *Kyoshi: A Haiku Master*) resembles the information-adding translation style often used in Japan to translate Chinese poems or old Japanese into modern Japanese without resorting to notes. In the absence of an explanation of *kozo-kotoshi,* the additional "which~" clauses are necessary. The last line uses two adjectives (*single+continuous*) to remedy the want of a perfect English verb for *tsuranuku,* which means passing from one state into another *and* continuing as is. But, pass through *what?* This famous *ku* is hard to grasp; and, because of the opinion that *haiku* should be read straight (*sunao ni*), not many people *dare* to interpret. My favorite haiku editor, Yamamoto Kenkichi did:

> He (Kyoshi) expressed his equally deep emotion felt towards both the old year and the new one with the words "a thing like a piercing/threading pole/bar" (*tsuranuku bo no gotokimono*). This is the sentiment of an old man who doesn't feel any special joy in the coming of what is called the New Year. (鑑賞俳句歳時記・冬・新年: 1997)

Years do not so much *pass through* (the "piercing" denotation), as *thread,* or *hold together* what *was* to what *will* be. To Yamamoto, this is far from the youthful hope for the new, or the traditional concept of the New Year as a time for re-creation. Iida Ryûta 飯田龍太 finds something altogether different:

> It is somewhat like Kyoshi's Taishô 2 (1913) *ku* "Years in tow / like one of the giant ilk / off he goes" or, "Year on my back / walking off feeling / like Atlas" (年を以て巨人としたり歩み去る *toshi o motte kyojin to shitari ayumisaru*) but, intended for radio broadcast, has a harder edge. One can feel the unswerving faith of a poet-aesthete cutting through the mist of natural and, even more so, social change in the poem. Five years after the end of the War, one can feel that Japan is finally starting to find its feet. (LR. I probably found it on the net.)

The first time I read Kyoshi's *ku,* I fantasized *a supernatural pole of time,* only visible to the mind's eye. This came from a vague (and, apparently, mistaken!) memory of hearing that people somewhere in Japan actually said *kozokotoshi* at midnight, much as my sisters and I chirped out the name of both states as our parents drove across state lines, and from an adult experience one New Year when the paper-thin division between past and future ripped and I felt connected to infinite ages. "Pole" in Japanese includes phallic connotations, so it also made me think of the jeweled spear thrust into the sea in Japanese Creation stories. As *haiyû* Tenki points out, the pole, *thick,* contrasts with the arrow of time, a concept found in the Sinosphere as well as the West. Genjô (-1607) plays with it, giving the "rebounding arrow of time" *fast legs* (high-speed) punned from the *ashi* part of *ashita,* the morning of the New Year (たちかへるとしの矢はやきあした哉 玄仍 発句帳 *tachikaeru toshinoya hayaki ashita kana*). Does he imagine an arrow picked up and shot back, or was he so happy with his pun that he just didn't care if he used a verb better used to describe a rebounding wave? I once managed to *experience* the arrow concept, the red (soon white)-hot tip of the arrow of time coming my way: *"What target / this blazing arrow? / First sunrise."* Have you, reader, ever sat back and played with metaphors of time?

去年今年縫い合わせてゆく時の糸　敬愚
kozokotoshi nuiawasete yuku toki no ito　keigu 1951-
(last year – this year, sew together proceed time's thread)

this year *that*
each another round
stitch in time

The term *kozo-kotoshi* dates back to holiday *haikai* jam-sessions where participants did pairs of poems, one for the passing year and one for the coming. The spiral (hem) stitch describes it well. If Keigu actually participated in such an event, the *ku* might be worth something.

立ちかえる波にもあるや去年今年　尋香 or 静澗 文久五百
tachikaeru nami ni mo aru ya kozo kotoshi　jinkô 百家類題 or seikan 1860's
(stand/appear-rebound/ing wave/s-to-also is/are/has/! [a] last-year-this-year)

are they found even　　　　　　　　　　　　do even waves
in the waves rebounding　　　　　　　　rebounding have their new
last-year this-year?　　　　　　　　　　　　and old years?

Imagine a rocky shore or sea-wall. It's sunrise. This creation of the old year by rebound seems sheer metaphor and, as far as I know, lacks soul, but like Kyoshi's pole, it might hold meaning.

初空に去年の星の残りかな 子規 明治廿八
hatsuzora ni kozo no hoshi no nokori kana　shiki 1895
(first sky-in last-year's star/s remain/s 'tis/!/?)

the new sky:　　　　　　　　　　　　　　　so those stars
are those stars hold-overs　　　　　　　in the first sky are
from last year?　　　　　　　　　　　　last year's survivors?

In most saijiki, *First-brightness* (*hatsu-akari*) and *First-sun*/day (*hatsu-hi*) come *before* the *First-sky* in the 天, or *Heavenly phenomena* section of the *New Year*. As *Sunrise* was traditionally *one* starting point for the year, the *First-sky* implied day-light. But midnight year-change is also found in Japan previous to its adoption of the Gregorian calendar. Shiki probably refers to morning stars or planets, but may be up before dawn?   It is easier to be sure about the sky in olde *ku* like the next:

中垣や梅にしらける去年の空　鬼貫
nakagaki ya ume ni shirakeru kozo no sora　onitsura 1660-1738
(inner fence/wall/hedge!/: plum[apricot blooming]-to brighten last-year's sky)

the inner wall
last year's sky fades behind
the budding plum

The idea of dawn as *shirakeru* or a "white-out," turning the sky into a blank sheet, or *tabula rasa*, is untranslatable, but it suggests the obliteration of the past and improves the idea of the new dawn. Note, the plum blossoms are also white. As with the dune *ku,* Onitsura is too subtle (there is probably a reference to a certain tree associated with an ancient romance where one party was in a castle) here for me.

去年の星長居をけさは霞みけり 見志 大三物
kozo no hoshi nagai o kesa wa kasumikeri   kenshi 1697
(last year's star long-stay [+contradictory/regret]: this morn-as-for mist[+emph])

last year's stars
stayed up only to meet
this dawn mist

The mist makes it clear that "this dawn" means New Year's. The "long-stay," (*naga-i*) is an expression used for a guest who has outstayed his welcome or stayed up waiting to enjoy a woman's charms at a pleasure quarter. The particle "o" suggesting disappointment favors the latter meaning. It is sweet to see such sympathy, though facetious, for the stars!

今朝の春有明月を見つけたり 子規
kesanoharu ariakezuki o mitsuketari   shiki 1892
(morning's spring has-light[dawn]-moon find/found/see[+etc.])

ari-ake

spring dawns: this morning
what have we here?   new year's day i found
a waning moon   a waning moon

Japanese poets used to know *exactly* what the moon was up to, every day.[1] Everyone did. The name=number of every day of the month gave the age of the moon. The traditional New Year began with the new moon,[2] not actually seen but calculated by the Japanese, as the Chinese did for over a millennium (versus the more subjective *sighting* of the two or three-day moon in the evening sky by Muslims). In Japanese, the moon has names indicating the time of day it is seen. The waxing moon is the evening-moon, while the *ari-ake,* lit. "has-light," is the dawn-moon, one that has seen its better days. By the traditional way of thinking, it does not belong up there at the dawn of the New Year. Before the Western calendar sundered sun and moon-time (when Shiki was a boy), this would have been *unthinkable*. While the original *ku* is as understated as the second reading, I believe Shiki, a traditionalist at heart, felt that the waning moon, at a time when all should be fresh and/or waxing and, therefore, auspicious, was inappropriate. The *"~tari"* on the end of the "find/see" in the original implies other old things also out of place in the New Year. That is why I include it in this chapter on the Old year in the New. Three years later, Shiki expressed himself more clearly: *"Well, I'll be! / New Year's day sets to / a six-day moon"* (おもしろや元日暮れて月六日　子規　明治廿八*omoshiro ya ganjitsu kurete tsuki muika*).

~~~~~~

1. Remembering *What Moon is What*. Readers who don't mind a vulgar mnemonic device might borrow from Swift's poem about cancer-causing cosmetic powder, which equates a streetwalker and the moon (whose face is slowly eaten, as womens faces were by the cancer caused by the white-lead=mercury), out early when young and proud to show her face in daytime, but, once over-the-hill, not appearing until the wee hours of the morning, when men are drunk and lights are dim.
2. Another New Year's Moon. I simplify Japan's calendar history. An alternative, possibly older, Japanese New Year may have begun with the *full* moon. I am saving this for the last theme, "Woman's New Year" (*Onna-Shôgatsu*) in the fourth book of *The Fifth Season*.

元日や月見ぬ人の橋の音　其角　五元
ganjitsu ya tsuki minu hito no hashi no oto　kikaku -1707
(original-day: / moon not-watching peoples' bridge-sound)

new year's day
the bridge sounds like people
out moon-viewing

it's new year's
i hear men *not* moon-viewing
on the bridge

The moon on the first day is would be so tiny a sliver as to be practically invisible yet the grammar allows a positive reading (people view the moon), so I make the possible metaphor a simile to be safe. The second translation, logically silly yet impeccable, takes the more likely negative reading, the people waiting for the first sun-rise do *not* view the moon; but, the metaphor implied is the same.

去年今年雪は其のまゝ明けにけり　潮水
kozokotoshi yuki wa sono mama akenikeri　chôsui 1860's 文久五百
(last year-this year snow[=went(year)?] just as-is dawns/open/sun-rises [+fin.])

new year dawns
the snow remains just as
last year left it

old year new
it dawns with the snow
just as it was

Here, we are back to the last-year-this-year expression, though I failed to use the phrase *as-is* in my translations. The snow may be *old* and not *new*, but this brilliant blank slate is a fine gift from the Old Year for the New Year to fill in. While snow is an obviously left thing, anything that doesn't disappear with a poof at the end of the year is, likewise, *left*. New snow is far more fitting: *"'Snow! Snow!'/ Yesterday is forgotten; / The year[old age's] flower"* 雪よ／＼きのふ忘れし年の花　鬼つら *yuki yo yuki no kinô wasureshi toshi no hana*　onitsura - 1738). The untranslatable equivalence of "year" (the New Year) and "[old] age" might suggest a new idea of the New Year that would cheer white-haired old men.

そのまゝて去年と今年や麦と雪　魯堂　文久五百
sono mama de kozo to kotoshi ya mugi to yuki　rodô c1860
(this/that-same-as, last-year-and-this-year:/! wheat and snow)

just as it was
our last-year-this-year
barley & snow

Including the wheat with the snow is good though I am unsure as to why.

元日や草の戸越の麦畑　召波 -1771
ganjitsu ya kusa no togoshi no mugibatake　shôha
(original-day:/! grass-door-crossing-wheat-field)

the first day of the year
through the door of my hut,
a field of barley

(blyth trans.)

Blyth, as always, has *excellent* taste. This subtle *ku* says what the last one did, but more attentively. Note: you should not stand in the door but look out from within to frame the scene. The best thing to view through a door is a river – believe me, it is magical – but a wind-rippled field is not bad.

春かせや野はおしなべて去年の草　多代女
harukaze ya no wa oshinabete kozo no kusa   tayojo 1775-1865
(spring-breeze/wind! field-as-for mostly last-year's grass/plants)

the wind of spring!
while the fields are mostly
last year's weeds

Last year is not only stars and snow. It is almost *everything*. Weeds (or, grass) expected to grow afresh in the Spring are especially worthy of comment. The wind helps us see them. Tayojo's *ku* is not so much a New Year's *ku* as a spring one I put here for the "last-year" reference.

物と我皆去年なから初日哉　観水
mono to ware mina kozo nagara hatsuhi kana   kansui 1687
(things and me, all last-year while/when/yet first-day=sun[maybe+rise?] 'tis)

first sunlight on things and me of the last year		the last year things include me the first day
	things and i all just as last year: the first sun	
for all things of last year even me this new sun!		first sunshine illuminates the old including me

The *day=sun* identity in Japanese frustrates accurate translation. *Which* are we talking about? Can we, reading in English, think of both as one? I think the clever "things and I" (if all were new from the start, could the novelty be experienced?) may pun "*mono toware,*" (諸君、いかがでしょうか) or "questioning stuff," as in "Can this be?" The dreaminess of New Year's gives birth to the hyper-logical.

吹きゝやすともしにもあり去年今年　二葉
fukikiyasu tomoshi ni mo ari kozo-kotoshi   niyô 百家類題 19c?
(blowing-extinguish lamp/s-too/even has/have last-year-this-year)

the night light i blow out also knows last year - this year	to think this lamp i blow out has both, too a past and future

At first, I imagined the existence of a candle meant to last a single night and translated: *"Blown-out / the one-night candle gets / two years."* There is no evidence for such a candle. Something about blowing out a lamp or candle reminds us of our mortality and *its*. Even the lifeless does not last forever. Things have *their* life-spans. This lamp has at least two years, maybe many more.

我富り新年古き米五升　芭蕉
ware tomeri shinnen furuki kome go shô　bashô -1694
(i wealthy/prosperous! new year old rice five *shô* (about a peck = 8 qts)

        wealthy me!　　　　　　　　　　　　　i am rich
 a whole peck of old rice　　　　　　a new year with old rice
    and a new year　　　　　　　　　　　　　five quarts

Bashô redid the poem in two versions, beginning, respectively: "spring's here!" (*haru tatsu ya*) and "how fitting!" (*niawashi ya*). The first of these other versions is obvious; the second, meaning the little he had fit his ascetic life – according to a contemporary, the total possessions of his cottage were ten tea cups, one vegetable knife and one gourd (named "four-mountains") holding five *shô* of rice – is fulsome. I think we can assume a tea pot and a bowl for that rice, but be that as it may, Bashô would seem to be thanking or reassuring friends on his supply of rice while humorously boasting of his poverty.[1] One charm of having little is having less that is old to corrupt the New Year.

元日も立のまんま（まゝなる）の屑家哉　　一茶
ganjitsu mo tachi no manma no (or, mama naru) kuzuya kana　issa -1827
(original-day! beginning/standing-even-as [or –is] rubbish/trash-house 'tis/!/?)

new year's day
my hovel
the same as ever

trans. blyth

初空に向た儘なる(or まゝの)山家かな　素樸
hatsuzora ni muita mama naru [or, mama no] sanka kana　sobaku -1821
(first-sky-to facing as-ever is [the same] mountain-house!/?/'tis)

facing the first sky
my mountain hut
the same as ever

Issa and his contemporary Sobaku wrote almost identical poems. Did one copy the other? Was it chance? Or, are *both* a take-off from some popular expression? To better show the similarity, I follow the same syntax Blyth does for Issa's *ku*. Blyth explains that " 'hovel' is perhaps too serious a word; there is neither contempt nor self-pity in the *bottom* of Issa's mind." It may be true that the word is a bit over (written with a different character, 屑家→屑屋 *kuzuya* means a *junkman*) and may be little more than rhetoric for self-deprecation in Japanese serves where the pronoun "my" or "our" might in English, but hovel is fine, for Issa played up his poverty, which, unlike Bashô's, was involuntary. Issa's Japanese plays on *tachi*," which first means the *arrival* of the New Year, then, as one reads on, the literally (though barely) *standing* hovel. It may also stand for him. Another version, makes it explicit:

↑ **1. Boasting?** *A Lot of Rice or a Little?* Stewart translates: *"Grateful Granary // Spring has begun, and in my gourd I clear / A peck of rice to start the coming year."* In the "notes" he wrote that this rice poured into the gourd by Bashô's "grateful disciples" were "riches indeed for a haiku poet." That's a bit off, for most of the poets of Bashô's day were wealthy. It was, more properly, riches for a man whose poverty was central to his philosophy.

あばら家の其身其まゝ明の春　一茶
abaraya no sono mi sono mama ake-no-haru　issa -1827
(ramshackle-house's that body/content/soul that/just as-is dawn's spring)

<blockquote>
this ramshackle house
and me just the same as ever
the first day of spring

(trans. blyth)
</blockquote>

<blockquote>
inside the shack
everything is the same
as spring dawns
</blockquote>

<blockquote>
spring dawns
the same old shack
same old me
</blockquote>

The original does not specify what the contents (*mi*) of that shack are. I think Blyth guesses right and he improves the poem by making it the house *and* poet. I copy it in my second reading.

元日の日向ぼこする屑家 (or つぶれ家) かな　一茶
ganjitsu no hinataboko-suru kuzuya (or tsubureya) kana　issa
(original-day's sunshine-bask-do trash/junk-house!/?/'tis)

<blockquote>
the old shack
soaking up the rays
on new year's
</blockquote>

<blockquote>
my old shack
basks in the sunshine
of new year's
</blockquote>

<blockquote>
basking in the first
sunshine of the year
my old shack
</blockquote>

<blockquote>
sunbathing
in the new year's light
my old shack
</blockquote>

This, my favorite version (not so well known) of Issa's New Year's shack takes the fantasy angle further. *Hinataboko* (sun-bathing) is a word generally used only for *animals*. Used for a shack, it does not seem so much zoomorphic as endearing. We feel affection rather than affectation.

元日や反古も机も去年の儘　松尾
ganjitsu ya hogo mo tsukue mo kozo no mama shôbi 18-19-20c?
(original-day: scrap-paper-even desk-even last-year as-is)

<blockquote>
new year's day
the desk and bits of paper
just as last year

(trans. blyth)
</blockquote>

I suppose the desk was the poet's most familiar landscape; it most certainly is mine. There is pathos in the scrap-paper remaining (note: Blyth pronounces the poet's name Matsuo). There are many desk *ku*.

すゑてあるまゝに机も今年かな 祖卿 百家類題
suetearu mama ni tsukue mo kotoshi kana sokyô 19c?
(placed-is-as-is desk, too last-year-this-year!/?/'tis)

    the desk, too   left as is
    with all in place   my desk, too, joins
    another year   the new year

                a new year
              for my desk my
              messy desk, too

Shôbi's specification of desk and scrap-paper beats Sokyô's more abstract *ku*, but I find Sokyô's mention of "this year" – "another year" and "the new year" in my readings – better than Issa's more obvious "just (the same) as last year."

撫て置机の塵やけさの春 山河 百家類題
nadete oku tsukue no chiri ya kesa no haru sanga (-1958?) 19-20c?
(stroking-place/leave desk's trash/scraps/dust:/! morning's spring)

              nudged and left
            this crap on my desk
              and it's spring

    what a mess   new year dawns
  my desk barely touched   all that crap i nudged and
    my new year   left on my desk

              i barely touch
        the mess on my desk and
              hello, spring!

The "nudged and left" detail in this *ku* is touching. Now, to one of the most common types of New Year *ku*, the generalization, something more acceptable for the new Year than any other time.

元日や古き姿もあたらしき 吟江 古き姿
ganjitsu ya furuki sugata mo atarashiki ginkô 1775
(original-day!/: form/shape/appearance also/too/even, new)

              new year's day
           even old appearances
             are novel now

    the first day   the first day
  old forms you know   even the things that are
    are also new   old are new

              first day
         even our old things
              are new

The five-syllabet "new" (*atarashiki*) in the original left space hard to fill, while "New Year's Day" and "new" are redundant. Hence the stilted "novel" and (for English) less natural "first day."

元日や昨日に遠き朝ぼらけ　移竹
ganjitsu ya kinô ni tôki asaborake　ichiku 1764-1831
(new year's! yesterday-to/from distant, dawn)

去年といへば遠きやうなる旦哉　泥牛
kozo to ieba tôki yô naru ashita kana　deigyû 1697
(last year said-if, far-off-seems-becomes dawn.new-year!/?)

it's new year's
how far from yesterday
the early dawn

last year?
it seems far away
this dawn

春といへば去年も昨日も忘れけり　素檗
haru to ieba kozo mo kinô mo wasurekeri　sobaku 1758-1821
(spring-said-if, last-year-too/and yesterday-even/and forgotten [+emph.])

spring? yes,
last year *and* yesterday
forgotten

"Only a few hours ago and everything was paying bills,[1] work, quarrels, greed; now, all is peace and smiles," writes Blyth about Ichijiku's *ku*. I felt tempted to follow him and the commutative law, changing the original to *"The dawn of New Year's Day; / Yesterday, / How far off!"* but kept the forward movement of the original, to preserve the contrast with Deigyû's *ku* that makes Last Year = *yesterday* rather than New Year's Day = today far off: The Chinese character makes the *ashita*, phonetically "tomorrow" *or* "morning" (in this respect, like the Spanish *mañana*) meaning the New Year in the original, itself a hybrid of two older poems: *"Last year? / it's partitioned off! / spring mist"* (去年といへは遠きへたてや春霞　紹巴 *kozo to ieba tôki hedate ya harugasumi*　jôha -1602) and *"Last year? / Yesterday! The curtain fell: / this morning mist"* (去年といへは昨日やをちの朝霞　宗砌 *kozo to ieba kinô ya ochi no asagasumi* sôzei -1455). Which do you prefer, the *physiological* metaphor of separation in the old poems or the *psychological* metaphor of the newer ones? The "*and* yesterday" in Sobaku's *ku* is clever new twist. The "and" cried out to be italicized, but the original did not stress it.

去年の事忘るゝけさのけしき哉　鴎歩　大三物
kozo no koto wasururu kesa no keshiki kana　ôho 1697
(last year's thing/s forgotten morning's=ny's view/sight!)

what a dawn
last year and all in it
are forgotten!

i can forget
the old year seeing
such a dawn

the old year
easy to forget looking around
this morning

~~~~~~

1. Paying Bills. The end of the year, called *shiwasu* (IPOOH winter 1) was a debt-paying marathon for most people. This worked as a foil for the New Year. Here is an old haiku supporting Blyth's explanation: *"Because of shiwasu / this dawn is so interesting / eternal spring!* 師走ありてけさ面白き千代の春　意計　大三物 *shiwasu arite kesa omoshiroki chiyo-no-haru* – ikei 1697). The eternal spring – lit. "a thousand ages" – evoked slow-motion, while *shiwasu* was identified with frantic running about. Hounded by time, the poet is relieved to find himself in a timeless sanctuary. How tough *shiwasu* could be for some is revealed by this *senryû*: *"On New Year's / he is still too afraid / to open the door"* (元日ハまだこわいから戸を明ヶず *ganjitsu wa mada kowai kara to o akezu*　– Yanagi. 1758)

seasonal decorations

<table>
<tr><td>

getting over
last year is easy with
this beauty

</td><td>

the old year
fast forgotten amid
new year sights

</td></tr>
</table>

Here we have some detail, if the *keshiki* is taken concretely. An attractive sight helps us forget what we should forget, i.e. *get over*. I first thought the *keshiki*, or "picturesque sight," referred to the sunrise but, on deeper thought, realized it included the New Year decorations.

正月のけしきになるや泥に雪 一茶
shôgatsu no keshiki ni naru ya doro ni yuki   issa -1827
(new-year's scene/sight/panorama is/becomes!/: mud-to/with/on/and-snow)

real life

<table>
<tr><td>

this becomes
our new year's image
snow and mud

</td><td>

snow on mud
the very picture of
the new year

</td></tr>
</table>

Keshiki again. Issa doesn't mention the last year at all, but mud, at least, is not made in a day. We will have more of Issa's mud elsewhere. If snow offers a blank slate to the New Year, mud holds the seeds of Spring.

春正月また白紙そ四方のあけ　淡々
haru-shôgatsu mata/mada shirakami zo yomo no ake   tantan -1761
(spring-correct-month=ny, again/still white-paper[+exclam.] foursides'[all-directions']dawn)

<table>
<tr><td>

spring new year
a blank sheet once again
posted at dawn

</td><td>

spring new year
north south east west still
draw a blank

</td></tr>
</table>

The "Spring New Year" is a [New] Year that follows the Solar Spring, i.e., falls within the Spring rather than the Spring falling within the [Old] Year as discussed in chapter I (*Toshi-no-uchi-no-haru*). They are ultimately different takes on the same phenomenon. Does the *ku* mean that whether or not the Solar Spring jumped the gun, the New Year is a purely fresh start? The first reading plays on "post/paste" as a homophone for *haru* (spring), a pun not necessarily deliberate. The Japanese view of dawning as a fade out – something like developing a photograph in reverse – makes the "white-paper" natural rather than forced. The four-sides (*yomo*) means *all around*. The "still" reading is slightly more likely than "again."

能いものやきのふには似す明けの春　正
ii mono ya kinô ni wa nizu ake no haru   tadashi 安永四 1775
(good thing! yesterday-to/as-for resemble-not dawn's spring=ny)

<table>
<tr><td>

a good thing
the dawn of spring is
unlike yesterday

</td><td>

how good
spring's dawn is unlike
yesterday's

</td></tr>
</table>

Yesterday is yester*day*; it is also yester*year*. A weather change is welcome. Another poet wrote *"Just to say / 'Yesterday' on New Year's / is funny"* (きのふとはいふもをかしやけさの春 祇有 明和2 *kinô to wa iu mo okashi ya kesanoharu* – giyû (1765)). Or, is *"interesting."*

年毎にめでたき春のけしき哉 貞吉 大三物
toshi goto ni medetaki haru no keshiki kana   teikichi 1697
(year-each-with joyful/celebratory spring's/new-year's image/sight/s!/'tis)

every year
what a joy to take in
spring scenery

spring sights
every year are worth
a celebration

the same spring
a sight to celebrate
every year

The original does not say specifically that the *keshiki* (image/picture/landscape/etc.) is "the same," but I think that is what the "each year" suggests.

God does not send strange flowers every year,
When the spring winds blow o'er pleasant places,
The same dear things lift up the same fair faces,
The violet is here.

A Violet. Stanza 1 (more in *Bartlett's Quotations*)

Unlike Adeline Dutton Train Whitney (1824-1906), we are not talking flowers alone. Imagine beautifully dressed people, clean houses, evergreen Gate-pines (*kadomatsu*) and other New Year decorations, some described in this book.

年の荷をおろせば輕しけさの春 得之 霞ふくろ
toshi no ni o oroseba karushi kesa no haru   tokushi 1829
(year's=age's burden lower -when/if light: morning's spring=ny)

unburdened
with the year/s, how light
this first day!

having dumped
the old year how light
this spring day

What an imaginative metaphor! Are we not *all* Atlases, carrying our year/s upon our shoulders?

侘びつくし／\てそ花の春　士朗
wabi tsukushi wabi tsukushite zo hana-no haru   shirô -1813
(*wabi* [subdued/stark taste] exhaust [taken to the limit], *x2*[+emph.] flower-spring=ny)

just in time

colorful spring
after we take starkness
to the limit

bare living
all we can bear and
it is spring

when the world
cannot get any bleaker
spring blossoms

Shirô fuses the simple and quiet winter hibernation of the poet with the bleak winter landscape so it is hard to tell if this *ku* a somewhat affected aesthetic statement or a mere fact of nature expressed with hyperbole. A visual feast after a partially voluntary and partially season-induced fast.

日そ寒き去年とやいはん朝曇　満助 河越千句
hi zo samuki kozo to ya iwan asagumori　　mansuke 年付？
(day/sun [emphasis] cold! last year it call not morning overcast)

spring, you say?

today is cold
can't speak of "last year"
this cloudy dawn

寒の内は去年とやいはんけさの春　古軒 大三
kan no uchi wa kozo to ya iwan kesanoharu　　koken 1697
(cold within-as-for last-year [emph.] say-not, morning's spring)

spring has come
but who can say "last year"
in bitter cold?

Until one can think of the winter as last year, the New Year, or spring, is a calendrical fiction. These *ku* play on an old saw going back at least to the very first poem in Saigyô's famous *Sankashû* (mountain hut anthology 12c). Prefaced "When rain falls on spring-within-the-year"(*toshinouchi ni haru tachite ame no furikereba*), the *waka* asks, *"How can I / feel it is spring / with this / cold drizzle proof / the old year reigns?"* (春としもなほおもはれぬ心かな雨ふる年のここちのみして　西行 山家集 #1 *haru to shi mo nao omowarenu kokoro kana ame furu toshi no kokochi nomi shite*　　saigyô 1118-90). My "reign" is an attempt to mimic the pivotal pun where *furu* means "falls" (*ame furu* = "rain *falls*") coming – with what comes before – and "old" (*furu toshi* = "[the] *old* year.") going. The colloquial language of Mansuke and Koken's *ku* may fit the complaint better than the classical style of Saigyô's *waka*.

正月は奇麗過ぎたる寒さ哉　亀年 失出典
shôgatsu wa kireisugitaru samusa kana　　kinen lost ref.
(new-years-as-for, beautiful-exceeds/excessive coldness 'tis/!/?)

on new year's　　　　　　　　　　　new year's
this cold that is just　　　　　　　　a cold that is too
too beautiful　　　　　　　　　　　beautiful

spring freeze

on new year's
beauty makes me shiver
all the more

I imagined an overcast New Year for the previous two *ku* though only one mentions it. But the coldest days are usually *clear* with a brilliant blue sky. Note that the poet's name means "turtle year" or "turtle age." Is this the *nom de plume* of an old man so cold he wishes he could pull his head back into his body? *I joke*. Though there is no mention of the previous year – no ticket to join this chapter – the cold has a hint of the winter, *i.e.*, past year, and this *ku* is far better than any of those we have just read about weather unsuitable for the New Year. How could I *not* introduce it?

朝朗去年の塵はく柳哉　横山 大三物
asaboroke kozo no hokori haku yanagi kana   ôsan 1697
(dawn-light last-year's dust sweep willow/!/?/'tis)

       at daybreak
     a willow is sweeping
      last year's dust

I would think that the willow has little to sweep with at this time – which is usually not windy either – some left-over dust (unlike snow) hardly worth noticing, and, if the willow alludes to a woman, it is a poor metaphor because, in *haikai*, a metaphor should never work as a metaphor alone. If, however, we think of the dust as that stirred up by the heels of the departed year, the *ku* is saved, barely.

けさの春や先づ押しかくす夜のもの　成美
kesanoharu ya mazu oshi kakusu yoru no mono   seibi -1816
(morning's spring/new-year: first push[away]-hide night's things)

      the dawn of spring
   first, i push out of sight
      things of the night

Neither "this year" or "that" are mentioned in this *ku* found with the theme *kesa-no-haru,* or "dawn of spring (=new-year)." But, remember, in the Land of the Rising Sun, the New Year began at dawn. I simplify;[1] but is Seibi's *ku* really so different from the next *ku*, more explicitly *kozo-kotoshi*?

起されてたゝむ衾や去年ことし　素山 文久五百
okosarete tatamu fusuma ya kozokotoshi   sozan 1818-92
(woken up [i?] fold up futon/ quilt: last-year-this-year)

    woken up   awakened
i put away my quilt   this year, i fold up last
last-year! this-year!   year's *futon*

       kozo-kotoshi

      awakened
 i fold up last year:
     my *futon!*

Here, I prefer the more imaginative translations to *that-year-this-year*. The *fusuma* is not the perfectly rectangular *futon* we know, but a quilt with sleeves that is *worn* to sleep, called a *kake-futon*.

去年今年我家はなれず風邪の神　百艸 改造社
kozokotoshi wagaya hanarezu kaze no kami   hyakusô early-20c?
(last year this year my house separate/depart-not cold's god)

     holiday visitor

     the cold god
stays over from one year
     to the next

↑ **1. Spring at Dawn?** While the old year was thought to depart the evening before and midnight officially signaled the change of year, the rising sun settled it. Take this elegant *ku* by Sôshun : *"The scent of plum / before the rooster's call / pre-dawn spring"* (梅か香や鳥より先の夜半の春 宗春 三籟 *umegaka ya tori yori saki no yoha no haru* 1734). The "spring" here is not entire; the plum tree (the scent of its blossoms) are a sort of advance for Spring-as-New-Year, who arrives for good with the day = sun's appearance.

This "cold" is not "cold" in Japanese, but *wind,* and means anything from the sniffles to influenza. Allegorized like this, a cold rises above complaint. The poet must have been happy to at least get *something* from his family's misfortune: a *ku*.

新年の柩にあひぬ夜中頃 子規
shinnen no hitsugi ni ainu yonaka goro shiki -1902
(new year's coffin-with meet midnight-around)

around midnight
i meet up with a coffin
for the new year

I put this in *kozo-kotoshi* because someone who died in the old year will be buried in the new. Blyth translates *"I met a coffin / at midnight / in the new year."* The PC (*poetically* correct) haiku world might frown on my dramatic "for." But "*in* the new year" is dead compared to the original "new year's coffin." Neither Blyth's nor my translation is precise. Mine may be more faithful to the original, which I feel cannot avoid a touch of metaphysical humor. Indeed, Shiki's *ku* even moved me to think of the New Year as a proverbial Chinaman (or medieval European noble), who keeps his own coffin on hand! Finally, the *ku* plays subtly against the last year, for *it* is what one might expect to bury.

去年の人霞わかてりけさの人　法久 大三物
kozo no hito kasumi wakateri kesa no hito hôkyû 1697
(last year's person mist split/ting this morning's person)

someone from   a last-year man
last year parts the mist   parts the morning mist
a new person   a this-year man

A person who only exists to us as memory traces from the previous year materializes from the mist.

去年今年片足に鸛の眠り哉　舞石 大三物
kozokotoshi kataashi ni kô no nemuri kana buseki 1697
(last year this year one-leg-on white-stork's sleep 'tis)

as stork sleeps
on one leg, the new year
and the old

The solemn movements of the white stork are identified with the magical slow-motion New Year we shall see in ch 5. The giant bird is also a Time-master, a being that can live a thousand years. This makes it embody the New Year, for all propitious symbols (especially those connected to longevity) are evoked on that day. But it is really the contrast between that single leg and the two years that makes the poem. *What* exactly it means, however, I do not know. It may be a reference to the subject of Chapter 1, solar spring falling in the winter, for there is a *ku* that says: *"Year-within: / A fine Spring Day stands / on one leg"* (年の内は片足で立つ春日哉 光有 毛吹草 *toshi-no-uchi wa kataashi de tatsu harubi kana* kôyû 1645). Or, it might reflect the balancing act of that last night, which, as far as I can tell, belongs to neither year. I only know that, like Kyoshi's continuous pole, *I like* it.

~~~~~~

A Couple Modern *That-year-this-year* Ku

Eメール地球は狭し去年今年 はな 右脳俳句
E-mehru chikyu wa semashi kozo-kotoshi hana 2001/1/1
(e-mail earth-globe [world]-as-for narrow/cramped, last-year-this-year)

                                with e-mail
                           the world's too small
                               that-year-*this*

my calendar yours   *it's a small world*

e-mail in/out   side by side
two years shout: what   the new year and old:
a small world!   that's e-mail

                                e-mail, e-mail
                            our world has shrunk
                                   that-year-*this*

The world's modification in the original, *semashi,* or "narrow," *may* mean only *"small,"* but "cramped" is the common connotation. I have contributed haiku to websites on the correct date for a given seasonal theme (such as a holiday) in the USA, only to be a day late in Japan. I even missed my own birthday! For better or worse, E-mail, by making an instant record of the time and date of letters from correspondents around the world, brings home the size and shape of our earth. Yet, let us recall a mid-19c *Peanuts* episode where it was already noted that there can be no End of the World, for the date is never the same everywhere, and, further, that the idea goes back *at least* as far as Twain's early-20c travel reporting!

今生きることを知りたる去年今年 江連晴生 夜半亭の録
ima ikiru koto o shiritaru kozo-kotoshi ezure seisei contemp.
(now living thing[obj]knowing this-year-last-year)

kozo-kotoshi

that-year-this   *this-year-that*
you feel you are   you feel you are
living now   living now

There is an unstated paradox here. The future and the past, or rather, the past and the future, if we would put things in the proper order, make us aware of the present. Considering the fact *this* year makes last year *that,* the more natural-sounding reverse translation seems permissible. I am afraid there were also sad events in the previous year, but do not know if it matters for the *ku*. (オマケ＝「去年今年だんだん耳の遠くなる」 江連晴生。年々遠くなるのが生理学だが、物理のドップラー効果のスローモーションと思えば面白い。敬愚の場合、＜重なれば耳鳴りならぬ去年今年＞ ＜耳鳴りに初静けさや除夜の鐘＞となる。）

吹く風のゆるみ心やこそことし　峰秀 文久五百
fuku kaze no yurumi-gokoro ya kozokotosni   hôshû mid-19c
(blow/ing wind's slacking/lull-heart/mind: last-year-this-year)

that year this
like a sudden lull
in the wind

I think this older *ku* may convey something similar to Ezure's without actually saying it. I could not fit a feeling/heart/mind into the translation and traded it in for a "like." To me the metaphor (not a simile in the original) is *exquisite*. There is no "sudden." I added it to fill space and because the onset of the lull we feel is always sudden.

Chapter Note on R.H. Blyth. This chapter has a higher proportion of *ku* translated by Blyth than any other. His small selection of New Year's related haiku includes more than a representative number of *ku* that look back. Blyth has an uncanny ability to find – or had a Japanese acquaintance with such sense? – the top *ku* on the few New Year subjects he covers, so we cannot help overlapping on occasion. When that happens, I prefer to mention it and quote him as far as possible rather than to pretend I am the first to introduce the *ku*.

See This? It is a Calendar!

What, exactly, is that Calendar?

Do you see the Chinese characters meaning big 大 and small 小? It is *them*. They are all needed to work out the rest by oneself. First, they show it is a twelve-month year, and not the thirteen-month year needed once every three or four years to keep the lunar New Year from wandering too far from the solar spring. Second, they show the order of the Big 30-day months and Small 29-day months. This year, you will note it is sBsBBsBsBsBs. Oddly enough, the modern calendar from which I borrowed the picture says it dates to 1861 which features a year animal as far from the Hare as could be. Either something Yin-yangy is going on, calendars were made for each birth-year, hares were charms for going uphill (against adversity) with those big hind-legs, or the proverbial hare in the moon was thought to know something about the same. The big *daikon* roots pun into "great-resolve," while the red sea breams with protruding eyeballs pun into a felicitious year.

十二支尽し
jûnishi-zukushi

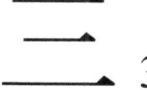 3

Playing With The Animals

けさたるゝつらゝやよたれ牛の年　貞徳
kesa taruru tsurara ya yodare ushinotoshi   teitoku 1570-1673
(this morning drips/hangs icicle/s!/?/: slobber/druel ox year)

synchronicity

<table>
<tr><td>this morning
the icicles slobber
year of the cow</td><td>dripping icicles
today, call them *slobber*
year of the ox</td></tr>
</table>

Every year in the Sinosphere comes with, or as an animal. Far Easterners identified themselves with these twelve creatures, as Occidentals do with their more eclectic (human, animal and chimera) monthly birth signs. Aside from prejudice against women born in the Year of the Horse (either because the horse, at high-noon, is uppity or because it is too spirited), there was, and is, less astrologizing with Year-animals than with the Zodiac. They were, however, used more extensively to demarcate time (i.e., as hours) and directions. The Chinese characters used for these animals are different from the usual ones and originally stood for the twelve stages of growth of a plant, but Teitoku's *ku,* above, uses the usual character for "cow" to enhance the animality(?) of the image. Today, the twelve animal signs 十二支(*jûnishi*) enjoy a strong visual presence, if nothing else because everyone in Japan buys or makes New Year's cards (see *nenga,* ch 7), most of which are adorned with them. Pre-Bashô poets *reveled* in these animals and, even today, every child and adult with a child in their heart *should* enjoy reading or writing haiku about them. Yet, most *saijiki* slight this practice by failing to give *jûnishi* enough space.[1]   Why? I believe it is because Bashô held up a *ku* about the year-animal as an example of what was wrong with the *haikai* of his day. *The above ku on the Year of the Ox, by Teitoku, was that poem.* Since Bashô ridiculed it as contrived, or nominal play, the *ku* has stood for what we might call *Teitoku's slobberel*. Had Bashô been writing in English, he might have found a *Year of the Dog* poem to criticize as "doggerel," but, seriously, too much has been made of this criticism. Teitoku may well have seen a melting icicle and found the coincidence worth noting – as most coincidences are – but, even if he just imagined it, *why not?* Melting icicles are a representative part of Spring. Their dripping was traditionally associated with romance-shed teardrops on sleeves, and there are at least three in the Shin-Kinkonshû anthology (1205) alone. Song #31 where *"The tear icicles / of the nightingale / start melting . . ."* (*uguisu-no namida-no-tsurara uchi-tokete furu-su nagara ~*), song # 633 with its virtual bed of icicles: "On my pillow and sleeves, icicle tears ~" (*makura ni mo sode ni mo namida tsurara ~*), and this:

---

1. ***Year Animals in Saijiki***   Shiki's *Categorical* has a number of *ku* for each year animal, but they are under separate headings between 40 year-old (四十の年) and the solar spring *risshun* (立春). They are not gathered under a heading such as my *Year-Animals*. In modern *saijiki,* they must be satisfied to lurk within the *New Year's Cards*.

年暮れし涙のつらら解けにけり苔の袖にも春やたつらむ 新古今集
toshi kureshi namida no tsurara tokenikeri koke no sode ni mo haru ya tatsuramu shinkokinshû #1,435
(year ends/ended, tear-icicle/s melt[+finality], moss-sleeve-to-even spring arrives[apparently])

a year ends
lachrymal icicles
melt down:

has spring come
to mossy sleeve?

icicles made
of last year's tears
have melted

could spring come to
even a monk's sleeve?

The ex-minister became a monk, hence moss-colored sleeves reminding one of likewise mossy rocks below which poets heard spring in gurgling water, but not to get lyrical here: my point is that even if Teitoku's *ku* is far from elegant and the Year Animal an artificial construct, finding something bovine in dripping icicles is not just a delightful image for the Year of the Ox; *it is surely an irreverent poke at the precious icicle tears of classical poetry.* Could Bashô have missed that humor? Personally, I prefer Teitoku's *haikai* wit to pretty, description such as: *"The first sun: / the icicles on the eaves / melt away"* (日の始軒の氷柱の解にけり　不得　大三物 *hi no hajime noki no tsurara no tokenikeri* futoku 1697) or, *"Spring rises / from the drops of icicles / on the eaves* (春立つや氷柱の軒の雫より　希因　古選 *haru tatsu ya tsurara no noki no shizuku yori*　kiin -1748). Perhaps that makes me a haiku heretic; but I think readers should bear in mind the fact that the idea of turning icicles into slobber is actually a fine creative leap, easy only in retrospect. While I find the philosophical complaint of Bashô *et alia* misplaced, Teitoku's poem *does* have *one* problem. *It is poorly written.* Keigu would have made it a question:

丑年　今朝たるゝ氷柱やたれの涎らん　貞愚
ushidoshi: kesa taruru tsurara ya dare no yodare ran　teigu (teitoku+keigu)
(ox/cow-year: this morning dripping icicle/s:/! whose slobber[+exclamatory interogative])

"year of the ox"

the icicles drip
whose slobber is it
this morning!

But let us see *ku* for each Year Animal in turn, including another ox/cow in its proper place, right after the rat. (オマケ：素丸の貞徳翁忌：この翁の書たまひし「天水抄」を開きて　天水の氷柱しぼらん硯にも)

~~~~~~

Rat · Mouse

宿の猫蓬莱山を守りけり　八重桜
yado no neko hôraisan o mamorikeri　yaezakura 1879-1945
(inn's cat/s hôrai-mountain guards [completely])

year of the mouse

the inn's cats
keep guard by the foot
of the *hôrai*

Nezumi includes both the rat and the mouse. Rat has a bad connotation in English not found in the Japanese, but there is a tradition of Englishing *nezumidoshi* Year of the Rat. I use both words. Despite the mouse/rat being the first animal in the cycle, auspicious for its connection with the underground and identified with prosperity (because *multiplying like rabbits* is *rat/mouse arithmetic* in the Sinosphere), I have found few good year-mice *ku*. Instead, I arbitrarily added a title to the above *ku* about a *hôrai*, the New Year decoration symbolizing a magical *Mountain of Youth* (ch.3). There are, however, more real mice in New Year haiku than any other mammal other than man; we will come back to them later in the magical mountain *Hôrai* and Princess Bride (*yome-ga-kimi*). If I find a good old year-mouse haiku, it will be added to a later edition of this book. For now, we'll make do with some January 1996 haiku.

年玉はかんべん子年猫寝なさい　敬愚
toshidama wa kanben nedoshi neko ne nasai! keigu

<table>
<tr><td>

no gift, *please*
cat, go back to sleep!
year of the rat

</td><td>

my cat's gift
auspicious or not
the rat is here

</td></tr>
</table>

year of the rat
thank you! no thank you!
i tell my cat

The irregularities of the New Year Season terrify cats. The excess nervous energy born from this increases their hunting activity, while the insecurity makes them ply their patrons with presents. But, is a dead red-mouse – the *ku* I wrote on that dead mouse are lost in my notebooks, so Keigu made one in Japanese and several in English – lucky (*For you, the year in a platter!*) or unlucky (*That is no way to treat the Year Animal!*)? We do not need to ask that of the following *ku*, contributed to the Shiki online internet forum on 1 January, 1996. How elated the poet must have felt at such splendid synchronicity!

two hands at midnight
on my mickey mouse watch
year of the rat.

jane reichhold

The modern equivalent of Teitoku's slobber? A *ku* that could have been written by a child? That is not criticism. It is *praise*. As we shall see later, childishness is one thing the New Year is all about.

~~~~~~

<center>

Ox

車座でいはひそむるや丑の年　吉林
kurumaza de iwaisomuru ya ushinotoshi　kirin　毛吹草 1645
(wheel=circular seating-arrangement-with/by celebrate-start! ox's year)

sitting in a wheel
we celebrate its coming
the year of the ox

</center>

We speak of sitting around a round-table. The Japanese, lacking large tables, called sitting in a circle, a wheel-sit. The "wheel" also meant, as it still means, a wheeled vehicle. Upper-class Japanese generally were carried in palanquins by men, but when they relied upon wheels, the cart was pulled by oxen. Following the prescription of the above *ku* would be a metaphysically suitable way to bring in the Ox! Another, by Soô: *"The long calm – / Still to shake its horns, / Year of the Ox"* (長閑さや角ぶりもせぬ丑の年 祖翁 毛吹草 *nodokesa ya tsunoburi mo senu ushinotoshi* 1645). The original is wittier because the syntax keeps the action not taken and the ox in direct contact, pegging on the year (*toshi*) last. It also fits the ox to a weather phenomenon considered typical for that time of the year and day (dawn). Finally, a *ku* that depends on un-Englishable homophones: *"From today / nose=flowers bloom=opening pass through! / ox's year"* (けふよりは花さき通せ牛の年　利重　鷹つくば *kyo yori wa hana-saki tôse ushinotoshi* rijû 1642).

Tiger

さほ姫の手飼成らし虎の年 定時 鷹つくば
sao hime no tegai naru rashi toranotoshi　teiji 1642
(sao-princess' hand-reared [pet] is-seems: tiger's year)

year of the tiger

raised by none
other than princess sao
annus tigris

Teitoku's *"Even the mist / is rising in patches / year of the tiger"* (霞さへまだらに立や虎の年 貞徳 *kasumi sae madara ni tatsu ya toranotoshi*) resembles his ox poem in finding an attribute of the year-animal in Nature, but is weaker because "patches" seem more fitting for a leopard than a tiger. Teiji's poem is more removed from modern haiku for it deals completely with fictions (readers who skipped earlier chapters should know that Sao is the [goddess of] Spring). A modern Year of the Tiger *ku* by Keigu:

大和撫子賛 内股も考え直す寅詣 敬愚
uchimata mo kangae-naosu tora môde　keigu
(inner-thighed [pigeon-toed]too, think-over tiger [shrine]visit)

feminine, you say?

toes pointed-in	women walking
first trip to the shrine	toes-in, the first shrine
this tiger year	visit of tigers

The pigeon-toed stance and walk of Japanese women in traditional footwear seems modest if not meek. But, come to think of it, don't *tigers* prowl with paws turned-in? 大和撫子賛・内股も恐い恐いや寅詣 敬愚

Hare

卯の年に　早く越る年やうさぎの上り坂　秀重 毛吹草
hayaku koyuru toshi ya usagi no noborizaka　shûchô 1645
(quickly crossing year/s!/: rabbit/hare's up/climbing-hill)

    the old tiger   hare's up-hill
quickly left behind   the year starts quickly
   hare's up-hill   time stands still!

rabbit man

the years pass
so quickly, a hare
going uphill

The saying "a hare's up-hill (*usagi no noborizaka*)," means *easy-going*, or *made for doing well in adversity*, because the hare/rabbit has longer hind-legs than fore. Did the year jump the gun, with Solar spring occurring in the tail of the Tiger? The lack of number in Japanese also allows for the possibility that the poet, born in the Year of the Hare, fused the saying and the conventional lament to create an upbeat observation about how fast the *years* go by.

年波を兎もけふや走り初　重次　鷹つくば
toshinami o usagi mo kyô ya hashirizome　jûji 1642
(year-wave/s[emotive "o"] hare, too, today run-start)

new year surf
today, the bunnies, too
off and running

The year as a huge wave is an old conceit and the moon-lit white-caps are thought to look like white hare/rabbits. The moon at the start of the month would not be visible, but it would indeed be starting to wax, or, in this *ku's* idiom, *run*. Since "year-waves" also refer to the wrinkles of old age, my wild-card B-side reading imagines a 48, 60, 72 or 84 year-old, white-haired fisherman, launching his boat for the first time that year.

Dragon

夜の雨にけさのほる日や辰の年　道宅 毛吹草
yoru no ame ni kesa noboru hi ya tatsunotoshi　dôtaku
(night's rain-in, morning rises sun!/: dragon's year 1645)

the sun rises
up from a rainy night
Dragon Year

Presumably watching the sun arise from the sea on the *Year of the Dragon*, Shinan wrote *"What else! / Dragon Years always rise / up from the sea"* (尤ぞうみの中よりたつのとし　信安　鷹筑波　*mottomo zo umi no naka yori tatsu-no-toshi*　shinan 1642). Unlike Dôtaku's *ku*, it is untranslatable *as a poem* for it depends on a pun: "dragon=rise/arrive" (*tatsu*). As someone who grew up by the sea, I can't help noting the Chinese zodiac is heavily biased toward mammals, having only one reptile, one bird and one fish to represent the rest of the animal kingdom. The dragon is the King of Fish and identified with moisture rather than dry heat, as is the fire-breathing Occidental variety.   Hence, the rainy night.

田の中に棒たつとしの始哉 是三 夢見草
ta no naka ni bô tatsudoshi no hajime kana   korezô 1656
(field-within/middle-in, stick stands/comes/dragon year's first!/?/ 'tis)

in mid-paddy a standing stick: the dragon year is here	year of the dragon incarnate from the stick stuck in my plot

If the poem is little more than a nominal pun on the verb *tatsu* (arrive/stand), the way the pun is set up from the stick is masterful. There may be an allusion here to the original stick, a halberd or spear that played a role in creating the archipelago, to the ancient practice of thrusting a stick into a field to indicate possession (has the poet just gained a field?) or it could be the marker for a *nagaimo,* a potato as long as burdock that will pop up a shoot when it grows warmer. *Though I have yet to solve it,* this is my favorite dragon-year *ku*. I made the *ta* a "paddy" because English has no good word specific to *a field or plot used for agriculture.* At this time of year, it could be muddy, but not full of water.

陽暦二千年の朝 辰年や玉子むく我世占い 敬愚
tatsudoshi ya tamago muku ware yo-uranai   keigu
(chicken/bird-year: egg/s strip/peel/ing i world-predict)

millennium madness

dragon year reading the future in a peeled egg	dragon year peeling the egg, i fly fast-forward

題宝玉 1 辰年や玉子取る指爪に成り 敬愚
tatsudoshi ya tamago toru yubi tsume ni nari keigu

dragon year
holding an egg, my nails
turn to talons

The Millennium happened to start (if 2000 is the start, for some think it 2001) in the Year of the Dragon when Keigu lived alone, without even gecko or cockroaches for company, in an artist's flat undergoing reconstruction in London. Mesmerized by a boiled egg in the glare of the bare light bulb (bare bulbs being common in the UK and Japan), he convinced himself that it was one of those crystal ball-like gems clenched in the talons of a dragon, and that anything but a perfectly shiny and smooth peeling would doom not only his year but that of the entire world! The egg peeled perfectly and Y2K went off without a hitch.

題宝玉 2 辰年や玉子のはだか光匂ふ 敬愚

dragon year
the egg i peel shines
in a new light

*S*nake

穴蔵はみの年祝ふあした哉 道節 滑稽太平記
anagura wa mi-no-toshi iwau ashita kana dôsetsu 1592-1642
(hole-storage/vagina-as-for, snake's year [I/we] celebrate this morning/tomorrow!/'tis)

our safe holes
today we celebrate
the snake year

at dawn a toast
for our crypts as this is
the snake year

It was necessary for the people in major Japanese cities to keep many of their valuables underground (or have such a space to quickly store them in) because of the frequent fires owing to wooden houses and earthquakes. The snake had good underground connections, and was associated with prosperity. The first day of the year was supposed to be concerned with gods, not goods, but there is a parallel with the dark cave of the beginning. As a foreign reader of Japanese, I was first taken by the *ashita* which on New Year's may signify the first morning, yet generally means "tomorrow." If there is a B-side (現代人には、まず思いつかぬ、出鱈目読みの) reading, taking advantage of that *tomorrow,* it is this:

year of the snake

hole of wealth!
your health is celebrated
tomorrow!

Yes, one of the three meanings for the *anagura* or hole-storeroom is a woman's private part. The first-sex (called *hime-hajime,* or "first-princessing!") of the year was supposed to wait for the worldly second day, when the mice, too, celebrated their nuptials. The Japanese hardly needed Freud to tell them what snakes and holes were about. The *prosperity* link is evident in the way Edo Era stripteasers, who allegedly let snakes in and out of their "warehouses," were made up and named after Benten, the Goddess of Prosperity! Though snakes shed in the summer, the new clothing metaphor is irresistible:

年はみなりみなりもそよぐきそ始 宗清 大三
toshi wa mi nari minari mo soyogu kiso-hajime   sôsei 1697
(year-as-for snake=body is/becomes, snake=body is/becomes-also sway dress-first)

the year a snake
swaying back and forth
first dress-up

this year the snake
our bodies undulate
first dress-up

Sorry. The pun on the homophonic "body" and "snake" (*mi*) does not work in English. Another depends on a homophonic pun (*fuku*=clothing=wealth): *"Year of the Snake=body? / wearing layers of clothing=wealth / first dress-up"* (みの年や御ふく重ねてきそ始　輕賤　大三物 *mi no toshi ya o mifuku kasanete kiso-hajime* keisen 1697). Snakes may shed but they do not *add* layers, hence the poem bombs as natural science; but the *body* pulls off the trick in the original. Note that if you were to call a snake a "*mi*" in a context other than the New Year (or traditional Sinosphere time-keeping), no one would understand you. The same is true for the rat, the hare and the boar. While not all year animal names are pronounced differently from usual, the proper character for writing their names is always different.

Horse

乗始めや殊にめてたき午の年　千河 <small>玉かづら</small>
norizome ya koto ni medetaki muma no toshi senka -1706
(ride-start! especially joyous/auspicious horse's year)

my first ride
a special joy this year
of the horse

This poem is suspiciously simple, but I believe it. A more languid poem brings out a different horse, possibly alluding to the poet: *"Knowing the road / spring comes: year of / the old horse"* (道しりてくる春や老の午の年　定時　鷹筑波 *michi shirite kuru haru ya oi no mumanotoshi*　teiji 1642). I only wish it would English better. Unlike the case with year-mice, easily translatable haiku year-horses abound.

来る年の午つなぎかや門の松　正平 <small>鷹つくば</small>
kuru toshi no mumatsunagi ka ya kadonomatsu shôhei
(coming-year's horse-hitch? /!/: gate-pine/s 1642)

a horse hitch
for the coming year
our gate-pine

The *kadomatsu*, or "gate-pine" decoration will be given an entire chapter in Book III. Here, suffice it to note that the use of small boughs of pine (or the lengths of bamboo in which they are stood-up) for an imaginary hitch is not so outlandish as poem #3843 in the *Manyôshû* (8c), where a bonzes are insulted for nostril hair thick enough to hitch a pony to! Another *ku* has the God of Prosperity coming on horse-back this year (福の神をけふのせくるや午の年 良徳 えのこ *fukunokami o kyô nose kuru ya muma no toshi*　ryôtoku, 1633), where this extremely obese god is usually depicted on foot; another allegorizes the opening of a new calendar with taking a look into said horse's mouth to ascertain its age (口あけて午の年見る暦かな 作者不知　毛吹草 *kuchi akete muma no toshi miru koyomi kana*　anon 1645); yet another explains the solar spring's lateness this year by its failing to overtake the quick steed (はや午の年に追つく春もなし　作者不知　毛吹草 *hayauma no toshi ni oitsuku haru mo nashi*　anon 1645), and so forth.

Ram

未年着初めに紙子おもしろき　敬愚
hitsujidoshi kizome ni kamiko omoshiroki keigu
(ram/sheep-year, paper-robe wear-first-if interesting)

year of the goat

first dress
why not put on
a *kamiko*?

Finding no interesting year-ram/sheep/goat *ku*, I let keigu try. The *kamiko* is a paper robe which was usually worn as an undergarment or as cheap winter clothing, but could also be as attractive as the best kimono. The idea is to humor the new year, *hitsuji* being noted paper-eaters. (The stock market in Japan thinks the *Hour* of the Ram/Goat unlucky for that reason!). Since we do not associate rams or sheep so much with eating paper, I used "goat" though "ram" and "sheep" are far more common translations. *Later*, I found a similar Year of the Goat *ku* that Keigu had possibly read and forgot/plagiarized:

年もひつじ紙だくさんに試筆哉　重頼 えのこ
toshi mo hitsuji kami-dakusan ni shihitsu kana　shigeyori 1633
(year-too goat/ram paper-plenty-with test-brush/writing 'tis/!/?)

the year's a goat
using reams of paper
for brush practice

the year's a goat
what piles of paper go
for brush practice!

Another *ku* from the same collection: *"Revolving / The New Year comes round: / a ram cart"* (めぐりくる年はひつじの車哉　氏重 狗子 *megurikuru toshi wa hitsuji no kuruma kana* shijû 1633). While my first thought is *B(l)aah! B(l)aah!* this *ku*, saying something of the nature of time, was the *only* Year-goat in Shiki's *Categorical*. I'll bet a page of Shiki's manuscript was lost. Eaten by a goat, perhaps? (Now, the dangerous thing is a freeze for "All my memory / rests in my computer / Year of the Ram.")

~~~~~~

Monkey

日の顔やけさあかねさす申の年　政昌 狗
hi no kao ya kesa akane sasu saru no toshi　seishô 1633
(day's face! morning red-color gleam monkey's year)

year of the monkey

the sun's face
so red this morning:
hello, monkey!

Red with drink would not have any bad connotations in Japanese, but such is not the metaphor here. The Japanese monkey – actually, a macaque – has a bright red face. This is the second most (in)famously bad year-animal *ku*. The standard complaint is "it is like a poem a child would make." *Sure!* It also loses to the icicle slobber because the sun always comes up red. But, *must all haiku grow-up?* Is there no room for slobbering icicles, red-faced monkeys and, Mickey Mouse watches? Is it not better to introduce children to fun haiku so they learn to like the form, than to expose them to better poems that may, by boring them, inoculate them against haiku forever? [1]

~~~~~~

1. Inoculation. My words (more or less repeated from the Foreword) are aimed more at Japan than the West. In Japan, children are liable to be shown haiku like *"Mountain road coming-to / how sweet! / a violet!"* (Bashô), or *"Young sweetfish / two-fingers-long / head up river"* (Shiki) or, *"On a far mountain / the sun is shining / [beyond the] withered field"* (Kyoshi). Even granted that the originals are far better than my transliterations, the subject matter is just not right for children. Luckily, some of Issa's fun haiku are included, too. (Shiki's fun haiku, on the other hand, are rarely given, for convention has it that only Issa wrote that sort of thing). From the examples given in chapters 4 & 10, you can see that some Japanese children, thank goodness, did get turned on in spite of this.

犬の子に目なかけそ申の年始　幸治　えのこ
inu no ko ni me nakakeso saru no toshihajime   kôji 1633
(dog-child [dog]-on eye-not-set! monkey's year-start)

```
        you better not                              dogs are best
   see any dogs at the start                    not seen as the monkey
        of monkey's year                             year comes in
```

In the Sinosphere, the dog and monkey get along like the dog and cat. To see a dog and worse yet, call or pet one, might incur the anger of the New Year. Or so, I imagine, the poet pretended. As some parts of Japan are more heavily monkeyed than others, we get some geographical chuckles: *"This spring must / have come up from Shikoku: / Year of the Monkey"* (四國よりくる春なれや申の年　正重　いのこ *shikoku yori kuru haru nare ya saru no toshi* - seijû 1633). Shikoku is where Imo, the young monkey (macaque) who discovered how to wash yams by tossing them into the ocean, hailed from.[1]   There may be another monkey connection I have missed, for a *senryû* mentions a "monkey pillar" at a Shrine in Shikoku (四国はおろか護国寺に猿ばしら　柳多留 115　*shikoku wa* ☆＝猿橋も猿梨も解るが、猿柱は初めて。情報求む).

~~~~~~

Cock

初渓もけさは合点か酉の年　里山　明和二
hatsukei mo kesa wa gaten ka/ga tori no toshi   risan 1765
(first-crow[cockledoodledoo] even this-morning-as-for agree? cock-year)

cockledoodledoo!

```
      no one minds                                the first crow
  the first crow this dawn                    on this day is welcome
     year of the cock                             year of the cock
```

Generally, poets hated crowing and the dawn it announced for it meant the end of a night of loving. Perhaps, others who preferred sleep to work hated it, too; but this day was the exception: *"It's New Year's / and not a soul hates / the break of day"* (元日や誰もきらはぬ朝ほらけ　定清　真木柱 *ganjitsu ya dare mo kirawanu asaborake* sadakiyo 1697); and the fact it was the *Year of the Cock/Chicken* to boot made the crowing desirable.

~~~~~~

1. **Imo's Lesson.** Imo also demonstrated how primate societies learn. For a long time, only the other even younger monkeys copied her until, finally, a high-rank monkey deigned to try it, and the practice caught on like wild-fire. [**Rant**: This does not support any magical 100-monkey "critical mass" theory. Rather, it means that until the wealthy leaders of our society choose to demonstrate responsible lifestyles (rather than collect cars & airlines & constantly travel about promoting and even celebrating literally astronomical waste by all who can afford it (including the dead), as they have for the past half-century), we will not budge one inch from our murderous +suicidal course. Most of the 'conscientious' hippies of the 1960's and 70's were bound to copy the leadership and turn into smart-ass yuppies. At least those who sport coats and vote Republican *know* what they are. Supposedly hip *entrepreneurs* – what rich people out of real ideas are called – who would shoot tourists into space make me sick. There are limits to growth; but there are, evidently, no limits to greed, whether it be for consumption or fame.]

けふ立や春もひょこのとりの年　光有 毛吹草
kyô tatsu ya haru mo hyoko no tori no toshi　kôyû 1645
(today stands/arrives/!/& spring too chick's bird=chicken-year)

Year of the Cock

hatched today
the spring chicken must
be a chick!

The year-chicken in haiku is generally easily sexed as an adult, for what crows is a cock and what lays is a hen, but the chicks would be a problem if it mattered. Luckily, in poetry it does not. "Arrive/rise/stand" (*tatsu*) is homophonic with "hatch," so we have many freshly hatched Spring *ku*. The chicken may be called (pronounced) simply *tori*, or "bird." Some poets take advantage of the ambiguity. I suspect the above *ku* may be about a late solar spring. Here is one about the calendrical spring, i.e. the New Year occurring after an early solar spring: *"Spring again today / so are we now parroting / the year of the bird?"* (今朝の春は鸚鵡返しかとりの年 正章 *kesanoharu wa ômugaeshi ka tori no toshi*　masaakira 1633?). The "*gaeshi*=parroting" (mimicking) probably parrots "*kaeshi*=hatched/ing." Here is a far better *ku*.

鳳凰も出よのとけき鳥の年　貞徳 えのこ
hôô mo ideyo nodokeki tori no toshi　teitoku 1570 -1653
(phoenix too, appear[positive imperative] calm/balmy/halcyon, bird-year)

phoenix, you too
show! this halcyon day
year of the bird

phoenixes, too
appear in this peaceful
year of the bird

what a serene
year of the bird – i almost
expect a phoenix

Tori is written with the character for "bird" in the version I found. It would be better to have it in the phonetic syllabary so as to maintain the ambiguity. Note that the *ku* is not *merely* nominal. Teitoku brings out the preternatural calm sometimes experienced in early spring. I first expressed this by adding a *cock-a-doodle-doo!* as a title, but on second thought decided it too much to assume roosters crowing brought out the silence in someone else's poem. Moreover, the Year Animals are theoretically the prime animal of their type, king of the tribe. Thus, we have a Tiger rather than house-cat and Dragon rather than the red snapper (though it is hard to say what Rabbits or Rats or Rams rule). A magical Phoenix might indeed be a far better choice than the rooster/chicken, though an old Chinese nursery rhyme asks *"Who is the lord that can open a thousand doors with one call?"* and the answer is *the mighty rooster*. Note, however, that the Chinese Phoenix, like the Chinese dragon (connected with water, not fire), differs from the Occidental one. It was – or, they were – an immortal chimera with a rooster's beak, crest and waddle, a fishy tail and more strange and beautifully colored stuff in between that lived on the fruit of bamboo (whatever that is!) and presaged the birth of an Imperial prince. No one imagined them burning up and rising fiery-eyed out of ashes, so, they are not ideal symbols of rebirth, which is good, here, for it would betray the delicacy of Teitoku's *ku*.

Dog

東よりござるべいかの犬のとし 由廷 毛吹草
higashi yori gozaru bei ka no inu no toshi   yûtei 1645
(east-from are [+polite] puppy[=vernac. emph.] dog-year)

      and hailing   *annus canis*
from the east we have   a red-eyed puppy harks
      the year-dog   from the east

The charming mix of the polite "to be" *gozaru* with the rustic emphatic *bei* does not translate. Remembering the way dogs, like talking drums, telegraph events ahead at 625 mph (they always beat the train), my first reading of the poem was *"Yessir, it is / out there to the east / that dog year."* Of course, the earth spins a bit too fast for that to work on flat ground, but if one is up in the mountains . . . Then, I came to conclude – with no proof whatsoever – the poet was mimicking the start of a dog-sumo match, after which I learned a *beika* (also *beka, bekainu,* etc.) means "puppy" *and,* according to one etymology, it should mean *a dog with red eyes.* That matches the morning sun, doesn't it?

しめ縄や春をもくゝる戌の年 無記名 狗
shimenawa ya haru o mo kukuru inu no toshi   anon. 1633
([thick braided straw] festoon: spring, too, slips through dog's year)

year of the dog

      canine spring   charmed hoop
slips neatly through   of health even spring
   a new festoon   slips through

Variable diameter (end-small middle-thick) spiral rice-straw rope festoons encircle sacred Shinto buildings and huge trees. They metaphysically protect the space and keep people from getting too close and damaging what is precious. The word used for these festoons, *shimenawa,* is homophonic for a lanyard or, in the case of dogs, a leash with a loop on the end. Moreover, dogs in Japan are identified with their ability to tunnel through hedges and whatnot, which is expressed perfectly by the verb *kukuru* (or, *kuguru*). I first imagined the Dog-year/Year-dog coming up to pay his respects by lifting a leg on what is sacred. Another *ku* has the dog messing up the snow remaining from the previous year (残る雪やけさけしかくる犬の年 一葉子 鷹づくば *nokoru yuki ya kesa keshikakuru inu no toshi*   ichiyôshi 1642), perhaps the same way, for the last snow tends to lie by the shaded base of trees. Still, I think the second reading of *shimenawa* as hoop-festoons passed through for good health the better one. Most year-dog haiku do not translate because they pun on a verb homophone of dog (*inu*) meaning "is not" or "not present." Eg. "The bird [*i.e.,* the last Year of the Chicken] / has flown and from this morning / is *not* = *dog*-year" (とりははや立てけさより戌の年　良継　鷹筑波？ *tori wa haya tate kesa yori inu no toshi*   ryôkei 1642).

~~~~~~

1. Speaking of what is not, Keigu was surprised *not* to find these *ku:* "Advice to the World" // *Howl out / at the new born sun / of the dog!* (戌年の勧め・吠えるのも微笑ましいぞ犬初日 *"inu-doshi-no susume" hoeru no mo hohoemashii zo inu hatsuhi*). ("First Walk" // *Barked at: / Damn! You think you / own the year?* (初散歩・吠えられて我が物顔か犬の年 *hoerarete wagamonogao ka inu-no-toshi*), *It's my year! / A shit-eating look on / Tray's face* (老犬の春・おらが年といわんばかりも犬の面 *"rôken no haru" oragatoshi to iwan bakkari mo inu no tsura*). *Good luck? / Stepping on dog shit / this Year of the Dog* (幸運かな戌年に踏む犬の糞 *kôun kana inudoshi ni fumu inu no fun*).

狼も上下で出よ戌の春 一茶
ôkami mo kamishimo de ideyo inu no haru issa -1827
(wolf/wolves too, formal-clothing-with/in come-out, dog-spring)

you wolves, too
put on your best tails!
it's canine spring

wolves, you, too,
put on your tails and show
for the dog year

This is the same Issa who shivered just to *see* wolf shit, according to one of his better known haiku. Evidently, the idea of a canine family including both wolves and dogs was around in Issa's time.

△ I found one sad Dog Year *ku* in Katô Ikuya's *City Well Cool* (in the chapter by the same name : 市井風流) by someone in the entertainment world, maybe a story-teller and pulp-fiction writer (Some of Katô's prose is too fine for me to follow), called Taisui (台水) that goes like this: *"It's New Year's: / This year, too, at our place / A Dog Year!"* (元日や今年も宅に戌の年 台水 *ganjitsu ya kotoshi mo taku ni inu no toshi*). I believe it is what I would call a *kyôku*, or crazy-verse, punning on the idiom "Like a dog grown old" (*inu no toshiyotta yô*) meaning *slowing down, getting old to no profit or purpose whatsoever*. The year before was evidently one where bad went to worse. Taisui had it down: if he lived a dog's life, he would soon die a dog's death – for he is said to have "collapsed on the road and vanished without anyone noticing." This would be in the early 20c.

Boar

亥のとしに 冬の亥の子そだちてくるやけふの春 信安 鷹つくば
fuyu no inoko sodachite kuru ya kyô-no-haru shinan [nobuyasu?] 1642
(year-of-boar-on // winter's boar-child/ren raising comes: today's spring)

year of the boar

the boars bring
their winter litter round!
it's spring today

Even without the coincidence, this is heart-warming for anyone who has seen a wild animal bringing its young along on their first scavenging expedition. My heart thumped aloud to see coon-faced foxes (*tanuki*) bring by their pups to show me to them or them to me for the first time. Our children, too, have a first time out but, unable to walk, they are not as ready to appreciate it as the rambunctious baby babirusa. My respondent adds that the youngsters are "spotted and cute." The haiku is low key enough, but what a party that spring day must have been! The *ku* is so good, the boars are through.

Most of the best year-animal haiku, *i.e.*, those that are strong enough to stand on their own merits regardless of the year they were composed, do not come right out and say what they are about. With nominal coincidence not thought highly of today, annotators who are remarkably good at finding earlier poems that are alluded to and, depending on the poet, investigating their lives and matching the circumstance to the poem, do not check the historical tables to see if these *potential* animal haiku do indeed match their year. So these undiscovered year-animal *ku* remain unnoticed here and there within other themes. Or, that is my belief, based on experience sufficient to convince me, but not, perhaps, scholars, all of whom would appear to hail from Missouri.[1]

閑古鳥

One Strange Bird

かんことりの卵かへすらん花の春 大江丸 俳諧袋
kankotori no tamago kaesuran hana no haru oemaru 1719-1805
(cuckoo/snark/nothing-doing's egg/s hatch-do/will! flowery-spring)

Year of the Kankotori?

a splendid spring	a splendid spring
this is when they hatch	my bird, the do-nothing
slow-time birds	already hatching

The *kankodori* is confidently translated by some as a "lesser cuckoo." Personally, I see it as one of the small grey doves that appear when the world is quiet. The Japanese themselves argue about its identity as a bird, but no one doubts its existence as a literary conceit. It stands for slow times off the beaten path, for miserable poverty or desired melancholy and people fiddling time away for lack of something better to do than, say, compose haiku. For the most part, they appear in the summer, when the water-saturated heat stills all but the most vigorous of the working population, but they pop up in all seasons. You will get no more example *ku* here for I hope to do a whole book on this fascinating creature, who, like all cuckoos, lays its eggs in other's nests; I put the *ku* in this chapter, for I bet it was written for the Year of the Cock/Bird. If Teitoku had a halcyon New Year call up the mythical Phoenix, this poet has it bear the legendary *kankodori*. In doing so, he out-haikai's Mr. Haikai, for this little bird includes a measure of something missing from the large one: the best part of wit, self-deprecation.

---

1. Latent Year Animals? Or *"Show me!"* It would be interesting for a Japanese-reading haiku lover to gather a large collection of New Year, early-spring and late-winter *ku* with any of the twelve animals that do not explicitly mention the New Year (or New Year's Day, First Sun Rise, etc.) in the poem or the preface, if it has one; and, then, check those that may be dated to see what percent of them match their year, or, when the content suggests it, the year before or after. I expect that the results will be far above chance (1 in 12). Of the dozen or so I checked, I recall getting more than half right, but only the most recent comes to mind. In that case, I wrote the group that annotated the work of Hajin (The famous poet Buson's teacher) and asked what might be the animal year when he wrote an end-of-the-year *ku* on a tight-roping monkey (一とせも暮たり猿の縄わたり 巴人 – *hito tose mo kuretari saru no tsunawatari* hajin (1672-1742), a perfect metaphor for the slow end of a difficult year for the poet and true to haiku realism, for the monkey act came to town and performed this trick at the time of the year. *Sure enough, it was* the Year of the Monkey, and the Kanôe monkey (We have skipped the fact that each year-animal comes in 10 types!), at that. This monkey signifies a state of *waiting and being held in suspense*. Now *that* is poetic synchronicity for you!. Hajin's *ku* already had two obvious layers, with this, it gained a third (or, fourth, if we include possible allusions to other *ku!*) 様々の句の内容に潜まれた年の動物＝十二支＝狩りの研究調査を、誰かしないか？

初日の出
hatsu-hinode

四 4

UP AND ADAM!

春立や誰も人よりさきへ起き 鬼つら
haru tatsu ya dare mo hito yori saki e oki   onitsura -1738
(spring comes: everyone others more-than early rise)

up and shine!

<table>
<tr><td>spring is here
and everyone wakes faster
than the other</td><td>the spring is here
all of us would awaken
before each other</td></tr>
</table>

My first translation was more logical: "and everyone *would* wake faster / than his neighbor." *Would*, meaning "intends to," or "wants to." But *this* is not just any dawn. It is the dawn of time. Relativity does not apply. The new world is magical, like that in the eyes of a lover. As strange as the original's logic may seem, Onitsura has it right. *Exactly*. Still, there are exceptions:

我愚雀に起つ初あした 桃水 大三物
ware oroka suzume ni okitsu hatsu ashita   tôsui 1697
(i [am] foolish sparrows-with awaken first morning)

foolish me
rising with the sparrows
on the first

Or, "woken *by* the sparrows." This is an elegant way to describe sleeping-in. Unlike the rooster or the crow, the sparrows aren't chipper until warmed up by the sun. The distress at missing sunrise is balanced by the magical warmth and quiet of a morning when sparrow chatter stands out.

春立やねらるゝといふ人もある 巣枝 俳諧五百
haru tatsu ya neraruru to iu hito mo aru   sôshi 19c?
(spring/ny!/: sleep-can [+attrib] says person/people also is/are)

<table>
<tr><td>new year dawns
and there are men who say
they can sleep</td><td>here comes spring!
to think there are men who
would rather sleep</td></tr>
</table>

Is the poet a man of robust constitution *(i.e.,* blessed with good absorption and excess energy), genuinely surprised to find people who think of New Year's Day as a good opportunity to sleep?

長寝士に蕣見せよ初朝　白英 大三物
naganeshi ni asagao miseyo hatsu ashita hakuei 1697
(long-sleep-warrior-to morning-glory show-let's-first-morning)

on the first day
show this slumber-knight
your morning glory!

From the neologism (?) *"long-sleep warrior,"* we know the poet generally misses the morning glory, but it is an early-fall flower, not found in the New Year season. I think the *ku* plays on Autumn *ku* about rising early enough to see the flower while actually alluding to the sun. Morning Glory is morning *face* in Japanese. If I read correctly, the *ku* jokes with the cloud-hidden sun: *"Today's your chance to show the slow-riser what you've got! Come on out!"* But, it is remotely possible the poem is third-person and the idea is that someone who regularly sleeps-in would not know it was the wrong season. Or, we can imagine a joke, showing the late-riser a painting of the morning glory or one of its metaphorical doubles – everything from a type of urinal to a type of cracker (today, anyway) – in Japanese.

朝起の徳や今年の初日の出　素十 玉かづら
asaoki no toku ya kotoshi no hatsuhinode sôtô 1751
(morning-waking-virtue:/!/? this year's first sunrise)

the virtue of
waking early: the year's
first sunrise

天地にあやまり初の朝寝哉　雅因 新選
ametsuchi ni ayamari-zome[or *-hatsu*]*no asane kana* gain 1773
(heaven-earth-in mistake/misstep-start's/first morning-sleep!/?/'tis)

the first slip-up   start of creation
on heaven and earth   call my sleeping-in
my sleeping in   a first misstep

Is the idea of the first *ku* that waking early is a virtue and he was rewarded on the first day this year when the sun also rose bright and early? The hyperbolic confession of the second poet is more amusing, and the concrete detail in the next *ku* so funny I hope it will not (mistakenly) be called a *senryû*!

春は曙己鼾に覚めてけり　正隆 失出典
haru wa ake[akebono?] ☆ onoga ibiki ni sametekeri masataka
(spring-as-for/the dawn/dawns[v.] own-snore/s-as/by waking[+emph.])

spring dawns   the best of spring
i am awakened by   is the dawn: i get up to
my own snores   my own snores

That men should sleep-in is not surprising. Common folk throughout the Sinosphere, worked hard and, naturally, were tired. Nobles and samurai (including most poets) traditionally were night owls. Luis Frois's multi-volume History of the Church in Japan, written in the late-16c, is full of anecdotes about noble Japanese tiring out clergy by visiting at midnight and keeping them up all night talking (For Japanese night-owl detail, see *Topsy-turvy 1585* item 13-25). ☆The character 曙 generally means, *the dawn, akebono*. Since that word seems too long, I wonder if it is oddly used for *ake* 明け, *to dawn* or *begin*.

はつ空や寝まきながらに生れけり 素堂
hatsuzora ya nemaki nagara ni umarekeri sodô 1641-1716
(first sky!/: nightrobe/nightdress-while born[+emphatic])

the first sky
wearing our nightdress
as it is born

the first sky
we watch the birth
in nightdress

むく起や蒲団の産しけさの春 夕歩 大三
mukuoki ya futon no umishi kesa no haru yûho 1697
(facing-waking: futon-born morning's spring)

springing up
full-born from the futon
the new year

Could the poet conflate himself with the New Year? The bright red sun *does* resemble the bloody head of a new-born. *Muku-oki*, not Englishable in a word, means *jumping up and flying out to immediately meet someone or do something*. I also imagine the *futon* left on the *tatami* with a vaginal hole somewhat like a cocoon left by a butterfly, while *also* wondering if the *futon* that the First-Sun=New-Year's -Day=Spring popped out of was a snowy mountain, for there are many such *futon*=mountains in haiku.

東山を眺望して嵐雪を思ふ
蒲団着て寝て居る上へ初日哉 其柳
futon kite neteiru ue e hatsuhi kana kiryû 1801 夢の猪名野
(futon-wearing-sleeping-above-to first-sun!/?/'tis)

the first sun
upon the futon-clad
sleeping man

falling asleep
in a futon upon which
the sun rises

the first sun
upon the futon i wear
still asleep

This is prefaced *"Gazing out upon East Mountain, thinking of Ransetsu."* Because the temperature rise lags the sun's return by a month or so, the Japanese New Year fell in the coldest part of the year. Snow was not only found on the mountain tops. This says it all: *"In bed, inside / I worship the Sun: / night snow"* (内に寝て天道拝む夜の雪 此筋 *uchi ni nete tentô o ogamu yoru no yuki* shikin -1735). People in Japan used their clothing for covers before they developed quilts for sleeping which had sleeves (If you wish to reading in bed in a cold house today, you must put leg warmers on your arms.) We cannot tell if the experience is first-person (the default reading for Kiryû's *ku*) or third-person, in which case it might well allude to Ransetsu (-1707), whose following *ku* was famous: *"East mountain / the form of one sleeping / in his futon"* (蒲団着て寝たる姿や東山 嵐雪 *futon kite netaru sugata ya higashiyama*).

元日と思ひまゝのひるね哉 蘭更
ganjitsu to omoinomama no hirune kana   rankô -1798
(original-day and/is think/wish-as-is afternoon-sleep[nap] 'tis/!/?)

new year's?
the day we are free
to take a nap

on new year's
we can take our naps
as we please

元日は誰に問ても宵寝哉 都貢 たてなみ
ganjitsu wa dare ni toute mo yoine kana   tokô 18c?19c?
(new year's day-as-for, who-to ask even evening-sleep 'tis)

new year's day
everyone i ask goes
to bed early

I suspect that half the magic of the New Year sunrise came from the fact that many if not most people never went to sleep, or, if they did, slept so little before being roused they were but half-awake. After sunrise, predictably, they are tired and either nap during the day or go to sleep early.

元日は豆腐屋が世の朝寝哉 露艶 第三物
ganjitsu wa tofuya ga yo no asane kana   roen 1697
(first-day-as-for, tofu-stores/makers' world's morning sleep!)

new year's day
the *tôfuya* has it made!
sleeping in

new year's day
i sleep while all the world
makes *tôfu*

I cannot say *tôfu*-man, for unlike our "ice-man" and "milk-man," the profession of making and selling *tôfu* was not a monopoly of one sex. English has *bakers* and *butchers* and *grocers*, but *tofuers?* No way! So, I use the Japanese term, as is. Before refrigeration, bean curd did not keep, so the *tôfuya* began work before dawn. On this day alone, they could, and did – or so the poet imagines – sleep in. The 3rd person seems *senryû*, but the grammar favors the first reading over the second, where *tôfu* is hay.

げにも春寝過ごしぬれど初日影 太祇 再現
ge ni mo haru nesugoshi nuredo hatsuhikage   taigi 1709-72
(really-even spring: sleep-in but [?] first-sun/sunshine)

quick dawn

spring's for real
the first sun shows up
while i sleep-in

sure is spring
i just keep in bed but
the first sun

There is another sleepy conceit that has nothing to do with the New Year itself. Spring, with its shortening nights and lengthening days, hosted the "sleep-demon" (*suima*), or sand-man. If I read Taigi correctly, he is quipping that Spring is not only a synonym for the New Year but *acts the season*, as his drowsiness proves (Even today, "drowsiness" is a proper spring theme). In the next *ku*, Buson may say the same in a more subtle way:

寝ごゝろやいづちともなく春は来ぬ 蕪村
negokoro ya izuchi to mo naku haru wa kinu bûson 1715-83
(sleepy-mind/feeling! wherence-even-not spring-as-for comes)

dawn of the new year

lying a-bed
some way i just know
spring's here

feeling spring
enter from somewhere
as i awaken

Negokoro means feelings/inklings experienced while you sleep, or lie in bed half-asleep. The perfect translation for the middle-seven syllabets *"from* nowhere in particular" was too long to use, so I made loose sense-translations. As the Japanese annotators write, the *ku* describes the delicious feeling of being half in dreamland as a spring day – either New Year's or Solar Spring – gently dawns.

sweet drowsiness!
spring is surely here
inside with me

There are many similar *ku*: *"Whether I stay / in bed or get up today / Spring's spring"* (= actually, the last 5 syllabets translate *"flower= gorgeous/celebratory spring"* 寝て居よが起て居ようが花の春 西吟 古選 *neteiyo ga okiteiyô ga hana no haru* saigin 1763); *"Lying in bed / My mind is still / of the New Year* (= *kokoro* could also be *heart* or *soul* ねころんでゐるゝも正月心かな 寄柱 文久五百題 *nekorondeiruru mo shôgatsugokoro kana* kijû mid-19c).   Similar rhetoric may be found for feeling the full-moon indoors on a rainy night.

予の朝寝礼者は春を告にけり 可不
yo no asane reisha wa haru o tsugenikeri   kafu 大三物 1697
(i/my morning-sleep greeters/callers-as-for, spring [obj]announced[+fin.])

i sleep-in
spring is announced
by callers

i sleep-in
and callers bring news
of the spring

This *ku* is found with the *reisha,* callers bringing New Year's greetings, in Shiki's *Categorical.* The bold first person *yo* and the callers *transmitting* (*tsuge*) the news to the poet makes what could be a sick-bed situation sound like a life of luxury.

日を人に問ふ正月となりにけり 茶静
hi o hito ni tou shôgatsu to narinikeri sasei 三日月集 1730
(sun/day[obj] person-to ask ny-into becomes[+finality])

this new year
a stay-in-and-ask-others
about-it day!

it turned out to be
an ask-others-about-it
New Year's Day

This is more subdued. Students of early modern haiku might recall the bedridden Shiki experiencing snowfall via reports from others. At first, I misread, imagining a recluse who lost track of time: *"Asking others / what day it was, it was / the New Year!"* but the grammar of the original disallows that reading. The "it" includes the sunrise and the weather that follows, which was thought to prognosticate the year to come. Were it not for the hint of negativity in the ~*nikeri* ending, the *ku* might also have meant this:

friend of the sun

    it's new year's   the time we ask
when we ask each other   about the health of the sun
    how the sun is   new year's here

1 of the 13 etymologies for *hito* (person) given by my OJD is, after all, *hi-no-tomo*, "friend of the sun." I *wish* I could believe in my translations right or wrong; but I lack Fitzgerald's *cojones* and extravagant readings went out with the last century, so, regretfully, I must agree with *haiyû* Tenki that if anyone's health is in question, it is the poet's and the "friend of the sun" reading is purely my invention.

霞む日も寝正月かよ山の家　一茶
kasumu hi mo neshôgatsu ka yo yama no ie　issa -1827
(misting sun, too, sleeping-new-year [+emph]! mountain house)

a sleeping new year

    the misty sun   mountain hut
also lies abed today   does the misty sun, too
    mountain hut   stay in bed?

There is a minor heading in modern *saijiki* called "sleeping-new-year" (*ne-shogatsu*). I assume the 70 and 80 hour work-weeks of 20c Japan are the cause of it, but the above haiku by Issa is the earliest instance of the word I know. Thoreau's *Journal* has some fine passages about the sublimity of life up in the rarified air of the misty mountains where one cannot tell dawn from dusk. Issa is not *that* philosophical.[1] He just notes that, in the mountains, there is liable to be haze over the sun, and a hermit, not having to answer to society, may sleep in. Perhaps, Issa New Yeared in such a hut. This may be a day for paying our respects to the sun, but *if the sun can sleep,* he asks, *can't I?* A slightly older *ku*, (facetiously) zoomorphizes the poet's digs more clearly than Issa did, yet remains superbly real:

元日も二日も眠き庵かな　沙門 大三物
ganjitsu mo futsuka mo nemuki iori kana　samon 1697
(new year's day and second-day, too, sleepy studio/hut!/'tis)

on new year's
the next day, too
my sleepy hut

By real, I mean that it captures the essence of what sleep-deprivation does to someone who is not among the lucky people with good digestion+absorption and, hence, energy to burn. The master's second day *ku*, reflecting heavy partying (and drinking) back with his countrymen, seems childish by comparison:

二日にもぬかりはせじな花の春　芭蕉
futsuka ni mo nukari wa sejina hananoharu　bashô -1594
(second-day-on/for-also, blunder/slip-up-as-for do-not's blossom-spring)

    on day two   on the second, too
i'd not slip up again   i'd better not botch it
    precious spring   this new year

1. Metaphysical Eternity. Issa may not have been as obvious a metaphysician (philosopher) as Thoreau, but some Japanese poets *were*. Here is a *ku* that would have made perfect sense to Emerson and his transcendentalists: *"The country's Spring / Mount Fuji at the dawn / of eternity"* (國の春不二は常世の朝朗 可都里 発句大業 *kuni no haru fuji wa jôyo no asaborake* katori -1817.) The word for "dawn" used here is one of many and it has a particularly bright but hazy quality. What I am forced to English as "eternity" is actually *"normal/regular/constant* world" (as opposed to the *impermanent & irregular* place we live). We generally call it "the other world" or "heaven," but neither word works *here*. The same 常= *"normal/regular/constant"* is pegged onto "road/way" to signify *the* road/way, or *Tao*. To grasp the challenge this simple word creates for translation and the ways it may be re-created in English, examine my scores of translations of the first six characters of the *Tao Te Ching* (4c? 5c? 6c?), *below*. The idea for doing it came from Alan Watts. In his autobiography, *Cloud-hidden, Whereabouts Unknown*, he claims there are at least eighty translations for the first six characters of this tract usually attributed to Lao Tzu's/Tse,

「道・可・道・非・常・道」 『道徳経』by 老子？
way-can-way-not-regular-way

The fifth Chinese character is the problematic "regular" that, in contrast to the transient world of appearances, becomes "eternal." For example, our *Rock of Ages* turns into a "*regular*-rock" – *tokiwa* in Japanese pronunciation.) Chinese is so skeletal the sentences may be fleshed out pretty much as we please. Watts found such freedom exhilarating. While he provided only a score of examples, "eighty" in the Sinosphere means *many*, so he can't be faulted on quantity. But most of his translations are too conservative to show the full potential of what I call *paraversing* and the charm of the poetic paraverse. Here are seven translations Watts introduced, including the best six and one bad example:

The Way that can be described is not the eternal Way.
The Course that can be discoursed is not the eternal Course.
The Go that can be gone is an emergency go.
The way that can be weighed is not the regular Way.
The flow that can be followed is not the real Flow.
Energy which is energetic is not true energy.
Force forced isn't force.

The first is straightforward and boring. The second, clever, but the fancy verb too far from the style of the original. The third is horrendous. The last three Chinese characters, as a *word* in modern Chinese and Japanese, can mean "emergency exit," but the pun does not English and the verb *go* does not noun well. The "weighed" is good pun. If "regular" were changed to "Real" the translation would *almost* make it; too bad "weighed" is always used in set phrases, like "weighed the possibilities," and sounds unnatural here. The "flow" is not bad, but a flow is not "followed." I agree about "energetic" "energy" but these polysyllabic words betray the simplicity of the Way. *Force?* The metaphor is a bit forced, and would be even if updated to: "Empowered power isn't power."

Watts and other translators do not take enough advantage of *our* way, The Way of English, where definitive articles, italics and capitalization may signify not only proper nouns but the sacred nature of something. Look at what a simple *the* can do:

The Way that can be described is not *the* Way.
The discoursable course is not *the* course.

We cannot match the original. Chinese is too compact for us. *If brevity is wit, we lack it.* But, we can achieve parity of sorts, by following the rhymes and rhythms of our tongue, and, most important, not forgetting to use rhetorical devices Chinese lacks. (☆With Japanese, English is not disadvantaged length-wise, but loses elsewhere, so the same advice holds true). Some of my paraverses:

Out of the way of ways is the Way.
Give way to all ways: that's the Way!

No way is the Way of Ways.
The Way of Ways is never *a* way.
Wayless is the Way of Ways.
The Way is not *this* way or *that*.
The Way is all ways and none.

The way you say is not *the* Way!
All ways lie in the way of the Way!
No ways lie in the way of the Way!
The Way of Ways lies out of the way.

No way is a way to The Way.
No way is the way to The Way.
The Way is away from any way.
To choose a way is to lose the way.

There is no way to find the Way.
All ways stray from the Way that stays.
All ways stray from Always
To take a way is to lose It.
All ways lead away from The Way.
All ways never lead to Always.
Forget all ways to find Always.
All ways lost means always found!
No way but The Way is all ways.
No way is Always.
No way is always the Way.
The Way is *always* – all ways are not.
The Way of Always, all ways is not.
All ways are not the Way of Ways.
The Way of Ways is weigh enough!
[a nautical term for "put up your oars"]
The Way is every which way but.

Only the Way is not in the way.
Get out of the way, if you would find It!

It has been about ten years since I did this exercise in what might be called exhaustive paraversing; and I can still remember the pleasure it gave me. I am not one to sit and meditate (unless composing haiku is so considered), but I feel like I meditated on that first line of the Tao and came away refreshed. Paraversing taught me how important it is to stick with the Way of our native tongue in order to gain a deeper understanding of what is written in another one. These examples will be cut from the second edition of this book. They link to the paraversing page of paraverse.org.

~~~~~~

The year after his sleepy sun, Issa slept-in again. Perhaps embarrassed about his anthropomorphic treatment of the sun (recall his Bashôite rant I quoted in the introduction of this book?) the previous year, he wrote a far plainer *ku*: *"New Year's day / Slept clean through it / mountain hut"* (正月を寝てしまひけり山の家 *shôgatsu o neteshimaikeri yama no ie*). We cannot tell if Issa, his hut (as per Samon's above *ku*), or all in his hut, sleeps. The year after *that*, Issa is back to his metaphysics, using a homophonic pun on plum, the first blossom, which he views, and birthing (both *ume*) to justify lying on his back (正月を寝て見る梅でありしよな 一茶 *shôgatsu o netemiru ume de arisho na*)! The plum is the calendar blossom – viewed as a natural alternate for our written one – and, here, may suggest a slangy *"Isn't this (a sleeping new year) great!"* (*umai*→*ume!*) Finally, at age 60, the year we are said to return to our original foolishness (see ch 11), Issa came up with his final, probably best, sleeping-New-Year poem:

正月やごろりと寝たるとっとき着 一茶 文政五
shôgatsu ya gorori to netaru tottokigi   issa 1822
(new year's! rolling about sleeping reserved-clothing)

semper paratus dormantum

it's new year's i slumber all day in holiday dress	new year's day i put on festive dress & slept it away

Well-prepared sloth. Issa, carefully dressed up to pay homage to the sun he would disrespect! Other poets slept-in or slept all day, but only Issa was so cheerful about it (Pardon my fake Latin). The next example of the season- word *neshôgatsu* (first found in Issa's earlier *ku*) I have seen awaits Chôi (1886-1930): "When the pine / raises its voice, how *wabishi* / a sleep-new-year!" (松風のつのればわび（わび？）し寝正月 蝶衣 *matsukaze no tsunoreba wabishi neshôgatsu*). I suppose *wabishi* here is somewhere between the "high lonesome" sound of bluegrass and dreary winter rain. This *ku* was written after the Gregorian calendar was adopted by Japan and the New Year moved to a time colder for being far from Spring's promise – i.e., January 1 – when no one in their right mind would *want* to get up early.

初日の出おがみたいけどおきられぬ 神保和成
hatsuhinode ogamitai kedo okirarenu   jinbô kazunari (tokyo)
(first sun-rise: worship/[pay] reverence/witness-want [to] but, wake-cannot)

first sun-rise
i would pay my respect
but slept in!

初日の出今年こそはといつも言う 小田晃子 *hatsuhinode kotoshi koso wa to itsumo iu* oda akiko (ôwake) (first sun-rise: this year at-last / more-than-ever , [i?we?] always say)	うるさいな正月ぐらいねむらせて 南佳子 *urusai na shôgatsu gurai nemurasete* minami kako (ôwake) (bother [me] not! new year's at-least sleep-allow!)
the first sun-rise like always, i say, this year i will do it!	leave me alone! can't i sleep in at least new year's day!

初日の出みんなそろってまいってる　松村美穂
hatsuhinode minna sorotte maitteru   matsumura miho (ôwake)
(first sun-rise: all together [are] dumbfounded/exhausted/saddened)

      first sunrise　　　　　　　　　　　　　　　the first sunrise
     everyone here　　　　　　　　　　　　　all of us who see it
       is beat!　　　　　　　　　　　　　　　　　overwhelmed

What did you think of the last four haiku? I did not want to give away the game too early by dating the names. All are *by children*, respectively: Jinbô Kazunari, 5th grade; Oda Kyôko, 6th grade; Minami Yoshiko, 4th grade; Matsumura Miho, 4th grade (*Kodomo Haiku Saijiki* (Kagyûsha: 1997)). In Japanese, some verb conjugations seem childish – and haiku tends to have particularly sophisticated conjugations – but in English this is not so obvious so the *ku* stand or fall on their content. The second and fourth *ku* are ambiguous. We do not know if they concern the difficulty of waking up early after an exhausting end of the year (and New Year's Eve television) or not. The second might concern New Year's resolutions and the fourth might mean that everyone got up early only to find the sun slept in or, more likely, that it was incredibly spectacular. The third unknowingly echoes an old *ku*:

元日やま一日あらはひるねせん　樨柯
ganjitsu ya ma ichinichi araba hirune sen   saika 1784-1840
(new-year's day: whole one day have-if day-nap do-will)

       it's new year's!
     i have a whole day
       time to nap

The only difference between Saika and Minami – besides the adult's freedom to decide – is that Saika knows that staying up all night or getting up early left him a longer day for a napping! But most adults have never been free. Someone (spouse, parents, employers) won't allow it. An earlier *senryû* made it clear that sleeping-in was a perk of being a big shot. My respondent favors the second reading.

寝て年を聞ぬ程にぞ成に鳬　武玉川 四編
nete toshi o kikinu[kikanu?] hodo ni zo narinikeri   mutamagawa 1752
(sleeping [new]year[obj] hear/listen[-not?] extent[+emphatic] become [+finality])

   becoming someone　　　　　　　　　　　becoming someone
enough to stay in bed and　　　　　　　enough to sleep all day and
  hear of the new year　　　　　　　　　　　ignore the new year

落付て春と知たる朝寝哉　桂双　類聚
ochitsuite haru to shiritaru asane kana   keisô 1807
(calmly/relaxed spring [that it is] knowing/learning morning-sleep 'tis/!)

    fully composed　　　　　　　　　　　　calmly knowing
knowing it is the spring　　　　　　　the spring came, i take
   that's sleeping-in　　　　　　　　　　　a morning nap

I never tire of poems about *not* starting the year right, though the second *ku* may not be one such, for the poet may have participated in dawn rituals and his calm is, itself, proper to the season.

十色程鐘かきこえて明の春 吟江 心の花
toiro hodo kane ga kikoete akenoharu   ginkô 1776
(ten-color-amount/about bells hear-can dawn's spring/ny)

      we can hear   the first dawn
  about ten bell colors   i hear the timbre of
      spring dawn   a dozen bells

"Color" can mean "tone" or *timbre* in Japanese. I like that, hence the first, direct translation. There is an old candy with ten colors (*toiro-ame*). It does not literally boast *that* diverse a hue. After all, who sees more than seven colors in the rainbow? But a connoisseur is said to be able to make out that many *flavors*. Because Kyôto is ringed by temples, I first thought of it. That is unlikely, for the national government only permitted one time-keeping bell in Kyôto (likewise for Ôsaka and Nagoya). Edo, where *nine* time-bells were officially allowed and a few others on the hilly outskirts winked at, is more likely, though it is possible other temples were allowed to ring bells on holidays. A much more famous poem by Kikaku claimed there was *not a day a (temple) bell was not sold in the Edo spring*. This speaks to the general prosperity of what was the world's largest city, but also reminds us of the fact that there was money involved in bells, whether it was the donations made at temples by people who rang them when they prayed, the taxes the time-tellers were permitted to take from those who lived within hearing range of the temple or the money they themselves paid for the monopoly right.

にっこりと鐘聞く春の旦哉 素外 句鑑
nikkori to kane kiku haru no ashita kana   sogai 1717-1809
(smile/grin-with bell hear spring's dawn)

      we hear bells   new year
  and smile at the dawn   the matin bells make
     of the spring   us smile

Sleep-proud people, farmers, and lovers reluctant to part all *hate* to hear the matins. But, on this day, they so not scowl, for the bells are welcome. They bring the ear into the new year. The psychological mimesis for smiling, *nikkori,* has a bright ring to it and even includes a touch of the sun (*ni* as in *nippon*).

柏拍手に岩戸開くや初日の出 祇山玉桂
kashiwade ni iwato hiraku ya hatsuhinode   gisan 1697
(clapping-hands-to cave-door opens [emphasis]: first-sun-appear)

drawing her out

  to clapping hands   the first sunrise:
  the cave door opens!   the cave door opens
    the first sunrise   to clapping hands

If the New Year is seen as a re-enactment of the mythic drawing-out-of-the-sun of the *Ancient Chronicles*, it makes good sense to clap as the sun comes up, or, rather, clap it up. The word used for hand-clapping here (*kashiwade*) specifically alludes to clapping for the gods! Creation in the Sinosphere (including many minority cultures) is a matter of opening holes: some in the earth, some in bodies, some in gourds and some in heads. *"Seven holes / opening eye-first / the first sun"* (七穴や目よりひらけて日の始 禾束 山 曉山集 *nana ana ya me yori hirakete hi no hajime* shizan 1700), as one *ku* puts it. (Compare this wit to this older 5-7-5-7-7 stuff: "Opening heaven's door, at last sunshine, a spring like that of the age of the gods comes" 天の戸をあくればやがて日の光神代のままの春やたつらん 正広 *ama no to . . .* shôkô 1412-1494 [See pg 273]).

元朝や祝ふ月日に並初　不角　花桂
ganchô ya iwau tsukibi ni narabi-some fukaku 1651-1743
(basic-morning!/: celebrate moon sun-with line-up-start)

    new year's dawn   new year's dawn
we line up with the honored   our first line-up celebrates
     moon and sun   the sun and moon

春は去←年→月日の三やけふの空　紹巴　大発句帳
haru wa kozo tsukihi no mitsu ya kyô no sora jôha 1523-1602
(spring-as-for, last-year-month-day's three: / today's sky)

spring came last
year, moon and sun make three
for today's sky

Respecting the first *ku:* 1) Households tend to line up in a horizontal row to view the sunrise; 2), It is the year-start for the sun, and the first moon-start; 3), The new-moon, unseen, does indeed rise with the sun. 4), The sun 日 and moon 月 side-by-side form the Chinese character for "bright" 明, which also means "to start," "open," or "dawn," *i.e.,* what the New Year *does*; 5), They line up on the calendar. Respecting the second *ku,* the early solar spring was not *telling*. The *real* New Year boasts all the items mentioned, *year, month* and *day*. In the Sinosphere, *three* settles a matter, any matter: 3 men make a market, 3 men make a tiger (prove its existence is no rumor), etc. The original's "year" is, first, "last ~" and, *then,* "new."

亀の背に海老ほのあかし初日山　鬼貫
kame no se ni ebi hono akashi hatsuhi yama onitsura 1660-1738
(turtle's back-on, shrimp [is] faintly red: first-sun mountain).

new year mountain

a faintly red
shrimp upon a turtle
the first-sun

The turtle is something rare, a symbol with international currency. It looks ancient to all of us. Imaginary turtle-mountains (a mountain on a turtle) are common to the Sinosphere and synonymous with the magical island of immortality Japanese call Hôrai (see ch. 8) In Japan, the turtle-mountain was not only connected with longevity, but folk belief (alternative to more anthropomorphic written myths of beginning) that the mountainous archipelago grew – the idea not so far-fetched, as coral *does* grow – on the back of a huge turtle (Note: This belief ties in with long debate about the extent of Southern, oceanic roots in Japanese culture/s and I am unsure of how widespread it was). A shrimp in the Sinosphere suggests a spry old man. The very characters for shrimp are "ocean海+old/elder老." They are hunch-backed, yet still spry, pink and healthy, or even red, like someone drinking (a celebratory, not shameful thing), and boast long whiskers. And the most venerable *elder of the sea,* as all Japanese know, comes from none other than Ise, the place where the Sun God came out of the cave. Since the Ise shrimp [1] was sometimes used to crown models of the magical mountain, the shrimp-on-turtle idea is not entirely fresh, but the allusion to a real mountain is. It is made by a pun on "turtle's back," *kame no se* with Kamenose-tôge 亀瀬峠 Turtle-shoals Peak, a pass to Nara opened by the beloved prince Shôtoku (the Empress's husband and regent who proclaimed what I would call the Golden Rule of the Heart). Maybe it is more than an allusion. Onitsura could have found the perennial spry elder on the back of that very mountain.

1. Ise Ebi The king of shrimp, the "Ise ebi," looks and tastes exactly like what we call a "crawfish" in Florida. It is no wee craw-daddy, but a clawless *lobster* with large spiny whiskers. My favorite shrimp poem is by Shiki: *"How interesting / the corpse of a shrimp / on New Years"* (元日に海老の死骸のおもしろや 明治二六 *ganjitsu ni ebi no shigai no omoshiro ya* 1893). *Favorite*, because, at first, I imagined a shrimp on the beach, for I grew up on the seashore and the winter sea provided a never-ending supply of dead sealife. So, would it be propitious to find such a symbol or ominous for being dead? But, in all likelihood, the *ku* refers to a salt-cured Ise Ebi adorning either Mt. Hôrai (ch 8) or discus-shaped sweet-rice-cakes (?) called *Mirror-mochi* (ch 16). The latter is more likely for the rice-cakes were generally simpler and would set off the crawfish well. Shiki, in a hyper-receptive New Year's mood has looked really closely at its fancy plate-mail and tiny black opal eyes for the first time since his childhood.

首上て亀も待たる初日哉　一茶
kubi agete kame mo machitaru hatsuhi kana   issa -1827
(head-raising turtle-too awaits first-sun 'tis)

raising its head
the turtle, too, awaits
the first sun.

I suspect the short-necked, perpetually cold Issa *is* the turtle. Issa may have observed a real turtle in a temple pond at dawn, but I cannot imagine one up so early on a chilly day at the start of Spring.

元日やからんとしたる海の面　且猷　霞袋
ganjitsu ya garan to shitaru umi no omo   soyû 1829
(original-day vacant/wide/open is/makes sea's surface/face)

tabula rasa

as spring dawns
how broad and blank
the ocean's face

出る日の外に物なし霧の海　士朗
izuru hi no hoka ni mono nashi kiri no umi   shirô -1813
(appearing/rising sun's other-than thing-not mist/haze's sea)

a sea of mist	there is nothing
aside from the rising sun	but the rising sun
there is nothing	a sea of fog

THE FLAG

In snow-white mist where sea and sky are one,
A single disc of red: the rising sun.

trans. Harold Stewart

Stewart included this poem in a trilogy of New Year's haiku elaborated in the appendix to his beautiful book, *A Chime of Windbells*. Unfortunately, it cannot be found in any Japanese New Year's *saijiki*. Perhaps, that is because it mentions *kiri*, "fog" or thick autumnal mist, and, unless someone made a mistake transcribing, belongs in the Fall section, not the New Year's! [1] ↓   That is too bad, because the picture is indeed metaphysically perfect for the New Year (as will become clear in the next chapter).

↑ **1. A Misplaced Haiku?** Stewart gives a magnificent page-long explanation of the history and metaphysics of the Japanese flag after re-introducing this *ku* in the Shintô section of his long and erudite "traditional background of haiku" essay. Three lines: *"The disc or sphere is red because it comprises in principle all the possibilities of manifestation, but in the latent state before they are actually deployed as rays. The ground is white because it represents the Unmanifest, which includes both the possibilities of manifestation and those of non-manifestation, just as white light synthesizes both red and the other hues of the spectrum. The whole heraldic device thus geometrically figures the first stage after the initial indifferentiation of the Void, the white mist or background alone, with its nondual relation between Being and Non-Being."* There is a miniscule chance Shirô wrote such a New Year's *ku*. More likely, Stewart was misled by Blyth's misty translation of what is definitely the same *ku* (Blyth gives it in the original, with one *furigana* づ added to modernize the spelling of 出る): *"The misty sea, / The rising sun, / Nothing else."* ("In the Poets of Issa's Time" in Blyth's *History of Haiku* vol.2: 1963). Blyth has "fog" in both the Japanese and its romanization, so he should have known it was a fall *ku*. But, the *ku* does seem a New Year poem (and is unexplained); so I wondered whether Blyth copied it from a source that was mistaken. The characters for "(fall) mist" or "fog" = 霧 (*kiri*) and (spring) "mist" = 霞 (*kasumi*) are, after all, close; and, old books often had tiny print. But the Japanese in Miyamori Asatarô's 1932/40 book is identical to Blyth's, and the translation includes "Autumn," in order to indirectly show he realized the convention, *i.e.*, "mist" by itself means *Spring*. The translation also includes a shocking mistake: *"In the sea wrapped in Autumn mist, / There is nothing / But the rising moon."* That's right, *"moon"*! I would guess a proof-reader who felt the moon was more suitable to the fall season inadvertently made the switch. The explanation, like the Japanese original, had it all right:

In haiku poetry, *kiri* means autumn mist.
The rising sun on a misty sea looks particularly large and scarlet . . . (*Haiku Poems, Ancient and Modern*)

To use a turn-of-the-century Usanianism, *you figure!* But, returning to Stewart, because the Japanese flag was not adopted until 1870 (after the *ku* under discussion), he defends his title, *FLAG*, by introducing the red sun on white background found on older banners, leading up to the metaphysical discussion quoted above. He also gives a haiku by Ontei: *"The clouds and waters now divide. The sun / Fans out its beams. The New Year has begun."* This *ku*, which I will not translate for lack of the original [if anyone reading is thinking of doing a book of translated haiku, do not dare do it without providing the original!] gets not one, but two full pages of explanation, of which this is the first line: *"Every New Year's Day is not only the first day of the annual cycle, but a re-enactment in time of the First Day of Creation in principio, that is to say in principle, outside of time and before time begins, and not merely "in the beginning."* Excellent! The third of Stewart's trilogy of New Year's haiku is "The Great Triad" by Meisetsu (pg. 300 in this book).

~~~~~~

海原へ心をはなつ初日哉 事紅 堅並
unabare e kokoro o hanatsu hatsuhi kana   jiko 18-19c?
(ocean-belly-to heart/mind/soul[+obj.] release/shoot first-sun 'tis/!)

mind released
o'er ocean expanse
the first sun

first sunrise
the sea quickens
with soul

my feelings
shoot across the sea
the first sun

In Japanese, "field/meadow" (*hara*) combined with "ocean" means the sea viewed as a surface, i.e., an *expanse*. It is also a homophone for "belly/womb." *Haiyû* find my last reading too much; but, look at this next 20c *ku*:

たちまち日の海となり初景色 鷹羽狩行 講談社現代
tachimachi hi no umi to nari hatsugeshiki   shûgyô modern
(suddenly sun's ocean into becomes, first view/sight/scenery)

suddenly the sea
is flooded by sunlight
first scenery

suddenly sun
light fires up the sea
my first sight

The original substitutes the *sun* (日) for the *fire* (火) in the common expression *hi no umi* "sea of *fire*". This makes me, at least, imagine the sun as a torch and the sea as oil.

明て春大魚浮む海の面　栗堂 句鑑
akete haru taigyo ukamu umi no omo   kyodô 1777
(dawned/ brightened/came spring large-fish[whale] float ocean's surface)

spring is here
whales float high in
a brilliant sea

spring dawns
and a whale floats
to the surface

初空やイルカ (魚+孚、魚+布) の優に風わたる 杙風
hatsuzora ya iruka no yû ni kaze wataru   kifû 1707 類柑子
(first-sky:/! dolphin/s elegantly/gracefully/gently wind cross)

the first sky
some dolphins gracefully
cross the wind

Dolphin and manta-ray tend to surface or leap up at sunrise, especially on holidays. Is this because we are more attentive then? Or, is it because other animals are curious about our presence on the beach?

奥州はいかにと思ふ初日哉　金月 安永四
ôshû wa ika ni to omou hatsuhi kana   kingetsu 1775
(outer-state/s(fiefs, etc)-as-for, how-so think first sun/day?/'tis)

~~the inner states~~
~~how do they celebrate~~
~~new year's day~~

the outer states
what do *they* think about
our first sun=day?

~~the landlocked~~
~~what do they think of~~
~~the first sun~~

I thought the poet wondered about *sunrise* way back in the hills . . . but my respondent pointed out that 奥州 was not all landlocked but the outlying regions (or, says my OJD, the peninsula of Tôhoku). I feel the question concerns the attitude of those out-of-power toward the New Year, with its claims to political continuity, my respondent thinks the poet is imagining the cold weather in those regions.

海のある國うれしさよ初日の出 蝶衣
umi no aru kuni ureshisa yo hatsuhinode   chôi 1886-1930
(ocean-is/has country delightfulness[+emph.] first sunrise)

i rejoice
this land has the sea
first sun-rise

how delightful
to be here by the sea
first sunrise

I grew up next to the sea. Even on ordinary days, I cannot abide seeing the sun rise up from anything but water. When Chôsui (-1769) boasts *"The sea so close / Edo is the very source of / the morning sun"* (海近し朝日のもとは江戸の春 鳥酔 *umi chikashi asahi no moto wa edo no haru*), I nod. Perhaps I should add that if the rising sun was preferred with the sea, the moon had its mountains. Moonrises from the water are wonderful but difficult to catch because they appear with little or no warning. Onitsura's red shrimp suggest his sun on turtle-back was seen from another mountain. Usually, that was not the case:

山里や初日を拝む十時頃　子規　明治廿八
yamazato ya hatsuhi o ogamu jûji goro   shiki 1866-1902
(mountain country: first-sun worship/pay respect/etc to ten o'clock about)

a mountain village
the first-sun is welcomed
about ten oclock

I made the "country" a "village" for it seemed right. The welcome would have to be a fast one, for by this time the sun would no longer be a shrimp. When Issa rented a shack in the low-side of Edo, he had only a tiny patch of sky to see. He probably made certain to sleep elsewhere for the New Year's. Later, back in his hometown with half-a-house of his own, he did little better, judging from this *ku:*

我門は昼過からが元日ぞ　一茶
waga kado wa hirusugi kara ga ganjitsu zo   issa -1827
(my gate=house-as-for, afternoon-from new year day hey)

sun-deprived	**lie-a-bed poet**
the new year? it don't reach my house 'til after noon!	at my house new year's day starts after noon

Two guesses. Knowing Issa and his wife drank a lot suggests the second reading. Issa did make an effort to see sunrise on some years. For that, he had to go outside. I found an earlier sleep-to-noon poem attributed to Buson (-1783) titled "New Year's Eve" – *"I can snore in peace . . . / the new year / won't confront me / till tomorrow noon."* (1960, anonymous editor). The original does not mention "noon." [1]

ぬかるみに筇つつ張てはつ日哉　一茶
nukarumi ni tsue tsuppatte hatsuhi kana   issa -1827
(quagmire/slush-in [walking-]stick thrust/thrust-out, first-sun 'tis)

planting my stick in the mud: the rise of the first sun	walking stick first i brave the slush to see the first sun

Blyth's translation, *"Planting my stick / In the quagmire, – / The First Sun of the Year"* is fine. I would have included it above but for being warned about copyright problems! He prefaces it with a warning that the poem is "not to be taken in any way symbolically." With the leading creation myths of Japan full of phallic sticks (in the ocean and up the crappers, but not in the mud), Blyth asks too much. But, he is right. Issa is not doing one of those rolls in the mud that Frazer has Christian preachers doing in *The Golden Bough.* Then he adds, "Issa worships the new sun standing in front of his house." We really do not know how far Issa had to walk before he planted that stick, but who cares? Let me, rather, take this

---

1. Noon New Year Buson's *ku,* which is actually an *End-of-the-Year* poem, *begins* a Peter Pauper Press haiku series III, "Cherry Blossoms," which has very few blossom *ku.* The original Japanese (いざや寝ん元日は又翌（あす）の事 蕪村 *izaya nen, ganjitsu wa mata asu no koto*) is more like this: *"Guess i'll sleep / the new year tomorrow / is another day."* The end of the year has so many deadlines (financial and otherwise), so many things one *must* complete that perfect closure was impossible. Buson plays on the old saw shared East and West: "tomorrow is another day," or *asu-no koto* "tomorrow's thing" (a matter for tomorrow) in Japanese. Whether the poet is left to snore in peace until "noon" or not is another story, which only Peter Pauper knows.

opportunity to proclaim how much I *hate* the word "worship." When we read it used with respect to the Sun, we feel someone does something childish or naive. *Imagine worshipping a burning ball!* Blyth does not think of it like that. He is thinking of the Japanese verb, *ogamu*. I prefer "paying respect to," because it does not seem condescending; but "respect" is too broad a term for one can pay it to almost anyone/thing, whereas one would only *ogamu* someone/thing greater than oneself. When it comes to discussing spirituality outside of the Judeo-Christian-Islamic tradition, English drives me crazy.

心よや真一文字の初日影 教無 明和二 1765
kokoro yo ya ma ichi monji no hatsuhikage kyômu
(heart/mind[+emph.] true "1" character's first sun-shape/light)

打たつる一の字うれしけふの春 共貞 大三
uchitatsuru ichi no ji ureshi kyônoharu kyôtei 1697
(punch/hit-out/set-up "1"-letter delighted today's spring)

　　　　　　　　　　　　　　　日

that's the spirit!
the first sun shows us
a perfect " 一 "

a joy to see
that " 一 " pop up
today's spring

I first noticed how often Japanese used "one" as metaphor for living a proper life, following one's first dreams, and being sincere when I compared the lyrics of country music and *enka* (like country full of weepers, but a bit more urban) around 1990. One heart, a single line (plot), etc. But the 1 in these *ku* is no abstraction; cloud wisps are horizontal. I have seen the rising sun make a perfect character for "one" (一) but never a vertical one (1) and, one Easter dawn, the sun even followed up its one with a perfect "two" (二)! Perhaps it is worth pointing out the fact that a 一 is found within the character for sun, 日.

今朝や猶大きく見ゆる初日の出 和角 玉かづら
kesa ya nao ôkiku miyuru hatsuhinode　wakaku 1751
(this morning!/: even larger looks first-sun-rise)

on this morning
looking even larger
the first sunrise

this morning
the first sun looks
even larger

心から大きく見ゆる初日哉 一茶
kokoro kara ôkiku miyuru hatsuhi kana　issa -1827
(heart/mind/spirit-from large see/n first-sun!/?/'tis)

the mind
makes it look big
first sun

Wakaku's *ku* is a bit odd. The *kesa, i.e.,* this-morning *by itself* means New Year's, so it seems redundant to write about the first sun; and while we may assume the comparison is with the usual sun which looks large at sunrise, the lack of a specified object of comparison is as illogical in Japanese as it is in English. Issa's poem, an objective description of a subjective experience, is far simpler. An older *ku* of a parallel nature, concerning scent rather than sight: *"From our hearts, / this morning (new year's) the willows / have a scent* (*i.e.*, are aglow with beauty) 人の気からけさは柳に匂ひあり　亀林　大三物 *hito no ki kara kesa wa yanagi ni nioi ari*　kirin 1697). Here *ki* 気 (feeling/spirit/heart/mood) is used rather than 心 ("heart/mind"), but the ideas are similar. If there is a difference, it is that the stress on sight in Issa's poem makes it possible to find an allusion to *hatsu-gokoro,* the first-heart of the young, alive with hope and pure intention, before it is warped and belittled by experience. Another older *ku* does not mention heart, mind or sun. It provides the reverse vector:

けふの足土あたゝかになりにけり 文句 大三物
kyô no ashi tsuchi atataka ni narinikeri   monku 1697
(today's feet, earth/dirt warm become[+finality])

new year's

    feet today
how warm the earth
    becomes

      at last bare earth
warmed up by the rays
      of this day's sun

    our feet today
have warmed the surface
    of the earth

At first, I thought the earth *felt* warm for the same reason the sun looked big. Then, thinking of all those people out running around paying their respects to the Sun and to one another, I recalled the *Peanuts* episode where Lucy demands Charlie Brown and the rest of the gang stop sliding between bases in order to prevent the earth from being worn down and I wondered if the earth might not have been warmed by all those hurrying feet. But, I think the correct reading is that the "today," meaning the New Year, evokes the written characters 今日, of which the second is the *sun,* and the "sun's feet/legs" in Japanese mean rays of sun-light, with the human feet only coming in as an association. Regardless, if we feel the earth warming up from below, this remarkable old *ku* warms up to us.

あたゝかに砂を敷日の始哉 攻幸 大三物
atataka ni suna o shiku hi no hajime kana   seikô 1697
(warmly sand[obj] spreads/carpets sun's-start/beginning!/'tis)

  warmly spreading
sand on the first day
    in the first sun

    the first sun
warmly spreading sand
    our first day

  warmly spreading
sand on the first day
   for the first sun

My word-for-word just cannot follow the original where the sun *almost* seems to spread the sand, though we know it is man that spreads – or, should I say *lays down,* for the *laying-down-the-red-carpet* idea of doing honor? – sand for the first day. If the poet is spreading fresh sand as the sun rises, the first reading is right. If it is spread to welcome the sun about to rise, the last reading is right. Or, could it be both? By removing the "in" and "for," the original ambiguity, which may or may not have been deliberate, can be regained, but the force is lost. Pardon the details, so much sand in the shoe for most readers, but such problems led me to this: *Could Japanese once have removed their geta and stood bare foot (or in their tabi) upon that sand, as if they were on the beach and less lyrically, but equally important, as was done before superiors?* (民俗歴史家求む。敷た真砂の上に裸足なって日を拝む習慣は？).

元日に田毎の日こそこひしけり はせを ☆
ganjitsu ni ta-goto no hi koso koishikeri   bashô 1689
(original-day-on paddy/plot-each's sun more-than-anything dear)

on new year's
nothing so dear as the sun
on each field

Though this is not, strictly speaking a *hinode* (sun-up) *ku*, we can imagine the rising Sun's first ray shooting out, first in a thin line and, then, spreading to fill the rectangular plots with the first light of the Year. Older *ku* feted the reflection of the *moon* in each paddy; but, this may be the first time the *sun* got such treatment. That moon, with its light representing the reach of Buddhist mercy and law, was easy to get to know. We all have *experienced* it moving with us (almost like a balloon on a string or a pet owl) in the night – we have become familiar with it, one-on-one. The seminal sun was, and is, too powerful for us to face. Even with sunglasses, we dare not, for the greater part of the day, even look at it. Only occasionally, in the early morning, when rays shoot across clear water or icy ground, do we notice how the sun, too, *comes to us* individually. Bashô's *ku* unobtrusively helps us enjoy a personal relationship with the sun. (★オマケ注 ― 前頁の濁点すらない「はせを」を、面白がっていたところ、加藤郁平の「俳林随筆」に次のことを読んだ。「はせを」が芭蕉の俳名ではなく深川早庵の号であって、西脇順三朗によれば、それを仮名に書いたのを「自慢なりとなり」も男茎の異名「をはせ」とのかけのためだと。（？）)

我物にして祝ふなり初朝日 夕浦 寶暦十一
wagamono ni shite iwau nari hatsu-asahi　yûho 1761
(my-thing-as make celebrate-become/is first-morning-sun)

i celebrate
the first morning sun
as my own

Going back up to Bashô's poem, he may also be responding to the ideas found in poems such as *waka* #5 of the *Shinkokinshû*: *"Today, forsooth, / this Spring that goes / clear to Cathay, / We feel has come / to our Capital alone!"* (*kyô to ieba tôdo made mo iku haru o miyako ni nomi to omoikeru kana*). Why stop at the capital, Bashô and Yûho ask? Don't we feel it comes to each of us alone? And, why the constant identification of the New Year with the capital anyway? With the old capital, it made some sense, for the New Year reflects the past, but the brand-new capital of Edo? One contemporary huffed *"What nonsense! / Out in the boondocks toasting /"Edo's spring!"* (愚いふ國々までも江戸の春　遊葉　大三物 *oroka iu kuniguni* [actually "countries," not "boondocks"] *made mo edo no haru*　yûyô 1697).

~~~~~~

日の光けさや鰯のかしらより 蕪村
hi no hikari kesa ya iwashi no kashira yori　bûson 1715-83
(sun's light/shine, this morning [+emphasis] pilchard's head-from)

new year of the dragon, indeed!

on this morning
the sun first shines
from a fish-head

正月の魚のかしらや炭俵 傘下 大三
shôgatsu no uo no kashira ya sumidawara　sanka
(new-year's fish's/fishes'head/s!: charcoal sack　1697)

the head of
the new year fish
a coal sack

大鰯生てすゐけりけさの春　示右
ôiwashi ikete suekeri kesanoharu　shiu 17-18c? 團袋
(large-pilchard alive-set-up[+emph] this-morning'spring)

a large pilchard
arranged life-like
the dawn of spring

Bûson's is by far the most commonly encountered *first-sun* haiku – one I have never *not* seen in a *saijiki*. Incidentally, it does not show the sun itself, only the shine. Blyth translates *"A day of light / Begins to shine / From on the heads of the pilchards"* and explains that "the pilchards are hanging from the eaves." [1] *More recent Japanese annotators of Buson's work have a different story.* The sunshine reflects from a single pilchard head stuck on the gate as a talisman to ward off demons on the *setsubun*, or "season-split," the day before the solar spring. On this year, the date fell on the first day of the New Year.[2] If a gate lacks a place for the sardine head, it would be put on the end of a stick. The coal sack in the second *ku*, would be black with coal dust and show off the silver head to great effect. In direct translation, the pilchard in the third *ku* could be set up *alive* (生きて), but this is not a fish that travels well, so the figurative meaning of an *arrangement*, as in flower arrangement, must be taken (活けて).

spring dawn is glinting
on a dew-wet garbage can
in a city street

Richard Wright
HAIKU 1998

Richard Wright's *ku* (pardon my parsing and decapping) is doubtless a response to Buson *via* Blyth, whose *Haiku* turned him to haiku in his last two years of life. Had Wright lived longer, he might have switched to 7-beat and re-written, say: *"Spring dawn / glints upon a dewy / garbage can."* I cannot say Wright was thinking of the New Year, but how could his *ku* not be included here?

腰照らす元旦里の眠りかな 鳴雪
koshi terasu gantan sato no nemuri kana   meisetsu -1926
(hips shine orig. day[ny] country/hometown's sleep/iness!/'tis)

how sleepy   hips shining,
the rural new year!   farm-belt new year
hips a-shine   somnolence

This beats Buson and the other pilchard heads as well as Wright's garbage can top, for it brings out the pathos of the hard life of rural people. On this day alone, when not asleep, they lay on their sides and gazed outside. Hips (covered by clothing or covers) shining in the sunlight. A masterful observation.

あら玉や鍬もかゝやく御手傳 笁女 花笠
aratama ya kuwa mo kagayaku otetsudai   chôjo early 20c?
(new-gem: hoe too shines [honorific+]servant)

the new sun   my good servant
the hoe too a splendid   the hoe also glistening
shiny servant   new year sunshine

---

1. Blyth's hanging pilchards. Blyth's mistake is not without reason. Dried pilchards were a staple at this time of the year: *"Dried pilchard / are what keeps the people: / my country's spring"* (干鰯民のもとなり國の春 扇子風＝雑中 *hoshiiwashi tami no motonari kuninoharu* senshifû).
2. The Date of Buson's Ku! The *Zenku* annotators neglect, however, to say that it was *also* the Year of the Dragon (*mizunoue tatsu*), chief of the marine tribe. I was able to check the date for Bûson's *ku* against the year-animal to confirm my guess that it would probably be the case, *which made me two for two*, as I had just confirmed a Year of the Monkey guess for Buson's teacher Hajin's *ku* (pg.90). There is only a 1/12 x 1/12 = 1/144 of a chance I was lucky both times. Many if not most Japanese haiku experts would probably find my claim preposterous, for they wrongly believe that sort of play stopped with Bashô.

Lacking an honorific, such as the *"o"* prefixing the "servant/help," English must use adjectives to convey the warm feelings it may sometimes express. To write "honorable" would be to betray the poem, for "honorable servant" would sound farcical rather than polite (See *Orientalism & Occidentalism*).

猫の鼻あたゝまる日のはじめ哉　忠門 談林2
neko no hana atatamaru hi no hajime kana　chûmon 17-18c
(cat's nose warming sun's beginning 'tis)

the first sunshine
begins by warming up
our cat's nose

Japanese houses are chilly. I imagine this cat following the sunlight as closely as our cats would a mouse. Unlike a dog, whose nose should be moist and cool, a cat's should be dry and warm. I do not, however, know if keeping their respective noses in such a condition does any good. I would love to find out whether or not this *ku*, which Buson might have known, dates to the Year of the Tiger. Because the poet is a virtual unknown, chances are we will never know for sure.

three i like

まづは左右に開きて通す初日哉　素丸
mazu wa sayu ni hirakite tôsu hatsuhi kana somaru 1712-95
(first-as-for left-right-to opening-pass first-sun!/'tis)

new sunshine   first opening
first opening left and right   right and left to pass
to let it in   new year sun

Because Japanese doors/windows often slide on two tracks, or the track goes into the wall, they are easy to open from either or both sides. It is odd not to specify what is opened in Japanese, too, so not to mind the awkward English! This *ku* could go with the sleeping-in *ku*. It also shares something with those alluding to the cave. I like to read it as the record of an improvised ritual. Somaru once called his atelier The Heaven & Earth Hut (天地庵). He clearly loved New Year themes. Perhaps he passed it on to Issa.

みいらともなりたがりてやはつ日の出 一茶
miira to mo naritagarite ya hatsu hinode   issa -1827
(mummy even to become-want! first sun-rise)

new year wish

the sun rises
and i would become
a mummy!

I wish I knew what you, my readers, think about the *ku* in this chapter. For me, the selector-translator, they are (with the exception of the children's *ku* and a few others) not especially interesting. They tend to be overly abstract and rarely surprise. I am afraid the same thing can be said for many *ku* in chapters 2, 5, 6 and 11. Apparently, the fact that the New Year called for a naïve (simple and trusting) frame of mind made the poets overly serious. There were exceptions. Truly interesting sunrise poems. This one was written at the beginning of Issa's 50th year, when he had just completed a standard lifetime (There are two standard lifetimes in the Sinosphere: the 5x10+50-year fortune-telling sign permutation and the 5x12=60-year animal-zodiac, birth-year cycle-based calculation). Is it a reflection of a totally unBuddhist desire to remain in this enchanted world, or simply to exchange soft flesh for something cleaner and eternal perhaps influenced by a wish to warm up and dry out from a cold wet influenza winter? Issa didn't write it until the end of the month, perhaps in compensation for his rather ridiculous "Hurrah for me!" (*onore yare* – see ch.11) and other *ku* too cheerful to be true to his situation (*unlanded, unmonied* and *unmarried*). The only poem I know of anything like it is by Shiki.

元日やとてもの事に死んでみん 子規
ganjitsu ya totemonokotoni shinde min   shiki 1893
(original(ny)-day: preferably/extreme/-thing-from die-try/would)

overwhelmed

new year's day
why not
die?

The title of the poem reflects the literal meaning of the middle part of the poem which is idiomatic for "rather/preferably." Shiki's *ku* seems positive. Current English (American) includes some very death-positive idioms (good things modified by the adjective "killer" or described as "*to die for*") , so this idea is not so outlandish as an unsympathetic reader might imagine. Still, it is hard to say how serious Shiki is. I imagine thoughts of leaving in the dream-time crossed his mind, but who knows!

this new year   it's too much
so fine i could almost   why not die happy
kill myself!   new year's day

After the First Sun Rises

元日の入相聞ん人も哉　成美
ganjitsu no iriai kikan hito mo gana　seibi -1816
(new year day's vesper [bell] hear/listen-would person wanted)

    oh, for a man
  who would hear the vespers
      new year's day

Everyone is so attentive to the *rising* of the sun. But who would witness its *setting?* Is Seibi, the consummate aesthete, simply noting something ordinarily ignored? Or, is there some Buddhism here, in both the attentiveness toward the end of things and in the memory of the vesper of the previous day, with its 108 strikes against various sins of the soul? Shiki once wrote more plainly: *"When the sun sets / on the Original Day / That's* aware*"* (元日の夕日になれば哀れ也　子規　明治廿七 *ganjitsu no yûhi ni nareba aware nari*). Aware (*a-wa-re*) is an untranslatable word meaning *beauty with a touch of pathos.*

元日の朝日一日朝日哉 班象 失出典
ganjitsu no asahi ichi nichi asahi kana　hanzô -1779
(new year day's morning sun one-day [all day long] morning-sun 'tis)

    the morning sun
  on new year's day, all day
    the morning sun!

This type of thinking, where the first sun, i.e. the first day, becomes a *dawn*, probably explains why we cannot find much interest in the first sunset. *Come to think of it, the last sunset of the year also gets precious little attention.* I must investigate *why* some day.

日／＼に新たなる日の始哉　北固
nichinichi ni aratanaru hi no hajime kana　hokko 1777
(day, day-on/by renews/new-becomes sun's [sun that renews] start!/?/'tis)

renewal

    the sun that   it's the start
  renews day after day   of the sun's renewal
     starts now!   day after day

I played a bit with translation, for the *ku* seems wrong with respect to the New Year – if *this* is true, why bother getting up to see it rise? Yet, it is also completely right. Every day *is* rekindled.

けふ見るや春は花さく梅の雨　昌叱 大発句帳
kyô miru ya haru wa hana saku ume no ame　shôshitsu -1603
(today see!/: spring-as-for, blossom-blooms plum's rain)

    today we see
  spring means flowering
    plums in the rain

民の戸の秋やけふふる春の雨　昌叱
tami no to no aki ya kyô furu haru no ame　shôshitsu -1603
(folks' gate/house's autumn!/: today fall/falling spring-rain)

fall for the folk
today falling, falling
spring rain

autumn roofs
rain falls on the folk
new year's day

The combination of the single day "today" (*kyô*) and the spring (*haru*) makes these *ku* New Year's Day poems. They also show that the sun did not always perform (?) properly on the first morning.

うれしかる子に元日の曇りけり　子規
ureshigaru ko ni ganjitsu no kumorikeri　shiki -1902
(delight[would] child/ren-to, new year's day's=sun's cloud-over)

new year's day
the dream of a child
clouded over

cheerful kids
how can the new year
cloud over!

the expectation
of children betrayed
a cloudy first-day

In Japanese, as in Chinese, the *sun* and *day* are the same. On the one hand, we imagine the clouding face of a child up early expecting to see the magical first sun-rise of the year or hoping to play outdoor games all day. On the other hand, we see *all* Japanese, *children of the sun*, mistreated by the same. Yet, this cloudiness is not nearly so gloomy, so sad as Santa not visiting the children of the poor.

人の日と思へはをしき曇り哉　梅室
hito no hi to omoeba oshiki kumori kana　baishitsu 1768-
(people's day [that] think if, regretful/[a]pity: cloudy!/'tis -1852)

clouded over!
a pity when you think
it's people-day

The new year's holiday splits up many ways. One has the 1st day for the gods, the 2nd for work (and sex), and the 3rd just for being. Another has the first 6 days for predicting the fortune of other beasts and the 7th for humans. This "peoples-day" was also the day young greens were gathered and eaten (See ch 19, 20), so clouds would not have been welcome. The poet also plays on the name for people, "*hito*." The "*hi*" in "*hito*" gives them a right to expect the "*hi*" (sun) to be out on *their* day.[1] At any rate, New Year cloudiness is meaningful because it is the reverse side of the New Year Sun.

---

1. The *Hi* in *Hito* The poet is probably not simply punning on a shared syllabet but alluding to a popular etymology for *"hito"* (people). Japanese have long enjoyed as many etymologies for every word as the Greeks in the time of Lucretius (c.99BC-c.55 BC) enjoyed theories for thunder (See his *De Rerum Natura*). When I have difficulty figuring out what makes an olde haiku interesting, I often dip into my OJD (*nihonkokugo-daijiten*) for the abundant etymologies. Some day, I hope to make a book of the most interesting basic words (those with the most, and most outlandish derivations). "Hito," *with no less than 13 different etymologies*, is one of them. Five of these explain the *"hi"* signifies "sun" of which my favorite combines *"hi"* and *"to"* (from *"tomo"*) to get "friend of the sun" (!) Unless we can repair the wall of ozone, this friendship may not remain green.

logical envoi

初景色整ふまでの二度寝かな 高橋睦郎
hatsugeshiki totonou made no nido-ne kana takahashi mutsurô
(first-scenery arrange/complete-until's second-sleep 'tis/!)

<table>
<tr><td>the first view
until it is complete
i sleep again</td><td>back to sleep
until the first scene is
fully composed</td></tr>
</table>

One expects certain things on the New Year. Was it too overcast to show Mount Fuji? Or, did the poet insist his wife and children wear their proper first-dress? I do not know the details, but this I can say: the *ku* is a masterpiece. It plays upon the idea first developed by Bashô who insisted on several props (?) being in place before admitting that spring was spring (Or was it summer, summer or fall, fall? – It does not matter, the *concept* does. I am not being coy. This *envoi* was added in exile from my Bashô and other books surrounded by 56 canine and bovine legs in the winter of the watermelon capital of the world.); but it is better than Bashô, for using the otherwise abstract idea as an excuse to gain a bit of shut-eye to grow on, and for its message (even if an apparent rationalization). All starts with ideals. If ours are not met, we should *do* something, even if it is only to go back to sleep. The second reading reversed the syntax but it managed to catch an important part of the original missed by the first reading. We are better able to imagine change occurring as the poet sleeps. This *ku* is brilliant because the poet succeeded in something no others (that I know of) did: he made a logical argument for not getting up. The *ku* is modern and I forget where I found it. *Hatsugeshiki*, or the first view/scene of the year that impresses you, is a popular seasonal theme today. If haiku are considered to be snapshots that manage to capture the ordinary and extraordinary magic around us, the *hatsugeshiki* is the first haiku, the *ur-ku*, antecedent to words. (日本文学大系の利用が拒否されなかったら、初景色の系譜をご紹介できたのに！)

joyous envoi

初晴を見上げて小さきくさめ哉 再現 青々子 右脳俳句
hatsubare o miagete chisaki kusame kana seiseiko (contemp) 2001/1/#3
(first-clear [day/sky] look/ing-up [at it], small sneeze!/'tis)

<table>
<tr><td>first blue sky
of the year, looking up
a tiny sneeze</td><td>looking up at
the first clear blue sky
a tiny sneeze</td></tr>
</table>

The "first clear sky" may imply an overcast morning with no visible sunrise, or an overcast day, in which case, this might be the second or third day of the Year. As noted before, openings, including the nostril, were associated with the "opening" of the New Year; but you need not know or even care to know that to immediately realize this is one of the sweetest New Year's poems ever written. Buson has a famous *ku* of a fox sneezing after sniffing a flower. I imagine a child, a cat or a young woman. And I think this unsung masterpiece is as good if not better than Buson's *ku*.

玉の春
tama-no-haru

五 5

THE FLAWLESS GEM

小便もうかとはならずけさの春　一茶
shôben mo uka to wa narazu kesanoharu   issa -1823
(pissing-even careless-as-for become-not morning's spring)[1]

omen

i even take care
with how i make water
on the first day

new year

even pissing
ia a matter for concern
this morning

Christian cultures tend to to be sober for Christmas and drunk for New Year's Eve. In Japan, it is the opposite. *Kurisumasu* is a time for outrageous partying – perhaps more "sararîmen" (salaried, i.e., white-color workers) see stripteases on Christmas than any other day of the year – while New Year's Eve is celebrated at home with the family and, let's be honest, the television. There may be some fire-crackers heard at midnight in addition to the bells, but that reflects outside (Chinese) influence.

初日の出身にあやまりのなきことを　原晃子 中1
hatsuhinode mi ni ayamari no naki koto o   hara akiko (contemp.)
(first sun-up self-with mistakes-not thing [+obj.(wishing/trying)])

the first sunrise
i pray i don't make
any booboos

world-watch

the first sunrise
i pray it goes off
without a hitch

first prayer

the new year's sun:
may neither it nor i
screw up!

This *ku* is by a middle-school student from Kôchi prefecture. It shows the ambiguity of Japanese forced into English is not a function of the poet's age. I suspect the child is most concerned with flubbing up some observance and being laughed at; but I remember reading of a Hopi girl concerned lest airplanes injured clouds.[2] This girl, like Issa making water in his sadly neglected masterpiss (岩波の『一茶句集』にもないぞ), may be thinking of more than herself in this time beyond time when everything matters.

~~~~~~

1. Issa's Concern may be for where he goes, for each year had a lucky direction best followed the first time out. Or, he may be worried about exchanging greetings (see ch.7).
2.The Hopi Girl was in a book of children's illustrations and words edited by Robert Coles, whose *Moral Life of Children* and *Religious Life of Children*, like collections of children's haiku, let the children themselves prove the depth of their understanding and natural goodness.

◎ 初春 ◎

明の春　今朝の春　千代の春　千ゝの春　代ゝの春　御代の春　國の春　神の春　神祇の春　年の春　今日の春　新しき春　新玉の春　**玉の春**　たちかえる春　君が春　公が春　民の春　三の春　新春　孟春　天の春　天地の春　天下の春　四海の春　雪の春　花の春　松の春　梅の春　日の春　曙の春　朝の春　。。。下馬の春　伽羅の春　諸事の春　自他の春　春を迎ふ　。。。。

The dawning of the New Year is not to be taken lightly by the anthologist either. It is called so many things that just listing their English translations would take pages. My Kaizôsha *saijiki* lists over 100 terms (I only had energy to type in about a quarter of them) under the general term初春*hatsu-haru,* or "first spring." Of these, who can say which should be jumbled together and which treated as separate themes, or whether they bear any resemblance to the theme I have quite arbitrarily, but not without thought, chosen to include haiku about, or suggesting *a gem-like quality* in this chapter. The word *tama* 玉, which includes the connotations *"gem/ball/precious/beautiful/perfect"* all rolled into one, was often used to modify the New Year. "Used" in the *past tense* because when I put the following haiku by Shiki on my Year of the Tiger New Year's Card for 1998, I was shocked to learn that most young Japanese were no longer familiar with the expression 玉の春*tama-no-haru,*[1] or gem-spring:

猫の顔もみがきあげたり玉の春 子規 明治二四
neko no kao mo migaki agetari tamanoharu   shiki 1991
(cat's face too polishing up gem/cat-name/precious/-spring)

tama the cat	***bright new year***
our gem, too pretties up her face spring-shine	even our cat polishes her face: this gem of a spring day!

In this very light verse, young Shiki polished the gem metaphor and, I believe, puns on the name of his cat. It is *her* spring. Proper names are generally not desirable in haiku because they make the *ku* ours; but Tama is so common a name for a pretty pussy cat that it *is* as generic as Tray is for a dog. The idea is that even cats appreciate and help to create the immaculate atmosphere of this day. The *ku* is convincing because cats are delighted with a clean house and, if secure in their place, the additional attention they receive from people off-work for the holidays, and express this by cleaning themselves.

---

1. *Tama-no-haru* The young Japanese can not be faulted for not knowing. The term is not included among the 17,000 odd terms in the Kôdansha *saijiki* index. Of the three *tama-no haru, toshi-no tama,* and *aratama-no toshi,*, only the last, meaning "uncut/new-gem-year" is included. Presumably, the editors felt only the last was the real thing and the others were abbreviated corruptions. I hate to stick my nose into foreign business, but the poets of olde used the *tama* gems as metaphors in ways that diverge from that of *aratama,* so they at least deserve a separate index listing. Issa's poem at the start of the chapter and the following 1765 poem by Minji ("sleepy-road") by themselves are enough to merit it: *"A bigarade / shadow-figure, look! / The Gem Spring"* minji (橙のかけほうし見や玉の春　眠路 明和二　*daidai no kageboshi miru ya tamanoharu* 1765), where the already huge bigarade (a grapefruit-sized orange, auspicious for reasons we will soon see) enlarged in shadow allows a pun on "spring=grow/swell" itself! The sun itself was seen as a gem: *"Our new gem! / The sack is unbound / to start the day"* (新玉や袋ほとけて日の始　帰的　桃首途 *aratama ya fukuro hodokete hi no hajime* – kiteki 1728).

初空や煙草吹輪の中の比枝（叡）　言水
hatsuzora ya tabako fuku wa no naka no hie　gonsui -1719
(first-sky: tobacco-smoke/spread ring's-within [mt.] hie[hieizan]=cool)

light blue haiku

<table>
<tr><td>

the first sky
i blow a smoke ring
around mt. cool

</td><td>

my first sky
mount cool within
a smoke ring

</td></tr>
</table>

The full name of this largest of the many small mountains surrounding Kyôto is Hiei. One nickname for it, Hie, is a homophone for "chilly," which is the one of its eight etymologies and a constant source for punning in *haikai*. The author, who once climbed it in the afternoon and stupidly ended up alone on top at night, knows it can indeed get *very* cold – but it is small stuff compared to Fuji. A visitor to Edo who saw Fuji at this time of year wrote: *"Spring! Today / Mt. Cool is like Fuji / in June!"* (春やけさ叡山富士の五月頃　由ト　大三物　*haru ya kesa eizan fuji no gogatsu goro* yûto 1697). Here, a different pronunciation of the mountain's name was intended, but the idea is the same, I think: *cool*. Be that as it may, Gonsui's *ku* is a "first-sky" (*hatsuzora*) poem, while the smoke suggests a parody on the first-mist/haze (*hatsugasumi*) theme – note that in the argot of thieves, tobacco was called *kasumi* (mist/haze). The mountain's name suggests a crisp, clear day that starts me singing (with apologies to Willie (and Nat)):

~ blue ~ sky ~
nothing but blue sky
all day long

Gem-like (*tama no*) in Japanese means *beautiful, precious* and *unblemished*. It can modify or stand for the first-sun, the brand new year, or a clear first-sky. A smoke-ring helps bring out the clear blue sky by contrast. The peace suggested by this "ring"[1] is playfully contradicted by the idea of smoke blemishing said gem. This will later be made explicit by Issa.

初空を拵へているけぶり哉　一茶
hatsuzora o koshiraeteiru keburi kana　issa -1827
(first-sky[obj] crafting/fashioning smoke!/?/'tis)

new year contribution

the first sky
fashioned right now
by my smoke

---

1. Smoke and Ring "Peace" and "ring" are homophonic in Japanese. The concept of tobacco smoke as a unifying element, a glue between souls (as found among the Amerindians originators of the practice of smoking), was quickly rediscovered in the Orient where waterpipes allowed it to be shared (Words on a Qing dynasty cigarette case *"sweet-smoke-exhale-threads-everyone-heart-share"* (甘煙吐絲皆心意).) By this time, the Japanese had settled on tiny pipes holding hardly enough tobacco for one smoker, much less a multitude, but the "ring" symbolism would still have worked. Tobacco was very *haikai*. A *ku* written before Gonsui's, *"Tobacco smoke / breaking in bits, drifting: / the morning mist"* zaishiki (朝霞たばこの烟　よこおれて　在色　談林十百韻 *asagasumi tabako no kemuri yoko orete* zaishiki 1675), was an appropriate follow-up for a poem where the exquisite nightingale wakes up vulgar (*sezoku*) sleep at the start of day for the Danrin, or "talking-forest" school of poetry haiku-jam! (I say *haiku*-jam rather than *renku*, because the chain is made entirely of 5-7-5 *ku*, with none of the usual linking 7-7 syllabet *ku*). I feel the *ring* makes Gonsui's haiku *less* vulgar than other tobacco *ku*, but you are free to disagree.

(or)

   it's forming
  the new year's sky
     .
    .
    s
     .
      m
      .
     o
     .
      k
     e

(↑ my re-formation of a david lanoue translation ↑)

初空を今こしらへる煙かな　一茶
hatsuzora o ima koshiraeru kemuri kana (diff. version of same *ku*)
(first-sky[obj] now crafts/fashions smoke 'tis/!)

the smoke
is now making
the first sky of the year

(trans blyth, centered and depunctuated)

Blyth explains: "He knows, somehow or other, that the smoke rising up and forming the first sky of the year has a meaning that can be expressed only by pointedly saying nothing about it."(*Haiku* vol 2 spring). *Half true*. Issa's choice of the verb *koshiraeru* says a lot, for it is only used for deliberate, intelligent action and, further, suggests the manufacture of fine handicrafts, such as polished gems. An older *ku* (初霞いつこしらへて四方の山　未聞　大三 *hatsugasumi itsu koshiraete yomo no yama* mibun 1697) has the mountains fashioning the first mist (or vice versa; it is hard to tell), but Issa's *ku* with the sky involved is more suggestive (to me, anyway) of the gem=*tama* idea. Perhaps I should add that Issa liked this verb and even used it with respect to a more explicit gem metaphor, *dew drops.* I do not know for certain that it is "my" smoke, but other poems Issa wrote that year suggest he made it himself, boiling water.

初空やはゞかり乍（ら）茶のけぶり　一茶
hatsuzora ya habakarinagara cha no keburi　issa -1827
(first-sky! hesitating [having scrupples about]-while, tea's smoke)

smoke pollution

the first sky:
feeling diffident about
making tea

Habakaru, a verb, means hesitating to do something for fear of doing damage, such as blemishing a gem. I am happy with my weak "feeling diffident," because Issa had mixed feelings on man's role in nature, or, at any rate, in the sacred time/place of the New Year. To me, the *ku* shares something with Chiyo's *morning glory*: it could be criticized as "precious" (as Issa once did to Chiyo: see the *Foreword*), though I, personally, would not do so. A less subjective version simply says: *"Tea smoke / trying to become / the first sky"* (初空にならんとすらん茶のけぶり *hatsuzora ni naran to suran cha no kemuri*). I do not translate it *as a poem* because I cannot find a decent match for the euphonious and somewhat humorous middle 7 syllabets *naran to suran*. Issa knew he had a good theme and wrote *ku* after *ku* on it.

初空のもやうに立るけぶり哉 一茶
hatsuzora no moyô ni tatsuru keburi kana issa -1827
(first-sky's pattern-as rises/appears smoke!/?/'tis)

we can make it

the first sky
rising smoke provides
its pattern

はつ空にはやきず付るけぶり哉 一茶
hatsuzora ni haya kizu tsukeru keburi kana issa -1827
(first-sky-in already/quickly wound/blemish/fall make/ing smoke!/?/'tis)

new year's qualms

the first-sky
already blemished
by my smoke

These positive and negative readings of a single happening also reflect contradictory metaphors of the year itself, as something blank which is filled in, or something perfect that is worn down. Even the single idea of a gem can be polished to perfection *or* blemished. As was the case with the earlier poems, the smoke is the *subject* in the original and not specified as "my."

初空を夜着の袖から見たりけり 一茶
hatsuzora o yogi no sode kara mitarikeri issa -1827
(first-sky[obj] night-dress's sleeve-from seeing[+so-forth+ emph.])

round-as-a-gem

the first sky!
i try looking through
my pj sleeve

It is easy to imagine a pale blue oval gem-of-a-sky through Issa's sleeve. I imagined him at home and wondered if a child might be looking through that sleeve, but when I checked his biographical data discovered Issa spent the New Year's at a temple that year. From what he writes, we know he was not up before dawn practicing *zazen* (meditation) and I would guess the priests would not make a big deal of watching sunrise. Since temples had large rooms and were on mountain slopes, they would be chilly and Issa, a self-professed hater of the cold, would not want to leave his futon-like nightdress.

青空にきずーッなし玉の春　一茶
aozora ni kizu hitotsu nashi tamanoharu issa -1827
(blue-sky-in wound/flaw one-not gem/beautiful/etc-spring)

true to name

in the blue sky
not a single flaw:
spring's a gem

In this, the last of Issa's sky-making/breaking *ku*, he finally makes explicit the *sky-as-gem* **metaphor**[1] only hinted at in his earlier poems. To my mind, it reflects his appreciation for the potential we are originally presented with. Issa's love for children and his *ku* come from the same place.

あら玉やくるりとまはるけふの春　貞継 毛吹草
aratama ya kururi to mawaru kyô-no-haru   teikei 1645
(rough[or new] gem: around rotates today's spring/nyday)

the new year   today the spring
starts spinning today: makes a revolution
a gem in the raw   a new *tama*

Issa almost surely read this abstract poem, probably treating *ara-tama,* as an "uncut/rough gem" *ku* but possibly as a new one like a ball or the circular *tamaki* of Kendô's *ku* (pg.32). If Issa's blue sky *ku* is the best plain *tama-no-haru* poem, he also wrote what must be the worst *ara-tama* poem: *"The year-gem / tossed over comes up / lice-ridden!"* (*aratama no toshi tachikaeru shirami kana* あら玉のとし立かへる虱哉). The compound verb *tachikaeru* first suggests a raw-gem turning and dropping inside a polisher [?] rotating on a horizontal axis, and later, after the shocking "lice" (*shirami*) suggests "white-caps" (*shiranami*), it "rebounds" with new meaning as the standard verb for what the "year-wave" does. In other words, the lice bound back like frothy waves off a rocky shore on the New Year, a time suggesting early Spring and slight warming.[1] The second worst New Year *tama* haiku is by Kiteki (1728). No pun, just a horrid metaphor: *"A new gem! / the bag is opened and /out pops the sun=day"* (新玉や袋ほとけて日の始 帰的 桃首途 *aratama ya fukuro hodokete hinohajime*). The equivalence of the first *sun* and *day* is lost in translation. Still, it is a sorry *ku*: *Who in the world brings and unloosens the bag, and who is left holding it?* Teikei's older *ku* beats this and Issa's crazy-verse, for it makes us wonder: *Does it take 365 revolutions to finish polishing the rough-gem, after which Time pockets it for good?* As far as where that raw gem *comes from,* a *ku* by Sôin (1604-82) suggests *The Mountain of Youth* (ch. 8).

〰〰〰〰〰〰〰〰〰〰〰〰〰〰〰〰〰〰〰〰〰〰〰〰〰〰〰〰〰〰〰〰〰〰〰〰〰

1. Types of Sky Art/Vandalism. The New Year sky is more crystalline today than in Issa's time, for the season is drier and colder. A January 2001 poem by Shôhei picks up on this seasonal aspect very well: *"The winter sky / has geometric scars: / vapour trail"* (冬天に機何学の傷飛行雲 正平 瑕 右脳俳句 *fuyuzora ni kikagaku no kizu hikôgumo*). It also makes us think about the nature of visual pollution. Compare the smoke wafting up from Issa's tea-fire with the long sharp slashes made by airplanes!

2. Waves and the New Year While "calm" (*nagi*) is far more haiku'ed, the new=rough wave concept is not without support: *"Spring comes, / and doesn't the sea / sound good!"* (春立つやさすがに聞きよき海の音 牧童 *haru tatsu ya sasuga kikiyoki umi no oto* bokudô -1715. I.e., *tranquility* is ideal, but *freshness* is fitting, too.

Note that the etymology of *aratama* has long been disputed. In the oldest anthology of poetry, the *Manyôshû* (8c) it is written with characters meaning "rough" or "unfinished," but it is nevertheless possible that it comes from a verb *aratamaru* meaning "renew."

たのもしや去年よりもあら玉の春　如幸 _{歳旦集}
tanomoshiya kozo yorimo aratama no haru　nyokô 1775
(promising!/: last-year more-than rough/new gem-spring[ny])

more promising than last year, spring this uncut gem	more promising than last year, spring a brand-new gem

With the purely phonetic *ara*, it is impossible to say whether the poet was thinking of what we might reify as a diamond-in-the-rough or a shiny, unsullied pearl; but neither the in/correct interpretation of the individual poems nor the details of the etymological debate argument need concern us here. The more important thing, to my mind *worthy of an entire book*, is the identification of a raw unfinished quality with precious newness in Japan. I cannot say that Japanese made a practice of appreciating unfinished gems, but they clearly appreciated unpainted wood and unglazed pottery; and this appreciation was not affected, in the manner of European nobility playing the rustic, but central to the celebration of beginnings, i.e. the sacred (This is not to say that Japanese nobles did not play make-believe. Some even had fake saltworks in their gardens, for the smoke was identified with bitter exile. But I talk of basic taste.). Important festivals and banquettes called for unpainted and unglazed service (cups and chopsticks), likewise, for the service used by important personages. Valignano, in the late-16c, marveled at this love for the crude and contrasted it to "our" practice of using only the best service of bejeweled precious metals on such occasions (For a long discussion, see *Topsy-turvy 1585*). It goes without saying that the Japanese were fine artesians and could bring out the best from precious metals; but they, unlike us, *also* had a mature enough aesthetic sensibility to appreciate the feel, look and smell of basic materials which tie us to our roots and, thus, literally embody what might be called our natural religion.

年もけふあら玉うてる子供哉　春盛 _狗
toshi mo kyô aratama uteru kodomo kana　shunsei 1633
(year/elder-even today new-ball/s/gem/s hit/s/hitting child!/?/' tis)

even the old are children at bat on new year's	today, new year's children are out hitting their new balls

This poem *plays on* the *aratama* New Year association, while describing either a New Year's game or the mood of the elderly. The poem is *much* better in Japanese where the word "year" (*toshi*) doubles as "old" (an elder) and the new *gem=balls*.

元日や小槌のこぐち玉の春　蕪村
ganjitsu ya kozuchi no koguchi tamanoharu　bûson -1783
(new year's day: small mallet's little orifice gem/s=beautiful spring)

The *tsuchi*=mallet is the *tsuchi*=earth: All things of creation are born from it.

new year's day
from the mallet's tiny hole
gem after gem!

Bûson's preamble 槌は土也。万物皆是より生ず literally translates as follows: *Mallet-as-for, earth/dirt is. Ten-thousand-things all this-from [are] born*). As far as I know, Buson is the first to point out the earth=mallet homophone. This enhances the *ku* as a just-so-story. Such stories are always justified by puns. The little mallet, one of the *Eight Treasures* [1] carried on the treasure ship, with each swing (if I understand right, it doesn't really have to hit anything) bears riches. The hole in the head is not visible, *but it must be there* because things just keep popping out. The metaphor is fabulous, as behooves the infancy of the year, while the earthy link reminds us of Ruskin on iron.[2] The *ku* is also a paraverse of a poem by Eu [?] read in a haiku fest Buson had participated in. Only the first five syllabets differ: *"The first day* [+obj?]*" tsuitachi-o.*[3] Depending whether the "o" is read as an object marker or an indicator of contradiction and surprise, Eu's *ku* either emphasizes the coincidence of lunar and solar calendars by making the first day a tiny hole, or singularity, through which all comes to us, *or* marvels that all this wealth pours forth though it is only the first day. Buson's paraverse avoids such intellectualizing by using *ganjitsu* (new year's day) a solid word fitting the hammering metaphor. Still, only the earthy spin provided by the preamble really differentiates his slightly amended poem from that by his predecessor.

雪の色やあら玉の年のあさ鏡 紹巴 大発句
yuki no iro ya aratama no toshi no asakagami jôha 1523-1602
(snow's color!/?/: new/rough-gem-year's morning-mirror)

the color of snow
morning mirror for
the *ara*-gem year

Both the new and rough aspect needs to be read into the *ara*. "Morning-mirror" is both the mirror used and the act of composing one's hair and applying make-up first thing in the morning. This poem is interesting for making us think about the color of the snow, something that will be done by later poets.

元日や雪を踏む人憎からず 也有
ganjitsu ya yuki o fumu hito nikukarazu yayû 1701-83
(original-day: snow treading/trampling person hate/d-not)

new year's day
i do not hate those who
trample on the snow

(trans. blyth, depunctuated and reparsed)

There are countless old *ku* complaining about sullied snow. It wasn't just a matter of aesthetics. When the aesthete winters in his hut, the unmarked snow serves as a hymen testifying to his triumphant (if humble) solitude. Moreover, as we have seen, snow on New Year's could, additionally, be seen as a mirror for the soul. At the same time, however, men on the New Year were broadminded and supposed to be above petty discrimination. That, and the fact the tracks were made by people out to witness sunrise or call on neighbors allowed Yayû to take a magnanimous view that seems to, but does not really contradict the view of the year as a gem. Here is another facet of the same:

---

1. *Treasures in Japan* The Sinosphere is full of magical treasures, the idea for which probably originated in India and became more fabulous to fit a civilization less religious but more child-oriented. Hence, parasols for floating up to heaven and cloaks to make one invisible (etc.) that would have delighted children as much as *anime* does today. Japanese, living on an archipelago, may well have taken the treasure ship more to heart than the Chinese from whom the idea came. I find myself thinking "cargo cult," with no anthropological research to justify it.

2. Ruskin on Iron Since reading that Ruskin destroyed Turner's erotic paintings, I have disliked him; but I still admire his advocacy of the aesthetics of common material. If you have not read it his once famous essay on Iron (far more important than precious metals for giving us our beautiful biosphere) you *must*.

3. Eu's Poem This obscure poet's *ku* is found in the *haikai* fest 寛保四年宇都宮歳旦帖 which 29 year-old Bûson participated in. Eu's *ku* itself may borrow from an older one (like the numerous *ku* on spring-within-the-year using Ariwara no Motokata's *waka*). The closest I have found so far is : *"The earth's wealth, / a sight that never bores: / spring blossoms* (つちのとみあかずながめん花の春 重宝 *tsuchi no tomi akazu nagamen hananoharu* jûhô 大三 1697 – actually, the last-5 is the usual "flowery spring," but I cannot help *trying* to improve things in translation). So, both Eu and Bûson may be paraversing Jûhô's *ku*. Since the magical mallet in question was held by the God of grain and wealth, Daikoku, the following 7-7 *ku* jokes: *"So, start with the sack / to draw a treasure ship"* (*mazu tawara-kara takara-bune kaku*) – Daikoku, you see, is always pictured seated upon his huge sack of grain.

青々と空の鏡やけさの春　蘆舟 玉かづら
aoao to sora no kagami ya kesa no haru roshû 1751
(blue-blue-as skies-mirror: morning-spring)

<blockquote>
the sky above
a bright blue mirror
spring's dawn
</blockquote>

The *aoao* is very *ao,* but *ao* is not quite the "blue" of English. It includes a pale, even blank element; but "pale" has a weak quality, while *aoao* has a positive, even vivid nuance. The mirror also has a spiritual side. It is not only reflective, in the deepest sense of the word, but suggests purity, for it must be kept free of dust to work, and dust is equated with the obfuscation of reflection by foul desire.

はつ空は欲なき人の鑑かな　素丸 一茶全集八
hatsuzora wa yokunaki hito no kagami kana somaru 1712-95
(first-sky-as-for, avarice/desires-not people's paragon[=mirror]!/'tis)

<blockquote>
the first sky   the first sky
paragon and mirror   a fine mirror for men
for pure souls   of pure heart
</blockquote>

The original of this aphoristic *ku* uses the Chinese character for "paragon," or "exemplar," but the pronunciation means it can not be read without also suggesting "mirror." In the chapter on *kagami mochi*, we will have more about the mirror, which is both a Buddhist symbol of the light of the Law in so far that it is equated with the moon, and the main symbol of Shintô, the Japanese Way of the Gods, analogous to the star of Judaism, cross of Christianity or sword of Islam. Back to the sky.

元日や世の息延る明の空　聞角 玉かづら
ganjitsu ya yo no iki noburu ake no sora bunkaku 1751
(original-day[ny] world[of humans]'s breath expands bright/dawn-sky)

<blockquote>
it's new year's
our breath expands
the dawning sky
</blockquote>

The original concerns a *breath-expanding-sky.* I improvised the middle line to avoid hyphens. Moreover, the idea of breath in Japanese has a magical, dreamy quality unmatched in English. Clam breaths are said to encompass worlds and Japanese illustrators tend to depict breath (especially that of sleeping people) as big balloons. Perhaps that is where I feel a *tama* quality.

元日や空にも塵のなかりけり　桃林 玉かづら
ganjitsu ya sora ni mo chiri no nakarikeri　tôrin 1751
(original-day! sky-in-even dust/trash [is] not [final])

     new year's day
    there is not a bit of dust
     even in the sky

The presence or absence of dust is a conceit common to the mirror and gem. The Shintô believer (if a religion without a catechism has "believers") is responsible for keeping his soul clean.

もろ／＼の見る物清し初日影　深雞 明和二
moromoro no miru mono kiyoshi hatsuhikage　shinkei 1765
(sundry seen things pure, first-sun-appearance/shine)

      everything
     we see is so pure
     first sunshine

This is mostly a matter of clean thinking – being sincere – but there was a vague concept of pollution and the corresponding practice of ablution in Shintô (as there is in Buddhism, Hinduism and more strongly in Judaism and Islam than in Christianity). Some poets seem confused about the relationship of the New Year to purity/pollution. The New Year, as the pure start of things (soul rather than material) antedates defilement, so it is *wrong* to write: *"New Year dawns / even the dust in the air / is purified"* (元日やまじはる塵も朝清め　湖月 安永四 *ganjitsu ya majiwaru chiri mo asa kiyome* kogetsu 1775). I can imagine dust from the clothing or lucky-straw floating in the early morning rays of sunlight, but that purification correctly understood, occurred the evening before. Somaru, who opined that one could live 9,000 years with the spirit of the New Year, expressed the absence of entropy on that day as follows:

器／＼すたる人なし君が春　素丸 同
utsuwa utsuwa sutaru hito nashi kimigaharu　somaru -1795
(vessel vessel dump [throw out contents of] person-not lord's spring)

  our lord's spring   no one at all
  not a soul empties   is out dumping stuff
  various vessels   the lord's spring

On this day, the vessels, i.e. our bodies are supposed to be filled with spirit and renewed. All the cleaning was done and food enough for the first three days of the New Year was cooked and the pots and pans scoured on New Year's Eve, so practically speaking, river and well-water would be reserved for ceremonial uptake. And, I imagine, old people with piss-pots would be very secretive about dumping them so as not to destroy the mood in the morning!

誰一人掃ともみえすけさの春　蓼太
dare hitori haku to mo miezu kesanoharu　ryôta 1707-87
(who/no one sweep even see-not morning's spring)

      not a single
    person is out sweeping
     the dawn of spring

元日の塵はつまんで投出され　武玉川 十一
ganjitsu no chiri wa tsumande nagedasare　mutama 1761
(original-day's dust-as-for pinched/ing thrown-out)

    on new year's　　　　　　　　　　　new year's day
    dust is pinched up　　　　　　　　trash is what we pinch
    and thrown out　　　　　　　　　　and chuck out

Does Ryôta indirectly explain the clean sky? The *Mutamagawa senryû* is hyperbole; but may be true. One would be as embarrassed to sweep on this day as a strict Christian on the Sabbath, but one might spy an overlooked speck of dust (or bit of trash) and pinch it up. We seem to have drifted off the subject of gems, but shiny things, including the pure, depend upon the counter-concept (対概念) of dust.

元日や埃をさまる日本橋　千驢
ganjitsu ya hokori osamaru nihonbashi　senryo 1751
(original-day! dust controlled [settles down] nihonbashi [japan-bridge])

    new year's day
    the dust finally settles
    on nihonbashi

The frantic dust-raising activities of the year's last day ends with sleep and the First Day, when the dust finally is allowed to settle. Nihonbashi, literally "Japan Bridge," was the center of Japan – the Point Zero for the mile-markers that extended throughout the realm – since 1603. This busy bridge was, and still is, in the middle of the Chuo, or Center Ward, of Edo, what is now Tokyo.

春立や浮て眼にたつ池塵 [原ママ] 卜峨　百家類題
haru tatsu ya uite me ni tatsu ikebokori　bokuga 19c?
(spring stands/comes floating eye-to stand[cut] pond dust)

    a new year　　　　　　　　　　　　my eyes caught
    dust floating in the pond　　　　by dust on the pond
    catches my eye　　　　　　　　　　spring is here

I first read the *ku* to mean "Spring is here / before my eyes up rises / dust in the pond" because the double *tatsu* or "stand/rise," neither of which made it into the translation, seems to play with a famous *waka* where the ruler looks over the nation from a hill-top and ritually observes the prosperity of his realm with its houses with their hearths' rising smoke and the rising birds (suggesting much grain?). Were it the full moon, we might imagine impurities floating up, but the New Year was in the dark of the moon. But wind-blown dust , common in spring proper – we will see it in cherry-viewing *ku* – was definitely not kosher on New Year's (If *kosher* sounds odd in a discussion about Japan, think of the common component here: *purity!*). No, it is left over from the busy year end and still floating because it is a calm windless day and the poet is equally calm and attentive. I wish I could have managed to keep the dust for last, as in the original, but it was impossible.

初空の心とけてや雪の雨　りん女
hatsuzora no kokoro tokete ya yuki no ame rinjo 1673-1757
(first-sky's heart/mind/soul melting/relaxing!: snow's rain)

<table>
<tr><td>the first sky
melting from the heart
snowy rain</td><td>is the heart
of the first sky melting?
a snowy rain</td></tr>
</table>

Why is this slush here with the dust? Because, the poet has found a way to put a positive New Year spin on it. The cold, cold heart of winter has melted. Better to celebrate *that* than bemoan the absence of a fine sunrise followed by a blue sky!

歳旦　福藁や塵さへけさは美しき　千代女
fukuwara ya chiri sae kesa wa utsukushiki   chiyojo 1701-75
(year-day // prosperity-straw: trash/dust even morning's beauty)

year-dawn

lucky straw!
even dust contributes
to this beauty

Japanese tend to be neatnicks. They are especially attentive to getting everything spic and span for the New Year. Yet this straw that is strewn about the entrance includes bits and pieces and dust. Taken in the wrong frame of mind, it might look trashy; but, shining in the first sunlight of the year, it looks like gold dust and adds to the enchanted beauty of this magical time. *"Lucky straw / On nunnery hems, / nunnery sleeves"* (福藁や御所の裾にも袂にも　千代 *fukuwara ya gosho no suso ni mo tamoto ni mo* chiyo-ni).

福藁に田毎の秋そ思はるゝ　乙由
fukuwara ni tagoto no aki zo omowaruru   otsuyû -1739
(lucky-straw-in field-each's autumn [+emph.] think/seems)

in lucky straw
we recall the moon-lit
autumn fields

I added the *moon* in translation, for "each field's fall" cannnot help but allude to Bashô's well-known *ku* (pg 107) or a *waka* (also well-known) on the omnipresent reflection of the moon. As moon-watching was a Buddhist rite, Otsuyû's *ku* gently exoticizes the Shintô New Year while giving it the patina of Autumn.

終年や佛の棚もかざり藁　吟江 ｱﾙｽ
shûnen ya hotoke no tana mo kazariwara ginkô 1775/6?
(ends year! buddha's/deceased' shelf too decorative straw)

spreading life

the year ends
even on the buddha shelf
ornamental straw

This year-end *ku* complements the last by turning a sacred Buddhist space into a Shintô manger. Issa wrote something close: *"It's New Years! / The crossroad Buddhas, too / wear red bandanas"* (正月や辻の仏も赤頭巾 一茶 *shôgatsu ya tsuji no hotoke mo akazukin*). To celebrate this time of cosmic birth, some of the cheerful spirit of life has been brought to the dark-side of the dead.

福藁に牛のめてたきねさめ哉　正常 大三
fukuwara ni ushi no medetaki nezame kana　seijô 1697
(lucky-straw-on, ox's/oxens' joyful/congrat./blessed sleep-wake!/'tis)

the oxen, too
are blessed to awake
on lucky straw

Almost a nativity scene! Another *ku* deadpans: *"New year's day: / The straw in the manger / is new, too"* (再現＝元日や牛部屋の藁も新しき　カコウ 安永六 *ganjitsu ya ushibeya no wara mo atarashiki*　kakô 1777).

福藁や暖さうに犬眠る　橡面坊 深山榮
fukuwara ya atatakasô ni inu nemuru　tochimenbô
(prosperity-straw: warmly[appearing] dog sleeps)

lucky straw
the dog sleeping
looks warm

Wherever it was strewn, so was the magical mood of the season. This is a modern (post-Shiki) haiku, objective. It is also *more*. Who cannot recall a drowsy moment of comfortable warmth as a child?

ふくわらに児のころひてほめにけら (り？) 鶯梭
fukuwara ni wara no korobite homenikera[ri?]　ôsa?　大三 1697
(prosperity straw-on/in [small]child falling, praised [+finality])

falling down
on the lucky straw, a kid
receives praise

Normally, falling is bad, but, here, it is auspicious. The lucky straw might even stick to the child. The *ku* found in Shiki's *Categorical* ends with an odd "ra" (ら) rather than the usual "ri" (り). A typo? Or a hint of laughing *kera kera?* The senryûesque *ku* is far better than this *haikai* doggeral: *"Lucky straw, / come to think about it / last year's washed hair"* (ふくわらや思へば云年の洗ひ髪 不求 江戸ヘンケイ *fukuwara ya omoeba kozo no araigami*　fukyû 1680). This next is no masterpoem either, but it is a fine epigram:

元朝にはくべき物や藁草履　風国 古句を観る
ganchô ni haku beki mono ya warazôri　fûkoku c1700
(original-morning-on wear-ought thing　straw zori)

roots

on new year's
we should start our day
in straw zôri

Everywhere, straw keeps ground warm and covers mud (Spring was often muddy) before the grass is well in, smells good, and reminds us of when we were closer to the ground and smelled it more often. In Japan, it is also wrapped around trees to protect them during the winter and, as noted already, used to create festoons encircling, or rather hallowing, sacred space. There is also something sensed by all: call it *rustic honesty*. In Japan, straw joins unpainted wood and unglazed clay as pristine material, as valuable as any precious metal, or more so for taking us back into pre-history. This challenges Occidental aesthetics, spoiled child of the human body and precious metals and rare minerals. *I repeat myself, for this cannot be overemphasized.* Yes, there is the straw in that manger reproduced in our nativity scenes, but that is as far as it goes. We may see the straw and even realize we love it when we think about it. *But who does?*

ざぶ／＼と泥わらんじの御慶哉　一茶
zabuzabu to doro-waranji no gyokei kana issa - 1827
(sloshily mud-*waranji* [straw-sandals]'s[honorific+] civilities!/?/'tis)

slish-sloshing
muddy *waranji* make
new year's greetings

Waranji is a rustic pronunciation of the *waraji*, crude straw macramé sandals worn by Issa and his neighbor. My dictionary gives *splish-splash* for *zabu-zabu*. A bird roughly shaking its wings in a bird bath does it; but *zabu-zabu* sounds harsher than *splish-splash,* and mud requires different mimesis.

だまって今日の草鞋穿く　山頭火
damatte kyô no waraji haku　santôka -1940
(silently[without speaking], today's *waraji* wear[put on])

      wordless
  i put on my *waraji*   lips clenched
     for today   i put on today's footwear

Santôka was a lost soul, "a drunken zen Buddhist" (Susumu Takiguchi), who wandered Japan in the early 20c. He is known for haiku of odd lengths (mostly short; sometimes long), often lacking a seasonal word, that still feel classic. Pilgrims wore *waraji*. Like the straw horseshoes (see *Topsy-turvy 1585*), they were dirt cheap and expendable. Since much of Santôka's walking was in the mountains, he is not exaggerating when he writes of "today's *waraji*." There is no indication that this is a New Year's *ku*. Indeed, it is not, and will not go into the poem index in the back of the book (I changed my mind, it is there, anyway). Yet, in combination with the *waraji,* it takes us back to the origin. Starting off his *day* with a fresh pair of *waraji!* Santôka reminds us of the enchanted life of *the traveler who starts each day as we start the New Year.* The verb for *being silent* used in the *ku* refers specifically to *not speaking*. I imagine a hung-over Santôka, in the entrance of a temple dorm or inn, composing this seasonless *ku* many would not even consider a haiku that, nonetheless, teaches us something about both the New Year and haiku.

道ばたの土めづらしやお正月　一茶
michibata no tsuchi mezurashi ya oshôgatsu issa -1827
(road-side's dirt rare/precious! [honorable] right-month(ny))

how rare this
dirt by the roadside
new year's day

Everything in this magic time beyond time was considered "rare," and the word "rare," in Japanese, meant *precious*. While Issa broadens the conventional idea of New Year rarity by adding dirt – we have seen this rarity=beauty applied to other's wives, etc. – here, he is not just playing with New Year conceit; his country, Shinano, was famous for heavy snowfall that was the first to come and the last to leave – from *snow* to *mosquito* and back again, to paraphrase another Issa *ku* – so this dirt really was new, a *discovery*, if I may borrow a word and idea from the ebullient Russian, Mikhail Prishvin.[1] Could the roadside dirt have been bared by the heavy traffic of New Year's callers?

元日やこの曙はサァいくら 柏筵 雑談 古選
ganjitsu ya kono akebono wa saa ikura hakutei 1763
(original-day: this sunrise/dawn-as-for, well, how much?)

new year's day
so, tell me, then, how much
this dawn is worth!

The answer, of course, is that it is *priceless*. But the poem is not only catechism. The colloquial "saa" suggests it is meant to be a chuckle at the metaphor of Spring as a gem.

Making the Sky Revisited

初空やよろこぶ雲の置処　鳥酔
hatsuzora ya yorokobu kumo no okidokoro chôsui -1769?
(first-sky:/! delighting cloud/s' placed/arranged place/location)

the first sky!
this the proper place for
clouds o' joy

the first sky
this is where the clouds
of joy are kept

the first sky
the clouds placement
delights me

our first sky
so where should we place
the clouds of joy

---

1. Spring Discovery When the Russian scientist+essayist, Mikhail Prishvin, standing on his doorstep, spied the first black earth rising from the snow, he felt like Columbus discovering the New World and shouted *"Land Ho!"* (*Nature's Diary*). I believe it was in *his* sixteeth Spring (a partial translation, with Updike's intro., was published by Penguin America as part of the Hoagland ed. *nature essay* series; the full book – much of the ethnographic parts of the book are missing in the Englished version – & other bks are available from editions Papyrus, in Japanese translation).

I was happy with Issa's concern about *fashioning* the gem called the sky. To some, such concern may seem as precious (meaning *reprehensible*) as Chiyo's morning glory seemed to Issa. Call it vain if you wish, but I find even the idea of taking responsibility for the state of the world a good thing. It is slightly possible the above *ku* may also be about fashioning or designing the first sky but seems more likely to play with the Chinese idea of "joy-clouds" (*yorokobu kumo* being an oddly direct Japanification), those propitious, stylized tufts of cloud gracing magical peaks in Chinese landscapes. The third reading is a result of my having seen many extraordinary arrangements of clouds as precious as any gem and as beautiful as any flower. To see something especially good on the First Day of the Year is a blessing, something to rejoice over. While my last reading, like the first two, refers to the Chinese clouds, I am not certain if I mean to say that Chôsui (Bird-drunk) has started to paint or that he is reflecting on the relationship of Chinese symbols to the cosmos of the Japanese. (出鱈目ですね。専門家よ、御意見下さい！)

The August Spring?

日の春をさすがに鶴の歩み哉　其角
hinoharu o sasuga ni tsuru no ayumi kana kikaku -1707
(sun's/day's-spring[+contadict./emphat.] as-expected crane's-walk!/'tis/?)

the young sun
yet it moves as befits
an august crane

a day so young
yet moving in majesty
like a crane

day to day
the majestic spring's
crane-walk

I put Kikaku's *ku* in this chapter because the slow-motion is both caused by and a cause of the attentiveness we have seen and because it is appropriate to lead the next chapter, when we find time virtually suspended. I was also lost for another way to squeeze this *ku*, one of the most enigmatic haiku to be often anthologized, into this book. The juxtaposition of the crane's legendary age (a thousand years), its august gait and the balmy days of early spring make it irresistible to anthologists though they cannot say exactly what it means. To leave it out would be to risk protests from those who protest such things (if there are any: no one has yet chastised me for leaving out a favorite sea cucumber *ku* from *Rise, Ye Sea Slugs!*). The "sun's (or, day's/s') spring" (*hi-no-haru*), a phrase of Kikaku's coinage (the usual being "this morning's spring" (*kesa-no-haru*) and "this day's spring" (*kyô-no-haru*) may be intended to bring out the youthful spirit of spring the better to contrast with its great age, evoked by the solemnity of the crane's movement, viewed against the vertical axis of time. This sun in Kikaku's *ku* moves slowly but pleasantly through the sky (It has no truck with the melancholy variety of time that goes *"a crawlin' by"*). Likewise, for the *day*, rather than the sun – though both are one in Japanese – in the second. The third, takes a longer view. One might think this a Spring *ku*, rather than a New Year's *ku*, but the auspicious crane pretty much demands the Fifth Season. Harold Stewart's well-considered translation:

TIME RENEWED

As New Year dawns, the stork with stately grace
Begins the spring by its initial pace

– Kikaku (from Stewart's *A Chime of Windbells* 1969/87)

元日・初日
ganjitsu • *hatsuhi*

THE ORIGINAL DAY

春立つや障子にあたる日の匂ひ 省我
haru tatsu ya shôji ni ataru hi no nioi shôga LS 失出典
(spring comes: shôji/paper-door-on hit sun's smell/glow)

spring is here
the smell of the sun
on the shôji

The *shôji* are the paper-doors that are repapered at the end of the year, so that they would indeed give off a new paper smell when heated by the sunshine. Such faint, pleasant scents are the stuff of day-dreams and help make the New Year so enchanting. Yet, because smell/scent in Japanese includes a connotation of glowing beauty, the poet *might* be describing the visual beauty of the sunlit paper.

はつ春によごれの見ゆる障子哉 樗堂
hatsu haru ni yogore no miyuru shôji kana chodô -1814
(first-spring-in, dirtiness seen shôji (paper-door)!/'tis)

at first spring
marks of soiling seen
on the *shôji*

Our attention is drawn to the purity of the new *shôji* by our own senses, fine-tuned in the New Year season. Within a month, the paper will have so many fingerprints none will notice them. Why begin a chapter on the Original Day with two *ku* that do not even include the term? Because, if you are like me, they take you back to your childhood, even if it was not in a country with paper doors.

初春やけさの心をいつまでも 桃里 玉かづら
hatsuharu ya kesa no kokoro o itsumademo tôri 1751
(first-spring[new years]: / morning's heart[+obj] forever)

first-spring
this morning's mind
forevermore!

元日や此心にて世に居たし　蘭更 1726-99
ganjitsu ya kono kokoro nite yo ni itashi　rankô 1726-99
(new year's day: this heart/mind-with, world-in be-want)

first wish

new year's day
i would stay in this
state of mind!

first wish

new year's day
that the world will ever
be this way!

Imagine how a young child feels on this day combining the magic of Christmas, New Year's, Easter, Independence Day and a birthday! Grown up, most Japanese must still feel that magic, amazement, hope and shared love very strongly and fall into a different state of consciousness – a space located in time-zero – every New Year. What Tôri and Rankô want is not only the unspoken desire of all Japanese but, an openly acknowledged, and I think *good*, philosophy, summed up in a popular saying my dictionary translates: "Be always as naive as you were when a novice" (*sho-shin wasururu bekarazu* = first-heart/mind forget ought-not). In other words, *"Never lose your original naïveté,"* which is to say, *your original openness, enthusiasm and dreams.* (Note: English-speakers have perverted the meaning of "naïve." In Japanese, naïve = *naibu* still means someone who is not cynical, but trusting of others and free of excessive mental-armor, is graced with a sensitive (receptive to the natural and human environment) and kind nature.) As we work, we tend to narrow our target, temper our enthusiasm, and lose track of, or grade down our dreams. Perhaps, this is inevitable, but, on some deeper level, it is not and should not be. We should believe in our *shoshin,* our first-heart. This *ku* has many seconds, and *they* have seconds:

元日の賓客なれや我心　左簾 句鑑
ganjitsu no hinkyaku nare ya waga kokoro　saren 1770
(original-day[n year]'s treasured-guest become, my heart)

heart of mine
become a treasured guest
on new year's day

元日は一日朝の心哉　卯雲 新選
ganjitsu wa ichinichi asa no kokoro kana　uun 1773
(original-day[n-y]-as-for, one/all-day, morning-heart 'tis)

on new year's
all day long we have
a morning mind

願くは常も元日の心哉　和城 安永六
negawakuba tsune mo ganjitsu no kokoro kana　wasei 1777
(desire/grant-if, ordinarily even/too new-years' heart 'tis)

heaven grant me
a new year's heart!
all year-long

わすれめやいつも此氣を花の春　橘旭
wasureme ya itsumo kono ki o hana no haru　kyôkyoku 1751
(forget-not! always this feeling[+obj] flower-spring 玉桂)

don't *ever*
forget! this feeling
of spring

Ganjitsu, the "original" or "principal-day," is the most common word for New Year's Day in Japanese.

初空や物を学ばゝ此心　津富 1770 句鑑
hatsuzora ya mono o manababa kono kokoro　tsuhô
(first-sky: things[what counts][+obj] learn-if, this heart)

ah, first sky:
to learn anything
this is the mindset!

the first sky
all learning begins
just like this

地を替えて初日を植える心哉　滄浪
chi o kaete hatsuhi o ueru kokoro kana　sôrô　1760
(earth/dirt [+obj] changing/ed first-sun[+obj] plant heart!/ 'tis)

changing the soil
we plant the first sun
in our hearts

the idea is this:
change the soil and plant
the first sun

All these *ku* are similar to Tôri and Rankô's at heart. Only the last, by Sôrô, shows any originality.

世の中は心なりけりけさの春　宗因
yo no naka wa kokoro narikeri kesanoharu　sôin 1604-82
(world-among [whole world]-as-for, heart/mind becomes [+emph.] morning-spring [ny])

as spring dawns
our world is nothing
but mind

"The world is mind precipitated" writes Emerson. On this first day of the New Year, mind is not yet precipitated. All is still Atman, the godhead: pure potential.

何事も心のまゝや（よ）けさの春　蔓甕 or 鹿貞 大三
nanigoto mo kokoro no mama ya[yo] kesanoharu　man__? or katei?　1697
(what/all things,too heart's/s' as-is/was [emphatic] morning-spring/new-year)

as spring dawns
everything remains
purely spirit

all things go
where the spirit leads
spring's dawn

in all things
we do as we desire
spring's dawn

The first reading is similar to Sôin's last. The others take *kokoro no mama* to mean "as desired." This is the saintly state of mind, where one is so pure, morality is meaningless.

けさの春何の心もなかりけり　由誓　百家類題
kesa no haru nan no kokoro mo nakarikeri　yûsei 1788-1859
(morning's spring [ny] any heart/mind/sign/intent/awareness even not [+emph])

spring dawns
and i have nothing
on my mind

new year dawned
and i felt nothing
nothing at all

new year's day
and i feel *nothing*
in particular

Blyth would have written *"all mind and no mind are ultimately the same"* and been done with it. I keep thinking of possibilities. One more: *"Spring dawned / and i had forgotten / all about it!"*

有様は命ちゞまるけさの春　来山
ariyô wa inochi chijimaru kesanoharu　raizan 1653-1716
(have-appearance=reality-as-for life shrinks this-morning's spring)

spring dawn:
having form is what
shrinks life

to have form
means life shortens with
each spring

spring dawns
the reality is that our
lives shorten

133

Perspective is everything. Do we *get* a New Year? Or, does each New Year's arrival mean there is one less remaining for us? There is a good reason most New Year *ku* focus on the immaterial. Only the material ages. The figurative meaning of *ariyô* is "in reality," but, literally, it means *"have-appearance/ form."* Years can hardly burden *nothing*.

何事となくてうれしき初日哉 城仄
nanigoto to nakute ureshiki hatsuhi kana   jôsoku 1767
(anything-not[there being nothing]delightful, first-sun/day 'tis)

<blockquote>
i'm happy
for nothing at all
the first day
</blockquote>

<blockquote>
the first day
happy about nothing
in particular
</blockquote>

Haiyû Oruka reminds me that the maverick folklorist Origuchi once exploded, "Without giving it real thought, don't you *dare* go calling the New Year something to be joyful about!" (「お正月だからって考えなしにおめでとうなんて言うな」). But, the New Year is, *by definition*, a time of joy.

元日や何となく気の改まり 百夫
ganjitsu ya nan to naku ki no aratamari   hyakuo 1765
(original-day: what-&-not[sorta, in some way] mood/spirit/ energy's renewing)

<blockquote>
new year's day
in no particular way
we're renewed
</blockquote>

<blockquote>
new year's
we're just sort of
recharged
</blockquote>

The word *ki* 気 usually pops up in English as *ki* or (the Chinese) *chi,* an esoteric energy flow. Combined with other words, it means: *genki* = 元気 = "original-*ki,*" i.e., "well" or "healthy;" *byôki* = 病気 = "sick-*ki,"* or "ill;" *kimochi* = 気持ち = "*ki-*holding," or "feelings;" *kûki* = 空気 = "empty-*ki,"* or "air;" *tenki* = 天気 = "sky/heaven-*ki,"* or "weather;" *kibun* = 気分= "*ki*-part/division," or "mood;" *yôki* = 陽気= "sun/bold/ yang-*ki,"* or "cheerful," and *inki* = 陰気 = "shade/yin," or "gloomy," etc.. In Japanese, it is a plain, familiar character. In this *ku,* though, it does have a touch of the magical, spiritual (Oriental?) quality Occidentals so like to dwell on. Be that as it may, the New Year renews our *ki*, renews *us*.

寛さを何にたとへん明の春 祇江
yuruyakasa o nani ni tatoen ake no haru   gikô 1765
(looseness/relaxation[+obj] what-as metaphor? bright/dawning-spring)

<blockquote>
the dawn of spring
what can compare to this
generosity?
</blockquote>

<blockquote>
what should stand
for generosity itself?
the dawn of spring
</blockquote>

<blockquote>
what might
we call *liberality?*
the new year
</blockquote>

Yuruyakasa is defined as "generous," "lenient," "lax," "slack," "loose." Could it be the gate of birth opening wide? The character used for *yuruyaka* is not the most common one (緩) but 寛, a character with the additional meaning of *tolerance*, so the metaphor the poet has in mind, if he had one in mind, is that of the Cosmos-as-a-generous-ruler (I would write "a *liberal*" but fear the significance of this word changes so quickly it is practically useless), providing yet another beautiful spring to us.

湯上りの一くつろぎや花の春 多代女 再現
yuagari no hitokutsurogi ya hananoharu tayojo ♀ 1775-1865
(hot-water-up-from's one[a] relaxation:/?/& flower's/precious/celebratory spring/ny)

that languid feeling
right after you leave the bath
oh, luscious spring!

i get a moment
to relax after my bath
then, it's spring

The character for *"kutsurogi"* (寛ぎ) is the same as the one used in the previous *ku* for *yuruyaka*. My respondent favors the first reading, where it is part of a metaphor of the New Year. In Japan, baths are so hot they leave you in a pleasant stupor, appropriate to the New Year. The metaphor reflects reality: working like a dog at the end of the year, we finally get a moment of respite. Using Christian mythology, we might say this is the First Day of Creation *and* the Seventh. The literal reading is less likely.

我なから元日ハ気の広き哉　巾声 大三物
ware nagara ganjitsu wa ki no hiroki kana fusei? 1697
(me-being[even for me], original-day-as-for, *ki*'s broadness 'tis)

portrait of a poet

even curmudgeon
is surprised at his ease
on new year's day

despite myself
i'm so broadminded
on new year's

我ながら心のひろしみよの春 保義 文久五
ware nagara kokoro no hiroshi miyo no haru hogi mid-19c
(me-being[even for me], heart/mind's broad [honorific+]realm's spring[ny])

despite myself
broadminded in the spring
of our realm

So much New Year's vocabulary does not translate. "Realm (*miyo*)" stresses *this particular* Spring or New Year. Broad/wide (*hiroki/shi*) has the same tolerant/mellow=good connotation in English and Japanese (Only English has the reverse (bad) side, *i.e.* "a loose broad."). "Spring" (*haru*), as we already know . . .

正月や心はひまていそかしき 一且
shôgatsu ya kokoro wa hima de isogashiki ichigi 百家類題 19c
(correct-month[new years]: heart/mind-as-for, free/[have]leisure-from/by, busy)

the new year's
our minds, free
are very busy

A rare one-of-a-kind *ku*? The New Year's frame of mind is, according to all other poets, slack if not still. But, the fact of the matter is this: when we have time off from work, most of us think *more*, not less. Consider the irregular state of mind called *love*. English speakers tend to associate it with the loss of reason, but the traditional Japanese word for "love," *mono-omoi* or "thing-thinking," reflects the way we are flooded with thought (fantasies, what-ifs, how-to's, fears, regrets, etc.). In other words, for all the jubilation, we can bet that in Japan, as everywhere, the suicide rate goes up over New Year's. The intellectual's ideal of *a blank mind* is appropriate for many reasons, but, I think, unrealistic and seldom realized.

元日は心にもある重み哉　新甫 文久五百
ganjitsu wa kokoro ni mo aru omomi kana　shinho 19c
(original day-as-for, heart even-in/on is weight/heaviness 'tis)

                  on new year's
                  even the mind
                  matters

on new year's   on new year's
we even take spirit   even our thoughts
  seriously   carry weight

                  on new year's
                  even the intangible is
                  real as can be

This *ku* is remarkable for not dwelling on the absence, or openness of the First Day. We are reminded of the *Logos* of the Genesis, though the spirit/mind here is not that of a God or idea *out there*, but what is within us, and the vagueness of Japanese with respect to number and definite articles allows it to be shared by one and all. Giving reality to spirit suggests a material world waiting for the re-creation.

こゝろまで枕になるやけさのはる　一瓢 玉山人歌集
kokoro made makura ni naru ya kesa no haru　ippyô - 1840
(heart/mind/soul-until, pillow/bed-into-become!/?/: morning's spring)

                  spring dawns
                  even mind becomes
                  her epithet

even our minds   even *kokoro*
serve as its epithet   can be a pillow word
  a new spring   the new year

                  the heart itself
                  serve for poetic conceit
                  as spring dawns

At first, I read the "pillow/bed" (*makura*) literally, and imagined an avowed sleep-a-bed who didn't even *nod* in the direction of duty toward the Rising Sun, or a pillow offered to the Goddess of the Spring; but, on second thought, realized there were far better ways to express either idea than "even [my/our/the/a] mind/s become/s [my/our/the/a] pillow." Considering the number of New Year's *ku* with a *kokoro* (mind/heart), Ippyô probably meant that said *kokoro* qualifies as what Japanese call a "pillow-word (*makura-kotoba*)," *i.e.*, a word, or phrase serving as a "set epithet" for "this morning's spring." These pillow-words typically connect a place with a historical association or natural features (like state mottos in the USA). As such, *kokoro*, *i.e.*, heart/mind/spirit, is exceptionally abstract.

元日や稚き時の物覚え　湖十 新選
ganjitsu ya osanaki toki no monooboe　kojû 1773
(original-day [new years]: childhood-time's thing-memory)

on new year's   remembering
i remember things   childhood things
  of childhood   it's new year

正月の子供に成て見たき哉 一茶
shôgatsu no kodomo ni narite mitaki kana issa
(new year's child-into/as become-try-want!/'tis -1827)

    on new year's   how, oh, how
    we wish to become   i'd like to be a child
    a child again   new year's day

Issa has some good early childhood memories. But not enough, for his step-mother behaved like the stereotype. He deserved to enjoy more years of magic. Unfortunately, Issa did not enjoy a long dotage.

春はたつよこしまもなき年初哉 貞繼 毛吹草
haru wa tatsu yokoshima mo naki nensho kana teikei 1645
(spring appears/stands evil/dirty time-even not year-start)

    spring rises
    without a trace of sin
    a year old!

Tatsu ("appear/rise") suggests a baby (*nensho* punning on *nenshô* = of tender age?) standing up and "year-start" could mean "first birthday." To compensate for the unEnglishable, I took great license translating.

日の本はさかやき青しけさの春 柳几 新五百題
hinomoto wa sakayaki aoshi kesanoharu ryûki 1819
(sun's origin-as-for, shaven-brow pale/blue: morning's spring)

    a clean pate

    this spring dawn
    the origin of the sun
    freshly shaven

The color *ao* does not share the bad connotation of our beard "shadow." Pale blue-green, it suggests young things like new leaves. Hence, "*freshly* shaven." That part of the crown, the *sakayaki,* may allude to the invisible new moon, for it includes the character "moon" (月代). A less poetic, but understandable *ku* has the *sakayaki*=moon/ths cover the poet's age: *"The first morning / bare pates help hide / our years."* (元朝の月代年をかくす哉 可曲 大三物 *ganchô no sakayaki toshi o kakusu kana* kakyoku 1697).

元日の人や無弦の琴のをと 大江丸 俳諧袋
ganjitsu no hito ya mugen no koto no oto ôemaru -1805
(original-day's human/men: no-string zither's sound)

    on the first day   on the first day
    men hear the music of   we are the sound made by
    a stringless harp   a stringless harp

The second reading is safer, for lack of a verb suggests identity. Chinese philosopher Zhuangzi's idea of a stringless zither – the sounds of the natural world – as the best music of all and the Japanese idea of the New Year as pure *kokoro,* or mind/heart, fuse. The *ku* before it in the *Haikaibukuro* (*haikai* bag) is *"This year, too / I declare my no-mind! / blossom lodge"* (ことしも又御無心申さう花のやど 大江丸？俳諧袋 *kotoshi mo mata gomushin môsô hananoyado* ôemaru 1719-1805). A *blossom lodge* usually means an inn for blossom viewers. Here, it means one where the New Year is passed, or, possibly, the spring, itself. There is a metaphysical match in a temporary abode where one is not at home and the no-mind which *declared* also means "begging," i.e., *This year, too / I throw myself on the mercy / of a beautiful spring!*

人毎に妖直しけりけさの春　嘯山 葎亭集
hitogoto ni yônaoshikeri kesanoharu　shôzan 1717-1801
(person-each-in/by beauty/witchery/sensuality renews this-morning's spring)

    the voluptuous   to every body
in each person reborn   charm returns to roost
     spring arrives   spring dawns

Though the difference between *yo* and *yô* in Japanese argues against it, I believe the original puns on *yo-naoshi*, "world-correcting," a term used both for what we might call Buddhist millennialism (though thousand-year units have nothing to do with it), and riots against price-gouging wealthy merchants. Issa wrote a number of *yo-naoshi* haiku. Here is one he wrote when an earthquake struck on New Year's,

世の中をゆり直すらん日の始　一茶
yononaka o yurinaosuran hinohajime　issa 1824
(world-among[obj] shake-renew/fix[emph.], sun/day's-start)

hoh, shake up
and fix our world!
the first day

Synchronicity found! Had naturalist John Muir, who was *delighted* to experience a large earthquake in the Yosemites and astounded to find others (whites and indians alike) terrified rather than thrilled, written a *ku*, it would have been something like this: *"An earthquake, whee! / Mother Nature bounces baby / New-Year on her knee!"* But to return to more conventional New Year's metaphor:

あら玉ハ皆よい男よいおんな　永語 初代川柳
aratama wa mina yoi otoko yoi onna　eigo 18c *senryû*
(uncut/new-gem[=ny day]-as-for/on, all good men, good women)

potential beauty

on new year's day
all men and women are
worth looking at

on new year's day   *original equality*

    in the rough   on new year's day
every man and woman   every man and women look
     a diamond   as good as new

The three paraverses hint at the meaning of the original's *aratama* pun, but are not as good as a single *gem* of a poem. I like the *senryû* better than the following haiku with common content: *"All people / look good to each other / on New Year's"* (あひ見るに皆よい人そけふの春　定直 大三 *aimiru ni mina yoi hito zo kyonoharu*　sadanao 1697); *"Even on New Year's / some women look good / some bad"* (元日も女は眉目のよし悪し 原水　大三物 *ganjitsu mo onna wa mime no yoshi warushi*　gensui 1697).

はつ春や男はかりもうつくしき 月守 新五百題
hatsuharu ya otoko bakari mo utsukushiki gesshu 1819
(first-spring!/: men[males] just/only too/also beautiful)

it's new year's
even men by themselves
are beautiful

"Men," as in male gender. Are they transformed by their behavior or their dress? I imagine an all-male group of poets, but it could be about first *kabuki*.

元日や同じやうなる人の顔 成美
ganjitsu ya onaji yô naru hito no kao seibi -1816
(original-day: same appearance/manner becomes/is people's face/s)

on new year's the faces of people look alike	new year's day appearances converge: people's faces	new year's all people share one face

Earlier, Rankô wrote: *"New Year's! / Today people share / One mind"* (元日やけさはひとしき人心 蘭更 *ganjitsu ya kesa wa hitoshiki hitogokoro* -1799).   One mind, one face. Platonism is not limited to the Classic West. Seibi avoids the "good/beautiful" trap by using the "same." Shiki went even further:

元日は是も非もなくて衆生なり 子規
ganjitsu wa ze mo hi mo nakute shujô nari shiki 1866-1902
(original-day-as-for, good/right and bad/wrong not: humans/sentient-beings are/become)

our first day there is no good or bad just being		on new year's no good bad right wrong just sentience

new year's day;
nothing good or bad,
just human beings.

trans. Blyth (my parsing, etc.)

Blyth notes, "there is no distinction between higher and lower, respectable and criminal, men and animals." So, Blyth was aware that the term used by Shiki, *shujô*, means *all sentient beings*, not just *our* species. Why, then, "*human* beings"? Is this an editing error? Did Blyth intend "*fellow* beings"? Shiki also wrote a *ku* that was a direct challenge to both the ideal of equality and pure spiritualism:

元朝や米くれさうな家はどこ 子規
ganchô ya kome kuresô na ie wa doko shiki 1892
(original/ny-morn.:/! rice/meal give-seems house-as-for where)

the beggar
< 乞食 >

it's new year's now where is a house that will feed me?		new year dawns now where's a house to give me rice?

Rice can mean meal, or it can mean rice, the most desirable meal. But let's return to the equality which Issa expands to clearly include sentient beings other than us.

古郷や馬も元日いたす顔 一茶
furusato ya uma mo ganjitsu itasu kao   issa -1827
(hometown/country!/: horse's/s' too orig.day[ny] doing/making face)

my hometown
even the horses look
new yearsy

back home where
even horses seem to know
it's new year's

What expression, exactly, marks *a face having a New Year*? I'd bet on the figurative second reading.

牛馬も元日顔の山家哉 一茶
ushi uma mo ganjitsu-gao no sanka kana   issa
(cow horse too, orig. day [new years]-face mountain-house)

a country house
even cows, horses boast
new year mugs

But, other *ku* show that Issa really wants to express the animals' awareness through their *faces*.

何となく人むつましきけふの春 浮輕 大三
nan to naku hitomutsumajiki kyô-no-haru   yûkei 1697
(whatnot[vaguely] people-affectionate, today's-spring)

today's spring
in some vague way
seems dear

today's spring
i feel a vague love
for people

Japanese respondents vote for the second reading. But, why "*today's* spring," rather than the standard "*this morning's* spring"? To show it is the daytime and warm? Because it is People's Day, the Seventh, rather than the First, or puns on the *Sixth* (*mutsubi*), as an affectionate (*mutsumajiki*) day? Who knows!

元日や何やら人のしたり顔 春雷 新選
ganjitsu ya nani yara hito no shitarigao   shunrai 1773
(orig.-day!/: what huh [for some reason] people's did-it=smug-face/air)

on new year's
our faces seem to say
we did it!

Compare this to "*People's faces / all cracking smiles / on new year's*" (人の面皆にこ／＼と明の春 翠山 明和2 *hito no tsura mina nikoniko to ake no haru* suizan 1765); "*On New Year's / no one on the road / looks seedy*" (元日や行かふ人に貧相なき 祇徳 *ganjitsu ya ikikô hito ni hinsô naki* gitoku 1765), for every one is rich of heart; or, "*All people / have relaxed faces: / spring dawns*" (皆人の和らぐ顔や明けの春 千蝶 玉桂 *mina hito no yawaragu kao ya akenoharu* sencho 1751). Nothing is even close to Shunrai's *ku*. The others just rehash old ideas. (「百顔もけさ和らおふ」 春日哉 道無 大三1697 など見れば、やはり、春雷の句がうまい！)

& the gods

元朝や神代の事も思はるゝ　守武
ganchô ya kamiyo no koto mo omowaruru   moritake 1473-1549
(original morning/day:/! gods' age's thing-even thought-of)

>   new year's day
>   the world of the gods
>   remembered

My translation is affected by my fondness for "remember," a magical word if taken literally. Excluding the placement of the verb, Blyth's prosaic translation is more accurate: *"It is New Year's morning; / I think also of the Age / Of the Gods."* Blyth's capitalized "Of" bothered me at first, but I came to like the way it allows one to ponder the *Age* before proceeding to *Of the Gods*. For any other poet, the "I" might better be *we*, but Moritake, as hereditary High Priest of the Shrine of Ise, the top shrine of Shintô, was himself in charge of god/s-things (*kamigoto*) for the nation. *Hokku* anthologies and haiku *saijiki* often start off with this *ku*, not only because the right theme is suitable, but because (if I have it right) Moritake is sometimes considered the first *haikai* master of the lineage that blossomed with Bashô.

元日は法師目なれぬ神代哉　溪石
ganjitsu wa hôshi me narenu kamiyo kana   keiseki 1774
(orig. day/ny-as-for, law-teacher [budd. priest/s] eye become-not gods-era!/?/'tis)

>   new year's day
>   not a bonze to be seen
>   it's the age of the gods

Nothing in mind, the horizontal equality of all, and, now, a vertical connection with the Age of the Gods. This Age, in one form or another, was shared by all humans before theocidal cults swept out of the dry cradle of civilization to run down and strangle their far-flung ancestors and spread monocultures of God (And Shintô goes back even further to include animistic abstraction preceding named gods).

正月や實に人の気も天の橋　幸賢　反故集
shôgatsu ya jitsu ni hito no ki mo ama no hashi   kôken 1810?
(correct-month[ny]: really, people's/s' spirit/s to heaven's bridge)

>   the new year
>   human spirits cross
>   heaven's bridge

元日や神路へもどる人心　峯島　安永四
ganjitsu ya kamiji e modoru hitogokoro   hôtô 1775
(orig.day[ny]:/! god-path/road-to return person-heart/mind)

new year's day the minds of men retrace the way of the gods	new year's day our minds travel back the gods' path

天の戸も明初にけり神の春 其道 宝暦十一
ama no to mo akesomenikeri kaminoharu kidô 1761
(heaven's door also open-begins [finality] god/s-spring)

> heaven's door
> also begins to open
> the gods' spring

Does *heaven's door* mean the firmament and "also"(*mo*) the blossoms of "the flower's spring" (ch.11)? The "door" was a boulder-blocked mouth of a cave in Ise which the Sun Goddess had to be lured from. So Ise was not just a place, but the source of the Sun, which was to say, time itself. Another poet wrote: *"New Year's Day / to be born a human / and in Ise!"* (元日や人と生れて伊勢の國 丘高 題業名所 *ganjitsu ya hito to umarete ise no kuni* kyûkô 17?18?19c?). One is lucky to be born human for it is closer to the level of a Buddha than a "lower level of reincarnation;" and doubly lucky to be born in Gods' Country.

> the new year   the new year
> our spirits soar across   when people really
> heaven's bridge   reach heaven

Two more translations of Kôken's *ku* on the previous page. Not wanting to break up the three *ku* reading cluster, I saved them for here. Unlike the cave and its entrance, the bridge is not common in New Year haiku. As a physical metaphor, it usually refers to the Milky Way, but here it is figurative.

天満宮御修復出来しに 天の御戸猶きら／＼しけさの春　宗春
tenmangû goshûfuku dekishi ni ama no mito nao kirakirashi kesanoharu sôshun c1730
(tenman-shrine [honorific] restoration completion-for// heaven's [hon.]gate still shiny morning's spring)

for the completion of the tenmangû shrine reconstruction

> heaven's gate
> even more brilliant
> this new year

As is true for all-too-many celebratory *ku*, the original is boring (and the translation is worse). I include the poem *for its idea:* namely, the parallel of the renewal of the year and the tradition of deliberately taking apart and rebuilding a shrine. Bernard Rudofsky claimed this practice reflected a Japanese "propensity for destruction ... sometimes worked off in rituals" and connected it to a "web of pathological streaks," including "ceremonial lunacy" and "the elementary destructiveness of the problem child" (*The Kimono Mind*: 1965). Though an artist, this condescending Occidental oddly failed to recognize how enchanting a practice it is: *de- and re-construction is the way to keep a structure young forever.*

日本紀や天地一枚明の春　旧室
nihonki ya tenchi ichimai akenoharu kyûshitsu 1682-1764
(japan chronicles [*nihon(sho)ki*]: heaven-earth one-sheet open/brightening spring)

> the dawn of spring
> earth and sky one sheet
> our chronicles!

The *Nihon-shoki,* like the *Kojiki* (*Chronicle of Ancient Matters*), tells the creation myths of Japan. The name of the former, having *ni* (sun) and *hon* (origin) in it, rather than the un-New Year "old/ancient" of the latter, is more suitable here. Imagine the gleaming surface of the ocean, viewed through the haze as it is illuminated by a ray of sunlight and quickly expands clear to the horizon!

元日を天地和合の始哉 子規 再現
ganjitsu o tenchi wagô no hajime kana   shiki -1902
(orig.-day=ny[obj] heaven-earth harmony/union's start!/?/'tis)

new year's day
the harmony of heaven
and earth starts

new year's day
when heaven and earth
start to fuse

This *ku* is pure philosophy, or *definition*. I put it here, for it reflects the idea of creation-as-union rather than separation, as do many of the older *ku* we saw in *That-year-this* (*kozo-kotoshi*).

元日の話や人のめつらしき 氷壺 文久五百
ganjitsu no hanashi ya hito no mezurashiki   hyôko mid-19c
(original-day's speech/talk/topic/s: peoples' rarity/preciousness)

the first day
our topics have little
of mankind

speech
on the first day
people are different

The first reading follows the concept of Day One belonging to the gods. On that day, it was a tradition to tell old tales where the Gods would figure more than mankind, which would indeed be rare. The second reading is more likely. *Difference* is "rare" (*mezurashiki*) in the additional Japanese sense of being attractive and reminds us of ancient times when unknown strangers were thought of as visiting gods.

正月言葉皆軽薄の世界哉 未存 大三
shôgatsu kotoba mina keihaku no sekai kana   mizon 1697
(new years words all light-thin (frivolous/shallow) world 'tis)

a world where
all words are frivolous
the new year

the new year
a world where all our
words are light

new year's day
a world where all we say
feels shallow

My first assumption was that *keihaku* (light-thin) here, had a good meaning for once – after all, what are greetings and civilities if not "light"? – but respondents doubt it. We will return to this *ku*.

正月は正月だけの咄かな たゝ女 新五百題
shôgatsu wa shôgatsu dake no hanashi kana   tayojo 1819
(new year's-as-for, new-year's only talk/topic!/?/'tis)

new year's
our only talk
is new year's talk

元日やつく／＼神のありがたき 魚淵 か 魚潤 文車
ganjitsu ya tsukuzuku kami no arigataki nabuchi 1755-1834 or gyokan 1772?
(original-day: keenly/intensely gods' grateful[thing]/obligation)

> new year's day
> how real the blessings
> of the gods

Arigataki describes a thing or state we are extremely grateful for. The root is the same as that of *arigatou*, "thank you;" it literally means "being-difficult." This combination of *difficulty* and *gratitude* is also found in the other Japanese "thanks," *sumanai*, literally, "un-ending," and reminds me of something my grandfather frequently said in English: *"Much obliged!"* This friend of Issa's (if it is Nabuchi's *ku*) did well by his gods. He had a prosperous peony nursery and lived long. He *should* be grateful.

唐のものさして（はあって）用なし神の春　調和
kara[tô] no mono sashite [wa atte] yônashi kaminoharu chôwa 1637-1715
(chinese-things emphatically [or, -as-for being] use-not gods' spring/ny)

> we have no use
> for chinese things on
> this, gods' spring

This poem sabotages itself. On the one hand, New Year's, as a celebration of roots, was purely native; but it was also supposedly *a time beyond discrimination* (see ch 11). I think of Christian zealots who would ditch the Christmas tree, but this ethnocentric boast is more ridiculous, for, unlike Buddhism, which, bells aside, can be left out of this day, Japanese dress, etiquette and the writing system, not to mention the luni-solar calendar, were *all* largely Chinese. Many Japanese recognized this:

けさの春李白か酒の上にあり 杉風 卯辰
kesa no haru rihaku ga sake no ue ni ari sanpû 1646-1732
(*this morning's spring, li po's wine-upon is/exists*)

> dawn's spring
> rests upon the wine
> of old li po

Chinese poet Li Po (701-62) loved his wine as much as Japanese loved him. His lyrical yet logical romanticism translates well. The *ku* may refer to part of the "Song of Hsiang-yang," to wit: *"There are thirty-six thousand days to a hundred years, / And each day one must drain three hundred cups, / From afar, the mallard-green of the Han River / Resembles grapes about to ferment. / This river could be turned into spring brew . . ."* (tr. Joseph J. Lee in the *Sunflower Splendor* anthology of Chinese poetry). The New Year was a time for drinking and celebration, to Li Po, one and the same thing.

元日や仏法いまだ注縄の外 蓼太
ganjitsu ya buppô imada shuren no soto ryôta 1707-87
(original-day: buddhist-law still festoon[thick twisted straw rope]-outside)

> on the first day
> buddhist law is still
> beyond the pale

"Beyond the pale" is beyond the pale, but we lack a word for roping off and designating areas as sacred (only a boxing ring comes to mind!)? This is a good *ku* and does not insult Buddhism. It just describes the way it is. The first day celebrates the *birth* of this world, not dying and going to another one!

大佛の心也けりけさの春　一之 大三
daibutsu no kokoro narikeri kesa no haru　isshi 1697
(large-buddha[collosal]'s mind/heart becomes[+emph] this-morning's spring)

    spring dawn
the heart of the *daibutsu*
    is what it is

    this morning
spring fills the heart
    of the buddha

    the very mind
of our big buddha
    gods' spring

    what's this dawn?
the emptiness of daibutsu
    the colossal heart

    what's the heart
of the colossal buddha?
    new year dawn

    my mind empty
as a colossal buddha:
    the spring dawns

The *kokoro* is "mind" only in the last reading because the hollow inside of the colossal Buddha statue is largely belly and English, gut feelings or not, can not put *mind*, empty or not, in there. The third reading has the *ku* fuse Shintôism and Buddhism. The *kokoro* in the *ku* may also mean the reply to the riddle of *what something is*. The first 12 syllabets would seem to be the solution for the final 5, but the vector of the riddle is hard to tell. I bet on readings 1, 4 and 6. The next *ku* is better known. The style is plain, but the presence of real feeling (I think my second reading correct) makes it better, period:

生まれなから僧にもあらす花の春　北元 紙つひえ
umarenagara sô ni mo arazu hananoharu　hokugen 1775-1838
(born-as monk-as is-not flower's/luscious/precious/celebratory spring)

here to flower

    ah, spring!
no one is born to
    be a monk

    ah, spring!
i was not born to
    be a monk

The untranslatable *hana* (flower's, or "flowery," as it is often translated, though "gorgeous" or "beautiful" might get more of the meaning) modifying the spring says it all. Nature in the spring votes for life. To become a monk was to give up having a wife, which is to say, a life as most understand it; and New Year was about *bearing* things, not *burying* them.

花の春といふもまれなる浮世哉　痩菊 新五百題
hananoharu to iu mo mare naru ukiyo kana　yasegiku 1819
(flower-spring [it's] said but rare/beautiful-is/becomes-floating-world [of woe]!/'tis)

    called splendid,
spring is still but a rare type
    of floating world

    how sad now
we rarely say the phrase
    flowery spring

    woeful world!
perfect springs are really
    a rare thing

Perhaps, as another poet opined, *"On New Year's, / it hardly seems a world / of suffering!"* (元日や苦の世界とは思はれす 圓風 安永4 *ganjitsu ya ku no sekai to wa omowarezu* enfû 1775), but the above *ku* seems to deny the idea of the New Year outside of Buddhist cosmology. The *floating world*, Japanese for the false world of appearances (*maya*) that seems a very real world of woe, may not look quite the same on New Year's but, this poet, Skinny Chrysanthemum, suggests we are still there. The middle reading is possible but unlikely. The use of *floating* (浮) instead of *troubles* (憂) for *uki* might also suggest that the pleasure quarters is particularly luscious on the New Year, but I prefer the broader reading.

四海皆兄弟なれやけさの春 南溟 俳諧名録
shikai mina kyôdai nare ya kesanoharu   nanmei 18c?
(four-seas all brothers become! this morning's spring)

    spring dawns   from sea to sea
across four-seas all ye   may all ye, brothers be!
     brothers be!   this spring dawn

Corny stuff. An extension of the open mind idea. I only include it to show Japan had cosmopolitans even when it was closed to the world (See Ueda Akinari in Tsunoda *et al: Traditions of Japanese Thought*).

元日は何國も春の名所かな 嵐外
ganjitsu wa nangoku mo haru no meisho kana   rangai -1845
(first-day what-country-even spring's famous-place!/?/'tis)

on the first day
what country is not
a famous place?

"Country" here means various *kuni* in Japan. On New Year's, every hill and dale is a place for sight-seeing. The equality simply voiced in this poem may reply to a couple centuries of boasting by Edoites (Think of them as New Yorkers or Parisians if it helps).

古き世の人に見せはや江戸の春 完来 五元?   ひんかしの京とは爰よ江戸の春 富長 洗濯物
furuki yo no hito ni misebaya edonoharu kanrai 1747   *hingashi no kyô to wa koko yo edonoharu* fuchô 1666
(old-world's people-to show-wish[if only!]: edo's spring)   (east[in dialect]'s capital-as-for here[+emph.] edo's spring)

     i wish i could   the eastern capital
show it to the ancients   that's right here, man,
     yedo's spring!   yedo's spring!

海近し朝日のもとは江戸の春 鳥酔 五元
umi chikashi asahi no moto wa edonoharu   chôsui 1747
(sea close morning-sun's origin-as-for edo's spring)

the sea's near
the origin of the sun is
yedo's spring!

I used the old spelling of Edo here, for it just looks a bit more impressive with the "y." All I could do to match the *hingashi* (Edo dialect for *higashi* = East) and the *"yo"* emphatic that dress up the original of the second *ku* was to add the hip *"man."* The last *ku* is a repeat translation (see pg. 104).

ちとの間に雪もほこりや江戸の春 旭富 文久五百
chito no ma ni yuki mo hokori ya edo no haru kyûhô 1819
(a bit of while-in snow too pride!/?/: edo's spring)

a sudden snowfall
that too is the pride of
an edo spring

Not all Edo springs are this conceited. One poet correctly points out *"If I may say, / it could use a lake: / Yedo spring"* (まゝならは水海ママほしや江戸の春 右茶 大三 *mama naraba mizuumi hoshi ya edo-no-haru* ufu? 1697) Edo was the known as the water-city, but it was the sea, the rivers and the canals. A *mizuumi* is a large lake. *That* Edo lacked. Another, presumably living outside of Edo, was fed up with *"Foolish talk / about the Yedo new year / in the country"* (愚いふ國々まても江戸の春 遊葉 大三 *oroka iu kuniguni made mo edonoharu* yûyô 1697). The *country* is "countries," and means the various regions of Japan.

親に似た顔見ぬはかり江戸の春 草鋸 五元
oya ni nita kao minu bakari edo-no-haru sôkyo 1747
(parent/s/master/s-to resemble face/s see-[not?] only edo-spring)

all the people	edo spring: here	edo's new year
resemble their masters	i see everything but faces	every face i see shows
edo's new year	like my parents'	a proud parent

The last reading assumes the concept of a parent-face (親顔 *oyagao*) is expressed in an odd way. A fourth, noting that many single and adopted Edoites meant few look-alike families, took *minu* as negative (see-not), like the second reading. But, considering the prevalence of matching liveries and the possibility of reading *oya* as master, the first reading seems more likely, though not so likely as the last.

家根の窓一度に引や江戸の春 一茶 文政五
yane no mado ichido ni hiku ya edo no haru issa 1822
(roof's window one-time-at draw[open] edo's spring)

roof windows
all open up at once
edo new year

Given a free horizon, what a fine place to view the first sunrise! This *ku* was my first introduction to roof windows. Edo was a crowd-culture, where men could shift like fish in a school; I can well imagine the simultaneous opening of thousands of such windows. Thinking of the faces popping out reminds me that Japanese solar spring falls on what we call Groundhog Day. Today, one hears the collective clap of the *amado* (heavy shutters to keep out night-air, rain and wind) opening, *i.e.*, slamming into their stops as they are slid fully open in the morning, so Issa's observation might be aural as well as visual.

元日の一日は鐘のなくも哉 菊雄 文久五百
ganjitsu no ichinichi wa kane no naku mogana kikuo mid-19c
(original-day's one[all]day[long]-as-for, bell/s bells-not/none desired)

on new year's	new year's day
i'd hear not a bell	how i wish it could pass
all day long	without bells

As Japan has always had many bell-lovers, there is a slight possibility *naku* is a misprint for *naru* and Kikuo means: *"On New Year's / I'd hear bells toll / all day long!"* But, as discussed already, bells are rung a 108 times on New Year's Eve and I would think it far more likely Kikuo heard enough of them for a year and wanted some quiet. He may also have had metaphysical objections. While Shintô shrines include a gong, bells were most strongly identified with Buddhism, a religion that came to Japan long after the Age of the Gods and was, as already mentioned, identified with burial rather than birth.

元日や近う聞ゆる瀧の音　丹頂 安永四
ganjitsu ya chikô kikoyuru taki no oto   tanchô 1775
(orig. day[ny]: close sounds[verb] waterfall's sound)

new year's day
how close the sound
of the waterfall

new year's
the waterfall sounds
very close

Because of the quiet *and* our heightened receptivity, time and space have collapsed into a singularity and the water trickles into our ears. This is also why we always hear the crows caw in Japan on the morning of the New Year and we hear them so plainly they could be sitting on our shoulders. (We will take up crows in Volume II, first-sounds). It is another reason bells might not be welcome.

にぎやかに静かなる日の朝哉　曲水 大三
nigiyaka ni shizuka naru hi no ashita kana   kyokusui 1697
(busily/bustling quiet become/is sun's morning [new-years]!/ 'tis)

the first dawn
of the sun how cheerful
in a quiet way

a morning
of quiet animation
new year's

a bustling
silence this dawn
of the sun

what crowds
and how quiet the birth
of the sun

There is a refreshingly brisk quality to the movement of the people going out to see the Rising Sun, make their first Shrine visit or scoop up "young-water, etc., yet such activity is not *frentic* as at the Year's End. It is quiet and dignified, in a word, solemn. It bears close resemblance to a peony-viewing, colorful yet sober compared to the famously raucous cherry blossom-viewing.

けさの春淋しからざる閑哉　冬松 あら野 1689
kesanoharu sabishikarazaru itoma kana [nodokesa ya?]   tôshô
(morning's spring lonely-not quiet/lull/idleness?/leisure!/'tis)

on new year
a tranquility that is
not lonely

spring's dawn
tranquility that's far
from lonely

This "not-lonely tranquility" is almost the same as the "bustling/animated quiet" of the previous *ku*. It differs from the next *ku*:

正月や内気な人か淋しがる　山本 新葉
shôgatsu ya uchikina hito ga sabishigaru　sanbon 1856
(new-year's!/: inner-spirit/feeling people-the lonely[as a verb!])

new year's　　　　　　　　　　　　　　　　　　it's new year's
the timid at heart　　　　　　　　　　　　　retiring dispositions
feel lonely　　　　　　　　　　　　　　　　　　grow lonesome

new year's
bashful men and women
feel empty

Uchikina, literally "within/inside/inner-spirit/feeling," reminds me of the modern term "inner-directed."

元日やおもへばさびし秋の暮　芭蕉
ganjitsu ya omoeba sabishi akinokure　bashô 1644-94
(orig. day[new years]: think/remember-if lonely fall's end/evening)

new year's day　　　　　　　　　　　　　　new year's day
i think of a lonely　　　　　　　　　　lonely when you think of it
autumn dusk　　　　　　　　　　　　　　　like late-fall dusk

As one might expect from the master, this is a better way to address holiday loneliness,. Blyth introduces lines from Wordsworth's *In Early Spring*: "In that sweet mood when pleasant thoughts / Bring sad thoughts to the mind." *Wonderful*. Japanese commentators note the extraordinary quiet of New Year's Day reminds Bashô of an equally quiet time. I think of how we simultaneously feel *more alone* and *more dependent* on community at these times. The earliest autumnization of the New Year was by a link-verse-master in a less serious *haikai* style: *"This morning / the fall of the moon and / spring of the bloom"* (月のあき花のはるたつあしたかな　宗祇 *tsuki no aki hana no haru tatsu ashita kana*　sôgi 1420-1502). "This morning/today" (*ashita* is ambiguous), means *The New Year*. I believe Sôgi's *ku* plays on the tendency of Japanese to play with the metaphorical *fall* and *spring* (A good example would be the "bamboo fall" in the spring when the leaves shed – there are more examples, but I only recall this because I lived like a panda in a bamboo grove – just in time to let sunlight fall on the new shoots!). The time when the moon is feted is Autumn. The New Year starts in the Spring, its clear contrary. So, if Spring is idiomatic for flourishing and celebration, Fall is the Moon's Spring and Spring its Fall. Although Bashô knew and loved Sôgi, I do not know if he read this *ku*, and it would not matter, for poems with emotion and those without it are different animals altogether.

嶋つなぐ海静か也浦の春　江山 大三
shima tsunagu umi shizuka nari uranoharu　kôzan 1697
(islands-connecting ocean calm/quiet becomes/is bay's spring/new year)

the isle-binding　　　　　　　　　　　　the isle-binding
ocean is still: spring　　　　　　　sea now calm, spring
comes to the bay　　　　　　　　　　　is on the bay

No ships, for the sailors are home. The whole world waits with bated breath for the new Sun/Day to show. "Isle-binding" refers to a particular scene: small islets scattered in a bay so calm sunrise resembles moonrise on a clear night. When the glow on the water spreads out to encompass all the islands, the binding – rather than the separating – quality of the sea is felt: *enchantment*. I am terribly impressed with Kôzan's *ku*. How many of us can see the sea as a bridge rather than a moat?

のどけさよ只などやらんけさの春　宗春
nodokesa yo tada nado yaran kesanoharu　sôshun c1730
(calm [+emph.] just etcetera do [say?]-not, morning's spring)

how still this dawn!
spring's arrival is
self-evident

glorious calm!
no *ifs, ands* or *buts*
this spring dawn

spring dawn
no *ifs, ands* or *buts*
what calm!

the first dawn

what peace!
no need to embellish
this spring

The "just *etcetera* do [say?]-not" in the original had me puzzled. The second and third readings were my *Eureka!* solution. But, the word *tada,* in this context meaning "just" (as in "just [what about] this or that?") has other obsolete idiomatic possibilities hard for me to grasp though I read and reread the examples in the dictionary. The first and last readings cover what I feel *tada* might mean, though I cannot explain by a direct translation of the middle-7 syllabets of the original.

長閑さや皆我家のみよの春　宗因　三ふえ集
nodokesa ya minna wagaya no miyonoharu　sôin 1604-82
(calm/tranquility! all[everyone] my[their own] house's realm's spring)

how tranquil!
each house tending to
its own spring

what tranquility
the spring of the realm
in every home

a tranquil realm
everyone thinks spring
visits his home

a peaceful time
everyone lays claim
to this spring

English must throw up its hands before "everyone *my*-home's realm's spring." The use of "my/mine" as third-person as well as first in Japanese allows *my-ism* to be universally applied (so personal computers are called *maikon* (*my com*puter), etc.). The "my" used here, *waga,* warrants comment, for Japanese has many ways to say it (Indeed, the "my this and thats," once awkward but now ubiquitous, may have begun in Japan, where "our" *mai* was adopted for product naming). *Waga* is egoistic yet warm. That, however, is only a start at reading this simple *ku* by the top haiku-master of the Osaka school. The first reading between the lines is Confucian: the non-action of everyone keeping to his own house, the micro-cosmos of the larger polity, brings peace. The second reading credits the peaceful reign with a situation where every home is able to enjoy the spring. The third imagines people so content with the calm day that they each think Spring pays special attention to them. The fourth combines and exaggerates the second and third. This calm of the first day, which we encounter in many New Year's themes, may not have existed as a New Year's theme in its own right until modern haiku turned it into one: "first-calm," (*hatsu-nagi*) or, more loosely, "calm" (*nodokesa/nodokasa* – it can be pronounced either way) on the New Year's.

初凪や潮引き砂のつぶやける　阿部みどり女
hatsunagi ya shio hiki suna no tsubuyakeru abe midorijo 1885-1990
(first-calm: wave/tide/surf-pulling/dragging sand's whispering)

the first calm surf-pulled sand is murmuring	rolled up and down sand murmuring the first calm

On a quiet day, ground swells gently but still powerfully roll up the beach and settle back down. I do not know if the sound is really sand (including pebbles) rubbing against itself, air-pockets (foam) in the water, or the soaking up and drying out that accompanies each breath. I just know that, on days like this, the sound stands-out. It is not well enough known to merit a name. Perhaps we may call it a *sand-murmur*. We may find more "first-calm" *ku* with other "firsts" in volume II of the *The Fifth Season*. There is a reason why *"Calm"* by itself is not a New Year's theme. It is a *Spring* theme and we do not find themes belonging in two seasons. (This poses a problem for Floridians. What can we do about the Hurricane Season, which includes summer *and* fall?) I probably should not have included Midorijo's "first-calm" *ku* in volume I, but, growing up by the beach, it is *my* beginning.

我が国のものとこそ思へ初日影　鳴雪
waga kuni no mono to koso omoe hatsuhikage meisetsu 1847-1926
(my/our country's thing [empathic *koso*] think! first-sun-shadow/form/light)

think it a child of your own country the first sun	know that the first sun is native to your nation

The "child" I invented sounds sweet enough, but the date of this *ku* makes it highly likely that the "country" means "nation" and it is a relic of what is now called neo-Shintoism and, if I may be pardoned the use of a critical word in a season where it ought not appear, *chauvinism*. On the other hand, "country" (*kuni*) in Japanese is as ambiguous as it is in English. When Japanese within Japan speak of going back to their "country," they mean their hometown. So, there is a wee possibility it is a perfectly innocent *ku* promoting what might now be called thinking locally!

人々の上にこそあれ神の春　西馬
hitobito no ue ni koso are kaminoharu saiba 1803-1858
(people x2-on-top-of more-than-anything is/are ought gods' spring)

be above humanity, spring of the gods	gods' spring it really must be above men

Could this have been written after Perry's black-ships came (1853) to express his hope that the Imperial Court of Japan would reassert itself (against the Shogunate and Buddhists?) as a transcendent power? Or, is it a naïve wish that the magical spring of the gods not condescend to settle in the secular world, but remain always something transcendent? As with the previous *ku,* we are left with a question.

The Meaning Of Forever

九億劫以前も同じけふの春　仏頂和尚
kuoku-kô [酉年だったら、どう？] *izen mo onaji kyô no haru*　bucchô -1715
(nine hundred-million eons/kalpa before-too same today's spring)

a whack for the newly distracted

even nine hundred million eons ago
the same thing, today's spring

Bucchô is the Zen priest, Bashô, haiku saint, practiced under. While some sects of esoteric Buddhism did unite with Shintô, it is still surprising to find Buddhist interest in the New Year for reasons already discussed. But one thing about the New Year was of interest to a religion originating in India. The New Year spanned ages and Buddhism reveled in numbers. That much survived the passage through China and Korea to Japan. *Nine hundred million* seems an odd number. Not so in the original, for a hundred-million is a numerical unit in the Sinosphere (20c Japanese often referred to themselves as "one *oku*-strong") and *nine* is the largest integer. The *kô* 劫 following the nine *oku* fooled me at first, for I read it on the road (actually, on a train) and had to guess the meaning. At that time, my readings were:

today's spring
nine million blessings ago
the very same

the same thing
nine million gifts ago
our new spring

new year's day
the same as that before
a million blessings

Since the book said that in 1691, the *ku* was published with a poetic pure *kanji* preface/title 春色新来一棒頭, to wit: *"Spring-color-new-come-one-rod-head,"* with the last three characters seemingly a reference to the whacks a Zen-master gives students practicing meditation (usually on the back) to help them concentrate on nothing in particular, I jumped to the wrong conclusion that *kô* meant "blessings" – students of Zen are very grateful for those whacks – and recalled the smack on the rump of a newly born. Back at my desk, I quickly learned 劫= *kô* was short for 劫波= *kôha,* the Sinofication of the Sanskrit *kalpa,* and meant a period of time so long (exactly how so was debated by various schools) that it was *as good as infinite.* I like that, for Shintô dating, like Judeo-Christian dating, tended to short-change the world. Be that as it may, Bucchô *may* have meant that when the Spring came to steal the attention of his students, he reached for his rod (あるいは？). According to Buddhist catechism, for those who know there is nothing new under the sun, even in the Spring, except enlightenment. For those of us who belong to the willfully unenlightened majority, the following wish suffices:

いつまても又いつまてもけふの春　高茂 大三
itsumademo mata itsumademo kyô no haru　kômo 1697
(until-when= forever, again until-when= forever today's spring)

forever more
again forever more
today's spring

御慶・礼者・年賀
gyokei, reisha and nenga

七 7

GREETINGS IN PERSON AND ON PAPER

年の賀やいふ門なみのかさり哉　笑水 大三
toshinoga ya iu kadonami no kazari kana　shôsui 1697
(year's greeting/tribute: say, gate all/same's decoration!/?/ 'tis)

<blockquote align="center">
the year's tribute?
that decoration found
by each gate!
</blockquote>

The various gate decorations tend to be made of pine, fern, bamboo, braided straw and white paper. While they are as central to the celebration as wreaths and trees are to Christmas, I am saving them for vol.II, which, hopefully, will be well-illustrated. Shôsui's *ku* is the only one where I translate *ga* 賀 in the old-fashioned way as "tribute" (the character comprises "money貝+ increase加") rather than "greeting." Doubtless, it came to mean "greeting" – not any greeting, but only the seasonal felicitation – because tributes were once paid yearly.[1] Today *ga* is most commonly known as the middle character of three = 年賀状*nen-ga-jô* = meaning New Year's card. Greeting was generally something humans did to humans; and this "greeting of the year," where Annus Novis is treated as an intelligent being, was the only *ku* in the entry (*toshi-no-ga*) in Shiki's *Categorical* or Kaizosha's *saijiki*.

新春の御慶は古き言葉哉　梅翁
shinshun no gyokei wa furuki kotoba kana　sôin -1682 or baiô -1825
(new-spring's [honorific+]felicitation/formalities-as-for old words 'tis)

felicitations for the new spring traded in old words	our new year: how old the words we use for greetings!

The words "New Year" are not in the *gyokei*, but the expression is only used for the New Year, so I sometimes translate it as "New Year's Greetings." The traditional expression, or "old" words, are longer and more formal than our "Merry Christmas!" or "Happy New Year!" and its nuances include *greeting, felicitation, civilities, thanks, request* and *supplication*. Here is the standard version:

---

1. *Almost Tributes:* Japanese companies still send out presents every year. After I joined a well-known linguist and the editor of a pr magazine for the world's largest liquor company, I got a box of liquor every year (*Suntory Malts,* with its flavor remarkably close to Ballantine Ale, was best) until I left Japan.

Akemashite, omedetô-gozaimasu! Kyonen [or, *sakunen*] *wa taihen osewa ni narimashita! Kotoshi mo yoroshiku onegai-itashimasu!* (この表現の歴史ご存知方の欄外注を求む)

[It (the year)] brightened/opened [is here], congratulations! Last year, you were helpful [to me/us]! This year, too, [I/we] entreating [are counting on you to help me/us]-am/are!"

All of this is ornamented with polite and honorific verb forms English cannot reproduce! I describe it as "standard" because Japanese has diverse dialects.

初禮の聲迄和歌の姿哉　友和 大三
hatsurei no koe made waka no sugata kana　yûwa　1697
(first-greeting's voice-until *waka* (gentle/japanese-song/poem[=young?])'s form!)

spring greeting
even the voices are
pure *waka!*

The character *wa* in *waka* – classic poetry – is generally construed to mean Japanese (*wa*) as opposed to Chinese song, but I cannot help wondering if it may not reflect the fact these songs/poems were read in a distinctive *sing-song* voice (judging from modern readings). Moreover, *waka* is homophonic with "young," so the last part of the haiku may *almost* be read as "even the voices *cut a young figure.*"

挨拶の七夕ならん御慶哉　嵐光 安永四
aisatsu no tanabata naran gyokei kana　rankô　1775
(greetings' seventh-eve[fest. of stars] become-would: felicitations!)

felicitations　　　　　　　　　season greetings
like the festival　　　　　　　like the stars who do it
of the stars　　　　　　　　　but once a year

A more direct translation: *"Call it / the seventh eve / of greeting."* On the 7th night of the 7th month – early September by the traditional calendar – the herder and the weaver cross the Milky Way for a night of loving. Everyone (excluding lonely souls such as Lady Ukyô Daibu (12c), who complains that *she* should be so lucky!) makes a big deal out of the poor lovers, who were turned into stars because they couldn't keep their minds on their work, meeting only once a year; the poet adds: *but what about social intercourse?* Or, so I interpret the *ku*. My second reading makes this explicit.

この艶は物にさわらぬ御慶哉　鬼恋
kono en wa mono ni sawaranu gyokei kana　kiren　1775
(this bewitchery/voluptuousness-as-for thing/s touch-not greetings!/?/'tis)

all this beauty　　　　　　　　spring greetings:
without any touching　　　　　this voluptuousness
our felicitations　　　　　　　without things!

The word *en* 艶 may be the single most erotic Chinese character. It combines others meaning "plenty" 豊 (itself beans 豆 with a melody or curve 曲 above that may also be a stew-pot) and "color" 色 (derived from doggy-style intercourse 参考＝白川静「漢字類偏」). The people all dressed up to exchange felicitations *look good*, which is to say charged with erotic energy, yet there is nothing vulgar, nothing physical about it (unless crisply starched clothing turns you on).

女にも詞四角に御慶哉　千珊 玉かつら
onna ni mo kotoba shikaku ni gyokei kana　sensan? 1751
(women-to/with-even words square/stiff/formally greetings 'tis)

even women formally addressed felicitations	new year greetings we use square words for women too

In most cultures, women are the sex more likely to play fast and easy with language, while men bind themselves to formality. In Japan, women have ever been linguistic pioneers and, even today, the mass media pays careful attention to the new speech mannerisms of school-age girls. My first reading was *"Even women / speak in stiff words: / felicitation."* Yet, the grammar and *all* my respondents demurred. Men were legally and culturally superior to women and generally spoke to them in rougher language than women would dare speak to men, except on formal occasions such as the New Year's felicitation.

同じ皃おなじ事いふ今朝の春　道楽　談林２集英社
onaji kao onaji koto iu kesanoharu　dôraku 17-18c
(same face, same thing say: this-morning's spring)

the same faces
saying the same things
new year's day

I can't help but quote from the poem by Adeline Dutton Train Whitney: *God does not send strange flowers every year . . . The same dear things lift up the same fair faces . . . The old love shall look out from the old faces . . .* ("A Violet"). Here, humans do the divine work. The Danrin school to which this poet belonged continued the clever but light tradition of the Teimon school in the Osaka area for a while after Bashô tightened up to East (North, if you ask me). This *ku* can be read in a sincere vein *or* as a senryûesque poke at convention. Not that Bashô himself was beyond the latter:

元日 とし／\ (or 元日) や猿 (or 狙) に着せたる猿 (or 狙)の面　芭蕉
[ganjitsu] toshidoshi (or *ganjitsu*) *ya saru ni kisetaru saru no men*　bashô - 1694
(year-[after]year(or, original-day=nyday): monkey-on wears monkey's mask)

no evolution?

year after year a monkey wearing a monkey's mask	year after year monkeys putting on their own masks

This *ku,* which Bashô himself admitted was bad, is a good metaphor of despair. The editor of 赤冊子, a book with the *ku,* has the master bemoaning the way people stop growing and fall into the same rut year after year. Since this was Bashô's 50th birth-year, a time when it was conventional for men to take stock of their lives, it may also be read as self-criticism (which saves it from being as *senryû* as the Dôraku's *ku*). We will see more such in ch.11. Monkeys were brought around in the holiday season, mostly to bring good luck to the stables, but also just to entertain=beg. The monkeys and their master danced and performed short dramas. Yamamoto Kenkichi (芭蕉名句集) writes that it could be a human (entertainer or monkey owner), wearing the mask of a monkey or a monkey wearing a mask with a human face. He favors the latter, though it is no longer done and he does not know for certain if it ever was (猿の人の面を被った証ごぞんじなら、お知らせ下さい). Nose also writes (in Ueda: *Bashô and His Interpreters*) there is no record of monkeys wearing monkey masks and wonders if Bashô had in mind a Kyôgen play.

再現＝元日の愚痴世と共に無尽也　大江丸 俳諧袋
ganjitsu no guchi yo to tomo ni mûjin nari   ôemaru 1719-1805
(original-day's complaints world together-with inexhaustible become)

```
    while men exist                      grumbling about
  grumbling will persist              the new year, that, too
      on new year's                       will never end
```

We cannot tell if Ôemaru means grumbling *on* or *about* the New Year. An anonymous 1821 *ku* treats the former: *"One thing / about spring is not talking / about things"* (世の中を云わぬも春の一つかな 失出典 再現 *yononaka o iwanu mo haru no hitotsu kana*). And Santôka (-1940), the latter: *"New Year's Eve / is dumb and New Year's / even dumber"* (大晦日愚かなり元日なお愚かなり＝再現 山頭火 *ômisoka oroka nari ganjitsu nao oraoka nari*). But I must say that aside from a few *ku* by disgruntled would-be snoozers, I certainly haven't found much of this complaining which Ôemaru notes in the Edo era.

山里は梅の匂ひて御慶哉　　里川
yamazato wa ume no nioite [or *nioi de*] *gyokei kana* risen 1759
(mountain[country] place/home-as-for plum (blossom) scent-with greetings!/'tis)

```
    up in the hills                    in the old hollars
new year greetings with            a plum blossom fragrant
   the scent of plum                  "happy new year!"
```

In Japanese, *ume*=plum (flowering apricot), by itself, means the blossoms. A millennium of poets claim this scent fills up every crevice of earth, every cranny of wood. The truth is that the scent is not so strong as to capture much more than the noon shade of the tree in the city, a place with powerful competing odors. Because there is so much plum blossom scent in haiku, I, for one, have developed antibodies against it. But, I think this *ku,* with its initial qualification, is real testimony of a refreshing experience.

けさの春そのもの／＼の匂ひ哉 吟江 夢占
kesa no haru sono mono mono no nioi kana ginkô 1780
(this-morning's spring/ny this thing thing's smell/scent !/?/'tis)

```
     spring comes                          the scent of
 each and every thing                   thing & thing today:
      has a scent                          that's spring

                       spring comes
                   i find myself sniffing
                        this and that
```

Here, the *nioi* seems smell rather than glow to me, but *"has a scent"* can be changed to *"its own glow,"* if you sense differently. My last translation pretends the *ku* was written in a Dog Year. It would be good for making the *ku* a sort of greeting, too, but *very* unlikely (「〜を嗅いでみん」となっていないから！).

ざぶ／＼と泥わらんじの御慶哉　　一茶
zabuzabu to dorowaranji no gyokei kana   issa (1764-1827)
(splish-splash/slip-slop-with muddy straw-sandals felicitation!/'tis)

```
    mucky sounds                        mish-mush go
 from my muddy waranji             our muddy straw sandals
    spring greetings                   spring felicities
```

Waraji are crude macramé sandals worn about the farm or when traveling. The primordial touch fits the New Year, but they should be new and crisp. Issa's folksy "n" is added to the middle of the word and the mud challenge that ideal. Issa lost no opportunity to bring mud into the spring. One of his most famous *ku* is a snap shot of muddy *geta* (two-stilt wooden sandals [1]): " Spring has sprung / from the mud on the *geta* / at every gate" (門／＼の下駄の泥より春立ぬ *kado kado no geta no doro yori haru tachinu*).

上下で下た（駄）ぶらさげて御慶哉　一茶
kamishimo de geta burasagete gyokei kana   issa -1827
(top-bottom[formal male wear]-with *geta* dangling felicitations! 'tis)

<table>
<tr><td>

in formal wear
dangling their *geta*
felicitations

</td><td>

wearing a tuxs
with his shoes in hand
ny formalities

</td></tr>
</table>

Peasants and poets generally wore straw sandals, and straw, as we have seen, was itself festive at the start of the year/spring. I recall a retired Osumô-san (sumo wrestler) in my neighborhood who made them for a hobby and gave me a pair for the New Year. Evidently, the upper class had a set of formal wear that demanded fancy footwear. Rather than muddy his *geta*, someone – a well-off patron or patrons visiting the poet's hut? – has elected to carry them and walk barefoot.[2] That is my guess, anyway.

年礼や下駄道あちは草履道　一茶
nenrei ya getamichi achi wa zôrimichi   issa -1827
(year-greetings/call *geta*-road yonder-as-for [fine woven] straw-sandal-road)

new year greetings
a *geta* road and, yonder
a *zôri* road

Different road surfaces for the respective shoes? [3] Different roads for the house-to-house and town-to-town? When Issa writes "Gate greetings / each from his respective / *zôri* path" (門礼や片側づゝは草履道　一茶 *kadorei ya katagawa zutsu wa zôrimichi*), it is clear he is speaking of neighbors. It took a stroke of genius to focus on the footwear, another to notice the roads.

---

1. Translating *Geta* A hundred years ago it would have made sense to translate *geta* as "chopine" or "chappin," etc. Today, the word is obsolete to all but students of fashion history. Because *geta* are solid wood and chopine, cork, both are clog-like, but clogs are closed while *geta* are open, like sandals. Both, moreover, lift the foot an inch to a foot above the ground upon two stilts, if stilt is the proper word for tooth-like boards. (*Tengu*, or goblin *geta* with just one stilt are the exception. My *Random House* mistakenly claims they came from Turkey to Europe in the 18c.; Bulwer, in *Anthropometamorphosis* pokes fun at English Gallants titter-tottering along on these things in the mid-17c. It is *possible* reports of Japanese *geta* influenced this. It is also interesting that the Turks and Japanese should share both shoe-style and language (both of the Ural-Altraic family).

2. Geta In Hand A more well known *ku* by Issa has worshippers climbing a mountain road with *"geta* in/on their hands,"* which scholars, taking the "on" reading, had long explained it meant they are worn by crippled or legless people. Although I have never seen it noted, bk 29 of *Yanagidaru* (1800) has a *senryû* predating Issa's by a decade: "Worn on the hands / of cripples, *geta* / in their dotage" (*geta no oikomi izari no te ni hakase* uyu) – the original makes it hard to tell which are *old*, the cripples or the *geta*. It follows "Doing laundry, / *geta* may be worn / on your butt" (*sentaku no toki geta o shiri e haki* – tôchô). Tanabe Seiko, on the other hand, explains in the course of her huge novel *Hinekure Issa* (warped issa), that the *geta* are carried because of the muddy roads and I, aware of Issa's less famous *kamishimo* haiku, above, think the novelist is probably right.

3. *Zôri* and *Waraji* While *zôri* and *waraji* are seen as different today – the *zôri* has a neatly woven fine mesh, while the *waraji* is loose large macramé – olde ku sometimes blur the boundaries. If being finely dressed yet down to earth is one's aim, "straw-*zôri*" (*wara-zôri*) – *straw* being primitive – seems a good compromise.

元日ハおきそうにして礼をうけ 柳多留 五
ganjitsu wa okisô ni shite rei o uke   yanagidaru 1770
(original-day-as-for, awake-trying/tried greeting/s receive/ing)

on new year's
we are greeted as we try
to wake up

new year's
is pretending to be awake
while greeted

The lack of concrete detail is what makes this *ku* seem what it is, a *senryû*. It is true enough, however, and we will see how Issa would soon handle it, below.

むく起（の）小便ながら御慶哉 一茶
muku-oki no shôben nagara gyokei kana   issa 1824
(just-awakened-and-up-urination-while [ny]greeting/felicitations)

a shinano new year

half-asleep
we exchange courtesies
while pissing

as we piss
still barely awake
our greetings

両方に小便しながら御慶哉 一茶
ryôhô ni shôben-shinagara gyokei kana   issa 1825
(both sides/parties-from urine-doing-while[ny]greeting)

on both sides
courtesies exchanged
while pissing

making water
we hasten to exchange
first courtesies

I like "greetings," but hate more than one "~ing" per *ku*. Unfortunately, the other words are long. "Courtesies" is three syllables, "formalities" four and "felicitations," five! This is realism, but, properly read, cheerful: pissing outside is refreshing, a far better way to start the day/year than staring into a toilet in a little room. Issa's *ku* are modern in that they are matter-of-fact rather than being outrageous to be outrageous, as was often the case with earlier treatment of body-function, such as a sequence begun by Plum Elder (Baiô). After his *hokku* (opening *ku*) on the Second Day's *zoni* (soup) seeming far from the First Day and second *ku* on the auspicious direction (*ehô*) for a first outing, Migaku jams: *"Neighbors facing / each other nose-blowing / shitting, pissing!"* or *"Neighbors lacking even / a sneezing relation, face to face / doing their business"* (再現＝鼻もひぬ隣に向ひ大小便 未学 （和文なくしたから名前はあてずっぽ） *hana mo hinu tonari ni mukai daishôben*). Presumably, they, too, exchange formalities!

入替る雪隠の口の御慶かな 紀達 正風彦根体
irekawaru secchin no kuchi no gyokei kana   kidachi/kitatsu 1712
(enter-replace snow-hide[toilet]'s entrance new-year's greeting 'tis)

going in and out
of the wc exchanging
new year's greetings

As this *ku* antedates Issa, it is clearly not right to associate body functions with Issa alone. Issa just did more of them and, mostly, did them better.

かつしかや川むかふから御慶いふ 一茶
katsushika ya kawamukô kara gyokei iu   issa 1818
(katsushika [edge of edo]! river-across-from felicitations)

new year's

in katsushika
calling out greetings
across the river

The meaning of Edo (now called *Tôkyô*, or East-capital), the greatest city in the world, according to European visitors, is "bay-door," or, loosely, *watergate*. It was full of inlets and canals and Katsushika, where Issa lived shortly after going to greater Edo, lay in the lowest part, surrounded by three rivers. There was even the Katsushikabune, a small boat used by farmers to move between fields. Issa wrote the above, what I would call an ethnographic *ku*, from memory, decades later.

白髪の天窓をふり立て御慶哉 一茶
hakuhatsu no atama o furitate gokei kana issa -1819
(white-haired-head/s[obj]wagging-stand greeting!/'tis)

a white-haired   felicitations
head wags up and down   white-haired heads
felicitations   wag wildly

proudly wagging
my white locks, i perform
spring courtesies

"Head" is written in a rare way, now obsolete: *"heaven's window."* Issa had white hair from his forties and now he is almost sixty. He finally seems to enjoy it. Did he realize his snowy head had become propitious rather than a mark of premature aging? Or, does the *ku* describe his half-brother, too?

婆々連や打うなつきてみよの春 一只 大三物
babazure ya uchi-unazukite miyonoharu ichida? kazutada? 1697
(aunties[old-women]groups: hit[meet]-nodding [honorific+]realm/age's spring [ny])

aunties meeting   spring in our age
aunty heads bobbing   aunties meeting aunties
spring in our age   heads a'bobbing

groups of aunts
meeting bob their heads
a peaceful spring

Elderly ladies stand out in festivals. Groups wearing similar kimono scurry about. They always know where they are going and seldom raise their heads, so, if you are not one of them, you must take care not to get bowled-over. I have no doubt that a couple hundred years ago when this *ku* was written they were equally formidable. The *uchi-unazukite* is a perfect compound-verb to depict what can be no other than a spasm of energetic bowing when two groups of "aunties" bang into one another. In a nation which has suffered warfare and famine, one does not find groups of elderly people energetically moving about like this. I was tempted to end the last reading with a nod toward the good rulers: *Tokugawa Spring*.

影法師に御慶を 申す わらじ哉　一茶
kageboshi ni gyokei o môsu waraji kana　issa 1824
(shadow-figure-to felicitation/formalities [say[humbly]] straw-sandal!/?/'tis)

    a shadow figure   straw sandals
accepts the felicitations   say happy new year to
    of straw sandals   a shadow figure

The first reading imagines a poor man paying a New Year call upon a superior who remains behind a paper door or window. The second, less likely reading, which I prefer, imagines Issa noticing someone's shadow and his own sandals when he speaks bowing. (But, see ch. endnote: *Both* may be wrong!)

武士やいひわけ云てから御慶　一茶
samurai ya iiwake iute kara gyokei issa -1827
(samurai!/'tis excuse saying-from felicitations)

those samurai!
begging pardon before
their felicitations

Issa's 20,000+ haiku are a vast library of ethnographic as well as personal observations. This is one of the former. Evidently, the samurai said something like "*kajitsu wa, tsukamatsutta*" ("pardon [me] for [whatever happened or didn't happen?] the other day") before exchanging the New Year's-specific greeting. Since last year is supposed to be out of the mind, such apologies *do* seem odd. Other *ku* describe the strange, uptight samurai, who even splashed water to cool down the street in the summer – a common practice – in a manner Issa found literally "square" (*bushimachi ya shikaku-shimen ni mizu o maku*).

鶯や裏からはいる禮者あり　萬翁 新選
uguisu ya ura kara hairu reisha ari　manô 1819
(nightingale:/! rear-side-from enter (ny)callers are)

the nightingale
there are callers who come
from the back

I do not know if a nightingale (actually a certain warbler) has come to the garden which is behind the house or if a nightingale is seen in front and a guest, not wishing to scare it off circles around.

門の春雀が先へ御慶哉　一茶 文化十
kadonoharu suzume ga saki e gyokei kana　issa -1827
([my] gate's spring, sparrow/s front-to greeting!/'tis)

      my new year   spring at my gate
the first to bring greetings   sparrows are the first
     these sparrows   to call on me

No big thing. An easy haiku, except for the fact rural children were also called sparrows, so we cannot be certain which Issa means. Regardless, Issa may play off of the more plentiful *ku* about the classy singer, the nightingale (who could also be a human singer), *eg.*: "*Precious spring / nightingale, too, would bring / her felicitation*" (鶯も御慶申さん玉の春　紙長 *uguisu mo gyokei mosan tamanoharu* shichô 1764).

王子 御年初を申入けり狐穴　一茶 文政四
ôji // onensho o môshi-irekeri kitsune ana　issa 1821
(o-year-start speak/venture [to] put/offer [to the] fox-hole)

felicitations at oji shrine

    and i paid　　　　　　　　　　　　　　　　i called out
a new year's visit　　　　　　　　　　　　　"happy new year!"
  to the fox den　　　　　　　　　　　　　　　　the fox den

The verb "paid" formalizes the visit, but English gives us no way to do the same to the greeting itself. The same year, Issa writes *"Calling upon / one more fox den / "Happy New Year!"* (も(ママ)一ッ狐の穴へ御慶かな *mo hitotsu kitsune no ana e gyokei kana*). I imagine a fox had a den somewhere on the shrine grounds and that Issa, having lost one child after another, may have been trying to get in good with the fox spirits (Issa's notebook includes a method of telling whether the suspicious person passed on a mountain path is a fox or not. You peek back viewing them upside-down under your left arm-pit!); but he also wrote,

親里の山へ向て御慶哉　一茶 文政八
oyazato no yama e mukôte gyokei kana　issa 1825
(parent-country's mountain/s-to facing felicitation!/'tis)

facing the mountains
of my homeland i profer
my felicitation

If he was this reverent toward topography, Issa may well have paid his respect to foxes without ulterior motives.

梅よりも先御慶也福寿草　香凬 安永四
ume yori mo mazu gyokei nari fukujusô　kafû 1775
([blooming]plum before first-greeting/exchange is: lucky-plant)

  i pay my respect　　　　　　　　　　　　　　n.y. greetings
to the fortune-flower　　　　　　　　　　from the fortune flower
   before the plum　　　　　　　　　　　　　　before the plum

We will have a full chapter on the potted plant with golden yellow blossoms (*Amur adonis*) I translate as a "fortune flower," "prosperity-grass," "lucky plant" and other things. Because it was kept by the window inside the house, the poet, waking on the New Year would see it first. My second reading follows a respondent who felt the flowers might be taking the lead here. Regardless, I am curious to know how many Japanese extended their felicitations to what things, *i.e.* the extent of their animism.

古里は同じ聲なる御慶哉　蒼虬
furusato wa onaji koe naru gyokei kana　sôkyû 1760-1842
(home-land-as-for same voice becomes/is felicitations !/'tis)

    back home　　　　　　　　　　　　　　　　my hometown
they sound like me　　　　　　　　　　the voices sound the same
   felicitations　　　　　　　　　　　　　　　new year greetings

Do all sound the same as the poet? Or the same as one another? Regardless, we are pre-Babel: a hick-town with a single dialect versus the big city where everyone speaks with a different tongue.

題大黒　小槌より出たか御慶の人通　馬光
dai daikoku // kozuchi yori deta ka gyokei no hitodôri   bakô 1686-1751
(subj: daikoku (god of grain/prosperity) // small-mallet-from came? greetings' people-passing)

new year greetings
(subject: daikoku)

so many callers
you'd think they flow from
the little mallet

けさ春の小槌を出でたり四方の人 存疑 失出典再現
kesa haru no kozuchi o idetari yomo no hito   zongi 1701-82
(this-morn-spring's small-mallet-from emerge four/all-sides people)

this dawn, folk
on four sides flow out from
spring's mallet

As explained previously, the mallet is a magic one which pours forth riches from its "tiny mouth" hidden in the gavel, each time it is struck. In other words, people performing their civilities are the real prosperity of the nation. Corny? Perhaps. But, it still is true and always will be. (The original's *kesa haru* ("morning spring's") is rare if not awkward. *Kesa-no-haru* ("morning's spring") would be normal).

来る人の口もたからや玉のはる 祇道 歳旦帳
kuru hito no kuchi mo takara ya tamanoharu   gidô 1765 明和 2
(coming-people mouths/words-too treasure/s:/! gem[precious]-spring)

precious spring!
the words of the callers
are treasures, too

The idea that propriety is a treasure is hardly peculiar to Japan, but Gidô's haiku expresses it particularly well!

あらた也よろづことのはけさの春 宗因
arata nari yorozu kotonoha kesa no haru   sôin 1604-82
(renewed become myriad word-leaves, this morn.'s spring [ny])

today's spring   spring today
the myriad word-leaves   our myriad words turn
are renewed   a new leaf

In Japanese, words = 言葉 are traditionally associated with leaves = 葉. *Kotoba* (word) is etymologized as *kotonoha,* or "thing/word-leaf/leaves," and the oldest collection of poetry is called the *Manyôshû,* which transliterates as "10,000 [a unit in the Sinosphere] leaf-gather/collection." As new leaves sprout, so do words. And the first, needless to say, are greetings.

言の葉やのひ広がりて四方の春 乙州 大三物
kotonoha ya nobihirogarite yomo no haru otokuni 1697
(word leafs!/: expanding-broadening four-sides' spring)

our words like leaves
growing, spreading out to all
four corners of spring

Reading many of these celebratory *ku,* can the *senryû* boys be faulted for writing things like the following?

二ッ三ッいひきをかくと御慶也 柳多留 十六
futatsu mitsu ibiki o kaku to gyokei nari yanagidaru 1781
(two, three snores make and ny-greetings are/become)

new year's

two or three
snores and it's time for
felicitations

This may borrow from Ikkyû and Yayû's *ku* we read in the Preface, but coupled with the formal greetings rather than the less specific idea of the New Year's coming, the *effect* is different. Be that as it may, most Japanese were probably not so jaded:

春の禮己己の心かな 忠之 大三 1697
haru no rei onore onore no kokoro kana chûshi/tadayuki
(spring's greeting/felicitations self self's heart/mind!/?/'tis)

felicitations	spring tidings
for the spring: the mind	straight from one heart
of every man	to another

The equivalence of words and mind reminds us of the *logos* of the Genesis with the difference being that *human* words were held to have soul in Japanese (This may be true in some esoteric Judeo-Christian traditions, but not generally). The "every man" and "one heart" are attempts to cope with *onore* (oneself), a problem for the translator, because English insists upon saddling the "self" with a "my" or "your" or "his" etc..

元日は晩まで朝の言葉哉 流兎 大三物
ganjitsu wa ban made asa no kotoba kana ryûto 1697
(original-day-as-for, evening-until morning's words!/'tis)

on new year's
they stay all day long
morning words

The standard New Year's phrase begins *akemashite,* or "brightened/opened!" and refers to sunrise, the Dawn of the New Year. The words not only remain all day, but, for that matter, remain for days or even weeks, for they are used to address anyone you haven't seen since the last year. The general idea of the *ku* is the same as those we have seen where the *mind* stays dawn-fresh all day.

元日やはつかしさうな禮者哉　楽水 百家類題
ganjitsu ya hazukashisô na reisha kana   rakusui 19c?
(orig. day [new years]:/! embarrassed-seem callers 'tis)

it's new year's
the callers all seem
bashful today

This embarrassment is not that of the truly bashful people, but the reticence expected of people acting in a manner that shows respect for others according to the Japanese idea of respect.   In such a formal situation, alcohol was a great help. This *senryû* expresses everything so well:

再現＝四角に酔って歩行年の？礼　武玉川 確認失敗
shikaku ni yotte aruki?yuku toshi[no?]rei   mutamagawa? 18c?
(square/stiff/formally drunk-walk/ing year-etiquette/call/caller/s)

properly drunk   getting drunk
they stagger about   formally we exchange
spring-callers   our formalities

People politely exchange drinks with each call and continue on their way in a quiet and proper manner – exchanging smart bows and formal words. As anyone who has walked in a city knows, drinking makes the miles pass easier. Some may overdo it, as depicted by this next crazy-verse (*kyôka* 狂歌):

生酔の礼者を見れば大道をよこすぢかひに春は来にけり 四方赤良
namaei no reisha o mireba taidô o yokosujikai ni haru wa kinikeri   yomonoakara 18-19c?
(raw[piss]-drunk caller[of ny greetings +obj] see-when, big street crossing-by spring come[+fin.])

d r u n k
a n d a l l o v e r
t h e   r o a d
s p r i n g c a l l s
a t   e a c h
a b o d e

We met Sao, the goddess of Spring, in Ch I and will pursue "her" in vol. II. Here the trope is the reverse of what it seems, for, in reality, a man making New Year calls is being turned into a season. The view of a tottering man zigzagging up main street from a distance indirectly paints a halcyon first day of Spring.

堀の氷廻禮の酔や石を打つ 虚子
hori no kôri kairei no yoi ya ishi o utsu   kyoshi 1874-1959
(moat/ditch round-greet[er]'s drunkenness: stone[obj] throw)

the frozen moat
a tipsy spring caller
chucks a stone

In Japanese, drunkenness is not *bad* by definition. Since it *is* in English, I changed "drunken" to a word with more endearing qualities, *tipsy*. This haiku brings the piss-drunk Spring of the crazy-verse and the proper drunks (or, drunk caller *type*) of the *senryû* down to the particular instance, which is charming in its detail. We can almost hear Kyoshi, if it is Kyoshi,[1] saying "What's *that*? Ice! Hey, don't you know spring's here!" or something like that, as he hastened to put another break in Winter's back. Kyoshi is not on a one-house visit, but a round of visits (*kairei*); and, like some Christmas carolers, has doubtless sipped a bit with each call.

正月の下戸くゞり来る柳哉　乙二 滑稽
shôgatsu no geko kuguri kuru yanagi kana   otsuni -1823
(new year's low-gate[teetotaler]ducks/winds-comes willow 'tis)

the teetolalers
on new year's wind their way
through the willow

ducking carefully
through the willow sober
new year callers

Normal callers are tipsy and brusquely *pass right through* the willows that hang over the street or pathway. The sober minority stands out, for they think too much and have to *make* their way through the dangling branches.

元日やきのうの鬼が禮にくる　渓石
ganjitsu ya kinô no oni ga rei ni kuru   keiseki 1774
(original-day[emph]: yesterday's demon/ogre greetings-for comes)

on new year's
yesterday's demon pays
a greeting call

There is no devil on the New Year. Even the creditor who hounded you at the end of the year behaves like an angel. This haiku is more senryû-esque than many *senryû* (Do you recall the *senryû* in chapter 2 about someone still afraid to open the door? (ganjitsu wa mada kowai …)).

かびたんもつくばゝせけり君が春　芭蕉
kabitan mo tsukubawasekeri kimi ga haru   bashô 1644-94
(capitan=captain too, crouch-made[emph.] lord's spring)

even kabitan
must kowtow before
our lord's spring

The "lord's spring" once referred to the Emperor, but in Bashô's era meant the Shôgun, who, received an embassy of traders every Spring. The *kabitan*, or "captain" (of a ship) comes from Portuguese, but in Bashô's time, the visitor would be Dutch. While the visit was made in late spring, it was considered a New Year's visit/tribute. Issa, writing not long after a rogue Russian trader alarmed Japan by his activities among the Ainu to the North, causing problems for other good Russians (such as Golownin), echoed and amplified Bashô's nationalism: *"The scent of plum [blossoms]: / This reign when the Russians / are made to crawl"* (梅がかやおろしやを這す御代　*ume ga ka ya orosha o hawasu miyo ni au*)!

---

1. *Kyoshi the Stone Chucker?* Both Kyoshi and Shiki were always throwing rocks and haiku-ing it. There is nothing like the *bonk* of a stone on a tree or the *plunk* of a stone in the water and so forth to freeze a scene into a snapshot or, as was the case of Bashô's frog, to deepen the silence that follows. A stone brings us into closer material contact with our surroundings and, as our proxy, can go places we cannot.

名の高き遊女聞こえすみよの春　宋阿 古選
na no takaki yûjo kikoezu miyonoharu　soa = 巴人 hajin 1672-1742
(name-high play-woman sounds[like]: [honorific]reign/age's spring=ny)

miyo no haru

we hear nothing
about famous courtesans
on this new year

This *ku* is tricky. At first, I though it meant *"It sounds like / a high-class courtesan: / Miyo no Haru,"* and was a rare example of a Year *ku* that was *not* nationalistic. *Miyo-no-haru* is a respectful way to refer to the Spring or New Year *of the current age*, which is to say, *Imperial reign*, yet *sounds like* the name of a high-rank courtesan! But, Maruyama points out, the *ku* means courtesans were not lionized as much as in the previous era. So the *ku* seems to celebrate the Confucian (moral) reign of their Sovereign.

初禮や女夫つれたつ里つゝき　雲塵 大三
hatsurei ya meoto tsuredatsu satotsuzuki　unjin 1697
(first-greeting: <u>wife-husband</u> accompanying hometown-bordering)

new year greetings   new year greetings
a wife with her husband   wife and husband go from
side-by-side towns   his town to hers

Usually, only the men made New Year calls during the first few days. The wife's relations, the main objective of New Year calls, were often far away, and she was too busy entertaining people visiting her husband's house to leave for long. In some regions, women didn't even start making their rounds until "The Woman's New Year" on the full moon (the 15th). Once they did so, however, they took their time with it, so women need not be pitied in this respect. In the case of the above *ku*, the wife's hometown is contiguous with her husband's so they do something unusual, they make rounds together. Like the English "bride and groom," *me-oto* has the woman first. This does not reflect the social relationship of the sexes. Japanese women were not social equals of men at the time. They did, however, have more rights and more freedom than women in most of Europe. As the Portuguese Jesuit Luis Frois wrote in the late-16c, unlike the more restricted European women, Japanese women were free to leave the house and walk around without asking their husband's permission, they could initiate divorce and remarry and they could lose their virginity without losing their honor and right to marry, etc. (See *Topsy-turvy 1585*) .

里帰り母のなまりがいきいきと　北永智恵子 小4
satogaeri haha no namari ga iki-iki to　kitanaga chieko 4th grade
([home] country/town-return[visit] mother's accent lively)

a home visit
mother's accent
comes alive

Dialect differences in Japan are far greater than regional dialects in the United States. When a mother makes a visit to her home, her daughter gets to see and *hear* her supercharged with energy *on her own grounds*. This little girl's haiku reminds us of the difference of living at home – in one's *country*, in the Country Music sense of the word – or in another's home. The New Year visit tradition not only allows the wife to return to her roots, but allows her children to share them.

御子等子に向ふてうれしき花の春　濱藻女 題業名所
okora ko ni mukôte ureshi hananoharu　hamamo-jo/me? 19c?
([honorific=other's]children-toward facing. happy flower-spring)

      the kids happy   other children
    greeting other kids   thrilled to meet mine
       flowery spring   this new year

The use of an honorific before the plural children suggests others' kids. This *ku* is sweet and true. I recall seeing a boy too young to talk stand up on a table and *applaud* – clap his little hands together – when another baby was carried into the restaurant where I ate with his mother.

羽子板のうれしくあたる礼者哉　知辰 大三
hagoita no ureshiku ataru reisha kana　chitatsu 1697
(battledore delightfully hits caller/ny greeter!/ 'tis)

    a new year's caller   a new year's caller
    delighted to be hit   delighted to see clean hits
     by a battledore   at battledore

                       delighted to hit
                the shuttlecock before
                   a new year caller

     delighted to hit   a new year's caller
the new year's caller with   is delighted to hit
     her battledore   the shuttlecock

Battledore (a long ping-pong paddle-like stick decorated with pretty pictures) and shuttlecock (three feathers on a tiny ball of wood) is a New Year's game mostly played by girls. I would not swear to any of the five possible interpretations of the *ku*. The first is my favorite. Little girls are the sweetest thing on earth and any contact with them is delightful. My respondent also favors the first reading, but does not rule out any of the others. The second implies the visitor would be delighted not to have jinxed the little girls, but to have proved lucky for them. The third is most likely. A girl would be delighted to do well, especially in front of a male visitor. Note that the pretty picture on the battledore is often a handsome male actor. For the fourth, imagine a maiden of marriageable age and a handsome young visitor. The fifth, and least likely, has the visitor borrowing the battledore and showing off his or her skill. There is also the overall question as to whether this happens on the road as the caller makes his rounds or in front of a house (or in the garden of a house) he calls on. The poem is a bit too ambiguous to my liking, but I find the modern style – it has a fine realistic touch even if we are unsure what is happening – in this olde *ku* noteworthy. Vol. II will have more on games, including this one.

畑をめぐりて菊枯るゝ戸に年賀哉　句佛
ta[hata] o megurite kiku karuru to ni nenga kana　kubutsu 1874-1943
([cultivated] fields winding [through] chrysanthemum withering door-to/at year-greeting[*ku*-fest]' tis)

new year's greeting   ~~~~   **new year ku-fest**
                         skirting fields
   skirting fields   to a house with mummy mums: winding through
until i reach a door   new year *ku* fest   farm plots to the house of
 with dead 'mums   ~~~~   dry chrysanthemum

Cultured single-stalk chrysanthemums dry up and remain resolutely in place, an obelisk of withered leaves. There is an unstated "that year – this year" (*kozo-kotoshi*) quality in the poem. As a recognized late fall or early winter flower, the 'Mum says *"The year is dead!"* while the greeting replies *"Long live the year!"* Since the 'mum, associated with longevity, used for herbal tea and entered in competition (Think of our horse, cat or dog shows!) were ideal hobby plants, old gentlemen usually grew them, so we imagine the occupant of the cottage is an elderly man. The term for the greeting, *nenga* also means a tribute, so we might guess it was the poet's father or teacher. Another Meiji era (1868-1912) *ku* mentions a haiku master's hut being outside town (廻禮や師の家遠き町はづれ 寒樓 *kairei ya shi no ie tôki machihazure kanrô*. Both *ku* suggest unspoken New Year's advice from the master: *"Get out and see nature!"* Why the other "*ku*-fest" readings for Kubutsu's *ku*? Because *nenga* has yet another meaning, a haiku contest held on the first lucky day of the year. So the *ku* could describe the place where it was held.

廻禮や戸口々々に雪払ふ 炎子 ＋黄第一句集
kairei ya toguchi toguchi ni yuki harau enshi 19c? 20c?
(rounds-greeting: doorway [after] doorway-at, snow clear-off)

felicitations

new year's round
at every house i clear
away the snow

new year's day

personal greetings
gate after gate we get our
snow brushed off

My first reading is far less likely than the second, suggested by my respondent. With a mid-winter New Year from 1873, snow became common. No wonder people began to do less calling in person and rely more on mail. Today, the words *kairei* (going from house to house to exchange felicitations) and *gyokei* (the exchange of New Year's felicitations) are only known to antiquarians and poets!

蝦寶 山に入テ髭の塵とる禮者哉　雨柳　皮こすり
[*kahô? ebitakara?*] *yama ni irite hige no chiri toru reisha kana* uryû 1699
([shrimp-treasure] mountain-into entering, whiskers' dust remove caller 'tis/!)

a caller sets foot
on mount shrimp to dust
its whiskers

One reason I presumed a caller was cleaning off snow in the previous *ku* was because I read this one first. The *whiskers* (in Japanese) are the spiny *feelers* of an Ise shrimp (= crawfish)! The original's "Shrimp-treasure" is pegged on *mountain*, but I guess Shiki's Categorical is mistaken and it should be the subject for the *ku* which starts with "Mountain" (解説＝欄外注を求めております). The verb "entering" is standard for climbing a mountain, as dense vegetation must be parted to proceed.

正月や三日過れば人古し 蘭更
shôgatsu ya mikka sugireba hito furushi rankô 1726-99
(new years:/ three-days pass-if/when people age/old)

the new year
after three days
we grow old

after three days
our callers grow old
the new year

Visitors are fine, but after a while the parade grows tiring, if my second reading is the correct one.

年賀状
new year's cards

During the 20c, the New Year's card came to largely replace the New Year visit. People still exchange the formal felicitations when they meet, but they do not do as much formal calling, because people got spread out and the mail became inexpensive.

年賀状深雪にぬれて届きけり　巨籟 ホトトギス
nengajô shinsetsu ni nurete todokikeri　kyorai early-20c
(year-greeting-card deep-snow-by/with wet arrive/s[fin.])

> new year cards
> due to deep snow
> arrived wet

Although New Year's cards only go back to the Meiji era so there are no truly olde haiku, I will introduce a fair number of *ku* because I was impressed with the time Japanese take with them – the whole office shuts down for days as people write the company cards at work – the amount of good artwork produced at home and the fact that in Japan today, high school or university students?] deliver the New Year's cards on New Year's day – which is, after all, when they should arrive! – while the regular postman takes a vacation.[1]

年賀状書くにはなさぬ酒杯かな　南天樓 現代俳句大観
nengajô kaku ni hanasanu [2] *shuhai kana*　nantenrô modern
(year-greeting-card write-with/for part-not sake-cup!/'tis)

> always on hand
> for new year's card writing
> a glass of *sake*

Writing New Year's cards is a *Winter* activity and not a New Year activity, though people who failed to get off their cards on time sometimes are known to do so on the New Year's. Since this poem was included in the NY section of the Kaizôsha *saijiki*, it may refer to writing or to New Year's *sake*. In my opinion, some wine is absolutely necessary to expedite written greetings. Without it, one cannot avoid pondering the right thing to say at this time of year when everything – especially words – are fraught with meaning. The alcohol which usually slows things down is needed to speed things up.

---

1. Students Delivering Mail Can this be imagined in a country where the society is so sick that traditional festivities such as trick-or-treating can no longer be properly (children running about by themselves as we once did) enjoyed? In such a culture, union or business regulations would forbid the students to touch the mail, violence in parts of town would make it impossible the ensure the student's safety, their ability to deliver hard-to-read mail would be doubted, and people would worry about whether the student were casing their home for a future robbery, etc.. For all of its problems, fundamentally, Japan is still a much healthier society than the USA.

2. A Pun Untaken For readers fluent in Japanese: I do not know how the poet could refrain from writing *"kakasenu"* rather than *hanasanu* after *kaku-ni!*

賀状書いて炬燵の山を散らしけり　自得 ホトトギス
gajô kaite kotatsu no yama o chirashikeri　jitoku   early-20c
(greeting-card/s writing, kotatsu-mountain[+obj] scatter[+emph.])

    writing my cards　　　　　　　　　　　　　　　writing cards
i scatter the mountains　　　　　　　　　　　　i stripmine the surface
     on our *kotatsu*　　　　　　　　　　　　　　　 of my *kotatsu*

how i've littered
mount kotatsu, writing
greeting cards!

Just because this was in the New Year section of the Kaizôsha *saijiki* does not mean it *should* be. It really ought to be with Year-end *ku*, but I include it for the lamest of all reasons: I identify with the poet, whether in the first reading, where stacks of cards received the year before must be rummaged through creating a mess, the second, where a pile of manuscripts, books, letters, etc. must be dug up for addresses, or the last, where we imagine a clean (bare) rocky-top *kotatsu* littered with scrap-paper.

元日や硯の海も波静か　静茶 玉かづら
ganjitsu ya suzuri no umi mo nami shizuka   seisa 1751
(original-day: inkstone's ocean also waves quiet/still)

new year's day
the inkstone's ocean
is also calm

After the storm in the ink pool at the year-end (cards or letters were *de riguer*, even for courtesans), a preternatural quiet. The "also" implies correspondence to the real sea, such a calm being a common variety of New Year's weather, and possibly a tranquil old face, for wrinkles were called "waves" (*nami*). The calm waves in the ink stone pool may be metaphor; the inkstone was generally put away when not in use. So this could also be a self-portrait of a recluse who leaves his inkstone out.

ホ句一つありて名の無き賀状かな　虚吼 改造社
ho[k]ku hitotsu arite na no naki gajô kana   kyokô 1866-1935
(*hokku* one is, name's not greeting-card 'tis)

a greeting-card
with a single *hokku*
and no name

Was the sender so engrossed in his own brushmanship [1] he forgot to sign the card, or did he think the other party would immediately recognize it? Since a *hokku* was originally the start of a poetic sequence, it does seem the right thing for a New Year's card.

片仮名の幼きものの賀状哉　沙汀 現代俳句大観
katakana no osonaki mono no gajô kana   satei 20-c
(*katakana*[syllabary]'s childish greeting-card!/'tis)

a childish-looking
greeting card written
in *katakana*

1. *More than Calligraphy* A friend tells me he changed to a word-processor because he was so satisfied with his hand-writing that it hurt the quality of his writing! Konrad Lorenz's teacher invented a concept called *functionlust*, where an animal feels pleasure at repeating learned movements. The more complex the skill, the greater the satisfaction. Hence writing complex characters gives greater satisfaction than writing roman letters.

The stiff *katakana* カタカナ script is usually printed and seems more childish than the cursive *hiragana* ひらがな though most children first read with the latter. We can't help wondering who wrote the card. An uneducated relation? A soldier? (The military was big on angular script). The *ku* reminds me that *katakana*, which I have never liked, has a good side. Though invented *after* Chinese characters, it seems *primal,* like something that could be scratched on turtle shell for divination purposes.

伊勢へ送り伊勢より来るや年賀状　来布 最新二万句
ise e okuri ise yori kuru ya nenshijô　raifu early-20c?
(ise-to send ise-from comes year-begin -card)

i send a card
to ise and receive one
new year tiding

I use the word "tiding" because it evokes the tide and Ise is a peninsula. It is also home of the Japanese Gods including the Sun Goddess. As noted already, the cave she was lured out of is still there, and the idea of agelessness as represented by the famous Ise Shrine, *de-* and *re-*constructed every 20 years (note: *a concept of conservation at perfect odds with preservation*), assures that she will be reborn every year. How wonderful, then, to be in touch with someone in Ise!

友垣やいつか賀状も絶えにけり　挿雲 昭和一万句
tomogaki ya itsuka gajô mo taenikeri　sôun early-20c
(friend/s: sometime greeting-card/s too vanish[+fin.])

old friends
one year, greeting cards, too
stop for good

First visits grew infrequent, then the yearly greeting card stops coming. It happens.

ひとつ／＼打返し見る賀状哉　他石 現代俳句大観
hitotsu hitotsu uchikaeshi-miru gajô kana　yaseki early-20c
(one [by] one hit-re/turn[fire-back]-try/see greeting-card 'tis)

~~new method~~   like solitaire?

~~greeting cards~~   one by one
~~for each one i get~~   i turn over to see
~~one fired back~~   greeting cards

~~With gifts, it *is* better to give than to receive; but how discouraging to send more greeting cards than you get! It shows that people think less of you than you of them. This guy has found a sure-fire way to be even-handed, though it means other people will all be getting their cards late.~~ My respondent advises a second idiomatic reading of *uchikaeshi* and the verb *miru* strongly favors her reading. So, we have someone who methodologically looks at his cards one side at a time, thoroughly enjoying the process.

年賀状一番多いお父さん　劍持 志織
nengajô ichiban ôi otôsan　kenmochi shiori 20c
(year-greeting-card first-place-many father)

年がじょう小さいたばは私あて 本多由加
nengajô chiisai taba wa watashi-ate honda yûka 20c
(year-greeting-card small bundle-as-for me-to)

    new year's cards
    the greatest number
    are for father

    new year's cards
    the smallest bundle
    is for me

I like these *ku* from 子供俳句歳時記 (children's haiku saijiki), from a 5th grader and 4th grader, respectively, more than this older *ku*: *"New Year's cards: / two or three for the wife / mixed in"* 妻へ来し賀状交りぬ二三枚 風屼（山の下に「豆」もある）*tsuma e kishi gajô majirinu ni, san mai*　fûkotsu? 改造社俳諧歳時記). If there is a sending and receiving balance, there is also a ratio of cards received by each family member and even on this day where all are equal at the start of time, there are observable differences.

年がじょうことしはふえて十まいに　南大輔 子供俳句歳時記
nengajô kotoshi wa fuete jûmai ni　minami daisuke 2nd grade ôwake pref
(year-greeting-card this year-as-for increase ten cards-to)

    greeting cards
    this year mine are
    up to ten!

The total number of cards received tends to grow year by year. This kid is doing OK. I imagine most people get about as many as they are years old. There are surveys about everything in Japan. If I find one for New Year's cards, I'll put it in the foot-note![1]

いつになく添書のなき年賀状　長谷弘子
itsu ni naku soegaki no naki nengajô hase hiroko 季題別 1997
(exceptional/unusual accompanying-writing-not year-greeting-card)

    no longer rare
    a new year's card with
    no handwriting

"Accompanying writing" (*soegaki*) is not quite a "postscript," "marginalia" or even a handwritten note. *Something* personal was always added to the cards, usually hand-made until recently, unless hand-made by computer counts. The poet is disappointed not to get it on more than one card. Be that as it may, all of the remaining New Year's cards will come from a single book, the *Kidaibetsu Gendai-Haiku-Senshû*, published in Heisei 9 (1997) by the Haijin Kyôkai, the largest haiku association in Japan. While I will skip about a third of the 27 remaining haiku found in it, I will follow the original order with the rest:

酒すこし注ぎ足して読む年賀状　富士本秀峰
sake sukoshi tsugi-tashite yomu nengajô　fujimoto hideo 季題別
(*sake* a bit pour adding read year-greeting-cards)

    new year's greetings

    i pour out
    a bit more *sake* for each
    card i read

Must we exchange toasts in person? I *like* this. We *should* drink when reading New Year's greetings.

おめでたうたった五行の賀状かな　松宮美喜子
omedetô tatta go gyô no gajô kana　matsumiya mikiko 季題別
(congratulations only five lined greeting-card !/?/'tis)

a greeting card with but five lines

con	お
gra	め
tu	で
la	た
tions!	う

A very *shibui* (minimalist) card, indeed. In Japanese, each syllable is a single letter, or *syllabet* – one to a line – so it reads as naturally as it would horizontally. Today, the た (or タ) would be written と (or ト), but that is a minor matter.

どっと来て少しづつ来て賀状束　清水佳津子
dotto kite sukoshi zutsu kite gajô taba　shimizu katsuko 季題別
(plenty come, some at a time come, greeting card bundle)

thick bundles	first, a spurt
then, some at a time	then dribble dribble
greeting cards	greeting cards

The Post Office saves all cards mailed over the last two weeks or so of the old year for delivery in one swell sloop on the New Year's. After a day off, a second batch of cards sent by procrastinators or people too busy to write them earlier arrives on the third. Then the real laggards and those who failed to mail a card but felt obliged to respond to others. And, finally, the "moved, new address unknown" returns. The original poem is made by the psychological mimesis (sound-worthy adverb) *do'tto,* which means for something to happen or appear suddenly *and* powerfully making a heavy impact. It Englishes better with emotions that "burst out" or cattle that "stampede." I still remember the sound of a packet of New Year cards tossed upon my lintel. It was between a *plop* and a *thud*, but the beauty of this *do'tto* is that it communicates the psychological impact as well as the physical. Is there a translation I failed to find?

---

1. *Number of NY Cards.* A) On New Years Day 2000, 2,700,000,000 cards were delivered. 23/person. Note that half again as many come on the 3rd and more trickle in later. B) A Dec. 2002 blog reports that an average of 61 cards/person is received. C) To think that each person gets an average of 40 cards must be rare in the world. D) A drop in the card numbers were anticipated but in 1998, 4,160,000,000 post office New Year Cards were sold. In 2004, 4,447,800,000. Despite high unemployment, 30/person marvels one reporter. (*Note:* Many are now printed at home but still bear the special New Year stamps and, more important, the lottery numbers the post office prints on all New Year cards. Also note that a low but double digit percent of cards are not included in this figure, for they are on special store-bought or hand-crafted cards. E) Ishikawa Prefecture is 2nd in the nation in the number of postcards mailed, 33/person compared to the national average of 26.2/person and 1st (least) in the nation in the unemployment rate for men age 45-54 in 2002 (only 1.8% vs a national average of 4.3%) and paucity of noticeable earthquake tremors/year, only 74, as opposed to the national average of 393 between 1973-2002. (*Final comment:* I know the figures do not match. Perhaps, someone can improve this for a future edition.)

活字ばかりの賀状淋しくよみ返す　堀田ひさ江
katsuji bakari no gajô sabishiku yomikaesu　hotta hisae 季題別
(print-letters only greeting card lone/lack/lonely/sadly reading-over)

wanting something
i reread the new year's card
with print alone

The beauty of this *ku* is in *its* rereading. At first reading, we already feel a bit irritated at a card with no handwriting and no picture. Or, at least, I do. But this "lonely" feeling I try to recreate with the first line is much subtler. I do not know if the poet reread it right away or later in the day, or another day, when all the cards were in and she felt too tired to do any work or was ready to sort out and put the cards away; but, when she did, the card just did not satisfy her, so she reread it, trying to find *something* heart-warming in the dry print.

吉野より手漉しの和紙の賀状来る　奥田智静
yoshino yori tekoshi no washi no gajô kuru　okuda tomoyasu 季題別
(yoshino[place]-from hand-made[?] japanese-paper greeting card comes)

a greeting card
of thick hand-made paper
and from yoshino!

There are many ways to say "Japanese." The *wa* in the original is the most beautiful of them. I could not use the English word "Japanese" to modify the paper (*shi*). Japanese paper, as opposed to Chinese and Occidental paper, is thick and cloth-like. Yoshino is *the* place for viewing cherry blossoms in classic poetry. I see "from Yoshino" here as the esthetic equivalent of the spiritual "from Ise" seen in other *ku*.

教師たりし生涯の至宝賀状の嵩　宇山雁茸
kyôshi tarishi shôgai no shihô gajô no kasa?　uyama karitake 季題別
(teacher as/duty lifetime's cherished treasure: greeting-card peak/mountain)

i am a teacher	a teacher, my life's
the treasure of a lifetime	treasure is this mountain
mt greeting card	of greeting cards

If the poet had a 50-student home class for 40 years, he would have a 2000-card-high mountain peak to gaze upon. People with room, sometimes keep all their cards.

吾子よりの賀状一番上に置く　近藤けい子
ako yori no gajô ichiban ue ni oku　kondô keiko 季題別
(my/own child-from year-card first-place top-of place)

placed on top
the new year's card
from my child

The cards are delivered in one order and rearranged – some may be leaned against something or pinned up, but as post-cards, they do not stand alone like our folded Christmas greetings – by the receiver. My own favoritism is not toward family or friends. I always place the cards in the order of their appearance, with the best-looking card on top.[1] This *ku* is a bit too simple, even for me. The next is better.

申の顔まこと品良き賀状来る　水口泰子
saru no kao makoto hin yoki gajô kuru　mizuguchi yasuko 季題別
(monkey's face genuinely classy/refined/genteel/dignified greeting card comes)

the monkey's face
on one new year's card
really dignified!

a card came
with a monkey boasting
a genteel face

A refined monkey! As a Greek philosopher pointed out, relativity does not apply to our relatives: we can accept a good-looking horse, but the apes are just too close for comfort and we cannot help but see them as deformed. So this is nothing less than a miracle. What type of monkey do you imagine?

絶筆となりし賀状の筆の跡　川筋渓水
zeppitsu to narishi gajô no fude no ato　kawasuji keisui 季題別
(sever-brush [last thing written by deceased] became greeting-card's brush mark/trace)

new year's

the brush strokes
on a card that became
memento mori

I translated around the untranslatable "trail/mark/trace/remnant" (*ato*) found in all too many haiku.

病む友の賀状の筆の張りもどる　松田知都 季題別
yamu tomo no gajô no fude no hari modoru　matsuda chizu
(ailing[long-sick] friend's greeting card's brush's firmness returns)

greeting card

renewed vigor
in the brush-stroke of
a sick friend

While a metaphorical brush is possible – as our pen is a plume is a feather still – here, most Japanese middle-aged or above write their New Year's cards, or at least part of each card – if only the address – with a brush. I must confess to cussing out my native tongue in the process of translating when I unsuccessfully sought a word similar to *hari*, for which I had to use the loose sense-translation "vigor," even in the literal rendition. The original can be *described* as "a healthy taut plenitude," but that is not the same as having a word for it.

---

1. *Card Art*. If you run an art gallery and have 12 years (one per animal) and a budget (say $10,000), I will gather cards from Japanese publishers – the cards tend to be good for authors and designers and bookstores are creative – and give you a hell of a show. Believe me, this stuff is a hell of a lot more interesting than 99% of what is called "art" and, for most people, infinitely more inspiring than the high culture exchanges of *noh* and *kabuki* and whatnot.

亡き人の去年の賀状や字の乱れ　御園英子 季題別
naki-hito no kozo no gajô ya ji no midare　misono eiko 1997
(deceased's last year's greeting card: letter's turbulence/messiness)

> last year's cards
> one from someone who died
> looks messy

The chief editor of a publisher I worked for received thousands of cards every year. There were always a few from, as she joked, the Other World! At first I thought *that* was what this *ku* was about and translated "The dead woman's greeting card / mailed last year / is messy" (And "Messy lettering / a greeting card mailed / by a dead man" and "A greeting card / mailed last year: the dead / write wildly). This is not the case with this *ku*. Imagine the poet looking over the previous year's cards (a quick way to get addresses and names right) as she writes her own, and coming across someone who died in the course of that year. Ah, come to think of it, the writing shows entropy. One reason I misread was that the *Kidaibetsu* collection had the *ku* in the *New Year* cards (*hatsu-dayori, nen-gajô*), not the *Winter* writing-the-cards (*gajô kaku*). The percentage of dead people in *Kidaibetsu* (under-represented in my selection) seems a bit high. Does this reflect the contrast of death and renewal, the high average age of the members of the association, or the understandable reluctance of an editor to turn down *ku* dealing with a grave subject?

余白なき賀状を海の男より　中納フミ子 季題別
yohakunaki gajô o umi no otoko yori　nakano fumiko 1997
(white-space[margin]-not greeting card[obj] sea's man-from)

> a greeting card
> with no margin from
> a man of the sea

I find this fascinating. *Why?* Because an inch-thick plank is all between the sailor and the sea whereas a home has thick walls and a yard? Because all the space in a boat is needed? Because the seaman sees water as *connection* and not *separation* and is not afraid to let the space beyond the card be the margin? Is there an unwritten *because* here? Most likely, the poet just felt there was *some* connection and wanted to share that with us. I once exchanged cards with the captain of a fishing boat. I remember well that he was an ex-yakuza who carved Goddesses of Mercy for contrition, just like the famous swordsman Miyamoto Musashi once did. But, hell if I can recall the design of his cards. Perhaps if I were deeper into haiku at the time I might. Haiku is good that way. It teaches you to be observant.

恋は遠し年に一度の賀状なる　豊竹春野 季題別
koi wa tôshi nen ni ichido no gajô naru　toyotake haruno 1997
(love/romance-as-for far, year-in one-time's greeting-card becomes/is)

> **the stars are not alone**
>
> how far my love!
> now just a greeting card
> one time a year

The annual nature of the New Year's greeting and that of the Stars meeting come together here as in the 1775 poem given earlier. The direct reference to romantic love (*koi*) makes this a *tanka*-like haiku.

盲ふてふ母へ寄り添ひ読む年賀　川口登子　季題別
mô fuchô? haha e yorisoi yomu nenga　kawaguchi nobuko 1997
(blind unwell[?] mother-to draw-sidling read year-greeting)

i draw up close to
my blind mother to read
her greeting cards

There is little worth *reading* in greeting cards, but some picture-dependent wit could be *described*. A cheese-like moon depicted for the Year of the Rat/Mouse (the brainchild of a clever editor at the publisher I worked for), a botanical illustration of a variety of mungo-grass called *ryû no hige,* or Dragon's Whiskers (a name known by perhaps one in ten Japanese, including a friend with an interest in botany) showing its tiny round beads on the Year of the Dragon . . . This sort of thing can be put into words. And, I suppose the old woman would appreciate the sort of brief personal news (babies born, pets acquired, new jobs, marriages, deaths) that mostly bores me. But this *ku* excites *me,* for I look so closely at the cards that I imagine the delight I always feel from the grain of the brush stroke and details of the pictures that cannot be put into words.

旧姓を小さく書きし賀状かな　長野多禰子
kyûsei o chiisaku kakishi gajô kana　nagano taneko 季題別
(old-[family]name[obj] small[as adv] wrote/written greeting-card 'tis)

her old name i find written small: new year's card	new year's card i write my old name in tiny letters

In other words, she got married and adopted a new "sir name" (pun by respondent OM). Until I had to translate this, I never noticed that English cannot *adverb* smallness gracefully. "Written tinily" might work, but not well. I had to resort to an idiom. That was the last greeting card haiku in the *Kidaibetsu* 季題別 collection. The first reading is less likely from the grammar but supported by the *ku's* placement in the New Year (rather than year's end) section. A final *ku* from the early 20c Kaizôsha *haikai saijiki* to wrap up the chapter.

水引に束ねて仕舞ふ賀状かな　鳥不関
mizuhiki ni tabaneteshimau gajô kana　chôfukan early-20c
(two-tone-paper-chord-with bundle-up greeting-cards 'tis)

the new year's cards
bundled up and tied
with mizuhiki

Mizuhiki is two-tone paper cord (red and white) made especially for tying envelopes or packages containing announcements for auspicious occasions (marriage, award ceremonies?). It is not very strong and tied in special loose decorative bows, so it would not normally be used for tying up piles of what will be old New Year's cards as soon as they go into the closet – or wherever they will be stored. But, when you think about the enchantment these cards represent, it does seem sad to think that most end up with rubber-bands or cheap string around them, or loose inside a shoe-box until, someday, they are unceremoniously thrown away. This *ku* shows how we *should* treat them.

正月言葉皆軽薄の世界哉 未存 大三
shôgatsu kotoba mina keihaku no sekai kana mizon 1697
(new year's words all light-thin(frivolous/idle/shallow) world!/?/'tis)

                      on new year's
                  our world of words all
                       immaterial

the new year   the new year
do our words today   a world where empty
end in play?   words rule

                       new year words
                 on this day all we say
                      is for display

the new year   new year speech
in this world all words   a world where heavy
are superficial   words are taboo

                       new year's day
                 a world when words
                     lack substance

new year's day   new year's day
a world where no word   when saying something
is good enough   says nothing

                       the new year
               when we can see through
                      our own words

I had intended to end this chapter with the greeting cards neatly bundled up, but felt misgivings about failing to do the same for this confusing *ku* with only three translations and two lines of explanation in the previous chapter, where it was set within an essay into *nothing*. The problem is it is hard to tell if the *ku*, by a poet whose name (probably adopted for this *ku* alone) means "pre-existence," describes words actually said on the New Year, in which case it belongs in this chapter, or the nature of the world we now live in, as opposed to the mythical one where words and deeds were one in a literal sense we can only understand in dreams today. The connotation of the double-character word "light-thin" (*keihaku*) is almost always bad, but, I cannot help wondering whether it might not allow a positive nuance in this magical time. Could the poet be extolling the freedom of pre-existence, when *lacking body, words fly?* In my blossom-viewing book, I defend the apparent banality of skeletons in costume as *an epiphany*, experienced with a shudder while sitting below leafless cherry trees in full-bloom. Here, I imagine myself listening to the greetings of New Year's Day callers, or, to my own voice, and suddenly feeling how shallow – ghostly – the words were, while dropping into a deeper reality.

☆**Issa's Shadow-Puppet.** On page 160, I explained that straw sandals greeting a *kageboshi* depicted a rich man greeted behind blinds or Issa looking down at his sandals as he greeted a superior's shadow; but two other shadow-figure *ku* suggest this may be a one-man puppet show. One does not mention greetings: *"My shadow, too / up and about this morning / New Year"* (*kageboshi mo mame-sokusai de kesanoharu*). Another, prescripted *"Traveling alone (一人旅)"* does: *"My shadow / seems chipper, too, so / I greet it!"* (*kageboshi mo mame-sokusai de gyokei kana* 発句鈔追加). Note, however, neither original has a clear "my," though the prescript for the latter makes it *likely*. *Mame-sokusai*, is identical in both *ku*, though I translated it "up and about" in one and "chipper" in another.

蓬莱
hôrai

八 8

MAGIC MOUNTAIN

蓬莱に我身ちぢめてはいらうよ　子規
hôrai ni wagami chijimete hairô yo   shiki 1866-1902
(hôrai-into, my/one's body/self shrinking enter let's!)

magical invitation

let's shrink
ourselves down and play
on mt *hôrai!*

My Japanese-English dictionary defines *Hôrai* as 1) [China's legendary] Isle of Eternal Youth; 2) A *shima-dai* [an ornament on a stand representing the Isle ~]; 3) A stand piled up high with seafood, vegetables and fruit, as a New Year's festive decoration;" 4) Formosa [for paradise was to the South?]. In haiku, all but the last apply. Although said dictionary has over 2000 pages, it skips an important fact: *the island is a mountain*. Indeed, there is a separate entry for *Hôrai-san* (*san* = 山 = mountain), but it only refers the reader to the above "*hôrai*" and fails to translate "*Mount* Hôrai," which additional sources say was one of three main magical mountains of Chinese legend and is pronounced Feng-Lai.

蓬莱や升の中から山か出る　来山 類題名家集
hôrai ya masu no naka kara yama ga deru   raizan 1653-1716
(hôrai! masu's inside-from mountain appears/sticks-out)

mt. feng-lai
a mountain rises from
a cedar box

It is tempting to use the Chinese name Feng-Lai rather than *Hôrai*, but considering the fact it is the Japanese rather than the Chinese who model this mountain, I will use their pronunciation from now on. The *masu* is a square open box made of aromatic cedar. I had imagined a reflection of the Hôrai in cold *sake* about to be drunken from it – I enjoy drinking such *sake* – but my more knowledgeable respondent sees a Hôrai of rice literally rising from the box which was originally for measuring grain rather than for drinking it. A *masu* is metaphysically appropriate for growing a mountain because the element earth is four-square in Chinese philosophy and *masu* is a homophone for that growth, or, "increase." The box serving as base of the *hôrai* is not, however, generally called a *masu*, but a *sanbô*, or "three-sides," a shallow square box on a large box, with decorative holes in three sides serving as its legs. It is also quite a bit larger than the typical *masu*. There was a preface to the *ku*, but I have not yet figured it out. At any rate, Raizan wrote many Hôrai *ku*. If his last miniaturizes the mountain, the next monumentalizes it:

踏み分けて我が蓬莱に出にけり 来山 再現
fumi-wakete waga hôrai ni ide ni keri raizan -1716
(tread-part [open a trail] my *hôrai*-to arrive [+finality])

new year pilgrimage

blazing a trail
i finally reach the foot
of my *hôrai*

Should I add that the poet's name transliterates as "come-mountain?" The wit is in the compound-verb *fumiwakete*, literally "tread-part" and used for one having to make a way through dense brush on a wilderness trek – and what we call "wilderness" was called "mountains" in the Sinosphere – in conjunction with the micro-cosmic *Hôrai*. I assume this means the *tatami* "plain" around Raizan's mountain is swarming with family and servants, or the lucky straw is especially bountiful, or he has found a ready-made *hôrai* in a market crowded with them. It is hard to say whether or not Raizan had a *me-on-my-Hôrai* thought as expressed by Shiki in the wishful lead *ku* of the chapter.

蓬莱に夜はうすきぬもきせつべき 言水
hôrai ni yoru wa usuginu mo kisetsu beshi gonsui -1719
(horai-on, night-as-for, light-silk don-should)

mist for a mountain

at night
the *hôrai* should wear
light silk

A *hôrai* usually doesn't much resemble a real mountain (Neither, for that matter, does Mount Blanc). In Japanese, any pile of stuff is called a mountain (*yama*) even when it is not high enough to merit the word in English. Still, the poet imagines that this "mountain" of plenty could use some spring mist and suggests how to create the illusion. Such an illusion beats the "morning mist" created by a pot of boiled what-is-not-said by another poet: 蓬莱や煮えたつ釜の朝霞 吟霞 萬題 (*hôrai ya nietatsu kama no asagasumi* ginka __).

鶏鳴いて宝飾の山明けんとする 子規 明治廿九
tori naite hôshoku no yama aken to suru   shiki (1866-1902)
(rooster crows *hôrai* mountain brightens/dawns[=opens] tries/fixes to)

new year

rooster crows	rooster crows
mount cornucopia	*open sesame! open*
nears dawn	*mount hôrai!*

Hôshoku is another word for the *hôrai*. The *hô* means treasure and *shoku* decoration. The rooster puts the magical mountain into the country and hints at *opening it* – a homophone (brighten=open) suggests this – on this magical day. Note that in the Sinosphere one rooster's crow was said to "open ten-thousand [*i.e.,* all] doors," and Japanese had – and still have – official dates for "opening" the mountain and the sea (for hiking and for swimming).

蓬莱は富士に人なき心哉　器水 大三
hôrai wa fuji ni hitonaki kokoro kana   kisui 1697
(hôrai-as-for,[mt] fuji-on/with people-less heart/essence!/?/'tis)

      the *hôrai*
    like mount fuji
      minus man

Today, Fuji is almost always written with the Chinese characters "wealth+warrior" 富士. Throughout the Edo era, it was written in other ways, too: "Un-exhaustible"(unexhaustible 不尽) and "un-death" (immortal 不死), "un-two" (unique 不二). All of these show it was indeed an icon, a huge *Hôrai*. One of the "false (*gi*) Bashô" *ku* in the Iwanami Bashô selection put it like this: *"It's Hôrai! / You go out to see Fuji: / Edo Spring"* (蓬莱や不二を見て来て江戸の春　疑芭蕉 *hôrai ya fuji o mitekite edô no haru*).

富士山を蓬莱にして庵の春　雄梧 続紅_集
fûjisan o hôrai ni shite io no haru   yûgo 18-19c?
(fuji-mt[obj] *hôrai*-into make hut's spring)

  mount fuji   cottage spring
serves my cottage   i make mount fuji
  as a *hôrai*   my *hôrai*

There were also mock-up Fuji's, but I prefer to imagine a painting or the real thing seen out the open door. Metaphorically speaking, the only problem was that people actually climbed Fuji, while the legendary mountain-isle was unapproachable; boats either sank or were blown away by a great wind. The pleasure quarters was the only "paradise" mortals (wealthy males, anyway) were allowed into. By being small, the model *hôrai* was, like the legendary original, inviolable. But, the spirit, on this magical day could get there none-the-less:

元日や蓬莱山もよそならす　笑子
ganjitsu ya hôraisan mo yoso narazu   shôshi 1775
(original day! mt *hôrai* even, outside/strange/exotic/standoffish is/become-not)

 it's new year's   on new year's
even the isle of *hôrai*   even mount feng-lai
 is reachable   is climbable

But one shouldn't be too familiar. A Meiji era (1868-1912) haiku by a poet whose name translates as "can+mountain" describes the proper attitude toward this model mountain:

かしこまる蓬莱山の麓哉　可山 明治一万句
kashikomaru hôraisan no fumoto kana   kasan late-19c
(behaving politely/respectfully/formally *hôrai*-mount's base!/'tis)

    we
  behave
 ourselves
 at the foot
of mount *hôrai*

I am afraid we cannot say the same for our Christmas trees. Perhaps, if we lived in pagan times, when a tree vandal might have his navel nailed to it and intestines wrapped around the trunk, we would hush. Japanese, like most people of the pre-modern world, revered trees and mountains.

蓬莱に南無／＼といふ童(or 子供)哉　一茶　文化八
hôrai ni na[n]mu na[n]mu [1↓] *to iu warabe* (or *kodomo*) *kana*   issa -1827
(*hôrai*-to *"namu namu"* [title for amida buddha sutra[?] says child!/'tis)

cosmopolitan spring

a child prays
namu namu namu
to the hôrai

The child in Issa's *ku* has one thing wrong. Grown-ups pray "*namu-ami-dabutsu . . .*" toward *Buddhist* objects, not magical mountains, which, Chinese roots or not, belong to the native half of Japanese religion, Shintô. Japanese pretty much reserved, and still reserve Buddhism for endings, in a word, death, and keep birth, marriage and other beginnings – such as New Year's – for the Way of the Gods. As one poet baldly put it, *"The gods are / more precious than buddha / spring dawn"* (佛より神そたふときけさの春　とめ　大三物*hotoke yori kami zo tôtoki kesanoharu*　tome 1697).[2↓]   Shiki expresses the same indirectly:

蓬莱や南山の蜜柑東海の蝦　子規　明治廿七
hôrai ya nanzan no mikan tôkai no ebi   shiki -1902
(hôrai! south-mountain's tangerine, east-sea's shrimp)

sources of spring

our *hôrai*, lo!
oranges from the south
shrimps from the east

These are not the directions Buddhism was identified with. The orange (*tangerine* had too many syllabets) is also a symbol of the rising New Year sun, while the shrimp embodies spry longevity.

蓬莱や額で折らす海老の髭　梅室
hôrai ya hitai de orasu ebi no hige   baishitsu 1768-1852
(hôrai! brow-by breaks-not shrimp's moustache)

~~our new *hôrai*!~~	mt *hôrai:* here	shrimp whiskers
~~my brow has just broken~~	we do not break at the brow	are free to stretch out
~~a shrimp's whisker~~	shrimp whiskers	on mount hôrai

I first imagined a myopic poet, but my respondent favored a negative reading of the verb and it occurred to me that this "shrimp" was an Ise Shrimp, which, like the Florida crawfish (spiny lobster), has two long hard feelers that double back over its "forehead" and may have been trimmed by chefs in Japan. Huge "shrimp" and tangerines were only the most eye-catching decorations. I will not even *try* to list all the items, edible or not, possessing symbolic significance, primarily based on puns, making their names auspicious.[3↓]   One of my favorite poets, perhaps noting an overly elaborate mountain, piled high with goodies far beyond the call of symbolism, dared to write a haiku that is very *senryû:*

1. *Namu namu* Some versions of this *ku* use Chinese characters (south+nothing), usually pronounced "*na-mu*," but others use the phonetic syllabary to write *nanmu nanmu*, a more mumbly childish pronunciation. Coincidentally, There is a line, once well-known, from an older Buddhist book, where the "south+nothing" *namu* is immediately followed by *sanbô* or "three+treasure/s" which was, as earlier explained, the name for the three-legged stand forming the base for the *hôrai*! That is then followed by four-characters *"one+inch+light+shade,"* alluding to a bit of gold found in an otherwise sandy desert, and meaning this: *"that special moment in time should be treasured."* So the poem *may* also be saying to the parent, doubtless a friend of Issa's, to treasure this magical time in your child's life which will soon be past.

2. Precious Gods Another version of the poem from the same collection: *"The Gods are / more precious than Buddha / New Year's inn"* (佛より神そたふとき宿の春 乙子（加生妻）大三~ *yado-no haru* – *otsushi*?). See IPOOH NY vol 2. Both versions of the *ku* are clearly emphatic in the original, but *"The gods, by God, / are ..."* would not work!

3. Auspicious Items According to Blyth, a standard *hôrai* includes: "some dried persimmons" [while a fall fruit, they turn the color of powdered sugar because of their natural sweetness when dried], "a mandarin orange" [the *mikan*, the standard Japanese orange, is a tangerine], "a bigarade (bitter orange)" [seems closer to a grapefruit to me, and the name, *daidai*, sounds like "big-big," or "generation (after) generation"], a *tokoro* ("a kind of vine folded up in paper of a certain shape") [lost me completely here, but the name puns with "place"]; . . . "a devil's apron" (a kind of sea-weed); *noshi* ("a thin strip of sea-ear") . . . Obviously, this sort of thing needs illustration (and I could use assistance for it)!

蓬莱に見るや浮世の欲そろへ　也有
hôrai ni miru ya ukiyo no yokuzoroe　yayû 1701-83
(*hôrai*-in/on see!/?/: floating/sinful/sad world's desires gathered/[a]set)

<table>
<tr><td>

in the *hôrai*
our world has gathered
all its desire!

</td><td>

all the avarice
of the world, is it found
here on *hôrai*?

</td></tr>
</table>

The *horai* is a cherished illusion, while the real world is a woeful for being an illusion. Wishes are good, desire is bad. A cornucopia is sacred *and* it is vulgar. Magic is paradoxical. Another poem by Shiki marvels at the *"Huge hôrai / [that] can be seen in / town houses"* (大なる蓬莱見ゆる町家哉 子規 明治三十 *ôi-naru hôrai miyuru machiya kana*). A "town-house" in Japan meant flats for the working people with the mindset the West associates with middle-class. We can readily understand why these towns-men like large *hôrai*. The wealthy tend to live on the hill-sides above them. Shiki also depicts *"The sod hut / a straw raincoat and hat / for the Hôrai"* (蓑笠を蓬莱にして草の庵 子規 *minokasa o hôrai ni shite kusa no io*). It is hard to say whether the somewhat conical hat sitting upon the thatched coat was *deliberately* made into a *hôrai,* or, Shiki's poetic eye, simply read the interior of the cottage that way.

蓬莱に貧乏見ゆるあはれなり 子規
hôrai ni binbô miyuru aware nari　shiki -1902
(*hôrai*-in poverty seeing piti/beautiful becomes)

aware

finding poverty
in the *hôrai*, it seems
more touching

Does English have a single word for "plaintive beauty?" Japanese does: *aware*. Forced to chose, I dropped the *beauty* for "touching." Shiki wrote a somewhat similar Christmas haiku: *"On Christmas / a small chapel / is touching"* (クリスマスに小さき会堂のあはれなる = 再現 子規 *kurisumasu ni chiisaki kaidô no aware naru*). Note: the same *aware*.

蓬莱の橙赤き小家かな　蒼虬
hôrai no daidai akaki koie kana　sôkyû 1760-1842
(hôrai's bigarade (orange) red small-house!/'tis)

a small house
the hôrai's bigarade
bright orange

A small house would be cold and dark without holiday spirit. I made "red" "orange" for the cheer. My respondent adds that bigarade color (*daidai-iro*) *is* "orange" in Japanese. More on this huge citrus soon.

貧しさに蓬莱二つ作りけり　青々
mazushisa ni hôrai futatsu tsukurikeri　seisei -1937
(poverty-from, hôrai two make[+emphatic])

my poverty	out of poverty
made me make	i end up making
two hôrai	two hôrai

"Out of poverty" can be "out of money" if you would be more concrete than the poet. I think you have to be poor or have been poor for *decades* (the poverty of a student does not count, for the young can take comfort in the future) to come up with such a *ku,* so I added the "my" and "me" not specified in the original. I did not feel it necessary to add pronouns to Issa's older, more cheerful:

蓬莱や唯三文の御代の松　一茶
hôrai ya tada san mon no miyo no matsu　issa -1827
(*hôrai*! just three mon [two bit]our time=reign's/age's pine)

mount *hôrai*	ah, my *hôrai*
with only a modern	just one two-bit pine
two-bit pine!	the current price

my hôrai pine:
what a time! eternity
for just two-bits

It helps to know that, in the Sinosphere (to steal a phrase from a diamond dealer), *a pine tree is forever.* Just three *mon* buys *that.* Blyth went whole hog translating this *ku,* the only *hôrai* in his anthology: *"Elysian fields be mine! / O age of glory! – / For a three-halfpenny pine branch."* The Occidental metaphor and complex phrasing – the "for" in the third line follows the first – is rare in Blyth. But he may have a point. Did my first two readings take the *miyo* (lit., "honorable reign," but often meaning "nowadays") too lightly? Blyth also has a wonderful description of Hôrai and two other islands in the Chinese Sea. He speaks sages living forever in golden, crystal, ruby and Jade palaces, and notes they look like clouds from a distance, but close-up appear under water! I cannot argue with that, but I must protest when he writes "It is to these islands that the above offerings are dedicated, but to such lofty beings [The sages living in the palaces?] Issa offers only his miserable little pine branch, with humour, and *in so far as it is humour,* with sincerity, with natural piety . . . ." The humor is, indeed, there. The problem is that the pine is generally not laid down, but stood up on the *hôrai,* or, in cases where there is nothing else, serves *as* the main body of the *hôrai,* which is, itself, more a re-creation, at most an object of sympathetic magic, or talisman, and at least a reified wish. The pine is not an *offering*.

吉桃の箸蓬莱の竹とせむ 角川照子 角川俳句歳時記 第三版
kittô no hashi hôrai no take to semu   kadokawa teruko 20c
(auspicious-peach chopsticks, *hôrai's* bamboo make)

sleight of mind

our mount *hôrai*
my lucky peach chopsticks
do for bamboo!

The pine, peach and bamboo were the three standard plants connected with sages and longevity in the Sinosphere. I can't say all are usually found on the *hôrai*. The young pine, with its fresh green is irreplaceable one.[1] The poet has made the remaining two with a single ruse. My ten-set dictionary shows no such chopsticks. But it is easy to imagine that someone makes peach chopsticks for easy birth (*momo* is a homophone for thighs), or a healthy child, because the legendary "peach-boy" Hercules, Momotarô, was born from a peach found floating down a river. But, here, the poet has found new auspicious properties in her chopsticks. Peaches (the fruit) were associated with long life in the Sinosphere. There was a legendary peach tree on top of a legendary mountain planted by the Western Queen Mother. It took 3000 years to flower and another 3000 years to bear a peach that would give you 600 years a bite. A picture of a piece of Qing Dynasty lacquerware [2] *shaped like a peach* shows a bowl-full of magical treasures from which the character "spring" wafts up surrounded by the dragons of ongoing creation. Another Qing Dynasty picture shows a boyish looking man astride a *kylin* (a chimera with a little elephant head, horse legs and turtle-plated skin as far as I can see) [3] bringing a *"peach-present- thousand-years"* from one world to another. In Japanese, peach (*momo*), is also a homophone for "hundred" or "myriad" and eons are called <u>*momochiyo,*</u> literally "hundred-thousand-ages," [4] while bamboo = 竹, with its many joints and similarity of character, has generally been associated with a thousand = 千 years. So, by poetically grafting the two plants, Kadokawa Teruko created something immortal, and literally charming for her family's *hôrai*. She may also have coupled mountain-islands, for the "Peach-Original-Home" 桃源郷 paradise is not the same as the *Hôrai;* but, enough detail! Let us just say that *"In the Hôrai / we see the sparkling / form of spring!"* (蓬莱にきりゝと春の姿哉 鷺十 *hôrai ni kiriri to haru no sugata kana* rojû 1765). Some models are minimal, the microcosmic in shorthand. Others burst at the seams, their plenty promising the spring (and fall!) yet to come. Still, for all its elements – and I have mentioned only a few – the *hôrai* was generally far smaller, and far less glittery than a Christmas tree. And, objectively speaking, this abstract mountain is a far more mature "installation" than a manger Nativity Scene with its dolly or wax museum-like quality. Only the fact that food predominates among the goodies ensures its popularity with children.[5] I wonder if I'm the only person who finds a hint of oral gratification in the sound of the words *namu namu* uttered by the child in Issa's *ku*, who some translators *assume* was his beloved Sato, though the *ku* dates back to three years before he was married.

1. *Pine vs Fern.* While the pine seems *the* most important item on a *hôrai,* because they are found on mountains, long-lived, and pun on "wait-for," some *hôrai*-like New Year decorations depend heavily on *fern*. I will give the fascinating fern (*shida*), a full treatment in Volume II.

2. *Why Qing Dynasty?* I happen to have on hand a huge, exquisitely printed book with the above-mentioned illustrations, because I translated it at the behest of the Japanese publisher for whom I once worked. Thanks to this work, I learned once and for all that *"longevity,"* as I spelled it for years, was too long! The book, mostly by designer Sugiura Kohei, is called *Moji no Shukusai (A Celebration of Letters)* and was published in 1995 to celebrate the 75 anniversary of the publishing house Shaken.

3. *Yes, the Kylin* is one and the same *Kirin* of **Kirin Beer**.

4. *Another 1000-year Hypothesis.* Bamboo I examined in Japan had about 50 joints (standard years for a lifetime) and the reign of an emperor was probably about 20 years, with each joint symbolizing an age, or era. **20 x 50 = 1,000.**

5. *Hôrai versus Christmas Tree.* Today, when every local store is a candy mountain, food counts for less. Japanese children are probably more impressed with Christmas trees. Moreover, a large *hôrai,* as is the case for so many traditional Japanese things, is ridiculously expensive. The first one I found on the internet was about $1000!

蓬莱の天窓をシャぶるをさな哉　一茶
hôrai no atama o shaburu osana kana　issa 1818
(hôrai's head[+obj] sucks infant 'tis/!)

    my infant girl
    sucks on the head
    of mt *hôrai!*

This *ku* about Issa's girl, Sato, takes the cake! I am not certain what exactly the "head" was. It may be a round-topped piece of *mochi* (sweet-rice-cake). Or, it could be a *daidai,* "bigarade," or big "Seville orange," according to my dictionary. The *daidai* is not only propitious for being bright and round but for being homophonic with both "generation-generation" (代々 = predictive of the long term well-being of the family) – and "big-big" (大々 = suggesting success at building a big name and large fortune).

橙や蓬莱に得る如意の球　半眠 大三
daidai ya hôrai ni eru nyoinotama　hanmin 1697
(bigarade! hôrai-to/on/from gain cintamani[budh.])

    the bigarade
    a wish-fulfilling gem
    on mt *hôrai!*

The only English for *nyôi-shu* (*nyoi-no-tama* is the poetic way to say it) in my Ja>En dictionary is a Buddhist (Sanskrit) word *cintâmani,* which is not in my biggest Eng>Eng dictionary. Luckily, the function of the gem (crystal?) was easily translated! Another poet (Fukaku, -1753) celebrated the 90th birthday of 千翁 by declaring the bigarade on the *hôrai* was none other than the (Chinese) legendary Queen of the West, who found the peach of eternal life (橙や組蓬莱の西王母　不角 *daidai ya kumihôrai no seiôbo*).

橙をくはぬ物かと児の問ふ　焦笠 大三
daidai o kuwanu mono ka to ko no tou　shôryû 1697
(bigarade[+obj] eat-not thing? so infant/child's asking)

    the bigarade
    but can we eat it?
    asks a boy

Eventually, they did end up eaten, although Japanese do not appreciate the flavor as much as a grapefruit-lover might. But, first – I read somewhere – they were tossed high into the air, or back and forth, over the head of such a kid I would bet! *Enough on the bigarade!* As I cannot imagine *ever* finding time to essay bigarades again in *this* lifetime, I indulged myself. Now, back to that magic mountain!

蓬莱に児はひかゝるめでたさよ　山店 続虚栗
hôrai ni ko wa haikakaru medetasa yo　santen 1687
(hôrai-to child crawls-up lucky/joyfulness[+exclam.])

sweet sight

    a joyful sight
    my child crawling up
    to mount *hôrai!*

The *medetasa* I turned into "a joyful sight" is, like *aware* and *kashikomaru*, one of those wonderful Japanese words English cannot match. I have no idea if the child is "my" child or not, but "the" would be odd and I did not want one "a" after another. *See how English forces us to make stupid choices?*

蓬莱を引とらまへて立=泣子哉　一茶
hôrai o hittoramaete naku ko kana   issa 1818
(hôrai[obj]pull-take/obtain-not-letting cries child 'tis)

pure desire

the *hôrai*
pulled from his arms
a boy cries

not allowed
to have the *hôrai*
a girl cries

This reminds me of the time I pulled a watermelon away from Hurtzel Rackety Masquerado Gill. Before I had time to savor my victory, she sank her sharp raccoon teeth into my calf. Children do likewise *by crying*. But, for those who love them, even tearful memories can be strangely endearing. The *hôrai* also drew smaller visitors:

蓬莱に鼠のうからやから哉　子規 明治三三
hôrai ni nezumi no ukara yakara kana   shiki -1902
(hôrai-in/on, mouse/mice's ~~scampering~~ clan !/'tis)

~~the *hôrai*~~
~~just hear the klutziness~~
~~of mice!~~

so is that
a whole clan of mice
on our *hôrai?*

~~from the *hôrai*~~
~~the scimper-scampering~~
~~of mice~~

蓬莱の麓へ通ふ鼠かな　鬼貫
hôrai no fumoto e kayou nezumi kana   onitsura 1660-1738
(hôrai's foot/base-to commute/s/ing mouse/mice!/ 'tis)

The foothills
of the *horai* crossed
by mice

back & forth
across the hôrai's foot
house-mice

To even a non-Japanese ear, Shiki's *ukara yakara* perfectly catches the sound and behavior of riotously scuttling mice. Another of his *ku* provides evidence for my *klutzy* interpretation of his creative mimesis: "*Misstepping / mice fall off the fern / on Mt Hôrai*" (蓬莱の羊歯踏み外す鼠哉 *hôrai no shida fumi-hazusu nezumi kana.*). *Sounds good,* but I was wrong on that *ukarayakara*. It is a multi-generation paternal+ maternal clan! My translation of Onitsura's *ku* is not wrong but the lack of a more poetic – i.e. general – word, for "commute" in English does not allow me to communicate what I believe to be the allusion:

spring bride

by the foot
of mount *horai*, mice
courting mice

In Chapter 18, we will see where some of this idea of *courting mice* comes from. First, a couple more:

喰摘へさそひ出るやまめ鼠 米翁 __明山荘__
kuitsumi e sasoi-ideru ya mamenezumi   beiô 1723-92
(food-pinch-to enticing come-out!/: miniature/diligent mice)

<blockquote>
enticing others
to the food-pile, tom thumb
romeos, these mice!
</blockquote>

Mame literally is "bean" and, as a prefix, generally means either "mini-" or "diligent." At first, I translated "Sharing news / about the food-pile / diligent mice." *Tit-mice* always do this, but mice mice? I doubt it. Then, I learned that a *mame* man (*otoko*) was "a diligent wooer of women." Since such wooing was traditionally nocturnal, I bet the poet coined a new phrase for mating mice, *mame-nezumi*. Finally, the poet may have been inspired by a *mame-otoko* stealing in like a thief from the ceiling in the Jôruri drama of the time (天井の上にてうかがひけるに、例のまめ男来て。。。（米沢本沙石集）)

蓬莱に鼠のえみ見る朝哉 未辨 大三
hôrai ni nezumi no emimiru ashita kana   miben 1697
(*hôrai*-on mouse/mice's smile/s see tomorrow/[new year's]morning!/'tis)

<blockquote>
in the *hôrai*   new year dawns
the smiling faces of mice   on the *hôrai* we see
tomorrow   happy mice
</blockquote>

The *ashita* can mean tomorrow or New Year's morning. Shiki, for all his espousal of "objective realism," was, at heart, a romantic, who would have lived a full life if his body had only followed his soul. He must have chuckled at Miben's *ku*. He, himself, wrote:

宝飾の陰や鼠のささめ言 子規 明治廿九
hôshoku no kage ya nezumi no sasamegoto   shiki 1896
(treasure-decoration's shadow! mice's whispering/sweet-nothings)

<blockquote>
soft nothings
in the shadow   in the shadow
of the *hôrai*, how sweetly   of the *hôrai*, the mice
peep the mice   peep sweetly
</blockquote>

The *hôshoku*, literally, "treasure-decoration," is not necessarily the same as the *hôrai*, but it does include it, and "in the shadow of the decorations" does not scan. A straighter *ku* from the same era notes *"On Hôrai / the mice squeek away / by our bed"* (蓬莱に鼠なくなり枕元 把栗 *hôrai ni nezumi nakunari makura-moto* haritsu?). It could get crowded in small houses where living rooms became bedrooms at night.

元日や置所なき猫の五器 竹戸 続猿蓑
ganjitsu ya okidokoro naki neko no goki   chikuko 1698
(orig.-day[new-years]: putting-place-not, cat's bowls)

<blockquote>
new year's day
there is no place for
the cat's bowls
</blockquote>

This is one reason why cats may go crazy over holidays.

蓬莱の麓に寝たる夫婦かな 子規 明治廿九
hôrai no fumoto ni netaru meoto kana shiki 1896
(*hôrai's* base/foot-at sleeping husband-wife)

dream-mates

sleeping
at *hôrai's* foot
a couple

If it is New Year's day, the couple, if they are human, are only dreaming, for sex was taboo. If it was the second night of the year, they may be making love along with the mice. That was my first, romantic take; but, it is more likely children, who had moved out, or guests are sleeping over and this was the only space available, or the couple live in a one-room home, something not as bad in Japan as in the West because the bedding is put away into closets by day, turning bedrooms into uncluttered living-rooms.

三宝に登りて追われ嫁が君 虚子 再現
sanbô ni noborite oware yome-ga-kimi   kyoshi 1874-1959
(three-treasures [a *hôrai* stand/base]-on climbing/ed chased bride-noble)

taboo or no taboo?

the little princess
is chased off when she climbs
on mount *hôrai*

In so far that the mountain was a symbol of prosperity as well as everlasting youth – indeed, the prosperity element achieved prominence, for wealth was a more attainable wish than youth – it is only fitting that mice are present. They are familiars of the God of Prosperity, Daikoku, who sits on sacks of grain so huge he could well afford to share the plenty with them.[1] *Nezumi* (mouse) was taboo during the first three days of the New Year so euphemisms such as "little-princess" were used (see ch 18). But there were limits to what they could get away with. Love-making is fine, but as Kyoshi notes, not all Japanese took kindly to mice enjoying the fruits of *their* mountain.

蓬莱やあるじになれて鳥の来る 涼兎 皮こすり
hôrai ya aruji ni narite tori no kuru   ryôtô 1699
(*hôrai!* owner/master-to accustomed, bird/s come)

peace

the *hôrai!*
used to its owner
birds visit

This is a simple and warm haiku. While "bird" is just *tori,* the character used is not the one used for "chicken" earlier in the chapter. It is simply "bird" as in English.

~~~~~~

1. ***Daikoku's Mice.*** Daikoku *nezumi,* or Daikoku mice/rats are white mice. Although mice may have come *with* prosperity, people knew the grain brought them rather than vice versa. An early haiku jokes about having to *"wade through / rat shit on the trail / through Ikuno"* (icho[一朝] 談林十百韻) because the previous verse mentioned a granary in the area and the structure could pun on an old poem lamenting the heavy dew on the same road. A later haiku/senryû jokes: *"For a new year's present / they distribute white mice: / daikoku-ya."* (*toshi- dama-ni nezumi-o kubaru daikoku-ya* Y101-28). Daikoku- ya was a seafood restaurant near Edo. (The "white" is mine)

喰摘やみな海山の寶もの　風峨 親類題発句集
kuitsumi ya mina umiyama no takara mono fûga 1793
(eat-pinch!/: all/everything sea-mountain's treasures)

mountain and ocean at home

the pinch-pile
everything a treasure
from the wild

"*Land* and sea" would sound better, but "mountain" was needed to specify that the treasures came from the wilderness that belonged more to gods than man. The food angle was big in Edo, where the *hôrai* was called a *kuitsumi* generally written either "eat-pinch (snack, or pick up with chopsticks), or, more commonly, "eat-pile/mound." Yet, not all the decorations – sacks [?] of uncooked rice, raw chestnuts, and so forth stacked or piled upon the white paper, fern fronds, *yuzuri* (*Daphniphyllum macropodum*) leaves and sheets of kelp laid over the *sanbô* base – were readily eaten by people. Not raw, at least!

喰つみや歯にあひさうな物はなし　一具 断稿思藻
kuitsumi ya ha ni aisôna mono wa nashi   ichigu 1855
(eat-pile: tooth-with meet-seems thing-as-for, not)

food-mountain	the food pile
nothing there my teeth	nothing there looks
can handle	edible to me

This is generally true, and for a good reason. The "food-pile" would be pillaged immediately by children if it were too tasty! I would not be surprised if some families saw to it that they had plenty of edible food in the decoration and even resupplied it. As one old *ku* I am not sure I get seems to put it, "Our dwellings / make *us:* a *hôrai* / makes me hungry! (人は住所蓬莱喰気に成けるよ 千那 *hito wa sumika hôrai kui-ke ni narikeru yo*   senna 1651-1723 ◎ "people-as-for dwellings" → "make us" = my guess.)

ほつ／＼と喰つみあらす夫婦かな　嵐雪
hotsuhotsu to kuitsumi arasu meoto kana   ransetsu -1707
(leisurely eat-pile ravage/scavenge husband-wife 'tis)

kui-tsumi

l e i s u r e l y	taking their good time
strip-mining the mountain	husband and wife ravage
husband and wife	a food mountain

In some *saijiki,* these *kuitsumi* are included with the *hôrai*. In others, they are right next to *hôrai*. In others, they are separated – by dozens of pages – perhaps because one type of *kuitsumi* is nothing but a stack of fancy lunch-boxes. It seems to me the difference was one of degrees. The adverb in the above *ku*, *"hotsuhotsu"* is a challenge. It has nuances of leisurely action cheerfully undertaken and seems to contradict the savage verb *arasu,* for which "ravage" is perfect.

喰積や雀気に入庵の扶持　素樸
kuitsumi ya suzume ki ni iru io no fuchi/fuji   sobaku -1821
([the] eat-pile: sparrows like [are satisfied with] hut's stipend=[mt]fuji?)

little snack-fuji
the sparrows approve of
my hut's stipend!

mount snack
my stipend is popular
with sparrows

I am unsure if a pun on Mt.Fuji was intended in this sweet *ku* by Issa's (at the time) more well-known contemporary, for the rice-stipend was called *fuchi[no mai]* more often than *fuji*. Be that as it may, you would think the food-pile was set up specifically to satisfy the sparrows, or, at least, that is how they saw it, and including Mt Fuji is entertaining.

喰積に一色多し白鼠　龍尾 玉かつら
kuitsumi ni isshoku ôshi shiro-nezumi   ryûbi 1751
(eat-piles-on single-colors many [are common]: white-mouse)

before fashion

in *kuitsumi*
monochrome dominates
white mice!

White animals, being rare, were thought auspicious everywhere. Daikoku's mice were generally white. So was the sweet-rice-cake. My title is added because stripes and other multi-color designs were pretty much equated with fashion in a culture where *form* was comparatively stable.

喰積や祝ふ名のみをいつあつめ　千慶 玉かつら
kuitsumi ya iwau na nomi o itsu atsume   senkei 1751
(eat-pile/s! celebrate-name/s only [obj] five[?] gather)

kuitsumi

mount edible
five foods, all names
to celebrate!

the food-pile
we gather five names
to celebrate

In Italy, I am told, all eat lentil soup because they resemble and are called the same thing as *coins*. Japan is like that. Chances are these foods are the same as those found on the *hôrai* proper. Most English-speakers associate some foods with certain celebrations but go no further.

蓬莱の汐たるゝ程匂ふかな　竹人 年間俳句集
hôrai no shio taruru hodo niou kana   chikujin -1764
(*hôrai*'s brine/ocean dripping degree smell!/?/'tis)

a mountain of sea-food?

the *hôrai* smell
so strong you can almost see
the dripping brine

the more brine
drips the more splendid
the *hôrai*

Auspicious or not, the emphasis on seafood in most parts of Japan must have made the house smell like iodine. Since Japanese houses had no central-heating, the Ise-shrimp placed on top of the fancy *hôrai* – such a crawfish was expensive then, as ever – could even be alive as suggested by the next two *ku*:

伊勢海老や蓬莱山の興がしら 渡邊氏 大三
ise ebi ya hôraisan no kyôgashira   watanabeshi 1697
(ise-shrimp[crawfish]: hôrai-mountain's excite-head)

ise shrimp
our mount hôrai has
a float-master

The *kyôgashira* is the man who directs a float, or rather the scores of men shouldering it. The Neapolitans have a word for it, *capo paranza*, but English, as far as I know, has none. So, *float-master* it is.

蓬莱の海老はめてたくかしく哉 小船 大三
hôrai no ebi wa medetaku kashigu kana   kobune 1697
(*hôrai's* ise-shrimp [crawfish]-as-for, luckily/joyfully squeaks!/?/'tis)

tidings from ise?

how auspicious	joy, oh, joy
mount hôrai's crawfish	a crawfish squeaking
is squeaking	on mt. hôrai

A crawfish can sound like it needs oil. It may suggest vigorous old age, but one wonders whether the lingering death of anything can be auspicious! Is the *ku* an inspired interpretation of the following one?

蓬莱にきかはや伊勢の初便り はせを
hôrai ni kikabaya ise no hatsudayori bashô -1694
(*hôrai*-from/on hear-would! ise's first-tiding)

i'd hear it
from my hôrai, the first
tiding from ise!

Bashô puts his mind's ear up to his *hôrai* to hear the tidings from the peninsula where the sun and years came from. He also claimed to borrow a few words from a *waka* poem by a priest about the delight of receiving a visitor from Ise. Could Bashô have meant to bring a hint of Buddhism into what seems to be a purely Shintô New Year with that reference? Does Kobune's *ku* imply that an "Ise shrimp" caught Bashô's ear? (Note: I may be wrong: red was so desirable that I suspect these crustaceans were usually cooked!)

蓬莱に松のみ残る日数かな 蝶夢
hôrai ni matsu nomi nokoru hikazu kana   chômû -1795
(*hôrai*-on, pine only remains day-number!/ ?/'tis)

strip-snacking

how many days	days pass
until only pine remains	and only pine remains
on mt. *hôrai*?	on the *hôrai*

the old *hôrai*

How many days
did we need to eat down
to the pine?

At the end of the year, cooking stops and doesn't resume for several days. People eat pre-cooked food saturated in soy sauce, sugar, salt and vinegar. Guests are offered lucky food from the *hôrai*

蓬莱（喰摘）にくふべきものを探りけり 子規
hôrai (kuitsumi)ni kuubeki mono o sagurikeri   shiki 1866-1902
(*hôrai (foodpile)*-on eat-able-things searching/groping[+emph.])

the bachelor's new year

i go hunting   & off i went
for something to eat   to mt *hôrai*, in search of
on mt *hôrai*   something to eat

When Shiki's mother and sister were out, he may have been reduced to eating off the *hôrai*. The emphatic suffix ~ *keri* suggests Shiki describes his own circumstances and not the behavior of a visitor. Shiki's *ku*, combining aspects of Chômu's *ku* and Ransetsu's earlier one with the *hôrai*-ravaging couple, seems more plaintive, yet witty, which it wouldn't have been with "foodpile" rather than the mountain.

蓬莱の小さき山を崩しけり 子規
hôrai no chiisaki yama o kuzushikeri   shiki 1899
(*hôrai*'s small mountain [=obj] breakdown[+emph.])

living off the promised land

disassembling   the *hôrai*,
a little mountain   my little mountain
our *hôrai*   taken apart

Don't ask me why I stuck on the "and" and the "our" for the second reading. Poets don't always know what they do; must the translator?

再現＝蓬莱に年はあら玉の在所哉 宗因
hôrai ni toshi wa aratama no arika kana   sôin 1604-82
(*hôrai*-on/in, year/s/elderly-as-for, new/uncut-gem/s/soul/renewal's site!/?/'tis)

mount *hôrai*   in *hôrai*
forever ageless home   the old have a home
for the aged   of youth

mount *hôrai*
home to fresh souls
for each year

mount *hôrai*   for mt *hôrai*
the year has a new   a year is just another
place to stay   place to stay

The *hôrai* wet more than the appetite for food that drew 2-, 4- and 6-legged animals. The appetite for life it reifies made it precious for those who most felt their mortality, the elderly. The *toshi* in the original *may* refer to the elderly and not just the year/s. Sôin's *ku* was difficult to English: too many puns – more equal signs than a math book! – and ambiguous grammar. A later *hôrai ku* shares something with Sôin's: *"Bundle another / in the Hôrai: / a precious=gem=tama spring"* (蓬莱に真ひとつ つまん玉の春 琴考 安永四 *hôrai ni mahitotsu[tsu]tsuman [maido tsutsuman?] tamanoharu* kinkô 1775). Is this just about Spring, or is it *one to grow on* for the aging poet?

蓬莱の山はさながらしらげ哉 種圓 大三
hôrai no yama wa sanagara shirage kana shuen 1697
(*hôrai*-mountain-as-for, nevertheless white-hair!/?/'tis)

    mount *hôrai*   *hôrai* but why   *hôrai* indeed
is right here but still   white hair on this   a mountain, but snow
      white hair   mountain of youth   white hair?

How strange men are. Knowing our magic doesn't work, we keep faith anyway. Has the poet noticed how funny it is that both white hair and youth signify agelessness?

蓬莱にかけてかざるや老の袖 去来
hôrai ni kakete kazaru ya oi no sode kyorai 1651-1704
(*hôrai*-for alone, decorate, yes! elderlies' sleeve/clothing/appearance/heart)

         the *hôrai*   *hôrai:* one thing
old folk care about   we old folk really
       how *it* looks   like to do up

The translation was *extremely* difficult to come up with because I am unsure of my reading (Once we are over the hill, only Vanity continues to put much effort into self-adornment. Instead, we decorate our magic mountains. Cosmetics, again, becomes cosmology.). *Sode* (sleeve/clothing/appearance/heart) has just too many connotations to shake a sleeve at (御異見求む). Only the availability of italics in English – and the marked case it indicates (i.e., *it*, not *them*) – saved what seemed like a lost cause.

ほうらいの山まつりせむ老の春 蕪村
hôrai no yama matsuri sen oi-no-haru buson - 1783
(*hôrai* mountain festival/party-do-let's/would elder's spring)

mount *hôrai*
just the place for old folk
to celebrate spring

Unlike young men and woman, who would, if I read between the words correctly, head for the woods to fest *their* spring. The above translation was done *before* checking Buson's age. As it turns out, he wrote it on his 60th birthday=Spring=New Year. This was the end of his fifth 12-year-animal cycle and the age where a man was supposed to return to infantile foolishness, at least on New Year's Day. So, the *ku* really deserves the first-person singular or, perhaps, plural:

        old in spring   *spring for the old*
let me then fete   *let's have our festival*
      mount hôrai   *'round the hôrai*

Moreover, a mountain-*matsuri* (festival) is not quite the May Day event my "young men and women" comment might lead one to assume. It means that a mountain deity or deities are celebrated, generally at a Shintô shrine. There is an element of worship in it, but I hesitate to say "worship" for the English term is so damn strong it trivializes all it touches that is not Christian by turning it into an idol. Right? So, there are echoes of the Taoist practice of seeking longevity by approaching the gods of the mountains. (With this in mind, reread the lead *ku* for the book!) Finally, there is a reason why this Mt *Hôrai* should have exercised particular fascination for elderly *Japanese*, as opposed to others in the Sinosphere. The reason is found in a legend, delightfully played by Kyoshi:

蓬莱に徐福と申す鼠哉　虚子
hôrai ni jofuku to môsu nezumi kana　kyoshi 1874-1959
(*hôrai*-in/on "Jofuku" [it is/i am] called mouse!/?/'tis)

and, who are you?

<blockquote>

the mouse
on mt *hôrai* spoke
"i'm jofuku!"

does that mouse
on the hôrai declare
himself jofuku?

</blockquote>

Jofuku, or Jofutsu, as the Japanese call him, was a Chinese regent (whatever that means) in the era of China's First Emperor – the conceited ruler who destroyed previous history to realize his self-assumed title. Trying to escape from a hopeless political situation and gain immortality at the same time, he set off with a selected party (usually described as 500 young men and women of great beauty) to find the Mountain Island with the elixir of immortality. They ran into a storm, and rather than reaching Mt Hôrai, which some identify with Formosa (Taiwan), ended up in Japan, where the cultural infusion was much appreciated. If you don't believe this story, we are told, you can visit Jofuku's grave in Wakayama prefecture and tell him so yourself.[1] (Other prefectures, most notably Yamanashi, also lay claim to the honor, but I like the favorite, Wakayama, because the *Waka,* written identically to the old poems (peace +song), is a homophone for *"young,"* and evokes *Youth*-Mountain. There is humor in Yamanashi, written mountain-*pear* but sounding like "mountain-*less*," as well, but it is irrelevant.)

<blockquote>

on mt. feng-lai
someone says, "i'm xu fu"
it's a mouse!

</blockquote>

Kyoshi's Jofuku *ku* is delightful and deserves a hundred translations. It is our "Night before Christmas" when all through the house it is so quiet we do not even hear the peep of a mouse, which is to say quiet enough to hear one, too. Yet, I read it and feel a wee bit sad. For Kyoshi's closest friend, the man who wrote more *hôrai* poems than anyone, was doomed to spend most of his short adult life dying. Yet, aside from his haiku prefaced "in sickness" or "sick-bed," you would never guess Shiki's condition. This next *hôrai-ku,* written three years before his death, is a testament to his spirit, healthy to the end.

---

1. *Jofuku Legend.* Yamanashi prefecture makes the same claim. While the locations in Japan differ – there are three main "nihon-san-hôrai,"i.e., made-in-Japan Mt Hôrai (all claiming to be where Jofuku settled) alone, and Mt Fuji, which was once surrounded by water on three sides, *itself* is in the running. The legend's general claim is substantiated by Chinese historical reporting on Japan. I believe the story/ies, because I grew up on Key Biscayne, which, according to my mother who wrote the book on our island, is the place Ponce De Leon came ashore to begin his search for the Fountain (rather than *Mountain*) of Youth. It *is* a small world, isn't it! (There's a great song by Chris Chandler & Anne Feeny called *St. Au- gustine* which turns the legend into a just-so story by fusing it with the peninsular shape of the state and the Canaveral moon-shot (Too bad that location is not quite right, unless Florida has, to use 300 year-old English adopted from a letter by Cotton Mather found in Chadwick Hansen's sage book on Salem witchcraft, (I corrected the Japanese translation), *a hole in his its yard.*)

蓬莱に一斗の酒を尽しけり 子規
hôrai ni itto no sake o tsukushikeri   shiki -1902
(*hôrai*-to/with a gallon [actually half-a-gallon] of sake finishing-off)

holiday hors de oeuvres

we drink up
a gallon of wine, eating
mount hôrai

first-erosion

washing down
mt hôrai with a gallon
of good sake!

ode to plenty!

toasting hôrai
we end up with an empty
bottle of wine

the sacrament

a gallon bottle
of spirit all spent
on mt hôrai

Reading this *ku,* my first thought was that Shiki *made* a *hôrai* from nothing but a single large bottle of *sake*. [1] With drawings of auspicious things and fancy strings tied around them, some bottles I have seen would certainly seem worthy of the honor. And, as we have seen, Shiki had written of a *hôrai* made from a straw rain-coat, perhaps placed in the *tokonoma*.[2] But, the *sake* bottle *ku* was next to a food *ku* and the grammar did not hold up to a closer reading.

蓬莱や梢はるかに酒の海 重正 大三
hôrai ya kozue haruka ni sake no umi   chôsho 1697
(*hôrai*!/: limbtops far off, wine [*sake*] sea)

the *hôrai*
through the pine, a distant
sea of *sake*

Old haiku are often criticized for being nominal, but how often are they praised for being surreal? I am not certain what the first haiku refers to. Probably, a wealthy household has a keg of *sake* open (the whole top is removed) to ladle out fuel for New Year's callers. (New Year Volume 2 will include the Year-*sake*.)

蓬莱の瀧より出るやとその酒 清重 大三
hôrai no taki yori deru ya tosonosake   seichô? 1697
(*hôrai*'s waterfall from comes-out!/?/: *toso* sake)

the waterfall
on the *hôrai*: the source
of *toso* sake

1. *A Sake Named Hôrai* We can cry rivers, right? Why not name a *sake* "hôrai" so we may drink a mountain? Come to think of it, I *have* seen such a *sake* (Google it!)
2. **Tokonoma?** Had Japanese invented this *one* cultural treasure, and nothing else, their culture would have proved its greatness. The *tokonoma* is a novel architectural concept, a space dedicated to art alone, built into houses, not as an extra, but as a fundamental part of the interior. It is a public (being in the living room where the guest can see it) shrine for the beautiful and exhibits only one or two – in that case, mixed media such as a flower arrangement in front of a hanging picture – works of art at a time. *If I were the Minister of Construction in Japan, I would not permit new apartments to be constructed without them.*

Magic mountains always have waterfalls. Fancy *hôrai* make them from white silk. The only *real* fake waterfall *I* have seen was by the gate of a house with a wake for the grandfather, a sumo wrestler, who was the oldest tall man (the short outlive us) I have ever met. I had some *sake* inside, and I hope the kind old Osumô-san (who gave me macramé sandals) – is on Mt Hôrai now.[1] Since the main longevity-related *sake*, Chrysanthemum, was drunken in the fall, we do not have many *ku* combining the *hôrai* and alcohol as might be expected. *Tosozake* was *sake* in which Chinese medicinal herbs were steeped, conventionally drunk on New Year's Day to stave off serious disease.

蓬莱や神の産たる國の数 文川 玉暦十一
hôrai ya kami no umitaru kuni no kazu bunsen 1761
(*hôrai/s-the god/s' birthing countries' number*)

prolific spring

all these *hôrai!*
one for every country
the gods bear

busy gods

mount *hôrai*
to think of the number
of places created

hôrai galore
as many as there are lands
born of gods

We are not going to look at the great variety of *hôrai* in this brief review. Let it suffice to note it. "Country" (*kuni*) in Japanese can mean just about anything. The American may sing of "coming from the country," but when he speaks of "my country" – unless he is talking C&W – he means the larger nation state. Not so in Japan. There, a *kuni* can be any size. Even a hometown might be loosely called one's "country." A *ku* by Shinrô finds "On the *hôrai* / nuts and berries from / a local mountain" (蓬莱にところの山の木の実哉 蜃楼丁卯句 *hôrai ni tokoro no yama no konomi kana* shinrô). The magic mountain has indigenized itself. And – if a homophonic pun is intended – perhaps, this is a matter of individual *konomi*, "taste," too. The second reading of Bunsen's poem, above, assumes the obviously foreign origin of the *hôrai* set the poet to thinking about the abundance of places, i.e., countries beyond Japan.[2] In Japanese mythology, gods do create by birth, though not only through the usual orifice.

松はかざり蓬莱ならぬ山もなし 清春 大三
matsu wa kazari hôrai naranu yama mo nashi seishun 1697
(pine-as-for decoration *hôrai beomes-not mountain-even none*)

spring

decorated
with pine, every hill
is *hôrai!*

---

1. Funeral *Hôrai* Since death is not seasonal, nothing in *saijiki* mention the use of *hôrai* at wakes. I may be wrong to associate the fake mountain + waterfall with Hôrai. Merhu, another mountain of eternal life, is more likely, as its water was symbolically connected with the underground Yellow Spring and the Elysian plains there. I do not know whether it means that Buddhists have incorporated a Chinese or Shinto idea into their funereal services to meet their clients' needs despite the obvious contradiction with Buddhist theology, or if such items are brought in by the bereaved family as an additional Shinto element. (専門家のご意見乞います).

2. How Japanese *Hôrai*? If the legendary mountain is a Chinese creation, the origin of *the model* is not so clear. It was first used for auspicious decoration at the banquettes (*shuen*) of nobles and only became standard New Year's decoration in the Muromachi era (14-16c), when it was also used at wedding feasts. So it spread roughly the same time as *haikai* did. How fortunate for both of them!

With Japanese hills (*oka*) loosely called "mountains" (*yama*), I thought the switch for alliteration justified. "Not a hill not *hôrai*" – What better way to express the eternal promise of Spring present in the annual resurrection of the world? And if every hill was *Hôrai* (or, "a *hôrai*" – Japanese is ambiguous on this distinction) and vice-versa, what could be done with hills could be done with *hôrai*.

蓬莱の手際を我は岡見哉 青石 安永四
hôrai no tegiwa o ware wa okami kana   seiseki 1775
(*hôrai's* craftmanship I [consider it as] hill-seeing[ceremony/rite]!/?/'tis)

hôrai

looking over
a finely wrought hôrai
i geomance!

looking over
this hill i made, call me
the emperor!

I invented "geomance" as a verb; but what the hell! We are talking about a very confused practice. In Japanese, according to the etymology of *oka-mi* in the OJD, a compound verb meaning "to inquire" became conflated with "hill" and "look," so "hill-looking" came to mean "inquire," but in a fortune-telling way. Before or after that happened – the OJD is bad with dates – there was a folk custom of putting on a straw raincoat inside-out, going outside, climbing a hill and spying the top of one's house over the tree-tops on the last day of the year to prognosticate the coming one (how such a view would partake such knowledge the dictionary forgets to say) because there was an old *waka* about looking over treetops as the old year passed by when the word-spirit (*kotodama*) was hard to catch (*obôtsukana*). The second reading assumes the poet is mimicking the *kuni-mi,* the Imperial Rite of overlooking the *country* undertaken for the prosperity of the nation every Spring, as first mentioned in the second poem of the *Manyôshû*, Japan's oldest anthology of poetry (8c) I believe the original encompasses *both* readings.

蓬莱や飾るものみなさざれ石 窓布 己未元除春遊
hôrai ya kazaru mono mina sazareishi   sôfu 1799 一茶 全集8
(*hôrai*!/'tis/: decorate/ing-things all pebbles)

our *hôrai*
all its decorations
are pebbles

our *hôrai*
every decoration
a baby stone

Hôrai here is plural and "our" means everyone's, not just the poet's household. This is a good example of a poem that must be explained to non-Japanese. The reference is to a famous *waka* poem that provided the words later to be part of Japan's national anthem, where the pebbles (*sazare-ishi*) grow into venerable moss-covered boulders, *i.e.* everlasting mountains (see ch. 16, *kagami-mochi* for more). The metaphorical allusion turns the *hôrai* into a dynamic cornucopia, a fount of fertility.

廊に蓬莱重きあゆみかな 友静 元禄
watadono ni hôrai omoki ayumi kana   yûsei late-17c
(hallway-in hôrai heavy walk/progress!/?/'tis)

if mohammed

heavy footsteps
mount hôrai walking
down the hall

199

We began the chapter looking at where the *idea* of *the hôrai* came from. How about the *thing* itself? This *ku* is one reply. Before the tree came to us, we went to the tree. Japanese did the same for a mountain. Here, the poem brings it a step further: right into the reader's mind. I imagine a man walking alone – perhaps it wasn't right for the household to see the magical mountain until New Year's Day – while other people behind paper walls hear the floor-boards squeak with the extra weight. I do not know how far the *hôrai* was bought ready-made and carried in, or constructed in place. I imagine it was generally set up late New Year's Eve. One haiku mentions a house that made their hôrai at 3:00 AM, but I suspect that would only have been mentioned for being extracrdinary. (蓬莱も飾る我家の三の朝　吟長　明和二 *hôrai mo kazaru wagaya no mitsu no asa*　ginchô 1765).

蓬莱や我物数奇を現わせり 佳園 大三
hôrai ya waga monozuki o arawaseri　kaen 1697
(*hôrai!*/: my things-like[eccentricity/taste] revealed [+emph])

behold

mount *hôrai!*
my eclectic taste
is revealed

fanciful

my eccentricity
comes out of the closet:
mount *hôrai!*

Like our Christmas trees, even a ready-made one would surely be trimmed by the household [?]. Poets might make odd *hôrai,* but there were regional and household differences, which is to say, traditions. Every *hôrai* is the last of a historical line of mountains copied from generation to generation.

家にある蓬莱作り覚えけり 沾徳
ie ni aru hôrai-zukuri oboekeri　sentoku -1726
(house-in is *hôrai*-design/making learn/remember[+emph])

mountain-making

the *hôrai*
at home is the one
we learn

A Meiji-Taishô era (early-20c) *ku* by Kôchiku (1881-1952) further personalizes the tradition: "*Hôrai-making / passed down from / mother's mothers*" (蓬莱作り母の母より伝わりけり　鼓竹 丁卯句錨 *hôraizukuri haha no haha yori tsutawarikeri* ★ 敬愚だったら、こうなる：＜母母の蓬莱山も笑ひけり). To me, to most of us, decorating for the holiday is a domestic if not humble activity; but that is not universally true. To balance the picture, here is a different *hôrai:*

蓬莱の沙汰きく松の木の間哉 素檗
hôrai no sata kiku matsu no ki[ko?] no ma kana　sobaku -1821
(*hôrai*'s progress[-report] hear pine-tree-room [daimyô's room]!/ 'tis)

***a daimyô's* new year**

progress reports
from the *hôrai* front
to the pine-room

The "pine room" was the room in a castle where the "big-name," ie. *daimyô*, head of the fiefdom, or country (in the sense that Texas is a country) lived. The word "front" is not in the original, but the use of the term *sata* or progress report, suggests a war situation. I suspect the "daimyô" is a comical allusion to the old poet himself sitting back letting others do the New Year preparations. Sobaku has another *ku* that suggests he has that perspective: *"Gramp and gram / say the wait was worth it: / pine decorations"* (ぢゝ婆が待甲斐ありて松飾 素檗 *jiji baba ga matsukai arite matsukazari*). There is also a pun on pine (*matsu*) as "wait," as in *waiting for the next world*, by keeping alive here.

蓬莱の役目も重し禄毛亀　志骰子 元除春遊
hôrai no yakume mo omoshi minôkame　shikôko 1799 in 一茶 8
(hôrai's duty-also/even heavy, edge-hair[seaweed-covered green sea]turtle)

is mt. feng-lai
a burden? so much grows
on this sea turtle!

it's not easy　　　　　　　　　　　　　　　　　　　a heavy duty
being mount feng-lai　　　　　　　　　　　　the sea turtle hôrai
mossy turtle　　　　　　　　　　　　　　　　　　　bears a forest!

A *hôrai* is literally a heavy role to play. The turtle in question is usually written 蓑亀 (*minokame*). The *mino* is a straw cape, but the allusion is to an old green sea turtle with sea-weed growing on its back. English is not a maritime tongue. The need to prefix "sea" to turtles and vegetation proves it. The turtle, a symbol of longevity, was generally given a taste of *sake* and released by Japanese fishermen. Respect for the aged?

手のくぼに蓬莱のかげ匂ひけり　素檗
tenokubo ni hôrai no kage nioikeri　sobaku -1821
(hand-hollow-in, *hôrai's* shadow/essence smell/sniff [v.+emph])

condensation

eau de hôrai
sniffed from the hollow
of an old hand

young water　　　　　　　　　　　　　　　　***one night stand***

how splendid　　　　　　　　　　　　　　　　　　how sublime
the hôrai's reflection　　　　　　　　　　the hôrai's shadow cast
in my hand　　　　　　　　　　　　　　　　　　　upon lovers

untitled

one night love
by the hôrai, how it
comes alive!

In the first reading, the *ku* plays on older poems of elderly poets cupping plum blossoms to sniff the tiding of spring. The contrast between the Mountain of Eternal Life and the bent back of the old man having to cup his hand to smell the pine and crawfish combines with the image of a mountain shrinking down to table size, then, down to the hollow of the palm of the hand and up his wizened nostrils . . . The second reading takes the smell (*nioi*) figuratively as (glow/beauty) and the shadow (*kage*) literally.

Older *ku* have water in one's palm doing the good deed of reflecting the moon and it is possible the poet cups young-water (see ch. 15) in it. The third reading takes the idiomatic reading of "hand-hollow" (the slight pocket of one palm), which is *a passing love affair or a single tryst* (滑稽本・鬼娘伝「其の方が胎内に今孕たるは、のうてん鬼が手の窪の塊なり」OJD). It was hard not to title the reading "Making Mountains." We may have a young couple imagined here, the poet's servants, or . . . mice! If it is *many* mice, could they be Jofuku's five hundred? Are those beautiful young men and women still making love? Pardon some foolishness:

LOVETERNALIFE

the squeals of mice
how the hôrai
comes alive
tonight
!!!

~~~~~~

Skipped One

蓬莱や日のさしかかる枕もと　釣壺か蝶羽か
hôrai ya hi no sashikakaru makuramoto   kinko or, chôu c.1700
(*hôrai*'tis!/: sun's shining-touches pillow/bed itself/by)

<blockquote>

ah, the *hôrai*
touched by sunlight
by my bed

sunlight and
the *hôrai's* shadow
on my bed

the *hôrai!*
sunshine lights up
my pillow

it's a *hôrai*
this bed struck by
rays of sun

ah, *hôrai*!
the sunlight reaches
my pillow

this *futon*
warmed by the sun
my *hôrai*

mt. feng lai
some rays of sunshine
strike my bed

</blockquote>

The relationship of the *hôrai,* sunshine and pillow (or bed) in this *ku* is so ambiguous that I didn't even *try* to translate it until I delayed too long to fit it into the main body of the text. It would take hours to redo the pages (I handcraft each), so I will just leave it here. Why not skip it? Because, the *ku* has a subtle charm, enough so that I would feel bad about having left it out every time I ran into it again.

And One More, With an Argonaut!

蓬莱ありや身は蛸船のうかれ行　千那
hôrai ariya mi wa takobune no ukareyuku　　senna -1723
(hôrai [+emph.] body/self-as-for, octopus-boat=argonaut's=float/drifting-goes)

<table>
<tr><td>this hôrai
an argonaut adrift
on its bark</td><td>hôrai! hurrah!
i feel afloat, giddy as
an argonaut</td><td>hôrai, ahoy!
like argonauts we float
around it</td></tr>
</table>

No *Jason &* ~ here. The metaphor is the female argonaut octopus (or, "brown (Hians) paper nautilus") that grows an eight-inch shell for her boat and carries the male as her tiny first-mate (but *that* is another story!). They were known to squirt out brine (bilgewater) as they "rowed" with two tentacles. The first reading alludes to the way this mountain island was thought to float itself and puts the poet's heart in the hôrai. The second and third readings seem more likely. There may be an allusion to a magical ship (ch.13), too.

和歌即蓬莱
a *waka* hôrai

慶賀　尋ねみよ蓬が島ぞ和歌の道心をのべて人は老せず　正広 松下集
keiga // tazune miyo yomogigashima zo waka no michi kokoro o nobete hito wa oisezu　shôkô 1412-1494
(greeting: visiting see! hôrai-island[+emph.] waka[57577poem]'s way, heart/mind-stretching/speaking person-as-for age-not)

New Year's Greeting

<table>
<tr><td>the way of waka
or way to? either means
the isle of xu!

a man that sings aloud
never grows old</td><td>ask me the way
to the blessed isle of youth
it's waka, i say

gentlemen who sing out
keep death at bay</td></tr>
</table>

"Boldly sings" is my way of getting around a pun on *stretching/relaxing* the heart/mind and *expressing* it. Since the word *waka* includes "song" and the old poems are often called songs, I do not feel it too far removed from the original meaning. The excessively complex *of* and *to* stuff was the only way I could find to translate the ambiguous nuance of "*no*." The need for a *to* as well as an *of* comes from asking the way. There is probably an allusion to a late-10c or early-11c poetic exchange where a pilgrim asks the way back to Wakasa, a place name that puns on "youth" (*wakasa ni kaeru michi ga shiritai*) *after* a young man notes in the form of an opening stanza that a "chickadee got into the pilgrim's traveling trunk," using words that could also be understood to mean that we "grow old from forty" (*shijûkara wa oi no naka ni zo irinikeri*). Hiroaki Sato notes this anecdote was related by Fukui Kyûzô (1867-1951) as one of the oldest examples of linked verse (renga). Strangely enough, neither theJapanese annotators of Shôkô's *waka* (online) nor Sato (*One Hundred Frogs*) mention the obvious puns on *youth*.

chapter notes

the Chinese Guy *and the* Hôrai

Xu Fu

This chapter raises the type of questions I would hope to encourage others to investigate further and contribute glosses for an expanded version of this *saijiki* or, eventually, an illustrated book on *hôrai* (for any publisher who will deign to pay me a reasonable advance). What is needed?

First, we need to gain a visual mastery of the *hôrai* from various parts of Japan including contemporary photographs and old artwork.

Second, we need *a full summary of the historical evidence.* There is lots of writing out there, mostly historical claims by various places in Japan connected to the legend. If this first edition is to be (provisionally) finished, I cannot take the time to sort the rice from the chaff, edit and translate the material. I can give you a quick tour of goodies found on the internet translated by *machine*, actually, artificial intelligence software of various types The result is not as informative as my *Good Readers* might want, but probably far more entertaining than anything I could write for my *Bad* ones (following H. Belloc, I do not mind owning up to both). I will not cite sources for reasons that will be plain to see. Some translations are from Chinese, some from Korean and some from Japanese. The [ ] s are mine:

> 1.The Xu luck crosses the sea ["Luck" is a literal translation of the last character of Jofuku's name. The computer should have translated **Xu Fu** and, recognizing a name, not supplied a "the"]. China has the first navigation which the history records explores. [= subtitle. Another Chinese website puts it like this: "Xu Fu is China has the exploration first person which the history records."].
>
> The archaeology lost the mark and the fable confirms the Xu luck wandered Japan, the modern anthropology also provides the evidence for this. In 1954, the Japanese scholar lasted 5 years, dissected the confirmation with the human body, Japanese's cranium index are greatly many and the Chinese Zhejiang, Jiangsu, Anhui, the Fujian person is completely same [thus, proving some Chinese came to Japan from parts of China Jofuku was said to hail from].
>
> No wonder that the Japanese Hirohito emperor of Japan's imperial younger brother three coolie hats palace [Mikasa, the name of the Imperial Palace in Japan means 'three-hats' of the type shaped like an upside-down salad bowl] in gives "the Hong Kong Xu luck meeting" in the congratulation speech gets excited he says: "Xu Fu is our Japanese's father." [Not for all Japanese, I would think, but perhaps for the Imperial line?]
>
> If really is this, the Xu luck compares him the older generation and the later generation many big navigations explorers comes, to humanity's contribution on the completely book,

he discovered with difficulty the Japanese chain islands, created one great nation. [A Columbus and Washington all in one!]

2. Seeking the non-old age [anti-aging?] immortal medicine, the Xu luck which crosses the sea. It probably is to be the passion which burns certainly in the inner part of that chest and boils. [Again, much like Columbus, who burned with passion, but far less vulgar, for Xu Fu, like Pounce de Leon, loved life more than gold.]

3. In addition, even the non-old age immortal secret medicine that it is said, Xu luck chased after, 'heaven stand crow medicine brown' and so on the stand which is sold is in. [This from a site giving pr for Kumomoto (Japan) . Besides medicine, the shrine Niimiya had various Jofuku memorabilia including "large carp of non-old age." This medicine is said to be good for treating some kinds of cancer as are the Yongji mushrooms bearing the name of a mountain Xu Fu climbed in Cheju (also Jejudo), Korea, where he is said to have engraved "Xu Fu visited here" on the rock wall. It remained visible until the 1950's. Knowing nothing of Xu Fu, I visited the island in the 1970's and saw the caves up the mountain where the ancestral gods were said to be born. I had entirely forgotten about that cave until I read the following passage in item #12 in the *Chapki* (miscellany) of Ô Sukkwôn (fl.1525-54), translated by Peter H. Lee:

> In the beginning, Cheju Island was inhabited not by men, but by spirits who emerged from the ground. This was a Mohûng Cave, North of Mount Halla [which Xu Fu climbed] . . . During the Cheng-te era [1506-21], one Ko filled a post in the Palace Guard (Naegûmwi). When a certain military official named Yi returned from a trip to Cheju, Ko asked him if he had seen Mohûng cave. Yi replied, "I saw it and utrinated into it." Ko was speechless.
> (A KOREAN STORYTELLER'S MISCELLANY Princeton 1989) [Abbrev. and bracketed words, mine].

[According to its bureau of tourism, Cheju has "the only waterfall in Asia in which the water falls directly to the sea." It also has a park with driftwood that looks like other things, one of which, I recall, is a dead-ringer for the immortal beagle, Snoopy. Anyway, even the Koreans admit that Xu Fu left the island and headed East to the Land of the Rising Sun.]

4. As for the person who does not know this "Xu luck legend" with the person who has interest in the Japanese ancient history it will not be. Especially, they arrived to Japan truly, in for the person whose interest is deep "rope sentence March age", whether or not is, it is the expectation which is the story which greatly is stimulated interest. [The Jômon age (10,000-300 BC) is literally *rope-pattern*, for the markings on the pottery, and Yayoi, 300BC-300AD, is indeed the Spring of Japan as a civilization and the name of the second month of the year].

One group where the legend, B.C. 219 year, it includes child man child woman [i.e., youths and maidens] 500 to the age of Qin's beginning emperor and pulls the group entire spirit 3000 and accompanies, seeks the 仙 [sage] person and the non-old age immortal 仙 [sage] medicine and goes on a journey to pink source home village Japan east from the Chinese continent was. . . [the "accompanies" were top-flight artesians, who brought the advanced continental material skills, and horses (?), to the Stone Age people of Japan.]

5. Xu luck to cross the sea, aiming toward the national 蓬 莱 [hôrai] of the large originator of the world and, the plain, finding the wide 沢[marsh], there . . . And, as for the area, unique high heaven field Cipango Mizuho [Old Chinese pronunciation of Japan as used by Marco Polo; the *mizuho* is a "water-blossom"] from Chinese country You [This is an interview with an author] say it was called. Very that, the Japanese starting point, being the place where well, also starting point of the world should call, It probably will be [Columbus thought he found the same when approaching the mouth of the Amazon].

As expected, does the unique high heaven field probably exist somewhere? And, as for the area of today It probably is the area where it has some kind of meaning for the people? In this report, of the Xu luck It searched out, it probably will approach to the truth "the country of the 蓬莱[hôrai] of the" unique high heaven field. . . . but as for this extending history 19 years (800 years) 4 Month, Mt. Fuji caused large explosion, eruption as much as 35 days had continuation being. As for this large eruption It is recorded even in the "Japanese period abbreviation", but according to handing down the high heaven field is destroyed, flatters the ancestor/founder mountain large shrine It disappeared.

Then, the shrine authorized personnel to immigrate to Sagami country, in the estuary nearby Koza Gun of the Sagami river, high heaven field Being associated with the name of the river which was flowing, you say it founded the Samukawa shrine, kept the document of transmission. Because of this you say the "Samukawa document" you could attach the name which becomes. As for the present document, the areola shallow source under the shrine Osamu shrine of the between shrine husband justice benevolence, visited the Samukawa shrine thickly Occasion, being frightened in serious characteristic of the document, is something which copies the all sentence, shallow it conveys to the between shrine the question . . . As for the Samukawa shrine, Koan 5 years [Kôan 5: 1282] because of the large flood which happens, the company building flows out, you say Damage was received, also the document disappeared. But as for the contents, because source under the shrine the husband copies thickly, it remained.

My survey might be summarized as follows:

> *"the figure which becomes in the first place Xu luck has been wrapped in the image which ambiguity dimly is done, it depends on also the fact that the concrete figure does not float."*

Third, we need to know *how seriously Japanese take this stuff* Does anyone really feel that a *hôrai* adds years to their life? Most Christians don't think their Christmas trees, evergreen though they may be, will help them stay young. And *hôrai* are not that colorful or pleasant smelling, either. They seem closer to a nativity scene, with less eye-candy for children (unless they stay up to watch the mice!). But, unlike the nativity, the Hôrai is not directly connected to the major religions. It can only be tied into Taoism in so far that some Taoists seriously sought immortality. I would like to see a survey of what might be called *Hôrai consciousness*.

Fourth, we need to investigate how the *hôrai* legend and concept relate to the Treasure Ship, something closer to a cargo cult. We will board the *takarabune* in chapter 13.

Fifth, we need a global survey of variations of this legend and related legends.

~~~~~~

Corny? Yes. But remember the New Year Connection!

蓬莱やこゝが命の置きどころ 明庵
hôrai ya koko ga inochi no okidokoro meian 1892
(hôrai:/!/'tis / here's life's placing-place[repository])

山
mount feng lai
here is the place where
life itself is kept

the *hôrai*
is a repository
for life

a *hôrai*!
the very place life
is kept

初霞
hatsu-gasumi

九 9
THE MAGICAL FIRST MIST

上下て見る人多し初霞　何力 明和二
kamishimo de miru hito ôshi hatsugasumi　kariki 1765
(above-below[formal-dress]-in see people many, first mist)

many see it
wearing formal dress
the first mist

Though the premiere sign of the Spring, the mist is not itself a deity revered like the Sun. Kariki's *ku* describes a fact. It is interesting for looking at the lookers rather than the looked at, and humorous for seeming to suggest that formal dress is worn *in order* to pay respect to the mist when that is not the case.

山　里　に　春　た　つ　と　い　ふ　こ　と　を
山　里　は　霞　みわたれる　けしき　にて　空　に　や　春　の　立　つ　を　知　る　ら　む　西行
yamazato ni haru tatsu to iu koto o = (mountain-homeplace-as-for, spring-stands[=new year comes] thing[+obj.] [poeticize])
yamazato wa kasumi watareru keshiki nite sora ni ya haru no tatsu o shiruramu　saigyô 1118-90
(mountain-homeplace-as-for, mist/haze spans landscape/picture-as sky/air-in springs comes[obj] know-would/should)

asked to compose a poem on the new year in hill country

in the hills　　　　　　　　　up in the hills
where landscape　　　　　where mist is all
is solid mist　　　　　　　　you can see

the sky knows that　　　　how spring may be
spring is this!　　　　　　　born of air

Spring was usually thought to come from over the horizon and not from the sky. Saigyô cleverly takes the perspective of someone living *within* the mist usually seen in the distance. The Spring mist in the mountains or haze in the horizon was observed by many for two reasons other than the mere fact it was there. First, people out to witness the rising sun noticed it if nothing else because it could get in the way. Second, it both resembled the anticipated blooming trees of Spring and blocked viewing them. While most old poems mentioning mist are *Spring* proper rather than New Year, this element, neither air nor water, common to the timeless hills and more mysterious than the warming rays of the sun, melting ice and quickening rain, all of which are almost exclusively Spring themes, was often associated with Spring-as-New-Year. (わが西行英訳に対して自信まったくない。専門家の「正誤」助を求む。).

たちかはる春を知れとも見せがほに年をへだつる霞なりける　西行
tachikawaru haru o shire to mo misegao ni toshi hedatsuru kasumi narikeru　saigyô -1190
(substituting spring[obj] know-as-if-to showing-face-as year/s[obj] separate mist/y becomes[+emph])

by keeping year
from year apart, the mist
helps us to see

auld lang syne has really
been replaced by spring!

Saigyô was the most creative of all the *waka* poets, but when it came to making the mist a prop in the New Year's drama, his efforts still seem dull (*unlike my translation!*) compared to what was to come:

古年の夢の行へや初霞　吟江 夢うら
furutoshi no yume no yukue ya hatsugasumi ginkô 1780
(old year's dream/s' destination! first mist)

. . . . . .　　　　　　　　　　　　*whereabouts unknown*

so where has　　　　　　　　　　　the first mist:
last year's dream gone?　　　　　　a year of dreams
the first mist.　　　　　　　　　　went where?

This is a perfect example of how *number* kills poetry. The original poem is better than either translation for not forcing the choice of *dream* or *dreams*. With long poems, ambiguity tends to confuse, but with haiku it can only enrich us. We need the dream/s of Japanese.

再現＝年喰ふ鬼の行方や初霞　大江丸 俳懺悔
toshikurau oni no yukue ya hatsugasumi　ôemaru 1719-1805
(year-eating demon's/demons' destination!/?/: first-mist)

smoke-screen　　　　　　　　　　*soul train*

spring's first mist:　　　　　　　　this year-glutton
ho, the year-eating fiend　　　　　can see his destination:
covers his tracks!　　　　　　　　the first mist!

After Ginkô's subtle dream *ku,* this seems crass. I still like it. The first translation plays with the literal meaning of the original. I have not yet encountered such a year-eating demon/ogre in Japanese folklure, but some types of supernatural creatures did disappear in puffs of smoke. "Year-eater" (*toshigui*) is someone who has lived many years. Years are typically "taken" in Japanese, but ingested? If the additional "demon" is idiomatic, it is uncommon enough not to make my OJD. The second reading takes *yukue,* or destination, more seriously. While *clouds* (*kumo*) rather than *mist* were generally considered manifestations of cremated souls, these phenomena are similar enough that some poets dared to tread on the latter.[1] If Ôemaru wrote this in his old age, it may be a chuckle over his own fate.

~~~~~~

1. Kasumi as Soul Train. Issa, riding on his Pure Land Sect faith, asks in a haiku *not* belonging to the New Year:　"The West Mountain: / Which mist is the one / I'll mount?" *nishiyama ya onore ga noru wa dono kasumi*).

春につれ春をさそふや朝霞　宗因
haru ni tsure haru o sasou ya asagasumi   sôin 1604-82
(spring-with accompanies/follows, spring[obj] entices: morning-mist)

trailing spring yet drawing her out morning mist	inviting spring and attending her morning mist

God knows what was in the poet's head. I imagine Chinese goddesses with loose long-sleeved robes and ribbons swirling about them like the "new gymnastics" in the Olympics. Not that it matters. Poems of this type *always* charm. I think of Issa's kitten chasing and being chased by leaves.

立つとしも見えぬやよもの朝霞　宗祇　大発句帳
tatsu toshi mo mienu ya yomo no asagasumi   sôgi 1420-1502
(stand/arriving year even see-not: four-sides' morning mist)

sign of spring, you say?

you can't see the new year's here morning mist	new year's here i know for i can not see it in the mist

The first 12 syllabets can also be punned as: "Even if you *stand* you cannot see (*tatsu to shi mo*, rather than *tatsu toshi mo*). At first, I thought this purely pun, not one of Sôgi's better *ku*; but when we recall that mist was a sign of the Spring=New Year, the idea of it hiding the same is ironic. And with this irony, the pun, lost in translation, revives (with the help of the "here" replacing the verb, "stand/arrive" (*tatsu*)). My second reading brings out the logical paradox more clearly than the original.

雪霞年をあらそふ高ね哉　宗祇
yuki kasumi toshi o arasou takane kana   sôgi 1420-1502
(snow mist year-over struggle high-peak/s!/'tis)

possession

mountain peaks where the snow and mist fight for the year	snow and mist the peaks are fighting over the year

Does Sôgi depict two natural phenomena fighting *over* who gets to be the face of the New Year, trying to pull the year back into the Winter or forward into the Spring? Or, is he thinking of peaks vying for the year, as mountains fought over maidens in the *Manyôshû* (8c)? The *ku* is put in *Saitan* (one name for New Year's Day) rather than *New Year's Mist* in Shiki's *Categorical*. Organizing haiku themes can be every bit as taxing as biological trees, and the haiku equivalent of the human genome project is still far from realization.

霞まく旭新し四方の春　信勝　大三
kasumi maku asahi atarashi yomonoharu   shinshô 1697
(mist seeding/scattering morning-sun new four-side/directions' spring)

the mist-sowing sun brand new spring in all directions	the sun sown by mist the spring fresh on all sides

This literal mist-icism may be influenced by ancient Chinese symbolism known to all educated Japanese: propitious stylized wisps of cloud. But we can not tell *what* sows *what*. There is no explicit tie between the sun and the new (the "brand" was thrown in for the meter).

山の気のけさいき／\と霞哉　法三　大三
yama no ki no kesa iki-iki to kasumi kana　hôsan 1697
(mountain's spirit's this morning[ny]'s animated[=breath]: mist!/?/'tis)

new year's　　　　　　　　　　　　　　　　　　　　　　　*first mist*

morning mist　　　　　　　　　　　　　　　　the lively spirit
the breath of animated　　　　　　　　of the hills this morning see
mountains　　　　　　　　　　　　　　　　　　their exhalation

Iki-iki means lively, but it hints at breath (*iki*). To my mind, the image resulting is of a number of mountains, each with their new mist. The landscape is coming alive with the dawn of Spring. And let me confess that without all this lively poetry, I would not be as inspired by the first-mist as Japanese have long been.

立春の朝よみける　年くれぬ春くべしとは思ひ寝にまさしく見えてかなふ初夢　西行
risshun no ashita yomikeru **toshi kurenu haru kubeshi to wa omoine ni masashiku miete kanau hatsu yume**　saigyô -1190
(comes-spring-morn-read=write// year-sets, spring-comes-ought longing-sleep-in just-that seen comes-true first-dream)

written new year's morning

the year ends　　　　　　　　　　　　　　　　*my first dream*
longing for spring　　　　　　　　　　　　*fulfilled: for this eve*
i fell asleep　　　　　　　　　　　　　　　　　*i closed my eyes*

and what i dreamed　　　　　　　　　　*longing for spring and*
came true, she's here!　　　　　　　　*woke to this surprise!*

The original seems boring, but *think of it*, dreaming of the coming of Spring = The New Year! Did people really *do* that type of thing? How often are *your* dreams of the natural world? "When he opens his eyes, sure enough," writes an editor, "[as per his dream,] the mist is on the mountain/s." I agree. *It must be mist.* Plum blossoms are possible but unlikely here, because a New Year's dream suggests large vistas such as mountains, not eyes zooming in on blossoms. I cannot help trying to make a philosophical *haikai* of the *waka*: *"Life is but / A dream of spring to come: / And, yet, this mist!"*

大空を仰きてそしる春霞　宗因
ôzora o aogite zo shiru harugasumi　sôin -1682
(big-sky[obj.]facing up[emphatic]/know spring mist/haze)

gazing up　　　　　　　　　　　　　　　　　　you must look
at the sky i know　　　　　　　　　　　up at the sky to really
spring haze　　　　　　　　　　　　　　　　know spring mist

Could Sôin have New Yeared at a Mountain Temple and found mist *above* him? The standard idea is looking *out* upon the mountains. Wondering if Sôin might be upset with the haze for blocking his view, I first thought "*zo shiru*" was "*soshiru*" (curse) and translated *"Gazing up at the sky / i cuss out / the spring mist."* But, not knowing Sôin well enough to justify so outrageous a *ku*, I left out that reading.

けさ神代はや人の代や初霞　梅郊 句鑑
kesa kamiyo haya hitonoyo ya hatsugasumi　baikô 1777
(morning god-era, already/quickly peoples era: first mist)

    cover lost   *clarity lost*

the age of gods   lo, the first mist!
so soon the age of men   already the age of man
first mist of the year   succeeds the gods'

                      the first mist
            the age of the gods burns off
                      we remain

On the one hand, obscurity can draw us back in time, on the other, it can block out the past. Sometimes it is hard to tell which metaphor is intended. Loving humor (moisture), I prefer the first reading, but the second is *more* likely to have been the poet's intention. When "this morning" (*kesa*) alone is mentioned, the presumption is that we are talking about the New Year's Day, but the *ku* may depict a first haze that came on the seventh day of the season which was officially People's Day. Two more readings:

    act two   *paradise lost*

the first haze: night's naked hills
the way of gods already   so quickly clothed by mist
lost to man!   the age of man!

The last reading, or, rather, paraverse, owes more to Christianity than the original. There is no mythology of naked people in Japan. The first parents of men, *i.e.* the gods, were clothed and you can be sure men were, too. (Why? I think because no one made a big deal of naked bodies.)

神の代や酒の霞に角とられ 敬愚
kami no yo ya sake no kasumi ni kado torare　keigu
(gods' age: wine-mist-by hard-edge taken [softened])

                mountain mist

              the age of gods
           so quickly humanized
                with wine!

Most New Year's *sake* is cold, but Keigu imagines warm *sake* creating mist on a cold New Year's day. Here is a genuine haiku showing Japanese, too, had *sake* on the mind:

年もけさこすや霞の濁酒　春可 狗猥
toshi mo kesa kosu ya kasumi no nigorizake　shunka 1633
(year too this-morning [we] cross (from last year) =filter: mist's cloudy-*sake*)

                 spring dawns

              the year filters
           at this time: the mist
            is cloudy wine

In the original, idiom for *crossing* from one year to another morphs into the filtering or straining of crude rice wine. Old-fashioned opaque white *sake* was called "mist" (*kasumi*), and we find poets wishing for wine cups large enough to gulp down mountains of it![1] This wine was notably good for clouding memories, and therefore appropriate for leaving the old year and one's blues behind.[2] The crystal clear *sake* created by straining, on the other hand, would have been perfect for New Year's time-travel.

東都 元日や人の世人にあらはるゝ 長翠 題業名所
ganjitsu ya hito no yo hito ni arawaruru chôsui -1813
(original-day: human world humans among appear)

new year's day
man's world appears
among men

the origin day
a world of humans born
among humans

the new year
when the human world
comes to man

The original has a prescript "Eastern Capital," *i.e.,* bustling Edo. The world reborn on the New Year is our human world, the only one we can know inside as well as out, and this is sensed more strongly in the big city than in the country. That does not necessarily tell us where the poet is coming from.

天地のはしめもけさの霞哉 昌叱
ametsuchi no hajime mo kesa no kasumi kana shôshitsu -1603
(heaven-earth's beginning too, this morning [new year's] mist!/?/'tis)

in the beginning
of heaven and earth this
morning mist!

is it the start
of heaven and earth, this
morning's mist?

Despite lacking the word *hatsugasumi,* this *ku* is clearly about first-day mist. In Japanese mythology, the world begins as a chaotic soup or sea of curd – not creation from nothing (or a vacuum) – from which islands congeal when it is poked. A mist-shrouded beginning fits such a scenario.

来る春や四方へ霞の衣くばり 休音 毛吹草
kuru haru ya yomo e kasumi no kinukubari kyûon 1645
(coming/came spring! four directions-to mist's robe-hand-out)

in four directions

the spring's here
handing out new clothing
made of mist

Kinu-kubari is a Winter theme, for clothing, mostly used, was handed out at the year's end, in time to help the poor clothe themselves for the New Year. But, here, it serves as a metaphysical explanation for the first-mist's appearance: *the world has been re-dressed.*

---

1. Mist-drinking The author of the *Kanazôshi* style story "sleep-talk weed" (*negoto-no-kusa*), laments *"Ah, me! / if i only had a [big enough] wine cup / i would drink the mist=sake!"* (*aware kasumi o noman sakazuki o mogana*).

2. Cloudy Sake I found the idea cloudiness= forgetfulness and clear=eternal/memories developed indirectly prior to haikai, and think it no accident that the poem in a series of 13 paeans to wine in the *Manyôshû* (c.780) that specifically advises us "Don't *think* (about [probably] romantic troubles), *drink*!" specifies cloudy/raw wine. (See the note on Ôtomo Tabito in *Orientalism & Occidentalism* for five of the translated poems). Even at that time (~800 AD), the upper class to which the poet belonged had clear *sake*, too, so the point (perhaps the poet's invention) is that cloudy wine is metaphorically/metaphysically the correct choice for such an occasion.

> spring arrives
> handing out new clothing
> right and left: *mist*

It is hard to keep the cosmic overtones and elegance of *yomo*. "Four-directions" is too formal, "on all sides" too prosaic and this, "right and left," pleasant but slangy.

春のくる跡を見せたる霞哉 玄仍 失出典
haru no kuru ato o misetaru kasumi kana   genshi 17-18c?
(spring's coming trace/trail/mark[obj] show mist 'tis/!/?)

this mist	it reveals
shows the trail	the route of spring
of spring's coming	that mist

Ato is a translator's nemesis. It means traces, marks, trails or any indication that something or someone has been somewhere.

たつ年のうちぎすがたか春霞 貞室 再現=失出典
tatsu toshi no uchigi sugata ka harugasumi   teishitsu 1609-73
(standing=leaving year's hit-clothing (house-wear) appearance? spring-mist)

~~spring haze~~	right at home	~~just-so story~~
~~what happens~~	then, is that	~~it's old man winter~~
~~when the leaving year~~	sir new year's house-wear?	~~dusting off his butt before~~
~~dusts his butt?~~	spring haze	~~he goes: spring mist!~~

Boy, did I blow the translation the first time. Unless Chinese characters indicate differently, *tatsu* can mean *leave* as well as *come*, and clothing can be beaten clean, but it is far, far more likely that my respondent is correct and the *uchigi* refers to clothing that is neither the colorful outer layer nor the underwear but that in-between which is typically worn at home. (The previous explanation included this: Teishitsu doesn't specify the old year's *buttocks* here – the original says "dress/clothing" – but the rear is typically what is dusted, so I did not make it up, either (I *did* add *Old Man Winter*, a figment of the European imagination).

二度立つや霞の衣のうら表 重方 毛吹草
nido tatsu ya kasumi no kinu no ura-omote   shigekata 1645
(two-times stand/arrive: mists/haze-clothing's back/inside-front/outside)

Spring

coming twice
she shows both sides of
her misty dress

Teishitsu's teacher Teitoku is known for his gross image of a micturating Princess Sao (Standing to make water, she wets her dress, hence the mist). The above *ku* is not risqué; it means mist was seen on both the early Solar Spring and the New Year. The next *ku* by Teitoku is. It suggests the precocious Princess was quick, if not gravid when she brought her trousseau to Old Man Winter's house (see ch. 1):

佐保姫も子を生み山のむつきかな 貞徳 再現
sao hime mo ko o umi yama no mutsuki kana   teitoku?
(sao princess, too, child bears mountain's diapers!/?/'tis)

first installation

princess sao's
a mother: see! swaddling
on the mountain

This is the only *ku* I know of to make the Princess a mother (Of *what?* The New Year? Spring blossoms?). More commonly, she was infantilized, or the little princess of the slow-to-blossom Spring who is also her father by pun, though Spring was usually female, in one *ku* by Teitoku (1570-1653) which Issa jotted down (*saohime wa chichitaru haru no himeko kana* 一一茶留書(全集より)). I may be wrong when I put a swaddling *ku* in the *New Year's Mist* section rather than with the *Spring Mist*. But surely a case can be made for this next *ku* written shortly later by another poet of his school:

佐保姫の生著かけふの朝霞 政公 毛吹草
saohime no ubugi ka kyô no asagasumi   seikô 1645
(sao-princess's infant clothing? today's morning-mist)

the dawn of spring

this morning mist:
is it the baby clothing
of princess sao?

"Today" (*kyô*) may mean the dawn of spring: Day One. Babies grow up: *"Princess Sao / has worn out / her infantile name"* (*sao-hime wa osana gamashiki na o tsukite*) claims one *ku*, perhaps alluding to the cherry spring; but she was generally seen as a maiden forever, for which another old *ku* concluded she must be the "Blue-Sun-Mother" (年よらぬ佐保姫ごぜや青陽母 忠のり？崑山集＝再現 *toshi yoranu saohime-goze ya seiyôbo* tadanori? 1651), elemental source of spring's alchemical (?) color: "blue."

佐保姫の寝姿見せぬ霞かな 仙布 丁巳元除春遊
saho-hime no nesugata misenu kasumi kana   senpû fl.1800
(sleep-form's princess:/! hidden, morning mist)

morning mist

never surprised
by mortal eyes: the sleeping
princess saho

初空は山ことごとく見知りけり 声疑 大三
hatsuzora wa yama kotogotoku mishirikeri   seigi 1697
(first-sky-as-for, mountains without-exception shy[before strangers])

the first sky   the first sky
the hills without exception   the mountains bashful
are bashful   as little girls

An indirect reference to the mist or haze hiding the faces of the mountains? The word translated as "reticent" is used to refer to the stage in the life of a young child when they are terribly shy before strangers. I find it remarkable that English lacks a common term for this. My grandmother told me that the Pennsylvania-Dutch (the Amish) had a word for it. They called such children "strange." She described the grandchild of my father's second wife that way and shocked everyone listening who assumed she meant the child was abnormal whereas she only meant *bashful before strangers*.

たばこ呑口より春は来にけらし烟もかすむはなの先哉 正長 古今夷曲
tabako nomu kuchi yori haru wa kinikerashi kemuri mo kasumu hana no saki kana seichô 1666
(tobacco drink=smoke-mouth-from spring comes[+fin.+?] smoke-too mists-over nose-tip=flowers-in-front!/?/'tis)

Spring comes
from the mouth that held
a tobacco pipe?
There's the mist, smoke
o'er his blooming nose!

Spring came out
of this tobacco-puffing
mouth of mine:
See all that mist hiding
the blossoms? – Smoke!

One source of the Spring mist in Japan was *American*. This crazy-verse found in Issa's notebook does not English well for lack of the homophonic pun "nose=flower." We will enjoy more tobacco metaphor in the summer when "clouds" are in season (i.e., a haiku theme). I added the "pipe" to avoid a *smoking* mouth making *smoke*. In Japanese, tobacco is "drunken" or "sucked" rather than "smoked."

天の原ふしの煙の春の色の霞になひくあけほのゝそら 前大僧正慈円 新古今集
amanohara fuji no kemuri no haru no iro no kasumi ni nabiku akebono no sora shinkokinshû #33
(heaven's plateau fuji's smoke's spring's color's mist-with/as spread out dawn sky)

where gods live
fuji's smoke takes on
the color of spring
under the mist spreading
in the sunrise sky

While tobacco did not arrive in Japan until the 16c, as *waka* #33 of the 13c *Shinkokinshû* shows, the idea of smoke turning into spring mist goes way back. Another thing brought to Japan from the West:

三文が霞見にけり遠眼鏡 一茶
san mon ga kasumi minikeri tômegane issa -1827
(three mon [unit of money] mist see-done far-glasses)

new year's close up

two bits
for an eyeful of mist
the telescope

for two bits
i got to see the mist
a spyglass

This well-known *ku* is usually put with the *Mist* of Spring proper. Annotators describe a typically placid day (in Japan, unlike England, it does not come in "like a lion!") with nothing going on, and, nothing much to see. Can I help it if I imagine Issa, diligently catching the mist, which one is supposed to see – but cannot always see in reality – to confirm Spring's arrival? Indeed, the desire to see the mist on New Year's Day was so great, one wonders if some poet's eyes didn't cloud over in anticipation.

我院に御慶申さん初霞梢風尼 再現
waga in ni gyokei môsan hatsugasumi shôfû-ni 1668-1758
(my convent*-in, [new-year's] greetings say-would first-mist)

in my convent
exchanging greetings
the first mist

would it bring　　　　　　　　　　　exchanging greetings
greetings to my convent?　　　　　　in our convent we make
the first mist　　　　　　　　　　　　the first mist

The first reading is not so dull as it might seem, if you recall the tenuous relationship between the New Year as a Shintô ritual of life and Buddhism as a religion identified with death and the other world. Moreover the mist, with its warm Spring connotations plays with the life of a nun which is by definition Autumnal. My respondent bets on the first reading, I bet on the second reading, and Keigu bets on the third because he himself once experienced this, though the mist did not come from his mouth.

汲取に小便すれば初霞　敬愚
kumitori ni shôben sureba hatsugasumi keigu
(scoop-take [toilet]-in, urinate-when, first-mist)

pissing into
an old-fashioned john
my first mist

Urinating outside in the cold always makes mist, but doing so into a cesspool in a small unheated bathroom makes more. Visibility dropped to less than three feet and the lonely bachelor Keigu thought, *so much for your romantic New Year's mist!*　Back to *traditional* mist.

むらさきを諸事に補ひ初霞 支考
murasaki o shoji ni oginai hatsugasumi shikô 1731
(purple[obj] all-things-on/to/with supply/complement first-mist/haze)

new year's aura

all things
blessed by purple
first haze

purple enough　　　　　　　　　　　all things are
to ennoble our world　　　　　　　　repaired with purple
the first haze　　　　　　　　　　　　the first haze

the first haze
today all things get
to wear purple

In Japan, as in many parts of the world, purple was a hard color to dye and restricted to nobility, or depending on the shade of purple, the highest ranks of nobility (Hence, the English proverb *"An ape will be an ape, by kind as they say, / Though that you clad him in purple array."*). My *purple haze* feeling is more along the lines of Jimmy Hendrix's electrifying guitar performance, but here the idea would seem to be that the patina of purple graces all with nobility or even divinity, for the Imperial line was a link to the Age of the Gods and, in a sense, therefore, immortal. Since Shikô was a convoluted character and the verb *oginai* suggests the *official supply* of apparel (something done at the end of the year), it is possible he meant this in a light vein as per my creative last reading. That would make the *ku* closer to the *haikai* we have seen, as opposed to the next two:

赤紅や水うつくしき初霞　鬼貫 1660-1738
akabeni ya mizu utsukushiki hatsugasumi onitsura
(vermillion lipstick/rouge!/: water beautiful first-mist)

first mist	what rouge!
the beauty of rouge	the water beautiful
and water	through the first mist

I guess *mist* just sounds better than *haze*. I am back to it. The *ya* taken as an exclamatory break, as per the second reading, would be standard. But my first reading treats the *ya* as a mere "and" (the usual vernacular meaning, but not likely for a haiku) and is, I think, better. But, to tell the truth, this poem bothers me. It is too subtle. Is it about the red sun and lightly misted-over water or rouge on the cheeks of a woman scooping up "young-water," a theme we will see later?

初霞掘り残されし芋を掘る　蓼?杖 大正新俳句
hatsugasumi hori-nokosareshi imo o horu　ryôjo? early-20c
(first-mist dig/dug-remaining/left potatoes/yams[+obj] dig)

the first mist
i dig up the yams
i didn't dig up

The ground thaws enough for digging. This combination of c/rude food and magical mist is a fine one. Still, if Kaizôsha's *saijiki* did not include this (with other new-mist *ku*) in the New Year's section, I might have my doubts, for digging yams is a highly unlikely New Year's activity. Issa, who mixed his yam farts with the scent of plum blossoms, would have loved it. I imagine the poet a hundred or two hundred yards up a mountain, because yams grow best at the height where there is enough rain and moisture for quick growth but not enough to cause rot. It is also pleasant to think of a poet (the printing in my 改造社の俳諧歳時記 is smeared, so his name is a guess) who notices a yam growing at this time.

音もなく香もなく立や春霞　昌叱 大発句帳
oto mo naku ka mo naku tatsu ya harugasumi　shoshitsu -1603
(sound, too, not scent-too not stand/appear: spring-mist/haze)

it appears
without sound or scent
spring mist

Because the subject of the verb is not clear in the original, it could be the New Year, the Spring or the Mist. This is why I do not feel the subject is simply the spring mist, but the arrival of Spring=New Year. There are many old *ku* concerning the *sense* with which particular seasons announced themselves. The Fall wind is first heard, spring breeze is first felt, etc. This poem may mean only that if mist is *the* indicator of Spring, the eyes get the notice.

霞の音聞ゆはかりに明にけり 未及 大三
kasumi no ne kikoyu bakari ni akenikeri   mikyu 1697
(mist's sound hear-not[打消?] only, brighten/dawn [+fin.])

    the sound of mist   we almost hear
   can almost be heard   the sound of the mist
     as spring dawns   as spring dawns

How silent the dawn on this day when no one works or commutes to work. The *ku* does not make explicit what day dawns, but I think it not only is a New Year's poem, but a very good one, for it powerfully expresses the anticipation we feel as a holiday dawns.

春に明て天の戸わたるかすみ哉 宗牧
haru ni akete ama no to wataru kasumi kana   sôboku -1545
(spring-in/for opened heaven's door crosses mist!/?/'tis)

clouds of mist
pass by heaven's cave
open for spring

The "door" Englished but not translated is the legendary one to the cave where the Sun Goddess once holed up. What a wonderful moving image! And what a fine way to reify the emptiness felt after the First Sun has arisen!

年玉
toshidama

 10

PRESENTS WITHOUT SANTA CLAUS

お年玉ポケットに入れ走り出す　針ヶ谷直希
otoshidama poketto ni ire hashiridasu harigaya naoki 5[th]grade
(o+year-gem=ny-gift, pocket-in put, run-start/off)

the new year's present

putting it
into my pocket,
i burst out running!

When I started writing this book about *olde* haiku, I never dreamed a chapter would open with a child's poem. But rereading this *ku*, it occurred to me that for all the delightful *toshidama* (literally: *year-gem*) *ku* by adults – Issa alone wrote no less than 28! – none came close to this perfect picture of joy.[1] It is about the gift of a nest-egg of money (coins) on New Year's, and may describe a younger sibling –

pure joy

pocketing it
he bursts out running
new year's gift

But chances are it is a self-portrait, for ambiguous subjects, as a rule, *are*. Neither translation does justice to the original which is a perfect gem. The coins, usually *go-en* (five *yen*), pun as "your-luck/fortune." They are presented in envelopes, not red as customary in China, but white, and paper "because" paper is a homophone for the *gods=kami* said to have begun the practice of gift-giving.

1. *Best Haiku by a Child?* The nature and selection of haiku and that of longer and more structured poems should be different. To produce a good sonnet requires practice and discipline unlikely in most would-be poets, much less a young child; but, with haiku, it is possible not only for a poor poet, but for a neophyte to occasionally come up with a masterpiece. *For this reason, people interested in collecting the best haiku on various subjects cannot restrict themselves to well-known poets.* Unfortunately, because of the tendency on the part of critics in Japan to downgrade most *ku*, especially *olde* haiku as worthless (*tsukinami*), and concentrate on the few poets whose taste meets their approval, the vast majority of haiku are completely ignored. I agree that most *ku* are not worth printing, much less reprinting; but I beg those who can still read the handwritten style of print to at least put *all* the olde *ku* that can be found *on-line and accessible* (the largest extant collection, the Iwanami *Nihon Taikei*, is, or was, on-line, but for inexcusable bureaucratic reasons, denies access to independent scholars), so that we may sift through them and select poems from minor poets, which, like this child's *toshidama* haiku, may well be unrecognized masterpieces. I should add that the editors of the fine collection of children's haiku in which this poem appeared did not dare play favorites. *They should have.* As I wrote in the introduction, *selection is the heart of haiku.*

去年の子の玉持初し旦哉　立松 大三
kozo no ko no tama mochi-someshi ashita kana risshô 1697
(last-years' child's gem=gift carry-starts morning/new-years!/'tis)

  last year's child   last year's child
gains his/her first year-gem   holds his/her/its first gift
   this morning   this morning

Birthdays for all were on the New Year (ch.11). Children were given New Year's gifts from their second birthday, their first by Western convention where a new-born is not *in* its first year but *before* it. The *tama,* or "gem," as we have seen, is associated with year and gift. This olde *ku* also hints of a year-progression metaphor, namely: "the child of last year (Kozo) *takes the ball* this morning." Yes, "his/her/its" is ugly as hell (You may share the pain of translators who are forced to choose between them).

年玉や童心の玉手箱　嘯山 再現
toshidama ya warabegokoro no tamatebako shôzan -1780
(year-gem/s[gift/s]! young-child's heart's gem-hand-box [?])

the *toshidama*
a box full of surprises
for the child at heart

First take: Once, the present was not limited to money as it is today. So there was the surprise element implied by *tamatebako,* a word lacking a good English equivalent. My *Kenkyusha's Japanese-English Dictionary* says "Urashima's casket," "the apple of Sodom," and "Pandora's box." Or even "a Dead Sea apple (opening one, you are disappointed)" An important *tamatebako*: "a treasured casket." None are right for the poem. "Jack in the Box" comes closest. The surprise element is perfect, Jack can mean money (in Australia, at any rate) but the "present" part is missing. My "box full of surprises" is not wrong but lacks the New Year's and gift connection (why I left the Japanese word as is). *Second take:* After reading over the legend of Urashima Tarô and reflecting further on the generally sad meaning of the treasure box and the tendency of this poet to be a wit, I came to the conclusion that the haiku probably means this:

year after year

with each present
the child grows older
urashima's box!

Urashima Tarô was a fisherman who freed a turtle and was taken to the Dragon Palace on the bottom of the sea as a reward. After three years in that paradise, he came back to discover 300 years had passed and everyone he knew was long dead. Before his mother's and his own headstone, his grief grew so strong that he ended up opening the box (the *tamatebako*) he was given to "open only when deeply troubled." In an instant, he grew white-haired and, dying, transformed into a crane and flew off. So the crane and turtle, symbols of longevity, are often seen together . . . ." (Obviously, the story came after the auspicious critters. The turtle looks old and the long legs of the crane . . .). Each time the gifts were given, the poet marveled how quickly the children were growing up. And, perhaps, he also associated the desire for treasure with the inevitability of growing old. Even little children are human, they are not innocent from the get-go.   Then, suddenly, the tables are reversed.   A modern *ku:*

年玉を孫に貰ひて驚けり 相生垣瓜人
toshidama o mago ni moraite odorokeri aioigaki kajin 20c
(year-gem[gift][obj] grandchild-from received/ing surprised[+emph.])

        i have received
     a present from my grandson
         surprise indeed!

I made the gender-neutral *mago* a boy because granddaughter would be too long for the *ku*. But, considering the sweetness of girls, the surprise would be greater to receive a present from a boy, so grand*son* is better for the poem. Before long, the grandson will be the bread-winner and grandpa the dependent.[1] Part of the surprise may be that the poet suddenly realizes he himself has aged.

元日霰のふりければ くる春の年玉ならん霰哉 親重 狗
ganjitsu ni arare no furikereba // kuru haru no toshidama naran arare kana shinchô 1633
(ny's-on hailstones fall-when // coming spring's year-gems/balls/gifts become/are! hailstones!/?/'tis)

hailstones on new year's day

  so call this hail   so call this hail
new year's presents   new year's presents
   from the spring   for the spring

       new year's hail:
  spring says, have a ball!
     a million of them!

Hail is *not* what one wants on New Year's. The poetic justification for putting on a good face does not work in translation because it is based on ball/gem=present. The idiomatic pun in my last translation approaches the spirit of the original but, unfortunately, "having a ball" is not the same as *getting a gift*.

年玉を皆千両の初日哉 富春 宝暦九
toshidama o mina senryô no hatsuhi kana fushun 1761
(year-gem/gift[+contradic. or obj.] everyone 1000 ryô [monet. unit]'s first-sun!/'tis)

  why these presents?   new year's mint
don't all of us get this   worth a million to all
   priceless first sun!   our first sun!

The "gem/ball" in word for a New Year's gift is matched by the roundness and shine of the sun. That, and the subtle classical "o" of contradiction makes the original less tedious than the translation. The second reading takes "o" as an object marker. Either way, there is precedent for *the year itself* (possibly envisioned as the sun) being the real gift: *"The year-gem=gift / tightly gripped, in comes / the Dragon-year"* (年玉をつかんでくるや辰の年　俊屋　鷹筑波 *toshidama o tsukandekuru ya tatsu-no-toshi* shunya 1642). Dragons were typically pictured gripping gems called *hôgyoku* (宝玉) in their talons.

---

1. *Dependency Reversal* Japanese traditionally retired in their middle-age and turned their business over to their children, content to become dependents rather than remain patriarchs to the end (hogging most of the house and commanding others) in the typical (?) Occidental manner. Since the children were *expected* to remain dependent up to that time, rather than forced to stand alone, after the reversal, the child felt obliged to care for his parents out of love, rather than social obligation. (See Alice Mabel Bacon's observations in *Topsy-Turvy 1585*).

年の玉ひろふ心のあした哉　吉白 大三物
toshinotama hirou kokoro no ashita kana　kippaku 1697
(year's gem/present pick-up heart/mind's morning/tomorrow!/?/'tis)

with the mind
of a beachcomber i find
my new year!

this morning
like a child i'm ready for
my year gift

this morning
i'm delighted to collect
another year

The metaphor *suggested* by the verb *hirou*, ("pick up" or "collect,") is that of finding a treasure on the beach. It is a way to express the poet's delight and links to the *tama* in *toshi no tama* ("year-gift") because *tama hiroi* is a poetic expression for *shell-collecting*, but cannot be linked logically to the year. The last reading assumes the poet is an old man who normally complains that the chariot does not come for him if it were but on this day is swept up by the magic mood and ready to pick up one more year.

年玉に梅折る小野の翁哉　言水
toshidama ni ume oru ono no okina kana　gonsui 1646-1719
(year-gem=gift-as plum [branch] breaks small-field [[?]location] master!/'tis)

the small-field master
breaks off a plum branch
for a new year's gift

I am not sure who this Small-field (Ono) Master might be. There is an old-man of Ono somewhere in the *Manyôshû* and there is an Ono One-sword school, too. Perhaps it is just a gentleman with a small plot with some plum trees. Regardless, a plum branch, with gem-like buds soon to bloom, is a superb gift. A single tree may have scores of shoots, each of which makes an excellent New Year's present. I have received a few and still treasure the memory over ten years later. Today, with global warming, the plum sometimes blooms in time for even our mid-winter New Year. As the first flower/blossom of the year, it symbolizes the first-heart/mind, as a homophone with birth, the first creation, and its bloom is white blank innocence or, more rarely, celebratory red. Here is an earthier equivalent:

糞とりの年玉寒し洗ひ蕪　許六
koetori no toshidama samushi araikabu　kyôroku -1715
(shit/fertilizer taker/s' year-gem/gift [is] cold: washed turnip)

what a cold gift!
from the night-soil man
washed turnips

cold year-gifts
from the honey collector
washed turnips

The "honey wagon" in Japan was a man or two men using a pail dangling from a bamboo stick. He would not come on New Year's Day. I guess this "visit" was made on the third day of the year. "Shit-collector" would be too crude, but "fertilizer" would be too vague. In Japanese, the *character* for "shit" is used, but *vocalized* as "fertilizer." Japanese turnips (*kabu*) – peach-sized round turnips, not the huge *daikon* sometimes so translated – are not like any I have eaten in the USA. They are succulent, sweet, and taste best raw! (especially sliced and mixed with a lesser portion of sliced persimmon and a little mayonnaise). Since the earliest New Year gifts were reputedly round balls or "gems/souls" of sweet rice cake (*mochi*), these round and shiny, freshly washed turnips seem oddly appropriate. And, like *daikon*, the great radish, they grow in cold weather and are one of the few fresh yet inexpensive gifts available at the start of Spring. I found the *ku* by Kyoroku (a poet, ethnologist and editor whose death at age 50 was a greater tragedy than Bashô's death at the same age) only in Kodansha's large *saijiki,* which gives another *ku* of turnips (with their leaves attached) carried as if they were very light indeed by a firewood vendor. At first, I thought that Kyoroku gave the night-soil man the turnips in exchange for his service – the original does not say who gives/gets the gift – but I forgot something important. Kyoryoku was the *customer* of the nightsoil man who bought his product to sell and/or trade it to farmers who needed the fertilizer.

年玉や杓子数そふ草の庵　太祇
toshidama ya shakushi kazu sou kusa no io　taigi -1772
(year-gift/gem: ladles numbers together[?] grassy hut)

ladle after ladle
new year's presents
for a grass hut

Did grass-hut poets live on reheated stew (or cold stew warmed by hot water) as I do? Stew can be made once every few days and one's cooking is done. Of course, stew pots need ladles. That is *one* guess. Another would have visitors scooping out presents or *sake* with the freshly made ladles (正解を求む). Either way, a *shakushi*=ladle is fitting for the start of the year because it also means *"tamajakushi,"* or tadpole, the gem/soul-ladle that grows and *returns* (like "frog" *kaeru*). Taigi also described a gift of medicine – common because salves were put into pretty painted clamshells! – that doesn't work from a third-generation doctor (年玉やきかぬ薬を医三代　太祇＝再現 *toshidama ya kikanu kusuri o i sandai* – It could be from the "quack doctor" category of *senryû!*). Even the useless survives from year to year.

年玉や抱ありく子に小人形　召波
toshidama ya daki ariku ko ni koningyô　shôha -1771
(year-gem=gift! hugging-walk-child-to small doll)

the year gift   the year gift
a child in its mother's arms   a little doll for the child
gets a doll   i carry about

This is the oldest *ku* I know of specifying *a child* as the recipient of a New Year's gift. Children do not appear in the earliest *haikai* on *toshidama*. This is not surprising, for in the Sinosphere, where aging was collectively celebrated with the New Year, more attention was paid to the elderly than the young. After all, *they* are the ones who have made it so far. The children haven't accomplished anything much. Why do *they* deserve gifts? [1] The *ku* could well be first-person. About a century after Shôha's death, Europeans were astounded to find Japanese men willing to carry babies or toddlers with them when socializing with other men while the mothers dyed their teeth, worked, or went to a play. In the Occident, men would have been ashamed to participate in what was considered a strictly female activity.

---

1. **Presents to Children.** While most children are more delightful than adults who deny their own childishness, our culture is *crazy* to value *potential* humanity as much as that which has become a caring person. It is a mistake to hold a fetus of equal humanity – with an equal "right to life" – as an adult human, or, for that matter, to pity the death of a "cute" baby seal more than that of its mother, who cares for it. It will not do to simply repeat the mantra "a woman's choice," for "choice/ no-choice" is a lower level of morality than "life/death." Unless we (*people who really love people*, not an abstract concept of "life") outgrow our *cult of the infant* and reflect deeply upon *what makes some life more precious than other life*, we cannot successfully challenge the unreasonable and harmful morality of fundamentalists (including some Justices), much less demonstrate the fundamental error in their reasoning.

年玉やわび寝の庵の枕上　召波
toshidama ya wabine no io no makura ue shôha -1771
(year-gem=gift: rustic/simple/quiet-sleep's hut/atelier's bed/pillow-upon)

the bachelor

new year's gift
it remains on the pillow
of a lonely bed

There is something touching about a gift on one's bed. In my case, it is because I opened my Xmas stockings and set my Easter basket on my bed in childhood. In Japan, beds not in use are either hung outside to beat and/or dry or folded it up and stored in the closet. If a gift is on a bed, it means the bed has been left out for holiday snoozing, someone is sick, or leads an unkempt solitary life. Could this gift be a jug of *sake* left by a visitor in a place suggesting it would be good for a night-cap? Who knows!

年玉を並べて置くや枕もと 子規
toshidama o narabete-oku ya makuramoto   shiki 1901
(year-gems/gifts [+obj] lined-up-left: pillow/bed-side)

invalid new year

all my gifts lined up, remain still by my pillow	i just line-up all my new year gifts on my bed

A prescript to this *ku* says Shiki was "gazing upon the gifts brought by Sokotsu." The context for these bed-presents may be different from Shôha's, but the warmth is the same.

我庵やけさのとし玉とりに来る 一茶
waga-io ya kesa no toshidama tori ni kuru   issa -1814
(my cottage! this morning=ny's year-gem/gift take-for come)

santa in bed

at my shack
the new year presents
are picked up

New Year's or not, in Japan, presents are generally passed out by the person who pays a call. In Issa's *ku*, it is backwards. Doubtless, a relative or a maid – for even the peasant poet Issa did occasionally employ one – were itching for their presents while, if I am not mistaken, the hung-over poet slept in. Years later, Issa complained about "lacking someone to help hand out the presents" (*toshidama o kubaru sewanaki iori kana*   issa 年玉を配る世わなき庵哉 一茶), so it may have been customary for the well-off giver to have underlings deliver presents, while they stayed home. Issa also haiku'ed going *out* to *receive* a gift/gifts – for himself or for his wife and child – and exchanging New Year's greetings (年玉を貰ひに出る御慶かな 一茶 文政四 *toshidama o morai ni ideru gyokei kana*); however, that day, he *also* wrote he was "pulled awake by the first call of the cock" and "set out for the East Mountain to greet the Gem-spring, polished to completion by the rising sun." So *this* may be the present referred to. Issa had just regained his voice and ability to walk, which he had lost for most of the winter and felt "reborn."

かくれ家や猫（に）も一ッ御年玉　一茶
kakurega ya neko ni mo hitotsu otoshidama   issa -1827
(hidden house: cat-to-also, one year-gem/gift)

on new year's

in my old hut
each of the cats, too,
get a present

the hide-away
i bring an extra gift
for their cat

a hidden hut
i bring presents for
my illegal cats

Issa's *toshidama* poems are remarkable in that 9 of 28 include non-human animals. The "old hut" is a "hidden house." Reading one, favored by a respondent, assumes Issa refers to his own house's lack of popularity, as proven by a dearth of visitors. The second reading imagines he refers to a hovel (usually occupied by kind, ugly people), magically overgrown with lush vegetation, keeping a variety of animals. The third assumes Issa aids and abets unwanted cats by encouraging them to hide out in the bush rather than approach people who might not appreciate them (something I once did in Japan). /

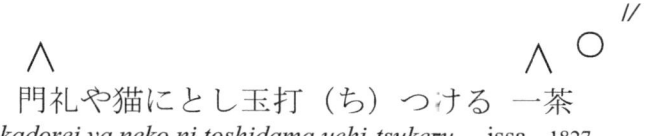

門礼や猫にとし玉打（ち）つける　一茶
kadorei ya neko ni toshidama uchi-tsukeru   issa -1827
(gate/door-greetings: cat-to/at year-gem/ball/gift throw-hit)

happy new year!   **the gift-tosser**

greetings exchanged
by the gate, a present
tossed at the cat

happy new year!
then i hit the cat
with a present

hitting the cat
with a new year's gift
i bow my head

Issa did not invent the practice of tossing New Year's gifts to cats. In the following poem, the cat gets a gift with a *noshi* (long thin strips of dried – pounded and stretched? – "sea ear," which is to say *scallop* which was attached to ceremonial gifts and came to be identified with them. It seems extravagant if not odd to give a cat so formal a gift. Unlike Issa's obvious with, this wit is in the untranslatable *noshi*.

熨斗なから猫の玉うつ朝哉　真宝 大三
noshi nagara neko no tama utsu ashita kana   shinhô 1697
(abalone-strips[=formal gift]-while, cat's gem[gift] toss morning'tis)

a formal present
is tossed to the cat
new year's day

In his second year back in his hometown, middle-aged Issa received an airborne New Year's gift himself: *"It's the street-boss / something's chucked in my window / a toshidama"* (番丁や窓から投（は
ふ）御年玉　一茶 *banchô ya mado kara hôru otoshidama*). There would seem to have been a lot of

throwing going on! Another *ku* that year: *"The NY gift / tossed into the window / of a not-at-home"* (とし玉や留守の窓からほ（は）ふりこみ 一茶 *toshidama ya rusu no mado kara hôrikomi*). Or, the poem might mean that while Issa is out lobbing gifts about town, someone lobs one into *his* house:

new year's exchange?

a gift for me
tossed through the window
in my absence

Why so many thrown gifts? I think it is because the idea of throwing them is particularly outrageous to Japanese because in there is a clearly established etiquette for handing someone a gift: with both hands and a bow. Another pre-Issa gift-throwing *ku*:

打玉に鳩は飛けり老の春 何云 大三
utsu tama ni hato wa tobikeri rônoharu katen? 1697
(toss/ed/ing gem-by/at dove/s-as-for fly[+emphatic] elderly-spring)

doves fly off	i tossed presents
when gramps tosses them	to the doves: they flew off
a new year's gift	my old spring

Doves are one of the few creatures with less significance in Japanese than English. For a start, they could also be pigeon, for they are both *hato*. I think the old poet tosses some beans out for the pigeons who mistake his intent. (可云は「なにいふ」か？) Issa's best animal gift *ku* has no action:

とし玉の上にも猫のぐる寝哉 一茶 文政四
toshidama no ue ni mo neko no gurune kana issa 1821
(year-gem/gift/s'-on-top-of-even cat's curled-sleep!/?/'tis)

new year's still-life

right on top
of the presents, our cat
sound asleep

It is in the very nature of cats to sleep on what people pay attention to. No doubt it gives them good dreams. The next *ku* is far less poetic, but still worth noting for its ethnographical value.

江戸衆や庵の犬にも御年玉 一茶
edoshû ya io no inu ni mo otoshidama issa 1821
(edoites! dwelling's dog-to-also o-year-gift)

new year's custom

those edoites!
even the dog at my shack
gets a present

Issa wrote a cherry-blossom viewing poem that wonders if a dog shits gold, but that would be about a pampered lap-dog owned by a wealthy person; here, he would seem to be talking about a phenomenon common around the world: dogs are treated better in the city than in the country, where they were treated as . . . dogs. Apparently, Issa's Edoite friends brought presents for him and his dog. Edoites were famous for spending their money as fast as they made it and for gifts. Speaking of ethnography, Issa has one New Year's present *ku* in a rough country dialect: *Just chuck it / over yonder, gramps! / The New Year's present* (こりよそけへいつけて置けよお年玉　*koriyo soke e itsukete-okeyo otoshidama*). "Gramps" is my invention. It seems to fit the untranslatable atmosphere. Even if an underling were to deliver a gift, urbane etiquette required one to accept it in a respectful manner. But let us return to Issa's animal-present *ku*. Knowing he had a subject other poets had not covered well, he composed many.

年玉を犬にも投げる御寺哉　一茶
toshidama o inu ni mo nageru otera kana　issa 1824
(year-gem/gift[+obj] dog/s-to throw [buddhist]temple 'tis)

new year's munificence

at the temple
presents are thrown
to the dogs, too

The "too" is significant. Alms are generally thrown to people. Issa may be indirectly calling our attention to that here. Or, he is simply impressed with the largesse that extends even to dogs at temples?

年玉をおくやいなりの穴の口　一茶
toshidama o oku ya inari no ana no kuchi　issa 1824
(year-gem/gift[+obj] place: fox/fox-deity's hole/den's mouth)

i leave a gift
for the new year in front
of the fox den

The fox is a playful Shintô deity, a jokester somewhat like the Amerindian Coyote. I think it interesting to contrast presents thrown to dogs at Buddhist temples and left for – offered to – Shintô foxes. As this *ku* was written in the Year of the Monkey, the enemy of the canine race in the Sinosphere, we might also see the Buddhist temple helping the underdog and Issa pulling the fox's tail (should it trust a gift received in the Year of the Monkey from a primate?). *Ignore me, reader, I think too much*. But, the cat as usual got the lion's share of the gift poems. This year Issa also did a paraverse of his cat-on-gifts *ku* of three years earlier.

ばか猫や年玉入れの箕に眠る　一茶　文政七
baka neko ya toshidama-ire no mi ni nemuru　issa 1824
(fool/damn cat! year-gift/gem-entered winnowing-basket-on sleep)

that silly cat   our fool cat
sleeping on a basket   asleep in the basket with
of *toshidama*!   the year-gifts

The cat has chosen to sleep in the only place where it will be in the way. "Baka" is the most common insult in Japan even today. It means "fool," and is written in Chinese characters for "horse+deer." Since there is no "damn" (*i.e.*, no derogatory or even angry adjective originally related with thoughts about going to hell and calling on God in vain) in Japanese, *baka* in this context could have been translated as "damn." But Issa liked the word and used it in a score of poems – usually modifying cats or crows – and, if I am not mistaken, in this context, it is *affectionate* and improves the *ku* by giving it a heart! (But, take care! I must confess to picking up this *baka* from Issa and using it lightly on someone dear to me who was not amused.)

年玉やかたり猫に（ぞ）打つける 一茶
toshidama ya katari neko ni [zo] uchitsukeru issa 1824
(year-gem/gift: swindling/fooling/crooked-cat-to[+emphatic?] throw-hit)

the *toshidama*:
feline crook i'll pitch it
right at you!

Since *tama* also means "ball," throwing it makes good figurative sense. Or, for that matter, it can mean a "bullet," and *utsu* can mean shoot! "Katari" is an adjective for something that fools something else. This is a cat that has at one time or another swiped food from Issa. The original also threatens to throw the gift *so it hits the recipient*. It is not interesting in translation, so I made it more of a matter of intent. You better be good, or Santa will *brain* you with presents!

年玉や猫の頭へすで [=住んで?] の事 一茶
toshidama ya neko no atama e sude [=sunde?]no koto issa 1824
(year-gift/gem! cat's head-to already (or, narrowly[missed])-thing)

new year's conversation

the cat's present?	the cat's present?
sure, he already got it	sure, it barely missed
plunk on the head!	hitting his head!

An idiom in dialect allows the second reading. *Don't get Issa wrong.* Only a real cat-lover descends to the cats' level and engages them in their own rough-housing. Personally, I prefer shooting a pea-shooter to throwing things because it is more accurate. The cats usually came into heat around New Year and the fact that this was when food was left around, as we have seen with the *Hôrai*, must have made it a time of great human-cat conflict. But Issa's deservingly best known gift-poem sub-theme is human:

とし玉を二人前とる小僧哉 一茶
toshidama o futarimae toru kôzô kana issa 1821
(year-gift[+obj] two-person-portions take small-bonze[little boy]!/'tis)

merchant-monk

a little boy
claims his new year's present
twice

That is to say, he pretended he had not gotten one yet in order to get two from the poet. A very young child has his hair shaved (except for a tiny tuft in back), so he looks like a monk (See the transliteration). Issa loved to depict children and cunning ones most of all.

とし玉のさいそくに来る孫子哉　一茶
toshidama no saisoku ni kuru magoko kana　issa 1823
(year-gift's pressing/dunning-to comes grandchild!/ 'tis)

new year's creditor

coming over
to dun for his present
the grandchild

The term *saisoku* is usually used to describe creditors pressing debtors to pay up. The word "dunning" is practically obsolete, so the translation may be a bit stiff. In Japanese, it is particularly funny, coming right after New Year's Eve, when creditors made life miserable for the debtor majority.

年玉や懐の子も手ゝをして　一茶
toshidama ya futokoro no ko mo tete o shite　issa 1824
(year-gift! pocket's child even/too hand-hand [begging] does)

want upon want

new year's presents
even the child on her back
starts begging!

The "pocket-child" is generally one carried in a shawl-like cloth on the back. I imagine the carrier is herself a little girl. "Begging" is not as good as the picturesque Japanese *te-te-o shite*, which shows us the little hands reaching up. Still, it was the closest equivalent available. The term is used when asking a dog to "beg" in Japanese. Issa's sweetest gift haiku may be this.

とし玉を天窓におくやちいさい子　一茶
toshidama o atama ni oku ya chiisai ko　issa 1823
(year-gift[+obj] head-on place! small child)

placing the gift
on top of his head
a young child

Perhaps because my parents had us jumping for sardines (like dolphins at the seaquarium), I first imagined Issa putting it on *his* head to make the tiny child jump for it, but then, recalling Issa's poem about his girl's mistaken praying to the Hôrai, realized that this child was imitating the most polite adult manner of receiving a gift – raising it up to forehead level while bowing slightly so that it did seem to be over the head for a moment – and ended up actually setting it on top of his head.

一番のとし玉ぞ其豆な顔　一茶
ichiban no toshidama yo sono mame no kao　issa 1821
(first=best year-gift/gem=roundthing, hey, that diligent/healthy face)

my best present	my best gift
is to see your attentive	this year is yours: that fat
gem of a face	and happy face

First=best, gift=round=bean=attentive-&/or-healthy. Englishing this fairly well-known *ku* is hopeless. According to some commentators, Issa expresses his thankfulness for his wife, Kiku, I wonder. The year *before* he married, Issa wrote *"A gem is a gem / what a year-gift=gem, / your attentive face!"* (玉も玉御とし玉ぞまめな顔　一茶 *tama mo tama otoshidama zo mame na kao*). This could describe a faithful *dog*, or child, intent upon getting said gift. Emily Dickinson was wrong to think sincerity was confined to the deathbed. *Pure expression of honest emotions* can be found in *dogs intent to serve* or *children intent to have*. Both are pleasant to see. But, it is also possible Issa intended another meaning of *mame*, "fat and happy," rather than "attentive." Anyone raised in poverty would appreciate *that* and the delight is better for being pure (Isn't the least admirable side of "our" Judeo-Christian-Islamic God his insecure craving to be worshipped and obeyed?). Another version of the *ichiban-no ku* makes it seem like a trade:

とし玉に見せ申也豆な顔　一茶
toshidama ni mise môsu nari mame na kao issa -1827
(year-gem/coins-for show[me] ask-am beany/diligent/healthy face)

for *my* NY present
i beg you to show me
your *mame* face!

This would surely be a child, for bashfulness is cured by age. Substitute "fat" or "chipper" for *mame* (literally, "beany") as you wish.

いく廻り目だぞとし玉扇又もどる　一茶
iku mawarime da zo toshidama ôgi mata modoru issa -1827
(how many circles is it, hey/hell, year-gift fan again return)

new year's present

how many times
around? that fan we gave
is back again!

Japanese, who are buried in gifts, must recycle or go broke. Today, there are professional gift-brokers to help by paying for gifts and trading so that the same gift does not end up returning home.

とし玉茶どこを廻て又もどる　一茶
toshidama-cha doko o mawatte mata modoru? issa -1827
(year-gift-tea, where circulating again return?)

new year's circulation

my present of tea
just whom has it visited
before returning?

Why so many Issa ku in this chapter? As noted, he left us 29 to chose from. By contrast, the Kaizôsha *saijiki*, which usually serves me well, has only 8 *ku* by Shiki or earlier poets, and the largest *saijiki* of all, Shiki's 200,000+ *Categorized* Haiku anthology, boasts but 17! I do not know why there are so few. Perhaps there are abundant *toshidama* in anthologies I am not lucky enough to own.

お年玉小さいじゅんにくれました　尾崎亜紀子
otoshidama chiisai jun ni kuremashita   ozaki akiko, age 10
([honorific+]year-gem/gift, small order-in received[as gift])

post-war order

new year's presents
we got ours in order
of smallness

Which is to say – the Japanese is likewise ambiguous – *starting with the smallest child*. My title reflects the fact that prior to the American Occupation, the order of the present reception would most likely have been the opposite in many if not most houses.

徐に徐に出すお年玉　一夜　右脳俳句
omomuro ni omomuro ni dasu otoshidama   hitoyo late-20c
(gradually, gradually, take-out/give [hon.+]year-gem [present])

little by little
i come up with their
otoshidama

This haiku was found on a haiku site (mostly in Japanese) called "right-brain-haiku." I wish I could translate it better, for it is the only haiku by an adult that I feel is up to the child's haiku with which I began the chapter! Can't you imagine the elderly poet stretching out the giving process, to gain more time with the adorable children and, perhaps, make them beg a little? Outrageous as it might seem to readers who deny their natural feelings in obedience to the dictates of egalitarian philosophy, *such begging can be very endearing* and the honest confession of the poet is a perfect complement for the kick of joy felt by the child who pockets his or her present. As I have noted many times, the New Year is marked by the paradoxical co-existence of proper etiquette *and* honest feelings.

BOOK I

Postscript

Unlike the holothurian haiku with their clear metaphors (paradoxically, including *ambiguity* and *formlessness*), that made me confident my first book of translated haiku, *Rise, Ye Sea Slugs!* would be well received by all readers boasting something noticeably lacking in the animal subject, *i.e.*, a brain, I am afraid the abstract nature of many *ku* in some of the initial chapters of *this* book may bore not a few readers and that worries me, for my nature is that of a child at Show & Tell: I want to share my delight and entertain. I can only hope my effort to fill the apparent vacuity of those *ku* with humor made most of them passable if not interesting even to readers who are not soulmates of those Germans described by Nietzsche as enamored of "clouds and all that is obscure, evolving" and think "everything uncertain, undeveloped, self-displacing, and growing is 'deep'" (*Beyond Good and Evil*).   BOOK II, with the exception of its first chapter, *the New Year as Birthday for all,* will be more *substantial* and, I dare say – to use a term learned in the course of researching *Rise* – provide a more satisfying *mouthfeel.*

However, my favorite chapter in this whole volume (Book I+Book II) was in this BOOK I. The *Mountain of Youth* everlasting, Hôrai, enthralled me. I am afraid I will have to return to Japan to finish sorting out the various images and names which are just too hard to make out at a distance – or find a student of the subject to help me gloss the next edition – but I am satisfied that I have done my best, for I have already been rewarded . . . *with a dream* the very night I finished that chapter.

> I was standing in my mother's 10th floor condominium overlooking the Atlantic. I was perhaps 20 feet back from the plate-glass windows and the room was full of people. There was a party. A banana leaf in the larger of the two banana trees standing just outside the windows suddenly began to quiver as if it were being pulled by an invisible dog shaking its head as it tugged, or a fish trying to pull its head from a clam (The memory is visible, not the metaphors which I make now) and, before the shaking got violent, it parted from the tree and shot up into the air like a bottle-rocket at about 70 or 80 degrees. As it went higher and higher, it slowed and I could see the vivid green leaf as clear as if it were a foot away against a crystal clear blue sky (I ate tofu and umeboshi that night, if you wonder). It made wave-like motions (dolphining like that Japanese Olympian, underwater) to keep going even higher, and the moment it dissappeared, suddenly appeared again. The tiny mote fell slowly at first (doubtless the perspective since it came from far away) and as it

came close enough to be noticeably green I believe I saw, barely, for it picked up so great a speed as it neared to become a swoosh of motion, that it had not turned around but merely reversed course, i.e., it was stem, or butt-first. At the instant its speed made it invisible, the leaf shot right through the window and the building, for otherwise the angle doesn't match, and landed next to my left foot, stem-butt *thumping* on the black slate floor. I reached out and caught it and, as I did so, *saw*: the stem had a neat half-hitch in it and, more amazing yet, the leaf was perfect, without a single tear. Then, I noticed an Indian guru near to the window in a white robe and I thought, with a measure of the skepticism that remains even in my dreams, that a certain French yogi who had lived downstairs from me but was in France at the time had cleverly thought to challenge my lack of belief in miracles by showing me one concocted by said guru whom she had sent for that purpose into my dream. *Clever, Janine, clever,* I thought. At the same time, I was grateful for the sensory experience – I had never seen colors that intense – and honored by being honored, though I can not recall if anyone else in the room even noticed it. And, I came to the conclusion (still within the dream, mind you) that I was being thanked by the plant spirits for my good deeds, for my love. Months before, I dug up the banana trees in a garden where they were imprisoned behind a tall wall and got almost no sunlight whatsoever. Now, they enjoyed a 10th floor ocean view and a healthy dose of sun. I also rescued some hibiscus plants from a trash pile and, for a moment, recall thinking as I did so that it was odd we had a *Society for the Prevention of Cruelty to Animals* but nothing for *plants*. Where are our shelters, nurseries, for abandoned flora? Is *that* fair?

The Magical Mountain did not actually appear in my dream, but the mood it created made it possible. I do not know if any charm does much good for our waking, or outside lives, but I can testify to their influence upon the stream of dreams within. ☆

the new year's here
all the wealth in my house
this star-lit sky

☆ A <u>star-moon night</u> is one with a clear sky when the stars shine brightly, as brightly as the moon, which is absent. Kikaku may mean his house lacked even have the few sacks of rice mentioned by Bashô. Because Kikaku was noted for his heavy drinking, I cannot help hoping to discover there was a <u>sake</u> with that brand name. (いかがでしょう？) New Year's come! / Everything I own / is in the stars! ★ This starry night: / all I own & all I bring / to the New Year!

new year's here!
a plump bale of rice on the tatami
元日やたたみのうへに米俵　北枝
ganjitsu ya tatami no ue ni komedawara   hokushi -1718
(original-day:/! tatami-upon rice-bale[such as prosperity sat on])

new year's here
neat on my *tatami*
bales of rice

my new year
on the tatami, one
bale of rice

bales of rice
upon green tatami
our first day

a
plump
bale of rice
on the tatami:
happy new year!

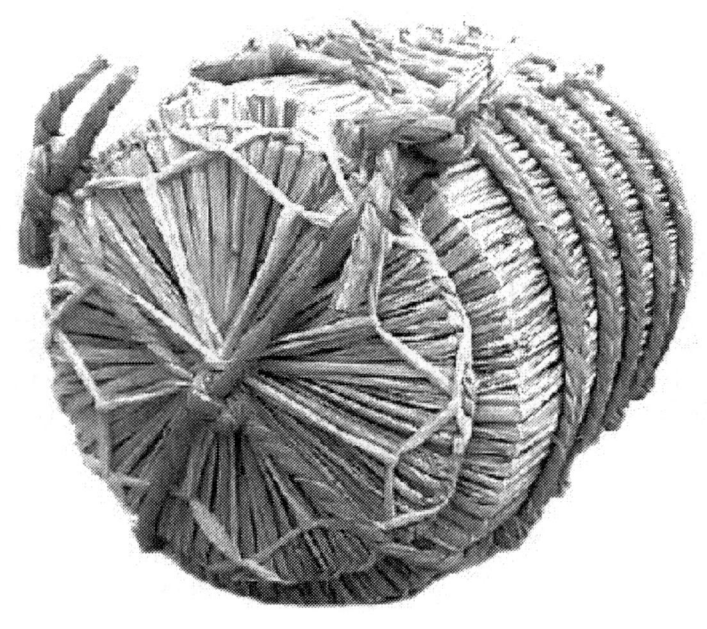

Can anyone find me some good *tatami* to go under the bale of rice floated off the w.w. web?   よろしくお願いします！ rdg

Eventually, chapters 11-21 will be a separate

Book

II

of

4

of

The New Year

And all books will have illustrations and larger print, or narrower margins.
For now, I must print them together to offer abundance at a decent price.

元日や我も一人と数へられ 芳洲 新葉
ganjitsu ya ware mo hitori to kazoerare   hôshû 1856
(new-year's!/: i too one[person]-as counted/included-am)

♪ ***Oh, when the spring . . .*** ♪

it's new year's
count me in as one
of that number

一切の祝ひはしめや玉の春 牛長 俳諧人名録
issai no iwaihajime ya tamanoharu   gyûchô / gyûan 牛庵-1693?
(all celebrating/celebration-start:/! gem/precious-spring)

    this is the start   precious spring
  of all celebration: this is the start of all
     precious spring   our celebrating

元日や玉に角ある人心 梅室
ganjitsu ya tama ni kado aru hitogokoro   baishitsu -1852
(orig.day[ny's]:/! gem=ball-upon corners/keenness has human-heart)

it's the new year
our hearts beautifully round
with keen corners

草も木もめてたさう也けさの春 良春 狗
kusa mo ki mo medetasô nari kesa no haru   ryôshun 1633
(grasses/shrubs/flowers and trees happy/celebratory-become today's spring)

    even the trees   even flowers
and shrubs seem joyful   and trees seem happy
     spring today   today's spring

~~~~~~

The first *ku* is a wonderful summation of the Japanese idea of the New Year as a joyous communion, a celebration in which all the world participates. We will develop one way of experiencing this, New-Year's-as-birthday, in chapter 11. The third *ku* on this page requires a word of explanation. While mellow, *i.e.*, psychologically speaking, *as round as a gem*, we are also full of hope and keen to read significance into everything. Hence, the sharp "corners," the contradiction of edges on a ball/gem (*Diamonds are forever?*).

日も人も松も新たな春也けり 好水 大三
hi mo hito mo matsu mo arata na haru narikeri kôsui 1697
(sun and people and pine new/afresh spring becomes[+emph.])

the sun, people
and pines: to each
a new spring

spring is new
for days, for people
for pine trees

春立や翌へと延す事斗　都貢
haru tatsu ya asu e to nobasu koto bakari tokô 18c?
(spring rises/comes/! tomorrow-toward stretch things only)

today all things
stretch for tomorrow
spring is here!

蛤の口より伊勢の初日哉 子規 明治三十四
hamaguri no kuchi yori ise no hatsuhi kana shiki 1901
(clam's mouth-from ise's [place with sun's cave] first-sun/day!/'tis)

from the mouth
of an ise clam balloons
the first-day

first-sunrise
at ise from the mouth
of a mollusk

かしこくも月日の童べ三の朝 素外 句鑑
kashikoku mo tsukibi no warabe mitsu no asa sogai 1777
(politely/smartly/fearfully-even moon-sun's child/ren three's morning)

moon sun year
one for all and all for one
this morning

天地の和合らく也三の朝 一十 安永四
ametsuchi no yawaragu nari mitsu no asa ichijû 1775
(heaven-earth's soften/fuse-become three's morning)

the tri-morning
when heaven and earth
blend together

heaven & earth
soften at dawn, when
three are one

The third *ku* is a bit odd, but if we are to have birthdays, we must have *births* and that is one way to do it. We have discussed Ise – remember Bashô's *ku* with the salty tidings and spiny lobster? – but not the clam. It was thought to exhale the mysterious mirage worlds that appeared in the horizon. Associated with the body part from which we all come into this world, it also evokes the cave the Sun Goddess was enticed from . . . We met the three children, Sun (day), Moon (month) and Year together in a *ku* (*haru wa kozo . .*) in chapter 4 (*Up and Adam*). The penultimate *ku* only mentions the moon and sun as "kids," but the-morning-of-the-three means *year+moon+day*. The last *ku* suggests to me that *becoming* is not just morphing but combining Fusion.

おらが春・花の春
ora-ga-haru, hana-no-haru

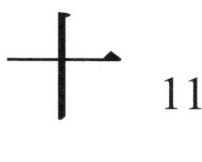 11

EVERYONE'S BIRTHDAY

ぬけて出る夜着よりすぐに花の春　成美
nuketederu yogi yori sugu ni hananoharu　seibi　1748-1816
(slipping-out-nightdress-from immediately flower/y/beautiful/festive spring)

popping out
of my nightrobe, right
into the spring

just outside
the pajama cocoons
flowery spring

slipping out
of her night-dress
spring blooms

splendid spring
as soon as we shed
our nightdress

It is fun to imagine pajamas on the *tatami* (straw-mat flooring), empty legs resembling a snake skin; but you *should* imagine a robe and, unless this *ku* can be dated to the year after the Year of the Snake, the better metaphor would be *an abandoned cocoon*. The poet, or all of us (the third reading is unlikely), immediately don/s his/our "flower/floral," which is to say, *celebratory*, garb and leave/s the nightwear as is. This scenario would be impossible in the Occident where the departure of the Old Year and arrival of the New Year is celebrated at midnight alone and there is no New Year's morning to speak of (unless we include *the year's first hang-over!*) To properly *feel* Seibi's poem, we must combine elements of *birthday*, *Christmas* and *Easter* mornings with *New Year's Eve* and (if Usanian) the 4th *of July*. In Book 1, we covered the respect paid to the rising sun; the timeless magic of the New Year and its greetings. Now, we will focus on the *New Year, or Spring-as-celebration*.

> . . . the poor little Japanese baby is ushered into this world in a sadly impersonal manner, for he is not even accorded the distinction of a birthday. He is permitted instead only the much less special honor of a birth-year. . . . *New Year's day is a common birthday for the community, a sort of impersonal anniversary for his whole world.* . . A communistic age is however but an unavoidable detail of the general scheme whose most suggestive feature consists in the subordination of the actual birthday of the individual to the fictitious birthday of the community. . . . *Then [New Year's day] everybody congratulates everybody else upon everything in general, and incidentally upon being alive.* Such substitution of an abstract for a concrete birthday, although exceedingly convenient for others, must at least conduce to self-forgetfulness on the part of its proper possessor, and tend inevitably to merge the identity of the individual in that of the community. (Percival Lowell: *Soul of the Far East:* 1888, my *italics*)

While it is true that individual birthdays as we know them were rarely celebrated in Japan until Japanese Westernized in the 20c, Lowell's splendid generalization – incorporating the prejudicial idea of the individual as real and the collective as fictitious – fails on two accounts. First, Japanese pay far more attention to *death*days than we do.[1] This speaks more to awareness of true individuality than *birth*days do, for we have less responsibility for our birth than our death. And second, from 16c Portuguese writings, we know the Chinese – the very soul of Lowell's "Far East" – celebrated individual birthdays (on the proper day and month, too) *before* the West paid them much account. Perhaps the biggest difference between such birthdays and those we celebrate today is that birthdays counted *more* with each passing year rather than *less*. Since we are born utterly worthless (except as potential) and only acquire our character and humanity with the passage of time, this makes sense.

親の年を子に祝ひけりけさの春　鴎玉
oya no toshi o ko ni iwaikeri kesa no haru　ôgyoku 18c?19c?20c?
(parent's age[obj] child-by/to celebrate/congratulate[+emph.]: morning's spring=ny)

the parent's age	congratulating
celebrated by the child	a son for his parent's age
today is spring	a new year's here

What at first glance might seem evidence for feting the aged in Japan, could contradict it – for what poet would describe the normal? Let me back-step and qualify the assertions made in the last paragraph. The most broadly celebrated *collective* birthdays were those of children, more specifically, those of 3, 5 or 7 years, who dressed up for special visits to shrines and other ceremonies. Excluding coming-of-age ceremonies, which in sparsely populated ruralities could include several year-cohorts, individual birthyears were modestly celebrated once every twelve years (when one's year-animal came around), until one reached a venerable age when they began to matter. Old *ku* mention turning 50 or 60 and, more rarely, for obvious reasons, 80 and 88. So, a more balanced view would be that both the young and old were celebrated. This seeming contradiction parallels that of the New Year itself, a time to think ahead *and* bond with the past. Grammar suggests my first reading, allowing the *ku* to allude to something larger, that we humans are the children of the cosmos, is likely to be wrong.

けふよりや咲ける咲かざる花の春　宗因 再現
kyô yori ya sakeru sakazaru hananoharu　sôin 1604-1682
(today-from blooms blooms-not floral/happy/celebr./beautiful spring)

it's from today	whatever the year
bloom or no bloom	should bring, let's cheer:
flowery spring	spring is spring!

The *hana-no-haru* with which the original ends, literally translates as "flower-spring," "flowers' spring," "floral spring," "spring of the flowers" or "flowery spring." Blyth usually used the last. I prefer to use one of the connotative meanings, such as *precious* or *beautiful*, but in this poem the "bloom" or "bloom-not" plays along with the literal meaning, so I use it for the first reading. If this *ku* were modern, I would guess it was a cold year and the plum was slow to bloom.   With an old *ku*, the

---

1. ***Death-days in Haiku.*** People in haiku circles know the death-day of any number of poets and it is common to write *ku* mentioning one's favorites (and, today, posting them that day on the internet). While a deathday itself is seasonal (so, strictly speaking, no other seasonal item is necessary), there usually is something seasonal also reflecting the character of the poet or his/her work in the *ku*. The New Year's section has no such *ku* for they are anthologized with the Spring and the New Year is a time for celebrating life not death.

blooming may only be figurative, as per the second reading, or have been intentionally both. English is not dead to the figurative flower, for we speak of men being in the "flower of their youth" and, less obviously, of a *flourishing*, i.e. "flowering civilization;" but, generally speaking, "flower" as an adjective in English conjures up images of flowers, while the same in Japanese modifies *anything connected with celebration or extravagance.* And, the New Year was, as a matter of fact, a celebration of a real flower (the bloom of the flowering plum (apricot)). Lowell, again:

> If the anniversaries of people are slightly treated in this land of the sunrise, the same cannot be said for plants. The yearly birthdays of the vegetable world are observed with more than botanic enthusiasm. The regard in which they are held is truly emotional, and if not actually individual in its object, at least personal to the species. Each kind of tree as its season brings it into flower is made the occasion of a festival. (L:SOFE)

Lowell's main contrast between an individualistic West and an impersonal (dehumanized?) Far East, a Japan that took a primitive level of civilization to its full development but missed growing up like the West did, is a debatable – and in some aspects, reprehensible – piece of Orientalism; but I can find no fault in his remarks on flowering trees. It is a fact: in Japan, the flowering tree identified with the New Year, the *ume* (plum/apricot), may be thought to share its "yearly birthday" with other Japanese.

木の母をたが云初（いいそめ）て花の兄　慶友 いのこ
ki no haha o taga iisomete hana no ani   keiyû 1633
(tree-mother[obj] who said-first flower-elder-brother)

a flower with seniority

who first said you
were the mother of trees
big brother plum

The Chinese character for "plum" 梅 has a *mother* 母 radical next to the *tree* 木 radical because the two dots representing nipples resemble little plums. I do not know if that is the correct etymology, but it is what the poet might have thought. While parents do precede their children, they are themselves someone's child and hence unsuitable symbols for unquestionable seniority. So the (Chinese) label "elder brother [1] of flowers-[2]" was thought more appropriate by this poet.

去年咲て今年や二つ花の兄　由廷 毛吹草
kozo saite kotoshi ya futatsu hana no ani   yûtei 1645
(last year bloomed this year two, flower's big brother)

Happy New Year

blooming last year   blooming last year
this year, big brother   he's now two years old
plum turns two   big brother plum

The first reading assumes the plum blossomed early, just before the New Year. Being "born" in the last year makes it a year-old already by the Sinosphere's inclusive count,[3] and with the coming of the New Year, two years old. The second reading assumes the young plum bloomed for the first time the previous Spring, and the poet is fond enough of it to note it is now gaining another year. Either way, flowers, *the* symbol of celebration, are themselves celebrated in this *ku*.

1. Elder Brother. English lacks separate terms for elder and younger brothers or sisters. This handicaps translation. "Elder/big/younger/little brother/sister" is too long for most haiku and description makes poor poetry.

2. The Plum is a Flower. In Japanese, *a flower is a flower is a flower,* whether it is a little plant close to the ground or a huge tree. In Spring, "flower" tends to mean a flowering *tree* in bloom, whereas, in the fall, it means the wild-flowers of the field. I usually abide by the English speaker's common practice of calling tree flowers "blossoms," but sometimes use "flower" to make a point about the Japanese connotation. When the Chinese influence on the literary culture of Japan was strongest, the word "flower" (*hana*) by itself was applied to the plum blossom or plum tree; but over the centuries it came to mean what it almost always means in haiku, the cherry blossom or tree. (For details, see *Cherry Blossom Epiphany*). There are some cherry blossom *waka* that seem to conflate the New Year's Cele-bration and individual birthdays. For example, *Kokinshû* (905) *waka* #349, which fetes a man's fortieth birthday, asks the *cherries* to scatter their petals in clouds to hide the way to old age. Annotators call it a *nenga* 年賀 or year-greeting/tribute, something suggesting a New Year's Birthday, but it must have originally been composed later in the Spring at his real birth-date, or anticipated date, though composed on the New Year. More on the birth-date problem at the chapter's end may repeat some of this.

3. *Inclusive Count*. A large unit comprised of many smaller units may be counted before or after the small units are expended. The reason a baby is "born a year old" in the East is not so much because the pregnancy is included (as is often noted), but for the same reason Japanese gain a year the moment the New Year arrives, which is why we now live in the Twenty-first rather than Twentieth Century.

這へ笑へニッになるぞけさからは 一茶
hae warae futatsu ni naru zo kesa kara wa   issa 1764-1827
(crawl! smile! two-to become [exclam.] this morning=new-year-from-as-for)

to my girl

crawl! laugh!
from this morning
you are two!

The original was prefaced with a line: "celebrating *zôni* (gruel for a healthy year eaten on the New Year's) with my daughter born last May, *like other people*." It is hard to know whether this means Issa was proud of his daughter eating like a grown-up at so young an age or happy to at last enjoy a normal domestic life at his advanced age. As the reader may ascertain from what has already been written about age in the Sinosphere, children never *turned* one, for they were considered to be in their first year as soon as they were born. Had Sato been born only a day before, she would still have turned two with the New Year. Two *ku* ago, I made the poet directly address the plum tree, though he did not in the original. In the next *ku*, the original is direct and I had only to add the pronoun "you," because English demands it:

けふさくは年づよなれや花の兄 望一 狗猥
kyô saku wa toshizuyo nare ya hana no ani   môichi 1633
(today bloom-as-for, year/age-strong become! flower's big-brother)

advice to a plum tree

gain the age
advantage, big brother
bloom, today!

Toshizuyo means "born in the first half of the year." As someone born premature, underweight and toward the end of the year (the disadvantaged side of the age cohort), I know all too well what it means.

飛梅やかろ／＼しくも神の春　守武
tobiume ya karogaroshiku mo kami-no-haru moritake 1473-1549
(flying-plum[tree]: lightly/effortlessly even gods'=paper spring/new-year)

how lightly
flies the faithful plum!
gods' spring

Moritake was head priest of Shintô's head Shrine at Ise. Hence "god's/gods' spring." According to legend, the flying plum belonged to a historical figure, Sugawara no Michizane (菅原道真 845-903). After court intrigues forced him to move, Michizane wrote a poem which cursorily translates as *"When East Winds blow / send me your sweet scent / my blooming plum! / Though your master's gone, / Do not forget the Spring!"* (*kochi fukaba nioi okose yo umenohana arujinashi tote haru na wasure so*). The tree was so moved they say it flew over to his new garden. The fact Michizane was a seminal figure (even, "god") of Japanese literature made the *ku* a proper start for Moritake's 1000-poem volume some consider the start of what came to be haiku. Other eminent *haikai* poets found more perspectives on the famous tree:

飛梅や年飛び越て花の春　徳元 狗 1633
tobimume ya toshi tobikoete hananoharu tokugen 1558-1647
(flying plum[tree]!/: year/s fly-crossing-over flower/floral/festive spring/ny)

oh, flying plum
you've flown across years
the flowery spring

spring blossoms   dear flying plum
the flying plum has flown   across the years you bring
from year to year   the flowery spring

香は四方に飛梅（むめ）ならぬ梅もなし　貞徳 いのこ
ka wa yomo ni tobimume naranu mume mo nashi teitoku 1570-1653
(scent-as-for, four-directions-in flying plum is-not plum's not)

the flying flower

in all directions
flies the scent, no plum
but has its wings

Tokugen and Teitoku are right. In a sense, we all fly even when we don't move. We fly in time and we send out our scent or other tidings like the plum trees, through their blossoms. Still, Moritake's earlier *ku* beats both because the *karogaroshiku*, or "lightly" *feels* right. This lightness, I think, reflects the uplifting spirit of the New Year and reads Michizane's *waka* in an allegorical way to mean *follow your heart*. A third flying plum from the same *Enoko* anthology (1633) pokes fun at the old *waka* in the style somewhere between what would later become *senryû* and surreal poetry, depicting said plum *preening* its leaves/feathers in a grove, presumeably before greeting its old master. Without the *leaf=feather* homophone, translation is meaningless (飛梅の葉づくろひする木立哉　富沢 *tobimume no hazukuroi suru kodachi kana* fukuzawa).

梅にまづけさぞ開けし花の春　宗春 三籟
ume ni mazu kesa zo hirakeshi hananoharu　sôshun　1734
(plum-with/as/by/through/in first, this morn. [+emph] opened flower/precious/festive spring/ny)

it bloomed first
this morning in the plum
flower of spring

flowery spring
first blossomed today
my plum tree

How much freer the relationship of plum and Spring in Japanese, where the post-position *ni* means *with/as/in/through/by*, in English with its more specialized prepositions. So, the second reading . . .

去年からみし梅なれと花の春 岱年 百家類題
kozo kara mishi mume naredo hananoharu　tainen　19c
(last-year-from seen plum [blossom?] is but flower's/celeb. spring)

this plum tree
a familiar sight today
spring in bloom

plum blossoms
out last year are still
the flower of spring

the plum blossoms
an old sight seen anew
in spring's light

plum blossoms
seen last year refresh
new eyes today

Was the tree blossoming before or just there? If the latter, do we have an allegory for someone taken for granted who is appreciated on New Year's Day? But I think we are talking about blossoms.

梅かゝに力添たる初日哉　青巴 玉かつら
ume ga ka ni chikara soetaru hatsuhi kana　seiha　1751
(plum[blossom]scent-by/in/with strength-added/ing first sun/day!/'tis)

giving punch
to the scent of the plum
the first sun

I found it hard to tell *what* was fortified by *what*! Before consulting with a native Japanese-speaker, I had three readings. The other two: *"I'm fortified / by the scent of the plum / the first day"* and *"The first sun / waxing in the scent / of the plum."* Regardless, we are talking blossoms, not fruit.

人の気からけさは柳に匂ひあり 亀林 大三物
hito no ki kara kesa wa yanagi ni nioi ari　kirin　1697
(people's-spirit-from this-morning-as-for, willow-with scent/glow is/has)

new year spirit

from our *chi*
the willow this morning
has a scent

our senses
today give scent
to willows

I used the Chinese pronunciation of what Japanese pronounce *ki,* for it has made it into the vocabulary of some English speakers. Recall that *scent* in Japanese also means a beautiful glow.

峰／＼や雲をかさりて花の春　路及 三千花
mine mine ya kumo o kazarite hananoharu   rokyû 1725
(peak-peak:/! cloud decorated/boasts flower/festive-spring)

<blockquote>

every peak
blessed with a cloud
spring blooms

flowery spring
each and every peak
wears a cloud

</blockquote>

These are not miscreant mountain-hiding clouds, but pretty trimmings and gallant pennants. Auspicious clouds were portents of the New Year and flowery because they were stereotypically confused with blossoms. Since wild cherry (not to bloom for another month or two) and not plum was the big bloomer on the mountain sides, clouds were the only "flowers" visible from afar on New Year's. The peaks, too, were enjoying their birthday/year parties if it were.

春立ては雪さへ花のふゝき哉　宗碩
haru tateba yuki sae hana no fubuki kana   sôseki 1474-1533
(spring/new-year comes-if/when snow-even flower's/celebratory blizzard 'tis)

<blockquote>

with the new year
even the snow becomes
a blossom blizzard

as spring dawns
even a blizzard ends up
floral confetti

spring has come
even blizzards become
snow flowers!

</blockquote>

Blossom blizzard is standard idiom for a heavy petal-fall. This *ku* reverses the metaphor. Everything of the New Year, including the year/spring itself, was pretty, and this old *ku* expresses it well indeed.

春来ぬといへば花なる言葉哉　宗砌
haru kinu to ieba hananaru kotoba kana   sôzei -1455
("spring comes[elegant style]" said-when/if flower-become words!/'tis)

<blockquote>

having said
"spring doth come," words
become flowers

"spring is here"
we say and our words
are the flowers

</blockquote>

This vision of flowers everywhere seems almost psychopathic, but in a good way. Note that words are literally *leaves* in Japanese, so the relationship is not forced.

年の花富士はつほめる姿哉　糵塒
toshinohana fuji wa tsubomeru sugata kana   shiji 18c?19c?
(year's blossom, [mount]fuji-as-for, budding form 'tis/!)

<blockquote>

the year-flower
and fuji is the form
of its bud.

</blockquote>

春立や天に匂へるふしの山 可都里 題業名
haru tatsu ya ten ni nioeru fujinoyama   katori 1742-1817
(spring-appears/rises/! heaven-until smells/glows fuji mountain)

spring dawns
and the scent of fuji
mounts to heaven

Even a mountain "bud" turns into a flower and, blooming, participates in the annual celebration. Fuji may have released a bit of smoke that New Year, but it would not be necessary for a figurative reading.

曙の星からさくや花の春 泊楓 桃の首途
akebono no hoshi kara saku ya hananoharu hakufû 1728
(dawn's star-from blooms! flowery-spring)

it blooms
from the star of dawn
flower-spring

Venus is also called the "Gold Star" – *gold* being the color of Spring (not Goddess of Love in the Sinosphere). But that is enough full treatment for "flower=spring" poems.   Most are not worth it:

>Flower spring: / A whole year's bud bursts / into into bloom.
>(一年の蒼は今そ花の春   吟江 *hitotoshi no tsubomi wa ima zo hananoharu* – ginkô 1776?)

>Spring dawning: / Does a blossom bloom / in the heart too?
>(心にも花さくものかけさの春   吟江 心花 *kokoro ni mo hana saku mono ka kesanoharu* – ginkô 1776).

>The heart's blossom / is the first to open / Spring dawns
>(先開く心の花やけさの春 晴風大三/百漂 安4 *mazu hiraku kokoronohana ya kesanoharu* – seifû 1697/1795)

>It's New Year's! / Flower minds in the capital / and the country.
>(元日や都もひなも花心   良石 *ganjitsu ya miyako mo hina mo hanagokoro* – ryôseki 1795)

>The Year-flower / blooms with its bounty of / days and months
>(日月の恵に咲や年の花   梅郷 *nichi getsu no megumi ni saku ya toshinohana* – baigô 1759)

The last *ku* creates food for metaphysical thought – a year does not pop out of a vacuum but is fertilized or stuffed by the previous year – but all of these seem more like aphorisms than poems.

~~~~~~

<div align="center">
月雪にやしなはれてそ花の春 士朗
tsuki yuki ni yashinawarete zo hananoharu   shirô 1742 - 1813
(moon-snow-by nourished/raised [+emph.] flower's/floral/abundant/celebratory spring)
</div>

its nourishment the moonshine and snow blooming spring	'tis cultured by our poetry by god glorious spring

My "by god" in the second reading is the emphatic *zo* in the original. The buds on some species of trees do indeed form in the Fall when Buddhists and poets practice moon-viewing and quicken in the snow – so we might say the religion of death and the cold create the bloom of warmth. It is also witty to have the third of the poetic triumvirate moon-snow-blossom (*tsuki-yuki-hana*, meaning poetic *savoir faire*), a product of the other two. Shirô's *ku* may be a response to the following older one:

月雪は人の欲也花の春　雨声 玉かづら
tsuki yuki wa hito no yoku nari hananoharu　usei 1751
(moon-snow-as-for, people's-avarice/desire-become, blossom-spring)

<table>
<tr><td>moon and snow
reflect the greed of man
flowery spring</td><td>gala spring
adding poetry to this
is avarice</td></tr>
</table>

Unfortunately for readers who desire certitude, there are other possible readings of Usei's *ku*.: "**Scarcity** // *Flowers bloom: / now our desire is / the moon and snow.*" "**Avarice** // *Man would dress / the beautiful flower spring / with moon and snow.*" Snow would not be rare, but the New Year begins on the new moon and would *never* have moonlight. So the desire, read literally, is a vain one. As one *ku* puts it, *"How happy / I'd be for moon-light but / it's flower spring!"* (月の夜になるうれしさを花の春　屋烏 新五百題 *tsuki no yo ni naru ureshisa o hana no haru*　yau 1819). Or is it, rather: *"This joy like / a full moon night: / flower spring!"*?

Spring as a birthday-like celebration → flowery modification → the celebration of flowering trees → year-as-flower → its culture, and finally to the above exchange. Let us get back on track:

天地父母孤なるものなしけさの春　唱
tenchifubo hitori naru mono nashi kesa no haru　shô? 1775
(heaven-earth father-mother orphan is/become one not, this-morning's spring)

<table>
<tr><td>heaven and earth
two parents, no one's alone
on the new year</td><td>heaven & earth
we all have parents
on new year's</td></tr>
</table>

Family rhetoric fits the idea of the New-Year-as-birthday. In the original, the heaven=father, earth=mother are more clearly parallel, but the words would not fit in the translation.

春そけさ國にまゝ子の何あらん　易貞 同書入
haru zo kesa kuni ni mamako no nani aran　ekitei 18c?
(spring[emphatic] this-morning country-in stepchild what is-not)

this morning
is spring, not a stepchild
in the land

In *The Tale of Genji*, a book some consider the world's first novel, Murasaki explains that despite the children's stories about evil stepmothers, the reality was that most are not mean to their step-children, but a thousand years later, "stepchild" was still synonymous with being a lonely, mistreated outsider.

正直に生れ代わりてけさの春 休甫 類題発句集
shôjiki ni umare kawarite kesanoharu   kyûho 1774
(honestly/uprightly born-changed/ing morning's spring)

new year, new man

born again
honest to goodness
this morning

spring dawns
and we are reborn
righteously

The two characters for the Sino-Japanese word for "honest" are 正 "correct/straight" and 直 "straight/[right]angle/direct." This would seem to be a Confucian honesty that Englishes as *rectitude,* as opposed to the more Japanese (and Taoist) *sunao* which equates honesty with *going along gently with the flow of things.* Perhaps, English can come up with a closer match for the characters:

> on this, the dawn
> of the new year we are
> reborn upright

We have considered Lowell's idea of Japanese birthday/year as different from the Occidental birthday by virtue of being collective. Another difference would be that the Occidental birthday, excluding the *one to grow on,* is all about *aging,* whereas the old-fashioned Japanese birthday always includes *a strong element of rebirth,* of return to the naïve (meant in a *good* way) beginning before our minds became warped. Every New Year, we have an entire nation of *Born-again Japanese.*

元日や千代重ねても／＼ 酒笑 安永四
ganjitsu ya chiyo kasanete mo kasanete mo   shushô 1775
(original[new-year's]/first day:/! piled-up/repeated-even *ditto*)

new year's day
though countless reigns
should pass

the first day
though reign should fall
upon reign

The world, by virtue of constantly dying to be reborn, never ages and we may participate in that everlasting life through death. The character I translated as "first" is 元 "original" and the original is by definition "well" 元気 (the second character, *ki,* is the *chi* discussed earlier).

元日や先改まる雞の声 眉峰 安永六
ganjitsu ya mazu aratamaru tori no koe   bihô 1777
(original[ny]day:/! first renew rooster's voice)

origin day
rooster's crow is first
to refresh

it's origin day
the first reformation is
cockadoodledoo!

The verb *aratamaru* means to remake, renew or improve. It is generally applied to the year. As Thoreau wrote, nothing is so exhilarating or "all nature-compelling" as a rooster's crowing. I checked the year and, sure enough, this *ku* was written in the Year of the Cock!

先つ空に通ふ心やけさの春　嘯谷 俳諧五百題
mazu sora ni kayou kokoro ya kesa no haru shôkoku 18-19c
(first sky-in/with commute mind/heart:/! morning's spring)

first our minds
criss-crossing the sky
as spring dawns

first the heart
communes with heaven
spring dawn

new year dawn
first of all our feelings
fill the sky

The rooster generally crows before the sun actually comes up, so I was not sure whether the last poem was about the first crow heard in the lightening dark or one heard after sun-up. I suspect that what one woke up to was already the New Year by definition, but do not know. Likewise, with the above-mentioned sky: how dark/bright is it?

元日やされば野川の水の音　来山
ganjitsu ya sareba nogawa no mizu no oto raizan -1716
(original[ny]day:/! ah/aha, field-river/stream's water's sound)

what is this!

it's new year's day
from the stream in the field
the sound of water

it's new year's day
is that the sound of a stream
flowing through the field?

The *sareba* expresses both surprise at the unexpected and recognition of something expected, both of which are appropriate, for the sound of water was long associated with the coming of Spring yet one was not always lucky enough to hear it. As Blyth, who used an "*ah*" for his translation, wrote about this *ku* and New Year's Day, *"Everything is the same, everything is different."* Yes, it is seen with new eyes and heard with new ears.

元日や古き姿もあたらしき　吟江
ganjitsu ya furuki sugata mo atarashiki ginkô c1780
(original day! old figure/form/appearance too/also/even new)

first day
even the old
seems new

家内にも客ぶりのあり今朝の春　惟艸
kanai ni mo kyakuburi no ari kesa no haru isô -1853
(wife-even guest-behavior/appearance is morning's spring)

New Year's Day

even my wife
acts like a guest
this morning

even the wife
behaves like a guest
this morning

If the entire world is new, it is unfamiliar, hence exotic.[1] In Blyth's words, "even such a thing as his wife, than [sic] whom is nothing more unstimulating and flat, in her dress, her manner, her surpressed excitement appears like a new creature." (*Haiku* vol 2) [see ch 14, *kiso-hajime,* on *that* effect]. In other words, it is as if they had just met. A rebirth of *their* spring. But Blyth and I overdo the magic. Do you recall the *gyokei,* the New Year's greetings of chapter 7? Wife and husband would exchange the same. *Formally.* The "the" before the wife in my second reading comes from an ex-navy man with a Japanese wife living up the street in Palolo Valley (Hawaii) in 1977. I do not know how common an expression *"the* wife" is, but it seemed absolutely *perfect* here.

老の後は猶めつらしやけふの春　宗因
oi no nochi wa nao mezurashi ya kyô no haru sôin 1604-82
(aged-after-as-for, still rare/strange/precious! today's spring/new-years)

it's here today!

old, i still
do not take the spring
for granted

always rare   *everexotic*

though i am old   though i'm old
some things never jade   the spring today is still
today it's spring   full of curios

To say something or someone is *mezurashi,* or "rare," in Japanese is to say it/he/she is a welcome sight. The character "rare" 珍 written with "taste" 味 means gourmet delicacies, 珍味, with "thing" "curios/novelties/antiques."[2] The connotation in English is not as strong as in Japanese, so I used *gyakuyaku,* or inverse-translation (for *not-*jaded, *not* taken for granted).

それも應これも應なりけさの（老の）春　涼菟 俳諧古選
sore mo ô kore mo ô nari oi no [also, *kesa-no*] *haru*   ryôto (1658-1717)
(that too splendid! this too splendid is/becomes elder's [also, this morning's] spring)

that is good, *this* too is good
new year's day
in my old age

(trans. blyth, centered plus *italics* but minus punctuation)

---

1. ***Exoticization***   The exotic wife is an extension of the idea of the whole world as different on New Year's Day. An earlier poem: *"On New Year's / the second floor is seen / as strangers"* (元日や二階をよそにしても見る　一清　新草 *ganjitsu ya nikai o yoso ni shite mo miru* issei c.1845). Since proper etiquette in Japanese is called *enryo,* or "far-consideration," the association of formality and distance is obvious and we might say that while the New Year brings the nation together, it also puts a wall between every single person over which they exchange their greetings. Such is, of course, the real wall that keeps our friendship green. This sub-theme also fits well into the "magical" or "dream-time" spring/ny of ch.6 in New Year's Book 1.

2. ***A Rare Equivalent***   I had a married friend at Georgetown (SFS) in the 1970's who constantly harped on his overwhelming desire to "go out and get some *strange."* It was the first time I heard the word used like that. This "strange" as something rare, and therefore desirable shares something with the Japanese *mezurashii,* which is occasionally found in *senryû* where spouses enjoying each other in a different time or place than usual find it *mezurashii,* a "strange" – i.e. thrilling – experience.

Blyth beat my translation so badly I dropped it. The difficulty here is the word said to come out of the old man's mouth. The Chinese character used for "ô" means "wondrous/splendid," but the word itself would be used without thought of such meaning. An elderly man in Japan, even today, acknowledges his interest and approbation of things by letting out a long lasting "o" sound from deep in the throat. That is all. The closest equivalent in English might be "*Wow at this / Wow at that: the New Year / of an old hippy!*" Obviously, *that* wouldn't do. Lacking a word for an old man's expression of pleasure, Blyth did the best he could. He chose a simple word, "good," obviously better than either the "wow" or a "wonderful!" translation (which I cut). Still, *it is not the same*. The original haiku is a masterpiece for using just the right word (Blyth stuck on a page of commentary and poetry, and I can add what you now read, but *nothing* can compensate for the loss in translation!). One version of the original does not mention "old age." Because "oo" is an old man's expression, such information is redundant in Japanese; but, in English, it is needed. I imagine the poet's family pointed out his mannerism, for only someone younger would think it noteworthy. Keigu paraverses:

けさの春おもしろくない物は無し　敬愚
kesanoharu omoshiroku nai mono wa nashi　keigu
(this-morning's spring interesting-not thing-as-for not)

on new year's
nothing is taken
for granted!

よきことの目にも余るや花の春　千代
yoki koto no me ni mo amaru ya hananoharu　chiyo 1701-75
(good things eyes-to-even/too exceed! flower/floral/precious/celebratory spring/ny)

good things   flowery spring!
overflow the eyes, too   too many good things
this spring!   even for the eyes

Here Chiyo, the most famous female haikai poet, actually uses the word "good" (*yoki*). Not just the new bloom and mist gushing out for the mind's primed eye, but New Year's decoration, the well-dressed people and their games . . . I would guess she wrote this in her old age (千代全集お持ちの方、いかがでしょうか？), for this is when we come to realize that the Spring and all in it are our birthday presents if we would only think of them like that. This is one of the "solve-the-*mo*" type *ku*. So, why is it the eyes *"too"* (or, "*even* for the eyes")? My guess is Chiyo means *"as well as for the heart."* At the same time, I feel she may be alluding to a particular poem (*ku* or *waka*) I failed to catch.

古希
一つづゝものなつかしやけさの春　蒼虬
koki // hitotsu zutsu mono natsukashi ya kesanoharu　sôkyu 1760-1842
(old-rare[celeb. of 70ᵗʰ b'day]// 1 by 1 things cherished/familiar! this morning's spring)

celebrating seventy   *celebrating a new year*

one by one   seventy today
the things i love   i've seen it all and love
spring is here   seeing it again

my seventieth spring

one by one
all things appear
each an old friend
to eye, nose and ear
it's spring again
& i'm here

English lacks anything close to the wonderful *natsukashi* which expresses the joy at meeting something with which one is familiar but has not seen for a long time, that is to say, the *gratification of nostalgia satisfied*, or even the realization of having missed something that wells up when one is reacquainted with it, *in a single word!* I can not make up that loss, even with three paraverses.[1]

あちらむくもこちらむくもや花の春 即章 大三
achira muku mo kochira muku mo ya hananoharu   sokushô   1697
(yonder face-even here/this way face-even! flower's/floral/celebratory spring)

looking here
looking there, yes, spring
is everywhere

安〱と得たりや得たり花の春 秋守 霞袋
yasu yasu to etari ya etari hananoharu   shûshu   1829
(easy, easy got! got! flower's/floral/celebratory spring)

easy to find   easy as pie
and easy to get!   i got her! i got her!
pretty spring   pretty spring

ゆたかさやそよくもの皆花の春 千慰 玉かづら
yutakasa ya soyogu mono mina hananoharu   seni   1751
(abundance! swaying things all flower's/floral/celebr. spring)

what abundance!
whatever sways belongs
to blossom spring

The first *ku* needs no explanation. If the second reading of the second *ku* seems a bit risqué, it should. The *ku* is a parody of the *Manyôshû* song #95, which is little more than a puerile boast about winning the hand of the prettiest girl, named Yasumiko, 安見兒, meaning literally, *child-easy-on-the-eyes* and including the phrase *yasumiko etari* (Yasumiko [I] got/won). The "sways" in the last *ku* refers to the movement of plants in the wind and the sleeves on the New Year dress. There is also a hint of the voluptuous, for the verb was used most often for the willow, an allegory for a woman and her movement. Now, before the reader burps on all this richness, let us get *shibui*.

---

1. Paraverse Allusions   As before, I admit borrowing from "The Violet" by Adeline Dutton Train Whitney (1824-1906). Another line: *God will not put strange signs in heavenly places / The old love shall look out from the old places."* The nature-loving women of the late-19 and early-20c would have loved haiku!

侘住や一輪さしの花の春　紅葉
wabizumai ya ichirinzashi no hananoharu　kôyô 1866-1903
(simple/quiet/poor/tasteful dwelling: one sprig sticker[holder]'s flowery/beautiful spring)

singular sign

a simple life:
one flower, my spring
in one vase

plain living:
a small vase & one sprig
of the spring

The wit of the original lies in the equivalence of the blossoming branch and blossom-spring. First, we imagine the plum blossoms and *then,* with the final word, "spring," realize we are talking about the New Year. The second reading is closest to the original with its *one-spray/sprig-vase.* Unfortunately, I do not know if "sprig" is clearly understood as a single small blossoming branch of plum. I used it because it sounds good and small. The first reading recreates the poem which, in the light of this chapter, we may see as a single-candle in a cupcake standing for a birthday cake.

大名の氣に負もせずけふの春　昌察
daimyô no ki ni oi mo sezu kyônoharu　shôsatsu? 1734?
(daimyô [feudal ruler]'s spirit-to lose even do-not today's spring [ny])

second in spirit
not even to a daimyô
today is spring

目出度さもちう位也おらが春　一茶
medetasa mo chû gurai nari oragaharu　issa (1764-1827)
(joy/congratulativeness-too middle-level[so-and-so] amount becomes/is my spring/new-year)

how happy?
just about average!
my new year

my new year?
i guess you could say
pretty happy

The "not even to a daimyô" *ku* reflects the equality of spirit of the New Year. The "you are two!" *ku* we saw a few pages back was the second in Issa's *Ora ga Haru,* "My Spring [=New Year]." The first was this "just about average." It is one of Issa's best-known *ku,* and most misunderstood. Blyth, who translates *"A time of congratulation, – / But my spring / Is about average,"* dwells on Issa's grim life, including his lonely childhood and the death of his wife. Actually Kiku was still very much alive, as was his daughter Sato, who would die months later.[1] *Issa was expressing his delight at having finally gained a modicum of what late-20c Usanians call "a life."* "Chû-gurai" was used in a somewhat humorous vein to mean "neither here nor there." For that reason, I like Hass's *but*-less wit: *"New Year's Day – / everything is in blossom! / I feel about average,"* even if Issa's Shinano was probably still snow-covered and Hass's readers will have no idea what Issa is driving at. We might note that nine years earlier Issa wrote *"My Spring: / a block of coal and / a clutch of greens"* (わが春やたどん一ッにを菜一把 *waga haru ya tadon hitotsu ni o-na ippa*) five years earlier, Issa wrote: *"Not celebrating / a New Year like [that of] other folk:*[2] */ pretty wretched"* (ご所並の正月もせぬしだら哉 *yosonami no shôgatsu mo senu shidara kana*). *Shidara,* or "pretty wretched" was the title of the work it was in, as *ora-ga-haru,* ("my spring") the last line of the above *ku* was the title of his far more famous later work.

---

1. ***Ora ga Haru* and Sato-jo.** While "My Spring" was written after Sato's death, it did not begin with it. The book includes *ku* written in the happy days of old Issa's Spring when his adorable girl was alive.

2. *Like Other Folk* The term *hito-nami* (like every-one else) here suggests the little girl lined up with her adult parents, but it is also the same term used in the "pretty wretched" haiku above cited; and makes it clear that the "average" poem was indeed a happy comparison to his earlier state. Issa would seem to be thinking, *perhaps asking for a good life would not be good for a Buddhist, but it is moral to want and even enjoy an average life, isn't it?* (Penniless and single at 55, the author takes heart in the fact that Issa had no a place of his own until age 51 and couldn't marry until he was a white-haired 52, down to his last tooth. Do I, too, have a chance of enjoy-ing average prosperity and happiness, if only for a few years, before passing on?). Issa's *ku* may be popular in Japan *for the wrong reason:* it seems to example the "we're all middle-class" mentality.

~~~~~~

世の人のいのちくらべぞけふの春 昌察 三籟集
yo no hito no inochikurabe zo kyonoharu   shôsatsu 1734
(world's peoples' life-comparing [emph.] today's spring)

spring is here
the people of the world
compare lives

This pre-Issa *ku* does not move us. More aphorism than personal truth, it is a *senryû* dressed as *haikai*. By personally owning up to "my" spring, Issa's comparison *is* a haiku. It is not that a haiku should be bereft of *self*. Haiku should not *dwell on* it and bore others (as much modern poetry does). Issa is good because nothing beats genuine personal experience. Today, *senryû* tend to be *more* personal than *haiku*. But, note: *originally, it was the other way around.* It would seem that nature has come to be identified with the objective and humans with the subjective, something patently ridiculous for we cannot help but see nature through subjective eyes, whether our own, or the shared lens of our culture.

何を足る身とはいふらん今日の春 弄香
nani o taru mi to wa iu ran kyô no haru   rôka 1694 蘆分船
(what [emotional obj.] sufficing body/self [you] say! today's spring/new-year)

new year's nonsense

today's spring
what's this talk about
having enough?

Is Rôka disgruntled because he was poor and fed up with reading *ku* about how everyone was wealthy and satisfied on the New Year? His *ku* beats the one before it, but still lacks the presence of Issa's more personal *ku*. Issa was not the first complaining *haijin*, he just did it better.

元日や人の妻子のうつくしき 梅室 1768-
ganjitsu ya hito no tsuma ko no utsukushiki   baishitsu -1852
(original-day: [other] peoples' wives [and] children's beauty/beautiful)

new year's day   new year's day
others' wives and children   how beautiful the children
look gorgeous   and wives of men

If Issa's "average" is refreshing in the face of all the sweet *ku* about people *feeling* the same on the first day of the year when mind is beyond, or rather *before* discrimination, so is this *ku*, contradicting the idealism about people *looking* the same, by Baishitsu, his long-lived contemporary. *Or, do I misread from not knowing the poet better?* Could he be unusually proud of the beauty of his *own* family?

元日や年のよったる顔もせず 一澤 心一つ
ganjitsu ya toshi no yottaru kao mo sezu   ittaku 1706
(original-day: year's-approaching [aging] face/appearance)

it's new year's
and no one looks
their years

the new year
it doesn't look
its years at all

People don't look their years on the New Year, and neither does the New Year look like an agent of aging. Does the year here mean *ours,* or that of the calendar year (Like Bashô's [ever]Young [god] Ebisu)?

まゝそろよ年一つよるも花の春　季吟
mama soro yo toshi hitotsu yoru mo hananoharu   kigin 1623-1705
(as-is-is[+exclam.] year one approaches/ages even, flowery-spring/new-year)

that's life!
you age a year you
gain a spring

it can't be helped
you age a year but who
can hate the spring?

For all who would not age, every birthday party has an upside and a downside. I never could find out exactly what *mama soro yo* means, but for some reason think of Thomas Heywood's *"A fig for care and a fig for woe (if i can't pay than i can owe . . .)."* I suppose it irresponsible, but, sometimes, I like my readings too much to dare look at a dictionary and prove myself wrong.

我としの寄をも知らず花の春 巴人
waga toshi no yoru o mo shirazu hananoharu   hajin 1675-1742
(my/self's year's approach [gaining a year/aging] know-not flower's/celebratory spring/ny)

who cares
if they age: today
is spring!

a new spring
today i don't feel
my age at all

who can tell
they've gained a year?
it's spring!

This is a straightforward version of the last *ku*. Both are a reaction to our mixed feelings for the New Year. Maruyama introduces a *waka* by the outrageous monk Ikkyû (1394-1481): *"The gate-pines / are markers on the route / to the underworld / something to celebrate / and something not to!"* (門松は冥土の旅の一里塚めでたくもめでたくもなし 一休 *kadomatsu wa meido no tabi no ichiri-zuka medetaku mo ari medetaki mo nashi*). Or, Anglified: *Each wreath / on the door rests on the lid / of your coffin?* And he comments that Hajin is *not* agreeing with Ikkyû, as most who read the *ku* imagine[1] but is *whole-heartedly joyful.* Accidentally or not, the *ku* resembles a *waka* written for a "year-forget party" (see IPOOH winter vol. 1) that predates Ikkyû: *"Forgetting / my years just keep / piling up / so delighted to hear / that spring draws near* (*toshi tsumoru onoga toshi o ba shirazu shite haru o ba asa to kikuzo ureshiki* – minamoto no shigeyuki (*shûi-wakashû* 13c). The similarities in wording are greater than revealed by the translation, while the differences in style – the original *waka* is simply atrocious! – are far greater.

---

1. *As Most Might Imagine, or, Misreading a Simple Haiku* As noted earlier, Hajin's poetry is introduced by a number of amateur scholars under the late professor Maruyama's guidance. Unlike all other books of/on haiku that I know of (in Japanese or English, excluding my own), it is honest to a fault. That is to say, *the mistaken interpretations of the participants are left as is*, and even Maruyama, perhaps the most famous scholar of haiku in the second half of the 20c, is unashamed to admit when he is not sure and leave the interpretation open. With this *ku*, the three amateurs (all educators and editors of haiku magazines, etc) misread it to mean that Hajin had lost track of time and with the coming of the New Year became aware of his own aging. I find it interesting that I read it correctly from the get-go whereas they did not, despite knowing their native Japanese language far better than I did. Was it because I immediately look for the wit of a poem, or because my in-depth study of the New Year told me that *hana-no-haru* (flowery-spring) signifies the wonderful, celebratory, fun aspect of the New Year, and that suggested the rhetorical reading of the first part of the *ku*. Maruyama hypothesized that the stress on, or catechism of, simple straightforward observation of nature on the part of the fathers of modern haiku prevented a more complex reading of the *ku*. So, it is also likely that my contrariness helped me read it correctly. (日本語の解る方：『巴人の全句を読む』を、是非お読みになって下さい！。)

年よるは忘れはせねど花の春　たよ女 良材
toshiyoru wa wasure wa senedo hananoharu　tayojo 1775-1865
(year-approaches[i age]-as-for forget-as-for do-not but flower's/festive spring)

while i can't
forget it makes me older
sweet spring!

while i can't
forget the added year
sweet spring!

I have a feeling the previous two poets were almost, but not quite entirely, honest, while this long-lived female contemporary of Issa's described *exactly* how she felt.

とらせ度又物ほしき日の始　由平 大三物
torase taku mata mono hoshiki hi no hajime　yûhei 1697
(taken time again thing/s wanting sun's beginning)

thoughts at the sunrise of the new year

i want to give
and receive something, too
the first day

i want things
to give and to get on this
day we begin

This, too, is honest. From a Buddhist viewpoint *desire is bad*. But is the desire to *give* not a good thing? And, isn't the confession of wanting things *itself* exemplary? The character 度 generally means "each time" or any incremental thing that happens, and the verb *toru* (take) is associated with aging (taking, or being forced to take years) so, until my respondent put me straight about archaic uses of both that I had not imagined – the former a shorthand for ~*taku* or "wanting," and the latter, literally, "having take," or giving to an inferior – I (wrongly) thought the *ku* meant: *Each time / I lose a year I / want something.* Needless to say, I regret losing so entertaining – or, audacious – a *ku!* Let us keep it and call it a paraverse of the original based upon a mistaken reading.

元日の居心や世に古畳　太祇
ganjitsu no igokoro ya yo ni furudatami　taigi -1772
(original-day's being-heart/mind/feeling:/! world-in old *tatami*)

on the first day
i feel like old *tatami*
in a new world

The scent of green *tatami* brings nature home. Old *tatami* is not, like old shoes, comfortable, for it loses its spring, and tends to be riddled with fleas. Orca/oruka reminds me of a saying: "Get new *tatami* even if you must pawn your wife!" It is safe to say the *ku* is self-deprecatory. A similar *ku* focuses on something intrinsically old, the hoary sea cucumber (or artifacts named for the same) as symbolic of something out of step with the flowery spring: 御世にふる生海鼠なからも花の春　昔居霞侯 is poem #778 in *Rise, Ye Sea Slugs!* Sea cucumber means many things including *tatami* and a type of brazier, but I now think round-edge roof-tiles most likely because that is where blossoms tend to fall. Issa's contempory, Baishitsu (1768-1852) covers Taigi's old tatami: *"Beautiful spring: / the only old thing / is me!"* (古きものは我身はかりそ花の春 *furukimono wa wagami bakari zo hananoharu*).

春くれとめもはなもなき朽木哉　静壽 鷹つくは
haru kuredo me mo hana mo naki kuchiki kana　seiju 1642
(spring comes but bud/eyes and bloom/nose lacking rotten-tree!/'tis)

    spring has come　　　　　　　　　　　　spring is here
but this rotten tree lacks　　　　　　had i but the eyes and
    bud and bloom　　　　　　　　　　　　　nose for her

No bud implies no eyes, or none that still see well, and no bloom implies a nose that no longer smells well (or, has fallen off from pox). In Japanese, parts of plants and the face *sound* identical. Unless the poet really was in bad condition, the hyberbole is fulsome. Issa wrote a similar complaint on *his* 51st birth-day/year so dependent upon punning that translation in a poetic manner is impossible: "Even pestle-like gums [enjoy] flower/beautiful spring" (すりこ木のやうな歯茎も花の春 *surikogi no yôna haguki mo hana no haru*), where a "tree" (k[g]i) is in the pestle and the gum suggests "leave/s" (*ha*) and stems (*k[g]uki*). "Pestle-like gums" means he is toothless and the "flower spring" is appropriate to celebrate the start of his second life after finishing his fifth 12-animal cycle the year before. Issa's self-portraits further suggest the flower-spring puns his swollen proboscis (that, too, a perfect homophone!) in which case, we have thin gums set against fat nose. This *ku* is more attractive:

爺が世や枯木も雪の花の春　一茶 文政八
jijigayo ya kareki mo yuki no hana no haru　issa 1825
(geezer-world! withered/dead tree-even snow's flower/floral/beauty/celeb. spring)

    a geezer world!　　　　　　　　　　　blossoms of snow
withered trees with the snow　　　i fear this beautiful spring
    blossom of spring　　　　　　　　　　　is a geezer thing

beautiful new year me?

this snow white
spring: geezer bloom
on dead trees

Issa's describes a *white* New Year, pretending to put-down snow-blossoms while playing with a fairy tale about a kind old man who made winter trees bloom – an allusion for painting the town red? – and alluding to his own solid white locks. White hair does well with the New Year. A poet in the *Kokinshû* (c.905 *waka #8*) laments the blessing of spring sunshine (the ruler), leaving his head snowbound, while Ise no Ôsuke-in (♀), in the *Goshûi Wakashû* (c1086), finds a snowy head in the new sunlight delightful. Another by Kazan-in (花山院 nickname of an Emperor) cleverly notes the only thing that does not vanish by Spring is the snow building on his head, and an even wittier early-16c take by Shôhaku

(肖柏) regrets that the white snow on his head won't melt but wonders if bowing into the Spring sun (消えがたきかしらの雪をかこちても先やむかはん春の光に *kiegataki kashira no yuki o kakochitemomazu ya mukawan haru no hikari ni*) might not help, and, the wittiest of all, a *tanka* by 20c novelist Musha no Kôji Saneatsu 武者小路実陰, quips that his white hair is an illusion: it is really *the tip of a buried ember*, that is, like the white-hot charcoal poking up from the fine ashes of a *brazier* (向ふ中はかしらの雪もおもはでぞ春の光にあたる埋火 *mukou naka wa kashira no yuki mo omowa de zo haru no hikari ni ataru umorebi*).

春立や四十三年人の飯　一茶 文化1
haru tatsu ya shijûsannen hito no meshi　issa 1803
(spring-rises[new-years]: forty-three-years [other]people's meal)

another spring
forty-three years eating
what others grow

Issa is glad to have survived his forty-second year (dangerous for a man), but introspective. "Another spring" misses the original's *tatsu* 立, meaning "arrives" but literally "stand up," in contrast with the dependency confessed. Considering the long hours he scribed for wealthy poets, Issa had no call to feel guilt; but the farm-bred poet went to his grave unsure of whether the writing life was a moral one.

よしや春齢とはれて恥はしめ　如雲 雑中
yoshi ya haru yowai towarete hajihajime　joun 18c?
(stop, oh! [or, great!] spring: year/age asked shame-start/first)

whoa there, spring!　　　　　　　spring's just fine
asked my age: first shame　　but if you ask my age the
of the new year　　　　　　　　first shame's mine

Despite Confucian-influenced "respect for elders" in Japan, hanging around was thought poor etiquette. Desiring a long-life was shameful for the warrior who was not supposed to fear death and sinful for the Buddhist who was not supposed to believe in the reality of this world. The *ku* would be a rusty old saw but for the lively phrasing. "First-shame" is clever and makes the poem. We will look at hundreds of *first-this* and *-that's* in New Year Vol. II. As there are unlimited *first's*, this is one of the more troublesome themes – one that tells a lot about the editors – and the most fun.

元日にとはゞかくしそ人の年　二夕 古選
ganjitsu ni towaba kakushi so hito no toshi　jiyû 1763
(original-day-on asked-if/when hide-not person's age)

on new year's　　　　　　　　when asked
if asked, men should not　　on new year's, hide not
hide their age!　　　　　　　your age!

元日や年より若くなる心地　萬丸
ganjitsu ya toshiyori wakaku naru kokochi　manmaru 1843
(orig.-day/new-year's!/: young is/become feeling/mood)

it's new year's　　　　　　　　it's the new year
today, old folk are　　　　　the elderly feel they
young at heart　　　　　　　　become younger

Of course, age wasn't supposed to matter in the timeless present of that enchanted day (see ch 6).

雪のみか天からふった花の春 宗治 毛吹草
yuki no mi [nomi?] ka [ga?] ten kara futta hananoharu   sôji 1645
(snow's body/self [(or) only= *nomi*] ?[or !] heaven-from fell/befell flowery-spring/new-year)

is the bloom of spring only this snow from heaven?	snow alone fell from heaven this blossom spring	is snow all? flower spring also falls from heaven

Without spaces, we cannot tell if "*-no mi*" or "*nomi*" is intended. Regardless, I see a snowy New Year and a white-haired poet happy for another Spring. The meaningless "flower/y" (beautiful/ precious, etc.) pinned on spring hints of flowers falling from heaven in the original.

こんな身も拾ふ神ありて花 [の] 春 一茶
konna mi mo hirou kami arite hananoharu   issa 1763-1827
(this [deprecatory] body/myself, too pick-up/keep/save god is flower's/celeb. spring/ny)

there is a god who'd keep this body: happy spring!	blooming spring! there is a god who dared to save this man

"This body = self" not only had white hair and no teeth, but was *often* sick and lame and *always* poor. Should "body" be changed to "old man?" Issa was happy with his young wife when he wrote the *ku*. A respondent favors the second reading because "dared" brings out Issa's gratitude most forcefully. ↓

☆see pg. 270

八十の年に 伊勢蝦や八十瀬を越えて老の春 令徳 再現
hachijjû no toshi ni // ise ebi ya yaso se o koete oi no haru   reitoku 1674?
(eighty years [old]-on, ise-shrimp [big crawfish] eighty shoals crossing old[age] spring)

an old man's spring

an ise shrimp
who crossed eighty
sand-bars

If Reitoku died at age 68, as reported, this is not autobiographical. Again, note the way aging, the New Year and the flowery spring dovetail together. The number 8 (八) has infinite = ∞ qualities. These do not translate. A *ku* celebrating the big eighty for Seifu-ni (Starcloth-nun): *"80 years / starts 8000 generations / of spring"* must be improved to, say, *"Four score / the start of a million / more springs!"* (八十とせを八千代の春のはしめ哉 野川 春山集 *yaso tose o yachiyo no haru no hajime kana* yasen 1811). My favorite *ku* for Seifu-ni was *"The eightieth year / of her spring: on her wrinkled palm / the single letter* 寿*"* (八十とセの春や皺手に寿の一字 一蓉 春山集*yaso tose no haru ya shiwade ni ju no ichiji* ichiyô (1811)). The letter means "longevity;" and, doesn't it look a lot like wrinkles? The same collection included this misguided effort: *"A scoop for each of your years and spring water would run out!"* (君か齢くむと尽しはるの水 宝徳（宝の上に火二つ）*kimi ga yowai kumu to tsukushi haru no mizu*). We will splash in "young water" later. Yet, another *ku* anticipates the *rice* 米of another spring, but Seifu-ni did not make it to her 88th 八十八 (Can you see it in the rice = 米?).

元日やこの時人寿二万歳　大江丸 俳懺悔
ganjitsu ya kono toki hitoju nimansai　ôemaru 1721-1805
(original-day: this time, people-longevity two-ten-thousand years[old])

> on new year's day
> all people are twenty
> thousand years old

The unit *man* (ten-thousand) stood for eons. Perhaps two *man* stands for the ying-yang creative elements. While celebrating collective history has something to be said for it, I prefer more personal counts:

百までは三十九年はなのはる　大江丸 俳懺悔
hyaku made wa sanjûku nen hananoharu　ôemaru 1721-1805
(hundred-until-as-for thirty-nine years: flowery-spring[new year])

> thirty-nine years
> and i'll be a hundred
> one fine spring!

In 1682, Sôin, who was to die at age 78, celebrated "a New Year when all went well" (literally, it was *easy to stand*) with optimism: *"It was a snap / if this is all, I'll go / for a hundred!"* (立やすしこんなことなら百とせも　宗因 *tachiyasushi konna koto nara momo tose mo*), but Ôemaru's is the only *ku* I know with such a countdown. I wish he could have made it all the way, but he did live a long time, partly I would guess, because of his optimism. 60 (or 61) was also the appropriate age to make a foolish poem.

死ぬまではいきる筈なり千々の春　蝶々子息?二葉?あやにしき
shinu made wa ikiru hazu nari chijinoharu　chôchôshi early-18c 俳諧貴人伝
(die-until-as-for live-ought-to be thousand-thousand-spring/s)

1,000 x 1,000

> *no spring is the same*
> we ought to live
> until we die!

Am I wrong to find "Rye Whiskey" humor – *If the whiskey don't kill me / I'll live till I die* – in this *ku*? The thousand-thousand (*chijino*) here probably means very, very many (springs), but it can also express great variety, so there is a possibility (not quite a probability) that my first line is not entirely an invention. Here are two more served up the same way:

死ぬ迄は定めて生ん千々の春　一鐵
shinu made wa sadamete ikin chijinoharu　ittetsu fl 1675?
(die-until-as-for, settled live-would/let's thousand-thousand-spring=ny)

> spring variety   no spring is the same
> my die is cast to live   until i die by god
> until i die   i shall live

あすはあす命のうちの千々の春　西武
asu wa asu inochi no uchi no chiji no haru　saimu 1605-78
(tomorrow-as-for[is] tomorrow, life-within's thousand-thousand-spring/s)

live every day
like there is no tomorrow
a million springs

Spring may be the same, with all the familiar faces and all that, yet, it is infinitely various, never the same. Reason enough to live until we die.

春立や愚の上に又愚にかへる　一茶　文政六
haru tatsu ya gu no ue ni mata gu ni kaeru　issa 1764-1827
(spring/ny stands/comes: foolishness upon again foolishness-to return)

second sixty

spring is here
an old fool turns into
a new one

This is the best known silly-60 haiku. Oscar Wilde, who observed that "to get back one's youth, one has merely to repeat one's follies," would have loved it. Issa scholar David G. Lanoue simplifies: *"a new year begins – / nonsense / piled on nonsense."* Blyth tries to capture the circularity of the annual cycle with his grammar: *"Spring begins again; / Upon folly, / Folly returns."* The "again" in the original is not attached to the Spring but, all in all, Blyth's translation is closer to the original than mine. *Or,* could my turning *folly* into *fool* bring us closer to the significance of the *ku*?

（大欲は無欲に似たり、至誠は大愚のごとし）
嘘つかぬ顔にまづ照る初日かな　素丸
uso tsukanu kao ni mazu teru hatsuhi kana　somaru 1712-95
(lie say/make-not face-on first-of-all shine first-sun!/'tis)

the first sun
shines first upon
a truthful face

Somaru, one of Issa's first teachers, was big on aphorisms. The *ku* is boring (unless you think of Diogenes and his lantern), but the prescript good: "Great desire is like no desire and sincerity is at heart great foolishness." I recall a grook by the Danish poet-scientist Piet Hein that may have went like this: *"He who takes fun / and seriousness in earnest / neither of the two discernest."*

（善悪の中から年よぬけたやら）
今朝の春知恵も利口も棚へ上う　壺中
kesanoharu chie mo rikô mo tana e ageyo　kochû 18c?19c?
(this-morning's spring wisdom and cleverness too shelf-to lift-let's/try)

as spring dawns wisdom and clever words i'd do without	new year's day let's shelve all we know and what we'd say

The 17-syllabet prescript asks whether the (past?) year has freed itself of good and evil. While I understand that it makes sense to let go of our critical mind and go with *what is*, I cringe to read the *ku* because of the way the establishment in Japan came to take advantage of silence and badmouth rationality to enforce unquestioning obedience, and nationalist critics came to discourage cleverness as Chinese, artificial and bad, thus ignoring and belittling the natural wit of the folk. Anti-intellectualism is fine applied to the New Year, which is to say, used to help those who need it to get into a properly spiritual mood, but otherwise *stinks*. The positive attitude expressed in the next *ku* is better:

元日や一の密蔵の無分別　木因 本朝文選
ganjitsu ya ichi no mitsuzo no mufunbetsu　bokuin 1706
(original-day! first/favorite hidden-store/treasure's no-discrimination/prudence)

<table>
<tr><td>it's the first day
most precious of all things
nondiscrimination</td><td></td><td>the first day!
how precious to lack
my judgment</td></tr>
<tr><td></td><td>it's new year's
our secret love today
is foolishness</td><td></td></tr>
</table>

The "white-haired" poet, was probably 50, 51, 60 or 61. "In retirement, rationality is left outside, and inside, there is an inexhaustible treasure," says one annotation. Ideally, a retiree should always live in the first day, the original day of the year and of the world. And, to a degree, all of us should never have to go back-to-babyhood, for we should still be babies at heart. If a Greek philosopher was said to have refused entrance to anyone not versed in mathematics, the shingle for Hamada Chinseki's Sharakudô, warned "rationality is not allowed within these premises." (分別の門内に入ることをゆるさず). *In Christian terms, we are talking about the celebration of innocence, the state before a bite was taken from that apple, rather than the supposedly saved one, later.* **Additional note:** As Katô Ikuya notes, a book edited by Bashô's most disliked apprentice, Shikô, introduced the *ku* as a 対,or *complement* to *another* by Bokuin: *"New Year's Eve / In the mirror I see / another me"* or *"Year's End / for an old man: Who's that / in the mirror?"* (老の暮かゝみの中に又一人　加藤郁乎『俳林随筆』+『市井風流』より). There is a time for reflection and a time beyond, or outside of, reflection.

雪隠に分別はなしけふの春　紫之 宝普斉引付
secchin ni funbetsu wa nashi kyô no haru　shishi 18c?19c?
(snow-hide[wc]-in discrimination-not, today's spring)

in the crapper
there's no discrimination
today's spring

My first reaction to this *ku* was: "Issa's *ku* about taking care when he pissed seems more honest than this; but there is probably humor here, somewhere (A "snow-hide" crapper originally meant one with something soft below – not just water but leaves or sand can do this – to silently hide the defecation) and I suspect the poet was sick of New Year's bullshit." After reading another *funbetsu ku* by a Buddhist priest introduced by Katô with no explanation: *"It's New Year's / I've yet to <u>attend to</u> / discrimination* 元日や未分別に手もつけず　大施和尚 *ganjitsu ya mada funbetsu ni <u>te mo tsukezu</u>*　daishi-oshô 18c?19c?), I decided I had better try harder to understand what this *funbetsu* (literally "split+separate") was. I knew the common usage where it means the discrimination that allows us to think and act prudently. I did not know that in Buddhism the knowledge called *funbetsu-chi* (分別智) is synonymous with delusion, i.e., doing what ordinary folk (as opposed to the enlightened) cannot help doing, or the idiomatic usage as WC (short for *funbetsu-dokoro* 分別所), for everyone agreed the WC was a superb place for composing poems! (糞別臭いもかけて？). Moreover, I learned the idiom I translated as "attend to" in the Buddhist priest's *ku* is literally "hand-place/attach, and may refer more specifically to not yet grasping *the rope that dangled by the large hole in the water closet*, both to help support the elderly and to make it less likely for children to fall in. That rope was also called a *funbetsu* (short for *funbetsu-nawa* (分別縄)! Finally, the hairless pate of the elderly, who had, after all done a lot of thinking over the years, was called *funbetsu*-bald, or *funbetsu-hage* (分別禿), so – this is a long-shot – the priest could also have meant *he had not shaved or waxed up his pate*.

正月は分別もなき柳かな 奇木 東華集
shôgatsu wa funbetsu mo naki yanagi kana   kiboku 1700
(new-year's-as-for, discrimination-even-not, willow 'tis/!)

the new year
lacks discrimination
it's a willow

the new year?
the willow without wile
shows the way

on new year's
the way is no way
like a willow

Limbs blown back and forth violate boundaries. Does this refer to the way the New Year moves about year to year based on the relation of lunar and solar dates? Or, is the willow a paragon for being open-minded rather than fixed in our ways, letting go to be as before choice created the ruts that hold us?

誰言大人者不失正月之心者也 正月の心常ある赤子哉 一流 大三
shôgatsu no kokoro tsune aru akago kana   ichiryû 1697
(new year's heart/mind normal is/has baby 'tis/!/?)

it is said a great man is a one who has not lost his new year spirit

it never loses
a new year frame of mind
behold the baby

the spirit of
the new year is ever
a little baby

I bet on my second reading, but it could be either, Another baby New Year *ku* in the 1633 Enoko-shû puns on the literary name of the first month, *Mutsuki,* which suggests diapers: *"Having aged / today again in swaddling / infant month"* (老て今朝二たび児のむ月かな 貞継 *oite kesa futatabi wara no mutsuki kana*   teikei c1640). Is the poet incontinent? A more sophisticated approach by a contemporary of Issa has the poet allowing himself a total dependency in the same Mutsuki month (むつむつと身を任せたる 睦月哉 素檗 *mutsumutsu to mi o makasetaru mutsuki kana*   sobaku -1821). The month's etymology is not really "infantile," but Mutsuki *sounds* warm (*mutsumajii*) as well as swaddly (diaper=*omutsu*).

町人に誕生もあり玉の春 芝光 花笠
chônin ni tanjô mo ari tamanoharu   shikô 18c?19c?
(townsmen(commoners)-for birthday/s-also have, gem/precious spring/ny)

common folk
also have a birthday
precious spring

Poets were seldom commoners. Even poor Issa had a last name, proof his father the farmer had samurai blood. Though some townsmen had surnames – a mark of what we now call middle-class – most commoners had none. And, who ever thought of them as having birthdays! There is irony in this equality and information, for Japanese today are not generally aware that individual birthdays were observed for nobles – and some samurai? – before changing to the Gregorian calendar.

君の春民をいはふやかさりわら 從方 大三物
kimi no haru tami o iwau ya kazari wara   jûhô 1697
(the lord's spring folk/subjects [obj] celebrate:/? decorative straw)

    our lord's spring
  do we celebrate the folk?
     decorative straw

The "lord" is either the Emperor the de-facto ruler, the Tokugawa Shôgun. Japanese nobles had a long tradition of reproducing various rustic scenes – dressing up their retainers and hiring peasants as their European counterparts did – and Chinese did centuries earlier. Some, in retrospect, are comical: imagine a whole salt work on a Southern island (a melancholy place of exile), reproduced on a river bank in central Japan! But this *ku* is not about such pretense. Jûhô pretends something else. He pretends to know that the practice of strewing rice straw was meant to celebrate the common folk, when such was not necessarily the case. His mention of celebrated "folk" should, however, pose a challenge to the sociologist and make us think of how *we* celebrate *our* working classes. To my mind, the straw had more to do with evoking ancient memories, or an alternative aesthetic of beauty, where unglazed cups, unpainted wood and straw are given the respect and enjoys the affection which only shiny things enjoy in less mature cultures. As already mentioned, this was first noticed by the Jesuits, who found it topsy-turvy and odd because precious metals had proven "objective" value on the international market, while old tea cups and whatnot did not. But, remember, if you can, the *magic* in a straw manger or Easter Bunny hutch that you felt as a child. Who is to say *you* were deluded?

元日や蛤売も人は人 鳥睡 安永六 1777
ganjitsu ya hamaguri-uri mo hito wa hito   chôsui
(origin=ny-day!/: clam-seller-even person-as-for person)

  it's new year's:
 though a clam vendor
  a man's a man

下女までも前垂赤し花の春 勝山 大三物
gejo made mo maedare akashi hananoharu   shôsan
(maids-even front-bangs red blossom-spring/ny 1697)

 even the maids
boast red aprons
 spring is here!

The clam-seller made his rounds over the holiday season, for clams stay alive in the cool weather. Any left over from the end of the year would have to be unloaded as quickly as possible and I would not be surprised to find they were actually sold on the New Year's Day though it would be improper. I am not sure what the *ku* means. That, he deserves a proper greeting? The second *ku* is simple. Red was a propitious color.   Serving or not, the maids were part of the world's birthday party.

かけ鯛に猫の年とる我屋哉 清忠 大三
kakedai ni neko no toshi toru wagaya kana   seichû 1697
(decorative-snapper-to/with cat year-takes, my house 'tis)

  that's my house!
the cats take the snapper
  for their new year

  that's my house
the cat passes the new year
  fixated on the fish

The decorative snappers, or red sea bream (two, usually belly to belly), are roasted with plenty of coarse sea-salt. Either way, they seem shellacked and hold up surprisingly long. For obvious reasons, the practice must predate the acceptance of cats within the house. The original is better, for the year is "taken" and alludes to the same happening to the decorative fish. But it is not certain. The fish may have been out of reach of the cats, hence the second reading.

元日や牛部屋の藁も新しき 可候 安永六
ganjitsu ya ushibeya no wara mo atarashiki kakô 1777
(original-day!/: cow-shed/house's straw too new)

the first day
the straw in the cow shed
new as well

We saw this lucky straw earlier; I reintroduce it to show how all creation shares in the cosmic birthday.

遊ぶ身も民の数なりみよの春 かつら 文久五百題
asobu mi mo tami no kazu nari miyonoharu katsura mid-19c
(playing/idle bodies/people-even folk's number becomes [hon.]reign-spring)

our nation's spring

idle bodies
as many as there are folk
in the reign

This type of poem makes fine historical ethnography – or at least it makes us wonder how many servants got New Year's Day off (for the answer, see *yabuiri* in book 4) – but it is, more than anything else, yet another toast to the realm, *self-consciously at peace*, in the Tokugawa Era (1603-1867). More, below:

長閑さや皆我が家のみよの春 宗因
nodokasa ya minna wagaya no miyonoharu sôin 1604-82
(serenity/halcyon[ity?]! everyone my/own home's [hon.]reign's spring)

a halcyon day!	a halcyon day!
the spring of the reign	all think the nation's spring
is made at home	their very own

Balmy weather was considered so common a New Year occurrence, or, rather, so fitting a coincidence as to become a haiku almanac theme of its own, but the rest of this *ku* is a toast to the wide-spread peace enjoyed by the citizens who may all pass the New Year at home. This became a common theme: *"The lord's reign / we greet the spring sitting / upon tatami"* (君か世や畳の上の明の春 京馬 新選 *kimigayo ya tatami no ue no akenoharu* kyôma 1819); that is to say, better on *tatami* than on a warhorse. Some toasts to happy times were crass: *"Subject: Gold // Out of sight / ten-thousand bars of it! / Our lord's spring"* (題 黄金 目には見す一萬枚を御世の春 其角 *dai ogon // me ni wa mizu ichiman mai o miyonoharu* kikaku -1707) and some outlandish: *"What a bigarade: / lumbago turns tail in / our lord's spring!"* (橙や疝気をおさまる御世の春 李由 風俗文選 *daidai ya senki osamaru miyonoharu* riyû c.1700). Lumbago tended to flare up in the cold months and improve in the spring.

It seems to have been rife among poets who sat on their haunches most of the time. The bigarade, a citrus fruit described in the *hôrai* chapter, puns on long-lived "generations" or "realms" and was used for New Year's decoration. Herbal tea made of its skin worked on lumbago. Because lumbago was a subject popular in old *senryû*, and I have read tens of thousands of them, I was able to "solve" that *ku*, but there are still many New Year's toasts to the realm I do not get. Eg.: *"We can even / take a bath at night for / our Lord's Spring"* (夜の内に風呂もすましてみよの春　みとり　文久五百 *yo no uchi ni furo mo sumashite miyonoharu* mitori mid-19c). What is this poet boasting? It is evident from the grammar of the original that bathing was something one had to get done with before the New Year dawned, but: 1) Are people so busy in a prosperous economy that they have no other time to bathe but late at night? 2) Are more people bathing *at home* rather than public baths? Or, 3) Are the public baths newly opened late at night? Only a historian can read between such lines.

日の本や金も（or が）子をうむ御世の春　一茶
hinomoto ya kane mo (or, ga) ko o umu miyonoharu　issa 1825
(sun's source! money/coins, too children[acc], birth honorable-reign's spring)

    source of the sun   here in japan
 the lord's spring bears   spring is when money
     coins and kids   bears children

The nation in this happy reign pours forth wealth, human and metal, as befits its name "source of the sun." Does Issa, like others, celebrate the greater entity as his own at New Year, or does this, rather, reflect his jealousy about, or intense longing for, these things he was not blessed with (his children were dead by this time.) or, is something missing here? One version, with *ga* making money the subject, suggests that either children gathered for their New Year gifts of coins, the wealthy enjoy having far more of them than the poor, or there were rewards for child-bearing I do not know about.

今年はと思ふことなきにしもあらず 子規
kotoshi wa to omou koto naki ni shi mo arazu　shiki -1902
(this-year-as-for…think/concerned-thing/s-not-as do-too am-not)

      this year
it's not that i have
      no plans

I follow a brilliant translation by an anonymous American: "This year – / it's not that I have / no resolutions" (in an online article by Kyoshi's grand-daughter, Inahata Teiko). The original speaks of "*thoughts for*" the year, something between *wishes* and *resolutions*. Japanese have things they hope to do but do not generally resolve to accomplish them or else. Shiki, with his tuberculosis, was not kidding. The *ku* is a simple masterpiece and I, as a poor man, rather than a sick one, must admit to often feeling the same way. We may be equal in dreams but not in means. Note the equivalence of our wishes as we blow out the candles on our birthday cakes and the way we look ahead on the New Year. In Japan, up to Shiki, they were one and the same.

～～～～～～～～～～

八十の坂越てもおなし春の山　星布♀　春山集
yaso no saka koete mo onaji haru no yama　seifu-ni 1732-1814

The 八 in *eighty* looks like a slope up and a slope down. Well," *I climbed over the top and what do I see? The same mountains of spring.*" The original (*in italics*) is simple, and simply untranslatable.

TODAY

Most Japanese celebrate their birthdays in the modern Western style, birthday cakes and birthday song – unfortunately, the English one rather than the much more beautiful Mexican one (so saying, even other Latin Americans choose to copy the crass *Norte Americanos* rather than the Mexicans!) which shares something with the New Year spirit, for it is sung at sunrise around the bed of the birthday boy or girl. Still, thanks to the continued presence of the Year Animals (see ch3), Japanese remain aware of their birth-year age. This is particularly true for people turning twenty, for the New Year's becomes the official birthday of their adulthood, though the ceremony takes place on the 15th at the end of the New Year season. Unfortunately, "official" means little. The legal age for driver's licenses, legal drinking and whatnot are all determined by the same individual birthday method of the Occident. (As far as I know, this is even true in Taiwan and The Peoples Republic where the old New Year is still celebrated on the traditional Luni-solar calendar date.) Most of these young adults rent a kimono for the occasion, make a Shrine visit, and have their photos taken. In old Japan, the coming-of-age ceremonies for the common folk were irregular. If there were few youth in a given rural community (for most people were rural), they might only be held once every several years. And, as is the case with most cultures throughout the world, even teen-agers became full-fledged adults. For the last half-century or so, the age of adulthood has been nationally fixed at 20. Here is a *ku* from an anthology published (every few years) by the world's largest association of haiku writers.

脱皮せる成人の日の貌匂ふ　原はつ子
dappi seru seijinnohi no kao niou　　hara hatsuko　1997 季題別現代
(shed-do become-person's day's face smells/glows[with eros/beauty])

freshly shed
adult day faces
all aglow

Shedding skin in Japanese suggests a change of attitude, but here, we feel growth and I imagine the shiny beauty of a snake that has just shed (though the date of publication suggests it was not written in the Year of the Snake). These twenty year-olds are not just new adults, they are *mint*. The verb used to describe this glow, "smell" is one with an ancient sound-scent (indeed, the poet uses the *fu* for *u* in the old style), A more spectacular metaphor from the same Haijin Kyôkai collection:

水鏡割りて魚飛ぶ成人祭　金崎雅野 同
mizukagami warite uo tobu seijinsai　kanazaki masano
(water-mirror breaking, fish jumps adult-festival/ceremony)

adult day

coming-of-age
up through smooth water
jumps a fish

breaking through
the water mirror a fish
jumps into view

I made a lot of changes in the syntax of that *ku*. Is the fish is experiencing the world beyond water for the first time? Or, are we surprised to see it? We do not find attention given to the twentieth birthday in old haiku. Interest in individual birthdays generally skips from the first years of tiny children to the last ones of the elderly. Life at a remove from the ends does not bring the unbroken circle to mind.

欠伸して四十歳が夢のよう　時実新子 有夫恋
akubi shite yonjussai ga yume no yô   tokizane shinko (20c)
(yawn-doing/did forty-years-the dream-as/seems)

yawning
i pinch myself
me, forty?

When I tried to put the "dream" into my translation, the results (One example is enough: *"I yawned / and forty years passed / like a dream"*) were horrible because, I think, dreams do not occur within yawns and yawns do not end dreams. But when I use the English expression "pinch myself," which indirectly says: *"Is/Was this a dream?"* damn if it, whatever it is, did not *seem* to translate! This *ku* by a modern haiku poet picks up on Ikkyû and Yayû (and *senryû*) which prefix the coming of a new year with body functions (eat, sleep, poop, snore) and the night becomes a dream, which is not really a dream but a metaphor.

envoi

元日のこころのみこむ二日哉　素檗
ganjitsu no kokoro nomikomu futsuka kana   sobaku -1821
(origin-day's heart/mind drink-swallow second-day!/?/'tis)

the second day we swallow the heart of the new year	the second day we embody the mind of the first one

One could not bear pure witness to the birthday and rebirthday of all *and* make something of it. This second-day *ku* would be *After The Party,* without the negative connotations.

☆ **Issa's Delight in Being Accepted by Kiku, & Kikaku**. After putting the *ku* in alphabetical order for the index, I wondered if Issa's *konna mi mo hirou kami arite hananoharu* (pg. 261) might not depend slightly upon Kikaku's *konata ni mo nyobo motasen mizu-iwai kikaku,* for it mentions getting a wife directly (see pg. 349) and the first part might be similar enough to help someone who knew it read between the lines of Issa's *ku* figure out that it was about having found a wife. あるいは、わが考え過ぎでしょうか？

おまけ
JAPAN'S BIRTHDAY & NATIONALISM

紀元二千五百五十三年の春　子規 明治廿六
kigen nisen gohyakugojûsan nen no haru shiki 1893
(era-origen two-thousand-five-hundred-fifty-three year's spring)

spring of year
two thousand five hundred fifty three
annô japani

Shiki was to repeat the *ku,* with the appropriate change, other years. For example his *ku* for 1896, year-29 of the Meiji era, was 2,556. This makes the start of the reign of the first of the Imperial Line, descendents of the gods – the Imperial family was called 天子 = "heaven-children" – younger than that of the Judaic calendar but older than the Christian or Islamic ones. I have read debates about the correct dates which, like those in the Judeo-Christian world, tell us that all this precision masks pure guesswork. I am not interested in the details of such schemes. Suffice it to say that Japanese did not use such a long-count calendar at all until scholars used the *Nihonshoki* (日本書紀) – as "ours" did the Bible – to derive the supposedly exact date, February 11, 660 BCE. It is generally pointed out that this holiday, called simply Origin Day (*Kigensetsu* 紀元節 also translated as "Empire Day") until the end of WW II and National Foundation Day (*Kenkoku-kinenbi* 建国記念日) today, was established to bolster the legitimacy of the Imperial family following the abolition of the Tokugawa Shogunate by linking the Meiji Emperor with the mythical first emperor, Jimmu, and the Sun God/dess Amaterasu (there was debate on his/her sex). I think it is unfair to stop at this without pointing out that it was no accident this new holiday was celebrated the first time in 1873, when Japan switched from its lunisolar calendar to "our" solar one. We have already seen how the New Year held as much significance for Japanese as Christmas+Easter+July4+B'day+New-Year's for us. While other nations dated their polity to this or that day on this or that month, Japan celebrated its origin on New Year's Day, which, as we have noted already, is literally called the Day of the Origin, 元日(See the common 元?). Could we not, then, see this artifice as just compensation for the loss of the traditional Japanese New Year? Shiki may parade the numbers to show that Japan was no junior to the Christian West, whose calendar had to be adopted for Japan to survive in the world "we" ran. I could be wrong on Shiki's intent. He may have wished only to offer something concrete – seemingly *realistic* – to replace conventional conceits for hoary age such as "thousand-era" (千代) and "generation-generation" (世々), the purely symbolic generalities such as the 20,000 (two *man*) or 9 hundred-million *kô* we have read, or even the reasonable rounding-off approach of Ôemaru (1719-1805) who celebrated the birth of an Imperial Prince (王[皇]子の歳旦) as follows: *"Oh, unchanged realm! / Three thousand years of this / Spring dawn"* (かはらぬよ三千年のけさの春　大江丸 *kawaranu yo sanzennen no kesanoharu* Note: Ôemaru deliberately used a syllabic *yo,* rather than a Chinese character to keep all possible meanings alive: *yo* here is *reign/era,* the *world,* or merely an exclamation.) One thing is certain, Shiki does not grant his rulers the history of a sea cucumber to whom he gave 18,000 – symbolic of millions – years of the good life (doing nothing).

Leaving aside the intent of the poets with respect to individual *ku,* I think it beyond doubt that there is more than a touch of nationalism/ethnocentrism in many New Year *ku.* That is only natural when we consider the fact that this day celebrated the birthday of the Japanese people as a whole. Patriotic poems go back way before haiku. If the New Year is taken in the broadest sense of the season, including the first two weeks of Spring, one might consider the second song in the *Manyôshû* (8c) composed by the Emperor Jomei (593-41) where he climbs Kaguyama to ritually survey his land and ends up praising Yamato as a splendid (*umashi*) country as a nationalistic New Year poem. There are far more poems by poets celebrating the sovereign and the reign he or she (in ancient times, women could be Emperor) embodied. I have never cared much for them and, accordingly, did not pay close enough attention to tell just when the New Year connection was made. It is there in the famous *waka* #343 of the *Kokinshû* (905) wishing the sovereign lives a thousand reigns, *until pebbles grow into boulders and cover with moss* (an idea we'll return to in the chapter on sweet-rice cakes) and #344 wishing a thousand years, the multitude of which is illustrated by counting grains of sand on a beach – both this and the moss-growing trope found in Manyôshû poems dealing with eternal feelings of love. It is hard to be sure, though, for other wishes for the longevity of the Emperor, Empress or others of the Imperial line, that *seem* New Yearsy have disputed dates, such as Fourth-month-Thirteenth-day in #346, where the poet wishes he could add his own life to the thousand the sovereign will get, and Ninth-month-Thirteenth-day for #347, where the poet playfully wishes he also could be around for the sovereign's eighty-thousandth realm. The annotator doubts that date and calls this a *nenga,* which generally implies the New Year; but it was the seventieth birthday of the Empress and if the actual birthdates of the Imperial family were carefully recorded, they may have been feted. Moreover, #349, also called a *nenga,* for a Regent's fortieth birthday – the crossroads in life – calls on the *cherries* to shed clouds of petals to hide the way to aging. Since cherries did not bloom until a good month or more after the New Year, this suggests that the poem either ought to be with a real birthday later on, or was read at New Year's, while anticipating that birthday (something interesting in its own right).

The relationship of the nation and the New Year was, and was not, taken for granted. Sometime in his 90 year-long life (1114-1204), Fujiwara Shunzei (or no Toshinari) wrote: *"The Lord's realm / may it last as long as / the sky-door's open, / Provided the months(=moon) and / days(=sun) run not out"* (君が代は千代（ちよ）ともささじ天（あま）の戸や出（い）づる月日のかぎりなければ　藤原俊成 *kimigayo wa chiyo to mo sasaji . . .*) The door to the cave, as we have seen, evokes the first sunshine and hence New Year. By "Lord," we mean the Emperor. Another of Shunzei's waka *should be* famous:

> *This is the day / When we all believe / the spring / that goes clear to China / visits Kyôto alone!*
> *Is this the day / We all believe / the Spring / that goes clear to China / visits Kyôto alone?*
> 今日といへば唐土までも行く春を都にのみと思ひけるかな　藤原俊成「新古今集」
> *kyô to ieba morokoshi made mo yuku haru o miyako ni nomi to omoikeru kana*　shunzei skks 1205

Kyôto, as the capital (*miyako*), was the pride and identity of the Japanese ruling class and whoever felt part of the nation. While Shunzei, as an international Buddhist and/or rational Confucian, i.e., a relativistic cosmopolitan, chuckles at the absurdity of ethnocentrism, he *also* celebrates the natural joy of what might be called topographical egoism. He could have replied to G.K. Chesterton's pointed question: *"What can they know of England who know only the world?"* ("On Rudyard Kipling" in *Heretics*) without taking a purely "orthodox" line. Not well-versed in history, I cannot say how widespread his apparently reflective attitude was, or whether the Mongol-Chinese invasions helped to create the more strident, subjective nationalism found in the following *waka* by Shôtetsu (正徹 1381-1459) and Shôkô (正広 1412-1494), respectively (three each):

> *What is spring / but this mist, clothing / Born of the vows / between sky and earth / in the age of the gods?*
> 来る春は神代や契り天地の中の衣をたつ霞かな　正徹　*kuru haru wa kami yo ya . . .*
> *This is the land / where the gods first came: / The new year / too, must surely / descend from heaven.*
> 此地に神のきにける初とや立かへる年も天くたるらむ　正徹 *kono kuni ni kami no . . .*
> *A misty day / In China they will know / about spring / Gazing with reverence / at the sun's origin.*
> かすむなりけふもろこしに日本をふりさけみてや春をしるらん　正徹 *kasumu nari kyô...*

Heaven's door / Opening it, at last / sunshine; / Here comes the Spring / of the Age of the Gods!
天の戸をあくればやがて日の光神代のままの春やたつらん　正広詠歌　amanoto o akureba...
When the Sun / parting ocean waves / rises up; / The Spring of the Gods – / Has it not come back?
わたつ海の浪まを分けて出づる日に神代の春や帰りきぬらん　同　wadatsumi no...
It's light! / Today, dawn reaches / China, too, / Spring born in the Land / of the Sun is there!
明けにけり光をうけて唐(もろこし)もけふ日の本の春や立つらん　同　akenikeri hikari..

The first two *ku* of both poets seem ethnocentric (not necessarily a bad thing) but are not obviously nationalistic. Both of their third *ku*, alluding to Shunzei's humble observation, *are*. They specify that Spring derives or comes *from us*. My "sun's origin" is not obviously enough "Japan," while my "Land of the Sun" (land replacing the three syllable "origin") is too obvious, but the idea is clear. Yet even these poems – perhaps reflecting Japanese confidence after beating back 13c Mongol invasions with the help of the *kamikaze,* or God/s' Winds (typhoons or gales) – seem pensive rather than strident nationalism. Shôkô's last is gentle enough not to jar one's sensibilities: the original's *ukete* ("receiving [the sun]"), which I failed to fit in the translation, is *beautiful*. Fast-forward another hundred years and we find Shunzei's *morokoshi,* which is to say Chinese, New Year, gains a new twist:

> *Showing them / the light of the Land / of the Sun / Spring has come / to far-off China.*   Or,
> *Boasting the brilliance of the Sun's country even in China, where a new Spring stands tall!*
> 日の本の光を見せてはるかなる唐土までも春や立つらむ　細川幽斎＝玄旨(-1610)　衆妙集
> *hi no moto no hikari ...*

What has happened? The poet wrote this on New Year's day of the year Hideyoshi would invade Korea (with China in mind 入唐の御沙汰ありし年の元日に). This was shortly after Japan unified in the late-16c (For more about this failed attempt to conquer the world, start with *Topsy-turvy 1585*). This poem, then, may have influenced the far more famous 18c literary scholar and nationalist (or, *nativist*) Motoori Norinaga to write:

> *By the light / shining forth from this / Land of the Sun / Korea and China, too / may know the spring!*
> さしいづるこの日の本の光より高麗唐土も春を知るらむ　本居宣長　*sashi izuru kono hi...*

Norinaga's pioneering work on old Japanese texts and beautiful prose has earned him the love of most if not all Japanese, but this is as obnoxious as the things he wrote about foreign languages, whose more abundant phonemes were put down as beastly or corrupt as opposed to the pure and pleasant sound of his own tongue. After a couple hundred years of isolation, Japan became overcrowded . . . with nationalists. Arakida Hisaoyu (1746-1804) was, like Norinaga, a scholar of the *Manyôshû*. They quarreled and the tenor of his poem tells you why:

> *Hey, riff-raff! / Adore the august faces / of the gods / of the godland glowing / in the first sun of spring!*
> 初春の初日かがよふ神國の神のみかげをあふげ諸々　　荒木田久老　*hatsuharu no hatsuhi*

He does not say he addresses foreigners, but the word (*moromoro*) meaning "everyone" insinuates "various nations" or, if I am not hypersensitive, "riff-raff," and I sense an allusion to *morokoshi* in the *moro*. The original has a first (*hatsu*) before the spring. Even Norinaga would have found the overblown style and crude imperative a bit too much! "Adore" is *aoge,* a verb implying "get down" for it means to look up in a reverential, or worshipful, manner. I found the poem, if we can call it such, in a collection of a hundred patriotic poems (定本愛國百人一首) published in 1943. While the above poem was not the product of desperation, the poetry collection reflects the obvious unease of its editor.

Another collection of patriotic poems, modern poems by the legendary 20c lyrical poet Kitahara Hakushû written before Midway turned the tide on what seemed to be a run-away victory by the Japanese is very different. Take this poem evidently written for children:

> *Long live Japan! Long live the Prince! / New Year's Day! Hooray, hooray! / How early you awake; / Asia's night is dawning. // The bugles for your realm / are tooting in the mist!*
> 日本万歳、皇太子さま、/ 元日元日おめでたう、/ おめざめ早いな、/ アジヤの夜明。// 君が代のらつぱ / 霞に鳴るよ．

> *Long live Japan! Long live the Prince! / Happy New Year, Father, Mother! / We children are strong / we grow by leaps and bounds. // "Advance!" the bugle calls / and echoes in the clouds!*
> 日本万歳、皇太子さま、/ 父さん母さんおめでたう / 子供はつよいな、/ ぐんぐんのびる。// 進軍らつぱ / 雲までひびく。

> *Long live Japan! Long live the Prince! / Happy New Year to one and all! / Just wait! In a while / the age will be yours. // "Advance!" the bugle calls / and sounds thoughout the world!*
> 日本万歳、皇太子さま、/ みんなみんなおめでたう、/ もうぢきすごいな、/ 僕らの時代。// 進軍らつぱ / 世界はどよむ。

Long live Japan! is *nippon banzai,* literally, "Japan, ten-thousand years!" (Note: *Banzai!* is not a blood-curdling call, like *Charge!* but an innocuous wish for longevity, one heard at birthdays and other celebratory occasions.) The "Prince" is Crown Prince Akihito, born Dec. 23, 1933, the 8th year of Shôwa, the era meaning "Shining Harmony," which changed to today's more modest *Heisei,* or "Level/peaceful-becomes" with the death of Hirohito, postumously Emperor Shôwa, in 1989 and ascension of Akihito. In the last stanza, which I did not translate, the Japanese flag *hi no maru,* literally "the sun round," or the "SS Sun," waves in Asia and we return to the mist in the first stanza, which, if you recall is a New Year theme. So, I think you can see how these modern poems, which may have been sung in school, reflect the older ones, and how the New Year incorporates the patriotic. I do not translate the poems to criticize or make fun of Japan. We in the West have quite a tradition of patriotic verse, ourselves. In the USA, in particular, it got so bad in the early-19c that one British critic claimed our entire output said one thing and one thing only, that we were *"the smartest nation / in all creation"* (Yet, *we* make fun of Kipling!?). Part of Japan's problem may have been an inferiority complex vis-à-vis China, and, later, the West. In this respect, too, Japanese resembled Usanians (The name *Americans* belongs to the continent). This is not the place to try to make sense of the Japanese part of the tragedy called World War II in the West. Suffice it to say that horrible things, unforgivable things, were to happen; but many if not most Japanese wished well for Asia and the rest of the world. They really wanted to free Asia from the colonial=Occidental powers. Kitahara Hakushû got so caught up in Japan's early victories seeming to prove heaven's backing that he raved happily on about Japanese flags plastering the world and even wrote of the equator rearing up into a flaming pillar of (Japanese) justice (今は、その赤道をそのまま縦にしたほどの巨大な火の柱となつて、ああ、日本は興隆しつつあるのだ。), yet, in the same book, he also lauded Gandhi's quiet strength in a poem that ends:

Should Gandhi die, he'd only live!	ガンジーは死んでも生きる。
Gandhi is a faith:	ガンジーは信念だ、
India must and will be free!	インドは必ず独立する。
Gandhi has no arms to fight!	ガンジーに武器はない。
He has only the pure sound of a spinning wheel.	澄みに澄んだ紡車の音だけなのだ。
Ah, Gandhi! There on his long eyebrows,	ああ、ガンジーの長い眉毛に
Can you see the flecks of white lint?	しろい綿ぼこりがふつかかつてゐる。

福寿草
fukuju-sô

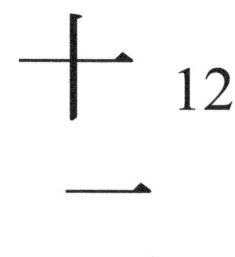

GOLDEN FLOWER OF FORTUNE

帳箱（面）の上に咲きけり福寿草　一茶
chôbako(-men) no ue ni sakikeri fukujusô   issa -1827
(ledger-box's(or, pad's) above-on bloom [+emph.] *fukuju-sô*)

blooming right
above the ledger box
a *fukujusô*

The dictionary tells us that the "prosperity/happiness/lucky+longevity+grass/weed/shrub/wild-flower" is an *"Amur Adonis"* or *Adonis amurensis*: a handsome young man from Amur (North China). This is interesting, but it tells English speakers nothing – unless "Chinese" made you guess the flower was *yellow* – and has nothing in common with the "prosperity+longevity" found in the Sino-japanese name.

黄金のけさ封きるや福寿草　千車 玉桂
ôgon no kesa fû kiru ya fukujusô   sensha 1751
(gold's this-morning=ny's seal cut/open /! *fukuju-sô*)

cutting the seal　　　　　　　　　　breaking the seal
on this golden day:　　　　　　　　on this golden day
a *fukujusô*　　　　　　　　　　　a pheasant's eye

Should we make up a name for the *fukuju-sô*? Gold can tie into both longevity and prosperity. How about *First-gold*? But gold would be *too* obvious on Issa's ledger box, and redundant in Sensha's *ku*. *Lucky grass* avoids the crass connotation of gold, but can we call an almost cactus-like plant with flowers "grass?" Then, how about *Lucky flower*? The repeated strong-weak beats sounds horrible and *lucky* seems so frivolous. Combining the flower's other name, *ganjitsu-sô,* "new-year's-day+grass/plant," with its slight resemblance to the chrysanthemum, gives us *Holiday mum*. I like it, but am afraid the absence of the propitious parts of the name is no help for translating the intent of the original *ku*. I found it translated "pheasant's eye" in on-line *saijiki*, but that turned out to be a slightly different plant, *Adonis annua,* and, worst yet, the flower was not gold but red, with a black center. So, here, as with *Hôrai,* the magical mountain, we will use the Japanese name, and remember what it means. After all, besides the fact this plant has an uncanny way of opening for the New Year, its main appeal – the reason why Japanese often presented it to one another – was its name. The entire Sinosphere is big on assembling auspicious things for the New Year, and this plant has not one, but *two* verbal charms in its name. A *fukujusô* by any other name is *not* a *fukujusô.*

福寿艸刀に近き置所 俳諧舩 彩色江戸物売図絵
fukujusô katana ni chikaki okidokoro   anon. 18-19c?
(*fukuju-sô* sword-by close set-place)

fukujusô
kept in a place close to
the swords

In a *buke,* or a *bushi* household, the sheathed swords are kept in open sight – samurai children evidently behaved themselves – in a neat little cranny, or a stand close to the *tokonoma.* Does the juxtaposition of sword and plant suggest that arms are needed to protect wealth, or that the warrior class has softened up and wishes for wealth, happiness and a long life? If the *fukuju-sô* in Issa's previous *ku complements* the ledger, here it *contrasts* with the swords.

福寿草一寸ものゝ始なり 言水
fukujusô issun mono no hajime nari   gonsui 1646-1719
(*fukuju*-sô: one-inch[long]things' beginning is)

fukujusô	*fukujusô*
one-inch is how	you are the start
things start	of little things

There is a wee possibility of things beginning head-first here, too, for *issun* (one-inch) was slang for a puppet's head. The Japanese can be read two ways depending whether the *mono,* things are modified by the inch or modify the start. Strangely enough, it makes little difference.

花よりも名に近づくや福寿草 千代尼
hana yori mo na ni chikazuku ya fukujusô   chiyo-ni 1701-75
(flower-more-than, name-to nears: *fukuju-sô*=grass/weed/shrub/wild-flower)

hardly a flower	hardly a flower
it's true to its name	it's true to its name
fukuju herb	*fukuju* weed

The *sô* 草 at the end of the name, usually translated as "grass," is used for most plants neither tree nor bush, including "herbs" "weeds" and "wild-flowers." If Japan's first woman of haiku refers to it as medicine for the soul rather than a merely decorative flower, it is an "herb." If she means it has little leaves only a botanist might find interesting on stubby shoots which look like they belong in stew rather than flower pots and flowers that fail to open fully, she may have "weed" in mind. I recall wondering what Japanese saw in this grubby-looking little plant. I was more impressed with the nice moss the flower-sellers had growing around it than the plant itself! Some Japanese share my first impression: *"Fukuju-sô: / the joyful color may be / more in the moss* (福寿草よりかも苔に喜色あり 後藤夜半 *fukujusô yori kamo koke ni kishoku ari*   gotô yowa) , as one contemporary *ku* put it.

天地のいでもの見せむ福寿草 巴人
ametsuchi no idemono misemu fukujusô   hajin - 1742
(heaven-earth's appear-thing [(first) production] show! *fukuju-sô*)

out with it!

so, let's see
the cosmic production!
fukujusô?

Hajin's *ku* is more ambitious and obviously wittier [1] than Chiyo-ni's simple observation. I *should* like it better, and don't know why I do not. Could I have a crush on the good-natured nun? Hajin's protégée Buson later wrote a more subdued but still clever *ku* on the plant: *"New Year's Day / and there in the grass [=among the grasses/weeds]/ Fukurokuju"* (元日や艸の中なる福禄壽 *ganjitsu ya kusa no naka naru fukurokuju*). The name of Fukurokuju, the Chinese deity of prosperity and longevity [2] and the auspicious plant contain each other. The precious is found in a lowly place. We find similar *ku* about the peony, "King of Flowers," as the embodiment of wealth humble for remaining close to the ground. Issa even praised it for blooming while seated if it were, unlike the epidemic of "Boy Prosperity" (Fukusuke) dancers – i.e., door-to-door (pushy) beggars – who plagued Japan at the time. Centuries later, Shiki would follow Chiyo and Hajin with an even blunter putdown of the *fukujusô*:

俗な名を色を形を福寿草 子規 明治廿八
zoku na na o iro o katachi o fukujusô shiki 1866-1902
(vulgar name! color! form! *fukuju-sô*)

a vulgar name
vulgar color, vulgar form
the *fukujusô*

But this has always been a minority view. Most Japanese, even intellectual poets, preferred to praise the little plant and what it stood for. Or, is Shiki playing with us? For a poet, particularly one in the *haikai* tradition, "vulgar" (and the same character means *folk/mores*) may be more interesting than elegant.

鉢植の形は蝸牛に似たれど触蛮の動きなき比花の曙を愛して、
あらそはぬ國いたゝくや福寿草 蓼太
arasowanu kuni itadaku ya fukujusô   ryôta 1707-87
(fighting/struggling-not country [i'll/it'll] take/accept: *fukuju-sô*)

Its pot, cochlean. Loving the still-horned dawn of this flower,

i'll take
a country without war
fukujusô

---

1. *Out With It!* Hajin's poem might also be mildly risqué. I have heard an appeal to show something to the world in a traditional comical story (*rakugo*), where a man in an antique shop confuses the term *chin-mono*, meaning "rare item," or "antique," with its vernacular meaning of "penis." The ten-minute routine ends with the shop owner demanding, "if you have one, out with it!" (*aru nara mise!*) The sprouts of the *fukuju-sô* are thin as wild asparagus and only a few inches long. Hardly, the big bamboo.

The preamble needs explaining. Ryôta refers to a Chinese proverb about the futility of nations struggling for power: *like warring armies on a snail's two horns* (the most instable flesh on earth). So the snail-like shape of the pot lets the poet show his contentment with the tiny plant and its modest flowers and joy for waking up in a country at peace with the world. At the same time, he may think the *fukujusô* fortunate to occupy its own little pot, as did the Japanese in this era of splendid isolation (For Japanese affirmation of the policy read Kaempfer and Golownin (quoted in *Topsy-turvy 1585*)).

神国や草も元日きっと咲　一茶
kamiguni ya kusa mo ganjitsu kitto saku   issa 1827
(gods' country! grass/es-too/even new-year's day surely bloom)

! for this is god's country !

even a weed	a mere flower
will surely bloom right	but you will surely bloom
on new year's	on the new year

In China, the *ume* (plum/apricot) may bloom by New Year's, but it – the capital, and hence main literary culture, anyway – is Northern and most plants (as opposed to trees) would not bloom until later. But, here, Issa's rhetoric seems to play the "we are special card" and is directed at a specific plant in the hope he can shame it into properly performing: *As, we agree, the gods are looking after us, prosperity will surely come with the New Year!* Our flower is not specifically mentioned, but the *ku* is placed with the *fukujusô* in the *saijiki* arrangement (vol 1) of Issa's *All-works* (*zenshû*), and an essay by a much younger Issa reveals he was highly *fukujusô*-conscious. Noting how happy everyone was with this plant, he got one himself and was not impressed with how it bloomed *until he realized that it must be one of those preternaturally sensitive plants, described in the classics, that completely change character and name to match the environment.* He describes what happened to the plant when it was introduced to his hovel in two haiku: *"Joining our brush / my poverty plant also / blooms in spring"* (藪並や貧乏草も花の春 *yabunami ya binbôsô mo hananoharu* 1808) *"My poverty plant / has enjoyed a most / felicitous spring"* (貧乏草愛でたき春に逢にけり *binbôsô medetaki haru ni ainikeri*.). While the reborn, renamed plant may also be pronounced *binbô-kusa*, I think *binbô-sô* best for the parallel with *fukuju-sô* and homophony-punning with impoverished *appearance* (*sô* 相).

色かはりなくてめでたし福寿草　梅室
irogawari nakute medetashi fukujusô baishitsu 1768-1852
(color-change-[does]not, cheerful/auspicious *fukuju-sô*)

the happy flower

neither fading
nor falling: all cheer
fukujusô!

Issa's long-lived contemporary celebrates the plant itself. While *irogawari* literally means a change of color (metaphorically, a lover's change of heart), it includes a change of place, a flower falling. As behooves a golden flower, the *fukuju-sô* does not fade or change color. Neither does it fall. I faintly recall mine shriveling up and disappearing. To me they seemed like a cross between cactus and a sea anemone. To properly appreciate the *ku*, however, we must jump ahead to the cherry blossoms and note that some poets claimed to find them a mixed blessing because their fate was troubling and even pretended to feel extremely relieved when their favorite flowers were done. A New Year's flower should not cause us to worry; and, with the *fukuju-sô*, Baishitsu notes, we *don't*.

善き鉢の殊にいやしや福寿草　子規
yoki hachi no koto ni iyashi ya fukujusô shiki 1899
(fine pot's particularly base!/: *fukuju-sô*)

      a fancy pot
    is particularly base
        fukujusô

Why is a fancy pot particularly ignoble with a *fukuju-sô*? Is it the mismatch? Or did Shiki grow enough in the four years from Meiji 28 to Meiji 32 to come to appreciate the plant as a crude start, worthy for the time of celebration for the same reason bare wood and unglazed pottery are? [1]

万両の鉢もめでたし福寿草　冷泉　最新二万句
manryô no hachi mo medetashi fukujusô　reisen 19-20c? 改造社
(1,0000 *ryô* [large monetary unit]/spearflower even joyous/auspicious *fukuju-sô*)

~~million-dollar pots~~   my *fukujusô*   ~~with *fukujusô*~~
~~are also auspicious~~ the million pound pot ~~even a precious pot~~
   ~~*fukujusô*~~   is also lucky   ~~feels holiday~~

I thought this a riposte to Shiki's *ku*, arguing that the primordial appearance of the *fukuju-sô* is robust enough to withstand if not complement a *manryô*, or, million-dollar pot, but a last minute dictionary check uncovered a decorative plant from 3-6 feet high by the same name. Called a "spearflower" in English, the punning luck does not translate. Then, again, neither does *medetashi,* a joyful, auspicious, festive feeling, with a touch of the sacred. A lucky million pound pot was the best I could do.

小書院のこの夕暮れや福寿草　太祇
koshôin no kono yûgure ya fukujusô　taigi 1709-72
(small book-room's this evening! *fukuju-sô*)

ready for new year   *as day one closes*

  this evening   *this* evening
in my small study   in my small study
  the *fukujusô*   the *fukujusô*

Were this by Bashô or Buson, it would be very famous, for the *ku* has a certain mysterious subtlety that attracts us. When *sakura* (cherry) is mentioned in this way, the name itself suggests blooming (*saku*). In this *ku*, however, we can only complete the poem by asking, what *else* can this plant do but bloom? Perhaps, the plant's buds may open on the following day or have earlier that day. I can not even say whether this is New Year's Eve or New Year's day, but the little plants *do* look better at such a time – for the dusk, unlike the dawn, always has a lull and can itself magically turn into gold. This discriminating observation makes the poem something I call a "gourmet *ku*."

---

1. Bare Beginnings. I repeat for the fifth time: the Jesuits were astounded to find Japanese using unglazed pottery and unlacquered chopsticks on celebrative occasions when Europeans would have brought out all their precious metals. Did Shiki rediscover the idea of back-to-the-basics being *the* heart of celebration? Here is a better known *senryû*-like complaint: *"New year's day: / a household shrine praises / its craftsman!"* (元日や大工をほめる神の棚　水室　*ganjitsu ya daiku o homeru kaminotana* suishitsu 1765). Shintô, in particular, was associated with clean design. Such fanciness would be so much dust on its proverbial mirror of reflection.

間拍子も順に程よし福寿艸　白羽 宇都宮歳旦帖
ma byôshi mo jun ni hodo yoshi fukujusô　hakuu 1744
(spacing-rhythm, too, order-in amount good: *fukuju-sô*)

ny metronome

it starts neat
and keeps the beat:
fukujusô

I found this in an obscure New Year's haiku fest by a group of poets including young Buson. The group of Japanese old *ku* buffs who recently published it debated over whether the *ku* meant only that the plant bloomed on New Year's day or that the buds kept coming, one at a time. The senior scholar (Maruyama) voted for the former, but I think the wording for the rhythm, with the *ma* (spacing) and *jun* (order), and the *mo,* or "too," favor the second interpretation. It is not, however, either/or. Is it not possible it not only starts on time, but paces itself well? I remember being impressed the way my first stubby, then scraggly, shoot managed to keep up a sequence of blooms, one at a time. Just when you thought it all over, out popped another.

明行や時計の側の福寿草　秀山 同
akeyuku ya tokei no soba no fukujusô　shûzan 1744
(dawn-ing: clock's side's *fukuju-sô*)

spring-time-piece

as it dawns
right next to the clock
the *fukujusô*

This is a time-piece with three hands: an artificial hour-clock (probably a European style mechanism improved by the Japanese to begin and end its half-day of hours with the rise and set of the sun), the natural, solar diurnal clock, and the annual timer, *fukuju-sô*. Again, unless told otherwise, when we read of a flowering plant in a haiku, the assumption is that it is blooming, or, as here, just beginning to bloom.

歳月日三のかほりや福寿草　蕪村
toshi tsuki hi mitsu no kaori ya fukujusô　buson 1715-83
(year moon day three's scent/whiff/suggestion/mood/appearance=face!/: *fukuju-sô*)

year, month, day
all three bloom in one
plant prosperity

For this one translation, I renamed the *fukujusô*. Written three decades after the above-mentioned New Year's Fest, Buson's *ku* still shows the influence of the two *fukuju-sô ku* in it! He is celebrating the fortieth birthday/year (called the "first-old" (*hatsu-rô*), or the start of old age) of three poets in his school, with the pen-names Buy-mountain, Self-rare and Bridge-sage. The translation falls short. I could not allude to the poets' different styles by a middle line like "three different *scents*" because of the narrow connotation of "scent" in English, nor improvise with different "blooms," when such variety is not in the plant. Buson, a painter by profession, presented the men with a sketch of Daikoku, deity of grain and prosperity, wearing two masks beside his own: Benten, goddess of wealth and beauty and Bishamon, god of treasure. The three faces of the deity are punned on ("face=*kao*!" is in the scent=*kaori*/etc.) in this *ku* that basically praises the plant for blooming right at the time the cycles of time meet.

on time

keep that beat!
three rhythms meet:
the *fukujusô*

After reading Buson's *ku*, I went back two *ku* to Hakuu's New Year's metronome, and fit in the idea of permutation to get the above.

植木屋の内で咲ぬ福寿草 『初桜』三谷一馬著「彩色江戸物売図絵」より
uekiya no uchi de sakinu fukujusô anon. 19c? (in a book by mitani kazuma)
(nursery-man's house-at/in bloom/s/ing *fukuju-sô*)

the *fukujusô*
bloom inside the house of
the nursery-man

I think this *zappai* (something between haiku and *senryû*) depicts more than the paradox of a poor man with wealth symbolically blooming in his house. Unsold merchandize blooms in irony.

福寿草くさとは見えぬ影法師　梅室
fukujusô kusa to wa mienu kagebôshi   baishitsu 1768-1852
(*fukuju-sô*: grass/herb/plant-as-for appears-not shadow-figure)

plato would like this one!

fukujusô: its shadow
a shadow puppet so   shows nothing of plant:
far from grass!   *fukujusô*

In Japanese, a shadow puppet is a *kagebôshi*, lit. shadow [Buddhist]priest, and refers not only to those seen cast *upon* walls and other surfaces, but *through* them, for most doors, windows and internal walls (moving partitions) in Japan were paper. Since Japanese had few pictures hanging and little wall-paper, the whole house was a screen. Baishitsu makes a close observation. This plant/grass does not cast a shadow that says "flora." The half-open bloom resembles a beast, or a human with a big head, perhaps carrying some small bags on his back, the buds. Or a few figures, a cluster of travelers. If I have the right blog some day, I may ask visitors to send in photos of *their* plant's shadow-figures.

ふた（ひと）もとはかたき莟やふく寿草　召波
futa [kaizosha] hito [kodansha] moto wa kataki tsubomi ya fukujusô shôha
(cover/petals?(or, one?)-clump-as-for hard bud/s: *fukuju-sô* -1771)

tight-lipped   the whole thing
petals on these buds   a clump of hard buds
fukujusô   *fukujusô*

One version of this *ku* may be wrong. A photo in the Kôdansha *saijiki* shows a wild *fukujusô* with as much *leaf* as bloom, but the one I bought came out of its bulb with hardly a leaf. It was more a cactus-like stem bumpy with buds. Even when they opened, they did not spread wide but remained guarded.

蒼太く開かぬを愛す福寿草　子規
tsubomi futoku hirakanu o aisu fukujusô　shiki
(buds thick/stout opens-not[+obj] loving *fukuju-sô*)

guarded gifts	*ah, fukujusô*	*conservative*
such stout buds it doesn't like to open the *fukujusô*	i love how the thick buds hardly open	the thick buds try not to open: great! the *fukujusô*

Exactly. That is what I, too, observed. Isn't the *fukuju-sô* perfect for modern haiku? Cheap, anyone can buy one. Tiny, it fits on the window sill or desk where it can be easily studied. *Still-life, indeed.* Though the plant has been around in haiku a long time, Kaizôsha's *saijiki* gives 49 post-Shiki (including 4 by Shiki) *ku* vs. 16 olde *ku*, while Kôdansha's large *saijiki* gives 28 post-Shiki *ku* vs. 5 olde *ku*, or a dozen, if those in the explanation are included). Something contemporary:

福寿草家族のごとくかたまれり　福田蓼汀 講談社大歳時記
fukujusô kazoku no gotoku katamareri　　fukuda ryôtei (contemp)
(*fukuju-sô*: family-like[resemble] cluster/ing)

the secret of prosperity?

fukujusô
in clusters like
families

Shoots? Sub-shoots? Buds? Same questions for another contemporary *ku*: *"My favorite / number: seven / fukujusô"* (わが好きの数の七つの福寿草　五十反播水 同 *waga suki na kazu no nanatsu no fukujusô* igarashi bansui). I recall a cluster just the right level of complexity to suggest a family or tiny caravan that seemed eerily animal. So I would guess shoots. But "blossoms" is usually the default translation for a flowering plant. Such a number reflects both the nature of the plant and the way it is sold in small pots. In the wild, the *fukuju-sô* is said to rise up out of muddy snow-melt ground in *hordes*.

福寿草平均寿命延びにけり　日野草城 講談社大
fukujusô heikin jumyô nobinikeri　　hino sojô (contemp)
(*fukuju-sô:* average life-time grown[+finality])

fukujusô	*fukujusô*	*fukujusô*
does it work? our average life-span *has* grown	why popular? our average life-span has increased	odd bloom longevity outgrows our wealth

Finally, attention to the longevity side of the plant! Does the ~ *ni-keri* ending on the original imply worry for Japan's future? Later, I came to wonder about another possible reading, namely, that the old tend to buy this plant more than the young; so, its ubiquitous presence may not affect, but reflect aging.

膳について子等賑々し福寿草　久女
zen ni tsuite kora niginigishi fukujusô   hisajo 1890-1946
(table-to arrive children ~~clutch-clutch-do~~ boisterous: *fukuju-sô*大正新俳句)

<table>
<tr><td>at the dining table
children clamor with joy
my *fukujusô*!</td><td>~~at the dining table~~
~~children clenching their hands~~
~~my *fukujusô*!~~</td><td>before breakfast
the children excited about
the *fukujusô*!</td></tr>
</table>

~~Hand-clutching by an infant was considered a sign of incipient talent and good luck as a merchant in future life. This *ku*, by a well-known female poet, superimposes the table behavior of children and the clutches of buds, in this context all the more auspicious for the anthropomorphism.~~ My first explanation was right, but not for this *ku*, as it would require the characters 握々, not 賑々.

福寿草ひらきてこぼす真砂かな　橋本鶏二
fukujusô hirakite kobosu masago kana hashimoto keiji
(*fukuju-sô* opening spills true-sand!/?/'tis – 講談社大)

<table>
<tr><td>*fukujusô*
as it opens up
sand spills</td><td>*fukujusô*
growing, it spills
beach sand</td></tr>
</table>

This *ku* by a modern poet is my favorite of the chapter. When the bulb of the *fukuju-sô* starts throwing up sprouts, some begin under the soil and raise it up to the extent that sand on top is pushed over the edge of the pot. The magic of the plant, as already explained, is in its crude simplicity. The Japanese unconsciously understand this and put a layer of large-grained sand on the surface of the soil in the pot. Such sand is called "true-sand" (*masago*), and is not to be confused with dirt. Its clearly visible texture complements the texture of the sprouts and, metaphorically, suggests quantity *and* intensity of feeling, also suitable for wishes of prosperity and a long life. [1] A critic might say, no, the *ku* only describes reality; but, how can metaphorical spill-over be denied?

ひと雫するや朝日の福寿草　蒼虬 改造社
hito shizuku suru ya asahi no fukujusô   sôkyû 1760-1842
(one drop does [on point of drop dripping]! morning sun's *fukuju-sô*)

a drop of dew
lit by the rising sun
fukujusô

If the plant is inside, as is probable, one drop of dew was all the dew on the tiny plant. It comes from a soon to open bud and no flowers are yet open. Issa wrote The only *ku* of the plant *outdoors* which I have seen are by Issa:*"Between boulders / pushing up through debris / a fukujusô"* (岩がねや塵をし分て福寿草 *iwagane ya hokori [chiri?]oshiwakete fukujusô*) and, *"It stands up / wearing a thick snowcap / the fukujusô"* (大雪をかぶって立や福寿草 *ôyuki o kabutte tatsu ya fukujusô*). Alpinists will hate to hear this, but I appreciate this plant more where the other poets keep it, inside.

---

1. Sand and Intensity. Beginning with the oldest anthology of Japanese poetry, the *Manyôshû*, "the number of grains of sand" on the beach is a metaphor for intense desire and infinite love. English does not use countable things to measure intensity. *"I love you as much as there are grains of sand on the beach"* would be ludicrous. Likewise for a similar metaphor of countless *waves* in the sea; Japanese have no trouble with them.

何もなき床に置きけり福寿草 虚子
nani mo naki toko/yuka ni okikeri fukujusô kyoshi 1899
(something-even-not[i.e. nothing] bed/floor-on place/d [+emph.] *fukuju-sô*)

new year still-life

on the bed
with nothing else
a *fukujusô*

i place it
on the bare floor
fukujusô

an empty house
i leave it on the floor
the *fukujusô*

Japanese beds were ordinarily put away during the day. This is either a sleeping-New Year holiday or a sickbed (Shiki's). I would guess the former, for we have seen it in Issa with the "year-gem" present. The bed is a place of nostalgia and a place of mortality. What better place for a plant whose name includes "longevity"? The "nothing else" makes the poem, by turning the bed into a background, a canvas if it were. "Toko" can sometimes mean floor, hence the other readings.

福寿草影三寸の日向哉 子規
fukujusô kage san-zun no hinata kana shiki -1902
(*fukuju-sô* figure three inches' sunshine/facing/bathing!/?/'tis/!)

little things

fukujusô
just three inches
of sunshine

fukujusô
just three inches
sun-bathing

In Japan, where the sun is always depicted as red – for that is when you can actually see it – golden sunshine rarely makes it into print. No gold or yellow is mentioned here, but we can see the yellow flowers and feel the comfortable warmth of the sunlight. I feel a quiet joy, cheer, in this *ku*. An invalid spending most of the winter inside tends to get the sun bit by bit and the plant only *needs* three inches of sunshine. (A more direct reading: *Three-inches of sunshine: a fukujusô shadow puppet.*)

一鉢の福寿草おらが庵の春 夜濤 改造社
hito hachi no fukujusô oraga io no haru yatô 1880-1953
(one-pot's fukujusô, my-shack's spring=new-year)

shibui new year

a single pot
of *fukujusô*, spring
in my shack

a single pot
of *fukujusô*, my hut
has a spring

This is interesting next to Issa's *ora-ga-haru* (my spring) *ku*, with its "about average." Here we have a wee – i.e., smaller than average when it comes to New Year's decorations – prize, but it does stand for wishes to enjoy a better-than-average life. *Shibui* is "minimalist" without the overdone Latin.

日記まだ何も誌さず福寿草　遠藤梧逸
nikki mada nani mo shirusazu fukujusô   endô goitsu
(diary still nothing-even written-not, *fukujusô* ↑ lost source)

nothing yet
written in my diary
a *fukujusô*

Imagine plant and empty journal on a completely clean desk-top. Perhaps the former casts a shadow.

猫の居る~~榛~~縁の日~~南~~並や福寿草
neko no iru fuchi no hinami ya fukujusô   shiki
(cat's being veranda/porch/ledge's ~~sun south~~ haunt! *fukuju-sô*)

~~southern sun~~	our veranda	~~southern porch~~
~~on the veranda, our cat~~	usual haunt of the cat	~~cat, sunshine and~~
~~and *fukujusô*~~	a *fukujusô*	~~our *fukujusô*~~

Japanese houses have a skirt of wood, a shelf, not much wider than a running board, outside of the double-door-sized windows, open from floor ceiling to floor. One can sit on these ledges in a Zen meditation-like style, or, more casually, let your legs hang over. They are perfect for potted plants and sunning cats. The appeal of the *ku* rests largely on the sensations of temperature evoked. The chilly start of spring and the warm sunlight come together in the sparse yellow budded plant like a touch of warm chocolate syrup on ice cream. (Note: The explanation is based on a faulty version of the *ku*, but still holds true!) If there is a cold spell, Japanese homes get freezing cold, so accidents can happen: *"By the stove / a flower gets burnt / fukujusô"* (炉邊に置いて花こがしけり福寿草　九萬字　改造社 *robe ni oite hana kogashikeri fukujusô   kumanji* 19c?20c?). But, generally, there is just enough sun to save the day.

日のあたる窓の障子や福寿草　永井荷風 講談社大
hi no ataru mado no shôji ya fukujusô   kafû 1879-1959
(sun/sunshine's hit window's paper! *fukuju-sô*)

the paper window
glows white with sunshine
a *fukujusô*

The *fukuju-sô* sits prim in the delicately warm paper-window-side atmosphere. The comfortable feeling was captured by Buson before Shiki or Nagai Kafû, a modern author most famous (to me, at least) for a novel about pornographers. Here is Buson's well-known *ku*:

朝日さす弓師が店や福寿草　蕪村
asahi sasu yumishi ga mise ya fukujusô   buson - 1783
(morning sun pierce/shine bow-master's shop: *fukuju-sô*)

the morning sun
shines into the bow shop
a *fukujusô*

This *ku* leads off the *fukuju-sô* haiku in all of the *saijiki* I have. I avoided "piercing" the archery shop with "a ray" of sunlight because it would have ruined the suavity of the scene, to my mind something akin to the magical brown of drying tobacco leaves, touched with low rays of sunshine and highlighted by the tiny yellow flowers. The old master craftsman is there, too. This comfortable delicacy or sweet mellow feeling is probably more common in modern *fukuju-sô* haiku.

安らけく稚児の昼寝や福寿草 水明渓 改造社
yasurakeku chigo no hirune ya fukujusô　suimeikei 19-20c?
(tranquilly/restfully infant's morning-sleep: *fukuju-sô*)

an infant
restfully napping
fukujusô

I do not know *why* the baby, that I imagine breathing in sleep, and the plant go together so well, but it seems so natural you almost forget to think of any possible symbolism. The *ku* is far better than, this, next *ku* by a poet with the name of "pleasant-dream," *"It's New Year's / your smiling face, also / my fukujusô"* (元日や君の笑顔も福寿草　楽夢　明和2　*ganjitsu ya kimi no egao mo fukujusô* rakumu 1765)

福寿草見てしづかなる命かな 梲童 講談大
fukujusô mite shizukanaru inochi kana　kaidô - 1947
(fukuju-sô seeing quietly become life?/'tis)

fukujusô　　　　　　　　　　　　　　　　looking upon
looking at them　　　　　　　　　　　　fukujusô our lives
i'm quiet　　　　　　　　　　　　　　　　calm down

病室の湯婆の側や福寿草　八重桜 改造社
byôshitsu no yutanpo no soba ya fukujusô　yaezakura -1945
(hospital room's warm water bottle's next-to! *fukuju-sô*)

in the hospice
by a hot water bottle
a *fukuju-sô*

There is something sweet and comfortable in these *ku*. Still, a hospital is a hospital. This next is the most cheerful *fukuju-sô* I know:

酒の香に咲くうれしけれ福寿草　鶯池 同
sake no ka ni saku ureshikere fukujusô　ôchi? 19-20c?
(sake's aroma-to bloom delighted-be[or, emph.]! *fukuju-sô*)

i'll bet you love　　　　　　　　　　　　bloom joyfully
to bloom in wine's bouquette　　　　breathing in my *sake*
my *fukujusô*!　　　　　　　　　　　　　oh, *fukujusô*!

Alcohol is part of New Year, for giddiness is proper to a magical time. Because rice wine is heated, its aroma spreads further than that of grape wine. It also seems better suited to this plant, why I do not know! Since Japanese generally did not have house-plants (*bonsai* were kept on the porch of the house), the *fukuju-sô* was lucky to be inside with humans and their gods.

福寿草屠蘇を冷たく頂きぬ 波岑 同
fukujusô toso o tsumetaku itadakinu   hakon 19-20c
(*fukuju-sô: toso* sake [+obj] cold receive/drink)

> *fukujusô*
> i take my *toso sake*
> cold

I imagined the spare plant complemented by cold *sake* drunken from an unpainted square wooden cup. But the *sake* in question, a special auspicious medicinal concoction we will examine in another volume, is, according to my respondent, drunken from special lacquerware. So, rather than being a proper match for the earlier *ku* with the stark image of spilling sand, this seems Chinese. We feel a modest merchantile frugality behind/before middle-class good fortune.

日の障子太鼓の如し福寿草 たかし 講談大
hi no shôji taiko no gotoshi fukujusô   takashi -1956
(sun/shine's [window]paper drum-like *fukujusô*)

> the window paper
> sunlit and taut as a drum
> *fukujusô*

The windows, newly papered at the end of the year, remind the poet of a drum membrane, perhaps, partly because the tiny asparagus-like stems of the *fukuju-sô* resemble drumsticks. Reading this modern haiku, I felt the bracing, or tonic effect on the mood of the cold *sake* in the previous *ku*.

生きてゐる限り句作や福寿草 野村喜舟 同
ikite iru kagiri kusaku ya fukujusô   nomura kishû early-20c
(live-being while [so long as] haiku-compose [emph] *fukuju-sô*)

> *composition*
>
> so long
> as i live, i'll haiku
> *fukujusô*

Haiku are never "written" in Japanese. They are always "read" (*yomu*) or "composed/built" (*tsukuru/saku*). Presumably, this vocabulary goes back to the time when all poetry was oral and men and women wooed one another with clever words partly traditional and partly improvised. In reality, many Japanese, like many English speakers, think best with pen (or brush) in hand, or fingertips on keyboard. The beginning of the year was a time to start writing. The spare, small *fukuju-sô* helps the poet realize how great his or her love for haiku is and how haiku is, itself, the source of spiritual wealth and mental health.[1]

---

1. *Haiku as Healthy* I do not mean that haiku serve as catharsis in the manner of modern verse. Composing haiku takes our mind off ourselves, is invigorating in the way that crossword puzzles are, and can be done even when – or especially when – we feel too tired to do anything else. We need to be in good condition to edit and select our haiku, but there is something about composition (listening to the world?) that *gives* rather than takes energy. The brevity of the individual poems makes it possible for busy and sick people to find the time to write, where otherwise they might not, and the little triumphs resulting pick up the spirits.

けふさくは世のほめ草そ福寿草 昌意 毛吹草
kyô saku wa yo no homekusa zo fukujusô shôi 1645
(today bloom-as-for, world's praise-grass=topic *fukuju-sô*)

secular flower   *propitious start*

blooming today   blooming today
the *fukujusô* proves it   the *fukujusô* obtains
loves the world!   the world's praise

Not knowing which of the first two readings was intended, I created a third for both: "**Fukujusô** – *It blooms today / to praise the world / and be praised!*" As my respondent thinks the second is right, I'll add another version of that reading:

◎   *Because you bloom / and bloom today, we love you / little fukuju!*   ◎

まどろめるわれを見守り福寿草　阿部みどり女
madoromeru ware o mimamori fukujusô　midorijo 1885-1990
(dozing me[+obj.] see-guard[watch]ing *fukuju-sô*)

while i doze
my guardian angel is
a *fukujusô*

guarding me   *fukujusô*
when i nod off   looks after me
the *fukujusô*   as i doze

A creative *ku* by a well-known modern poet. I suppose the opening buds have a somewhat eye-like appearance, but I think it more simply the presence of this plant, the only one in the house. The first translation should be read figuratively. The Japanese have no concept of a guardian angel. The compound verb, *mi-mamoru,* or "watch-guard," is the behavior expected of a watch-dog, or the God Whom little children in the West are taught to pray to before sleeping.

これだけか見ないで買った福寿草　敬愚
koredake ka minai de katta fukujusô　keigu
(this all? see-not-with bought *fukuju-sô*)

a bit of yellow

so, *this* is all!
the *fukujusô* i bought
bloom-unseen

When I bought my first *fukuju-sô,* I had yet to see a single one in bloom. Since they were selling like hotcakes at the curbside flower-vendor, I just figured I was in for a real treat. Had I read all these haiku first, I might not have been disappointed. Some day, I hope to buy another *fukuju-sô* and see if my feelings are different. I titled the *ku* "a bit of yellow" for it seemed that a bit of yellow did not please me as much as a bit of blue or red might. But, had I been Chinese, where yellow was *the* color of celebration, even a bit of yellow might have satisfied me.

pROVSPERITY

福寿草貧乏艸もあらまほし 子規
fukujusô binbôgusa mo aramahoshi shiki - 1902
(*fukujusô poverty/poor-grass/flower too be-want*)

    prosperity blooms   prosperity grass
    i wouldn't mind a pot   it would be nice to have
    of poverty, too   poverty grass, too

prosperity grass!
dear me, where can i find
some *poverty*!

Since Shiki wrote this the same year he claimed the *fukujusô* was vulgar, at first, I thought he meant that *if this plant represented "prosperity," he'd hate to see what represented poverty;* but, the archaic grammar suggests something desirable, or even ideal. And, as *haiyû* Tenki points out, this is not merely a call for nominal balance between prosperity and poverty – in that case, the peony would be more perfect, for its name does not include the element of longevity – but a sort of idealism, perhaps the idea that we would live figuratively richer lives if we enjoyed a modicum of prosperity *and* poverty. This was, after all, the *haijin's* ideal since Bashô (who got it from Taoism and, if you will pardon mixing cultures, Franciscan schools of Buddhism). Shiki, living in a time when the nation was hell-bent on becoming prosperous, may have felt this mattered on a national as well as personal scale. Moreover, the Japanese New Year's Day was a time capsule, a trip back to the simple start of the world before there were many things or, for that matter, *any* things. If wealth can no sooner get to heaven than a camel can squeeze through the eye of a needle, it can also keep us from experiencing the immortality of the original day.

~~~~~~

Notes: 1) For Shiki's *ku,* I had to give up the policy (mostly) followed throughout the chapter of using the Romanized name of the plant and call it *Prosperity* to make the contrast work. 2) I did not translate the *longevity* part of the name because it had no bearing on the contrast, and because 3) There is a poverty *vine* already, so by calling for a "grass," I think Shiki means a small potted plant with flowers (What flowers I leave to your imagination). 4) Finally, this ↓ is less a note than a perspective:

> In the Edo era, people had a custom of eating well-boiled, diced *gobô* [burdock root] during the New Year, requesting "to live in a modest manner thin and long." (「細く長くつつましく生きる」)The gobô is full of calcium and fiber. It is best to choose one that is a uniform thickness for its entire length.

Searching for information about Edo era New Years, I googled upon this matter-of-fact item in a list of Holiday food. I love *gobô* (burdock)*,* which tastes as elegant as its closest Occidental equivalent, the carrot, tastes childish. Throwing out the "damn dock" as a weed only proves the immaturity of our food culture. Reading it, I knew I had to append it to this chapter on *fukujusô*. Why? Because it brings out another reason the *fukujusô* rather than a miniature *camelia, sasanqua* or other more spectacular blossom became the representative of good things. There is something to be said for a truly frugal life. This "thin and long" stuff may sound funny in English – and note the "thin" is used in a stanza of the Japanese translation of Elvis's *Love Me Tender* – but, it is true to life. Trees missing branches and rats with limited caloric intake outlive those lucky enough to indulge their vegetable or animal appetites more fully. As we grow older, we come to better appreciate the humble golden flower.

The first is a print by the most prolific and talented graphic artist of all time, Hokusai, and is as I recall *fukujusô*. It is not embossed and in color, with the golden yellow of the flower (and, with artistic license, the stem!) contrasting with the blue of the Chinese pot (as my respondent said). The wild (?) flowers in the second, borrowed from the web and redone in black and white (a free book for the photographer, whose name I cannot find, if he finds me!) are exceptionally wide open. Many if not most *fukujusô* found on the web often seem closer to prize Chrysanthemum than the grubby (?) *fukujusô* I was acquainted with! But, then again, mine, like Issa's, should probably have been renamed!

初夢
hatsu-yume

13

First Dream

浮橋の下につなぐや寶舟　青山 末若葉
ukihashi no shita ni tsunagu ya takarabune　seizan 18c?
(floating-bridge's below-to/by fasten:/! treasure-ship)

coming to moor
below a floating bridge
the treasure ship

The treasure ship (*takarabune*) was two things; *first*, an imaginary entity, a huge boat full of wealth and magical devices, and, *second*, a picture of the same sailing toward you, placed under the bed or pillow as a charm for propitious New Year's dreams to be seen on the solar spring, New Year's Eve, New Year's night or on the night after that (It varied from place to place and time to time, but eventually, Edo came to settle on the last, after people recovered from the busy end-of-year and the all-nighter). The picture generally included a palindromic *waka* with the first 5-7-5 asking all to awaken from their long night's sleep (*night* punning on distant times, too?) and the final 7-7 delighting in the pleasant sound the (arriving?) ship makes riding through the waves (ながきよのとをのねぶりの みなめざめなみのりぶねのおとのよきかな). The floating bridge – made by putting planks over boats facing into the current lashed together – alludes to a tenuous link between our floating (*i.e.,* imaginary woe-filled) world and a magical real one beyond or over it. *How can a giant ship squeeze under the planks?* That's easy: a fully-laden ship floats low. (はい、はい、出鱈目の説明です). Most *saijiki* moor the "treasure ship" theme either in front or behind the "first-dream" (*hatsu-yume*). I put it *inside* the first-dream – *i.e.,* unite the themes – because of its being a prop for said dream. For reasons beyond my ken, the above *ku* is the *only* "treasure ship" poem listed in Shiki's *Categorical!*

生れ子の分も買ハせる宝舟　俳諧一枝竹／全(三谷：江戸商売図絵)
umarego no bun mo kawaseru takarabune　anon. 18-19c?
([newly] born child's portion-also bought treasure-ship)

buying one
for her new-born as well
treasure ship

A sweet poem about a sweet mother. A charm for a child too young to even know it has dreams! This next *ku* would be its antithesis, proper for a New Year's book only if we take it as humor:

哀れいかに宝船売る人のさま 大江丸 俳諧懺悔
aware ika ni takarabune uru hito no sama ôemaru 1719-1805
(pitiful how! treasure-ship sell person's/peoples' appearance)

how wretched
the men look who sell
treasure ships!

how wretched
this man who sells
treasure ships!

If the poet describes only one treasure-ship charm peddler, this *haikai* is haiku, if plural, it becomes *senryû*. It deserves to become proverbial, for it beats the doctor who can't care for himself and the cobbler who can't keep himself well-soled. A more poetic sketch by Issa records: *"First-dreams / made and sold on this / chilly night"* (初夢を拵へて売る余寒哉 hatsuyume o koshiraete uru yokan kana). The "remaining cold" in the original is a seasonal term. It is Spring, while charm-selling is Winter.

袖抽斗や宝舟買ふ銭五文 露月
~~sode baka~~ hikidashi ya takarabune kau zeni go mon   rogetsu 1873-1927
(~~sleeve only~~ dresser/chest-drawer! t-ship buys money five-mon (monetary unit))

~~only enough~~
~~treasure ship for one arm~~
~~five bits~~

dresser drawer
enough for a treasure ship
five pennies

~~just enough~~
~~for a share of treasure~~
~~five bits~~

~~Because "sleeve" means an arm-pillow, I first thought the picture a small one rather than one large enough to put a *futon* on? But, on more consideration, I think "sleeve" here is idiomatic for a small bribe to get access to someone or something.~~ My cultured respondent saved me. A magnifying glass showed I had the *kanji* wrong. The corrected version is better. Is not the drawer itself a treasure ship? Another exact description of the cost in a treasure boat *ku* is actually about a courtesan. The amount makes that clear: *"For a crown / one can buy a good dream / the spring town"* (大判て能夢買ん春の町　沾峨　吐屑庵 ôban de ii yume kawan haru no machi   tenga 1776).

授かるや尼が手摺の寶舟 桐一 ホトトギス
sazukaru ya ama ga tezuri no takarabune tôichi (mod.)
(accept! nun's hand-rubbed treasure-ship)

i'll take it!
a treasure ship hand-printed
by a nun

A nun is a magical creature who pretty much lives on dreams, so any treasure-ship she made ought to work. I do not know if there is any historical evidence for nuns in the business of selling treasure ships – there is far more on fake prostitute nuns who plied their trade from boats (*funabikuni*) – but it is delightful to find someone in a Buddhist order participating in New Year activities. A bar owner once told me how her father, who owned and operated the Buddhist temple within which she grew up, kept a Christmas tree hidden inside the closet to delight the children who knew about them from the US Occupation's most powerful persuader: Hollywood. I think the *ku* by Tôichi beats the older one about the wretched men selling the charms. Yet, I think the next contemporary *ku* is even better:

華街のれん分け行き買ひぬ宝船 久保田月鈴子 講談社大 20c
kagai [hanamachi?]noren wakeyuki kainu takarabune kubota getsureishi
(flower/prosperous-street[gay-quarters=dict.] [shop]curtain split-go-buy treasure-ship)

      in old uptown   parting a *noren*
parting the *noren*, i buy   in the gay quarters to buy
       treasure ships   my treasure ship

The part of town in question has no good name in English. It generally boasts long-established artesians and shops that retain the old custom of stringing shop curtains across the entrance. These have tasteful logos, an indication of the product or simply something auspicious (eggplants and tops for example) and are usually indigo, *the* traditional dye of Japan which takes us back into the magical times of the past. These short over-head curtains are segmented and pushing between them calls to mind cutting through waves. Since most people no longer buy and sleep on treasure ship charms, I think the poet *had* to go to the old-fashioned (traditional Japanese) part of town to find one, or enough for her family. But, it may be a place where luck plays a big role in life, the red-light district, too.

やごとなき一筆かきや寶船 召波 改造社
yagotonaki ippitsu kaki ya takarabune shôha – 1771
(extraordinary/elegant one-brush[jotted]-drawn:/! treasure-ship)

   treasure ship   how important   one brush stroke
and the brush-stroke   this drawing in one stroke   this is the real thing
     has no end   my treasure ship   a treasure ship

First of all, *"yagotonaki"* (more commonly *yangotonaki*) means something done because it cannot be helped, so I imagined Shôha, having forgotten to buy a charm, drawing his own:

     having no choice   ah, the elegance
dashed out in a brush-stroke   of a treasure ship drawn
      my treasure ship   with one stroke

Looking up the term, I also found connotations of *extraordinary* and *elegant*. Hence, the additional reading. But, the Chinese characters by which it is written: 止事無 (*stop-thing not*) *do* evoke a drawing made without stopping to replenish the ink. I have been amazed to find Japanese calligraphy that seems to have been created by what we might call *a fountain-brush.* There is magic in a brush that never leaves the paper until its work is done. (Note: I have two letters from Shirakawa Shizuka, Japan's leading expert on Chinese characters and his ball pen (not brush!) *never* leaves the paper: the complex characters resemble *tornados!* – In case you wonder why I wrote him, it was to obtain his opinion about a *Shi-ching* poem where Waley and Pound have a woman delighted to have rolled a *man* in the dew, while Japanese translators have the sexes reversed.) It is a good way to draw pictures with your eyes closed. Be that as it may, there is a good chance Shôha may be praising his friend Buson's drawing rather than describing what he did.

老後とや藁で作れる宝船 加倉井秋を 講談大
rôgo to ya wara de tsukureru takarabune kagurai akio
(age-after! straw-with making treasure-ship 20c)

     in my old age   that's old age
making them out of straw   treasure ships made
     treasure ships   out of straw

This is a damn good contemporary *ku,* but my memory of an ex-sumo wrestler braiding straw sandals for gifts, as a hobby, is so strong that it is hard to read this *ku* as is.   There may be a hint of Thoreau here – or was it Emerson? – i.e., the bridge (or was it a rocket?) to the stars turned into a woodshed (Remember, "we" are translated into Japanese, though we translate almost nothing into English.). I have not seen a straw treasure ship, but I *have* seen straw festoons – two-strand (yin-yang) twisted rope – depicting the character for *longevity* and have no doubt but there *are* treasure ships out there, or could be. I also feel that, by using straw, the old poet returns to the old days before plastic turned much of Japan into modern camp, and that these are the dreams his ship brings, *as it is made*. To return to the more usual medium for depicting treasure ships:

つくづくと寶はよき字宝船 後藤比奈夫 講談大
tsukuzuku to takara wa yoki ji takarabune   gotô hinao 20c
(intently/exhaustively "treasure"-as-for good letter, treasure-ship)

tremendous care
taken with the letter "treasure"
on the treasure ship

The character for "treasure" is usually found in the center of the sail. This contemporary *ku* notes the perfectly drawn, exquisite thick strokes of the character, conventionally surrounded by a circle, a symbol of the harmony from which prosperity comes. In the nationalistic early-20c, the circle sometimes turned into the sun. *"The treasure ship / Drawing a great round / red sun"* (寶舟大日の丸を画きけり　月斗 *takarabune ôhinomaru o egakikeri* getto 1868-1949) Doubtless, it was red and stood for the poet's hope for the success of the national dream, i.e., the greater Prosperity Sphere of Asia. And, note that Japan's national anthem was first sung in a 19c song about *Hôrai* 薩摩琵琶歌「蓬莱山」.

いちにんの舸子の余地なき宝船 丸山海道 講談大
ichinin no kako no yochinaki takarabune   maruyama kaido 20c
(one person boat-child[sea man]'s extra-space not, treasure ship)

no room for
even one seaman
the treasure ship

The boat was so loaded that the seven gods aboard barely peek over the bounty or sit so close to the side of the boat one fears losing them overboard. And, the obese God of Happiness and Wealth (who causes problems for others because (according to *senryû*) he cannot reach his own you-know-what or (I had better skip *that* detail for a different type of book!), takes up so much room . . .

宝舟目出度さ限りなかりけり 虚子
takarabune medetaki kagiri nakarikeri   kyoshi 1874-1959
(treasure-ship propitious/joyful/celebratory limit [is]not[+emph.])

the treasure ship
for there is no limit
to joyfulness

I chose the *medetaki* with "full" in it for it fit the ship. Sometimes the treasure ship charm was given some assistance in the form of props. At least I think that is what the following poem is about:

蓑笠に庵の狭さよ宝船　蓼太
minokasa ni io no semasa yo takarabune　ryôta 1707-87
(straw-rain-gear-to[with respect to] hut's narrowness! treasure-ship)

my sea poncho
too big for the tiny hut
treasure ship!

Straw rain-gear was hardly worn by sailors alone. I go too far in calling it "my sea poncho," but the *ku* seemed to need it. Does the room become the magical ship? Another by Ryôta is equally ambiguous and fascinating: *"Treasure ship! / a mat/room that has never / known a storm"* (たから舟嵐のしらぬ一間かな　蓼太 *takarabune arashi no shiranu hito ma kana*). The *ma* can mean the room *or* a unit of *tatami* mat : The contrast of the room/mat and sea hints that the greatest treasure is already enjoyed: *peace*.

宝船こころすなほに敷いてねる　蜃楼 改造社
takarabune kokoro sunao ni shiite neru　shinrô 1884-1946
(treasure-ship heart/mind frankly/meekly lay/place/spread-out sleep)

going to sleep　　　　　　　　　　　the treasure ship
wishes openly laid out　　　　　　spreading it out to sleep
the treasure ship　　　　　　　　　without doubt

Sunao means honest/frank *and* gentle/soft, even compliant, a combination not found in English. I guess it refers here to the attitude of believing the traditional fiction and falling asleep hopefully.

宝船訳の聞こへぬ寝言かな　太祇
takarabune wake no kikoenu negoto kana　taigi -1772
(treasure-ship meaning hear-not sleep-words!/'tis)

the treasure ship
impossible to make out
this sleep talk

Taigi alludes to the Chinese spoken by the seven Chinese Gods on the treasure ship and alludes to the phrase "Chinese-sleep-words" which means "like Greek to me" in English. As far as I know, Chinese did not sleep on pictures of treasure ships like Japanese did. But, long before the Occident began to explore, Chinese sailed ships the length of two football fields (with watertight compartments and many other modern features) throughout the Pacific and this may have started something like the airplane-inspired cargo cults of parts of 20c Oceania. While this was no longer *known* to the Japanese, there was, I would guess (and, I mean it, it is *only* a guess!), a vague cultural memory.

いたいけに争ふ早寝や宝船　はぎ女 大全
itaike ni arasou hayane ya takarabune　hagi-jo 19-20c?
(innocently/sweetly compete/fight early-sleep!/: treasure ship)

the treasure boat　　　　　　　　　innocently
innocently competing to be　　　competing to sleep first
the first to sleep　　　　　　　　　the treasure boat

老ぬれば早寝ぬるなり宝舟 佐藤漾人 講談社大
oinureba haya inuru nari takarabune   satô yôjin? 20c
(old-becoming, early-sleeping-become treasure-ship)

growing old
i go to bed early
treasure ship

early to bed
my reward as a geezer
treasure ship

growing old
i hit the sack early
my treasure ship

At first reading, I preferred Hagi-jo's *ku*, probably depicting her children, to this contemporary *ku*; but, when I added the clear "reward" between the lines and considered what dreams mean to the elderly, I came to like them equally.

鼻息に飛んでは軽し宝船 子規 再現
hanaiki ni tonde wa karushi takarabune   shiki -1902
(nose-breath-by flying-as-for light/easy treasure-ship)

dream power

the treasure ship
how swiftly it sails in
a nose wind

寶舟敷いて寝し子の鼾かな 零雨 愛吟集
takarabune shiite neshi ko no ibiki kana   reiu 20c?
(treasure-ship spread-out sleep child/ren's snore/s 'tis/!)

ah, the snores
of a child sleeping upon
her treasure ship

ah, the snores
of children asleep on
their treasure ships

In Japanese cartoons, sleep is represented by a balloon protruding from the nose, which, in animation, expands and shrinks with each snore. Dreams, too, may be depicted within this bubble, rather than in bubbles coming from the cranium. That is what my "dream power" title means. Shiki's idea could be generalized: *Treasure ships / How swiftly they run before / a nose wind!* The second *ku*, in the accepted modern style, is far more subtle. Any *ku* can be given whatever number, sex or pronoun you prefer (My respondent prefers a singular *child*).

初夢や額にあつる扇子より 其角
hatsu yume ya hitai ni atsuru sensu yori   kikaku -1707
(first dream:/! forehead-on touch/rest/ing fan-from/out-of)

my first dream
from the fan resting
on my brow

This is one of the most widely *saijiki*-ized first-dream *ku*, but I can only guess what the idea is (在米の上、其角全句の解注書が高過ぎて買えないから、当てずっぽうだ). The first, most natural one would be that the fan is adorned with images of the three most desirable dreams, *Fuji*, *Hawk* and *Eggplant*, respectively; where *Mt. Fuji* is not only lofty but has more than one propitious name: *Wealth-warrior, Inexhaustible, Not-two* (*i.e.,* one and only, top); a hawk flies high, is far-sighted, a good hunter and a homophone for "high" (*taka(i)*); the *eggplant* resembles a black-bag full of wealth and, more important, is a homophone for accomplishing (*nasu*) something. But, I also wonder whether the fan is intended to provide wind to propel the treasure ship. (There is so much magic in the wind and in fans. According to a *senryû*, one famous Kyoto fan-shop did a good trade with Woman's Island (Nyogo-gashima), where the sea wind was the women's only lover. On still days, the fans served as dildos. I apologize for vulgarity, but dreams are dreams, and the fantasies of lonely men with their islands of women and children with their treasure ships are equally fascinating things of the air.)

吉原の眠らぬ床に宝舟　俳諧一枝竹／全（三谷：江戸商売図絵）
yoshiwara no nemuranu toko ni takarabune　anon. 18-19c?
(yoshiwara's sleep-not bed/floor-on/in treasure-ship)

<blockquote>
a treasure ship
under a sleepless bed
in yoshiwara
</blockquote>

The treasure ship may allude to the courtesan on the bed as well as the picture *under* it, for the women were sometimes called treasure ships. I could not gracefully save the allusion in the translation. The Yoshiwara was the very place of dreams, the *Pleasure Quarters*. I have read that the only day the women had off from work was New Year's Day, but even then, they would have had to greet their employers and any guests that visited to exchange formal greetings. If the *ku* dates from late in the Tokugawa Era (1603-1867), it might be the night of the Second Day when she would indeed be working.

宝ぶね明六ッからは捨小ぶね　童の的　(同)
takarabune akemutsu kara wa sutekobune　anon. 18-19c?
(treasure-ship dawn six(o'clock)-from abandoned small boat)

<blockquote>
the treasure ship
from six in the morning
a scrapped dingy
</blockquote>

寶舟旦一片の反古かな　橡面坊　改造社
takarabune asa hitohira no hôgo kana　tôchimenbo
(treasure ship morning one piece scrap-paper 19-20c)

<blockquote>
the treasure ship
in the morning, a piece
of scrap-paper
</blockquote>

The first *ku* might be an allegory for the courtesan left by her patron in the morning. The second is clearly no allegory. The charm, like an old betting slip, has simply lost its magic.

夢の跡皺になりけり寶舟　放江
yume no ato shiwa ni narikeri takarabune　hôkô -1930
(dream's trail/mark/trace: wrinkles-to become [emph.] treasure boat)

<blockquote>
the treasure ship　　　　　　　　　traces of dreams
a dream's wake turns　　　　　　　end up as wrinkles
into wrinkles　　　　　　　　　　the treasure ship
</blockquote>

宝船皺寄ってゐる目覚めかな　千原叡子 角川現代
takarabune shiwa yotteiru mezame kana   chihara eiko 20c
(treasure-ship wrinkles approaching eye-wake!/?/'tis)

treasure ships
wrinkles move together
as we awake

i awaken just
as my treasure ship
starts to wrinkle

treasure ship
ripples became wrinkles
as i awoke!

The paper charm wrinkles, for Japanese beds are not fixed, and ripples grow close as boats approach shore (or dock). In Japanese, waves can be wrinkles. The first *ku* can be overread as the summation of a life that began with great dreams and found out all that tangibly remains are wrinkles. The second *ku* is masterful both for capturing the moving dreams of dawn and the brow wrinkled by the light.

寶舟敷き寝の枕高々と　王城 ホトトギス
takarabune shikine no makura takadaka to   ôjô   early-20c
(treasure-ship, spread[bedding/paper-charm]'s pillow/bed high-up)

going to sleep
on the treasure ship
my pillow high

Another *ku* specifies a cottage-master (usually meaning a poet or retiree) sleeping with a bonze pillow, one generally made with the husks of buckwheat stugged into a cylindrical cloth (old sleeve?) and tied at the ends. (庵主の坊主枕や寶船　鬼城 *ionushi no bozu makura ya takarabune* kijô 1864-1938) I am not sure what it means, but this next *ku* suggests the metaphorical reason why a high pillow might have been in order (practically speaking, it was probably to preserve the holiday hairdo):

今朝さめて波濤跡なし寶舟　瓦全 昭和一万句
kesa samete hatô ato nashi takarabune   gazen 20c
(this morning waking, surf trace not, treasure-ship)

waking at dawn
no trace of the high surf
the treasure ship

Yes, a rough surf. I would guess this *ku* celebrates the ideal New Year weather, total calm.

Two Favorite one-of-a-kind Dream Ku

寶船われに知らさず敷きありし　雨丁 漁火
takarabune ware ni shirasazu shikiarishi   utei 20c
(treasure-ship me-to tell/inform-not spread-out-was)

a treasure ship
placed without notice
under my pillow

a treasure ship
i slept without knowing
it was under me

a treasure ship
no one told me it was
under my bed!

This is a one-of-a-kind, and I love it. The poet is blessed with a wonderful wife or child. Please, someone do a double-blind experiment to see if the dreams of people who do not know they are on a treasure ship are nonetheless improved! The next *ku* has no treasure ship but is a better *ku*.

おにんぎょとねてはつゆめをみましたよ 綱 宏美 小一
oningyo to nete hatsuyume o mimashita yo tsuna hiromi contemp.
([honorable+]doll-with slept, first-dream[+obj] saw[+emphatic])

i slept with a doll
and saw my first dream
i really did!

when i slept
with my doll i had one
a first dream

my first dream
it came when i was sleeping
with my doll

Varieties of Japanese are hard to reproduce. This *first-grade* girl's *ku* is, in the original, *a single sentence of prose*. I would not be surprised if an adult heard her say it and counted out those 17-18 syllabets. So, you might think, it can hardly be called a poem. But, it just so happens that the *idea* or *image* of the girl with her doll dreaming is more poetic than 99% of the poems in the world. Anyone with a decent eye can find natural productions by Mother Nature that beat almost all of the so-called art by recognized artists (including that in fancy galleries, sold for more money than some of us have ever seen) hands-down. In that sense, haiku is like the plastic arts. Like no other poetry, haiku may be *found*. This does not mean *ku* cannot be composed, but that *choice*, i.e., recognizing what is good or bad is what counts most.

A V*ARIETY OF* F*IRST* D*REAMS*

初夢や庭に富士見る松けしき 吉長 大三
hatsuyume ya niwa ni fuji miru matsugeshiki kichichô
(first-dream: garden-in fuji see pine-scenery 1697)

the first dream
fuji seen through pine
in my garden

If this is just the dream, the *ku* would be too thin, so I assume the good weather permitted the poet to fulfill his dream and actually see Fuji from his garden with the pine that not only is evergreen and long-lived but a homophone for "wait." *Lofty dreams will be fulfilled for all who wait?*

初夢の不二の山売都哉 一茶
hatsuyume no fuji no yama uru miyako kana issa -1827
(first-dream's fuji mountain sell capital!/?/'tis)

a mount fuji
for your first dream sold
in the capital

At first glance, Issa is chuckling at the idea of selling dream-mountains, either treasure ships to help you see the "best" dream or pictures of the mountain. Did Japanese knew how visualization could influence dreams? Read again, the chuckle turns into a laugh, for *capital* by itself means Kyôto, a city far removed from Mt Fuji. Again, and you start wondering how people in parts of Japan far from this mountain felt about it.

初夢に猫も不二見る寝様哉 一茶
hatsuyume ni neko mo fuji miru neyô kana   issa -1827
(first-dream-in cat too fuji sees sleep-manner/appearance!/?/'tis)

first dream
the cat, too, sleeps like
it sees fuji

We imagine Issa's cat lying on its back with its front legs stretched out over its head. Cats sleep on their back when they are feeling secure. This endearing *ku* is found in many *saijiki*.

元朝(元日)の見るものにせんふじの山 宗鑑
ganchô[jitsu]no mirumono ni sen[semu] fujinoyama sôkan
(original-dawn{new year's} see-thing-as do-let's fuji mountain1465-1553)

let's make it
our new year's sight!
mount fuji

Blyth's expansive translation is easier to understand: *"For this New Year's Day / The sight we gaze upon shall be / Mount Fuji."* Being a Sôkan fan, I have mixed feelings about his comments: "The excellence of this poem has caused many to doubt whether Sôkan, whose other haiku fall far below this, is really the author [1] . . . However, it is possible that the author meant the verse in a shallower sense than we now take it." Blyth also introduced *"The First Day of the Year: / One line of Emperors; / Mount Fuji."* [2] (元日や一系の天子不二の山　鳴雪*ganjitsu ya ikkei no tenshi fujinoyama* meisetsu 1847-1926), which he wrote "expresses the feelings of most Japanese about Japan on this particular day." If your country goes back to the beginning, New Year's rather than July 4, is the time to celebrate! The original calls the "Emperors" *tenshi,* or "heaven-child/ren," an expression that strictly speaking means the Imperial family but loosely interpreted covers all Japanese as the "children" of the same. And, it should be pointed out that the characters used for Fuji are not the standard "prosperity-warrior" but "not-two," emphasizing the unique nature of the mountain and making "one, not two" tie together the family and the mountain.

不二見よと起こされにけり今朝の春 素檗
fuji miyo to okosarenikeri kesanoharu   sobaku 1758-1821
(fuji see-let's/about/as/and woken[+fin.] this-morning's-spring=ny)

new year's day i'm woken up with "look at fuji!"	"look, it's fuji!" wakes me up at the dawn of the new year

First bet: the sky is clear and the people who are awake do not want the poet to miss his chance to get a good start for the year and get primed for dreams the following night. Second: The poet in his bulky sleep *futon* resembles said mountain. Third: a model Fuji has been carried into the room for a joke.

1. Sôkan's Poem? This poem credited to Sôkan is not found in collections dating to his lifetime, so it is possibly not his. Haiku are so short that authorship of individual poems are much harder to confirm than is the case with longer Western poems, where content and style may be almost conclusive.

2. Day, Emperor/s, Fuji The relationship of the parts of this *ku* is hard to grasp. Compare Blyth, above, and Stewart's *"New Year's Day, Mount Fuji's snowy cone, / One line of Emperors: each stand alone."* The equivalence of single Mt Fuji and the Imperial line, reflects the New Year upon New Year nature of the New Year.

~~~~~~

年のはじめに 一日の物おぼへなり不尽の山 素檗 1821
toshinohajime ni// ichinichi no monooboe nari fujinoyama sobaku
(year-start // one/all day's thing-remember beccme fuji mountain)

<center>our touchstone
for the entire day
mount fuji</center>

<center>***on the first day of the year***</center>

mount fuji	mount fuji
what we keep in mind	the only image i hold
the whole day	the whole day

Sobaku used the *Not-two* 不二 writing for Fuji in the first *ku* and *Not-exhaust* 不尽 (eternal) for the second. Were either *ku* about good fortune, he probably would have used the most common writing: "prosperity-warrior" 富士. The biggest question with the second *ku* is whether the more conceptual reading [1] – Sôkan's poem minus the prescription part – is right, or the more personal last reading.

明の春富士にうしろはなかりけり 列甫 春帖
akenoharu fuji ni ushiro wa nakarikeri   reppo 1806 滑稽
(bright/dawn's-spring, fuji-to back/reverse-as-for, not[emph.])

<center>spring's dawn
fuji has absolutely
no back-side</center>

The psychological connotations of *front* and *back* in Japanese are more powerful than in English, but let's skip that discussion. *The idea of a mountain as all out front!* This is the magical spirit of Japan's New Year. I tried to imagine which side of Fuji was seen at sunrise and, as I wondered, realized that it does not matter where the poet stands; the point is only that as he gazes, he feels (correctly) that countless other people are doing the same. As strange as it seems, it is normal for us not to be conscious of people on the far side of a mountain. Life is in the foreground. Call this an epiphany *ku*. Another *ku* suggests the way viewers from a broad area are drawn to face the famous mountain: *"In Musashi Field / Fuji is our lodestone / Edo New Year"* (武さし野は富士を磁石や江戸の春 風山 桜川 *musashino wa fuji o jishaku ya edo no haru   fuzan* 1674).

~~~~~~

1. Fuji in the Mind's Eye I cannot help but recall a *ku* calling Fuji the "nose-bridge" (*hana-bashira*) of Japan and imagine the poet meditating on his nation's nose: *"Tis the bridge / of the nose of our nation / Mount Fuji"* – takeraku (我国の鼻ばしら也不士（二）の山　岳連絡 茶の随斎筆紀より *waga kuni no hanabashira nari fuji no yama*); but I doubt Sobaku had the same thought! In Japanese, a "tall/high" nose is something to be proud of and "bridge" is literally "pillar," as in "pillar of the community." So a figurative reading would be: *"Indeed it is / the pillar of our nation ! Mount Fuji;"* but this loses the humor of mountain-as-nose. In the 19c, Edward S. Morse surveyed the Japanese image of Fuji, asking people to sketch its outline which he compared to the reality. Sure enough, it was depicted as a far steeper mountain than it actually is. This is still true.

元朝のふじ二つ見ん羨まし 乙二
ganchô no fuji futatsu min urayamashi otsuni -1823
(original-day's fuji two see-let's/would envious)

<table>
<tr><td>

new year's day
you can see fuji double
wish i could, too

</td><td>

how envious
to see two mount fuji
on new year's

</td></tr>
</table>

Some people have all the luck. If you have a pond between you and Fuji, you can see two mountains. If the date for the first-dream was the second night, seeing a lot of Fuji on the First would certainly heighten the possibility of an auspicious dream of the same. Regardless, this lofty mountain with a way of popping magically out of the blue sky is well worth gazing on for its own sake.

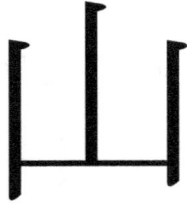

元日は余りに浅しふじの山 素檗
ganjitsu wa amari ni asashi fujinoyama sobaku -1821
(original-day-as-for, excessively shallow/low fuji mountain)

on new year's
it seems too low
mount fuji

Even if Fuji doesn't measure up to its image, to actually say so on a day where one was expected to see it as larger than life is truly extraordinary!

初富士や草庵を出て十歩なる 虚子再現
hatsufuji ya sôan o dete juppo naru kyoshi 1874-1959
(first-fuji: grass-hut[obj] leaving ten-steps becomes/is)

first fuji!
outside my grass hut
ten steps

Was ten steps out enough to see Fuji around the corner of the hut or around an evergreen? Was it enough to frame the mountain with just the right tree branches? Was it far enough away from the house to free the poet of his earthly shell? Or, far enough toward the mountain to count as a pilgrimage? This *ku* is generally the second one given in the modern *ku* category: *hatsu-fuji*, which ought not be conflated with dreaming of Fuji. The one before it is usually 初不二の雪を貢の日の出かな 千兵 玉かつら *hatsufuji no yuki no mitsugi no hinode kana* senhyo 1751 *first-fuji's snow[+obj] tribute'sunrise!/'tis*). I like to think it means:*"First Fuji: / Its snow a tribute for / the rising Sun!"* But the grammar and correspondent Tenki say a more likely reading is *"First Fuji / Sunrise brings us a gift / of new snow."* To my mind, First-Fuji *ku* should rise above words to include those *apparently* about First-Fuji – a good example would be Sobaku's *ku* – though the precise term, *hatsu-fuji* might be absent.

初夢や富士飛び越えて花に月 古白
hatsuyume ya fuji tobikoete hana ni tsuki   kohaku 1867-1895
(first-dream! fuji fly-over blossoms-and[=to?] moon[=arrive?])

<blockquote>
my first dream
flying over fuji, blossoms
and moonshine
</blockquote>

In Japanese, this *also* sounds like "flying over Fuji, I reach the flowers" or, "flying over Fuji, I land on my nose." This is not a plain propitious poem. Blossoms and the moon – not to mention the snow on Fuji – stand for poetry and make the dream the declaration of a poet. Shiki, who thought he would die first, was devastated by Kohaku's premature death by suicide.

初夢に大いなる海を見たりけり 花笠 明治俳句
hatsuyume ni ôi naru umi o mitarikeri   hanakasa 改造社
(first-dream-for/in large ocean[obj] saw [+emph.] late-19c)

<blockquote>
and for my　　　　　　　　　　the ocean grand
first dream i saw　　　　　　　is what i saw in it
a great sea　　　　　　　　　　my first dream
</blockquote>

Since Japanese think of the ocean as antonymic to the mountains; this may play against Fuji. Or, does the poet see the ocean from the vantage point of Fuji? Perhaps, the dream is patriotic: Japanese taking part in the global game and not remaining home huddled around their big mountain.

宇宙遊泳して初夢の覚めにけり 磯部石水 季題別平九
uchûyûei shite hatsuyume no samenikeri   isobe sekisui 1997
(space-play-swim[float] doing, first dream's wake [fin.+emph.])

<blockquote>
space-walking
i woke up from
my first dream
</blockquote>

Hoh, this *is* new! Does space-walking, then, trump visions of Fuji? The *~ni-keri* finality implies a reluctance to wake, but thank goodness he did. Otherwise, the dream might have been forgotten.

初夢の覚めてゆくへや小蓬莱 寒樓 late-19c
hatsuyume no samete yukue ya ko hôrai   kanrô 明治新俳句集
(first-dream's waking[-state]whereabouts/destination! small *hôrai*)

<blockquote>
my first dream　　　　　　　　　waking up from
its waking whereabouts　　　　　my first dream, i head for
the small *hôrai*　　　　　　　　the small *hôrai*

　　　　　　my first dream
　　　　　waking, i find myself
　　　　　　by the hôrai
</blockquote>

English's lack of one word for "destination" *and* "whereabouts," as well as its demand for pronouns works against the poetry here, for it is best *not to know* whether the dream, poet, or both, head for the magical mountain/isle. Fuji was sometimes identified with Mount Hôrai (pg. 181).

初夢やさめても花は花ごゝろ 千代尼 再現

hatsuyume ya samete mo hana wa hanagokoro   chiyo-ni 1701-75   (first-dream:
waking-even/though, blossom/woman-as-for, blossom/woman/springtime/ heart/mind/feeling)

first dreams
waking, all that magic
is still in us

first dream
even awake the gift
is in my heart

my first dream
even after waking
i bloom within

The extraordinary number of connotations of *hana* (flower/blossom) make straight translation meaningless. It is probably not enough to know flower could stand for a woman, the Spring and the beauty of the New Year. My first readings were as follows: **a nun's reflection** // *My first dream: / i woke up yet spring / kept blooming;*   "**night blossom** // *First dream: / waking, i am still / enchanted;* and, after Donegan and Ishibashi ("first dream – / even after awakening / the flower's heart the same"), *My first dream / even after awakening / a woman yet.* I wrote: *Even after becoming a nun, Chiyo felt her womanhood, her irrepressible eros, on the first day of the year. Enlightenment* [=waking] *is no match for the Spring.* But blossom *also* can stand for both the most precious offerings and outer appearances. Reading over and over, I came to think that if the subject of Chiyo's *ku* is the first-dream, she probably describes the nature of the New Year Season rather than her allegorical womanhood.[1]

はつ夢や正しく去年の放し亀 言水 講談社大

hatsuyume ya masashiku kozo no hanashi-game   gonsui
(first-dream: correctly/precisely last year's freed turtle   -1719)

my first dream
if it wasn't last year's
freed turtle!

first dreams
i'd call them last year's
freed turtles

The ritual practice of liberating animals once or twice a year is found in most Buddhist cultures. Turtles also have two special supernatural attributes. They were associated with longevity throughout the Sinosphere, and Japanese folklore credited them with repaying those who helped them. The legendary Urashima Tarô was taken to the underwater palace of the Dragon King by a grateful turtle; and fishermen who caught turtles traditionally treated them to *sake* before releasing them to put in a good word to the fish below.[2] I do not know exactly what my second reading means, but I like it.

願わくば鯨わくわく今朝の海   駄訳は敬愚

wishes filled
the New Year's sea
full of whales

Jane Reichhold (1/1/96 shiki site & see her *Dict. of Haiku*)

Dreams come in two basic types, direct or in need of interpretation. The first-dreams found in *waka* were usually of the first type. Spring mist or blossoms are dreamed of and, sure enough, the poet wakes up to find it true. In retrospect, this made a dream a *masa-yume,* or "true-dream." If we let "wishes" be dreams, Reichhold's fulfilling *ku* follows that classic school. Even the mist is there, whale spume wafting gently over the sea. I may joke, but the "i/we did it!" attitude *is* very *haikai*.[3]

1. Chiyo's "Flower's Heart" Donegan and Ishibashi do not come out and say the poem is allegorical, but how else can we interpret "the flower's heart the same"? Chiyo's style is said to be *pure* and *clear*, but she was playful and clever, so not a few *ku* are difficult for even modern Japanese to read. I think the work of this most famous female haiku poet deserves full annotation such as has been done for Bashô and Buson. Without such a book, we must rely on guesswork (as is true for Issa's *ku*, too, so it is not just a matter of gender discrimination).

2. *Drunken Turtles* Occasional drink has been associated with longevity & sea turtles, like many Chinese sages, clearly enjoy being drunk. In *The Erotic Ocean*, Jack Rudloe describes giant logger-head turtles swimming into "hordes of" Portuguese man-of-war and "eagerly munching away on the tentacles." Not immune to the stings "their eyes become puffed and swollen and red" yet they "go into a feeding frenzy and madly stuff themselves" losing their coordination and looking "terrible." He doubts man-o-war have much food value and notes drunk turtles do "not duck under water at the approach of a boat, the way turtles normally do."

3. *Reichhold's Haikai.* I also like the filfulling reversal, *w*-alliteration, whales, themselves, for many reasons, and the *"if wishes were fishes"* association. I realize my *mist* is far-fetched and a contemporary English haiku may be a bit out of place *here*. But, this chapter is on dreams, so what better place for odd associations? Or, is it really so strange? An old *ku* without the wishes: *"Spring is here! / A huge fish floats / upon the sea"* (明けて春大魚浮む海の面　栗堂 句鑑 akete haru taigyo ukamu umi no tsura kyodô 1777). His intent may be plural: a big catch *and* whales. The original has them "floating/ rising up" (*ukamu*). But see the *shitarigao ku* on p.140 for why J.R.'s *ku* is *haikai*.

初夢や梅に蛙のはふ所 正秀 大三
hatsuyume ya ume ni kawazu no hau tokoro   masahide 1697
(first dream!/: plum-on/in frog's crawling place/moment)

<table>
<tr><td>

first dream
a frog creeping to
a plum tree

</td><td>

first dream
a frog is crawling
up my plum

</td></tr>
</table>

The funny thing about the theme "first dream" is that it gives modern poets an excuse to put almost *anything* into their *ku*. But the above is an *old* poem. It should have *meaning*. The same character for frog is pronounced *kaeru* in prose and *kawazu* in poetry. The colloquial *kaeru* is homophonic with "return." Does this make the frog fitting for Spring's return, in the persona of the blossoming plum?

初夢に大いなる毬を貫ひけり みどり女 改造社
hatsuyume ni ôinaru mari o moraikeri   midorijo 1885-1990
(first-dream-in/as huge ball[obj] receive[as gift+emphatic])

first dream
i am presented with
a huge ball

This poet has been blessed with the new gem=ball (*ara-tama*) of the Year itself, the gem=ball Spring (*tama-no-haru*). Apparently, the homophonic *haru* meaning "swell" and the *haru* of Spring combined in her dream to create this appropriate, yet individual dream.[1] Perhaps she read or discussed the expression *tama no haru* before going to sleep.

1. *A Woman's Ball Dream* Japan's premier cartoonist of traditional (pre-*anime*) – especially humorous erotic – motif, Kurogane Hiroshi apparently turned this haiku into a story. Midori-jo, who is considering marriage interprets the dream as a prediction. While a *mari* is, narrowly speaking, a ball used for New Year games, a ball is a *tama*, or "gem/fine/perfect." This, plus the fact it was seen as the years passed over ([*toshi-no-*]*koshi*), suggest a *tama-no-koshi*, or a "gem of a pass-over" (marrying *up* to an attractive and wealthy man). So, she says *"Yes!"* to the first man who asks for her hand and, as it turns out, his only outstanding possession was literally his balls, the size of beach-balls. When I first read/saw the cartoon I did not know about the haiku; I doubt most Japanese do.

蓑虫の天女なりしを初夢に 吉本昇 季題別
minomushi no tennyo narishi o hatsuyume ni   yoshimoto noboru
(bag-worm/fagot worm heaven-woman become first-dream-as 1997)

a bag-worm
turns into an angel
my first dream

bag-worms
turned into angels
a first dream

Unlike the plum and frog, the figures in this contemporary haiku are not traditional to the New Year; but the symbolism is fitting, for the worm/s blossom/s like the floral Spring and, if singular, the angel is Princess Sao. In that case, this modern haiku *might* be considered a bit traditional.

初夢に大きな門をくぐりけり 名本喜美
hatsuyume ni ôki na mon o kugurikeri   namoto kimi
(first-dream-in large gate[obj] pass through[+emph] 1997)

first dream
i pass through
a big gate

Rebirth is also appropriate symbolism but seems to concern the individual, not the greater world metaphored by the frog in the plum tree, the ball and, perhaps, the angel. I feel the same way about such a modern haiku as I often feel about modern *non*-haiku poetry: it is all very good for the poet, but is there enough in the *ku* to make it interesting to *others?*

初夢の混沌吾の創世紀　船迫たか 季題別
hatsuyume no konton ware no sôseiki   funasako taka 1997
(first-dream's chaos: my genesis [=creation-]record [*book of genesis*])

my first dream
the chaos is my own
book of genesis

my first dream
such chaos: a record
of the creation

No complaint with this contemporary *ku*. Here, lack of a clear image to interpret has been cleverly interpreted in a manner appropriate to the season! Who hasn't heard of *ontogeny recapitulating phylogeny*, but this replay is something new . . .

初夢に古郷を見て涙かな 一茶 寛政六
hatsuyume ni furusato o mite namida kana   issa 1794
(first-dream-to home-country seeing/seen tears!/'tis)

misty eyes

first dream
i saw my hometown
and cried

This seems a modern first-dream *ku* – call it a *neochronism* – completely bereft of traditional conceit. While Issa's teary eyes might be said to hint at "misted over," it may well be pure coincidence. This was Issa's first first-dream *ku*. At age thirty-two, he had been working for survival wages as a scribe for haiku masters for over a decade and still had almost two decades to go before he could afford to settle – even then, on the road for half the year – in the half-a-home awaiting him in his homeland, a place which had not treated him kindly. His next dream *ku*, about ten years later is also blunt: *"My Dream True: / Bright and early in Spring / visited by Poverty."* (正夢や春早々の貧乏神 *masayume ya haru hayabaya*[or *sôsô*] *no binbôgami* 1811). The God named Poverty (*binbôgami*) was generally restricted to Winter haiku because the first month of that season was when the Gods left for, and returned from, a month-long caucus in Izumo. He was a common guest in Issa's haiku (Interested readers will find a chapter about him with scores of haiku in *HIC! = Haiku In Context*: tentative publishing date is 2008). His presence does not seem right on this day, when all bad words and ideas were taboo, but it is far better to complain than commit suicide, and Issa made it interesting for his readers by mentioning the ragged-looking god rather than just waving his own empty sleeves (pockets) in their faces.

隔て住むや子の初夢に吾のあり 乙字 改造社
hedate sumu ya ko no hatsuyume ni ware no ari   otsuji 1881-1920
(separated live:/! child's first dream-in i am)

living apart
i turn up in my child's
first dream

living apart
part of my dream turns up
in my child's

A touching *ku*. No traditional allusion or metaphor. A good example of what modern poets do best.

初夢の巴里に迷ひしままに覚む 中村将晴 季題別
hatsuyume no pari ni mayoishi mama ni samu   nakamura masaharu
(first-dream paris-in wandering/lost as-is wake-up 1997)

my first dream
i wake up still lost
in paris

This haiku, like the dream of the big Gate, does not grab me like the one before it. I am not satisfied by detail, no matter that it might be true. Perhaps the poet feels guilt at following French culture, thereby betraying that of Japan. Something is *there*. But, I still find myself asking *"So what?"*

初夢の麒麟に帽子とられけり 北村耕一路
hatsuyume no kirin ni bôshi torarekeri   kitamura kôichirô 1997 季題別
(first-dream's camelopard(giraffe)/kylin (legendary lional-flying-horse)-by hat taken [emph])

first dream
a camelopard takes
my hat!

first dream
my hat is stolen by
a giraffe!

Yet *this* detail I *do* like! The legendary kirin (kylin) has a sun-like image that makes it suitable for a New Year's poem, but it is also the more familiar giraffe which reaches down from on high to remove the poet's hat. To preserve the mystique of the original, one reading uses the giraffe's uncommon name, "camelopard." Could this lofty animal stand for the vertical depth of time felt on the New Year that demands respect by removing hats? Or does it refer to a bright child or grandchild? A child-prodigy may be called a *kirinji,* or kirin-infant. Unlike the case in most haiku, where the poet's word can settle most ambiguity, since a dream is a dream, the poet can not contradict my interpretation!

初夢のむかしの仕事しておりし　長島舟遊子
hatsuyume no mukashi no shigoto shiteorishi　　nagashima shûyûshi
(first-dream's old work doing [+humble-style]was 季題別 1997)

    my first dream　　　　　　　　　　　　　my first dream
      just doing　　　　　　　　　　　　　　just doing the work
    my old work　　　　　　　　　　　　　　　i used to do

I love the poet's name: *Long-island Boat-play-child*. If we assume he is retired and the dream is a memory of the good old days, however hard they may have been, this is a first-dream particularly interesting because it would not have been interesting on any other day of the year.

初夢の昔のままの夫に逢ふ　金龍あや子
hatsuyume no mukashi no mama no tsuma ni au　　kanetatsu ayako
(first-dream's old just-like husband-with meet 季題別 1997)

    first dream
    i meet my husband
    as he used to be!

Too perfect, perhaps, but beautiful. Today, there are far more poems about the return of the deceased than the young. Indeed, judging from the *ku* in the 10th *Kidaibetsu* collection of the *Haijin-kyôkai* (Japan's largest haiku association), the dead were the most common protagonists in first-dreams. *"How animated / the words of the deceased / in my first dream."* (初夢の故人いきいき物を言ふ 保田治代 季題別 *hatsuyume no kojin iki iki mono o iu*　yasuda haruyo 1997); *"The dead man / sure talked up a storm / my first dream"* 初夢の死者なかなかに語りけり　綾部仁喜　同*hatsuyume no shisha nakanaka ni katarikeri* ayabe hitoyoshi 1997). Yes, *haijin* tend to be old. I think this next by far the best of this genre:

初夢やあの世からくる夫と友　平松あさ子 季題別
hatsuyume ya ano yo kara kuru tsuma to tomo　hiramatsu asako 1997
(first-dream: that world [the other world]-from come husband and friend)

    my first dream
    my husband and a friend
    from that world

It is hard to appreciate another's dreams. But something about that friend coming with her husband opens me up to the poet's world. I even start imagining what her husband and his friend look like! There is no "my" in the Japanese. I hated having to put a "my" before both the "first dream" and the husband, but it is more natural that way. Every time I struggle to English a *ku* like this one, I resent the boorishness of my native tongue.

初夢のまめまめしさの哀しけり　小川幸子 季題別
hatsuyume no mamemameshisa no kanashikeri　ogawa sachiko 1997
(first-dream's servility/diligence/devotion's pitiful/sadness (emphatic)

    my first dream　　　　　　　　　　　　　my first dream
    such seriousness　　　　　　　　　　　　all work no play
    is just pitiful!　　　　　　　　　　　　　how sad!

初夢のあさきゆめみし憂ひかな 山田みづえ 角川
hatsuyume no asaki yume mishi urei kana   yamada mizue 20c
(first-dream's shallowness/baseness dream seeing distress/lament!/'tis)

the first dream
i see is so humdrum
i'm depressed

Some people are blessed with imaginative *soma* and some are not. I knew a Japanese school teacher who not only flew *every* night, but claimed the story thread always picked up where it left off. When she tried to share her pleasure with her husband, she was chastized: *"Can't you be serious even in your dreams!"* Complaint about boring dreams is found in old English diaries and essays (Pepys and Lamb if I recall). If the complaint is in olde Japanese literature (haiku included), I have yet to find it.

あまりよく初夢うそと云れけり 澤雉
amari yoki hatsuyume uso to iwarekeri   takuchi
(too/so good first-dream "[a] lie" said[+emph] -1693)

my first dream
it was so good they say
i made it up

I *like* the lack of detail in the *ku*, but would also like a line or two *of prose* about it! The "made it up" for *uso* (a lie) is borrowed from Blyth: *"It was such a fine first dream, / They said / I had made it up."*[1]

初夢や秘めて語らず一人笑む 松宇
hatsuyume ya himete katarazu hitori emu   shôu 1859-1943
(first-dream! concealing/subduing tell-not alone smile[verb])

first dream
i keep it to myself
and smile

Blyth gives a perfect sense-translation: *"The first dream of the year; / I kept it a secret, / And smiled to myself."* Does mine suffice? This dream, too, I – unlike Blyth, who preaches the benefits of not telling for "when we begin to explain ourselves, fools are confounded and the wise shut their ears." (*Haiku* vol 2, spring) – would like to know!

初夢を見てゐていはぬかなしかり 秋山巳之流 角川現代
hatsuyume o miteite iwanu kanashigari   akiyama minoryû 20c
(first-dream[+obj] seeing/saw say-not sad-am)

my first dream
the sadness of having
no one to tell
i am left with
an unspeakable sadness
my first dream

I can almost see a reverse Mona Lisa? This modern *ku* is beautifully vague, and better than older *ku* about dreams that could not be told because of their sexual nature, such as Issa's prefaced "the loves of a maid" (寄下女恋：初夢も御座に出されぬ寝言哉 *hatsuyume mo goza ni dasarenu negoto kana*).

初夢の嘘ついて人を喜ばす 露月 改造社
hatsuyume no uso tsuite hito o yorokobasu   rogetsu -1927
(first-dream's lie/s telling, people[obj] delight)

i lie about
my first dream
to delight others

Thank goodness Blyth didn't find this one, too. Or, maybe he did, but found it too shallow. I like it, for, as usual, it makes me wonder what dream the poet invented! It is also a rare *confession* for a poet in a genre that boasts simplicity and honesty.

初夢や富士にしておく山の形 佳棠 己酉初懐紙
hatsuyume ya fuji ni shiteoku yama no kata   kadô 1789
(first-dream:/! fuji-as make-put/decise mountain's shape)

first dream the mountain i take to be fuji	first dream deciding the mountain must be fuji

A questionable mountain turns into the desired one. The *ku* is not so much about Fuji as about dream interpretation. I like it enough to feel tempted to do a dozen more readings, but let me settle on one: *"My first dream / if the mountain's not Fuji / it should be!"* Here is another:

初夢や絵に画いてある不二ながら 牧之 秋月庵発句集
hatsuyume ya e ni kaitearu fuji nagara   bokushi 1830
(first-dream: print/picture-in drawn fuji while [it is])

first dream
though only a painting
fuji is fuji

first dream though my fuji was a drawn one	first dream though it was a fuji from a print

I think it no accident that Fuji in this masterfully observant *ku* is written "Not-two," and "Prosperity/happiness-warrior" in the previous *ku*.

初夢の吉に疑無りけり 清々 改造社
hatsuyume no kichi ni utagai nakarikeri   seisei
(first-dream's lucky [is] doubt-not[+emph.] 1869-1937)

a first dream no doubt it must be lucky	my first dream left no doubt that it was lucky

Entertaining may require some lying, as per the last *ku,* but dream interpretation hardly needs such help, for in the Sinosphere, even bad dreams can become good merely by being claimed as *gyaku-yume,* or "reverse-dreams." Hence the cynical first reading. The second is more likely the poet's.

初夢や至る処に青山あり 小蚯？最新二万句改造社
hatsuyume ya itaru tokoro ni seizan ari   kokoku early-20c?
(first-dream/s: every place-in/at blue-mountain/s is/are)

first dreams
wherever i look
a green hill

first dreams
wherever you look
a green hill

There is an old Sino-Japanese saying: *"When you die, any place is a green hill,"* i.e., any place is fine. I think the *ku* means that good omens can always be found if you only know how to search for them. If taken in the first-person, it is hard to tell if it is a good or a bad one.

女来よ初夢語りなぐさまん 子規 改造社
onna koyo hatsuyume katari nagusaman   shiki -1902
(woman/en come! first-dream tell [i'll?you?] console/amuse [you/me]-would/let's)

i'll console you:
women come 'round and share
your first dreams

women come
tell me your first dreams
i have none

let's console each other

women come here
tell me your first dreams
i'll tell you mine

I feel embarrassed not to be sure how to read what seems like a simple *ku*. My respondents doubt the second reading and favor the last. Shiki's must be the only *"Come, women!"* haiku ever made.

初夢や連歌鎖のごとつなぐ 佐々木久代季題別
hatsuyume ya rengakusari no goto tsunagu   sasaki hisayo
(first-dream/s: linked-verse chain-like connect 1997)

my first dream
it connects like a chain
of linked verse

first dreams
connected like a chain
of linked verse

This, like the Green Hills *ku*, can be read as a personal observation or as a comment on the nature of dreams. Though formal *renga* (linked-verse) includes rules about who does what verse (guest *vs* host, etc.) and the place in the sequence when a certain season should be mentioned, all of which is far from the freedom of a dream, it is still the best metaphor I have ever come across for describing the associative manner in which dreams, or, rather parts of dreams, flow. That is because poems do not link in the logical manner of prose, nor in the manner of the stanzas of a song, but in a manner that is loosely associative and often not even noticeable at a glance. There is a surreal quality to the best sequences. At the same time, since dreams have been around far longer than *renga*, this *ku* suggests that the poetic aesthetic takes after dreams. I prefer the latter translation partly because it can, itself, be read two ways. *Not only can parts of one man's dreams connect, but the dreams of all.*

初夢のおぼゆるとなく子の咄す 如露露 改造社 年鑑俳句集
hatsuyume no oboyuru to naku ko no hanasu   jororo? early-20c
(first dream/s knowing/remembering somewhat/not child talks)

the first dream
a child talks about things
half-recalled

not knowing
it was a first dream
the child talks

not really
recalling his first dream
a boy talks

This is a very ambiguous poem. I prefer the second reading because it seems more amusing for a child to be telling about his or her dream without knowing it has special meaning on that day.

獏 THE BAD DREAM EATER

初夢や獏が歯固枕の今朝　常可 雑中
hatsuyume ya baku ga hagatame makura no kesa   jôka 19-20c
(first-dream! *baku*[tapir]'s tooth-hardening pillow/bed's morning)

my first dream
the <i>baku</i> hardens its teeth
at my bedside

There are very few bad first-dreams reported. One reason might be the contribution made by the Baku, a fabulous creature poor dictionaries only translate as "tapir." It has a long association with dreams in China[1] and, according to Hashimoto Keiji (in the *Kôdansha Dai-saijiki*), it originally ate copper, iron and bamboo, so the folk decided it might as well eat up bad dreams, too. Note that this is a broader category than nightmares, for a dream can be ominous without being frightening. Perhaps as many people bought Baku charms as insurance as bought treasure ships, and some bought both. The *ku* also contains a literary pun, for the "tooth-hardening" characters may also be pronounced *hako* and a *hako-makura* or box-pillow (the pillow supported by a box with a drawer for personal effects) was the support for one's dream voyages *and* often had a *baku* inscribed on one side. Jôka's clever *ku* is found both in First-dream *and* with the Tooth-hardening (*hagatame*) themes in Shiki's *Categorical*. "Tooth-hardening" was generally the Solar Spring, once the most common time to see first-dreams. It is a theme that attracts humor. Issa, down to a single tooth by the time he married at age fifty-two, joked about hardening his gums on *tofu!* But, to return to the subject:

---

1. China and Dreams. We find dream interpretation around the world long before Freud took it up and found sex in everything because people in his/our culture happened to not have the sex their minds and bodies desired. What makes the Chinese unique is the attention given to manipulating dreams – undoing them or reversing them – through various devices. As a culture with a sweet tooth, they had many nightmares.

枕外す女夢なし獏の札　月斗 1868 -
makura hazusu onna yume nashi baku no fuda getto - 1949
(pillow/bed-removing woman/women dream/s not/none baku card/talisman)

when her head leaves
the pillow she's dreamless
baku talisman

a *baku* pillow
the woman leaves her dreams
behind in bed

This *ku* seems to suggest that women are more likely to fear bad dreams and take measures to prevent them or erase them (this point is not clear) than men. Another early modern *ku* makes the same claim: *When their dreams / go too far women use / baku pillows.* (女共が迷ひの夢を獏枕　句佛　獅子窟句抄　改造社 *onnadomo ga mayoi no yume o bakumakura* kubutsu 1874-1943). This dream may be neither nightmare nor related to the New Year. *Mayoi* (wandering/getting lost) suggests an adulterous dream: *"The romantic dreams / of women feed them: / baku pillows"* Placing the name of the monster directly after the dream with an objective "o," may have a mimetic "swallowing" effect, for the usual mimesis for devouring is *pakupaku* (hence, "Pakkuman" for the gobbling electronic game).

獏枕子のよき夢をつゆ知らず　赤尾兜子 講談社大
bakumakura ko no yoki yume o tsuyu shirazu akao tôko 20c
(baku-bed/pillow: child good dream dew(not at all) knows-not)

sleeping with baku
a child cannot remember
any good dreams

a child with baku
how little we know about
her good dreams

獏枕一睡にして夜明けたり　菰聖窟 木虫句集 改造社
bakumakura issui ni shite yoaketari   koseikutsu 19-20c?
(baku-pillow/bed/sleep one-water-to makes night-brightens)

when dawn breaks
nothing at all remains
sleeping with baku

Since nightmares tend to be recalled more commonly than good dreams which don't wake us, all this makes perfect sense, but it still seems the modern *ku* seconds the idea of the Baku's indiscriminately eating *all* dreams, as suggested in the older poem following it. If the *baku* was generally not used together with the Treasure Ship, this would explain why. Otherwise, we would find *ku* like these:

獏乗せむ寶一つば捨てちまふ　　敬愚
それとも：獏乗せむ寶一つを捨ててヨイ
baku nosemu takara hitotsu o sutechimau

獏のせば保険付きとや宝船　　敬愚
それとも：保険かな獏も乗せたる宝船
hoken kana baku mo nosetaru takarabune

make room
for *baku*: sacrifice
one treasure!

with the baku
aboard, a treasure ship
fully insured

I recently found an old painting with the character for *baku* instead of the usual *takara* (treasure) on the sail! Maybe a *ku* like Keigu's actually exists! Under *baku-fuda* (baku-card/charm), my *OJD* gives an example *ku*: *"Spring night / dreams, sold and bought: / baku charms"* (春のよの夢や売買獏の札

忠知　俳諧桜川 *haru no yo no yume ya urikai baku no fuda*　tadachi 1674) and a passage (*yumechigai no baku no fuda, takarabune-uri, nado*) from Saikaku's *An Amorous Man*, which haiku'ed might read:

see dreams pass
each other by: *baku* charms
and treasure ships

dreams good and bad
pass in the street, the monster
and the treasure ship

Combining the example *ku* and the passage, we get:

dreams bought
dreams sold: *baku* charms
and treasure ships!

treasure ships
and baku charms: dreams
bought and sold

Because the *baku* eats dreams, you might say that the vendor of *baku buys up your bad dreams*, though it is you paying him. Thought of as a free agent, the *baku* resembles a different profession, *the sin-eaters*, who used to get free meals at funerals in Europe in order to take the sins of the deceased upon themselves (I realize the "bought" might refer to wholesaling the goods but that is less poetic, so I skip it.).

獏枕夢にまで苦労したくなし　広瀬泣麻呂 季題別
bakumakura yume ni made kurô shitaku nashi　hirose nakimaro 1997
(baku-pillow/bed/sleeping dreams-up-to trouble/suffering/hard-times do-want-not)

a *baku* charm
in dreams at least i don't
want to suffer

If the poet thought to reinterpret the significance of first dreams, so that the quality of the first dream determines that of the dreams to come for the rest of the year, then this is a major *ku*. Otherwise, it is kinda sad. The poet's pen-name "Crying Marô" sadly suggests the latter reading.

空ごとと思へど捨てず獏枕　佐藤紅縁 講談社大
soragoto to omoedo sutezu bakumakura　satô kôroku 20c
(empty-thing/falsehood think-but dispose-not baku-pillow)

though i think
it hocus-pocus, i keep
my *baku* charm

though dreams
may be nothing, i keep
my *baku* charm

There is a book called *Faces In the Clouds* that guesses religion comes from betting on the safe side.

喰ひに来し獏を夢見ぬ獏枕　室積徂春 講談社大
kui ni kishi baku o yume minu bakumakura　murozumi sôshun
(eat-to-came baku[obj.] dream see[or, see-not!] *baku*-pillow 20c)

pillow with a charm

i do recall
the baku coming to eat
my dream

and i cannot
recall the baku who came
to eat my dream

Some advise us to get involved in our dreams and guide them. Being the Captain of your dream might appeal to one who believes that empowerment is an end in itself, but would it not also prevent pleasant surprises? Better to call a *baku* into action only after the dream is clearly a loss. The ambiguity of *minu* (see/not-see) permits different readings. Either way, the bad dream was eaten up.

三人に一人初夢見たりけり 青楓 改造社
sannin ni hitori hatsuyume mitarikeri seifû 明治一万句
(three-people-of/in one first-dream see [past+emphatic.] 19-20c)

<blockquote>
one person
in three seems to have
a first-dream
</blockquote>

<blockquote>
one person
in three remembered
a first dream
</blockquote>

初夢を見は見たりしが忘れけり 鶯池 明治一万句
hatsuyume o mi wa mitarishi ga wasurekeri ôchi 19-20c 改造社
(first-dream[obj] see-as-for saw[sort-of] but forgot[emphatic])

<blockquote>
my first dream
sure i saw it but then
i forgot it
</blockquote>

Did the first poet actually survey the percent of those who had a New Year's dream? The most common dream is identical to the most common type of fish: *the one that got away*.

夢もなき身の拙さよ寶舟 蝶衣
yume mo naki mi no tsutanasa yo takarabune chôi -1930
(dream-even not body/self/i/me's/people's wretchedness[+emph.] treasure-ship)

<blockquote>
how wretched!
life without even a dream
treasure-ships
</blockquote>

<blockquote>
treasure ships:
how miserable living
but dreamless!
</blockquote>

<blockquote>
what a bungler!
can't even get a dream from
a treasure ship
</blockquote>

The original is ambiguous for, with the treasure ship just plopped down at the end of the *ku*, we can not tell if the poet laments his sickness and lack of personal hope for his future, sees people in poor circumstances buying the charm and is depressed about their hopeless poverty and the worsening situation in Japan and the world, or if he composed the *ku* after it failed to deliver, and meant to say what my last reading says far more clearly. On that last note, I recall Bashô's *ku* claiming those who are *not* enlightened by a bolt of lightning are valuable. So, then, are those on whom charms don't work.

朝寝して初夢もなき男哉 青嵐 明治一万句
asane shite hatsuyume mo naki otoko kana seiran 1875-1943?
(morning-sleep-do first-dream also not/none man!/'tis // or 1857-1931?)

<blockquote>
this man who
sleeps in and lacks even
a first-dream!
</blockquote>

<blockquote>
sleeping in:
who says men even have
first dreams?
</blockquote>

Making dreamlessness male raises the *ku* over a line like: *"My first dream / i forget exactly / what it was"* (初夢何やらなりし忘れけり 続石 落椿 *hatsuyume no nanyara narishi wasurekeri* zokuseki 19c?20c?), or,

初夢の何も見ずして明けにけり 子規
hatsuyume no nani mo mizu shite akenikeri shiki 1897
(first-dream's something-even see-not brighten/dawn [+finality]).

while i waited
to see my first dream
the day broke

it has dawned
and i have yet to see
my first dream

not a glimpse
of my first dream
and it's dawn

On second thought, Shiki's *ku* has a saving grace. The combination of seeing nothing followed by the arrival of daylight parodies the loved one waiting up all night in vain for the visit of a lover, or, "night-crawler," to use the Japanese expression. Consider also that sleeping on a kimono inside-out to help attract a lover resembled sleeping on the treasure boat. But, was Shiki dreaming about waiting in vain for a dream or waking up now and then and thinking, damn, when will it get here and finally giving up as the sky began to dawn (lovers were not supposed to be spotted so they left when the cock called, before sunrise). Moreover, men and women were known to wait for lovers in their dreams, for one interpretation of a visit was that it was proof the other person cared for you . . . .

それらしき夢も見ざりき宝舟 相馬遷子 講談社大
sore rashiki yume mo mizariki takarabune sôma senko
(that seems-like dream-even see-not[?] treasure boat 20c)

a treasure boat
still i didn't see the right
type of dream

I think the poet means a few fragments of life in the office or other such spam does not count as a *genuine* dream. I agree. There are dreams and there are dreams. The last five words of the translation would make a great book title!

初夢と思ひき瞼覚めやらず 青木千代子 季題別
hatsu yume to omoiki mabuta same yarazu aoki chiyoko
(first-dream [i] thought, eye-lids waken let-not 1997)

my first dream
i had it but my eyelids
wouldn't open

How many times have you had a great dream and thought you'd remember it, but failing to open those eyes and wake up completely, lost your masterpiece? The Opium Eater complained, but chances are, had that much maligned visitor not interrupted his dream, Coleridge would have lost not only the ending but *all* of his famous Xanadu. The original beats the translation because Japanese "see" their dreams, rather than "having" (English) or "sleeping with" (Spanish) them. And, the place they are said to *see* them is supposed to be on the insides of their eyelids. *A twin-screen theater in the cranium!*

おもしろさ二日に夢を見そこない 柳多留 再現
omoshirosa futsuka ni yume o misokonai　yanagidaru 36-6
(interesting/funny second day-on dream seeing miss　early -19c)

      that's life!　　　　　　　　　　　a big to do
  having a good dream　　　　　about missing a dream
    a day too late　　　　　　　　　　on day two

While the first dream came to be viewed on the second once the practice of staying awake on the Eve became common, it was still the First Day that was supposed to prognosticate the year to come. The *senryû* has noted this cultural schism and I, please forgive me, borrowed the idiom of an English play to translate the chuckle in the second reading, which is the main one.

初夢の覚えのなきを吉とせり 川井城子
hatsuyume no oboe no naki o kichi to seri　kawai jôko
(first dream's memory's not [+obj] lucky make　角川三版 20c)

  my first dream　　　　　　　　　the first dream
no memory proves　　　　　　　"failing to remember it
   it was good　　　　　　　　　　means it's lucky"

        i make out
  forgetting a first dream
     to be lucky

The second reading is best because a poet consoling her child, or observing her husband doing so, is sweeter than rationalizing away her own loss. The last reading keeps the active sense of the verb.

初夢やうら／＼として金砂子 月斗 改造社
hatsuyume ya ura-ura to shite kin sunago　getto 1868-1949
(first-dream: glorious/serene [psycho. mimesis] gold-dust [paint])

   the soft glitter
of gold dusted lacquer
   my first dream

The psychological mimesis *ura-ura* was associated with the particular character of a sunshine on a halcyon spring day. Finding no match for its twin connotations of gloriously shining beauty *and* serenity, I used a description, "soft glitter." Has the poet chosen, *"to linger a-bed"* chewing *"the cud of a foregone vision . . . collect[ing] the rays of a brighter phantasm"* (Lamb[1])? Or, does he remember no details, but simply feels refreshed by whatever he saw? Likewise for this next contemporary haiku:

初夢の茫漠として余震あり 桃井克夫 季題別
hatsuyume no bôbaku to shite yoshin ari　momoi katsuo 1997
(first-dream's boundless/vague[psych. mimesis] after-tremors/reverbations are/have)

***butterfly effect*[2]**

  my first dream
vague and boundless
  after-tremors

1. Lamb's Essays. If you have not yet read Lamb's "Popular Fallacies," found in *The Last Essays of Elia*, run, don't walk to the nearest library. The above snippet is part of an essay disagreeing with the common advice *that we should rise with the lark.*

2. Butterfly Effect In reference to the proverbial butterfly of simulated climatology, whose wings, for aught we know, churn up enough air to alter global weather, maybe even touching off a hurricane. What could be smaller than the vague dream of one poet? And yet . . .

One of the most fascinating exchanges I have seen on haiku interpretation concerns a *first-dream* haiku that appeared recently (2001-1-#2) in the internet haiku magazine/salon Right-Brain Haiku:

初夢のとはずがたりやふたり膳 游 右脳俳句
hatsuyume no towazu gatari ya futari zen   yû contemp.
(first dream's' unasked tale/s: two settings/table[eating])

first-dreams
unasked but still told
at the table

first dreams
told at breakfast to
a silent spouse

The existence of a term for a story told to an un-interested party (*towazu-gatari*) – punning off the title for an old unasked tale (towazu *mono*gatari) – is itself remarkable. In Japanese, the listener *must,* I repeat, *must* make periodic grunt-like vocalizations while another person tells a story – novelist Tanizaki Junichirô wished he had a tail like a cat he could twitch so he would not feel obliged to respond that way – so it is easy to tell if someone is not responsive. One reader commented that, to the contrary, this was an *exceptionally warm* haiku about a couple who are so close they need not say anything (not even grunt)[1] – or, there is, at least, no need for those grunts. Yet another commented that the *ku* was testimony to the sorry relationship between old spouses who no longer have anything to talk about. So, not only dreams, but haiku *about* dreams can be interpreted in many ways! My discriminating respondent writes: "I agree with the first reader, *i.e.* a very warm couple who thinks alike; a spouse does not even have to worry about the other's critical reaction. 'Towazugatari' has a warm, natural connotation and has no acrimonious or cold feel to it." The readings may differ along generational lines; older readers tend to feel silence comes from a good relationship where only couples with problems exchange words while the happy ones no more talk to the other than they would to themselves (the implication being the couple *is* of one mind), while the young are suspicious of silence as an indicator of a lop-sided relationship or even oppression. (This is one of a small number of cases where I would like to *know* which interpretation is right. Hopefully, I can find the author of this haiku and ask someday!)

1. Interpreting Silence. 20c Japanese socio-linguists tended to explain elliptic speaking patterns and relative lack of conversation between spouses on the part of their compatriots as proof of a relationship closer than found in the "individualistic" West. This concept of silence was not simply created by Neo-Shintô facism. It has a long history in Japan going back at least to the mid-Tokugawa era. A *senryû* in *Mutama-gawa* bk2 (1751): *"A close couple, / they are more quiet / then dolls"* (*yoi naka wa ningyo yori mo shizuka nari*). I imagine young lovers are what the *senryû* has in mind. The silence of long-married spouses is not necessarily the same! (If this and other problems in socio-linguistics interest you, please see my *Orientalism & Occidentalism – Is the Mistranslation of Culture Inevitable* or, if you read Japanese, *Eigo-wa Konna-ni Nippongo*).

着始
kiso-hajime

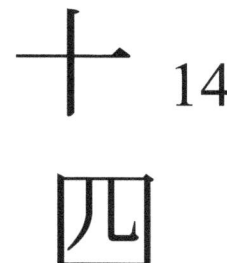

DRESSING UP FOR THE YEAR

粘こわき音揃ふなり著衣始　千得 玉かづら
nori kowaki oto sorou nari kisohajime　sentoku 1751
(starch stiff/loud/powerful/scary sound gather-is wear-dress-start)

the starch-stiff
sounds have assembled:
our first dress

hear the rustle
of starch, the new year
dress is here!

new year's dress
the awesome sound of
gathering starch

Kiso-hajime, or "dress-start" means new clothing worn for the first time on the luckiest day of the first three of the New Year (In the Sino-sphere, there is an ongoing parade of good, bad and so-and-so days, which are always consulted for deciding dates for weddings or signing deals, etc. *Kichi-nichi* is sometimes Englished as "red-letter day."). Evidently, this clothing was full of starch. Loudness (*kowaki*) is homophonic with *frightening*. I could not find a word to express the type of existential fear that wells up in the presence of a large number of stiff whispering garments. A hundred years ago, "sublime" would have been perfect.

上下の音より春の明る哉　可勝 大三物
kamishimo no oto yori haru no akuru kana　kashô 1697
(up-down[formal ♂ dress] wear's sound-from, spring brightens[dawns+emph.])

from the sound
made by formal dress
the light of spring

spring dawns
from the sound of
formal dress

Is this all who got up early to see the sun rise or, more specifically, to the "year-man" (year of his animal) up early to draw first-water and make tea. The *hakama* trousers men wear with formal kimonos, called "upper-lowers" (*kamishimo*), have broad culottes-like legs which brush together.

上下を着ると内でもかしこまり 柳多留 廿一・十七
kamishimo o kiru to uchi de mo kashikomari   yanagidaru *senryû* 1786
(up-down[formal male dress] wear and/when inside-even polite/respectful/behaving)

even at home
formal wear makes us
behave ourselves

formal wear
men behave themselves
even indoors

いささかの他人行儀も春着かな 飯田陀笏 角川現代
isasaka no tanin gyôgi mo harugi kana   dakotsu 1886-1962
(slightly stranger-behavior/etiquette too spring-dress 'tis)

spring dress!
a bit standoffish
but colorful

people keep
their distance but still
it's spring dress

No seasonal reference is needed for *senryû*, but *kamishimo* suggests the New Year. My respondent feels there is something in the formal *kimono* that makes her behave more gracefully while wearing it. I added the "colorful" to my reading of the haiku because Spring clothing, *harugi*, suggests the floral beauty of Spring in a way the First-dress-up, *kiso-hajime,* does not. Color in Japan was mainly associated with festivals, which could be explosive and remove barriers between people, but here . . .

福藁の塵はいとわしきそ始 春波 類題発句集
fukuwara no chiri wa itowaji kisohajime   shunpa [1] 1774
(prosperity/lucky-straw's dust/litter-as-for hate-not dress-wear-start)

no one hates
the bits of lucky straw
first dress

People in finery get upset about extraneous matter and frantically dust it off. But they are happy to let *this* straw's health and wealth stick with them.[2] While the starchy chapterhead is my personal favorite New Year's dress ku, this welcome lucky-straw is, perhaps, the most widely anthologized *ku* on New Year's dress, for it evokes the proper holiday spirit. The following, too, is well anthologized:

我裾の鳥も遊ぶやきそはじめ 千代尼
waga suso no tori mo asobu ya kisohajime   chiyo-ni
(my hem/s' bird/s too play/s!/?/: dress-wear-start 1701-75)

even the birds
on my hem at play
first dress

---

1. Shunpa's Name Half my books use the character for a *wave* for the "pa," and half *slope* (坂) One source places the poem after Issa's (making it 19c) while the above given source makes it 1774.

2. Sticky Luck In the 1980's, high-school students went to a zoo in Kyoto? Osaka? in the hope that a famous shit-throwing gorilla would hit them. "Shit" and "luck" (*f/un*) are homophones, so if the former sticks, the latter does too. As far as I know, no one approached the gorilla's cage wearing New Year's finery, though.

A sweet *ku*. This first-dress would not be the somber one with a family crest, we are talking about the colorful *harugi* (spring-dress) or what, at other times would be called *haregi* (clear [like a *clear* sky] dress). I do not know if the birds on Chiyo's dress are auspicious cranes, cheerful sparrows or uguisu (nightingale/warbler) among plum blossoms, but I would have liked to see them dance!

遥かなる春着こちらへ来ず曲る 山口誓子
harukanaru harugi kochira e kozu magaru yamaguchi seishi
(distant/way-off spring-dress here-to come-not turn)

<table>
<tr><td>

a distant kimono
heading this way
turns the corner

</td><td>

off in the distance
a spring kimono heading
this way, turns

</td></tr>
</table>

This is a masterpiece. It brings to life the perfect vantage point for observing the New Year, a long view from a hill; we feel refreshed even if the colorfully dressed figure does not come our way. I use the singular *kimono*, for one kimono, unless otherwise described, is color enough.

一軒家より色が出て春着の児 阿波野青畝 講談社
ikkenya yori iro ga dete harugi no ko awano seikei 20c /& 河出新
(one [solitary/isolated] house -from color comes out: spring-dress's child/ren)

<table>
<tr><td>

color pops out
from a lone house: a child
in spring dress

</td><td>

color flows
out from a lone house
spring kids

</td></tr>
</table>

Today, colorful kimonos are mostly limited to young women on their twentieth New Year (coming-of-age) or little children, especially girls. The second reading imagines a stream of children, not impossible, but unlikely from the grammar. English lacks a short word for *an isolated building*.

膝に来て模様に満ちて春着の子 中村草田男 講談社
hiza ni kite moyô ni michite harugi no ko nakamura kusatao 20c /& 河出新
(lap/knees-to come decoration/patterns filled [with, flowing-over] spring-dress's child/ren)

> a child in spring dress
> overflowing with patterns
> comes to my lap

This poem, like the last one, is in both of my modern *saijiki*. In Japan, where the man in the grey-flannel suit kept to his fashion (?) longer than in the Puritan culture that bore it, the colorful patterns of traditional clothing make a more powerful contrast to the everyday than one might expect in the nation of its birth. The man's traditional *hakama* trousers are usually dark and have no pattern.

母方（上）の紋めつらしやきそ始 山蜂（峰）続猿蓑
hahakata (or ue)no mon mezurashi ya kisohajime sanhô 1698
(mother's side's [family-]crest rare/nice: dress-wear-start)

<table>
<tr><td>

a rare sight,
mother's native crest!
first dress

</td><td>

how rare to see
our matriarchal crest!
the first dress

</td></tr>
</table>

1. *Sanhô* =*Mountain Peak? Wasp?* Three of my sources give the poet's name as "mountain-wasp" and one as "mountain-peak." Kaizôsha has it "peak" and puts the poem in *kokin mohan ichiman-shu*, Shiki's categorical collection has it "wasp" and cites *zoku sarumino,* a late 17 c work, while Kôdansha's large *saijiki*, also "wasp," puts it after Issa but before Shiki, which suggests the 19c. Katô Ikuya has the same as Shiki, so …

Japanese formal *haori* (light over-coat for a kimono) generally has a family crest on it. Aside from this day when time stretches back, the mother's family crest is not seen in the husband's house. On the same day Japanese celebrate collectively, husbands and wives enjoy a greater individual identity. The only *ku* under *first-dress* (*kiso-hajime*) in the 1997 Haijin Kyôkai's 32,205 *ku* anthology has that same crest: *"First clotheshorse: / taking over a woman's crest / from my mother"* (初衣桁母よりつぎし女紋　島田千鶴 季題別*hatsuikô yori tsugishi onna mon*　shimada chizuru. Note: The "clothes-horse" here is a clothes-hanger or rack specifically for a kimono.) This crest takes us back to the legendary matrilineal past.

うなゐ子が千はやふり袖きそ始　三人 宝暦十一
unaiko ga chihayaburi sode [= furisode] kisohajime　sanjin 1761
(infant child wildly/diyonesian? [=waving/long]sleeve dress/wear-start)

<blockquote>
an infant wildly
waving about long sleeves
his first dress
</blockquote>

The everyday robes worn by infants in Japan had sleeves extending far beyond the hands to prevent scratches, fingers in the eye, etc. It was a far more intelligent manner of restriction than the swaddling used by Europeans (See *Topsy-turvy 1585* for details). Is this little boy waving his arms up and down with glee at the pageantry or is he eager to escape the long-sleeved kimono? The powerful old word used to depict the wild action, *chihayaburi,* is perfect for the New Year for it suggests the primal energy of a god and punfully connects with the dress called a *furisode?*

三才の春着を翅のごとひらく 辻田 克巳
san sai no harugi o hane no goto hiraku　tsujita katsumi
(three year's spring-dress[obj] wings-like open 角川 20c)

<blockquote>
a three year old
spreads her spring dress
like wings!
</blockquote>

The flying image is heightened further by the way a little girl's *obi* is tied in the back in a large butterfly knot.

春着の子黒瞳いきいき畦を跳ぶ 律田清子 角川
harugi no ko kuroi me iki-iki aze o tobu　ritsuda kiyoko 20c
(spring-dress's child/rens black-eyes lively-lively levee[obj] jumps)

<blockquote>
in spring dress
a child with bright black eyes
levee-hopping
</blockquote>

I think of sparrows and a mother who could see the eyes of her child clearly from a distance. The *aze* are the ridges that run between paddies. Lacking a proper word in my English, I made them levees.

ゆきたけの猶長かれよきそ始 柳絮 安永四
yuki take no nao nagakare yo kisohajime   ryûjo 1775
(sleeve-length hem-length still long-let [it be]! dress-wear-start)

the sleeves and hem
may they be longer still
new year's dress

new year's dress
too long, my friend, is
just about right

Does this embody hope for room to grow on the occasion of the birthday of all creation? The emphatic *yo* may playfully fuse with the *ki* for dress to create *yoki,* or "good." My respondent noted that *room to grow on* misses the intent of the original: "The parents do not want their child grow too fast." Another *ku* dated the same year: *"How delightful! / the sleeves and hem suffice: / new year's dress"* (あな嬉しゆきたけの足る著衣始 百人　安永四　*ana ureshi yuki take no taru kisohajime* hyakujin 1775). Lacking the extra wish, this *ku* is lacking unless a B-side reading (*kisohajime* was slang for the first time a courtesan slept with a client [1] after he passed a round of preliminaries) is considered.

きそ始春風うごく被哉 古音 大三
kisohajime harukaze ugoku katsugi kana   koon 1697
(dress-wear-start spring-breeze move [a lady's] veil!/'tis)

the first dress
moving in the breeze
a woman's veil

a woman's veil
moves in the spring breeze
the first dress

Princess Sao in human form? The image in this quietly hypnotic poem is about as far from the wild infant as is possible. The veil may allude to the first-mist.

炬燵でる足袋の白さや著衣始 烏堂 卯堂 18c？再現
kotatsu deru tabi no shirosa ya kisohajime   udô _ 続春夏秋冬
(kotatsu [skirted-table with heater] leave tabi's whiteness!/: dress-wear-start)

how white the *tabi*
coming out of the *kotatsu*
new year's dress

The *kotatsu* is a skirted table with a hole in the floor under it for a stove and the legs. Today, the heating device is usually attached to the bottom of the table about a foot off the floor and there is no hole for the legs. Old or new-style, when people sit around these tables their legs are hidden, so they are noticed (and sometimes, I am afraid, smelled) when they are pulled out. The *tabi* is a stiff sock split between the big toe and the next, worn on the *tatami* or with sandals outside. Here, the *tabi* wearer got dressed up for the New Year and sat with his or her legs under the *kotatsu* to keep warm in the chilly morning. There may be an allusion here to the Sun Goddess coming out of the dark cave.

---

1. *Clothing Metaphor* For all his metaphysics of clothing, Herr Prof. Diogenes Teufelsdröckh ('god-born devil-shit') of *Sartor Resartus* may have missed the metaphor most common in the Japanese poetic tradition. *To wear clothing was to have sexual intercourse.* New clothing was a new mate and old clothing a mate of long-standing. In one of the funnier songs in the *Manyôshû* (8c), adultery is rationalized as acceptable, for borrowing old clothing would hardly damage it. As to whether I am right about this haiku having the B-reading, suffice it to say that the exclamation *ana* is homophonic with "hole" – as if to suggest she is, shall we say, *hole happy!*

身つくろひ残る事なし著衣始 浮石 大三
mizukuroi nokoru koto nashi kisohajime fuseki 1697
(body/self grooming remaining thing not: dress-wear-start)

> my grooming
> has left nothing undone
> first dress-up

あらたまの春著に着かへ用のなき 万太郎 講談社大
aratama no harugi ni kigae yô no naki mantarô 1888-1963
(new-gem-spring-dress-to dress-change business [have] not)

> changing into   all dressed up
> new spring dress i have   in new spring robes
> nothing to do   and for what?

The first of the above *ku* seems to have nothing to say but what it says *until you read the modern one* and wonder if the perfect cosmology of the First was meant to evoke a surrounding vacuum. Unless one is planning to pay a visit to a shrine or call on others, all this beauty stays at home. The poet is all dressed up with no place to go. And, *that is as it should be*, for the ideal New Year's travel is vertical (in time) rather than horizontal (in space). It is possible, however, that the second, modern *ku* is a lament by a recent widower not accepting New Year's visitors, as was the custom during mourning.

無衣 明ぼのの春早々に借着かな 一茶
akebono no haru hayabaya (sôsô) ni karigi kana issa -1827
(no clothing // dawn's spring fast-fast borrowed-clothing!/?/'tis)

> **my first debt**
>
> spring's dawn &
> i am already wearing
> borrowed dress

Good clothing everywhere is a burden on the poor. How many Japanese had to wear kimonos patched together from rags such as the clothing described by Dolly Parton in *The Coat of Many Colors (That My Mother Made For Me)*? With this *ku*, Issa throws a stone into the trouble-free spiritual and physical beauty of the New Year. "Borrowed" (*kari*) in Japanese also means a debt incurred. I substituted my title for the boring "no-clothing" of the original to better English that.

古頭巾烏帽子に捻ん花の春 清峨＝五車か 春来＝新選
furuzukin ebôshi ni yoran hana no haru seiga __ or shunrai 1773
(old head-cloth, crow-hat(noble headgear) into twist/form-would flowery-spring)

> old cloth-cap   why not turn
> shall i barnacle you?   my cap into a top-hat?
> posh spring   it's new year's

The formal hat was about two-feet high, black as a crow, and shaped like a thin barnacle named after it. Either Issa was not the first poor poet, or this man was caught away from home on the holidays.

うら返す其古衣の着衣始 子規 明治廿八
uragaesu sono furuginu no kisohajime shiki 1866-1902
(inside-out this old-robe/clothing's dress-wear-start)

inside-out
this old robe becomes
first dress

Shiki's imagination could alight anywhere. I first thought he applied the dream-inviting charm mentioned earlier (pg 316) to New Year wishes, perhaps with a nod toward foolish calends behavior or poetic poverty, but my respondent makes much more sense: *"Shiki may be referring to his new year's clothes made from the inverted material of the old kimono. Re-making new kimonos with material of the old kimonos taken apart, turned inside out, washed and pressed was a common practice up to my youth. My mother used to do it all the time – and we weren't particularly poor. . ."*

鳥虫の願ひは安し着そ始 巴人
chôchû no negai wa yasushi kisohajime hajin -1742
(birds-bugs' wishes-as-for easy: dress-wear-first)

first dress   birds and bugs
the birds and the bugs   have got it made: we make
have it easy   our new dress!

The second reading adds what I think is the point. We must *make, buy, beg, borrow* or *rent* a new dress. My loose sense-translation follows a Hajin study group that came to the conclusion the *ku* means the poet, speaking for humans, is jealous of the natural world which is naturally clothed. In that sense, his poem is an impersonal predecessor of Issa's. For readers who have not lived in Japan, I will add that the practice of renting dresses for the New Year is still common, because good kimono cost more than the items "we" (Usanians, at any rate) rent for the prom or, weddings.

きそ始山の梟笑ふらん 一茶
kisohajime yama no fukurô warau ran issa -1827
(dress-wear-start mountain's owl/s laugh/s yea)

first dress   first dress
the mountain owl   is that hoot owl
is hooting!   laughing?

Did an owl just happen to hoot right when Issa walked outside in his new dress? Does it "laugh" because men take such trouble to dress up the New Year while it is content with his old feathers? Or, does it think old Issa quite the sight? Is there wit in the owl's insertion in the middle of the standard conceit of a "mountain" (*yama*) "laughing/smiling" (*i.e.*, wearing its vernal dress)?

雲は寝巻山は霞をきそ始 方角 花(玉?)かづら
kumo wa nemaki yama wa kasumi o kisohajime hôkaku 1751?
(cloud-as-for sleep-wrap [nightgown] mountain-as-for mist[obj] dress-wear-start)

its nightgown
a cloud, mist is the mountain's
first dress

Looked at like this, rather than in contrast with other animals, man is just following nature. "Mist" alludes to a specific kimono design, where a color gradually fades out. The nightgown seems a bit odd, for it is rare that a cloud-covered dawn turns into mist; but note that the nightgown is really a quilt (which could have sleeves) and, thus, is far thicker than the day-time dress, so the cloud metaphor works better in Japanese.

曙や紫染をきそ始　政顕 大三
akebono ya murasakizome o kisohajime seiken
(dawn! purple-dye[obj] dress-wear-start 1697)

our first dress
this purple fabric
of the dawn!

it's daybreak
a plum purple sky
the first dress

The beauty is welcome, but let's hope it was not too extensive, for in Japan, too, "*Red sky in the morning . . .*" holds true (Japanese are always surprised to hear that the West *also* has such a saying! Actually, it dates back at least as far as to "our" *Old Testament*). As elsewhere, purple dye was costly and generally restricted to the Imperial family.

雪車引や揃小みのゝ着そ始　一茶
sorihiki ya sorou komino no kisohajime issa -1827
(sled-pullers: completed [full-set] small *mino* (straw-coats') dress-wear-start)

the sled-pullers
with matching straw-coats
their first dress

This *ku* is not found in as many *saijiki* as the borrowed clothing or laughing owl *ku*, but I prefer it. Issa, playing the ethnographer, probably depicts his cold home country of Shinano.

煮紙子を我代の春や釜の音　松洞 大三(?)
nikamiko o wagayo no haru ya nabe no oto shôdô 1697
(boiled paper-child(kimono)(+obj) my era's spring: stew's sound)

boiled kamiko

a bubbling sound
in the pot my paper dress
my new year

my own spring?
that bubbling sound
from my dye pot

While there was a time when wealthy aesthetes competed to show off their artsy paper kimono, the seemingly crazy idea originated in monks making clothing without the help of women – raising silk worms and weaving were women's work (and even noblewomen wove presents for their lovers and chewed sweet-rice to make them *sake*). The *kamiko* was famously good winter wear (paper being warmer than cloth) but, by the time the above *ku* was written, it was largely symbolic of poverty, for most *kamiko* were cheap, and old age. So this *ku* is yet another forerunner of Issa's poems of poverty which include the use of all sorts of old scraps to create beautiful *kamiko*. Aesthetic+ascetic makes this subject particularly attractive to haiku poets. I cannot find "boiled *kamiko*" in the dictionary and assume it refers to dyeing the paper in the color most common, a dark persimmon.

名所や絹商人の著衣始　子規 再現
nadokoro ya kinu akindo no kisohajime shiki -1902
(name[famous]+place: silk-merchant's dress-wear-start)

the place to see it silk merchants dressed for the new year	just fame to see the silk merchants out in their first-dress

A "famous place" was idiomatic for a sight-seeing spot, renowned for one thing or another. We know them from the prints of Hokusai, but there were countless such, some of which drew tourists for hundreds of years. Some combined the place with the time-of-year. I vaguely recall reading that Shiki lived or once stayed where there were many silk merchants. Doubtless, their first-dress would have been impeccable. Unlike the poorly shod cobbler, these merchants were wealthy men.

虱なき着物着にけり今朝の春　素檗
shirami naki kimono kinikeri kesanoharu sobaku
(lice-not dress wear [finality] morning's spring -1821)

the new year i put on a kimono without lice	the kimono i wear has no lice spring's here

At the very least, it would be nice not to itch in the time of the Gods! As long as we are low-browing:

犢鼻褌を腮にはさむ著衣始　汶村 古今模範一万句集
fundoshi o ago ni hasamu ya kisohajime bunson -1713
(loin-cloth[obj] chin-by sandwiched!/: wear-dress-start)

> my loin-cloth
> firmly gripped by chin
> dressing begins

The above, writes Shibata Shôkyoku, in his charming essay of obscure but fine old *ku* (『古句を観る』), is hardly representative of the spirit of New Year's dress, but worth introducing to set folk history straight. A man cinching up his loincloth in that manner was introduced in a contemporaneous drama (perhaps 'ukiyo-buro'?) and found in two *senryû* written later than Bunson's haiku. Since these and other *senryû* are cited by scholars to example folk custom, *Why*, he asks, *can't ku, such as this one proudly serve such a purpose?* It is a good question, worth asking as much today as in 1943. Haikai scholarship still tends to concentrate on the literary and biographical to the exclusion of other matters.

裸にも禮あり鬼のきそ始　方谷 宝暦十一
hadaka ni mo rei ari oni no kisohajime hôkoku 1761
(naked/ness-in-even etiquette/manners is: demon's/s' dress-wear-start)

first dress

> even the naked
> have manners: a demon's
> new loin-cloth

I had to shuffle the parts of the original to create a readable poem. The haiku may allude to a guardian demon at a temple presented with a new loincloth, or to the person in the house who plays the demon, throwing beans on the day before the solar equinox, for occasionally it falls into the New Year rather than occurring near the end of the Lunar Year. In that case, however, the "demon" usually wears a kimono with a mask.

靈夢から裸もあるにきそ始 團友 千鳥掛
reimu kara hadaka mo aru ni kisohajime danyû 1712
(spirit-dream-from naked-even is-although, dress-wear-start)

    divinely naked   divinely inspired
dreams not withstanding   dreams of nakedness: why
     our first dress!   begin with dress?

A *reimu* is a mystical dream of divine origin. I would guess this refers to a particular dream in the literary canon, but have not yet pinned it down; the implication would seem to be that the New World of the New Year should start *al fresco*.

安楽やわがきのまゝの著衣始 松吟 大三
anraku ya waga kinomama no kisohajime shôgin
(comfort/ease! my feeling as-is dress-wear-start 1697)

this is the life!
wearing what i want to
for new year's

I think this sort of *ku* is valuable for showing that there was no shortage of Japanese who favored comfort over culture. We can't help wondering what circumstances permitted Shôgin to do this.

世とともに身のきそ始思ふ哉 白雄
yo to tomo ni mi no kisohajime omou kana shirao -1792
(world together-with body/ies/myself's dress-wear-start think!/'tis)

   with all the rest   i guess i will
i guess i'll get dressed   go along with the world
    for the spring   new spring dress

This might mean the natural world, but it probably only means he is thinking of going along with other men (perhaps with a pun on *mi* (body/self) and the year of the snake). A picture of Shirao I have seen makes him look like a bulldog, so I don't know if his dress will be of much help.

腰替り人魚の幾代をきそ始 言水
koshigawari ningyo no ikuyo o kisohajime gonsui 1646-1719
(hip-change[style kimono design] doll's how many generations dress-wear-start)

   how old that   how long will
mermaid doll sporting   the merman sport a new
  her first-tail?   mismatch robe?

1. *Mermaids/Mermen in Japanese Poetry* Until more Japanese haiku & senryû are put on-line (where word searches are easy) it will be hard to get a handle on such a rare item. I have encountered only one other such ku so far: *"I see / mermaid fin in the soup: / my lord's spring"* (人魚のひれ吸物に見ん君か春　西斯 雜中 *ningyô no hire suimono ni min kimigaharu* saishi 18-19c?). This would refer to dugong meat.

---

koshigawari,
or first-dress *ala mode*

how long will we
play the mermaid dressing
for two in one?

At first glance, I imagined mermaids changing their scaly tails from the hip down – changeable heads, which may be pulled off from the clothing are common in Japanese dolls – but, even if the Far East not only knew of mermaid/mermen, but sold dolls to gullible Europeans, this didn't make sense for the poem as a whole. Was *ningyô* ="doll" = 人形 miswritten *ningyo* =人魚 = "mermaid?" Was there a mermaid doll that got a new change of dress or a new fish-bottom every year? Does the poet use the character "fish" (魚) to indicate a rare pronunciation (変) of the second part of "doll" as "*gyo*," while playing with the name of the fashionable design called *koshigawari* or, "hip/rear-change?" Divided in three horizontally, with the midriff section blank, the disparate upper and lower designs suggest the chimera. I would bet on my last reading – that the poet did not care for the fashion.

美しき唖の娘や著衣始　祥石 青嵐
utsukushiki oshi no musume ya kisohajime yôseki 19-20c?
(beautiful mute/dumb daughter/young-woman: wear-dress-start)

how beautiful
the mute young maiden
new year dress

If the first poem in the chapter concentrates on the sound of New Year's dress, this poem brings out the predominately visual element better than any other poem I know. And, if you, like me, know a mute young woman and have seen her in a flowery kimono, it is something you never forget.

抱きよせてつめたかりける春着かな 神保憙
dakiyosete tsumetakarikeru harugi kana jinbogai 20c 角川
(hug/ged/ging-close, [felt]cold[+emphatic]spring-wear 'tis/!/?))

spring kimono
when i hugged her
it felt cold

あたゝめて春着きせたり妹にかな女 early-20c
atatamete harugi kisetari imôto ni kanajo 大正新俳句
(heating/heated spring-wear dress [another party] little-sister-on/to)

first i warm it   warming up
helping my sister into   the spring kimono i dress
her spring dress   my sister

著衣始恍惚として親心　鱶洲
kisohajime kôkotsu to shite oyagokoro　shôshû
(wear-dress-first, ecstatic being parent-heart 19-20c?)

first dress
and no one so happy
as parents

若水
waka-mizu

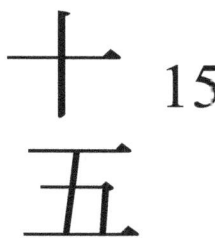

First Water, Young Water

先祝へ初曙の初手水　菰葉 明和二
mazu iwae hatsu-akebono no hatsuchôzu koyô
(first celebrate! first dawn's first hand-water 1765)

first celebrate!
the first water scooped
the first dawn

The "first-water" (*hatsu-mizu*) drawn on New Year's was thought to be good preventative medicine, serving to keep whoever drinks, washes and bathes in it young. Usually called *waka-mizu*, "young-water," it came from freshly melted snow and was, like "young-leaves" (*wakaba*), itself "young." "Hand-water" (*chôzu*) is a portion of that water used to wash the hands and face. This *ku*, standing alone under the theme "First Dawn" (*hatsu-akebono*), was *the first entry* in Shiki's 12-volume *Categorical*. You might say it *baptizes* the collection. Let me add one he missed: *"He starts singing / a song to the young water: / the holy man"* (若水に歌よミそめし聖哉　素月 (星布尼の四季発句集). *wakamizu ni uta yomisomeshi hijiri kana* sogetsu (c1800).) "Singing" usually means "composing" a *waka*, but, in this case, it seems others hear it, so "singing a song" stands.

天甘露地は若水の春日哉　吟静 大三
ten kanro chi wa wakamizu no harubi kana ginsei 1697
(heaven sweet-dew, earth-as-for young-water's spring-day!/'tis)

a fine spring day
sweet dew from heaven
young water from earth

A "spring-day" (*harubi*) is not *any day in spring*, but one that is magically clear and refreshing. Sometimes, the first day of the year was *that*. The poet, out early to scoop up Young Water (why we know it is New Year's), finds abundant dew, often the case with days that turn out beautifully. Japanese speak of dew as "descending," hence it comes from the sky. Sweet-dew is the Sinofication of the Hindi *amrta*, a nectar of immortality. The use of "from" twice saved an otherwise lost poem.

若水や汲まるゝ迄は去年の水　文瓜　新類題発句集
wakamizu ya kumaruru made wa kozo no mizu　bunka 1793
(young water!/: scooped-until-as-for, last-year's water)

young water
until scooped up
it's old water

若水や流るゝうちに去年今年　千代女
wakamizu ya nagaruru uchi ni kozokotoshi　chiyo-jo -1775
(young-water: flowing-within/while last-year-this-year!)

young water as it flows by last year becomes this!	young water even as it pours in another year!

Water was drawn at dawn and sunrise brought the New Year. As we bend for young-water, another year is piled on our backs. Chiyo's "flows" suggests a river, but may be a stream pouring from well-bucket to carrying vessel. I like the flow metaphor for *kozo-kotoshi,* or, *that-year-this-year* (see ch 2).

先けさは蛙見に行井出の水　言水
mazu kesa wa kawazu mi ni yuku ide no mizu　gonsui -1719
(first, this-morning-as-for, frog/s look-to go well-leave water)

this morning first i visit the frogs to draw water	first, at dawn i go to see the frogs in the well

I believe "this morning" and the well implies the "first water." I do not know how many wells had frogs, but having anti-bacterial properties in their skins, are good for the water. Gonsui jokes that the first rite of the New Year might well be called "frog-viewing." Of course, frogs are not the only thing people find in young water: *"Young water / the shadows of gold and / silverfish stars"* (若水や金魚銀魚の星の影　栗銘　元除遍覧　文化九 *wakamizu ya kingyô gingyô no hoshi no kage*　ritsumei 1812). Another *ku* has the bucket "draw up the stars" (星すくふ手水も玉の春なれや　満明　明和2 *hoshi sukuu chôzu mo tama no haru nare ya*　manmei 1765). Or, maybe only *the* Morning Star:

星一つ手にいただくや初手水　潤子　玉桂
hoshi hitotsu te ni itadaku ya hatsuchôzu　junshi 1751
(star[=year] one hand-in receive [as gift] first-hand(scooped)water)

one to grow on	*this, too, a gift*
my hands accept the present of a star in first water	first water my hands scoop up one star

In the moonless night, stars would stand out and reflect. Is the water sparkling? Or was it carried on a tray in a formal star arrangement (*mitsuboshi,* etc.) and the poet took one "star?" Metaphor may be the point: *star/s* can mean goals or years achieved, including *aging* (*eg., seisô* 星霜 for *saigetsu*).

若水や銀河と酌めば桶踊る　桜硯子 日本俳句鈔
wakamizu ya ginga to kumeba oke odoru　rokishi? 19-20c?
(young-water!/: galaxy and scoop-if/when tub/bucket dance)

   bucket dance　　　　　　　　　　　　scooping young
 young water drawn with　　　　　　　water with the milky way
  the milky way　　　　　　　　　　　　　my pail dances

The poet is drawing or scooping up water before dawn. I know that buckets dance and stars shine brightest in the cold (Jan. 1, if written after Japanese adopted the Gregorian calendar, a month or two later, if the Lunar calendar) but cannot vouch for the condition of the Milky Way. *Anyone?*

若水に鰹の躍る涼しさよ　其角
wakamizu ni katsuo no odoru suzushisa yo　kikaku
(young-water-as bonito's dance coolness[+emphatic] - 1707)

  cool indeed　　　　　　how refreshing　　　　　　young water
 a bonito is dancing　　to see the bonito dance　　so cool we can see
 in young water　　　　　on young water　　　　　　bonito leap

This poem is among the young-water *ku* in almost every *saijiki* I have seen. Yet, something does not make sense. First-bonito and coolness are *summer* themes. Is the idea that the water is so bracing one *thinks* of the smart smack of a bonito's tail on the water surface when it jumps? (こここそ専門家の説明を求む！)

若水や色なき星が桶の中　美柑みつはる 季題別
wakamizu ya ironaki hoshi ga oke no naka　mikan mitsuharu 1997
(young-water!/: color[sexuality]-less star/s pail's within)

  young water　　　　　　young water　　　　　　young water
 the stars in my pail　　no sex with the stars　　any stars in the pail
  are colorless　　　　　in this bucket　　　　　　are innocent

It is hard to believe this is contemporary. It is so *haikai!* The most commonly poeticized stars are the lovers (herdsman and weaver) who enjoy their annual tryst on the seventh evening of the seventh month. Unlike *those* stars, these are colorless, i.e. not sexually charged. Japanese did not think of sex as dirty, so the "innocent" reading is not quite right but would, say, "chaste" be better? Yet, people did refrain from sex on this night, so an association with a ritual sense of purity can be made. If I take that idea and add a verb to the poem, we get: *"Young water: / the stars we draw up / are all clean."* Or, am I wrong? Could these "stars" reflect the eyeshine of a self-consciously old poet? I hope not!

若水の底にも笑ふ初日哉　擧扇
wakamizu no soko ni mo warau hatsuhi kana　kyôsen 1765
(young-water's bottom/floor-in/on-also/even smiles/laughs/ing first-sun!/?/tis)

  also smiling　　　　　　　　　　　　　　new year's day
 under young water　　　　　　　　　we even smile underwater
  the first sun!　　　　　　　　　　　　　young water!

The "too/even" may also allude to water's topographical opposite, the mountain, for *yama-warai,* or smiling mountain/s, is a standard spring theme. I am not sure "underwater" is the right place for the smile, for Japanese sometimes claim what we assume is seen from the water *surface,* namely, a reflection, is on the bottom of the river, pond or whatever. Because English forces a choice between "sun" and "day," the ambiguity as to whether the smile is solar or human can not be kept in translation. Here is a *ku* that translates much more easily:

若水や移る笑顔を結ひあけ 素候
wakamizu ya utsuru egao o musubi-age sokô 1777
(young-water: reflect smiling-face[obj]cup/join-raise)

<table>
<tr><td>young water
smiling faces cupped
and raised</td><td>young water
i cup and lift up
a happy face</td></tr>
</table>

I imagine more reflections were seen in pails drawn up from wells, but the *idea* of cupping one's own smiling mug is more interesting.

手の内に春を見せけり初手水 楓鹿
tenouchi ni haru o misekeri hatsuchôzu fûka 1697 大三
(hand/s-within spring[obj] shows/shown[+emph] first wash-water)

<table>
<tr><td>***first-water***

scooped up
within my hands
the spring</td><td>**new scoop**

first water
the spring's right here
in my hands</td></tr>
</table>

behold spring
cupped within our hands
the first water

I imagine a reflection of the skyscape or landscape rather than the scooper's face. I failed to find a good translation with the "show/shown" verb found in the original.

若水のたるごとくなり年男 作者不知 毛吹草
wakamizu no taru gotoku nari toshi-otoko anon 1645
(young-water's dripping-like-becomes year's-man)

the year-man
an old sponge dripping
with young water

Unlike May Day in parts of Europe, where all girls desiring beauty go out to bathe their faces in the dew at dawn, in most of Japan, the young water was drawn and carried home by "the year-man." This *toshi-otoko* was the same man chosen to be the bean thrower at the *setsubun* ritual. If the man was only the "year man," chosen for being born in the year-animal (born in that year), we could say the young-water was indeed the first of the year, as it usually is considered to be today. But, men, or in some parts, women, too, were sometimes of a crisis year (33 for women, 42 for men), and it was once common to do the ceremony on the *setsubun* (season-divide-day), which was the day before the Solar Spring. In that case, the main point would have been *ablution,* i.e., to wash off the pollution of the

Old Year. Since it eventually became common to cover up a well on the last day of the year and have the Year Man open it early in the morning of the New Year, it would seem that the ceremony became more forward-looking with time. It is interesting to note that the bean-throwing most associated with the *setsubun,* which has elements pointing both ways, as some beans are tossed out that the bad goes and others tossed in for the good to stay, is today uniformly a Winter Theme while young-water is a New Year's theme.

若水や手桶枝杓の木の匂ひ　言友尼　改造
wakamizu ya chôzu hishaku no ki no nioi　koyû-ni late-18c
(young-water!/: hand-pail's ladle's wood's scent/smell)

young water
the scent of the ladle
of the wood

The ladle for distributing the water from the pail was probably made of thinly shaven cedar attached to a bamboo handle. Changing "the scent of the wood of the ladle" to "of the ladle, of the wood" saved the poetry in this *ku* by a Buddhist nun.

若水や井戸からものゝもらひ初　乙由
wakamizu ya ido kara mono no moraisome　otsuyû -1739
(young-water: well-from thing-/receiving/accepting[asgift]/borrowing-start)

young water!   young water!
from the well, our first   from the well we begin
gift of the year   our borrowing

That the water first drawn was not taken for granted is reflected in its special name (rare in *haiku,* for it seems too fancy), 井華水 (*seikasui*), meaning *well-flower-water.* The indebtedness may also owe to the well's being owned by another person.

井は一つもつべきものよけさの春　蓼太
i wa hitotsu motsubeki mono yo kesanoharu　ryôta 1707-87
(well-as-for one have-ought thing, yea: morning's spring/new-year)

your own well   spring morning:
everyone should have one   a well – each of us
it's the first   should have one!

I just love this type of *"Wouldn't it be nice if . . ."* haiku! And, I heartily agree and wish *I* had one.

大雪はたゝ若水の泉かな　望一　毛吹草
ôyuki wa tada waka-mizu no izumi kana　môichi 1645
(big snow-as-for, just young-water's spring 'tis/!)

heavy snowfall
why it's just a spring
for young water!

While the Japanese may not yet have figured out the science of artesian wells (as Erasmus Darwin had in England), a thousand years of poetic tradition spoke of melted ice-water running below boulders.

清る世やその若水も古井より 玉江 四季 in 星布尼
kiyomuru yo ya sono wakamizu mo furui yori gyokukô c1800
(purifying world!/: that young-water too/even old-well-from)

<blockquote>
the world purified
that young water, too
from an old well
</blockquote>

注連縄に古井の水も春めきぬ 春郊 句鑑
shimenawa ni furu i no mizu mo haru mekinu shunkô 1777
(warning-connect-rope-with old well's water too spring-like[as verb])

festoon-bound	properly decked
the water in the old well	the old well's water
joins the spring	becomes spring

"Festoon" here means the thick, twisted straw rope that removes a space from the secular world. Most wells were so decorated, including Issa's, about which he quipped in his characteristic self-defacing style:

庵の井もけさ若水と呼れけり 一茶
io no i mo kesa wakamizu to yobarekeri issa -1827
(hut's well, too, [this] morning "young-water" called [emphatic])

<blockquote>
this dawn, the well
at my hut, too, is called
"young water"
</blockquote>

We imagine an old, run-down well. Three years later, Issa describes what was done to improve the quality of the young water:

新桶は同じ水でもわか／＼し 一茶
araoke wa onaji mizu demo wakawakashi issa -1827
(new-pail/tub-as-for, same water-even/though youthful)

a new pail	our new pail
the very same water	the same old water wet
young, young!	about the ears

The Japanese had plentiful rain, better waste control than in the Occident, and not too many minerals in its volcanic land, so the water was, on the whole, better quality than it was in most of Europe. But it was still a pretty crowded place and much of the well water was probably not pristine. Another *ku* from Issa's time pointed out the obvious: *"Young water! / Though plain water / just yesterday!"* (若水やきのふハ常の水なから 里耕 四季 in 星布尼 *wakamizu ya kinô wa tsune no mizu nagara* rikô c.1800). I suppose doing the trick without a new pail is higher art, but most of us appreciate the aid. A more imaginative poet used a method symbolically apt but hygienically suspect:

わか水や揚る釣瓶に亀うかむ 湖月 四季
wakamizu ya agaru tsurube ni kame ukamu kogetsu c1800
(young-water!/: raising [well-]bucket-in turtle floats 星布尼集に)

young water
in the raised well-bucket
a turtle floats

若水を汲むや冥土へ通ふ井戸 杉岡せん城 季題別
wakamizu o kumu ya meido e kayou ido sugioka senjô 1997
(young-water draw!/: nether-world-to/with circulate/connect well/s)

young water

today the well
i draw from reaches
the nether world

just one spring
wakamizu drawn from
the elysian well

drawing young water
so, do our wells connect
with the yellow spring

This contemporary poem has the feeling of a *ku* older than Issa's! It could have been written in the 17 or 18c. When poets write an old-fashioned poem, the letter う is usually written ふ. *Meido* is the nether region, the Hades of Buddhism, the paradisiacal Chinese Yellow Spring, and more broadly "the abode of spirits." To be linked with all who have lived is a form of immortality. The many older *ku* we have seen connect to the Age of the Gods on the New Year; this poet feels a slightly different, more human, or perhaps biological, link with all who have lived. Or, I, at least, feel that link between the words of the spiritual metaphor.

The Sound of Drawing Water

元日や耳に井車眼に焚火 梅室
ganjitsu ya mimi ni iguruma me ni takibi baishitsu 1768-1852
(new year's day: ears-in/to well-pulley, eyes-in/to [an open-air] fire)

it's the new year!
a well pulley in the ear
a fire in the eye

The majority of young-water well poems mention the *sound*. Was this because most people (including the poet) heard it being drawn from their warm futons? The well-pulley is from a "pulley well," defined in my dictionary as "a well from which water is drawn in a bucket hoisted by means of a pulley." Many wells did not use pulleys; they relied on long poles with a weighted bucket on the far end – called *sweeps* or *swipes* in old English – which could be swung down thereby lifting the bucket from the well without cranking or hand-over-hand rope-work. The fire is the "new stove" (hatsugama) kindled by the "year-man" to heat tea and New Year's stew (*zôni*: ny book 3).

若水にのぞく井筒の響哉 草虫 大三
wakamizu ni nozoku izutsu no hibiki kana   sôchû
(young-water-at/in peek well-curb's echo!/?/'tis 1697)

<blockquote>
peeking to see
the young water! i hear
the well-curb
</blockquote>

The Japanese *izutsu* is obviously "well-tube" for any Japanese reader. That is what the old English word *curb* means here. Here, I imagine the bucket scraping the side of the curb.

若水に鶴の声有り車井戸 鯉遊 玉かづら　　　井戸闇く滴る音や井華水 鳴各子 改造社
wakamizu ni tsuru no koe ari kuruma ido   riyû 1751　　　*ido kuraku shitataru oto ya seikasui*   meikakushi early-20c
(young-water-to/in crane/s' voice is/has pulley-well)　　　(well darkly dripping sound:/! well-blossom-water)

<blockquote>
this young water　　　　　　　　　　a dark shaft
has the voice of a crane　　　　　　the sound of dripping
a pulley well　　　　　　　　　　　　well-blossoms
</blockquote>

I have no idea if "pulley-well" is a proper phrase. The otherwise noisy squeaking sound is propitious for resembling the symbol of longevity, the venerable "thousand year" crane. With the second, early 20c *ku*, the *blossoms* are, of course, propitious. I dropped the "~water" in "well-blossom-water" for in English it seems a separate word, while in the original it is but part of the agglutination. In Japanese, flying bits of matter may become *blossoms*. The most common usage is "wave-blossom" for bits of spume blown off white-caps. The metaphor is beautiful and, in the darkness, *deep*.

隣人と闇のつづける若井くむ 本多静江 講談社大
rinjin to yami no tsuzukeru waka i kumu   honda shizue 20c
(neighbor/s-to/with darkness continues young-well draw/scoop)

<blockquote>
darkness extending　　　　　　　　　darkness connects
from neighbor to neighbor　　　　　neighbor to neighbor
young well-drawing　　　　　　　　　drawing young water
</blockquote>

In the darkest hour, just before dawn, neighbors out drawing water would hear but not see one another. Imagine a chain of darkness linking neighbor to neighbor linking all Japan if you wish. The poem, chosen as the example poem for *young-water* in the Kodansha's large *saijiki*, is a masterpiece.

若水や升なき時の人心 蓼太
wakamizu ya masu naki toki no hitogokoro   ryôta 1707-87
(young-water: box/measure-lacking time's people-heart/mind)

<blockquote>
young water!　　　　　　　　　　　　young water!
overflowing with　　　　　　　　　　the mind of a man
nothing below　　　　　　　　　　　without measure
</blockquote>

A *masu* is generally known as a square wooden container which serves as a measure or a cup for drinking cold *sake*. Here I think it refers to 水を引く桶（ひ）の接続部分などに設けてある、大きな箱。 a large box that was fixed to receive the well-bucket. Without it, some water would spill over on the ground, and that, Ryôta feels is appropriate at this time.

けさの春水にうなづく我若し 如稲 大三
kesanoharu mizu ni unazuku ware wakashi   jotô 1697
(morning's spring water-in/to nodding/bowing me young)

new year's day　　　　　　　　　　　　　　new year's dawn
a younger me nods back　　　　　　　　　this face in the water
from the water　　　　　　　　　　　　　looks so young!

spring water
i can't help nodding i
do look young

The "young me" reflection seems to nod that you/i am/are indeed young. No single translation works.

顔の皺けさ汲水に譲りけり 丁眠 大三
kao no shiwa kesa kumu mizu ni yuzurikeri   teimin 1697
(face's wrinkles [this]morning scooped water-to concede/transfer [emph.])

a year younger?

wrinkles ceded
to the face of the water
scooped this dawn

I love mirrors that are not too cruelly exact. That would explain the young face in the previous *ku*. But what do you do with disturbed water? This poet comes up with a great play on the equation of ripples and wrinkles in Japanese. Rather than saying the waves *made* him wrinkled, . . .

若水は百千童子の鏡哉 言色 大三
waka mizu wa hyakusen dôji no kagami kana   gonshiki 1697
(young-water-as-for hundred-thousand infant-children's mirror/reflection/s!/?/'tis)

young water:　　　　　　　　　　　　　young water:
reflecting millions of　　　　　　　　the mirror for millions
infant faces!　　　　　　　　　　　　of its children

A poetic etymology of "young water." If any *ku* could be called adorable, this is it. All Japanese are born again on the New Year (See the frontpiece of Headland's *Chinese Mother Goose* (c.1900) for the very image!).

六十の春を祝して 汲〳〵てくむ程若しけさの川 百丈 安永四 1775
rokuju-no haru o iwaishite // kumi kumite kumu hodo wakashi kesa no kawa   hyakujô
(sixty year's spring celebrating // scooped, scoop [up] as much youthful this-morning's[ny] river)

celebrating my sixtieth spring

scoop! scoop!
the more the younger!
dawn at the river

A fine study – joking self-deprecation – of an old man energetically scooping up water. Like most of Japan's folk belief, "young-water" was only half-believed in. This is not to criticize Japanese. Lukewarm belief is common to gentle, rational people who would retain a modicum of magic in their world.

若水の鏡は老の始哉　沾峨 吐屑庵
wakamizu no kagami wa oi no hajime kana   senga 1776
(young water's mirror-as-for old-age's beginning!/?/'tis)

young water	*ripple effect*
we start aging from the moment we look into the mirror	does old age start when you see yourself in young water?

if you look

our first thought
of old age, reflected
in young water

The original says only "the mirror of young water is the start of old age." The question is whether it means that one starts feeling one's age the first time *in one's life* the ritual is engaged in; or, *every year,* if for no other reason that our doing something to remain young reminds us that we are *not.* One wonders what the young who generally want to be older, think about this!

若水よ　袖びちゃ／\の老の影 友吉 大三
wakamizu yo sode bichabicha no oi no kage   yûkichi 1697
(young-water! sleeves drippy-drippy [soaking]'s elderly reflection/face)

an old face with soaking wet sleeves young water	oh, young water! what's an old face doing with wet sleeves?

A *haikai* chuckle at old trope, using the rhetoric of incongruity. In the older song and poetry tradition, wet sleeves meant *romance*: someone longing for someone they couldn't meet, and these wet sleeves often reflected the face of the moon, which itself might mirror the image of the absent beloved. Here, the old poet's sleeves got wet while enthusiastically scooping up young water.

若水やこれも遊ものと知りなから 古山 類題発句集
wakamizu ya kore mo asobimono to shirinagara   kosan 1774
(young-water:/! this, too, play thing knowing-while)

yes! young water
though we know this, too
is only a game

Apologies for the late-20c Usanian slang *"Yes!"* I thought a better affirmation than an exclamation mark was needed. Doubt about the efficacy of this ritual is best couched in untranslatable puns: *"Young water: / An old man stretches out / the well-bucket rope"* (若水や老ひきのはすつるへ縄　素翁 大三 *wakamizu ya oi hiki-nobasu tsurubenawa* soô 1697). The middle of the *ku* suggests stretching out, i.e. extending, the old man's life (or it's signs, wrinkles) but it ends in a *senryû*-like chuckle over the full bucket of water by which the old man, perhaps the poet himself, would *like* to do so.

若水に前髪の跡撫にけり 一見 大三
wakamizu ni maegami no ato nadenikeri ikken 1697
(young-water-with/in front-hair's trace [place where it was] rub/stroke [+fin.])

coming of age   **a bald wish**

young-water   rubbing the place
caresses the place   my forelocks were
his hair was   with young water

I think "his" likely, for the "place/trace" seems visual. The front of the head was shaved for the coming-of-age, but samurai also did this, so it cold be "my." The second reading is unlikely, but . . . .

若水を幾度頬へ蟇 紹簾 古選
wakamizu o ikutabi hô e hikigaeru jôren 1763
(young-water many-times cheeks-to toad[=pull/draw]-back)

young water again
and again: still the cheeks
of an old toad!

To piss on the face of frog, or toad, was a metaphor for lack of response on the part of the other party. Here, the name for toad – a single Chinese character – is punned on. No matter how many times water is splashed on his cheeks, the poet remains an ugly old toad. It might be nice to imagine the poet playing with a toad met at the well, but I think the New Year was a bit early for them to emerge.

若水や冬は薬に結ひしを 野坂 類題発句集
wakamizu ya fuyu wa kusuri ni musubishi o yaba -1740 ↑1774
(young-water: winter-as-for, medicine[meat]-for/with cupped [+contra.+emph.])

this young water!
the same that washed down
meat in the winter

The original has *medicine*, not meat, but I believe it a euphemism for something people, especially old men in ill health ate in early winter barbecues for the express purpose of making it through the cold season ahead. The contradictory sigh, the "o" ending the poem, bemoans the guilt associated with the taking of life that spiritually pollutes the water now being invoked for youth and health, something brought out by the binding connotation of the verb used for cupping hands to drink in Japanese.

若水に皺影笑ふあしたかな 杉風 講談社大
wakamizu ni shiwakage warau ashita kana sanpû 1646-1732
(young-water-in wrinkled-reflection/shadow-smiles/laughs morning 'tis)

it's the spring
a wrinkled shadow smiles
in young water

If the reader can find a 19c or early 20c Aesop's in English, he or she will note that the *reflection* of the dog with the bone in the pond was called a *shadow*; so please indulge me in my syllable-saving choice! This *ku* combines aspects of *ku* we have seen: waves-as-wrinkles and a smile in the water.

若水に白髪吹かせて自慢哉　一茶
wakamizu ni shiraga fukasete jiman kana   issa -1827
(young-water-in/to/with white-hair blow!/?/ 'tis)

<table>
<tr><td>making a show
of my shock of white hair
for young water</td><td>of this i'm proud
my white hair reflects well
in young water</td><td>i guess i'm proud
of my white locks puffed up
by the young water</td></tr>
</table>

Issa was in his late fifties. His hair turned white in his thirties. Issa wrote a lot of his shame at living a long time; this is a happy exception. He would seem to have realized that there came a point where his white hair became a badge and he was proud of it. The same year, he wrote this:

欲どしくわか水つかふ女哉　一茶
yokudoshiku wakamizu tsukau onna kana   issa -1827
(avariciously young-water use/s woman/women 'tis)

<table>
<tr><td>greedily
using young water
women</td><td>greedily
using young water
a woman</td></tr>
</table>

Do women cling to life more tenaciously then men, who were not supposed to care? Or, are we talking about *beauty* here? While I cannot find a single *saijiki* explanation of "young water" *used as a beauty aid*, youth itself is a large component of beauty. Could this depict Issa's wife (in her thirties)?

わか水のよしなき人に汲まれけり 一茶
wakamizu no yoshinaki hito ni kumarekeri   issa -1827
(young water's reason-not (unsuitable/bad) person/s-by drawn [+emph.])

<table>
<tr><td>young water
drawn by people who
don't need it</td><td>young water
drawn by one who will
only waste it</td></tr>
</table>

Issa's journal has a preamble: "The well in Misaki-nonaka is a *memento mori* of the courtesan Kashiwagi" (三崎野中の井は遊女柏木がかたみ也). Does he mean that a courtesan needs her youth to attract clients while others who draw water from the well do not really need to worry about their wrinkles? Or, does he mean it is lost on him? (あるいは、他の読み方は？)

名代のわか水浴る雀哉　一茶 文政一
myôdai no wakamizu abiru suzume kana   issa 1818
(representative-as young-water bathes sparrow/s!/?/'tis)

my proxy
bathes in the young-water
a sparrow

Can you guess what happens to the sparrow the following year (next page)?

名代のわか水浴る烏かな 一茶 文政二
myôdai no wakamizu abiru karasu kana issa 1819
(representative-as young-water bathes crow!/?/ 'tis)

as my proxy bathing in young-water an old crow	my proxy bathes in young-water: that crow	as my proxy the old crow bathes in young-water

A couple versions of the sparrow precede the crow, and one mentions the coldness of the water (*kanmizu*). I agree with Blyth that Issa may have rewritten his poem without necessarily seeing a crow bathe the following year, but I do not think it just because Issa "*should have seen* a black, glossy crow;" or "thought the crow a stronger, more humorous "proxy" than the timid sparrow." The main advantage of the crow is that its black color makes it formal and its voice and stiff motions when walking, *suggests an old man* – such as the poet – whereas the sparrow (not necessarily more timid) is usually associated with children. Issa wanted a creature representative of himself.[1]

わか水や並ぶ雀もまめな顔 一茶
wakamizu ya narabu suzume mo mame na kao issa -1827
(young water: lined-up sparrows, too, diligent/faithful/chipper faces)

young water
even the sparrow family
looks diligent

The *mame* is the same untranslatable adjective Issa used to describe a human face in the chapter on New Year's Gifts. It is a patronizing term, fit to describe good servants, but also endearing, and the translation suffers without it. I think this *ku* depicts sparrowhood far better than the delegate *ku* does.

わか水(や)見たばかりでも角田川 一茶	わか水や土瓶一ッに角田川 一茶
wakamizu ya mita bakari demo sumidagawa issa -1827	*wakamizu ya dobin hitotsu ni sumidagawa* issa
(young-water: /! looked[at] only, still, sumida river)	(young-water: earthen-jug one-in sumida river)
young water it suffices to look at the sumida	young water a jugful of the sumida is enough

The first is even lazier than leaving young water to the birds. I recall my prescient cat, Han-chan, who *looking* out on the snow that fell during the night, raised a hind-leg and shook it before being forced out to do his business. The Sumida River was far from young looking even in Issa's day, but its name is a homophone for "suffices." This modified version – likewise punning – was written by 62 year-old Issa remembering his slumming days by the river in Edo. That year, he also wrote a version which did *not* pun: "I *look* at young water / to open my eyes: / the Sumida." (目覚しにわか水見るや角田川 一茶 *mezamashi ni wakamizu miru ya sumidagawa*). Issa loved New Year ritual, but he hated the cold.

---

1. Representation in Haiku There are more proxy *ku* in Japanese, but Blyth's translations introduced the idea in English. His "as representative" translations were picked up by the top sparrow and crow haikuist in English, Richard Wright, whose "delegate" *ku*, include: *"As my delegate / the spring wind has its fingers / in a young girl's hair"* and *"As my delegate / the scarecrow looks pensively / into spring moonlight."* Wright's "delegate" *ku* explore more psychological possibilities than Issa's, but Issa himself came up with one new twist: *"As proxies / for the nightingale / singing sparrows"* (*uguisu no myôdai ni naku suzume kana*).

わか水の歯に染み（し）のもむかし哉　一茶
wakamizu no ha ni shimishi no mo mukashi kana　issa 1764-1827
(young-water's tooth-on smarting also long ago!/ 'tis)

young water
once upon a time
it hurt my teeth

young water
the teeth that smarted
long gone

This is Issa's only *explicitly cold* young-water *ku*. Years earlier, he recorded the sorry end of his last tooth. How he continued to eat without a blender is beyond me. Well, at least cold water no longer smarts! Toothless Issa could still smile and managed to squeeze a dozen or more fun haiku from his missing teeth (See *Teeth-hardening* in NY Book IV, perhaps.).

麓には水のつめたき初日哉　一鼠 其雪かけ
fumoto ni wa mizu no tsumetaki hatsuhi kana　isso 1772
(foot-hills-in-as-for water's cold first-sun=day!/? /'tis)

how cold this
water in the foothills
our first day

in the foothills
it is a chilly water
new year's day

This is an observant *ku*. Though not specifically a "young-water" poem, it also makes clear why I, like Issa, would prefer a proxy bather on that day. The worst-case scenario:

雪に袖わか水重きしつく哉　昌叱 大発句帳
yuki ni sode wakamizu omoki shizuku kana　shôshitsu -1603
(snow-in sleeve, young-water heavy drop/s 'tis)

snowy sleeves
how heavy each drop
of young-water!

A *very* loose translation. The grammatical glue in the original is so weak, I had to invent the meaning.

若水をうちかけて見よ雪の梅　亀洞 あらの
wakamizu o uchikakete miyo yuki no ume　kidô 1689
(young-water throw-upon-try snow's plum)

try tossing
young water on that
snowy plum

"Snowy plum" *implies* a budding plum-tree wearing a layer of snow. This is my favorite young-water *ku*, for I enjoy a provocative approach to nature. The plum, first blossom of Spring can use some help. I'd have preferred a slow-blooming plum without snow, so the water's work would be deeper, but the idea is still a good one. And, it improves further if you imagine the snow as white hair, which, by an application of this water breaks into bloom.

梅挿すや春一番の桶の水　奇淵 俳句大全
ume sasu ya haru ichiban no oke no mizu   kien 1765-1834
(plum[blossom] insert/arrange: spring first-rank's tub's water)

this budding branch
what better water for plum
than spring's first tub

the first tub
of spring water: i stick
a plum in it

There may have been a blossom open but I mostly imagine buds because that is what I have experienced. Hopefully, it will be in full bloom in time for the Woman's New Year, i.e. the full moon.

若水やそóとつき込（む）梅の花　一茶
wakamizu ya sôto tsukikomu umenohana   issa 1762-1827
(young-water!/: quietly/secretly stick-enter/insert plum-blossoms)

young water
very gently i slip in
ume no hana

young water:
gently i slip in a limb
plum blossoms

"Plum blossoms" could mean buds about to bloom, for *ume-no-hana,* like *ume,* was used loosely.

三文の若水あまる我家哉（庵かな）　一茶
san mon no[ga] wakamizu amaru wagaya [iori] kana   issa 1764-1827
(three mon [small monetary unit]'s young water remains (over) my house[hut]!/'tis)

just two bits
of young water suffice
for my house

for my cottage
three-pence of young water
more than does

This comes a few years after Issa marries. Other *ku* suggest the house he shared (it was partitioned) had a well or access to a public (free) well nearby. Was young-water from special wells in Shintô temple grounds bought? Did it come with a new cedar tub? Or was the three *mon* for such a vessel alone? In either case, the warp of Issa's poetry was poverty and, luckily, the ascetic tradition in haiku established by Bashô not only allowed but admired it. Another of his doing-with-little *ku*: "One tub does / for young *mizu*, young *yû* / and young tea" (一桶をわか水わか湯わか茶哉 一茶 文政六 *hito oke o wakamizu wakayu wakacha kana* 1823). Because cold and hot water are both called "water" in English, I had to use the Japanese *mizu* and *yu*. A Yankee school teacher once recorded a less self-conscious woman in early-20c Appalachia, who used a single pot to allow a guest to wash her face, which was washed for cooking a meal and, then, washed once again to make tea.

新桶は同じ水でもわか／\し　一茶
ara oke wa onaji mizu demo wakawakashi   issa -1827
(new tub/pail-as-for, same water even, youthful!)

a new pail
makes the same water
very young!

This *ku* suggests Issa's three-*mon* (two-bit) expenditure may indeed have referred to the cost of the tub.

Perhaps it was wrong to include so many crude and plain *ku* by Issa in this chapter – and this one we see for the second time! – but the down-to-earth character of his *ku* is, itself, suitable for this back-to-scratch time of year. Which is not to say that more abstract poetry is not also welcome:

若水に心姿を洗ふ哉　幸悦子 大三
wakamizu ni kokoro sugata o arau kana   kôetsushi 1697
(young-water-in/with mind/heart form/figure/appearance wash!/?/'tis)

      in young water   young water   young water
we wash our bodies   when we wash away years   to cleanse the persona
    and our minds   with our mind   of our spirits

Not knowing the poet's work, I cannot tell if the poem is a psychological observation of wistful (wishful?) thinking, i.e., temporary cognitive dissonance, a philosophical one of mind-over-matter, or a metaphysical take on spirit. Regardless, such conceptual *ku* are now endangered species.

若水に知恵の鏡を磨うよや　嵐雪 玄峰
wakamizu ni chie no kagami o togôyo ya   ransetsu -1707
(young-water-with/in wisdom's mirror polish/hone let's)

       young water   good polish for
why not use it to clean   the mirror of wisdom:
     wisdom's glass?   young water

This is not just Shintô reflection but good philosophy. Youth may not know much, but as Thomas Jefferson once noted, a man who knows nothing is miles ahead of one who knows wrong.

天の川若水からんあした哉　擧扇 糸まき
amanokawa wakamizu karan ashita kana   kyôsen 1765
(heaven's river young-water spread-out/spiggot[?] morning!/?/'tis)

     this morning   on this morning   the milky way
young water all about   the spigot of the galaxy   turns into young water
    the milky way   pours young water   this morning

Young water in Japan goes back at least to the *Manyôshu* song #3245, where the poet wishes for a "long bridge" from heaven and taller mountains so the "moon-teller" (*tsuki-yomi*: moon-god) can descend to bring "turn-young water" to the aging master. The *long-bridge* suggests the Milky Way, or Heavenly River, speaking of which, here is another, probably wrong, version of a *ku* previously given:

若水や銀河と酌めば桶濁る　櫻磈子 日本俳句鈔
waka mizu ya ginga to kumeba oke nigoru   rokishi 19-20c?
(young-water:/! silver-river[galaxy]-with scoop/ladle/draw-if tub clouds)

      young water   the milky way
drawn with the galaxy   in the young water
   clouds the tub   clouds the tub

The *cloudiness* here may be my misreading of a smudgy "dancing" character (躍 as 濁) in Kaizôsha's reprint. It is an unlikely reading because, even if chaos is cloudy and a possible first-day theme, the metaphorical significance of "cloudiness" does not fit Young Water. Yet, it is not impossible.

若水や北斗の星のかけ清き 良湖
wakamizu ya hokuto no hoshi no kage kiyoki ryôko c.1800
(young-water!/: north-dipper's stars appearance pure/refreshing)

young water!
how refreshing to see
the big dipper

The original says the sight of said constellation is pure/clean, but I think I captured the feeling. There are more, less obvious stars: *"There's a man / scooping young water / from white-water"* (白川に若水をくむ男哉 忍山 大三 *shirakawa ni wakamizu o kumu otoko kana* ninzan 1697) Does this not evoke the galaxy? And, all of this takes us back to the longevity-oriented alchemy of China.

若水や流れの末の我等迄 吟江 古き姿
wakamizu ya nagare no sue no warera made ginkô
(young-water!/: flow's-end's us-until 1775)

the flow   young water
ends here with us   eventually reaches
young water   the likes of us

young water
from the milky way
down to me

A trickledown theory of rejuvenation? I think my second reading, or guess, where "us" means *we who draw it from downstream or lowland wells as opposed to the high-class people who draw off their young-water upstream* is correct; yet prefer my more lyrical readings. The Milky Way here is all mine.

砂金に若水むすふ朝哉 信雪 大三 1697
sunakane ni wakamizu musubu ashita kana shinseki
(gold-sand/dust-in young water cup/join[hands] morning!/'tis)

new year's morning
cupping young water
with golden sand

The *ni* (with/on) is not clear, but even in English "with" seems more poetic than "over" and a haiku has no room to spread the "gold-sand" on the bottom of the tub. In Japan today, bits of gold leaf are found in special New Year's sake. Did the wealthy put it in their young-water, too?

わかゆてふ水やたがため老の春 宗碩 宗碩発句帳
wakayu chôzu [or *chou = to iu?*] *ya ta ga tame oi no haru* sôseki -1533
(young *yu*=warm-water (for washing hands & face):/! whose purpose elder's spring)

warm young-water   *so who's it for,*   an old man's spring
who might *that* be for?   *this so-called warm young-water*   this warm young-water
an old man's spring   *a geezer's spring*   who might it be for

I believe that this remarkably modern 16c *ku* is a thank-you (and a chuckle) for young-water, meant for washing the hands and face, warmed up for the old poet who may have, like Issa later, been a cold-hater,. It is also interesting because feeling the bracing chill was the idea (sometimes contradicted by a bow toward spring warming). Or, maybe something else is happening. Since the water used to clean new-born babies (*ubuyu*), was warm, could this not have been the poet's 50/51st or 60/61th New Year, when he returns to start and is reborn in a big way? The *ku* has some of that foolish quality marking said year (see ch.11). The translation is weakened by the lack of a single word for "warm water" (*yu* in Japanese) in English. The original *is* original for taking the usual "*wakamizu*," or "young [unheated] water," and replacing *that* water (*mizu*) with the aforesaid *yu*, to coin a new word, "young [heated] water," *wakayu*.

THE WATER FETE

春王正月老・生死の昔男そと水祝　其角
[*haruô shogatsurô // ikijini no mukashi otoko zo to mizu-iwai* kikaku 1660-1707
(spring-king new year's-elder [?] // life-death [live-death?]'s old[fashioned]man [+emph.] water-fete)

spring king but new year's gramp

    i'm an ole boy   i'll risk my life
ready to die on my feet   i'm from the old school
   the water blast   the water blast

                    the water blast
             i'm old-school what's life
                without romance

There was a practice of "feting" men who married the previous year by dousing them with buckets of water. My "blast" is not inappropriate, for the fete could become so disorderly when the groom was jealously beset by other young men that the practice was outlawed for much of the Tokugawa era. I assume an older man has gotten married, so he is King of Spring, but is nevertheless old, and older yet for gaining a year on the New Year. The "old-boy" refers to the ladies man of the *Tale of Ise*, who risked his life for his amorous exploits. Remember that February could be freezing cold, so getting soaked could be dangerous even if not viciously pursued. Though young water could be used for the *mizu-iwai*, the fete is not properly included in the "first-water," or "young water." I allow it here in mid-chapter because it is exciting and I thought we could use a break. Since Kikaku died at 47, I am not sure the *ku* is first-person.

したしき友に・こなたにも女房もたせん水祝　其角
shitashiki tomo ni // konata ni mo nyobo motasen mizu-iwai kikaku
(close-friend-too: you-to/with/for too, wife have-would-not? water fete -1707)

to a close friend

how about you
do you too want a wife?
my water fete

water blasts
so would you, too
take a wife?

The problem here was how to read the "too" (I guessed that Kikaku recently took a wife in the other *ku*) and the intent of the verb which may be read in the affirmative or negative as one pleases.

逃しなよ水祝はるゝ五十聟　一茶
nigashi/nogashi na yo mizu-iwawaruru gojû muko issa
(flee/get-away-let-not! water feted, 50 [year old] groom -1827)

don't let him bolt!
a spring waterfet, the groom
fifty years old

issa, flee not!
what's water feting spring
for a groom of fifty

he mustn't flee!
a fifty year-old groom
meets cold water

This is dated a year late for the spring after Issa's marriage but could be autobiographical. A web print shows men in loincloths letting loose with buckets of water at one man in the middle who tries to dodge the worst of it. A *ku* titled "Stark Naked" has someone chased around what I took to be a big wisteria but actually alludes to a man in a Kyôgen Play who behaved cowardly when attacked (赤裸・追廻る大藤内や水祝　滄浪　宝暦11 *akahadaka oimawaru ôtônai ya mizu iwai* soro 1761). I do not believe men were ever completely nude, but wet loincloths probably showed whatever the cold water left:

脱かぬる裸の形や水祝　詩釣　大三
nugikanuru hadaka no katachi ya mizu-iwai shichô
(strip-cannot naked/ness's form!/'tis water-fete 1697)

a nakedness
you cannot take off
water fete

it won't do
to strip yourself of you
water fete

the water-fete
we cannot strip off
our bodies

the nude form
when stripping will not do
water fete

a water fete
what nudity looks like
when clothed

I would imagine most men were not thrilled to parade the discrepancy between the enormous phalli of erotic art and fertility festivals and reality. We have all seen the art but if you have not seen the enormous floats – wood, papier-mâché, straw, natural colors, bright red, veined, smooth, thin, thick, standing at attention or carried prone but so large one thinks of medieval battering rams and even wonders if any have actually been used for just that purpose and *all* with huge glans (unlike African and Mediterranean ones which pay scant attention to it) – by all means, do a web-search for fertility festivals in Japan! My respondent suggests either the last two readings, which do not need this explanation, or nakedness in the sense of the English "raw emotions," to wit:

        a water fete
        our naked emotions
        don't peel off

一生のはれの裸や水祝　祇川 類題
isshô no hare no hadaka ya mizu-iwai　gisen 1774
(one life's proper/gaily-dressed' naked/ness!/: water-fete)

  once in a lifetime   once in your life
  nakedness is splendid   ceremoniously nude
  the water-fete   the water-fete

        the water-fete
        for once well-dressed
        means naked

Without an English word like *hare*, antithetical to *kegare*, meaning dirtiness and pollution and attached to clothing means something good worn on celebratory occasions, the translation lacks the crisp wit of the original. So saying, I still do not think the *ku* as good as the one before it which was not only clever but compassionate. While the water fete occurred at the New Year and not at the date of the marriage and, thus, is a genuine seasonal phenomenon, most *ku* touching upon it seem *senryû*.

鼻たれの男なりけり水祝　虚子 1874-
hanatare no otoko narikeri mizu iwai　kyoshi -1959
(snot-dripping-man become[+emphatic] water-fete)

  turned into   snotty nose
  a snotty-nosed boy   becomes a real man
  water fete   the water fete

        dripping snot
        i became a man!
        the water fete

The expression "snot-dripping" (*hana-tare*) includes the idea of being a novice or greenhorn, and as in English, it is just not a good image. I believe that Kyoshi means the experience of being chased about makes one re-live childhood which, for boys, almost always includes being the recipient of cruelty. The original says "man," not *boy*. The boy is implied in the snotty nose. The "man" means that this experience is part of what turns boys into men. I might have failed to catch that nuance but for my familiarity with a wonderfully ironic *ku* by Issa, where men prove their manhood with the large teardrops that roll *poroporo* down their cheeks from eating hot chilies! While I used the first-person, Kyoshi was such a healthy man I would not have expected his nose to start dripping from the cold water. I shiver just to read these *mizu-iwai* poems because, even when "well," my head's circulation is so bad as a result of a high-school neck injury that cold pierces deep into my inner ear like an icy awl in temperatures even babies need no cap for. This practice, which was, as already said, outlawed, came back as a genteel ceremony, limited to relatives and others very close to the groom. But, from what Kyoshi writes, the water-fete retained some of its hazing element. Indeed, my respondent thinks the *ku* is third-person and "making fun of" the person described.

鏡餅
kagami-mochi

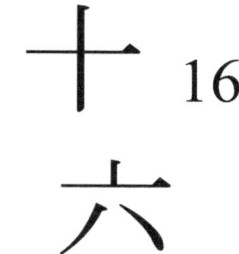

MIRROR & ROCK OF AGES

餅の出る槌のほしさよ春（の）雨　一茶
mochi no deru tsuchi no hoshisa yo harunosame   issa -1827
(*mochi*[sweet-rice-cake/dough]'s come-out hammer's desirability! spring-rain)

the spring rain and i
long for a magic mallet
to pound out mochi

Mochi is usually translated as "sweet-rice." The raw grains are round in the middle and pointed on the ends. Cooked, it is the stickiest of all rice, and of all food I know of, and can be pounded into cake unlike what we call cake, for it is not porous, but *called* cake for lack of a better word! The pounding process seems a cross between a dance and martial art. Between swings of a mallet boasting a head twice the size of one used for croquette, a second person (often the pounder's wife), bravely darts her hand in and out of the mortar, wetting and moving the rubbery blob of cooked *mochi*. These dances peak at the end of the year, but this *ku* is saijiki'ed with Spring-rain, as the magic mallet (which would not just pound but supply the *mochi*) is associated with the Treasure Ship, a New Year theme and a certain amount of "young sweet-rice cake" or *waka-mochi* was made during the first two weeks of the year which are shared by the New Year and Spring.[1] We will not elaborate on the making of *mochi*. The reader will have to wait for the Winter volume to attend to the birth of this strange substance which is wonderful eaten immediately, when still soft and more pliant than silly putty – it can even serve as an ear-plug according to one joking haiku (和餅をいはふや老の耳ふさぎ　壽信　洗濯物 *yamato mochi o iwau ya oi no mimifusagi*   jushin 1666) – but more often allowed to dry into what seems more like *white bricks* than "cake," which must, then, be either slowly boiled or roasted, when it expands like a marshmallow and once again softens. In Edo=Tokyo, the *kagami,* or "mirror" *mochi* of the New Year comprises two pieces (loaves?) of *mochi,* one about the diameter of a large frizbee but about twice as fat under another smaller of diameter but usually almost twice as fat, or high.

---

1. Spring Mochi? Mochi was not only a New Year food. It was also part of the Doll Festival (now called Girl's Day) on 3/3. It is possible Issa had a sweet tooth, for another *ku* has him has him taking a boxed lantern out into the Spring rain to buy *mochi* (餅買に箱でうちん（提灯）や春（の雨）一茶　文化8). If the mallet were not in the above *ku*, I would have saved the *ku* for the *spring rain* in another book.

元日大寒に入ければ けさの春おかん斗の餅ゐ哉 道可 虚栗 1683
ganjitsu daikan ni hairikereba: kesanoharu ogan bakari no mochii kana   dôka
(origin-day big-cold-to enter [fin.]: morning's spring worship-would-almost's *mochi!*/ is)

on a "big-cold" first day

spring is here
and i could almost worship
the *mochii*

This is a difficult *ku*. Were it by Bashô, there would be hundreds of commentaries to consult, but, as was the case with the last haiku, the author is a nobody. With the first *ku* of the chapter, the most important question (I did not address) would be the relationship of the *mochi* and the spring-rain. Here, it is what it has to do with the "Big-Cold" mini-season (a Chinese calendar-set date: for more, see Liza Dalby: *East Wind Melts the Ice*). First, I assumed the white skin of the *mochi* (called by its old name *mochii* in this *ku*) embodied the season, but, on second thought, it is probably the association of the *mochi* and the mirror, for a mirror was used to entice the Sun Goddess from the cave and the sun brings warmth.

子は親にすへてもちゐの鏡哉　徳元 狗
ko wa oya ni suete mochii[?]no kagami kana   tokugen 1633
(child parent-on[by] placed/ *mochi's* mirror=reflection[spitting-image]!/?/'tis)

child placed	mirror *mochi*
on the parent, the *mochi*	the child a spitting image
a mirror image	of the parent

These cakes are usually stacked two-high and called *kagami-mochi,* or "mirror-*mochi*" because the discus shape recalls traditional Japanese mirrors, with the associations already discussed. *Mochi* also *sounds like* "durable/long-lasting," a *nominal* trait, affirmed by the boulder-like appearance of the "cakes." Tokugen's haiku makes the smaller cake a "child" and image of the larger "parent;" and, by doing this makes the design symbolic of the perpetuation of life from generation to generation. The two are generally said to represent the Sun and Moon, with the smaller Sun – viewed from earth it *is* smaller and as a time unit sun-as-day is smaller than moon-as-month – above. One *ku* alludes to this by quipping about suns placed repeatedly on moons for millennia to create Spring (月に日をのせかけ／＼千代の春　元工　宝暦9　*tsuki ni hi o nose kake nose kake chiyonoharu*　genkô 1759). Translation is impossible, for the moon and sun in the *ku* must be read as both individual objects *and* months and days, something hopeless for English. *Mochi ku* about the sun and moon – or moon and sun are rare, reflecting, I think, metaphysical confusion. Edo era Japanese generally elevated male over female, so the Sun, traditionally a goddess, was increasingly called "Tendôsama," a name with masculine overtones. The West, with its female luna *and* man in the moon, should not find such a contradictory cosmology alien in any way.

餅につくる三の初のいはゐ哉　休音 いのこ
mochi ni tsukuru mitsu hajime no iwai kana   kyûon 1633
(*mochi*-in/with make three [year+month+day] beginning's celebra[boulder?]tion!/'tis)

out of two

in *mochi*	with *mochi*
we celebrate the start	boulders we celebrate
of all three	the triple-start

The editors of Iwanami's *Shôki Haikai Shû* (1991/5) write "*ku-i-fumei*," or "*ku*-meaning-unclear" and explain nothing. The title reveals my guess. In the Sinosphere, *Three*, the child, or start of all, comes from *Two*. Procreation is 1x1=3. Mongolians stress the *Two* as the creative principle, for their national musical instrument the horse-head fiddle – with a carved horse-head head, and strings as well as bow made of horse-hair – has only two strings for that reason, strings which fiddled create, if it were, the cosmos entire. In less metaphysically-minded Japan, where the relation of the *Two* and the *Three* was not dwelled upon, it seems unlikely the *ku* refers to the two-cake *mochi* alone. There might be three, rather than the usual two, cakes, for a couple hundred years later another poet would write "three layers / of *mochi*, could there be / a greater mirror!" (三重の餅や又なき大鏡　八重桜 *san chô no mochi ya mata naki ôkagami* yaezakura 1879-1945)   With three pieces, one may stand for the first day=sun, one the moon and one the year. The first day of the year was, after all, called "the morning of the three" (*mitsu no asa*). But, as the "year" is categorically different from the firmament, I think a *bigarade* or tangerine on top of the cakes as the fruit of the Two makes more sense – and 12 segments could be lucky – unless our *planet* was taken into consideration (My respondent thinks *three mochi* are "not uncommon," but I think it *was*). Regardless, the *iwai* (celebration) in Kyûon's *ku* may pun on *iwa*, or boulder, a distant relation to our "rock of ages" *and* evocation of the boulder before the solar-cave. . . . Or, eureka! Doesn't the character 三, or "three," *outline two stacked cakes!?*

鏡餅重ねて千代も八千代哉　千頂 玉かつら
kagamimochi kasanete chiyo mo yachi yo kana   sencho 1751
(mirror *mochi* stacked-up 1000 eras[long-lived reign] 8000 [eons]!/?/'tis)

mirror-*mochi*
once you start stacking
you never stop

Think of living in a highrise: if one floor is over you, or under you, there might as well be a million more. Japanese numbers are too full of significance to waste in translation. Where we would say *"Long* live the King!" Japanese would ask for "a *thousand* eras," and "*eight*," whether pegged on a *thousand* or a *ten-thousand*, time becomes what our 8 makes it rotated ninety degrees → ∞.

餅鏡ついたち頃のなかめかな　心成 大三
mochikagami tsuitachi goro no nagame kana   shinsei
(mirror-*mochi* first[of month]-around's sight/vista is 1697)

mirror-mochi	*mirror-mochi*
what we gaze upon	around the first day
the first day	it's our vista

This is ridiculously simple, but isn't that the point? The *mochi* is the clean-slate of the New Year as well as a mirror to see the past and a crystal ball. But, as repeated already, the New Year fell in the coldest part of the year. The *mochi* might look like the defoliated or snow-covered hills.

皆人の笑顔や向ふ鏡餅　千春 玉かつら
minahito no egao ya mukau kagamimochi   chiharu 1751
(all people's smiling faces face mirror-*mochi* fl 1670~)

the smiling faces
of all men now face
our *mirror-mochi*

English's ability to verb anything, including body parts like "face," is one of its best features, but here it is unfortunate, unless you happen to like such repetition.

不足なき姿やうつす鏡餅　文賀 玉かつら
fusoku naki sugata ya utsusu kagamimochi　bunga
(lack-not, form/appearance!/: reflect mirror-*mochi*　1751)

mirror mochi we see the reflection of nothing alack	the reflection is plentitude itself *mirror mochi*

This, like the *ku* before it, follows the pattern of the many *ku* of the New Year's contentment we saw in earlier chapters. While faces do not reflect well in the white *mochi*, the shape of the mochi (round) itself represents perfection.

おも影やしらぬ親しる鏡餅　止月 大三
omokage ya shiranu oya shiru kagamimochi　shigetsu 1697
(image/countenance! know-not parent/s know mirror-*mochi*)

i seem to see the mother i never saw *mirror-mochi!*	i see the face of parents i never knew *mirror-mochi!*

mirror-mochi
 we meet the parents <br> we do not know

The original does not specify the number or gender of the parent/s. Without knowing the personal circumstances of the poet, your guess is as good as mine. I suspect the poet meant ancestors and/or the Imperial family.

老の影うつさでうれし鏡餅　巴雀 類題発句集
oi no kage utsusa de ureshi kagamimochi　hajaku　1774
(old-face/appearance reflects-not-therefore happy mirror-*mochi*)

happy because it doesn't show old faces *mirror-mochi*	*mirror-mochi* delightful for not showing the ugly old

The poet may be joking about how kind this "mirror" is to his ugly old face, and/or he may be giving a facetious explanation for the tendency of old people to be cheerful in the presence of *mirror-mochi*, perhaps because it is a tangible reminder of their own childhood.

皺深い手も磨いたり鏡餅　敬愚
shiwa bukai te mo migaitari kagamimochi　keigu
(wrinkle-deep hand too polishing [and so forth] mirror-*mochi*)

mirror-mochi polished now and then by an old hand	an old hand strokes it now and then *mirror-mochi*

Old folk, especially women, get physical with food. In that, they resemble children; but there is more love in it. As our senses grow weaker, we come to appreciate sensation more. The elderly are our true materialists, *materialists* in the sense of the word used by Alan Watts in *Does It Matter?* In the original, there is a hint of polishing up a wrinkled old hand, but it had to be dropped in the Englishing.

若うなる我が影うつせ鏡餅　子規 子詢？
wakaunaru waga kage utsuse kagamimochi　shiki 1867-1902
(young-become my face/appearance reflect! mirror-*mochi*)

mirror-mochi
show me oh show me
my young self!

Shiki was far from good-looking even as a boy, but now he had tuberculosis. I think he longs not only for the past but the future that once was his, the hope as well as the innocence of youth. I imagine the *mochi* not so much as a mirror as a different kind of looking glass, one which can see *The Isle of Never-Come-True* of G.K. Chesterton (as described in his wonderful poem about a place where we still waltz with the love/s we lost and live the life/lives we could not lead, in short, fulfill the dreams chance and choice took away.)

思ひ出つ赤人にまで鏡餅　　言水 1646-1719
omoi-idetsu akabito ni made kagamimochi　gonsui
(remember/memory-appears: akabito-until [back to] mirror-*mochi*)

remembering all
the way back to akahito
mirror-mochi

Yamabe no Akahito is the most lauded poet in the *Manyôshû* (9c). It would seem like this mirror was a sort of time-machine. (OJD の 「鏡餅」の用例に「永縁鏡」もあるが、その語の見出はない。誰か助け！).

丸けれは千代も身安し鏡餅　　初子 大三
marukereba chiyo mo mi yasushi kagami mochi　shoshi 1697
(round-when, thousand-ages even body/[physical self] easy[living?] mirror-mochi)

if you're round	if you are round
what's a thousand realms?	an eon is easy as a day
mirror-mochi	*mirror-mochi*

Roundness is to form what gold is to material. It is happily inert. It is the soul. Still, this is an odd use of *mi,* for the body-self, implies something is alive. Is *mochi,* then, alive?

古歌に曰く千歳そ見ゆる鏡餅　　梅翁
koka ni iwaku chitose zo miyuru kagami mochi　sôin 1604-82
(old-song-in, to wit, thousand-years see-can mirror-*mochi*)

rock of ages

as sung of old
eons can indeed be seen
mirror-mochi

While the ability to see for ages suggests the clear looking-glass quality of the smooth, shiny round *kagami-mochi*, Sôin's *ku* simultaneously plays upon the stone, or rather *boulder*-like quality of *mochi* which was brought out by placing boughs of pine nearby, alludes to the early 10c *Kokinshû waka* that eventually mated with a depressingly slow medieval melody to become *kimi-ga-yo* (the ruler's reign), the national anthem of modern Japan. In the *waka* and the anthem, a wee pebble grows into a massive boulder covered with moss. So here we have the answer to the question, "Is *mochi* alive?"[1] Yes. And we ought to note as well that the smooth *mirror-mochi* often did in fact turn into the very model of a hoary boulder; as it aged, it cracked and buckled, becoming more rock-like, and growing mold modeled the moss. Issa, matter-of-factly haiku'ed: "A piece of *mochi* / turns into a stone: / spring rain" (餅欠の石と成りけり春（の）雨　一茶*mochikake wa ishi ni narikeri haru no ame*).[2]　参照：さされ石も岩となる御世也けり＝元日や我家も苔の生にける　茶静　みさこ集（美佐古鮓　文政元年）

股ぐらで淋しく削る餅のかび　武玉川 九
matagura de sabishiku kezaru mochi no kabi mutamagawa 1756
(crotch-with, lonely[as adverb] shaves/ing [off] *mochi's* mold)

his crotch for a vice
he forlornly shaves off
the mold on the *mochi*

forlornly scraping
the mold off of mochi
between his legs

The Japanese are non-plussed at the mold, but they don't like it enough to eat it. Scrapping it off while joking with one's family would be a cheerful activity, but doing so alone is depressing. This early *senryû* could be a haiku, for it has both season and sensitivity to detail. But, presented as it was in a collection containing many clearly dirty poems, we also think of the moldy neglect suffered by the privates of the bachelor, widow or widower. Note: *lonely* cannot adverb, hence "forlornly."

酒雫かび行餅を山路ならん　華鴬 新虚栗
sake shizuku kabi yuku mochi o yamaji naran kayo 1777
(rice-wine drops mold goes/runs *mochi* mountain-path becomes)

drops of *sake*
make the *mochi* moldy
mountain trails!

This old *ku* connects mold to something decorous, *sake* used as an offering. The *mochi* is not only a boulder but an entire mountain. A more mischievous poem from the same collection:

---

1. Strange Science? On January 4, 1947, the *Tenseijingo* editorial of the *Asahi Shinbun* took its national anthem to task. While the growing pebble may be rationalized away as coral, it still seems a "primitive idea" when translated into a foreign language and, besides, the moss is ridiculous: in a sultry climate it hardly requires eons to flourish, but can appear virtually overnight. "How do we expect to capture the minds of the new generation growing up in an atomic age?" laments the editor. About thirty years later, the Korean essayist Lee Oh Young contrasted the optimism of the growing Japanese pebble with the pessimism of the Korean national anthem, which contains the line "until Mt. Paekche turns to dust."
2. Issa's Rock A decade later, Issa named his second son Rocky (Ishitarô) and blamed his wife for his death because she gave him a bath from which he caught a cold despite his warning not to do so *"until the soft little pebble hardened into a boulder"* (100 days). The boy died shortly before the mirror-opening. Issa wrote: "A raven's croak! / To hell with celebrating / *mirror-mochi*" (*kagami mochi iwaishi kai mo naku karasu*). Issa puns like crazy verse (*kyôka*) when he is disheartened – here, the "no" in "of no worth" (my "to hell with") becomes "croak/call/cry" when followed directly by a crow. Issa named his next son Gold-child; he died even faster. So much for lucky names! My respondent notes: [boys were given] un-propitious names such as *sute-matsu* (abandoned pine)", etc. so that they wouldn't attract God's attention.

春の餅かびて嵯峨野の秋と誰レ 其流 新?虚栗
haru no mochi kabite sagano no aki to dare kiryû 1777(or 1683?)
(spring's *mochi*, molds/ed: sagano's fall and[says] someone)

spring *mochi*
molds and someone says it's
sagano in the fall

Light, but I love it! The fields of Sagano were famous for wild flowers and chirping bugs. This is the haiku equivalent of Lear, Doctor Seuss or Shel Silverstein depictions of human hair as a biosphere.

青黴の春色ふかし鏡餅 佐々木 有風 角川新
aokabi no haru-iro fukashi kagami mochi sasaki yûfû
(green mold's spring-color deep mirror-mochi 1891-1959)

this green mold
the very heart of spring!
mirror-mochi

The modern poet comes right out and celebrates the mold. The *ku* describes something fairly rare; the mold on *mochi* is usually grey, black or even red, a very propitious color, though I have yet to see it haiku'ed! Since the rice cake is eventually eaten, mold is not desired. *Mochi* was sometimes taken out to get air and sun:

鶯や餅に糞する縁（椽）の上（さき） 芭蕉
uguisu ya mochi ni fun suru en no saki bashô -1694
(nightingale/warbler! *mochi*-on shit-do porch/veranda-end)

a liminal salutation

it's a warbler   spring has come
pooping on the rice cake   is that nightingale poop
drying outside   on the *mochi*?

This poem is not, strictly speaking, *about* rice-cake. The pooping *uguisu*=nightingale (trad. transl.)/ warbler (scientific transl.) and drying *mochi* belong to the Spring, rather than the New Year. Drawn from the bush by balmy weather, the harbinger of spring has "dropped a compliment" on the ritual object. As explained in more detail by Hiroaki Sato (*One Hundred Frogs*), the *ku* was meant to open a poetic sequence and demanded a salutary nuance.[1] His translation dead-pans *"A warbler shits on the rice cake at the end of the porch,"* while Stewart, in a lush rhyming couplet, has the bird kindly make the "icing on the cake!" (Should we slice it up for Princess Sao's wedding?!). Bashô's emphasis on the end of the veranda (a punning association to a fruitful meeting) fails to translate. For my part, I cannot help but wonder if he *also* chuckles about the coincidence of *uguisu* shit, collected and sold for a beauty aid, falling on *mochi,* which was synonymous with a beautiful, shiny white skin! (*mochihada*) and imagine that the bird, seeing the *mochi's* skin began to crack in the sunlight, kindly dropped balm on it.[2]

1. Pooping a salutation? Look at what Occidentals do! Can you imagine how strange it must have been for the Japanese to hear a broadside of cannons greet (!) Francis Xavier returning from his walk about Japan decrying infanticide and idolism, etc.?

2. Beauty-aid Most if not all haiku experts think little of such additional coincidences. I feel this is because they labor under the mistaken idea that wit cheapens a haiku. I do not buy that. Good poems are not so easily hurt. Even puns improve them.

ひわれけり天神様の鏡餅　竹滞 改造社
hiwarekeri tenjinsama no kagamimochi　chikutai 春夏秋冬
(dry-cracked [+finality], heaven/sky-god-sir's mirror-*mochi* 19-20c?)

all cracked up!
this *mirror-mochi* belongs
to the sky god

Ugliness is not the only thing strong enough to shatter a mirror. The brilliance of the Mighty Sun can do it too. It was impossible to keep the *mochi* dry enough not to mold yet *not* crack. But, this was probably not *mochi* drying at home. My respondent thinks "the *mochi* here is probably an old offering placed in front of the statue" of *tenjin-sama* found by the road. But, who is this "sky-god?" Noh, following popular belief, depicts a demonical god, the wrathful ghost of the exiled scholar-poet and top government minister Sugawara no Michizane (845-903). His plight, expressed in poetry (see his touching poems for the trees he left behind in S. Carter's *Traditional Japanese Poetry*), and the fate of his rivals captured the hearts and imagination of generations who made him a god of scholarship. "Sky" evokes both sun and thunder, while "sky-god" also means wrinkled dry fruit. *Are the cracks/lines writing?*

餅の勢笑へばわらふ鏡哉　十哲 大三
mochi no sei (ikioi?) waraeba warau kagami kana　juttetsu 1697
(sweetrice-cake's power/energy/appearance, laugh/smile-if laugh/smile mirror!/'tis)

mochi power	that's a mirror	the *mochi*'s alive
that can make you smile	you laugh and the *mochi*	you laugh and the mirror
it's a mirror	gets crowsfeet	just cracks up

Sei (or *ikioi*) is word describing the very look of vigor, with too many connotations for the poor translator to shake a pen at. Couple that with the *warau/warô*, ambiguous because the former, in old Japanese (not today) can be read like the latter and you get at least three major readings. Because *warau* can mean *smile* or *laugh*, the reader is free to substitute one for the other in any of the readings.

風年や笑み割れそむる鏡餅　鬼城 改造社
kazedoshi ya emi waresomuru kagami mochi　kijô 1864-1938
(windy year! smile/laugh breaks-out mirror-*mochi*)

a windy year	a windy year!
the mirror-*mochi's* face	the mirror *mochi* cracks
cracks a smile	an early smile

Since cracks in fruit were "smiles" in older *ku*, and "mirrors," as we have seen reflected joy, there are older examples of *mochi* cracking smiles, but specifying that it was "a windy year," when all dries quickly, is new and might also evoke the roasted *mochi* puffing up with air.

鏡餅八萬ひびを作りけり　卯の吉 ホトトギス
kagamimochi hachiman hibi o tsukurikeri　unokichi? early 20-c?
(mirror-*mochi* eight-*man*[unit:1,0000] cracks=days[obj] make [emphatic])

in mirror *mochi*
the crack, crack, crack
of myriad dawns

Again, eight and ten-thousand (a counting unit in Japanese) have connotations of the plentiful if not infinite. The pun (*hibi*=crack, *hi-bi*=days) is a masterpiece which finally makes the cracks as propitious as cracks can be! It did not really work in English, for "dawns" is not meaningful enough. In the original pun, the *mochi* makes the myriad *days*. It is as if the Rock of Ages creates the time itself. I thought of an English "crack" pun, but the result was a completely different *ku*: "Is longevity / all it's cracked up to be? / mirror *mochi*." Moreover, the name of the poet, "hare's luckiness" is fortuitous: "the hare in the moon" is always depicted in the act of pounding *mochi* (my respondent adds he was probably born in the year of hare). The *ku*, from Shiki and Kyoshi's haiku magazine *Hototogisu*, or "Cuckoo!" proves that the classic punning haiku made it safely into the twentieth century.

鏡餅暗きところに割れて坐す 西東三鬼 角川
kagamimochi kuraki tokoro ni warete zasu saitô sanki 1899-1962
(mirror-*mochi* dark place-in cracking sits)

mirror-*mochi*
sits there cracking
in a dark place

This poet makes no effort to find something propitious in the cracks. This haiku is featured in two of my saijiki. The point, which I had missed until reading an explanation: the New Year activities have petered out – the green pine decorations are gone – and the *mochi* (which no longer is brightened by an offering candle in the vicinity) is all that remains.

鏡餅弁天池の石となれ 阿波野 青畝 角川新
kagami mochi benten ike no ishi to nare awano seihô 20c
(mirror *mochi* benten-pond's boulder become!)

become the stone
on benten's isle of wealth
o' *mirror-mochi*!

This poem is a bit perverse for turning a symbol of reflection into a talisman of wealth, but the creativity is cheering. Pictures of Benten's island, which is in the middle of her, the Goddess of Wealth's, pond, show a boulder with a single small pine behind it. The resemblance to some mirror-*mochi* arrangements is marked. Keigu would simplify the above *ku* (I feel is a charm-poem) as follows:

mirror
mochi on my shelf
become a magic stone of wealth!

~~~~~~

一村を鼓でよぶや具足餅 史邦 小文庫
hitomura o tsuzumi de yobu ya gusokumochi fumikuni
(one[whole]-village[obj] drum-with call armor *mochi*. late-17c)

call to arms?

a whole village
is summoned by drum
martial *mochi*!

There was more than one *mirror-mochi* in most houses. A small set was even placed in the bathrooms. The greatest treasure of a military class family next to its honor, was its armor. The main *mirror-mochi* for the samurai was not called such, but *gusoku* (a type of full body armor including a scary helmet) *mochi,* for it was placed in front of said armor. Evidently, some families summoned the whole village to see the display. Was the poet was irked, neutral, or humored by the practice? Regardless, the *ku* is evocative of the peaceful Tokugawa era when real call-ups for war were rare.[1] *Saijiki* usually put *armor-mochi* in a separate category from *mirror-mochi.* Both were, however, much the same thing; their shape was similar and both were broken up the same way before cooking.

鏡開き
Mirror Opening

具足開く手力祝へ老の春　冬葉　改造社
gusoku hiraku tajikara iwae oinoharu　tôyô 1892-1956
(armor[*mochi*]-opening arm-strength, celebrate old-man's spring!)

an old man's spring
hurrah for the arm-power
to cleave armor

bust that armor,
old man, celebrate
strength in spring

All the mochi cakes are "opened," which is to say broken up by hand – though I have seen moderns cheating by using hammers! – the martial variety makes for better metaphor. "Cleave" is not quite right. If you do not mind a long poem, you may change it to "tear apart.."

具足開阿吽の聲のひびきかな　鯱人
gusokuhiraki a-un no koe no hibiki kana　kojin 18-19-20c?
(armor-opening ahum[sanskrit]:expiration & inspiration) voice's echo)

ahum!
armor breaking
the sound of labored
breathing

The Sanskrit term *aun* (*alpha* and *omega?*) stands for *in-* and *exhalation.* Combined with the voice, it may mean labored breathing. Since grappling sumo wrestlers are said to sound out each others *a-un* when preparing to chance a move, a Japanese reader would imagine a protracted struggle with the *mochi.* Note that *mochi* is not mentioned in the original in this and the previous *ku.* The context is sufficient to add it to the armor. (蛇足：*aun* was the first pen-name for Sugawara no Michizane.)

相撲取の金剛力や鏡割　鬼城
sumôtori no kongôriki ya kagamiwari　kijô 1864-1938
(sumo-taker's steel-power! mirror [-*mochi*] tearing)

the steel power
of a sumo wrestler tears
open a mirror

↑ **1. Tokugawa Peace** Soon after Fumikuni's time, riots, some of which came close to civil war, became common; but even admitting this, the warring and casualties were nothing compared to the previous Warring Period and Issa, who reports riots first-hand, was, until his final decade, happy and proud to live in a peaceful age.

Here, too, note that "mirror" is not followed by *mochi*. I do the same in English the better to illustrate one of the reasons Japanese can fit so much in their haiku and because, even if such abbreviation is rare if not unnatural in English, it hints at a poetically better way of doing things in languages where such abbreviation is accepted.[1] There are many more sumo-wrestling "mirror openings." *"The old wrestler / uses his manual power / mirror-opening"* (老力自の手づから鏡開かな 碧泉 最新二万句 *roriki ji no tezukara kagami-hiraki kana* hekisen early-20c?) is good for reminding us of the strong-armed God at the Cave the Sun-Goddess was holed up in. But I have seen no really good ones except for this:

道場や鏡開きの新莚　春象 昭和一万句
dôjô ya kagamihiraki no ara mushiro   shunshô mid-20c
(*dôjô* [martial arts gym or arena]!/'tis/: mirror-opening's new-[straw]mat)

it's our ring!
for the mirror-opening
a new mat

place for a bout
this new mat will do for
mirror-splitting

Breaking dry *mochi* inside would leave a mess. But Japanese rarely sat on the ground and some of the *mochi* would be lost if it were broken outside. So, it was done over a mat. A new mat is appreciated for the crumbs will go into the soup and for the pleasant, fresh grassy smell.

塩なげてそれから開く鏡かな　敬愚
shio nagete sore kara hiraku kagami kana   keigu
(salt throwing/thrown that-from open mirror 'tis/!)

after tossing up
some salt, i'll grapple
with the mirror!

Keigu was inspired by Shunshô to take one step further and bring in a sumô purification ritual where the wrestlers toss up a handful of purifying salt (Some almost drop it on the sand, others heave it so high it showers spectators in the stands!)? If he ever gets back to Japan, he promises to actually do it!

鏡とて老力まだ取る独り相撲　敬愚
kagami tote rôriki mada toru hitorizumô   keigu
(mirror [saying], old power[sumo-wrestler] still wrestles one-man-sumo)

the old wrestler
grapples with himself
mirror-breaking

In Japanese, *fighting windmills* is called "one-man sumo." You will find the expression in a genuine *ku* (as opposed to those by Keigu) in *Rise, Ye Sea Slugs!* describing the poet's attempt to pick up slippery slices of sea cucumber. The bits of *mochi* thus obtained with great effort are toasted and added to sugary red-bean soup or used for "tooth-hardening" (*ha-gatame*). We shall skip that soup (I never liked it much, anyway) and save the latter, as noted twice already (very entertaining, for it is not just for teething babies but for everyone, even toothless poets), for another book.

↑ **1. Comparative Abbreviation.** I am not putting down English. If it does not abbreviate as much as Japanese, it is probably because it is, on the whole, more compact (this can be tested by reading translations aloud, taking care to use examples going both ways because what is written in one language tends to grow in translation) and didn't need to develop such a strategy. I find the pluses of any language balanced by a minuses and vice-versa. The pity of it is that these things are often tied into syntax and, consequently, not transferable to an exotic tongue. If an ideal language is one that combines the best features of all languages, it is by definition a total impossibility.

正月を出して見せうぞ鏡餅 去来
shôgatsu o dashite mishô zo kagamimochi kyorai -1704
(correct-month [ny +obj/on/over] take-out show [emph.] mirror-*mochi*)

let me take out
and show you the new year
mirror-*mochi*

That is to say, the *mochi* embodies the New Year. If we take the "Correct-moon/month" as the New Year and nothing else, this would be the most logical translation. But, if we take the "moon" in *shôgatsu* in a less common sense of literally being a moon, the reading changes to this:

where is it, you ask?

i'll show you
the new year's moon, i will!
mirror-*mochi*

Since the month began with the new moon, which was on the first evening, for all practical purposes, invisible, I can imagine a child asking the poet "Where is the New Year Moon? I can't see it!" The *mochi* here becomes the moon. Pointing would not do it. I imagine the poet pulling out the bottom mochi, the moon mochi, to show it to the child. Yet, I can *also* imagine the poet talking *to* rather than *about* the mirror-*mochi*, perhaps on New Year's eve:

the promise

on new year's day
i'll bring you out for show
my sweet-rice cake!

"I'll bring you out and show you off" is what I would have written had the syllabets allowed it. The "o" is grammatically problematic; I am not confident "on" is justifiable. My courage to make the poet talk to his *mochi* comes from reading this *ku* by Issa: *"I'll show you / a waterfall of pee! / o peeping frog! (shôben no taki o miseyo zo naku kawazu).*[1] Two years earlier, Issa wrote a stranger New Year *ku* "The new year! / The new year! cry / the frogs!" (*shôgatsu o shôgatsu o to ya naku kawazu*). It is strange because frogs are usually not out that early in the year and I only mention it because the *shôgatsu+o* suggests the waterfall pee *ku* the next year was influenced by Kyorai's *ku* and that gave me my wee pretext for the last reading.

---

1. Frog Pee Poems Reading Issa's journals I ran across enough haiku on peeing on or near frogs or on frogs themselves peeing to note a category. I suspect that the existence of the saying "like peeing on the face of a frog" – meaning something won't have any effect on the other party – gave Issa the excuse to indulge.

Three Telling Ku

学寮や祖師の鏡のあぶり喰　召波
gakuryô ya sôshi no kagami no aburigui shôha -1771
(student-dormitory: the founding-master's mirror's roasting-eat)

the student house
eating their master's *mochi*
that they roasted

the student house
they roast the *mochi*
of their teacher

Usually, the broken-up bits of *mochi* are roasted and put into soup comprising little red beans and sugar and sometimes bits of a kumquat-like fruit. Since the *mochi* in question would be that which sat by a picture of the (dead) founder/teacher – maybe Bashô? – do the students feel it is metaphysically wrong to toss it into the murky soup, and instead roast and partake of it in a drier (perhaps wet by soy sauce and wrapped in laver?) form? My respondent, more practically notes: "Just roasting takes less time, too. Making soup takes too long and is more involved. Perhaps, the students have to be discreet and quick." Regardless, there is something to this *ku* that did not impress me on first reading.

石に餅の香はなし伊勢の日の始　鏡樹 宝暦九
ishi ni mochi no ka wa nashi ise no hi no hajime kyôju 1759
(rock-to/with sweet-rice's scent-as-for not; ise's sun's beginning)

no scent of mochi
coming from the rocks of ise
as the year dawns

Is this a bad *ku* because no one, or no one sane, anyway, would *expect* rocks to smell edible? But, what if the poet actually went to Ise, the metaphysical fulcrum of Japan, and means to say that getting to the beach at dawn on Ise to see the sun rise over the giant male and female rocks at Ise was no cup of tea? Or, what if he did not, but wants to make the point that going out to witness wild rocks (or semi-domesticated rocks, for they do wear rope festoons) is not the same as sitting comfortably at home with totally cultured edible, aromatic rocks? Would *that* save the *ku?*

あるはなしある年毎の鏡餅　梅翁
aru hanashi aru toshi goto no kagamimochi sôin 1604-82
(certain story [or, is-as-for not/becomes?] certain year-each's mirror-*mochi*)

every year
a certain story and
mirror *mochi*

there is a tale
every year the same
mirror *mochi*

The reading is not settled. If "story" is correct, perhaps the reference is to the myth of the cave and mirror used to show the Sun Goddess the wanton dance outside, but my respondent writes: "I don't believe so. I first read *'aru hanashi'* as *'aru wa nashi;'* but, it does not make sense. I am mystified."

THE ROCK OF AGES REVISITED

古歌に曰く千歳そ見ゆる鏡餅　梅翁
koka ni iwaku chitose zo miyuru kagamimochi　sôin 1604-82
(old-song-in, to wit, thousand-years see-can mirror-*mochi*)

rock of ages

as sung of old
eons can indeed be seen
mirror-mochi

We saw this same *ku* nine pages back.　The translation is fine, but my explanation may have been a bit off.　I jumped on the hoary old rock, and that lead to moss and mold and an essay that was too much fun to break, so I just let it go.　The original *ku's* "old-song" probably refers to this *waka*:

千代までも影をならべてあひみむといはふ鏡の用ゐざらめや　源仲正　夫木集巻三十二雑部十四
chiyo made mo kage o narabete aimimu to iwau kagami no mochii-zarameya　minamoto nakamasa 1310
(thousand-realms-until form/s[+obj] lined up, each-other see[+link] celebrate mirror's mochi[=using], using not so?)

soul conference

and is not this	shall we not
mirror of mochii round	celebrate our mirrors
we toast with wine	of pounded rice
worth keeping for it keeps us	that bring us face to face
in touch with men of all time?	with men of all ages (& mice)?

The grammar at the tail of the poem escapes me, but I can say that *mochii,* an old pronunciation of *mochi,* often written with the character for *doing* or *business* (用) is cleverly verbed. This knowledge I owe to Yamamoto Kenkichi's explanation in Kodansha's large *saijiki*.　He also points out something I knew – round *mochi* can stand for the soul – and something I did not – that in Kansai (Osaka, Nara and Kyôto), disc-like mirrors are rare, for they have *balls* of *mochi* which, eaten, bring vitality and rebirth. Some say the shape is modeled on the heart.　Most importantly, he claims *mochi* is not called a mirror because of its shape but because, as a reification of our soul, it reflects us and came to celebrate/toast a person's thousand realms of life (*sono hito no senyo o kotohogu*).　I think it wrong to phrase it in *not-this-but-that* terms.　The round shape may have come more from the idea of the soul than the standard mirror shape, but the mirror connects with clarity (ironic considering the opacity of the *mochi*) and that, as we can tell from old *waka* mentioning pristine water together with everlasting memories, was important for the time travel, if I may, again, call it that.　I also doubt the idea is just the longevity of a person (*sono hito*).　It may be a single soul – Japanese have several types of souls and one is permanent, or recyclable if you prefer – but, I think we have a sequence of bodies, or persona, united.

let's celebrate	and why not
our mochi mirrors,	put to use our mirrors
line them all up	of pounded rice
to bring back the faces	we toast for uniting us,
of a thousand generations	a thousand generations?

Further Reflection on Mochi as Soul

Mirror-mochi was called simply *"kagami"* (mirror) at least as far back as the *Tale of Genji* (indeed, Yamamoto quoted such a passage); but, I have yet to read anything indicating that the same *mochi* was ever called *"tama"* or "soul" by itself. This, and the fact that mirrors were considered to be tools for soul-searching in Shintô and souls – especially female souls – popularly thought to reside in them, makes me hesitant to even think of trying to separate the two.

年の緒をつくやかがみの餅そくい　重治 鷹筑波
toshi no o o tsugu ya kagami no mochi zo kui   shigeharu 1642
(year's/s' string[necklace/bracelet] connect/fuse!/?/: mirror-mochi[+emph.] eat)

we'd tie together
the heart-strings of the years
eating mirror mochi

eat mirror mochi
it's how to repair the heart
string of the years

This is the closest any *ku* that I know of comes to playing with the *kagami-mochi*-as-soul. It was composed in an era of *haikai* where the poem-jammers main interest seemed to be making fun of the ancient poets' fixation on romance. The old conceit for losing a lover was busting one's "soul=heart-string" (*tama-no-o*). One particularly memorable exchange in the *Manyôshû* (9c) has a man offering somewhat rudely to string up a woman's soul that he heard was loose – imagine a pearl off its string, there is a hole in it and it is just rolling about – to which the woman replies he is too late, for another has already strung her up so to speak (Yes, it does seem risqué in the original, for "string-up" (*tsuranuku*) is more like "stick-through.") Shigeharu's *ku* offering to join/fix a newly invented term called the *year*-string (*toshi-no-o*) by eating *mochi* plays with the old conceit. Needless to say, it both justifies eating the *mochi* and eroticizes it, if only in jest. Depending on the context of the *ku* in the anthology – it is probably part of a sequence of linked verse – the "we'd" or subjectless second reading might be changed to "he" and the "year" might double as "age," for the elderly, with their sweet-tooth taste, were known to like *mochi*. In that case, the *ku* might *also* mean that joy to be able to eat *mochi* was one thing that kept the elderly stringing along, even if the pounded sweet rice is so glutinous that many people, most elderly, choke to death on it every year! (◎注「鷹筑波集」に句の前後を見れば本来の連想がもう少しよく理解できよが、在米、しかも田舎で図書館もない、無所属貧乏の吾は、首尾アテズッポ仕舞い。)

Mochi Mallet, called *Kine*, and Mortar called *Usu*

The mortar is a tub made of fragrant wood with a thick bottom and a hole that grows a bit deeper every year. The pestle is a mallet so it can be swung. Some people think the mallet is very heavy. I do not. But it is hard to use for another reason. The handle cross-section is narrow and *round* (my embossing of the photo is misleading) *as a dowel*. Only a very powerful grip and rough calluses can wield it with ease. All it would take to change this would be to make the handle like that of an axe or a tennis racket. So why does it never change? Is the round cross-section lucky? Or, do Japanese like to make things hard? You should see the traditional Japanese 3-string fiddle (only used now for Court music called *gagaku*). Though light, it is played balanced on a point, rather than resting between hip and belly as the Chinese fiddles do. Perhaps an arguement could be made that the alarming ease with which the head swings from side to side allows for some sort of control by a powerful expert. 名人の証言求む。

餅花
mochi-bana

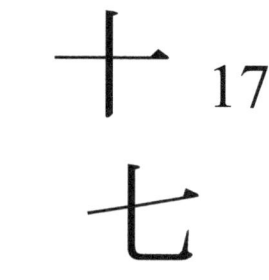

flowers to eat

餅花の木陰にてうちあはゝ哉　一茶　文化十
mochibana no kokage nite uchiawaba kana issa 1813
(sweet-rice-flower/blossoms' tree's shade-in caucus-would!)

the invitation

under the tree
where the *mochi* blooms
let us converse!

Mochi balls were stuck on real or artificially constructed branches. This being the year Issa, age 51, finally returned to his home-town, there may be a touch of magical regression here. I imagine he remembers his beloved grandmother who cared for him when his step-mother did not.

餅花や火鉢に倚りて淡き恋　墨水　改造社
mochibana ya hibachi ni yorite awaki koi bokusui -1914
(mochi flowers:/! heater-by approaching/ed fleeting/fragile)

mochi blossoms   a fragile love
drawing 'round the stove   sits 'round the heater
fleeting love   *mochi* blossoms

mochi blossoms
gentle love leans over
the finger stove

The *hibachi,* usually translated "brazier," is a thick clay or iron pot with a thick lip where hands can be rested. It is full of fine light-colored ashes within which a burning piece of hardwood charcoal smolders for hours. I imagine its dim light shows the white *mochi* blossoms dimly, like on a night when the moon is less than half-full. While the *hibachi* is still used in early Spring which, thanks to the slow warming quality of our Earth can be as cold as Winter months after the solstice, it is a winter theme. And, to tell the truth, these *mochi* blossoms are hard to pin down on the calendar. In most *saijiki*, they are purely New Year, but many have a separate section in the Winter for *ku* such as the above. A few *saijiki*, such as that for Issa's *ku* (Zenshû 1), put *all* of them into the Winter (This was presumably because most were found in the twelfth month in his journal, but a couple are in the tenth month between some New Year *ku* – Issa's journal was not kept in perfect order.)   Some regions of Japan, or some households, had a tradition of making the blossoms in the last month, which makes sense considering that mirror *mochi* was made then.   Still, the four *mochi* blossom *ku* by Issa in the Kaizôsha *saijiki* are placed with the rest in the New Year volume; I will do the same.

餅花に春を促す一間かな 蝶衣
mochibana ni haru o unagasu hitoma kana   chôi -1930
(*mochi*-blossoms-by/in/with spring[obj] prompt/encourage one-room!/?/'tis)

my one room
with *mochi* blooming
primes the spring

drawing spring
into a single room
mochi blossoms

This *ku* makes the *mochi* blossoms a force of Spring, while "prime" suggests they precede it. Note that it is a modern haiku which expresses the nature of the New Year after the Gregorian Calendar pulled it back into the heart of Winter. But the point is not so much the precise place in the calendar as the attitude. If you think of the blossoms as bucking the dead of the winter, it is a winter *ku*. If you think of them as a draw for the Spring, it is a New Year's *ku*.   There is something too easy about the *ku*, but the active verb *unagasu*, or "prompts," which I translated as "primes," invigorates it.   I can remember reading about Amerindian practices where it was believed that without human help, the New Year's sun would not come up.   The same can be said for *everything*; I think most of us feel it is both true and absurd, a humble idea and the ultimate in hubris.

餅花のともし火春となりにけり 八重桜 俗春夏秋冬
mochibana no tomoshibi haru to narinikeri   yaezakura -1945
(*mochi*-blossom's light/torch/lamp spring becomes [+finality])

the lamp placed
for the *mochi* blossoms
becomes spring

This contemporary *ku* is more subtle for not speaking causally, but I think it means about the same thing as the last.

餅花や鼠が目にはよしの山   其角 -1707
mochibana ya nezumi no me ni wa yoshino yama   kikaku
(sweet-rice-flower/blossoms! mice/rats' eyes-in, yoshino mountain)

mochi blossoms
to the eyes of all mice
mt goodfield!

for the mice, this
is their mount yoshino
mochi blossoms

Yoshino, the mountain whose name I Englished as "good-field" ("good" being a homonym of "yoshi") for the Candy Rock Mountain effect, was and still is famous as the place for the best cherry-blossom-viewings, a sort of floral heaven on earth.   There is no mistaking that this *ku* metaphorically puts the "blossoms" into the Spring.   Note that real cherry blossoms do not bloom until late in the Spring.   Let's compare Kikaku's *ku* with the following one by Bashô.

餅花やかんざしにさせる嫁が君　芭蕉 歯がため
mochibana ya kanzashi ni saseru yomegakimi　bashô -1694
(sweet-rice-blossoms: hair-pin-as stick-in bride-ruler)

mochi blossoms!
they'd make a good hairpin
for a mouse bride

If Kikaku's *ku* is imaginative, Bashô's is surreal. If Kikaku sees the *mochi* blossoms and mice as a miniature model of Yoshino, Bashô gives us a mismatch of scale that prevents our visualization. The *mochi* blossoms were often stuck on what seems like a miniature willow, and the whole thing does bear a resemblance to some of the elaborate hairpins worn by Japanese women (who, on the whole wore less accessories than European women did). We already mentioned the mouse-bride on Mt Hôrai and will be giving her a whole chapter. There are anthropomorphic depictions of mice on the picture scrolls going back hundreds of years before Bashô, but I think you need to see the real thing in Japan to know just how cute mice can be. [1] I think the following is as good as Kikaku or Bashô's *ku*:

餅花の奥や鼠の嫁入道　仙魚 役者の俳句
mochibana no oku ya nezumi no yomeiriji　sengyo 1745-53
(*mochi*-blossom's depths/far-side:/! mouse's/s' bride's[marriage]-procession-route)

mochi blossoms
behind them the route of
the mouse bride

This will do for the mouse bride here. We will have a whole chapter soon enough.

民の戸や松に餅咲く百代　柳興 虚栗
tabi no to ya matsu ni mochi saku momokaeri　ryûkyô 1683
(folk's door/gate:/! pine-on/plus *mochi* blooms hundred generations/realms)

the gates of the folk　　　　　　　　a hundred returns
a hundred realms of *mochi*　　　our gates all boast pine
blooming on pine　　　　　　　　　and *mochi* blooms

かまけるな柳の枝に餅がなる　一茶
kamakeru na yanagi no eda ni mochi ga naru　issa 1819
(take care not [?] willow's branches-on *mochi* becomes/grows)

so, why work?
why worry? *mochi* grows
on willow trees!

---

1. Cute Mice In the essay on mice by *haijin* Kyorai (1651-1704), published in the collection of folk essays by *haijin* Kyôroku (1665-1715), he writes "One name is *yome-ga-kimi* (bride-ruler). Another, [simply] *yome* (bride). . . . Eyes like on a [Japanese *sansho*] pepper [tiny, shiny=cute]. Nose like an *adzuki* bean (tiny, round and reddish). Teeth that could be threaded for fine needle-work. Ears like a leaf bud barely open." Exactly. They are incredibly finely wrought works of art that make us humans look crude by comparison. Further in the essay, Kyorai did not neglect mentioning the way mice/rats piss and poop on Buddhas and [Shintô] Gods alike – and, medical historians, take note – spread disease (*byô o umezu[?]*)! (*fuzoku-bunsen maki-dai*-3 c.1700)

While the *mochi* was called "blossoms," it was not only stuck on the branches of blossoming trees such as plums and dogwood, but on the never-blossoming branches of the Chinese nettle tree and the willow. The pine, hence the second reading of the first *ku*. Why did Issa choose to specially celebrate willow? The Kaizôsha saijiki mentions people visiting the Turtle Well Esoteric Shrine in Tokyo at the First Hour of the Hare (*hatsu-u*, about 6 AM) to buy *mochi* blossoms (called cocoons, as we shall soon see), fastened to a willow branch, together with other charms. This was brought home and set in the proper place to celebrate and pray for wealth. I thought to check the date, and sure enough, Bunsei 2, or 1819, was the Year of the Hare. So we may have a *ku* about a charmed charm. Then, again, Issa's *ku* was in the winter. Could he, rather refer to the very real pussy willow catkins?

木に餅の花咲く世にも逢にけり 一茶
ki ni mochi no hana saku yo ni mo ainikeri issa -1827
(tree-on mochi flower blooms world-in-even meet [+fin.+emph.])

i live to see
a world where *mochi*
flowers bloom!

Issa wrote a first version ("I [live to] see the *time* when *mochi* . .") after he finally won his half of the house from his step-brother (by threatening the town he'd appeal to higher authorities) and the above *ku*, later, when happy with his wife and daughter Sato. Since *mochi* blossoms were standard New Year decoration/charms, Issa's expression of joy to encounter such a fantastic world reveals the long cultural starvation of a poor bachelor to whom domestic joys were but a dream. (As a poor man with likewise modest dreams long unfulfilled, I feel I know Issa's joy, though I have yet to experience it).

もち花を咲かせて見るや指の先 一茶
mochibana o sakasete miru ya yubi no saki issa 1824
(*mochi* flower bloom-make-try: finger-tip)

digital new year?

finger-tips, it's		trying to make
time to make *mochi*		*mochi* blossom i find
flowers bloom!		my finger-tips
	trying to make	
	mochi blossoms bloom	
	these old fingers	

This last haiku may be better in the first-person, in which case Issa becomes the fabled *hana-saka jijii* (花咲かせからの変化？), or, flower-blossoming grampa (old man), rewarded for goodness with the ability to make trees come into bloom in the winter. While Issa probably means no more than that he kneads and sticks the *mochi* balls on the branches. The *mochi* "blossoms" I have seen in photographs are just large marshmallow-sized balls (or, more kindly put, large buds). Nothing fancy there, unless it is the little red criss-crosses of cloth attached (how I do not know) on one end of some I have seen (in a photograph) hung up in a shrine in Kyôto. As is true for most of Japanese ceremonial art there is no realistic imitation of flowers. Still, there is a slight possibility that Issa plays with them – makes some look real – after his wife stuck them on the branches. Or, so I like to imagine. But my best bet is the allusionless second reading, where making the blossoms draws our attention to our finger-tips. The last reading assumes that old Issa is laughing at his own klutzy fingers. There might be a pun on "tongue tips" which could figuratively make word "leaves" bloom.

もちはなをていねいにつけしかられる 柳多留 20-8
mochibana o teinei ni tsuke shikarareru   yanagidaru 1785
(*mochi*-flowers[obj] politely placed/stuck-on scolded)

taking care to
place the *mochi* blossoms
she's scolded

In Japanese art and, for that matter, placement is everything. There is so much that is – or once was – well arranged that Westerners with good aesthetic sense have always loved Japan. Ideally, this arrangement is not done in the slow and considered manner of a Western interior decorator, but quickly, artlessly, even brusquely. Careful work would look artificial. But I doubt such aesthetic considerations would explain why she=wife (my guess) is scolded. More likely her husband thinks she is wasting time or considers such caution, or small-heartedness, belies the spirit of prosperity which is broad, carefree and rough, rather than stiffling and fastidious. That is to say, she sabotages the metaphysical side of the decoration. In my opinion, this "senryû" is a fine observation and deserves to be included with the best haiku on the subject. [1]

Mochi Cocoons

Some *saijiki* have *mochi* blossoms and *mochi* cocoons together, with either one of the two serving for the main heading for the theme. Others keep them separate. While they tend to be conflated in the cities, *mochi* cocoons were apparently an invention of the farmers who raised silk-worms, who wished for a productive year. My OJD claims the small balls of *mochi* were first stuck on branches of mulberry – this makes sense for the leaves of this tree fed the silk-worms – and red oak (akamegashiwa), and only later on leafless willow and small bamboo. I would suspect an older origin among the nobles, for the women sometimes raised the silk-worms as part of their hobby of weaving cloth for their lovers/husbands, but cannot find any old haiku mentioning *mochi* cocoons. All are about the blossoms. It would seem that the *mayudama* and the haiku about it only became widespread at the end of the 19c or early 20c. (☆ The character for *cocoon* 繭 has *thread* 糸 next to *bug/worm* 虫 under *plant*!)

1. *Senryû* in *Saijiki* I have yet to see a *senryû* (as determined by the book it first appeared in) included in a Japanese haiku *saijiki*. This is a shame, for, I think that content should count, while source should not. I am delighted with W.J. Higginson's inclusion of *senryû* in his international haiku almanac *Haiku World*. Of course, most *senryû* should not be confused with haiku. A rice-flower example: "Because the tree / bears *mochi,* mother / is troubled" (*ki ni mochi no naru no de haha wa mayaka sare (zorori zorori to)*). The tree (*ki*) is a homophone for "virgin/pure [young girl]" and *mochi* a homophone for "carry [a child]," which is to say a daughter perhaps promised to a man who would be a desirable in-law, has been knocked up. The *mochi* flower reading by itself is meaningless – that is to say, this is purely allegory – so this can not possibly double for a haiku.

繭玉の小判照り合ふ火影かな 佐登女 同人俳句集
mayudama no koban teriau hikage kana   satôjo   early-20c
(cocoon-ball's [oval gold]coins shine-meet/back firelight!/'tis)

gold pieces glow back and forth: cocoons in the firelight	gold pieces in the cocoons glow with the fire

繭玉や小判光りて俗ならず 瓦全 年刊俳句集
mayudama ya koban hikarite zoku narazu   gazen   -1911
(cocoon-balls!/: [oval gold]coins shining vulgar become-not)

mochi cocoons
gold pieces shining
are not vulgar

The *koban* is an oblong oval gold coin which, unlike round ones, can be comfortably handed from one person to another finger to finger. These coins hung with the *mochi*. I doubt the coins in these decorations were solid gold. Most would be decorative. I failed to find a way to translate the compound verb "shining-meet/face" in the first *ku*. I do not know if the coins are glowing back and forth between themselves, or with the fire, which, if burnt down to the embers, would be an equal.

繭玉を買ふに塵銭なかりけり 雪人
mayudama o kau ni chirizeni nakarikeri   setsujin   -1918
(cocoon-balls[+obj] buy-for dust-money[small-change] not[as verb+emph])

mochi cocoons buying them took the last of my change	*mochi* cocoons and here i am all out of small change

My respondent, who is usually right, takes the second reading. Is he a poor bachelor who bought food first, so no money remained for decoration? Or, is he a rich bachelor, who only had large coins?

繭玉の映る金庫を拭ひけり 龍雨
mayudama no utsuru kinko o nugoikeri   ryûu - 1934
([silk]cocoon-gem/balls' reflect safe[deposit box] [+obj] wipe off[+emph])

double talisman

and the safe
reflecting the *mayudama*
is wiped clean

A good *ku*. This coincidence of charm and physical protection is almost too good to be true, but the reflection and the wiping make the physical reality of this safe beyond question: we feel the poet has made an actual observation and is not purely conceptualizing.

BACK TO THE BLOSSOMS!

餅花や灯たてゝ壁の影 其角
mochibana ya tomoshibi tatete kabe no kage kikaku
(*mochi*-blossoms: light/lamp stood-up wall's shadow -1707)

mochi blossoms!
i set up a lamp for
shadow-viewing

I found branches of budding and blooming plum in my room made very enjoyable shadows. The fine filaments in the blossom make for details missing with the *mochi,* but these solid round "blossoms" would lack cast crisper and very spectacular shadows. My preference is for the natural style where the *mochi* blossoms are here and there on the smaller branches, but all too many of the "blossoms," are strung up serially on willow branches and the effect is, rather, geometric. To each his own.

餅花や壁におぼろの影もなし 蝶衣
mochibana ya kabe ni oboro no kage mo nashi chôi -1930
(*mochi*-blossoms: wall-on unclear/hazy shadow/figure-too not)

mochi blossoms
no shadow on the wall
looks hazy

mochi blossoms
not one hazy shadow
on the wall

Chôi's *ku* plays off the stereotypically hazy spring moon, which presumably made hazy shadow figures. For the stereotypical modern critic, it is a better *ku* than Kikaku's, for it makes a fine distinction and the poet observes rather than does. I, too, like it; but Kikaku, deliberately setting up his lamp, gets *my* vote.

賑やかや米積む上の餅の花 炎天
nigiyaka ya kome tsumu ue no mochi no hana enten 1883-1963
(busy/prosperous!/: rice packed up above's *mochi's* blossom)

what prosperity   such bustling
above the piled up rice   on the mountain of rice
mochi blossoms   *mochi* in bloom
                    this is bounty
                 rice mountain erupts
                    mochi-blossoms

The last reading is obviously too much. Something about all those balls of mochi reminded me of a volcanic eruption... Big sacks of rice or bales of rice – thought our "bales" cannot begin to describe the wonderful rice-straw wrapping – are part of the New Year decoration. A *mochi*-blossom "tree" was often set up just behind the bale/s or thrust into one to stand as a tree growing on a mountain.

散(also: とる)事を待とはおかし餅の花　千代女
chiru koto o matsu to wa okashi mochi no hana　chiyojo 1701-75
(falling thing [obj] wait-as-for, funny/strange: *mochi's* blossom)

it might be fun	how strange
to wait for them to fall	waiting for them to fall:
mochi blossoms	*mochi* blossoms

The second reading is grammatically closer, but my loose translation "*It might be fun*" seems more appropriate for the playful Chiyo. I cannot make much sense of another version of the poem beginning *toru-koto*, "take/remove thing [obj] wait." If one *does not* wait for someone to remove the blossoms, what *does* one do? Take them off yourself and roast and eat them? Or, is it mice doing the taking? Issa has some *ku* which suggest *mochi* blossoms enjoy a natural cycle:

もち花の盛も一夜二夜かな　一茶
mochibana no sakari mo hitoyo futayo kana　issa
(*mochi* blossoms peak, too, one night, two night 'tis)

mochi blossoms
they, too, peak only
one night, or two

They behave like real blossoms. But, why count *nights* rather than days? I first thought it was because they were inside and observed more closely at night, but there is more. They were generally made on the night of the 14th, eve of the full-moon, always the 15th day of the month. So the *mochi* would look best at night not only because it was new and yet to be cracked or eaten by mice (or people) – *sakari* (peak) also hints at such night activity (see *Cherry Blossom Epiphany*) – but because of the moonlight.

もち花のぽたり／＼とちる日哉　一茶
mochibana no potaripotari to chiru hi kana　issa -1827
(*mochi* blossom's plop/thud plop/thud-with fall/ing day!/?/'tis)

so is this it,	*plop! plop!*
the day the *mochi* blossoms	i hear the *mochi* blossoms
tumble down?	fall today

もち花やいつちるとなくちるとなく 一茶
mochibana ya itsu chiru to naku chiru to naku　issa
(*mochi*-blossoms: when/sometime[?] fall-and-not [vaguely] x2)

mochi blossoms	*mochi* blossoms
not that it really matters	who cares? who cares?
when they fall	when they fall

One would think the glutinous blossoms would shrink up and cling to the branches forever, but apparently, they sometimes fell if they were not eaten and sounded more like little fruit *dropping* than "flowers" *falling*. Between the lines, I sense another contrast between the *mochi* and the exemplar of flowers in Japan, the cherry blossom. Issa saw the latter behaving like religious Buddhists, showing little attachment for this earth and admirable trust in Buddha by readily falling.

もち花や母の心の闇の梅 言水 俳諧五子橋
mochibana ya haha no kokoro no yami no ume gonsui -1719
(*mochi*-blossoms:/! heart's mother's dark [pitch-black-night]'s plum [blossoms])

    mochi blossoms   *mochi* blossoms
the spirit of my mother   the plum in the dark,
  a plum in the dark   mother o' my heart

mochi blossoms
like a plum in the dark, the scent
of mother's heart

This *ku* is almost magically beautiful, but the mother (*haha*), heart/mind/spirit (*kokoro*), dark (*yami,* as that of a moonless night) and plum (*ume,* imagine white blossoms) linked by nothing but the triple *no* ('s, of) cannot be read with certainty. Note that "darkness's plum" suggests either a plum blossom invisible in a pitch black night or a plum blossom visible in the dark, as a white heron is exceptionally visible in the dark (*yami no shirasagi*). Note also that the Chinese character for plum includes "mother" (母). I first thought the *ku* meant the white *mochi* blossoms visible in the dark manifest the pure heart of his mother who made them, but on second thought, went for the scent of the *mochi* in the pitch black room.

餅花や都しめたる家ざくら 言水 俳諧五子橋
mochibana ya miyako shimetaru iezakura gonsui
(*mochi* blossoms:/! capital occupies house-cherry)

mochi blossoms
the capital is occupied
by house cherries

The cherry, as a flower that blooms in mid-late Spring is not a good metaphor for a New Year blossom. But, there is no "house-plum" while *ie-zakura,* or house-cherry is a common term for a cherry tree in one's own garden that may be viewed at the pleasure of its owner. With the *mochi* in bloom if it were, we have something akin to house-cherries in every house. There may also be an allusion to the woman-of-the-house.

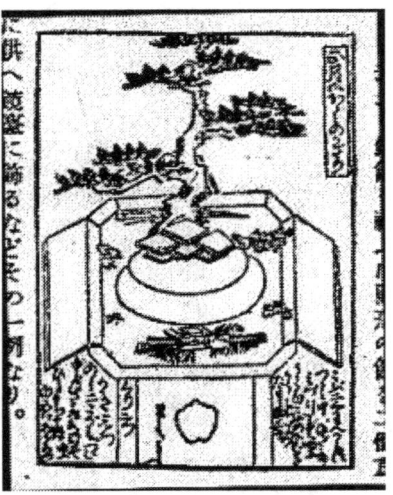

Above: An odd drawing of *kagami,* or mirror *mochi* from the Kaizôsha *saijiki*. Odd, because if there is something resting upon the sun (small *mochi* cake), it is usually a citrus fruit, and the pine seems to have grown from nowhere! The drawing should have been in chapter 16, but will be useful to give an idea of one stage for the peeping nuptials of the Princess Bride in the next chapter. In the picture, from an 1885 "Japanese Fairy Tale Series" translated as "The Mouse's Wedding," **below**, we see the Bride doing the same 3x3 drink of *sake,* and wearing the same "horn-hider" as a human bride would.

嫁が君
yome-ga-kimi

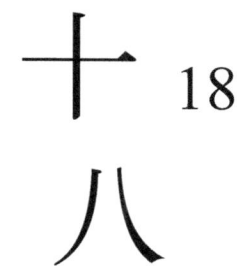
18

PRINCESS BRIDE WITH A TAIL

新世紀の通ひ路急ぐ嫁が君　王？五？玲子？　右脳俳句
shin seiki no kayoiji isogu yomegakimi   ôreiko?↑ name scribbled illeg., but found↓)
(new century's commuting-road hurries bride-ruler-mouse/rat 2001/1/3, right-brain haiku)

princess-bride
scuttles down the alley
of a new age

It need not be the Year of the Rat for a poet to appreciate rodents sighted on the New Year. The first three days of the year, rats and mice are not rats and mice but "bride-ruler" or "princess-bride." How delightful that not only this lowly creature, but "her" taboo term, virtually obsolete outside of the world of poets, has survived! If I translate *yome-ga-kimi* many ways in this chapter, it is because there is no good translation. To me, at least, the chapter-lead *ku's* main merit is bringing out the complex mind-life of the little creature by so simple a description. Note, the princess-bride is *not chased but in a hurry* to get home as the day – and, coincidentally, our new century and millennium (depending on your calculations) – dawns. If the New Century was not specified, I might have wondered if the poet was thinking, *She better hurry, for this is the year of the snake!* As it is, that is unlikely. I may well be the only person in the world to make that reading. So let us focus on the "bride." She is *thinking about something*, something beyond the behaviorist's limited choices. I take strong exception to another modern *ku* smugly claiming: *"Princess-bride / she's never dreamed of Fuji / or anything"* (*yomegakimi fuji no yume nado mita koto nashi*　角川＝俳句歳時記第三); as Loren Eiseley wrote, every day, animal dreams pass beneath our feet unnoticed.[1] A more conventional post-modern *ku* published in 1997 observes Princess-bride commuting through an iron [building] frame (鉄骨の中を通ひ路嫁ヶ君　石川昌子　季題別 *tekkotsu no naka o kayoiji yomegakimi* *ishikawa masako*); I prefer – or, perhaps, should say, *need* – the dramatic "new age" and "hurrying" of the *ku* I scavenged on the web.

---

1. *Animal Dream Web.* In *Night Country*, Loren Eiseley describes a field-mouse uprooted by a bulldozer, attempting to create his or her (I forget) dream-den in a large house-plant pot. Eiseley essays further, imagining a vast web of these tender dreams carried by little creatures crossing our lives unseen, in sewage pipes, along culverts, etc.. True, seeking an ideal and dreaming while asleep are not quite the same. But either way, rodents dream. Maybe not about Mt. Fuji (unless they are literally more far-sighted than we might imagine), but, neither do I.

One reason I began with a recent haiku is that, for an obsolete word and even more obsolete concept, our princess-bride has remained remarkably popular with late-19c and 20c poets, who, judging from the *saijiki* I have seen, were more taken by this olde theme than were their Edo era predecessors. Or, perhaps, it is more accurate to say that, previously, the princess-bride made her appearance in various themes, but was generally not herself a theme. In Shiki's huge *Categorical* haiku anthology (c1900), we find only two *ku* under the "princess-bride" (*yome-ga-kimi*) heading. The slightly later Kaizôsha anthology (c1930) gives *fifty*, including two by Shiki. Of those, only two were Edo era (1603-1867) *ku*. The first, by Kikaku, may well be found in every *saijiki* published which includes olde haiku:

明る夜のほかにうれし嫁が君　其角
akuru yoru no honoka ni ureshi yomegakimi　kikaku 1660-1707
(dawning night's slightly/dimly/faintly/delicately joyful/satisfied/happy bride-ruler)

in dawn's glow	as the dawn comes	dawn comes
i think i saw a blushing	some cheer from the faint glow	with this delicate joy
princess bride	of a princess bride	princess bride

This may well be the first haiku to feature the princess-bride (Bashô's *ku* we saw in the last chapter features the mochi-blossoms, not the princess-bride). It is hard to tell if the slight/delicate/faint joy belongs to mouse or man. As a mouse seen at this time would be lucky, I assume it is shared. The ambiguity of the original in this respect caught the eye of Kikaku's contemporaries. Shikô, who was, as per his name, which translates as "support-thought," a logic-monger, found the *ku* made more sense if it was about *another thing* altogether, a special New Year's lamp once called a *yome-ga-kimi* (参考=改造社の俳諧歳時記). *I.e.*, as the night began to dawn, the faintly perceived lamp made the poet feel good: my middle reading. The second of the two princess-bride *ku* given in Shiki's *Categorical*:

物の化の雛にあれけり嫁か君　如風 未来記
mononoke no hina ni arekeri yomegakimi　jofû 1661-1740 ↑ = 1765
(thing-change/monster's doll among?become?ravage?[+finality] bride-ruler)

is there a spook
among the new year dolls?
princess bride

While the Doll Festival is late Spring (3/3), there were New Year dolls, too. The most popular set for the New Year was the eight Chinese deities found aboard the Treasure Ship. This plays on the fact that the mouse's taboo name, Princess-bride has a doll-like ring to it.

三日月を出てみるあとは嫁が君　乙二 改造社
mikazuki o dete miru ato wa yomegakimi　otsuni 1754-1823
(third-day-moon go-out see after-as-for, bride-ruler)

after going out	the three-day moon
to see the new moon, it's time	goes down, your time is nigh
for princess bride	oh, princess bride!

The moon starts each lunar month at dawn, setting at dusk. By the third day, it sets shortly after nightfall. The poet sees it off and returns home. This third night is the end of the mouse-as-princess-bride period, high-time for her wedding. Perhaps, the poet means that when the moon sets the mice will come out on this, their last night of charmed existence before they turn back into ordinary rodents.

In classical Japanese poetry, the thin crescent moon was *the* metaphor for a quickly glanced feature, a single pretty eyebrow, that turns the poet into a moon-struck lover. This gives a faint scent of romance which fails to translate. And, with that, our supply of olde Princess Brides dries up. If only Issa's curious girl, Sato, lived a little longer, I'm sure he would have written something like, say:

嫁が君むこはむこはと女子かな　敬愚
yomegakimi muko wa muko wa to onago kana　keigu
(bride-lord groom-as-for groom-as-for, girl-child 'tis)

princess bride:
what of the groom, her groom?
asks my girl

If there is a bride, where, then, *is* the groom? Keigu is not the first to have asked this, for the existence of the taboo term (a word used in place of usual one) "bride" for mouse led painters and story-tellers to come up with an entire wedding procession. The most well-known story is about a Mouse King searching for the most powerful husband in the world for his daughter. First he went to the Sun, who admitted that Cloud could block him out any time; then, he went to Cloud, who said, *You had better go to Wind, he's always pushing me around*; but Wind said, *Yeah, but Earthwork can stop me cold*; so the Mouse King finally asked Earthwork if he was, indeed, the most powerful of all. His reply was that there was someone who could bring him down by digging holes. *That* was *Mouse*. So, the Mouse Princess got married to a fellow Mouse. Be that as it may – need I elaborate on the moral? – I have met people in 20c Japan who, in their childhood, waited up in the hope of spying the wedding procession of the mice (*nezumi no yomeri*), much as we might try to catch Santa Claus! Sengyo's 18c *ku* is the only old one I know specifying the procession, so the idea may have been minor and local.

長き尾を隠しおほせず嫁が君　疎香 昭和一万句
nagaki o o kakushi ôsezu yomegakimi　soka 20c
(long tail[+obj] hidden/ing/covers-not bride-lord)

she can't quite
conceil her long tail
the princess-bride

There are many tales of animal brides marrying men in Japan. Foxes are more common brides then mice in these tales, but mice are by no means the strangest. We even have snake and dragon brides! All tend to have some magical power that helps the man who treated them well gain a fortune and one thing the man promises never to do (*No, dear respondent, I need not reveal what it is!*), which, eventually, he does, causing her to turn back into her original form and leave forever. Though merely an observation of a mouse whose tail was first noticed, this *ku* plays on that magical idea. If you have the anthropomorphic concept of a "bride," you might expect them to hide their tails for their betrothal.

ほの暗き偲び姿や嫁が君　碧梧桐 同句集
honoguraki shinobi sugata ya yomegakimi　hekigodô -1937
(dim-darkness sneaking-form/figure:/! bride-lord)

in the dim light
something sneaks by
princess-bride

The verb *shinobu* in classical poetry meant to restrain ones love or to creep about to avoid attention as one carries on an affair.   The *hurrying* in the chapter *ku* is fresher.

行燈の油なめけり嫁が君　子規
andon no abura namekeri yomegakimi　shiki -1902
(lamp[in a paper covered box]'s tallow lick/ed-up bride-ruler)

our lamp oil licked up in the night princess bride!	licking away at the lamp tallow! it's the bride

Princess-bride bloomed in the Meiji era (1868-1912). Never married, childless, Shiki was strongly attracted to sweet themes, such as the doll festival and the princess-bride. My respondent reminds me that lamp-oil-licking fox and cat changelings often figure in horror stories and wonders whether Shiki, too, has dark thoughts here. I doubt it. Mice and lighting devices go together. English-speakers have their mouse jumping over the candle-stick and a popular Chinese nursery rhyme features little mice having trouble getting down from the candles they climb up.[1]   Richard Wright notes how

on winter mornings
the candle shows faint markings
of the teeth of rats

By Shiki's standard of photo-realism, his own *ku* is less pure than Wright's (with apologies to his editors for my centering, etc.), but the contrast of vulgar licking and noble bride makes it more interesting to *me*. Another *ku* about damage by mice:

若餅と契りにけりな嫁が君　　蝶衣
wakamochi to chigirinikeri na yomegakimi　　chôi 1886-1930
(young=master rice-cake-with troth/tryst=tear-up[+finality] ~~not~~ ? bride-ruler)

~~oh, troth not~~ ~~with young *sir mochi*,~~ ~~princess bride!~~	hoh, princess bride have you now trothed with young *sir mochi*?

"Young *mochi*" is the smaller, upper loaf of the mirror-*mochi,* or a separate one, set out for the New Year, or on the last day of Princess Bride's nominal reign. Like the Princess, *Waka-mochi* is a word born of taboo: "young" replaces "small," inappropriate to the New Year. In that sense, they are a good match. The son of a lord or wealthy merchant was called *waka* + family name, or young+ master. He was stereotypically spoiled and occupied in womanizing. Can the reader imagine a nicer way to ask a mouse to lay off the decorations? *But,* says my respondent, *the first reading is wrong.* (I misread a quizzical *na* as "not."). ☆ Later, I found a the groom's father was named Kanemochi (*Rich*, with a pun on rice-cake?) in a fairy-tale picture book the poet would have read in his childhood. Kudos to its translator, David Thompson, who had the marriage *"consum-mated . . . and much to be congratulated!"*

---

1. Chinese Tallow Mice   From I.T. Headland's CHINESE MOTHER GOOSE RHYMES (c1900): *"He climbed up the candlestick, / The little mousey brown, / To steal and eat tallow, / And he couldn't get down. / He called for his grandma, / But his grandma was in town, / So he doubled up into a wheel / And rolled himself down."* The color of the mouse and the whereabouts of grandma are born of rhyme. This rhyme has many variants and reflects the affection Chinese have long had for mice (the cloying high notes of the fiddle in old-fashioned Peking Opera would only please mouse-lovers). Starfield=CZ=Hoshino mentions less common variants where Brother Cat happens by, or Sir Toad croaks a dirge for the poor trapped mousey. Princess-bride, however, is a Japanese invention.

楽人の夢想のひまや嫁が君　渓水 明治一万句
rakujin no musô no hima ya yomegakimi   keisui late-19c
(ease/leisure-person's dream-thought's sparetime: princess-bride)

a day-dream
of the leisure class!
princess bride

Not held back by science-fearing Christians, most Meiji intellectuals were able to adopt a rational worldview *much* faster than their counterparts in the Christian West, most noteably Usania (See Edward S. Morse: *Japan Day by Day*). This poet may not have known about the taboo name origin of the princess-bride and, as a modern man in a scientific world, felt righteously upset with the anthropomorphism inherent in it. Or, he may, rather, have longed to return to a time where men had world enough and time to indulge in fantasy. One cannot tell which side he is on. Most poets, like Shiki, were definitely delighted with the princess-bride's existence.   But electricity was to change things:

嫁が君古人は心ひろかりし　富安風生
yomegakimi kojin wa kokoro hirokarishi fûsei 1885-1979
(bride-ruler: old/ancient people-as-for, heart broad)

"princess-bride"
what broad minds people
used to have!

This poet was a scientist-administrator of electronic communications. He must have been familiar with the science of extermination, for rodents have a strange attraction for weak current which makes them gnaw through telephone lines and short wiring in cars, causing so much damage that even those who do not begrudge the loss of food or mess, might find it hard to bless the blushing brides!

嫁が君出て貧厨のめでたさよ　孤峰
yomegakimi dete hinchû no medetasa yo kohô ホトトギス early-20-c
(bride-ruler appears poor[impoverished] kitchen/cupboard's festive/cheerful/ auspiciousness!)

princess-bride
my bare cupboard gains
a holiday spirit

bringing cheer   how cheerful
to a poor man's cupboard   one princess bride makes
princess-bride   a bare cupboard!

princess bride!
one can be lucky to have
a bare cupboard

From long years of material poverty, I can say that little creatures, even lacking such magical names, do more for the poor than well-off readers can possibly imagine. What kept my spirits up when writing this book? Too poor to keep a cat or dog, I depend upon progressive radio (someone voicing my anger at the self-serving liars running "my" country) and . . . *geckoes*. Hearing them vocalize, I look up from this screen to watch them facing off (like cats, they rise up, turn broadside, wag their tails in a menacing way and vocalize) and carrying out attacks so novel and decisive one is reminded of Miyamoto Musashi (See William S Wilson's biography of the great lone-swordsman). ☆Half a year later, circumstances forced another move on me & I had to exchange these wall warriors for farting old dogs.   Kohô's cheerfulness beats conventional objectivity, such as: *"At night, a sound / from the bare cupboard / princess-bride"* (貧厨に夜ひと音あり嫁が君　守水老　改造社　*hinchû ni yoru hitone ari yomegakimi*　shusuirô 19-20c?).

餅の粉に化粧やすらん嫁が君 夢幼 明治新俳句集
mochi no ko ni kesho ya suran yomegakimi　muyô late-19c
(sweet-rice-cake's powder-in/with make-up do! bride-ruler)

sweet-rice flour
is what she makes up with:
our princess-bride

a mouse's toilette

your make-up?
try the flour on the *mochi*,
princess-bride!

mochi-flour:
let it stay, princess bride
needs make-up!

The flour is something like that used to dust dough when rolling it. Like bread, the whole loaf of *mochi* may be dusted with it, so it is also on the upper surface where it is not really needed. Women in the Sinosphere did not powder their faces to touch them up or surreptitiously assume a paler shade; they *white-washed* their faces, letting the edges of the make-up show as clearly as a bikini line.[1] Brides were powdered up as bright as Snow White. Could Princess-bride do any different?

嫁が君手形足型炉灰かな 師竹
yomegakimi tegata ashigata rokai kana　shichiku late-19c?
(bride-ruler: hand/paw-prints foot/paw-prints stove-pit-ashes!/'tis)

cinderella

princess bride
handprints and footprints
in the stove-ash

The old-fashioned *irori* stove cooks things over ashes that serve to anchor the butt-end of skewers with small fish and vegetables. Japanese lacks the just-for-animals word "paws," but it does *usually* call *these* "hands" *mae-ashi* or, "front-legs." While the poet *has* deliberately humanized the mouse, who is, after all, a bride, the anthropomorphism in the original is less outlandish than in translation. The hands *and* feet evoke the interspecies mindset of Issa's famous *ku "Don't hit the fly / He rubs (=prays/begs with) his hands, / he rubs his feet!"*[2] At the same time, the strange wording pulls our minds-eye down for a close-up of the paw-prints, themselves, fairy cute to all good-hearted men.

1. Powdered Brides   The human bride in Headland's CHINESE MOTHER GOOSE uses no less than 200 layers of powder, as does a character depicted by the Japanese playwright+*haijin* Saikaku (d.1693). The West associates make-up with wantonness but, as Edward S Morse explained in an 1894 lecture at Vassar, *make-up can serve modesty rather than show*, for not to apply it would be tantamount to boasting "she possessed so fair a complexion" she did not need it. *Artificial beauty, by and large, is an equalizer.* See *Topsy-turvy 1585* for more.

2. Anthropomorphic Animals   Blyth correctly pointed out that most criticism of "the pathetic fallacy" misses the mark, for true anthropomorphizing (versus figures of speech, satire, farce, etc.) is very rare. If anything, it is more common for other animals to be robbed of the emotions *they* have. Still, many poems do seem juvenile in translation because the differing connotations of our mutually exotic vocabulary make it *seem* the poet has his or her species confused. I pursue this problem together with Issa's untranslatable *ku* in *FLY-KU!* chps.1- 4.

嫁が君の通ひ路狭し升落し 子規 明治三十
yomegakimi no kayoiji semashi masu otoshi   shiki 1897
(bride-ruler's commute-path narrow[is] measuring-cup-dropped [mouse]trap)

~~princess-bride~~   a narrow aisle   ~~i hear a cup fall:~~
~~is your path too narrow?~~   for our princess bride   ~~is your aisle cramped~~
~~a cup falls~~   mouse traps   ~~princess-bride?~~

Shiki has no "too," but pointing out the path is narrow suggests such sympathy. In Japan, brides traveled to their groom's house; I used "our" word *aisle* for the effect. My respondent explained that *masu-otoshi* was a trap. Bait was tied to a stick placed under the square wooden measuring cup, resting on one edge.

今宵また橙おとす嫁が君 九斤子
koyoi mata daidai otosu yomegakimi   kukinshi 19-20c
(this evening again bigarade [huge orange] knock-off bride-ruler)

princess-bride
tonight, the bigarade
will roll again!

The *daidai*, as we have seen, was put on the *hôrai*, which could be a *mochi* cake, or on top of the moon and sun "*kagami=mirror=mochi*," or even tied into a type of hanging decoration. The mice in this house are obviously very rambunctious. Or, maybe they are *rats*, for it is not easy to move a fruit the size of a grapefruit even if it is round. Princess-bride is taking full advantage of her honeymoon period!

子を二つ連れて居ますや嫁が君 笑月 明治一万句
ko o futatsu tsurete-imasu ya yomegakimi   shôgetsu late-19c
(children two, bring-together-is: bride-ruler)

two children
right there, by her side
princess-bride!

In Japanese, rapid reproduction is called "rodent-addition" (*nezumizan*); but, really, princess, you jump the gun! *I joke*. But, note how fantasy serves reality. If you were to read only of a big mouse with two little mice seen in a house, those mice would slip through your brain like they never entered it.

嫁が君この家の勝手知りつくし 轡田進 角川三版
yomegakimi kono ie no katte shiritsukushi   kutsuwada susumu
(bride-ruler, this house's kitchen know-exhausts 20c)

princess-bride
she knows our kitchen
inside out!

Long before haiku, the bride in Japan moved into her husband's house, where she underwent what we would call a long hazing. But here is this little bride, right at home! Again, a fantastic depiction of something as real as real can be. How many of *us* can remember what is where in our cupboards?

臆面もなく夜遊びの嫁が君　森上 涼 季題別
okumen mo naku yo-asobi no yomegakimi　morikami ryô 1997
(shame/embarassment-even-not, night-play's/playing bride-ruler)

no modesty
on her night to sport
princess bride

how cheeky!
princess-bride plays
all night long

人見知りして影見せず嫁が君　塚月 凡太 季題別
hitomishiri shite kage misezu yomegakimi　tsukazuki bonta
(people-see-know[=shy/bashful], figure shows not: bride-ruler 1997)

just too bashful
to show your pretty face,
princess-bride?

These contemporary *ku* show opposite sides of mouse behavior, which varies according to the design of the home, behavior of the people and, perhaps, the age of the Princess-bride.[1] The term used for "shy," *hitomishiri,* is one usually applied to toddlers who shy away from strangers and hide their faces between their mother's legs, or in her skirt.   Ideally, here is what the princess-bride *should* do:

嫁が君出番深夜の時計鳴る 神保奈美子
yomegakimi deban shinya no tokei naru　jinbô namiko 河出新歳時記
(bride-ruler appearance[time for duty/ to go on stage]: late-night's clock rings 20c)

princess bride
her stage call is the strike
of midnight

The untranslateable word *deban* makes the poem. "Appearance" is too broad and "stage-call" too narrow. *Deban* includes the proper time to appear in a parade, a party, a sport's event, a jam session or a wedding. It just so happens that midnight is struck in the middle of the two-hour-long hour of the mouse/rat according to the traditional scheme of time. So, our mouse makes a double *deban* as a princess-bride and as the proper animal in a sequence of hour-animals.

一人起きて居るとも知らず嫁が君　皆川 白陀 河出同
hitori okite-iru to mo shirazu yomegakimi　minagawa hakuda 20c
(single/alone/one-human awake-is even knows-not bride-ruler)

princess-bride
doesn't know someone
is still awake

And she doesn't know she is a "princess bride," either. The "someone" *should* seem human, because the "alone" was written with the Chinese characters "one-human." The content of the haiku is so simple and so good that I would not be surprised to find another just like it. It is also a perfect example of the Japanese grammar most troublesome for English. My translation is direct, yet the subject of the poem in the original comes at the very end of the sentence, rather than the front. I like the quiet consciousness in this *ku* but identify more with the next, slightly older *ku*:

↑ **1. Shy/Forward Mice** I once knew a Japanese mouse – a red field-mouse caught by one of my semi-feral cats – that time after time came out of the book-pile to walk on my *futon* among the sleeping cats. I had to sit up with a water pistol to defend said mouse against the cats, who weren't really sleeping. After nodding off and barely closing the window on a cat who decided to take the mouse out to play, I *trained* the mouse to come out when I scratched the *tatami* and climb up my leg and trunk to my hand to lick soybean powder and showed this trick to a neighbor, who showed it to her mother and got permission to adopt the trusting creature before it got itself killed. The mouse was no baby, but must have been young, for such behavior would surely not have allowed a long life. So "shy" mouse brides are old, and "forward" ones are young – just the opposite of our species.

~~~~~~

この翁かくて在るぞや嫁が君　露月
kono okina kakute aru zo ya yomegakimi   rogetsu -1927
(this master/oldman like-this is[+emphatic]: bride-lord)

<table>
<tr><td>

this old man
is right here with you!
princess-bride

</td><td>

ah, princess-bride
there is this old guy
here, as you see

</td></tr>
</table>

兼好が寝顔のぞくや嫁が君　夏風 明治新俳句集
kenkô ga negao nozoku ya yomegakimi   kafû late-19c
(kenkô's sleep-face [it] peeks[at]:/! bride-lord)

ah, she peeks at
the face of sleeping kenkô!
princess bride

I am not sure *what* Rogetsu means to say to Princess Bride. Some will welcome the chance to fill in the blank; others will not. Kenkô is Yoshida Kenkô, a 14c Buddhist priest from a family of hereditary Shintô priests, whose *Essays in Idleness* (*Tsurezurekusa*) contributed to the formation of what became *the* Japanese aesthetic (I like the way Kenkô noted that the reason for some old New Year customs escaped him. An author, he did not pretend to authority). A great proponent of treating animals kindly, he criticized keeping wild animals. But, he also put house-mice right between *the lice we endure* and *the robbers that plague the countryside*, as an example of "things that attach themselves to something else, then waste and destroy it." (D. Keene trans.) *Is the Princess trying to figure him out?*

闇に出て闇に消えゆく嫁が君　前野聖子 季題別
yami ni dete yami ni kieyuku yomegakimi   maeno seiko 1997
(darkness-from appear, darkness-from disappearing-goes bride-ruler)

purple mouse

out of the dark
into the dark she goes
princess bride

This is easier. My title plays on the name Murasaki, literally, *purple*, because a cultured Japanese cannot write of "going from dark to dark" without thinking of Murasaki Shikibu's *waka,* introduced, with a similar poem about the life of sea cucumbers, in *Rise, Ye Sea Slugs!* Anything associated with Murasaki is romantic; her novel *Tale of Genji*, might well be renamed *The Romances of Genji..* Maeno's *ku* is such a natural that I half-expect to find the same one written (independently) hundreds of years earlier. Let me go further, chances are the *ku* was *already* written by someone else!

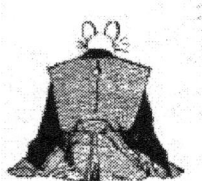

Let me take advantage of this chapter on mice to propound a strongly held opinion on Chinese characters. In mid-20c Japan, when the Occupation Authorities decided that some limitation of the number of characters would further literacy in Japan (though Japanese were probably already as literate as we were), lists of characters deemed proper for teaching in school or use by the mass media were prepared and promulgated. In the first, the *cat* = 猫 and the *mouse* = 鼠 were left out. Eventually, a revision brought back the *cat,* perhaps because it was unfair to favor the *dog* = 犬, or because *cat* = 猫 is not really a very complex character. In a public debate in the Japanese popular bi-monthly magazine *Aera* (in the 1990's), I argued that the mouse = 鼠, too, deserved to be saved. The character is a bit complex, but my point was that even if it is hard for many to *write*, it is easy to remember for *reading* purposes, as it reminds us of the fine-featured, timorous creature and there are no characters at all similar. I argue that the list for *reading* and *writing* should be separate and that even though both have traditionally been taught together, for some characters, a separate approach is called for. If one is taught to read 鼠, eventually one may come to write it, too; but, if it is removed from newspapers so that people rarely come across it, they will never learn to read or write it. Be that as it may, *look* at that character. Isn't it cute? Can't you see the wee legs and, perhaps, even the whiskers and tail?

若菜摘み
waka-na-tsumi

19
十九

PLUCKING YOUNG GREEN

the proposal

pretty basket, pretty maid!
picking greens of tender blade!
pretty scoop, in pretty hands!
guess ye who before thee stands!

confess thy clan, confess thy name!
i'll tell mine first, just do the same!
they call me lord of this whole land
for man and god know my command!

but you, alone, i deign to ask
what i could, by right, demand!

This is a *very* loose sense-translation of the first "song" of the 4,516 poem *Manyôshû*, Japan's oldest anthology of poetry. A more direct rendering would be: *Basket! Pretty basket holder! Scoop, too! Pretty scoop holder! On this hill, child [=young woman [1]] picking greens! Tell [me] your family! Tell [me] your name! All of the country of Yamato, all of it is my reign, and I, on my part announce my family and name!* There is some debate in Japan about the meaning of the last part, but I incorporated it into this translation and added the title and last two lines because asking a girl's name is said to be tantamount to a proposal of marriage, [2] and the politeness of that proposal – if the last line is correct, and granted the middle part seems a bit pushy – seems out of character for the brusque and, according to some historians, cruel, Emperor Yûryaku (5c). Some day, I may yet write an entire book on this first song of Japanese poetry; here, let me just note what the maiden addressed by the Emperor is doing. She is not necessarily a farm girl. Chances are she is a noble child (they married, or at least were promised for marriage young) engaged in the ancient ritual of picking the first greens of the year=spring. This event is thought to have included wooing in the form of song-exchanges. The term used for picking greens in the ancient poem, *na-tsumasu*, is, excluding the conjugation of the verb, identical to the later *na-tsumu*. Since *na* was a homophone for "name" and *tsumu* or "pluck," was slang for "intercourse," the ritual activity could not help but be erotically charged, nominally speaking.

↑ **1. *Child=Woman*** Critical female reader, before this upsets you, *please* note that in old poems Japanese women call their boyfriends and even husbands *waga seko,* literally "my back-child," which is to say the dear little thing they carry on their back. I have seen many translations of old poems (*my love, my sweet-heart, my darling, my man,* occasionally, *my boy*), but none seem to have found the natural translation of this: *my papoose!* Men call girlfriends and loved wives *imo,* or "little sister" (Japanese has a different term for an older sister). So, on the whole, it is men who are infantilized the most!

2. *Proposal of Marriage.* While this poem, like most in the *Manyôshû*, is written in solid Chinese characters chosen primarily for their pronunciation, the fact the "pretty scoop holder" (*mi-fukushi-mochi*) is written in Chinese characters 美夫君志持 meaning "beautiful-husband-ruler [you?]-wish-have" (I call this "stereo script") suggests the "name-asking=proposal" interpretation of the scholars is correct. I assume that if a ruler knew a girl's family and name he could find her again and, as she, or, rather, *they* could hardly refuse his advances, she would have no choice but to become one of his wives.

古へもこんなものかははッ若菜 素樸 俳人藤森
inishie mo konna mono ka wa hatsuwakana sobaku -1821
(olden-times, too, this thing like? first young greens)

was it like this
in the days of old?
first young-green

Na, "greens," are usually preceded by *waka,* "young." The question with this *ku* is whether it celebrates the thrill of finding the first edible new thing or bemoans the let-down – as in, *that's all?* If the former, does Sobaku feel the primal experience connects him with the past? If the latter, does he miss the singing young men and women of whom he read? Either way, it is hard to speak of *one* past. Even if it simulated peasant living as a a form of aesthetics, the aristocratic culture which created *waka* (5-7-5-7-7) poetry, had different practices than the folk.¹ The upper class tended to pick greens for presenting to their lords and masters, whereas the folk picked for themselves and their families. One 18c *ku* asks *"For whom / do you pluck these young greens, / little beauty?"* (誰が為めに若菜摘むらん小傾城　五明　大全 *ta ga tame ni wakana tsumuran kokeisei* gomei -1803). The term used for pretty girl here, little *keisei* (literally, "little tip[i.e. topple]-castle") generally referred to a young harlot, so the poem is less romantic than touching. We think of her far-from-storybook life. Be that as it may, the idea of romance was always part of the plucking:

傾城になる子もあらん若なつみ 逸雅
keisei ni naru ko mo aran wakanatsumi itsuga 黄昏日記 1760
(beauty/harlot-into/become/is child/girl-even be-might[surmised] , young-rape-plucking)

i hope to find
some real beauties out there
green-plucking

green-pluck day
i'll bet there're some real
beauties out there

will any of them · end up selling herself? · green-pluckers
even harlots · are not harlots plucking · young-green

1. *Aristocratic Greens* One of the first *waka* in the *Senzaiwaka-shû* (1188) appears to mean : *"I envy you!* [or, is it: "I envy *her"*?] */ rustling your hands through / the soft grass / beneath the snow and who is / your Tobuhi young green?"* (*urayamashi yuki no shitagusa kakiwakete tare o tobui no wakana naruramu*) Tobuhi means "Flying-fire." It is a slope on the outskirts of Nara that centuries earlier had been readied with fire-hurling devices to fight off invaders. The poem by 治部＿通俊(助け求む) seems very risqué. But, it is prefaced by comments to the effect that so and so's wife sent greens to the wife of the poet who dutifully waited at home. (And, I have not read enough in that period of Japanese history to tell any more about what was going on, if anything!)

A "castle-toppler" generally meant a beautiful courtesan, but could mean just a prostitute or just a beautiful girl, so it is tough to settle on one reading. My last two de-parsed readings are paraverses where I allowed my heart more freedom than the grammar did. I first imagined a fatherly-like concern for young pluckers, and then, that even harlots might be out plucking greens *and,* while doing so, was probably not a harlot at heart but a maiden dreaming of love. You might note that with this *ku* and some others when "young-green-plucking" is too long to fit, I may drop the "young" or the "pluck."

つまとりや傘をさゝせて若菜つみ　暁台
tsumatori ya kasa o sasasete wakana tsumi　gyôtai - 1792 大全
(~~mate-taker~~[long kimono's] hem/taking:/! parasol[+obj]thrusting young-green-plucker/ing)

~~out for a mate~~　　　　plucking greens　　　　~~trying to pick up~~
~~his umbrella thrust over~~　holding up a long hem　~~girls picking young greens~~
~~a green plucker~~　　　　and a parasol　　　　~~with a parasol~~

~~This makes it apparent that the picking up was informal~~. The pun was more obvious to me than the reality, based on an idiom I only found when proofing. Someone has her hands full while plucking.

有るものを摘め来よ乙女若菜の日　虚子
aru mono o tsume ko yo otome wakananohi　kyoshi 1874-1959
(have-things [obj?/emph?] pluck-come! girls/virgins/maiden/s young-green day)

the invitation

young-green day　　　　　　maidens, just pluck
pluck what there is and come　what you can, and come!
my young maids　　　　　　young-green day

By Kyoshi's day, the maiden of old and the ancient song-fest element of green picking was long-dead. But romance lives forever in the hearts of men, and, to a man, a "maiden" – the connotations of *otome* and *maiden* are remarkably close! – is always exciting. And, even if the festival was not all it once was, it was a good day for men and women to get out and flirt, though one wonders what the young things thought of the idea of plucking and bringing rather than meeting half-way! *Aah,* I misplaced a simple but excellent modern *ku* wondering if the man next door would find a bride on this day.

Sobaku's chapter-head *ku* wonders what it was like in the days of classic poetry. Here is a fine contemporary young-greens *ku* which touches upon an even more ancient past in a novel manner:

古事記には海なる野辺の若菜摘　赤松薫子 講談社大
kojiki ni wa umi naru nobe no wakanatsumi　akamatsu kaoriko 20c
(old-things-record-in, ocean becomes field[-border?]'s young-green-pluck/ing)

young-green-plucking　　　　　　in the old book
in fields where the old book　　these fields were ocean
put an inland sea　　　　　　young-green day

once upon a time
we would have been at sea
picking youngreen

Reading the *ku,* I first imagined Japanese as sea people plucking seaweed from rocks, but rereading more carefully ruled that out. The first translation explains what is what. Place names and other geo-archeological evidence show that large inland bodies of water mentioned in the *Kojiki* (early-8c), generally translated as *The Ancient Chronicle* or *The Record of Ancient Matters* – I shortened it to "the old book" – are now undoubtedly *terra firma*.

若菜摘む人を知る哉鳥静　暁台

wakana tsumu hito o shiru kana tori shizuka　gyôtai -1793
(young-green plucking people[+obj] know 'tis/!/?/: birds quiet)

they know us		they know
out picking greens!		we are plucking greens
quiet birds		quiet birds
	the birds silent	
	they know people pluck	
	young-greens	

From time immemorial, birds have watched us go about our silly business. I (think I) have observed old crows that knew about the quiet dawn of the New Year in Japan explaining things to young crows who unnerved by the silence; and I can imagine that back in a century when the flood of people out into the fields pulling up plants was the more observable anomaly birds of all ages had to take account of it. There are more people-watching birds than bird-watching people.

鶏に一葉ふるまふわかな哉　一茶

niwatori ni hitoha furumau wakana kana　issa 1821
(chicken/s-to/~~with brandish~~ give [a gift, beneficiently] young-leaf 'tis)

~~the chicken~~	one big leaf	~~dancing from~~
~~brandishes one leaf:~~	i give to the chicken	~~hen to hen, a leaf~~
~~young green!~~	young green	~~of young green!~~

Baishitsu, Issa's long-lived contemporary, has *sparrows* cheeping *chiyo chiyo* ("a thousand generations, a thousand generations") to celebrate young green (千代々々と雀もいはふ若菜哉　梅屋 *chiyochiyo to suzume mo iwau wakana kana* -1852), but it is a *ku* to celebrate the birth of a child and not bird-centered. Chickens are hungry, curious and competitive. Reading *furumau* as "brandish," I first imagined a spinach-like leaf moving between chickens with flapping wings and flailing legs. But that was more *me* than Issa. *Furumau* means treating someone to something: *"Young greens / I treat the chicken / to a leaf."* Regardless, it plays against traditional courtly poems as did this next older *ku*.

此門を名乗してゆけ若菜摘　暁台

kono kado o nanori shite yuke wakanatsumi　gyôtai -1793
(this gate[house=family+obj.] name-ride[announce]ing, go! young-green-pluckers/ing)

go thee forth	call out the name
announce our name to all	of this gate as you go forth
youngreen pluckers	green-pluckers

Na-nori is the ancient practice of nobles announcing their names before doing man-to-man combat, as there was no glory in fighting an inferior. Off the battlefield, a martial air is always humorous. I imagine Gyôtai lazily playing general to the rest of the family and servants heading out to the fields to compete for the greens, the young men wearing twisted cloth headbands trussed up smartly.

松かげにならびてうたへ若菜摘　暁台
matsukage ni narabite utae wakanatsumi gyôtai -1793
(pine-shade-in, line-up sing! young-green pluck[ers]!)

new-green day

young pluckers
line up in the pine tree shade
and sing away!

Gyôtai barking orders again! So he followed them out into the field and wants some music as he watches? There were traditional plucking songs, so this, like the last *ku* is also a nod toward the past. I see two pines, one male (black) and one female (red), under which pluckers of their respective genders gather to sing back and forth. I may imagine too much.

とゝははやすめば聲若し若菜歌　嵐雪 -1707
toto haha ya sumeba [yasumeba?] koe wakashi wakana uta　ransetsu
(papa mama:/! finish [or, rest/take-a-break]-if/when] voice/s young green-plucking-song)

papa and mama	when mom and dad	mom and dad
sound youthful after plucking	take a break, youthful voices	their voices youthful after rest
young green songs	young green songs	young green songs

Sumeru (*sumeba*) seems oddly formal here, while *yasumeba* means a 4-8-5 syllabet rhythm. If the latter, the voices could be that of youths or of parents plucking in the morning.

一とせに一度つまるゝ菜づなかな 芭蕉
hitotose ni ichido tsumaruru nazuna kana　又若菜哉　bashô 1644-94
(one-year-in one-time plucked/picked *nazuna* [shepherds-purse/mother's heart]!/'tis)

the *nazuna*
picked only once
per year

The *nazuna* (more on the name in translation next page) was only edible at the beginning of spring, when it was tender – or, at least, tender enough if chopped up and cooked – and, after that, was nothing but a weed. So Bashô is accurate but, according to commentators, discarded this verse (being Bashô, it still survives) because he feared readers might take it in a maudlin way: *"Pity poor Nazuna, only valued on one day per year and otherwise ignored!"* True, but there is also some saving wit. *Nazuna,* as we shall soon see, is strongly identified with "seven," so there is an allusion to the Stars who cross the Milky Way and refresh each other (Twain called *it* "refreshment" in his *Letters From the Earth*) only one night per year, the Seventh Night of the Seventh Moon.

若菜摘野になれそむる袂哉　樗良
wakanatsumi no ni naresomuru tamoto kana chora -1780
(young-green-plucking field-to accustom-start sleeve-bag!/'tis)

young greens	young greens
sleeves touch the field	sleeve bags learning
the first time	about the field

If the poet used the word *sode,* or "sleeves," the *ku* would be a *renga* looking back to *waka* – which is to say, taken as an allusion to a young lover – but the *tamoto* is the lower corner of the sleeve, which served for a pocket. In this sense, the *ku* is for real. Having a part of clothing grow used to something is another story. In old haiku, it is not uncommon for things to have hearts like this. Note that because the *tamoto* is not flush to the body like other pockets, it does not overheat what it carries.

畠から頭巾よぶなり若菜摘　其角
hatake kara zukin yobunari wakanatsumi　kikaku -1707
(garden-from cap[=old-man] calls out young-green-plucking)

old young spring

a capped-head
calls from out in the garden
plucking greens

This *ku* is found in many *saijiki,* for it is subtle yet rich, as good *ku* are supposed to be. The poet has called on an older man's house – perhaps Bashô, never without his cap – and is first noticed and called by the man who was out in the garden plucking greens alone. By cutting out all that romantic old stuff, Kikaku was declaring his new (post-Bashô) poetics: *Get real!* with the contrast of the old-man (indicated by the cap) and the young-green providing *haikai* humor. A garden nearby could save one from traveling to farther fields. Do you recall Kyoshi's *ku* with ten-steps to see sunrise (pg 302)?

炬燵から十足出て摘む若菜哉　也有 改造社
kotatsu kara toashi dete tsumu wakana kana　yayû 1701-83
(heat-table-from ten-steps departing pluck young-green 'tis/!)

c/old spring

taking ten steps
from the heater, i pluck
young-greens

Today, most *kotatsu* are skirted tables with a heater attached beneath but, in Yayû's day, most houses had a pit below the table for the heater and for legs to hang down. They are so comfortable we can see why men stayed still. Issa, who constantly harped on his discomfort in the cold, has his own solution.

温石のさめぬうち也わかなつみ　一茶
onjaku no samenu uchinari wakanatsumi　issa 1763-1827
(warm-stone cools-not during-is young-green-plucking)

young-greens   while my stones
i pluck until my stone   are warm i keep plucking
cools down   young-greens

This pocketable heater was the forerunner of the 20c *kairo,* a little bag of something that is shaken up and stays warm for a half-hour or so, after which it is discarded. Here is another way to stay warm:

君火をたけ我菜をつむも藪の中 沾徳 失出典
kimi hi o take ware na o tsumu mo yabu no naka   sentoku -1726
(you fire[obj.] kindle, i greens[+obj.] pluck-even/though thicket-within)

almost romantic

you kindle a fire
i pluck the greens and all
this in the bush

you light the fire
i pick the greens but the sticks
is still the sticks

There must be some old song or scene where one person kindles while another plucks; the scene is a beautiful valley, not some god-forsaken place. This might be about camping as per the first reading, but it is probably self-deprecation, the saw Issa would later play until the teeth wore off:

酔た手で若菜つむべき雪間かな 萬子
youta te de wakana tsumubeki yuki ma kana   manshi 1653-1719
(drunken hand's-with young-green pluck-ought snow-while!/'tis)

advice for plucking

drunken hands
pluck young greens best
in the snow

we ought to pluck
young greens with drunk hands
under the snow

Not only would *sake* be warming, but the drunken state might help one loosen up and follow the intuition when searching for greens under the snow (something we shall return to later).

七草や油障子に雪の音 庭後 江戸発句集
nanakusa ya abura shôji ni yuki no oto   teigo 18-19c?
(seven grasses!/: oiled [paper] windows/doors-on snow's sound)

seven herb day
on oiled window panes
the sound of snow

Young-greens, not always limited to seven varieties – the number is lucky and alliterative (*nana*) – were gathered on the sixth day of the year, or early in the morning of the seventh, to eat on the seventh day. With the New Year usually coming in what would now be February, just after the coldest part of the year, many early young-green poems mention *snow*, including Akabito's early-8c lament, *"Yesterday, snow, / and now it just keeps falling / upon the fields / we marked for plucking / spring greens, today!* (*asu yori wa~ Manyôshû* #1427) and the most famous plucking *waka* of all: *"For my Ruler's sake / I go out into the fields / where the snow / gets into my sleeves / as I pick young-greens"* (*kimi ga tame haru no no ~* in both *Kokinshû* (early-10c) and the 100 famous songs collection, *Hyakunin-isshû* (13c)) The sassy diva of good taste, Sei Shônagon (born c 965), likewise mentions snow:

> I also enjoy the seventh day, when people pluck the young herbs that have sprouted fresh and green beneath the snow. It is amusing to see their excitement when they find such plants growing near the Palace, by no means a spot where one might expect them. (*The Pillow Book of Sei Shonagon* trans. Ivan Morris)

The snow provided the cover for the herbs to encroach upon the palace, for, as Morris notes, Japanese kept the nearby grounds clear of all wild growth, and that even included grass, considered a weed. [1]

昔より雪を詠みける若菜哉 鶯池
mukashi yori yuki o yomikeru wakana kana ôchi 19-20c?
(oldentimes-from, snow[+obj] read[+emphatic] young-green!/'tis)

from olden times
we have sung of snow
young-greens

霜は苦に雪に楽する若菜かな 嵐雪
shimo wa ku ni yuki ni rakusuru wakana kana ransetsu -1707
(frost-as-for, pain/ snow-in/to pleasant/comfortable have young-green!/'tis)

frost is a bane   frost is a pain
snow is comfortable   snow makes it easy
!young-greens!   young greens!

for young greens
the snow man sure beats
cruel jack frost

Frost not only marks a cold day, but is the kiss of death to most plants it touches. Snow, on the other hand, can be kind to both the pluckers and the plucked. The last translation is clearly over-englished.

つみつみて枯野を戻る若菜かな 蓼太 講談社大
tsumi tsumite kareno o modoru wakana kana ryôta 1707-87
(pluck plucking withered field return young-greens!/'tis)

all plucked out   after plucking
then, back through brown fields   young greens, back through
that's young green!   withered fields

This bleak scene chills more than snow. Haiku aficionados will recall Buson (1715-83) carrying spring onion (a winter crop, but English demands "welsh" or "spring" for such onions), walking down a road by a row of leafless winter trees. On a cold year, the young greens would only be found on south-facing slopes and well-manured plots, so some may have had to do a lot of walking to find them.

雪の戸や若菜ばかりの道一つ 言水
yuki no to ya wakana bakari no michi hitotsu gonsui -1719
(snowy-gate/entrance! young-green only's road single)

a snowy gate   one snowy path
one path for one thing   for young greens alone
young-greens   from my gate

---

1. *No-Lawn Culture* When I lived in Japan, I was surprised at the extent to which my landlord would go to kill all the weeds – including what Usanians would call "grass" – around my cottage, leaving only dirt that turned to mud when it rained. I thought it reflected the desire to keep tenants naked before the landlord's proprietary eye and a farmer's (many landlords in Japan are land-rich farmers) weed-pulling (and poison-sprinkling) instinct, which allows nothing to grow the farmer himself doesn't plant. Reading Frois' 611 contrasts of Japan and Europe written in 1585, I found that the Europeans already liked grassy plazas, where the Japanese pulled up every last bit of green on them. On the whole, I prefer the Japanese approach because I hate the roar of the lawn-mower!

Either the poet spent his New Year as a recluse, or it snowed the night before.

青し青し若菜は青し雪の原　来山
aoshi aoshi wakana wa aoshi yuki no hara   raizan -1715
(blue/green/pale/fresh[x2] young-green-as-for blue[+ditto!] snow-field/belly)

salad days

how soft and green!
young rape soft and green!
on snowy slopes

beautiful green	tender blue
tender young-green	pale young greens
snow meadow	a snowy hill

The proper English for *na* is "rape." I used it once to avoid repeating "green." Because of the obvious problem with this word, today in the USA, it is usually called *rapina* or *canolla*. I trust the reader will understand why I write "young green" rather than "young rapina" or "young canolla!" The *ku* is faintly erotic in Japanese, for "meadow" is *hara,* a word homophonic with "belly." English body-language does not include a topological "belly." As "field" seems too barren, I added some curves. *Ao* (*aoi/aoishi*) cannot be fully Englished. It is light blue or green, the standard color for new leaves.

若菜摘む手や袖縁の紅の色　支考
wakana tsumu te ya sodefuchi no beniniro   shikô -1731
(young-green plucking hand: sleeve-edge's vermillion color)

a hand plucking
young greens – her sleeve
of crimson hem

A white hand and forearm darting in and out of a crimson opening. Sexual allusion can not be denied. But it is less important than the fact that the red color will make the faint green of the young plants brighter and more visible to onlooker poet and plucker alike! Since many Japanese turn beet red when they drink, Manshi's advice to drink when you pluck may also owe something to this effect.[1]

---

1. *Red and Green.* The Sinosphere has long had a more sophisticated understanding of color physiology than our psychologists, with their faulty tests showing the effect of individual colors, and of color aesthetics than our well-meaning architecture of "natural" earth-colors. While it is a fact that if red or green (or other colors) are allowed to fill your visual field, they will indeed affect you as scientists say they will (raising/lowering blood-pressure, heart-beat, adrenaline, etc.), it is *also* a fact that a little bit of one color can enhance its opposite. A hat with a red rim will make nature look greener, not deaden it, as our hats with supposedly "soothing" green inside do. Our environmentalists (?) tend to paint railings and other trimmings green "to blend in with nature," with the result that the less perfect green of the surrounding landscape looks pale, while traditional design in the Sinosphere uses red or vermillion trimmings which enhance the appearance of natural green. We know about complementary colors, but oddly fail to realize the *significance* they have for color-psychology, clothing design and landscaping!

草履道一筋明けてつみ菜哉　三徑 桃首途
zôrimichi hitosuji akete tsumi-na kana sankei 1728
(zori[grass-sandal]-road one-line open/ed/ing pluck-rape!/'tis)

a vein opens
this sandal path must be
for the greens

a single lane
open for sandal traffic
green-plucking

若菜摘けふより花の道廣し　千代女
wakanatsumi kyô yori hana no michi hiroshi chiyojo -1775
(young-rape-plucking/ers today-from blossom-road/s wide)

young
green pluckers
from today, the path
to the blossoms is broad

The word "blossom" here can only mean one thing to Japanese, cherry blossoms and that means cherry-blossom viewing and, after that, the end of spring. Chiyojo depicts the young-green pluckers as *seasonal trail-blazers*. Another version has "close" (*chikashi*) instead of "wide" (*hiroshi*).

足にまだふむ草はなし若菜摘　也有
ashi ni mada fumu kusa wa nashi wakanatsumi   yayû 1701-83
(foot/feet-to still-tread/ing grass/herb-as-for not, young-rape-plucking/ers)

plucked-out

no more herbs
for our feet to tread
young green

In some places, the first edible herbs were pretty much the only thing underfoot.

硝子に酒の減る日や若菜摘　玉波 鶉たち
biidoro ni sake no heru hi ya wakanatsumi gyokuha 1751
(glass-flask-in sake's reduce-day:/! young-green plucker/ing)

i see less *sake*
in the bottle today
green plucking

I am not sure this *ku* suggesting possible inebriation should be capped with the next:

転んでも目出度いふ也わかなつみ 一茶
koronde mo medeta iu nari wakanatsumi issa 1822
(falling-even festive/joyous becomes: young-green plucking)

the best part of plucking

taking a tumble
is something to celebrate
young green day

Because both "pluck" and the word for "falling/stumbling/tumbling" have sexual connotations, this might be called a facetiously sexual poem. Issa wrote it at age 60 (I guess breaking your hip this way would be something like dying while doing it.). A couple years later, this aging goat (The number of refreshments Issa and his wife enjoyed, as recorded in his journal, are impressive) found a butt-print and declared it belonged to [Ono-no] Komachi, the famous poet of love poems and slang for a high-strung, or should I say, *snotty*, young beauty, out plucking greens! To wit:

尻餅の迹は小町がわかなつみ 一茶
shirimochi no ato wa komachi ga wakanatsumi issa 1824
(butt-rice-cake[rump]-print-as-for/? / komachi [is] young-green-plucking)

this butt print? i'd say a classic beauty plucked greens	this butt print looks like a spoiled beauty plucking greens

There is an idiom, "to hit one's rear/buttocks' *mochi*," meaning to slip and fall. It normally has no especially erotic connotation; but when a print is involved and that is coupled with the name of the long-dead poetess (who legend has it died a virgin, some say for lack of a tenth hole to consummate the love she poeticized), or idiom for a young beauty, the white skin of the sweet rice-cake and whoever made that print come alive. We also must imagine that the print is in snow rather than mud. This is more surreal and erotic than most of Issa's *ku*.

爪紅の雪を染めたる若菜かな 泉鏡花
tsumabeni no yuki o sometaru wakana kana kyôka -1939
([finger]nail-crimson/polish snow dyes young-green!/?/'tis)

fingernail rouge
has dyed the snow
young-greens!

Until reading this poem, I had not known of a nail polish that, like rouge, could run! Since the mere mention of snow and young greens makes it clear we are not talking about farming, the "plucking" need not be stated. I would have preferred a first-person poem, but such romantic mannerism was, as astute readers might guess, largely a male thing. If you see the woman in the act of plucking there is little difference between this and Shikô's crimson sleeve-mouth we read earlier. It is best to imagine the poet puzzled at some red in the snow, and pleased to solve the mystery!

★

大雪の旦若菜をもらひけり　白雄
ôyuki no ashita wakana o moraikeri   shirao 1735-92
(big[heavy]snow morning/holiday young-greens [i] receive(+emph))

a heavy snowfall
this morning i'm *given*
my young greens

There are many *ku* about young greens obtained by other ways than the correct one (finding them in the field), for *haijin* enjoyed confessing their sins against tradition.

七草や八百屋が帳のつけはじめ　汶村 松風彦根体
nanakusa ya yaoya ga chô no tsukehajime   bunson – 1713?
(7-herbs!/: 800-shop[green-grocer]'s ledger's mark/account-start)

seven herbs:
the green grocer chalks up
his first sale

While the ideal was getting out into nature and finding greens for oneself, it was probably rare if not impossible for anyone to find all seven herbs.

我がために出る春の野や若菜売　千代尼
waga tame ni deru haru no no ya wakana-uri   chiyo-ni 1701-75
(my=his/her-ownself-for go out [into] spring field/meadows: young-green-seller)

for her own sake   for her own sake
plucking in the spring field   out in the spring field
the *wakana* seller   the *wakana* seller

This is a made-to-order poem on the theme "young-green-sellers," but gutsy for playing with the first line from the famous plucking *waka*: "for *[my] ruler's sake*" (*kimi-ga tame* pg.393). At first, I thought the "my" meant for Chiyo's sake, but, in that case she would probably have used a more polite form of the verb, so I changed my reading to "her own sake." Still, I cannot tell if Chiyo means the young-green-seller is out there plucking for him- or herself (or themselves) or that they are out there selling the greens for the same. I prefer the former reading, which makes this *ku* similar to the one about the plucking harlots. It is more enchanting that way. A *Mutamagawa senryû* from the same period:

我が春を二本は残す小松売　武玉川 十七
waga haru o nihon wa nokosu komatsu uri   mutamagawa *senryû*
(my spring[+obj] two-pieces leave-over *komatsu[na]*-seller late-18c)

the *komatsu* girl
sets aside *nihon* (two)
for *her* spring

Komatsu(na) is one name for a radish-bottomed Chinese cabbage (*Brassica Rapa var. pervidis*), one of the seven herbs. It also happens to be written "small-pine" and that suggests the two pines stood up at the gate for the New Year and the counter *nihon* sounds the same as the sun's origin.

もらっても済むべきものを摘む薺　梅室 アルス
moratte mo sumu beki mono o tsumu nazuna　baishitsu 1768-1852
(received[as gift]-even suffice/end-ought-thing[+contrad.] pluck mother's heart/shepherd's purse)

receiving them
as a gift should do, but i pick
shepherd's purse

i am presented
shepherd's purse, why then
pick one myself?

Was Shepherd's Purse, or Mother's Heart, as *nazuna* is translated, particularly lucky to pluck because the two *na* combine as *nana*, or "seven"? I hope the pun I could not resist was not too vulgar.

七草や数を合せに隣から　多代女
nanakusa ya kazu o awase ni tonari kara　tayojo 1775-1865
(seven-herbs!/: [full]number[+obj]gather/match-to/for neighbor-from)

seven herbs
including a number
from next door

seven herbs
with the neighbor's help
they add up

Getting an herb or two next door isn't really like buying them. Who could criticize this?

摘みに出たあとに買ひおく若菜哉　梅室 アルス
tsumi ni deta ato ni kai-oku wakana kana　baishitsu 1768-1852
(plucking-to left afterwhich, buy-keep young-green!/'tis)

while i'm out
plucking, she buys a set
of young-greens

after going out
to pluck them you buy
young greens

while she's out
plucking, i buy a set
of young-greens

At first, I thought the *ku* suggests both a lack of confidence in the plucking ability of one's partner, and consideration for them (a sort of insurance policy). But, the middle reading is also possible.

小わらはの物は買ひよきわかなかな　召波
kowarawa no mono wa kai yoki wakana kana　shôha -1771
(small child/ren's ones-as-for, buy good, young-green 'tis)

the best thing
is buying from a tyke
young greens

if you'd buy,
buy from a little child
young greens

It is more auspicious, for a small child metaphysically fits the start of the year, *and* who doesn't want a poor child to sell out quickly and return home?

賤が子は薺見る目のかしこさよ　杉風
shizu ga ko wa nazuna miru me no kashikosa yo　sampû 1646-1732
(impoverished child/ren shepherd's purse looking eye's intelligence!)

what intelligence
in the eyes of poor children
spotting young greens!

The tiny "shepherd's purse" or "mother's heart" is distinctive. Lying flat on the ground, it is the perfect plant for a child to spot. I wanted a shorter *"How wise / a poor child's eyes / spotting greens!"* but "wise" seemed too deep. "How clever" or "how cunning" / the eyes of . . ." would err in the opposite direction. So, I stuck with the unpoetically long word "intelligence." I was tempted to pun *"How bright the eyes / of a poor child picking / shepherd's purse,"* or something worse with the "mother's heart," but felt that so specific and dramatic a name would detract from the overall idea. Both this and the following *ku* by Issa bring out the Easter egg hunt-like search element that made it a game for most involved. Even, I would guess, for children who did it as work.

負た子が先へ指すわかな哉 一茶 文化十一
ôta ko ga saki e yubi sasu wakana kana   issa 1763-1827
(carried[on back] child ahead finger points young-green!/'tis)

piggyback
a child points ahead
young green!

We don't know whether this child's mother was picking for herself and her family or for extra income.

きのふ迄毎日見しを若菜かな 一茶
kinô made mainichi mishi o wakana kana   issa 1763-1827
(yesterday-until every day [i] saw [+contrary emotive] young-green!/'tis)

damn!
until this morning
i saw them every day
young greens

Issa saw them everywhere when he didn't need them, but now, when he wants them, he either cannot recall where they are, or has lost them to an early-bird.

わかなのや一葉摘んでは人をよぶ 一茶
wakana no ya hito ha tsunde wa hito o yobu   issa -1827
([a] young-green field! one-leaf plucked-as-for people[obj] call)

wakana field	a young green!
i pluck one leaf and	he plucks one leaf and calls
call everyone	the world to see

Or "*she* plucks one leaf / and calls the world." Please translate as you see it. The first-person is the default reading for a haiku, and Issa does have good *ku* about his public (?) behavior, of which my favorite has him, self-declared man of leisure, walking down the street announcing the arrival of . . . the mosquitoes! But, I like this *ku* in the third-person. Regardless, the question is whether calling out is an altruistic act by one who has discovered a patch of green in an otherwise bleak field or a boastful one, advertising one's prowess as a hunter of vegetable matter, or a scavenger without equal?

摘む人の傍に寄り若菜摘む　温亭
tsumu hito no katawara ni yori wakana tsumu   ontei -1926
(plucking person's side-to-approaches, young-green plucks)

<blockquote>
pulling alongside
of a plucker to pluck
young greens
</blockquote>

Is searching for young-greens like gold-mining (if it looks like someone has hit pay-dirt, you stop looking around and stake out a claim next to theirs)? An Easter egg hunt (properly done with the eggs well-hidden; not a race to grab plastic eggs littering the ground such as I saw in a park on Key Biscayne in 2005)? Or, fishing (you take interest in the catch of others and enjoy the comradery, even as you compete)?

七くさや欲にもけふのよくばかり　千代尼
nanakusa ya yoku ni mo kyô no yoku bakari   chiyoni 1701-75
(seven herbs:/! desire/avarice/greed-to-even, today's desire only)

the seven herbs among the various greeds only today's		the seven herbs our desires are many but today just one

seven herbs

<blockquote>
in greed too
one greed at a time
pluck today
</blockquote>

Chiyo's *ku* was written after she became a nun; but even before adopting the cloth (gaining the freedom to travel and be her own woman), she would have been able to list the various types of *yoku* desire/ greed, Buddhism had evolved on paper – less *primitive* than the crude coveting-your-neighbor's-home-ass-and-wife stuff carved into the stone of Judeo-Christian-Islamity (one must wait for the writings of some saints to find mature analysis of morality in Occidental monotheism [pardon my generalizing]). Had Chiyo-ni only noted that there was greed in plucking greens, the *ku* would be so-and-so, but here she implies either that we have room for only one desire – *Does that make it "pure" and does such monomaniacal behavior free us of other desires?* (Remember Somaru's prescript for his New Year's Day *ku* (*It shines first / on faces that don't lie . . .* = page 263), *i.e.,*: *"great* greed resembles *no* greed"?) or, that this desire for health was the only *acceptable* desire. Regardless, I admire Chiyo's guts, for, even in her day, thought in haiku, *haikai,* or whatever you call it, was subject to criticism, yet she did not censure her hyperlogical mind.

雪の下にある七草や七ふしぎ　重頼
yuki no shita ni aru nanakusa ya nanafushigi   shigeyori
(snow's below-at are seven-herbs! seven wonders 1601-1680)

seven herbs underneath the snow! seven wonders	seven wonders: seven herbs growing below the snow

It is indeed surprising to find tender green things alive under the snow. The sap of some leaves has sugars that serve as antifreeze. These leaves not only bear up to the relatively kind snow but even frost, which has the strange ability to cling to and wither many leaves at temperatures above freezing. In Japan, Seven Wonders were generally of this or that locality rather than " ~ of the World."

こゝらかと雪にこと問若菜かな 千代
kokora ka to yuki ni koto tou wakana kana   chiyo -1775
(here-abouts? snow-to ask: young-greens!/'tis)

i ask the snow
if i'm getting warmer:
young-greens

'round about here?
today, we question snow:
young greens!

Perhaps I should have resisted the English idiom used in the first reading, but considering the wit lost in translation, I do not feel it is completely uncalled for. This *ku* and the next few show the personal style that makes Chiyo, like Issa, *exceptionally lovable*.

七草や雪を払へばそれでなし 千代
nanakusa ya yuki o haraeba sore de nashi chiyo-ni
(seven-plants: snow brush-off when, that [it is] not)

young green day

one of the seven?
when i brush the snow off
it's something else

The version in the Kaizôsha *saijiki* ends *sore-de yoshi,* meaning "that's fine/enough." I think it is wrong, but it could plausibly be understood as *"All seven greens: /brush off the snow / and* voila!*"* where she has bought them and put them out to catch just enough white-stuff to look natural. Or as *"Seven greens / i'm happy just to brush / the snow off them,"* where she would just enjoy the hunt without actually plucking her vegetable game. But any *yoshi* reading is unlikely when we consider her other poems, such as

行かばあるやうにいそぐや若菜摘 千代
yukaba aru yô ni isogu ya wakanatsumi   chiyo -1775
(go-if are[exist] like, hurry: young-green-plucking)

spring pluckers

so off we rush
as if those young greens
are really there!

Or, more baldly: it is *"Nothing at all! / You talk about a snow job! / young greens!"* (置かぬものたつねて雪乃ワかな哉 千代*okanu mono* [1] *tazunete yuki no wakana kana*), where the Japanese idiom more appropriately connotes things like searching a shelf/dresser for something that turns out not to be in it.[1] Yet, for all of that, or *because* of all of that (people, like pigeons, play longer when there is some chance element, i.e. failure, rather than purely positive re-enforcement) plucking greens was, in a gentle way, thrilling. Chiyo once pouted *"These legs that / would wait for blossoms: / young greens!"* *"These legs that / even hate walking to blossoms: / young greens?"* (花までは（消：花にまで）出惜しむ足を若菜哉　千代*hana made wa de-oshimu ashi o wakana kana*) – the last part, possibly puns on *baka-na kana* or, *how foolish!* Chiyo was nicely rounded, corpulent perhaps, and evidently did not like to walk very far. But she could not help going out on plucking day. Her many young green *ku* prove she really got into the activity.   This next *ku* is my favorite of her many plucking *ku*.

1. *Okanu mono: Placed-not-shelf-search* I believe a modern translation (the first translation of this *ku* to date?) is off: *"Not having planted them / I must search for young greens / in the snow."* I assume the translators could not find the *okanu tana sagashi* idiom, and assumed the verb *okanu* "not placed/situated" meant "not planted." So did I in an earlier translation, and my respondent, not knowing that, wrote: "I felt the poet was amused that she was seeking something she did not place herself." When we search desperately, it is usually for things we, ourselves, lost. Perhaps, her wit can be captured like this: *"Trying to find / something I did not misplace / young-greens in snow."* However, haiku poets rarely take idiom in vain. Chiyo probably means this particular search was futile.

雪礫返す間もなし若菜摘 千代
yukitsubute kaesu ma mo nashi wakanatsumi chiyo 1701-75
(snowball return space[interval/time] even not, young green plucking)

raincheck

plucking greens,
i've no time to return
your snowball!

young green

just too busy
to return fire: the pluckers
eat snowballs

young-play, anyone?

my snowball's
only response: "we're busy
plucking greens!"

The first interpretation makes the poem a spontaneous response, perhaps shouted aloud to the culprit, but I suspect my second interpretation is the most likely. Still, I *want* to think our witty nun is the one throwing the snowball as in my third version. The original voice/quote *vs.* description

手の跡を雪のうけとる若菜かな 千代
te no ato o yuki no uketoru wakana kana chiyo -1775
(hand-print/s snow receive-takes [a receipt] young-green 'tis)

the snow accepts
our handprints when we
take young greens

voucher

the snow takes
our handprints for
the young green

your snow took
my hand-print for each
young green

Thinking of so-called primitives who drop gift gems or coins into holes left by pulled out plants as payment, I first read barter into this: *You take my handprint, I take your produce.* But the combination of the print, a common signature for goods bought on credit, and the verb *uketoru,* meaning to receive something in a formal, if not legal way, suggests a modern economy. The last reading imagines Chiyo plucked on private property. Regardless, I believe this a good example of the light humor in which she excelled. Bashô realized in his last years that *karumi,* or a light touch, was harder to master than one might imagine, and a respectable pursuit in poetry. Had he lived longer, Bashô might have pointed out the positive role of logic in composing such *ku.*

NOT ALWAYS SNOW

土べたに子を這せおく菜摘哉 素丸 アルス
tsuchi beta ni ko o hawase-oku natsumi kana somaru 1712-95
(earth-flush-on[?], child/ren crawl-allows-leave greens plucking!/'tis)

    letting children   a child allowed
crawl about in the dirt   to crawl on bare earth
      green picking   mother's heart

The young-green hunt was not always snowbound or cold. There was hospitable spring weather. Japanese, even children, usually *never* make direct contact with the dirt unless stepping in the muck of their rice paddies. They do not want to dirty the *tatami*. So this is primal indeed. My second reading takes extreme poetic license to turn the unspecified greens into *mother's heart*.

みどり子の土一つかみ薺かな 素丸 素丸句集
midorigo no tsuchi hito tsukami nazuna kana   somaru
(infant-child's earth-one-grab, shepherd's purse!/?/'tis)

an infant child
grabs a handful of dirt
mother's heart

The folk etymology for the representative herb of the seven, *nazuna* (shepherd's purse or mother's heart) includes "carress-green," "because it is so dear." Could that, rather than the appearance mentioned earlier, be why young green often come with a child? "Mother's Heart" is almost too good here! Is the child doing a poor imitation of adult plucking? Or, is the plant so tiny dirt predominates?

高低にわかるゝ道や芹薺 梅室 アルス
takahiku ni wakaruru michi ya seri nazuna   baishitsu 1768-1852
(high-low-into split/s road/s:/! seri [dropwort], nazuna [mother's heart])

the road splits
high and low, mother's heart
and dropwort

Seri, "Japanese parsley" or *Oenanthe javanica* according to my dictionary, is only found in soggy culverts. More aromatic than parsely, it is also called water-cress. Fresh as mint, it is more elegant than either. The beautiful shiny, straight and very strong white roots belie the muck they grow in as plainly as the flower of the lotus. I never threw away the roots without first standing them upside down in my coffee grinds and enjoying my kitchen sink installation for a day or two. I would write more, but if you know the plant, you don't need a description and if you do not, it might bore you (オマケ＝西行も芹根数寄＝「かつすぐ沢のこぜりのねをしろみきよげに物をおもはずもがな」).

The Big Two

high and low
all paths split
seri - nazuna

I will not try to describe all seven herbs, for only botanists care for what they have not eaten (pictures are the exception to this rule, perhaps we can do better in a future "dream" edition), but Chiyo did make one observation too obvious not to be interesting: *"Of seven herbs / the one that doesn't match / is the turnip"* 七草に似合ぬものは蕪かな　千代　*nana kusa ni niawanu mono wa kabura kana* -1775. A little turnip with an upturned root would be particularly auspicious for pun reasons, but it is true that it is the odd guy out of the set.

畠の門錠の明けりわかなつみ 一茶
hata no kado jô no akikeri wakanatsumi   issa -1827
(plot=garden-gate/s lock opened[+emph] young-green-plucking)

<blockquote>
the garden gate
is left unlocked
young-green day
</blockquote>

Most of Japan, like the rest of the land in the world, was occupied by someone, but Issa's haiku suggests that on this day the whole country was restored to its original undivided self, a beach, free to walk and hunt. The *hata* or *hatake* is larger than a garden and actually means a plot of land used for farming. English lacks such a word and can only speak of fields of corn or fields of wheat or watermelon, etc. But, in the early 19c, not all people had access to the fields:

江戸芥の山をゑりはりわかな哉 一茶
edo gomi/akuta no yama o eriwari wakana kana   issa
(edo trash-mountain/s[+obj] select-dividing, young-green!/'tis)

<blockquote>
divvying up   divvying up
edo's mount trashmore   the trash piles of edo
young greens   young greens
</blockquote>

Edo in Issa's time was the most populated city in the world and there were parts where people could walk miles with little greenery visible (most was behind walls). I assume this means many of the poor lacked gardens, and couldn't get to the country or afford to buy the greens. With Issa, realism even comes to the New Year. I borrow the name of the mountain in the first reading from the only literally natural high in Miami. Someone previous to Issa described a poor mother and child searching through refuge for the seven herbs, but I am afraid I have lost the *ku*.

大原や人留めのある若菜つみ 一茶
ôhara ya hitodome no aru wakanatsumi   issa
(big-field:/! people-jam is young-green-plucking)

<blockquote>
at meadowbig!
traffic comes to a stop:
green plucking
</blockquote>

Is Ôhara, here, the name of the largest meadow near Issa (Japanese natural features can, like "main street" in English, be a proper name), or *the* Ôhara of historical romance, with women known for their unique culture, heading huge bundles of brushwood and firewood for Kyôto? If so, do authorities stop them because there would be collisions on the trail with the amateur and professional greens vendors out to hunt greens, or block commoners and allow the nobles to monopolize the field? Or, is this a naturally made traffic jam? Less likely, Issa might mean "people-stopping women" (人留女), or women who sold their favors are out, too. Regardless, the number of people in fields near crowded cities must have been *huge*. Unlike blossom-viewing, which went on for weeks, here they had only a day or two. If the weather was good, I imagine *everyone* headed for the fields on the morning of the 6th. What an exodus that must have been! Chiyo notes *herons* fled the field (人あしに鷺も消るやわかなの野　千代 *hito-ashi ni sagi mo kiyuru ya wakana no no* [the *hito* written "people" and combined with "leg" meaning large numbers of us but punning *hito-ashi* = "one-leg," what herons often stand on]) and of *cranes* drawn by the human presence/commotion (人音を鶴もしたふて若菜かな　千代女　改造社　*hito-oto o shitôte wakana kana*). Here is another bird *ku*, though, as you will see in the next chapter, the image may have been a figment of my imagination (I was delighted this reading and explanation, and leave them as is):

七種や跡にうかるゝ朝からす 其角
nanakusa ya ato ni ukaruru asagarasu　kikaku -1707　講談社大
(seven-herbs:/! afterward floating/excited/crazed/tipsy morning-crow/s)

<table>
<tr><td>

seven herbs
followed by a tipsy
morning crow

</td><td>

i am followed
by an excited crow
seven herbs

</td></tr>
</table>

A crow is an animal requiring as much if not more thrills than your average human. Hence they roll in ant-hills to get high. Seeing people swarming about and pulling up things revealing bugs and roots and dropping trash and whatnot, they would be delirious with excitement and follow about in the fields like dolphins playing on the wake of a ship. The verb in the original is a form of "to float" that is used for cats in heat or for anyone crazed with passion.

我が事と鯲の逃げし根芹哉　丈草
waga koto to dojô no nigeshi nezeri kana　jôsô
(my thing, loach flees/fled dropwort!/?/'tis -1704)

thinking he was game
the loach flees:
dropwort!

Today, this *ku* is generally found in the Spring, not New Year section of the *saijiki*, but the *seri*=dropwort is one of the seven herbs and the fact people are out pulling up the plant where that is not usual (hence the surprised fish) suggests a New Year, i.e., Young-green Day designation would be better. My dictionary calls the *ne-zeri,* or root-seri, "a parsley whose roots may be eaten," but my large *saijiki* simply includes it with the other *seri*. For now, I will just let it be *dropwort*.

おもひかね階子をかけて根芹哉 素丸
omoikane hashigo o kakete nezeri kana　somaru 1712-95
(think-cannot, ladder placing/leaning[on something] dropwort!/?/'tis)

it boggles the mind
using a ladder to go
after dropwort

We think of ladders as useful for reaching things in high places; but, here, one serves to descend into a riverbed. The surprise shows that Somaru did not invent it but observed a professional dropwort hunter, someone with big baskets full of it, carrying a ladder and asked him or her what it was for.

かすむ程たばこ吹きつゝ若菜つみ 一茶
kasumu hodo tabako fuki tsutsu wakanatsumi issa -1827
(mist-over enough tobacco smoke-while young-green-plucking)

    smoking enough   *we smoke enough*   plucking greens
to make a fine spring haze   *to make our own spring haze*   she smokes enough to make
     i pluck my greens   *plucking young green*   a spring haze

Mist or haze, as noted in Book I, is a sign of Spring and the New Year. Before adding the "our" reading, I titled it *"Young Weather"* as the "young" did not fit before the greens. Were young-greens so plentiful Issa (who dabbled in tobacco sales), his wife, or both, could afford to fiddle with his/her/their pipe/s? Or, was going slow the whole idea?

精出して摘むとも見えぬ若菜哉　野水
sei dashite tsumu to mo mienu wakana kana yasui 1657-1743
(energy/spurt-put-out pluck [at all] appears-not young-green/s!/'tis)

    no one picking   doesn't look like
seems too energetic   anyone is going all out
     young green   young greens

Most plants events, such as rice planting and buckwheat harvesting, or even more informal *daikon* (5 lb radish) pulling tended to be *competitive*, but this, alone, was done in a leisurely way. Could the poet, who lived into his eighties, be suggesting that the secret to staying young is taking one's time?

朝の間に摘みてさびしき若菜かな　白雄
asa no ma ni tsumite sabishiki wakana kana shirao -1792
(morning-within plucked lonely young-greens!/?/'tis)

     young greens   ***the long wait***

   plucking done   plucked early
by noon: how lonely   the young green has
the rest of the day!   a lonely look

Have you heard of the proverbial Mexican peasant who refuses to sell all of her wares to a rich gringo for it would leave her in the market with no goods to enjoy squabbling over for the rest of the day? Some poets neither slowed down nor quit. But the *ku* is a bit better than that, for all who have gotten up early and accomplished things know that, despite feeling good about having done this, it is hard to avoid the lassitude that sets in about noon. Moreover, the plucked greens might themselves lose some of their green blush if they are unwisely taken inside. A wilting leaf is a good picture of loneliness. There may also be an ever-so-light allusion to a master-servant love affair, though it is unlikely.

竹かごにすこしあるこそわかな哉　一茶
takekago ni sukoshi aru koso wakana kana issa 1763-1827
(bamboo-basket-in [a] little/few are more-than-anything young-green!/'tis)

a bamboo basket
far from filled: *that*
is young-greens!

Coming from a farm background, Issa knew that farmers came in from the field with huge heaps of produce. *This* was not work. It was a different game. A bamboo basket looks good and would usually be used for heavy fruit because it is strong. The loose weave would allow some of the small greens to drop and that, too, might be seen as propitious: is not *affluence* a flow?

OLD FOLK AND YOUNG GREEN

おのれ老人なれば 女衆に出し抜れつゝつむわかな 一茶 文政一
onore rôjin nareba // onnashu ni dashi-nukaretsutsu tsumu wakana   issa 1818
(myself old-man becoming // woman-crowd-by passed (beat to the punch)-while pluck young-green)

myself, an old man

left behind
by the women i pluck
my young greens

women folk
beat me to the punch
plucking greens

老かつむ若菜を人のもらひける 士郎
oi ga tsumu waka-na o hito no moraikeru   shirô 1742-1813
(elderly picked young-greens [other] people receive [+finality])

others enjoy
the young greens plucked
by the elderly

others enjoy
the fruit of old hands
young green

young-greens
an old man plucks end up
with another

Old Issa sometimes had trouble walking – gout, lumbago, stroke or some disease I read about and forgot – so he would not be exaggerating. Yet, despite bad joints and worse eyes, elders could often out-pluck their children, for, unlike most fieldwork, which required brute strength, finding half-wild greens was a wisdom-intensive activity.   And, the old folk had something many of the young lacked: *time*. Shirô, a poet Issa briefly worked for, has done the old people of the world a service in pointing this out. At the same time, as per the last reading, he may be boasting about *his* success as a match-maker – and a bit jealous of the lucky groom! Shirô also wrote a more poetic *ku* on this subject:

若菜摘は鳩なくところ／＼哉 士郎
wakanatsumi wa hato naku tokorodokoro kana   shirô -1813
(young-green plucking-as-for dove crying/singing places-places 'tis/!/?)

young green plucking
the places here and there
where doves coo

The dove was, if I am not mistaken, associated with loneliness and calling (trapping?) doves was considered work for old men (it took no teeth to hoot). Doves, like cats, have an uncanny way of finding pleasantly warm, quiet spots. Men who live long may share some of that natural wisdom.

道くさも数（藪）のうちなり若菜摘　千代女
michigusa mo kazu (yabu?) no uchinari wakanatsumi chiyo-jo 1701-75
(road-grass[i.e.dawdling] too, numbers among become young-green-plucking)

getting off track
is part of tracking
young greens

diversion counts
as we fill our sleeves
with seven herbs

the diversions
are part of plucking
young greens

The idiom for dawdling around, "eating grass along the road," plays upon the fact young-green are also called "*nana-kusa,* or "seven grasses/herbs" and the idiom used to show the idea of "inclusion" plays on that "seven," by speaking of "number/s." Kôdansha's *saijiki* has *number* = 数 as *thicket* = 藪.

in praise of thickets

our diversion, too
found off the beaten track
young green plucking

This may be a typo, but there is some sense to it and Chiyo often had more than one version of her *ku.* Since the character for thicket has the "grass" radical over number, the typo might even be her joke!

此七日若菜より野のなつかしき　也有
kono nanuka wakana yori no no natsukashiki yayû 1701-83
(this seventh day, young-greens more-than field/meadow's [satisfying] nostalgia)

fields of nostalgia

this seventh day
the greens move me less
than the memories

on this seventh day
the young-greens mean less than
being back out here!

on the seventh
young greens are beaten
by memories

Specific "this" or not, Yayû's *ku* holds a general truth. For all but those people who love the meadows, this *is* what young greens are about! If Japanese lack a word like the English "miss" – as in *missing* home, some food, or a friend – English lacks a single word to express the joy of meeting up with or even hearing about something we miss, whether we thought about it or not. I wrote "[satisfying] nostalgia" for lack of a better term. The exclamation *natsukashii,* adjective *natsukashi* and state of *natsukashisa* cannot be translated. Moreover, because the order of the things compared is reversed in English and Japanese, in the original, the more *natsukashi* fields (*no*) come *after* the young-greens (*wakana*). Since the fields are less likely to be featured than the greens on the seventh, it is more interesting that way for keeping the surprise for last. Unfortunately, retaining the order requires "less than" rather than "more than" in English, which gives an ever-so-slight negativity to the *ku* which is undesireable for the New Year. "More than" can be kept by reversing the order:

this seventh day
i savor the fields more
than the greens

In language, unlike math, the Law of Commutation does not always work. The above seems to, but what about the next?

七草や内より春は外の物　桃仙 桃の首途
nanakusa ya uchi yori haru wa soto no mono　tôsen　1728
(seven-plants! inside-more-than spring-as-for outside-thing)

seven-green-day
less spring is found
inside than out

look *out* not *in*
for the thing called spring:
seven-green-day!

At first, I kept the order, translating *"Seven-green day! / Spring is more an outside / than inside thing."* It is not only boring but sounds bad. Then, I made "seven-green-day" the title and maintained the original order using a fancy construction of "less" to get: *"Not so much / an inside as an outside / thing: spring."* The last line's "thing: spring" is interesting, but, as a whole, the *ku* still fails. So I came up with the above creative readings to cover the loss inherent to reversing the order.

不断見る野なりながらわかな哉　一茶
fudan miru no nari nagara wakana kana　issa　1763-1827
(non-stop[ordinarily] see fields being-while/form-while: young-greens!/'tis)

these old fields
so familiar, but today
young greens!

This simple *ku* written less than two years before Issa's death is a natural. His hometown fields seem something more than the place where farmers shed their blood, sweat, tears and excrement. On this day, they are enchanted and the young greens are rabbits pulled like magic from the hat. The words "old" and "today" are not found in the original. I felt they were needed to give the right feel to the translation. When exotic tongues are involved and poems must be re-created from scrap, the translator needs the same poetic license as any other poet does.

七草や目に新たなる草の色　五空 改造社
nanakusa ya me ni aratanaru kusa no iro　gokû　-1928
(seven plants! eyes-in renew plants/grasses/weeds' color/appeal)

seven greens:
plant color is restored
to our eyes

Or, "~renewed / in our eyes." What we call "green" encompasses a rainbow of variations. By specifying the "seven" plants, rather than the collective "young greens," our mind's eye is drawn to this variety and the subtle shades of green. Since the term *arata-naru* (renew/restore/afresh) usually modifies the (New) Year, here, by association, it celebrates a sort of green New Year for the eyes, which complements the rising of the red sun of the first day. And, as always, the "color" contains a hint of something else that might be called eros, or appeal.

A PARADOX OF PLENTY

つみすてゝ踏付けがたき若な哉　路通 猿蓑
tsumisutete fumitsukegataki wakana kana　rotsû 1691
(pluck-abandoning tread-on-difficult young-green/s!'tis)

i find myself
not stepping on the greens
i, plucking, left

over-plucking:
ditched greens are hard
to step upon

a green plucked
and left stops my foot
in mid-step

At first glance, this *ku* seems what Chiyo's famous morning glory *ku* (see Introduction) is accused of being, *too* precious. I, for one, cannot recall ever getting carried away and harvesting more of anything than I could take home and eat. But, I can recall taking care not to step on something I had thinned, though logic would dictate that it would be kinder to put the plant out of its misery than leave it to slowly dry up and die. For some reason, you let them lie in peace or hope against hope that someone or something else – even your enemy the peanut-blossom gobbling rabbit – will get them while they are still fresh. So the *ku* is not precious, but simply a very fine observation and a classic example of what haiku are (perhaps, better to ponder than that damn frog plop).

戻りには目もふところやわかなつみ　千代
modori ni wa me mo futokoro ya wakana tsumi　chiyo 1701-75
(return-on-as-for eyes and pocket[=breast+sleeves]! young-green-plucking[=load])

satiated with spring

on the way back
eyes and robes stuffed
with young green!

Eyes can be bigger than pockets, even when one's entire garment above the waist is a huge pocket. [1] Chiyo is probably punning on the homophonic *tsumi*, where 摘み = "pluck" suggests 積み = "load."

買たほどこぼして行し若菜かな　梅室
kôta hodo koboshite-yukishi wakana kana　baishitsu
(bought as-much spilling-go, young-green!/'tis 1768-1852)

superfluous spring

walking home
i spilt as many as i bought
young greens

That is to say, Baishitsu plucked some and bought some. He also wrote the clearest description of spring plenty I have read: *"No trace remains / of plucking young greens / at every house"* (摘む跡もなくて家々の若菜哉　梅室アルス *tsumu ato mo nakute ieie ni wakana kana*). Superfluity is the mark of

1. *Robe as Pocket.* In 1585, Luis Frois, SJ noted that Japanese stuff their bosom with tissue paper, and "the more there be, the more gallant (*primor*)." A Tokugawa era Russian visitor wrote of kimonos turned into "entire stores full of goods" and the late-19c traveler Isabella Bird wrote "men sometimes carry their children in the fronts of their dresses, and I have seen as many as seven books and a map taken out of the same capacious reservoir." The hanging sleeves could even be filled with rocks for a drowning suicide. The closest equivalent in Europe were the early-17c breeches of the men, which, if Bulwer is believed, sometimes held as many personal effects as a large sized back-pack could today! (See *Topsy-turvy 1585*)

↓

abundance, a suitable start for a prosperous New Year. Spilled greens are only paradoxical when we consider the *ku* we read earlier where everything green was plucked. Different weather (a cold dry year vs. a warm wet one) creates different approaches to celebration. Centuries earlier, Jôha (1523-1602) wrote *"Left over / though plucked by all: / young green!"* (家々につミてもあまるわかな哉 紹巴 *ieie ni tsumitemo amaru wakana kana*). Baishitsu and Jôha's *ku* were more similar in the original Japanese (both *ie-ie*, i.e., "house-house"). But, here we must ask, *if there was such an abundance of young green, why is anyone buying it?* That is the second paradox of plenty.

七草も昼になりけり上手下手　太祇
nanakusa mo hiru ni narikeri jôzu heta   taigi -1772
(seven-herbs-too/even noon-as become[+emphatic] skillful/lousy)

seven herbs
by noon we know who
can and can't

seven-herb day
by noon, split into haves
and have-nots

some have it
and some do not: by noon
seven herb day

Taigi gives one answer: *some people are just incompetent.* But the following explanation-in-a-haiku by Chiyo supplies the primary reason that plenty is unavoidable.

七草やあまれどたらぬものもあり　千代女　改造社
nana kusa ya amaredo taranu mono mo ari   chiyo 1701-75
(seven plants: excessive but lacking ones also are)

seven greens
of most i have too much
of some too little

Some of the seven plants were found in most fields; others were not. *Nazuna*, ("shepherd's purse" or "mother's heart") was easily found in the meadow (and came in several varieties), *daikon* (huge white radish) and *turnip* seedlings (both called by other lucky names) would also be easily found in gardens and nearby fields, but some of the others would not. As we noted already, it was necessary to search out the high and the low. We can imagine that trying to get all seven plants by oneself would be like a scavenger hunt. A successful hunt might involve trading and, when necessary, buying whatever was unavailable in the region. Yet, even as I write this, I cannot help thinking about what I have experienced in Japan. I suspect that there is considerable preparation ahead of time: *You* go to the valley and get the dropwort. *I'll* go to the farm plot and get the *daikon*. I hope to find some prose dwelling on the actual circumstances for a future edition.

我庭に春七種の一つ欠く 阿部みどり女 角川三
waga niwa ni haru nanakusa no hitotsu kaku midorijo -1980
(my garden-in, spring seven-herbs' one lacks/lacking)

in my garden
one of spring's seven herbs
is missing

one of seven
of the herbs of spring:
not in my garden

That may sound like a lament, but 6 of 7 in a single garden is truly remarkable. Midorijo lived to be 95.

◎ One I almost missed: *"This withered field! / Waiting for rain we pluck / first young greens!"* 枯し野や雨をまつつむはつわかな 宗碩 *kareshi no ya ame o matsutsumu hatsuwakana* sôseki -1533. I have little doubt dryness was a bigger problem than snow, but this is the only *ku* I know who noticed it!

FAVORITE ODD PLUCKING KU

松ははや見かへる跡や若菜摘 也有
matsu wa haya mikaeru ato ya wakana-tsumi yayû 1701-83
(pine-as-for, already look-back trace/mark!: young-green-plucking)

the pine already
a landmark we look back on
young green plucking

There is no ocean mentioned in this *ku*; but the pine one looks back on, the *landmark*, evokes a sea journey, for such pine dotted the rocky hills on Japan's sea coast. It does not do this crudely, and our first vision is a ridge with a pine beyond which lie green fields, or mostly snowy fields, where the poet, who usually does not wander that far into the country, hunts for young greens. There are more direct links with the sea in young-green haiku. We have seen the contemporary one mentioning the sea of the *Ancient Chronicles*. Some even bring shellfish into the picture: *"The seaside field / among the young greens / some lover-shells"* (磯畠や若菜の中の妹背貝 禾水 大全 *isohata ya wakana no naka no imosegai* shisui? 19-20c?) – I have no idea what the shells are, and experience tells me that even if I were to look up the translation in the dictionary, chances are not one in a thousand readers (including me) would learn anything more from the Latinate name we would find. What matters here is that the name *imose-gai* combines *imo* (sister=girlfriend/lover) and *se* (back=papoose=boyfriend=lover) and *kai/gai*=shell. These words for boy and girlfriend are those found in ancient poetry and *that* evokes the romantic aspect of ancient green-plucking. Another greens and shellfish *ku*: *"River-dig Inn / we have young greens / with corbicula"* 堀河の宿は若菜と蜆かな 蝶衣 大全 *horikawa no yado wa wakana to shijimi kana* chôi - 1930). The *corbicula* is a tiny shellfish great in miso soup. Since *wakana* (young green) can stand for a young man or woman and *shijimi* (corbicula) was idiomatic for the sex of a little girl, the *ku* can not avoid an erotic undertone (See the *Lubricious Sea Slug* chapter of *Rise, Ye Sea Slugs!*). Note that the name of the place where the Inn was located translates as Digging-River. But that is small stuff. We want something bigger for the New Year. The next *ku* provides it:

天地のゆるむひまより初若菜 松宇 改造社
ametsuchi no yurumu hima yori hatsu-wakana shôu - 1827
(heaven-earth's relax/loosening freedom/play/space-from first-young-green/s)

the first greens
between winter and spring
heaven and earth

heaven and earth　　　　　　　　　　　　　　　from space born
relaxing, gave birth:　　　　　　　　　when heaven and earth let go
young greens　　　　　　　　　　　　　　　　first young greens

from the play
between sky and earth
the first plants

from the rest　　　　　　　　　　　　　　　　from freedom
of heaven and earth space　　　　　　given of heaven and earth:
for young green　　　　　　　　　　　　　　the first plants

born of heaven
earth and man at leisure
first-young-greens

The original *ku* is faultless. I cannot begin to match the verb *yurumu,* used when ice frozen solid in a stream begins to show some *slippage,* or a tight knot begins to *loosen* or we *let our guard down* after going on vacation, or the noun *hima* meaning *play, give, freedom, leisure, time-off* and simply *having nothing one has to do*. There may also be an allusion to a *Kokinshû* (905) *waka,* where the frothy waves breaking through the cracks in the ice made by the warm valley breeze are called "spring's first blossoms." (谷風にとくる (中略) 春のはつ花). I added the "man" in the last reading.

when heaven and earth give　　　　　　　the first greens
the first young greens　　　　　　　　when heaven and earth
fill the gaps　　　　　　　　　　　　　　　　give a little

Ridiculous! As many readings as a body has holes, yet not one half as good as the original.

土手の馬くはんを無下に菜摘哉 其角
dote no uma kuwan o muge ni natsumi kana kikaku -1707
(bank's horses' eat-not[or would?][+emph. contrad.] directly green-plucking!/'tis)

what the horses　　　　　green-plucking　　　　　going straight
would not eat on the bank　　i snatch one up from under　　for what the horses leave
green plucking　　　　　　　my horse's nose　　　　　　green-plucking

This *ku* I almost missed. At a glance, it has a crude, no, *rude,* quality that does not invite us to love it. But, if you were to look at a package of these greens, they do indeed seem hardly worth the attention of a horse. They are puny. Or, does *kuwan* mean the horse is *trying* to eat it (middle reading)? Either way, Kikaku makes us think about both the strange nature of culture and what it is to be human.

Identification

若草や形あるものの芹薺　素外
wakakusa ya katachi aru mono seri nazuna sogai 1717-1809
(young-grass:/! form-has-one/thing *seri* (j. parsley) [and] shepherd's purse)

young herbs
the only ones with form
seri and *nazuna*

young herbs
only two stand out
seri and *nazuna*

easy young herbs

seri & *nazuna*
leaves that don't leave
you guessing

The "leaves" is *my* guess. A turnip and daikon are recognizable enough by their roots, but these roots are not visible when the plants are tiny. A basket of growing young greens are pictured below:

策雲居酔歩　それそともしらで若菜を摘にける　士郎
sore zo to mo shira de wakana o tsuminikeru shirô -1813
(this-even know-not-with young-green[+obj] pluck[+fin.])

a drunken walk by the cloud-scheme hut

not knowing
what it was, i plucked
a young green

not knowing
one young green from
another i pluck

I do not know enough about Shirô's life to tell how big a role the drinking may have played in this or whether said hut was his own or that of another poet, but I love the *ku*. (↑ illus. is a stolen, redone color photo)

Trade in Young Greens?

初市や雪にこぎくる若菜舟 嵐蘭
hatsu-ichi ya yuki ni kogikuru wakanabune ranran -1689
(first-market!/:/and snow-in rowing-come/s young-green-boat/s)

>the first market
>rowing in, in the snow
>young-green boats

Not wishing to detract from the local green hunts, poor children with clever eyes, etc., I kept this reality-check *ku* for last. Did areas to the South grow the young-greens for the North, or was this just how things moved about? Expect more economics in a future edition. (研究者の方、どうぞよろしく！)

Between the Plucking and the Chopping

七草を打おさめたる空手かな 其川 蕪村発句集九部
nanakusa o uchi-osametaru karate/kûshu kana   kisen 18c
(7-herbs[+obj] ~~strike~~/chop-conquer/finish bare-hand/s!/'tis)

>seven herbs
>nothing in the hand that
>chopped them

>~~seven herbs~~   ~~seven herbs~~
>~~i captured all of them~~   ~~i tore them apart~~
>~~bare-handed~~   ~~without a knife~~

Uchi-osametaru can mean simply "conquer," *uchi* is a verb that functions as an emphatic as well as meaning "strike," "cut-down" or "chop-up." *Nanakusa* (seven herbs) probably puns with *ikusa* (rebellion), for *osame(ta)ru* used with the latter means *to quell*. *Karate* was not yet used to mean the martial art, so the words "bare-handed" are literal and work by contrast with *armed* to create a war metaphor. All of this is true, but such martial metaphor is only slightly present in the *ku*. As one respondent put it, 七くさを打つトントンというリズムが打ち終わって空手になった手に、なお残っている、ということかと思います。Oruka。(But, my respondents disagree on the pronunciation of 空手 *that is,* the empty hand just finished chopping away *ton ton* at the greens, that still quivers with the rhythm of the joyous task. Because this reading is far more poetic than mine, it is correct and the other wrong, though the allusion to triumphing over the herbs can remain. This *ku* really belongs at the end of the next chapter when we shall be –

>*empty-handed*
>*after chopping up all*
>*seven herbs*

七種打
nana-kusa tataki

20

BEATING (& EATING) THEM

七種や日出づる方に向い打つ　素水
nanakusa ya hi izuru hô ni mukai-utsu　sosui 1813-1897
(seven-seed/species: sun appears direction-to facing-hit/chop)

seven herbs!
chopping, i face where
the sun rises

The collected young-greens are chopped up and/or beaten on carving boards or in a pestle & mortar prior to being turned into a seven-herb soup, a charm against all sickness. The Chinese character used for the plant in the above *ku* was not the usual "grass/herbs" but one meaning "seed" or "species." It has a stronger medicinal nuance and the "seed" fits the propitious start of the year. While "seven herbs" can refer to the hunt, it usually implies the preparation or eating of the young greens on the seventh day of the year. *Seven*, of course, was lucky. How so, varied by locale. In North Kyûshû and North-east Japan, the seven-this-or-that soup (it has several names, all with seven in them) is carried by seven year-old children to seven houses in the neighborhood! (講談社大歳時記)

世わすれに薺打らん月と梅　士朗
yo wasure ni nazuna utsuran tsuki to ume　shirô 1742-1813
(world-forgetting-to shepherd's purse chop/beat hey: moon and plum [bloom])

forget this world!
chop your greens to the moon
and plum blossoms

"Camping out / green-choppers oblivious / to the time," says a *ku* in *Minashiguri* (empty chestnut), a *haikai* sequence famous for Bashô's participation (草枕薺うつ人時とはん　山川　虚栗 *kusamakura nazuna utsu hito toki towan* sansen 1683). Who knows the proper time for starting to chop! The six and seven-day moon rises early and sets before midnight. So, some people must have chopped before sleeping, as there are some who open Christmas presents at midnight rather than waiting for dawn. In some places, herbs are chopped at *both* times: 4x7 times on the evening of the 6th and 3x7 more at dawn. Did they wait to see the moon rise over the mountain or their neighbor's roof on the sixth and for the sunrise on the seventh? Shirô's *ku* specifies *nazuna*. This herb is relatively plentiful, includes a lucky "seven" (*nana*) [1] within its name (*nazuna*) and, evidently, feels good to chop, for it is mentioned more than any other of the seven herbs, *and sometimes stands for all of them*. Even if an English name would fit in the translation, already pressed for space because of the need to add "blossoms," the idea of chopping, beating or dicing a "mother's heart" appalls and a "shepherd's purse" would be little better. The plum blossoms are excellent in the *ku*.

隣／＼うしろ隣も薺の夜　白雄
tonari tonari ushiro-donari mo nazuna no yo　shirao -1792
(neighbor neighbor behind-neighbor, too shepherd's purse night)

<table>
<tr><td>my neighbors
right, left and even behind!
it's herb night</td><td>neighbors, too
on all sides, tonight belongs
to mother's heart</td></tr>
</table>

The reader can substitute *nazuna* for "herb." A later *ku*, probably by Seisei (1869-1937), also makes it clear that chopping could be done at night: *"A small house / goes to sleep after chopping / the seven herbs"* (七草を打ちて寝たる小家哉　青々　再現 (貧乏で引越し多く、入った歳時記、消えたよう) *nanakusa o uchite inetaru ko-ie kana*).

あかときの星に打ち出す薺哉　茂竹　青嵐
akatoki no hoshi ni uchidasu nazuna kana　mochiku 19-20c?
(dawn-time's stars-to hit/chop-begin/launch shepherd's purse 'tis)

the first chop

<table>
<tr><td>out comes
the *nazuna* to the light
of dawn stars</td><td>make a wish
on the night's last star
mother's heart</td></tr>
</table>

The compound verb *uchidasu* is too perfect for translation. It means "open fire," "go first," "launch" [an endeavor] "spark" [strike sparks from] and, here, hints at the literal "hit/strike/chop" starting up (*dasu*). I exchanged *nazuna* for "shepherd's purse" not only to kill the picturesque language that might detract from the sound and the sight, but because three syllabets are far shorter than three syllables and the inexplicable need to add "light of" to the English stars left the poem, even with part of the meaning of the compound verb put into the title, with no room to spare. The second reading is part invention, for I do not know of such a wish accompanying the first chop, though the whole ritual *is* a wish for good health.

---

1. Seven X *Na*. There are even a number of poems which introduce the "seven" sound (*na*) of the *nazuna* seven times! Shigeyori's *takusan na na wa nanakusa no nazuna kana* (たくさんななはなな草のなづなかな　重頼) quips that *nazuna* has the most *na*'s (homophonic with "names") of all the seven herbs. Another by the less well-known Shunka gets in the seven while saying that *wakana* is the classiest word of the seven (for it appears as a chapter head in the TALE OF GENJI. (ななつのなかになまめくわかなかな　春可 *Nanatsu na no naka ni namameku wakana kana*). These are in the 1633 Teimon classic ゐのこ集. A later *ku*, likewise with 7 *na* (なにごともなくて七草薺かな　菊狂　古今類範 *nani goto mo naku-te nanakusa nazuna kana* kikukyô?), translates as "Nothing at all except the seven-herb *nazuna*," which is clever, for *nothing to speak of* was everything by the Zen way of thinking and, as we have already seen, is appropriate New Year rhetoric.

きぬ／＼や薺に叩き起されつ 鳴雪 大全
kinuginu ya nazuna ni tataki okosaretsu　meisetsu 1847-1926
(silk-zilk[lingering-goodbye of lovers] shepherd's purse-by beaten awake)

lovers part
beaten awake by
mother's heart

beaten awake
by mother's heart,
lovers part

Kinuginu is a classical expression for the parting of lovers – which can include husband and wife, for once husband and wife lived separately – at or before the crack of dawn. We may have mentioned it when discussing the Year of the Bird, for the cock is the much vilified messenger of bad tidings (Strange that no one writes poems expressing their anger at their alarm clocks!). This modern poet is either thinking of ancient times or pretending that the ageless ritual of herb-chopping made even the so-called "night-crawling" practice still found in the country-side seem classical and, therefore, romantic.

薺打つ遠音こもるや明霞 八重桜
nazuna utsu tô ne komoru ya akegasumi　yaezakura -1945
(shepherd's purse chop/hit distant-sound fills/impregnated/holds-in dawn-mist)

herb day

filled with
the din of distant dicing
dawn mist

大雪に明けてしづけし薺打 六松 閑古鳥
ôyuki ni akete shizukeshi nazuna uchi　rokushô 19c? 改造社
(heavy-snow-to dawning quiet shepherd's purse chopping/beating)

a snowy dawn
how quiet the sound of
chopping herbs!

this morning
the herb chopping's quiet
a heavy snow

This is one of the most sound-centered human activity themes in the Fifth Season. What impressive human sounds are there today that are pretty much heard everywhere? I think of the fireworks at New Year, for even if one lives out of the way, chances are some children nearby will explode something. Otherwise, there is damn little collective noise that extends further than music in the park, a block party, or church-bells that do not count for they are heard every day. Imagine stepping outside and hearing a din of dicing (and songs as we shall see) from every direction! It seems like a little thing, but when you really try to imagine it, you can see how this exceeds anything done by the most ambitious monumental installation artists. Snow puts a damper on the sound.

七草を打つてそれから寝役哉 一茶 文化十四
nanakusa o uchite sore kara neyaku kana　issa -1827
(seven-grass/plant/herb hit/chop-from sleep-duty 'tis)

after chopping
seven herbs, i return
to sleep duty

While old man Issa was to turn his noontime naps into his "duty," at this time, Issa was only married for a couple years and may be thinking of his marital duty. Or, his wife, who had a brisk character, may have informed him that it was his turn to get out of the way of whatever chore she was doing.

七草や夜着から顔を出しながら 一茶
nanakusa ya yogi kara kao o dashinagara   issa 1823
(seven-grass/plant/herbs: sleep-wear-from face stick-out while)

seven herbs!
while i peek out
from my quilt

This is some years later. Issa's journal shows he drank and slept-in a lot year-round. And, as we also have seen, he hated the cold. He is almost surely in bed as his wife or a maid chops away early in the morning, but he might be in the kitchen still wearing his quilt (a *futon* with sleeves).

七草は隣のおとで置にけり 一茶
nanakusa ya tonari no oto de okinikeri   issa 1823
(seven-herbs-as-for, neighbor/s' sound-by awakened[+fin.])

seven herbs i wake up to the sound of my neighbor	seven herbs the day my neighbors wake me up

seven herbs
i'll let my neighbor's
noise be mine

The verb for awaken is written with the wrong *kanji*, one pronounced the same but meaning "to place." One of its idioms allows one thing to be put in place of another: the last (unlikely) reading.

若菜つみ包丁ならば牛のふん 朱拙 アルス
wakanatsumi hôchô naraba ushi no fun   shusetsu 1655-1733
(young-green-plucking, knife [preparation]-if/when cow-shit [1] [lousy])

young greens

oh, he can pluck! but back in the kitchen she's out of luck	oh, she can pluck! but back in the kitchen he's out of luck

While serious cutlery was male – there were professional carvers with ranks putting them into the upper-class society (see *Topsy-turvy 1585*) – men *let* women do most of the domestic dicing. But on this day, men got into the act for, as we shall see, there are many self-deprecatory *ku* on poor chopping.

---

1. Cow Shit. Since cows for milk were not part of Japanese culture, "ox" might be better; but that wouldn't scan. And "bull-shit" has too many connotations of its own. My OJD explains that because bovine cakes have a hard crust on the outside, but crumble easily, cow shit idiomatically means *someone who is far less competent than his or her exterior might warrant*. I have a sentimental attachment to cow-pies, for my first job as a translator for a commercial firm in Japan concerned experiments with feed and was titled: *nama-gyufun,* or "raw cow shit," which, considering my inexperience at the time, was exactly what I was producing!

へた／\と笑ふて下手な薺哉　壺角 其雪影
heta heta to warôte heta na nazuna kana　kokaku 1772
(poor (at something)! poor! poor shepherd's purse!/'tis)

man, you stink!
you really stink! i *do* stink
at dicing herbs

bad! bad! even
i laugh at my own *bad*
herb chopping

what a klutz!
what a klutz! klutzy at
nazuna, that's me!

The idiom for doing something poorly, *heta,* is a single word. If *wakana* by itself implied plucking, *nazuna* by itself implies "chopping" or "dicing"

笑はれて又打直す薺哉　景道 つつきの原
warawarete mata uchinaosu nazuna kana　keidô 18?19?20c?
(laughed [at] again hit/chop/beat-correct/again shepherd's purse!/?/'tis)

laughed at
he again starts beating
the *nazuna*

i'm laughed at
she chops up the *nazuna*
all over again

More chopping than "beating" is going on, but to translate "chopping" would lose all trace of the parallel with *beating* (as someone is *beaten,* not *chopped* in punishment) or *hitting* a person (as in a fight). Ostensibly, this is a straight depiction of a persevering person at the cutting board, but the wit is in the idea of being laughed at yet continuing to fight. Do you imagine wives laughing at husbands, their children's first efforts, or the contrary?

薺打中に女の笑ひかな　冠露 明和二
nazuna utsu naka ni onna no warai kana　kanro 1765
(shepherd's purse chop/ped/beat?ing? / while/included women's laughter/!/'tis)

while *nazuna*
is beaten, the laughter
of women

deep within
the green-chop din, women
laughing

the laughter
of women diced into
mother's heart

The past tense and laughter included in the product (not just process) in the last reading is my doing and the phrase "green-chop din" in the middle reading for brevity and rhyme's sake.

ならへ置膳に薺のひゝき哉　我峰 ありそ海
narabe-oki zen ni nazuna no hibiki kana　gahô 1695
(lined-up placed-[portable]tables-on shepherd's purse's echoes!/'tis)

tables in a line
the sound of *nazuna*
resounding

Is this a *ku* about a family doing it together? Or, are these bachelors? I must admit to cringing at the thought of what amounts to competitive dicing. I cannot for the life of me imagine why the number of emergency room visits and lost digits accruing from this activity is not tabulated and published every year as are the number of people who choke on their sticky sweet-rice cakes in their New Year's soup (See *New Year* vol.2, *zôni*)!

大方は笑はれてうつ薺哉 只丸 俳諧漢和
ôkata wa warawarete utsu nazuna kana   shigan 1639-1712
(most parties-as-for laughed [at] hit/beat/chop shepherd's purse!/'tis)

    most people
are roasted as they beat
    mother's heart

    most of us
are laughed at while we
    chop *nazuna*

The first reading is obviously my fun, created from the accidents of English. The original reads remarkably well for what amounts to a generalization. Besides, the obvious fact that many people doing the chopping on this day would not have been used to kitchen work, it was generally chilly. An aesthete might wish *"Oh, for snow / sprinkling the nazuna / on the cutting board"* (俎板の薺の上に雪も哉　林也 うらわかは *manaita no nazuna no ue ni yuki mogana*　rinya 1697) and a tough recluse advise *"Just chop it / all together! thin ice / on the nazuna* (それ共に叩け薺の薄氷　芙雀 *sore tomo ni tatake nazuna no usugôri*　fujaku late-17c), but I have had ice freeze in a glass by my bed just outside of Tokyo at this time of year (when I wrote a book in that room, I took to gripping a bare light-bulb whenever the pencil dropped from my cold fingers), yet I would not want to push my luck with a knife! And, note, also that many Japanese were thin, like me; the cold must have sunk straight to the bone. Even the generally brusque Kikaku (1660-1707) noted with amazement how –

さはらびの七種打は寒からん 其角
sawarabi no nanakusa uchi wa samukaran   kikaku -1707
(pretty/sweet/small-bracken's seven-herbs among-as-for cold[+probably/right?])

    bracken hands
chopping seven herbs
    look so cold!

    the maiden ferns
shiver with clutched hands
    seven herb beating

Maiden-ferns in Japan had their wee "hands" broken off and eaten. Bracken was standard trope for female hands+wrist thin to the point of fragility. To fully appreciate what might otherwise seem ridiculous anthropomorphism in the second reading, please read the history of this trope in *Fly-ku!* ch.III.

とはしり（る）も顔に匂へる薺哉 其角 炭俵
tobashiri[ru= kdd] mo kao ni nioeru nazuna kana   kikaku 1660-1707
(spray too face-upon smells shepherd's purse!/'tis)

    splashed with sap
my face too smells like
    shepherd's purse

我顔に薺とばしるうれしさよ 青々 河出
waga kao ni nazuna tobashiru ureshisa yo   seisei 1869-1937
(my face-on/to shepherd's purse sprays delightfulness[+emph])

    shepherd's purse
flies up in my face
    the joy of it!

    how delightful!
my face is splashed with
    shepherd's purse

Just imagine vigorous chopping with juice and bits of stem flying through the air! Compare Kikaku's *ku* with his contemporary's more boring description of the same: *"From the knife (=chopping) /*

his/her sleeves get wet: / shepherd's purse" (包丁に袂もぬるゝ薺哉 浪花 *hôchô ni tamoto mo nururu nazuna kana* rôka 1669-1703). I have never chopped up enough green matter, or chopped it finely enough to bring out the juices, but I have seen green-lipped cows and what blenders can do.

七種や俎板きよき木の匂い 靑生 靑々
nana kusa ya manaita kiyoki ki no nioi seisei 1869-1937
(seven herbs: cutting board pure/clean/bracing wood's smell)

seven herbs	seven herbs	seven herbs
the new cutting board	fresh from the cutting board	the new wood scent of
smells of wood	the smell of wood	my cutting board

English has no word like *kiyoki,* meaning *fresh, refreshing, pure, pristine, clean, bracing* and *lofty,* in a figurative way. The translations show how I tried to get around the lack of that word.

親と子の間にこぼるゝ薺かな 乙二
oya to ko no aida ni koboruru nazuna kana otsuni 1754-1823
(parent and child between spill/tumble off shepherd's purse 'tis)

dueling knives

shepherd's purse
spilling over between
parent and child

An exceptionally wholesome *ku*. Can you see the parent/s and child/ren facing off from their respective chopping boards, seeing who can get through their pile fastest, with the result that no little part of the total falls off the chopping blocks onto the table or floor? This was a family event, for a *ku* by Taigi (1709-72) explains: *"Seven herb day: / the children are all up / and assembled"* (七草や兄弟の子の起きそろひ 太祇 *nanakusa ya kyôdai no ko no oki soroi*). *Herb-beaters to your* (chopping) *blocks!* Does this remind you of anything we have seen before? Yes, this is similar to the way families lined up to witness the rising of the first, original sun. This time, the participation will be more active.

七種や粧ひしかけて切刻み 野坂 講談社大
nanakusa ya kehai shikakete kirikizami yaba 1663-1740
(seven-herbs!/: make-up[=commanding presence?]-put-on, cut-slice/chopping)

seven herbs	those seven herbs	seven herbs
barely made up, she	putting on make-up and airs	a decisive first chop
chops away	i cut 'em to bits	to psych-up

My respondent imagines a woman, barely made-up, rushing to the chopping board. I see a man, the poet, with his make-up helping him feel like a kabuki samurai. This attitude may be one reason Yaba made it into his eighties, as not a few playful *haikai* poets did. My last reading is based on *misreading* what was written in Kôdansha. But, who knows! First = 初 and cut = 切 are similar enough, the *saijiki* could be mistaken. The modern term "psych-up" is also odd, but Japanese have a way of starting things *decisively.* You can hear it in the fife style in *bon* (Japanese all-souls) dance music. Tito Fuentes could blast off his flute, but it is rare in Occidental music, where a song is more likely to *end* that way. A good *karaoke* singer is marked by his or her ability to *start* with a bang.

よもに打薺もしどろもどろ哉　芭蕉
yomo ni utsu nazuna mo shidoromodoro kana　bashô 1644-1694
(four-directions-in/from hit/chop/pound shepherd's purse, too, incoherent!/?/'tis)

from all sides

even chopping
nazuna our rhythm
just falls apart

Like so many of Bashô's *ku*, it is hard to tell exactly what he is driving at. Most Japanese commentators guess the subtle poet means that even with the loud sing-song chant accompanying the ritual, eventually the rhythm falls apart, and that is not only true on the poet's cutting board, but all over. The first reading takes *shidoro-modoro* as a process in time. Either people are beginning at different times, not singing the same song, or pooping out . . .

even chopping
greens the world sounds
out of sync

This reading emphasizes the echoes heard from all sides. Come to think about it, in a valley where a knife chopping on a heavy cutting board might be heard for a couple hundred yards, the speed of sound and the echoes would make concerted rhythm practically impossible . . . . It might sound right for a while because our ears search for meaning and create illusions of rhythm where it doesn't exist. Then, it would *seem* to fall apart though it was not really there from the start. Unlike Bashô's various annotators, I wonder whether the "too/even" (*mo*) in the original reflects relief on the part of Bashô that he is not the only klutz in town.   To wit:

still together, after all

chopping *nazuna*
others, too, seem not to keep
a perfect beat!

Though my reading may be unlikely, another poet did write what amounts to exactly that:

七草や余所の聞えも余り下手　太祇
nanakusa ya yoso no kikoe mo amari heta　taigi - 1772
(seven-grasses/plants/herbs: elsewhere's sound, too, just too poor/bad)

seven herb day
elsewhere, too, it don't
sound too good!

The original is as colloquial as my "don't." More important, we can't be sure if Taigi means the chopping, chant, or both. The words to the chant are, roughly rendered: *"Seven-herb nazuna! Before the Chinese birds cross over to the Land of the Sun's Origin! Seven-herb nazuna!"* (*nanakusa nazuna tôdo no tori ga nihon no tochi ni wataranu saki ni nana kusa nazuna*). Though it parses into 5 x 7 syllabets, I can not for the life of me get much rhythm from it! Nor, for that matter, meaning!

なゝ種に天（マ？）々国打し拳かな　素丸
nanakusa ni tengoku uchishi kobushi kana　somaru 1712-95
(seven-herbs-by heaven[x2=onomat. *tenten*?] hits fists!/ 'tis)

<blockquote>
seven grasses
our fists bang away
clear to heaven
</blockquote>

I have no idea why the sky part of heaven is repeated or why fists are mentioned. Is it the image of the hand clutching the handle of the knife? The broad meaning may be the range of the ruckus.

七種は唐土の鳥のすりえ哉　重頼　えのこ
nanakusa wa tôdo no tori no surie kana　shigenori 1601-80
(seven herbs-as-for, chinese-land's birds' ground-food [paste-feed]?/!/ 'tis)

<blockquote>
the seven herbs
are we pounding it into
chinese bird-feed?
</blockquote>

China, being generally to the North of Japan, birds in the Spring migrate *from* Japan, rather than toward it. Young Shigenori (1633) evidently found the chant, which hints at birds coming from China puzzling enough to poke fun of it. Apparently the greens were chopped up *very* fine, for one *ku* describes it as beginning as slices of bonito (I'd say five to an inch) and ending as *natto*, fermented soy beans which, when chopped up are pulverized into chunks the size of large sand grains held together by what can only be called *natto* slime (初薺鰹の叩き納豆まで　素堂　再現 *hatsu nazuna katsuo no tataki natto made*　sodô 1641-1716). A rough job was apparently not acceptable:

七草を敲き直すや昼時分　一茶
nanakusa o tatakinaosu ya hiru jibun　issa -1827
(seven grasses beat/chop-anew/fix: [noon]day-time)

<blockquote>
the seven herbs
i chop them up again
in the daytime
</blockquote>

The verb *naosu* is ambiguous, for it means both redo and/or fix. Imagine a hung-over young Issa (he was around 40) performed a cursory chopping to keep up (auditory) appearances, went back to sleep, and awoke later to discover he had not done a very thorough job. The question is whether he had the gall to do it loudly the second time. Issa admits to surreptitious chopping in one *ku:*

七草を内／＼に打寝坊哉　一茶
nanakusa o nainai ni utsu nebô kana　issa
(seven herbs[+obj] within within-in beat sleep-in-guy!/'tis)

<blockquote>
seven herbs
lie-a-bed chops
in private
</blockquote>

<blockquote>
seven-herbs
i beat mine in secret
sleepy-head
</blockquote>

<blockquote>
seven-herbs
the sleepy-head beats
his in secret
</blockquote>

sleeping in
i keep my seven-herb beating
to myself

"Within" and "beating" both are pronounced *uchi*, and *uchi-uchi* means secretively. The middle line of the last reading has an extra beat in the middle-line and the syntax is reversed, but I like it best.

はづかしき朝寝の薺はやしけり 淡路女 河出新
hazukashiki asane no nazuna hayashikeri awajijo 1890-1955
(embarrassing morning-sleep's shepherd's purse chanting [+emph.])

how embarrassing   how embarrassing
to sleep in yet sing out   to sleep-in and be roasted
the *nazuna* song!   by green-choppers

embarrassment
the herb-beating song of
this lie-a-bed

Had she *not* sung out, the neighbors would still notice her *not* doing it earlier in the morning. The term for a song with repeated choruses used here, *hayashi,* also means those poking fun at others (once done by groups of both sexes). My respondent thus favors the second reading. The "roast" may not be deliberate but is heard as such by the poet sleeping in. The *lie-a-bed* in the last reading is indeed obsolete, but "sleepy-head" isn't quite right. It would seem that English gave up a good old word for someone who sleeps-in, without finding a new one.

七草に鼠が恋もわかれけり 几董 改造社
nanakusa ni nezumi ga koi mo wakarekeri kitô -1789
(seven-herbs [chopping]-to/by mice love/love-making separates [+emph])

seven herbs
time for mouse lovers
too, to part!

The courtship of the mice, as we have seen, is a natural for the New Year because of the taboo term, "princess-bride." Taigi's oddly endearing *ku,* "New Year's Day / the mice show their faces / love peeks out" (元朝や鼠顔出すものの愛 太祇*ganchô ya nezumi kao dasu mono no ai* 1772) shows when it all starts. The *mo* or "too" usually signals what the poem is really about.[1] The seventh day concludes the rodent romance and the most important half (the *matsu-no-uchi,* or "within the pine" part) of the two-week-long New Year's Season. So mice and men enjoy the same magical period.

きぬ／＼や薺に叩き起されつ 鳴雪
kinuginu ya nazuna ni tataki-okosaretsu meisetsu 1847-1926
(sweet-parting! shepherd's purse by beaten/chopped awake)

time to part!
lovers beaten awake
by *nazuna*

Only a half dozen pages ago, I redefined *kinuginu.* I will do it for a third time, for it is entertaining.

1. *The Mo of It.* Considering the great amount of information on *kireji* (cutting-words) supplied even by translators(?) who cannot really read Japanese, it is unfortunate how little attention the *mo* gets. I believe it is because too much attention has been paid to form and too little to meaning. To understand what Japanese haiku are really about, one must become extremely attentive to the suggestive *mo*.

The term *should* be, but is *not* between *kinuge-nezumi* (lit. *silk-hair-mouse*), or "hamster," and *kinu-goshi*, or "silk-strained bean curd," in my large Japanese-English Kenkyusha dictionary. It is, or *was*, the standard poetic expression for that *sweet sorrow*, the parting of lovers at dawn (or earlier), because proper high-class love-making required men to leave before sunrise. A less violent older *ku* put it like this: *"It's dawn! / nazuna, too, is something / love hates"* (曙や薺も恋の憎みもの　麟上 *akebono ya nazuna mo koi no nikumimono*　rinjô 1759). Usually, the rooster is the bearer of the hated news, but, on this day, any man love-besotted enough to sleep at his sweetheart's home, will awake to a different alarm.

福引の貧（負？）腹たゝく薺哉　青羅
fukubiki no makebara tataku nazuna kana　seira 1739-91
(lottery-drawing's ~~poor~~ losing-belly[feelings/grudge] beat shepherd's purse!/'tis)

beating *nazuna*	the lottery loser
my revenge for losing	takes it out on the hide
at the lottery	of young greens

There was, and still is, a New Year's lottery on every local main-street. Most people use coupons collected while shopping, but some buy additional tickets. The "my" might be "her" if the poet was married. Issa's diary records huge losses by his wife (after which he had her attending Buddhist catechism for moral instruction! – what we call *therapy* today – and/or *punishment!*). There are more *ku* about less than pure motives for beating herbs, but I think the above one, by itself, interjects just the right amount of realism into our New Year.

DRIVING BIRDS BATTY

七草や跡にうかるゝ朝烏　其角
nanakusa ya ato ni ukaruru asagarasu　kikaku 1660-1707
(seven-plants! trail-in/after[it], intoxicated/carried-away/high/crazy morning crow/s)

seven herbs!	early crows
followed by a riot	set off by the noise
of early crows	seven herbs!

In the previous chapter, I read this as a *ku* describing how human activity *in the fields* excited the crows. Here, I read it as one where the sound of the chopping + songs are what drives them crazy. The latter reading seems *more* likely because seven herbs by itself usually means the chopping rather than the plucking, but *less* likely because the "after" (*ato*) is written with the character for "trail/mark" rather than that indicating temporal succession.

七草の音に負けじと烏かな 一茶
nanakusa no oto ni makeji to karasu kana   issa -1827
(seven-plants' noise-to lose-not, so crow/s 'tis)

<blockquote>
not <i>about</i> to lose
to seven noisy plants
noisy crows
</blockquote>

Issa's *ku* requires no guess-work. It is as clear as the caws of his crow/s and suggests that Kikaku's crows may indeed have been set off by the noise of the chopping. Keigu recalls a 2001 Easter Sunrise Service on the beach at Key Biscayne:

competition

<blockquote>
he is risen!
"but i rose first!" sings
the grackle
</blockquote>

The grackle sat right on top of the temporary cross stuck in the sand from start of service to end, doing his best to outsing the chorus and outpreach the priest.[1] A hymn to the Son is sung as the sun rises. And, as was the case with Issa's crows, the black bird got in the last word.

鶯も鳴くや七草はやす時 守水牢
uguisu mo naku ya nanakusa hayasu toki   shûsuiro 1835-1907
(warbler/nightingale[pro singer?], too sings: 7-herbs sing-out/chorus/kid time)

<blockquote>
nightingale, too
joins in when we razz
the seven-herbs
</blockquote>

When can a warbler – the correct translation of the *uguisu* – be a nightingale? When a bird with a particularly melodious voice is famous, for, in poetry, connotation overrules denotation. And we do not even know if the nightingale in the *ku* is a bird? It could be a professional singing girl, for they were called "nightingales," who joins in.[2] Can *hayasu* be "razz"? Since English has no simple word for the often nonsensical choruses which are usually, but not always, high-pitched female voices and provide rhythmical spice and a healthy erotic overtone to folk-song, much less further nuances of "making fun of by singing and noise-making," for which we have only a fancy French – or was it Italian? – term used by scholars that I would recognize but cannot recall, "razz" will have to do here.

七草の古き歌にてはやしけり たま女 年間俳句集
nanakusa no furuki uta nite hayashi keri   tamajo early-20c
(seven-herbs' old-fashioned-song-by razzed[+emphatic])

the seven herbs	the seven herbs
young things roasted	i razz my young leaves
by an old song	with an old song

1. *Key Biscayne Grackle*. The grackle piped up with special enthusiasm when the choir sang "Blackbird Is Singing" and clapped his wings behind his back, as male blackbirds do against strong challenges. Keigu's haiku was allowed because the Easter sunrise service is, in some ways, as close to the traditional Japanese New Year as any holiday in the USA. As a matter of fact, when the huge red sun first appeared that morning, it broke through the haze about a diameter above the Atlantic in a perfect imitation of the Chinese character meaning "one," (like a thick dash). This phenomenon was recorded in a New Year's poem published in 1765: *"It's the mind! / A perfect letter "one" / forms the first sun"* (*kokoro yo ya ma-ichi monji no hatsuhikage* – kyômu 虚無). As the K B sun rounded out, it put on one of the Jewish beany-caps! Keigu told himself, "haiku *that* if you can!"

2. *Uguisu With Breasts* A *waka* in the *Goshûishû* 1086 or *Shûigusô* 1216 notes *"The most difficult / ones to pluck and play / are those wild / young greens with voices / like nightingales'* (*tsumitamuru koto no muzukashiki wa uguisu no koe suru nobe no wakana narikeri.*) In the original, it is a bit more ambiguous in that it can also be interpreted to mean that the voice of the nightingale makes it hard to concentrate on plucking, but I think we have an old man trying to pick-up some chicks here.

3. *Old Songs in Old Days* Perennial wisdom/philosophy? Parallel to that is perennial *nonsense*. I once thought most nonsensical verses could be understood if only one went back into history, but, reading the Greeks, we find *them* lamenting over ancient ditties said on certain occasions for reasons no one any longer knew! Yes, indeed, it *is* turtles all the way down!

Most razzing that goes on in the world is done by new verses, for one must be up-to-date to insult people. Perhaps, I go too far. The "young" was added for contrast that, I think, was implied between the fresh first greens and a song so old no one knew what it had to do, if anything, with the greens.[3] ↑

宵薺囃せば踊る鼠かな 松宇 -1827? or ↓
yoi nazuna hayaseba odoru nezumi kana shôu 1858-1943?
(evening shepherd's purse singing/razzing-when, dances mice!/'tis)

night nazuna

when the herbal
chorus rings out come
the mice to dance

We know about those mice. I imagine a widower, using his drink to chop in the wee hours. 1707-87 ↓

沢蟹の鋏もうごくなづなかな 蓼太
sawagani no hasami mo ugoku nazuna kana   ryôta
(marsh-crab/s scissors too/even move shepherd's purse 'tis/!)

the marsh crabs	shepherd's purse
scissor their wee claws	even the marsh crab
shepherd's purse	pincers move

Was the chopping even heard by these crabs? And, were scissors as well as knives used to cut greens?

君が代の薺をはやす拍子哉 子規
kimigayo no nazuna o hayasu hyôshi kana   shiki 1866-1902
([the] imperial reign's shepherd's-purse/mother's-heart razzing rhythm 'tis/!/?)

mother's-heart

razzing greens
the whole country shares
a common beat

Sometimes translation has the advantage. Here, I could use the second name for *nazuna* in my Japanese-English dictionary, "mother's heart," for the title. But the original is better for the ambiguity of the final *kana*. The English is too sure. I wish I could say for certain *what* that beat was, but, to tell the truth, I could not find much rhythm in the song. Another *ku* saved by "mother's heart:"

一とせの心拍子は薺哉 無倫 其袋
hitotose no kokoro byôshi wa nazuna kana   murin -1723
(one-year's heart/mind beat/rhythm-as-for, shepherd's-purse hear 'tis/!)

yours is the beat
for the whole year
mother's heart!

mother's heart!   oh, *nazuna*!
the whole year gets   the heartbeat of the year
its heartbeat   is yours!

As the straight rendering shows, I have dramatized the *ku* considerably. But, even so, it is not as exciting an idea as Shiki's geographical extension, for what Shiki writes can be imagined. Even if the New Year is supposed to set the pace for the year, we do not feel this *nazuna* beating beat goes on.

~~~~~~~~~~~~~~~~~~~~~~~~~~~~~~~~~~~~

Here is the same *ku* I mistranslated and put at the end of the last chapter (p.416) in the *proper context*:

七種を打ちおさめたる空手哉 其川 蕪村俳句洲 9
nanakusa o uchi-osametaru karate kana   kisen   18c?
(7 herbs beat/chopping conquer/clean-up empty hands!)

<div style="text-align:center">
the seven herbs
beaten until beat, the victor
empty-handed
</div>

Now, the herbs are in the pot. So, let's get cooking.

~~~~~~~~~~~~~~~~~~~~~~~~~~~~~~~~~~~~

心いよいよ七草の粥にうつろなる 駒村
kokoro iyo-iyo nanakusa no kayu ni utsuro naru   kuson 1881-1943
(heart/mind/feelings/mood finally seven-herbs' soup-with/in empty/blank become/is)

my mind
and the world blanks out
herbal soup

our minds   herbal soup
finally settle down   my mind is finally
herbal soup   a-void-able

finally afloat
my mind a total blank
seven-herb soup

The *kokoro* in the original is, indeed, the *heart* of the poem. I hope *mind*, in one reading supplemented by the *world*, will do for the translation. I would guess the poet, tired from holiday activities in general, and the hunt for greens and chopping them up in particular, has caught himself gazing dumbly into his gruel, which I translate as "soup" to avoid the comical "green gruel" or the unwelcome sound of "herbal gruel." At the same time, because the New Year attitude was properly blank, it makes sense to find a return to blankness at the end of the first, important week.

天暗く七種粥の煮ゆるなり 普羅
ten kuraku nanakusa kayu no niyuru nari fura 1883-
(sky/heaven dark seven-herb-soup's boiling-is -1954)

a dark sky
the seven-herb soup
is boiling

Once the young greens are plucked and chopped up as seven herbs, a dark cloudy sky seems right, even welcome. The pot of gruel turns into a cauldron, the magic deepens and what green is not in the pot looks greener in the dark reflection of the sun. This *ku* may date to the dark days of World War II, or have some other association that only the poet could reveal, but none of that matters now.

俎に薺のあとの匂ひかな 鳴雪
manaita ni nazuna no ato no nioi kana meisetsu
(cutting-board-on/in shepherd's heart's mark/stains!/'tis 1847-1926)

how sweet the scent   i smell the scent
of the mark of mother's heart   of mother's heart staining
the cutting board   the cutting board

I'm sorry. I could not help mentioning this post-chop *ku* here. Though not about cooking, it is simultaneous to it. And I also apologize for taking advantage of that name. If you prefer, change "mother's heart" to *nazuna*. Back to the stove! Or, cooked greens, at any rate:

先づ春の匂ひも嬉し薺粥 二遊 改造社
mazu haru no nioi mo ureshi nazunagayu jiyû 19-20c?
(first, spring's smell/scent too delighted shepherd's purse soup)

first, happy
with the smell of spring
herbal soup

Whether this means the smell of the simmering gruel, or smelling it in one's bowl before drinking, it is equally pleasant to find the nose in front.

雑炊の名もはやされて薺哉 支考
zôsui no na mo hayasarete nazuna kana shikô -1731
(mixed-gruel's name kidded/ing nazuna [na-zu=naming]!/'tis)

the name game
is even played with gruel
that's *nazuna!*

The *nazu* in *nazuna* sounds like *naming*. When I asked for help with a *ku* by Somaru (1712-95) that I thought was about choosing a restaurant for eating seven-herb soup based on the lettering of the character (粥) used for another name for gruel, *kayu* (七くさや粥の名字の品さだめ 素丸 *nanakusa ya kayu no myôji no shinasadame*), Oruka pointed out that *kayu* was sometimes addressed as *Okayu-san*, or "Sir/Madam Kayu" and that the 名字, ot "name-letter," meaning first-names, was also written 苗字, where 苗 suggests *seedlings*, so we are talking about the members of the Okayu family, each having the name of a green. Pretty ridiculous, but fun. Could Shikô's older *ku* refer to this type of thing?

朝粥にみどり匂ふ早七日なる 竹の門
asagayu ni midori niou haya nanoka naru   take-no-kado 1895-1966
(morning soup-to green/fresh/raven smell/scent already [the] seventh becomes/is)

a green smell in my breakfast: it's the seventh!	i smell green in my breakfast gruel: already, the seventh!

Was the poet exceptionally busy at work after a short (three-day) New Year's break, or laying about so out of it, he didn't realize the date until it tweaked his nose? The "morning-gruel" in the original suggests this poet usually ate something porridge-like for breakfast. My desire for a decent sounding translation knocked out that detail and the "already" from the first reading.

酒荒れの舌に七草粥熱し 痴翁 改造社
sake are no shita ni nanakusagayu atsushi   chiô 19-20c?
(*sake*-irritation/chapping tongue-to seven herbs soup [is] hot)

herbal soup
a *sake*-scalded tongue
finds it hot

After hitting the *sake* too hard over the New Year, herbal soup should be soothing, but this "Crazy Elder" finds it smarts. As the attentive reader may have noticed, *all of the ku about the soup are Meiji era or later!* For reasons beyond me, earlier poets stopped short with the razzing and the beating/chopping. Could it be a case of competitive exclusion, *i.e.*, the first-gruel (*ozoni*) is too close? Be that as it may, two of the few exceptions, both by Mr. Haikai, himself, Teitoku:

うましとて口をもたゝく若菜哉 貞徳 ゑのこ
umashi tote kuchi o mo tataku wakana kana   teitoku -1633
(delicious says/shows mouth-too chops/beats/says young-green!/'tis)

greens beaten now eaten: well, you can't beat this!	now you find you smack your tongue young greens

つみたゝき後ははくひつく若なかな 貞徳 ゑのこ
tsumi tataki nochi wa kuitsuku wakana kana   teitoku 1570-1653
(pluck/pinch beat/chop after-as-for eat/bite-into/attach young-green/maiden/s!/'tis)

you pinch beat and, then, snap up young greens	pinch and beat young greens and they'll cling to you!

The metaphorical analogies in the first *ku* don't English perfectly, but combining the readings in your head, you can get it well enough. Teitoku's second *ku*, in the original, includes the compound verb "eat-attach," which means both to bite into something and to become firmly attached or cling to something as a parasite might. We are unsure whether to pity the plight of poor young-green, as per the first reading, or gasp at the colloquial expression of the horrid popular psychology that "women love it," as per the second. The transparent ambiguity of the bawdy allegory, and the humor antedates the style of the best of what later came to be called *senryû*. The *ku* is also an obvious improvement on one by Sôkan (1458-1586) found in Kenneth Yasuda's *The Japanese Haiku*:

A SERVANT CALLED WAKANA IS SCOLDED

Being picked and then
Being beaten up again
Are the young spring greens

Yasuda, like all too many who have written on haiku, fails to give even the Romanized original but the following poem from the Teitoku-edited *Konzanshû* collection includes what must be it:

摘まれてはまた叩かるゝ若なかな　宗鑑　再現
tsumarete wa mata tatakaruru wakana kana　sôkan 1651 崑山集
(pinched/plucked-as-for, again, beaten/chopped-up young-green 'tis/!/pitiful)

a sob for young green

pinched
then, beaten
poor wakana!

I added the "poor," for it is one of the connotations of the closing *kana*. The same could have been done for Teitoku's *ku* (and who can say but he pities the abuse of young green). There is no preceding caption about "a servant," for that is obvious to Japanese readers. Immediately following this *ku*, we find a much better one, by Teitoku or Sôkan (reference is not at hand). It is a fitting conclusion to the chapter, for it takes us back to the first poem of the *Manyôshû* and the salad days of Japanese poetry:

摘むおなごその名をとふも若なかな　宗鑑？貞徳？崑山集
tsumu onago sono na o tou mo wakana kana　sôkan? teitoku? 1651
(plucking girl that name ask too/also, young-green=wakana!/'tis)

a plucking girl　　　　　　　　　　the girl you pluck
and what is her name?　　　　　　　what is her name?
it's wakana!　　　　　　　　　　　　it's wakana!

the girl plucking?
i ask her name and only
get "young green"

The first two readings are possible. I would bet on my last reading – of which I am proud – where the *mo* does not mean "*also* like what she is plucking," but "*even though* I asked her" for her name, she only said her name was Wakana, i.e. she would not give her real name. Returning to the *ku* titled A SERVANT CALLED WAKANA introduced by Yasuda as an example of the *haikai no renga* "with its pervasive insistence on the amusing and witty," his only explanation was this: "The pun here is of course clear; the servant's name Wakana can also be translated as young spring greens." The reader may guess that *tsumu, i.e.* "pick," also suggests "pinched," or that which rhymes with "plucked." Unfortunately, Yasuda neglected to mention that it was standard to "beat"(chop) *wakana*. The same thing happens with his other example of "a Buddha of snow" that, having melted becomes "a true one." Yasuda notes that "The snow Buddha, having melted away in the early spring warmth, has attained the reality beyond form and matter," but forgets to explain that "snow-buddha" (雪仏) is vernacular for "snowman" in Japanese! Yasuda provides many quotes, passages revealing the intent of the pioneers of *haikai no renga,* but by failing to make clear the extent to which poems such as those on the young green and the snow-buddha are real and natural as well as facetious allegory, the wit dies and one is left with an unfairly low impression of the poetry. Such insufficient explanation is not unique to Yasuda. To a degree, *it is true with virtually all translation of Japanese poetry I have come across*. It bothers me, both because it indirectly turns wits into bores and because it normalizes poetry that is not entertaining.

若殿を抱て又打つ薺哉　牧童
wakatono o dakite mata utsu nazuna kana bokudô - 1715
(young-sir[+obj] embraced/hugging[=screw] again beats shepherd's purse!/'tis)

after embracing
young master, again beating
shepherd's purse

At a glance, this senryûesque *ku* might seem more of the same, but actually it is a reversal, for the one doing the beating is the un-named servant, who has returned from love-making to her celebratory chore of chopping up the *nazuna,* here translated as shepherd's purse to keep something risqué in the English. Since the "young master" (*waka-tono*), as a character, was famously lazy, it is fitting as well as splendid to find him, and not "young green," taking the objective case.

老の腰摘むにもたゝく薺哉　也有
oi no koshi tsumu ni mo tataku nazuna kana yayû 1701-83
(old-hip/back, plucking-with-even beat/chop shepherd's purse 'tis/!/?)

when i pluck   a geezer's back
is it *nazuna* i beat?   plucking i must beat
no! my back!   more than greens

the old man's young green

even plucking
throws it out of whack!
beat *nazuna?* no, my back!"

Here is a more indirect approach. Always the gracious gentleman, Yayû turned the poor girl Wakana's beating into something closer to home. After a gentle activity like plucking tender greens, Yayû's lower-back required one of those chopping massages. Or, maybe he walked along whacking at it between plucks. I had trouble making the "beat" pivot between two meanings in English (it is poor for chopping veggies and massaging backs) and dropped an important word to make space. In the original, the lower-back is described as "old," a contrast by allusion to "young green." This is a *bona fide* haiku that plays upon an old saw to make a personal complaint (bad back) entertaining.

★

GREENS & NAILS?

あすは元日の爪でもきらう　山頭火
asu wa ganjitsu no tsume demo kirô　santôka -1940
(tomorrow/morning original day's/ny's nail/s even cut-shall)

this morning i guess i'll clip the nails of the new year	i guess i'll clip my new year nails this morning

At first glance, I thought this *outrageous*. Imagine! The unorthodox and famously drunk Santôka was thinking of clipping his nails on the New Year's, rather than when he should have at the end of the year, and was also playing with the older conceit of nail-polish-red (actually, nail-*dye* in Japanese) sun-tinted mountains of the New Year's dawn![1] But, after discovering there was a ceremonial *nail-cutting ritual* on the 7th day, when the hands and feet were washed in water with a small portion of the seven herbs – or at least the representative herb, *nazuna* – to rid oneself of any bad spirits that might have made it into the Year, I realized that while the word-play is still there, the sanctity of the Japanese New Year has not been violated. By "New Year's nails," Santôka meant *the nails he has grown since New Year's Day*.

薺湯やきのふ摘みにし爪の土　鉢友 失出典
nazuna-yu ya kinô tsumi ni shi tsume no tsuchi　hatsuyû 17-19c
(shepherd's purse warmwater:/!yesterday picked nails' dirt)

nazuna wash dirt from plucking them under my nails	steeped *nazuna* the dirt from yesterday plucking them

washing the dirt
from my nails that plucked
shepherd's purse

While not as good as Santôka's *ku,* there is some humor in getting the dirt one ritually cleanses obtaining the main ingredient in that wash. Without a single word for "warm water" in English, I could not use it. The simplest of the various names for the ritual is *nazuna-zume,* or "*nazuna* nails."

垢爪や薺の前もはづかしき　一茶
akazume ya nazuna no mae mo hazukashiki　issa -1827
(crud-nails:/! shepherd's heart-before-ever embarrassing/ed)

dirty nails i blush to face even mother's heart	what dirty nails! even before *nazuna* wash, embarrassed me

Trite or not, there is wit here, too. The humor is in the *mo*, "even," for one would expect that for a cleansing ceremony, *the more dirt the better*. This is also the only nail-cutting haiku I have seen translated, though the translation (corrected after I pointed it out) was wrong: "dirty nails / facing my new year's soup / ashamed." Because the herb by itself can mean just about anything – and the original does not mention warm water – translation without first knowing what was what was impossible. Do you think it was irresponsible of me to take advantage of the name, Mother's Heart?

小鋏の付根の鈴や薺爪　梅屋 青嵐
kobasami no tsukene no suzu ya nazunazume　baishitsu
(small-scissor's crotch/fork's [jingle]bell:/! sheperd's-purse's nails)

that's the bell tied to the scissors! *nazuna* nails	is that jingling from a tiny scissors? *nazuna* nails

Japanese has not one but many names for bells, and this *suzu* is a tiny one that jingles rather than dings, dongs, chimes or clangs. It is what a cat might wear. The original specifies the location said bell is tied as the crotch of the scissors. This means the scissors are bladed tongs, or tweezers-like scissors with the crotch, or fulcrum at the far end rather than the middle. Such scissors are beautiful in their simplicity but relatively unwieldy, so most Japanese cut their nails with knives (See *Topsy-turvy 1585*). This *ku*, by Issa's contemporary (1768-1852), is interesting, for the news in it, and sweet. Who would guess that a jingling sound would conjure up a washing ritual!

今朝食ヘバ早夢に見る若菜哉　素檗
kesa kueba haya yume ni miru wakana kana　sobaku 1758-1821
(morning ate, already/soon dream-in see young-green [wakana!]'tis/!)

green reverie

sipped my soup fell asleep and saw her sweet wakana!	ate it this morning and i already dream of my *wakana*

I love this *ku*. Since I cannot imagine the poet dreaming of his food, I imagine he dreams of a pretty young thing, if you will pardon my objectifying vocabulary. It has been my experience that when you eat something you have not eaten in a long time, interesting dreams are common. So, I believe that Sobaku[2] is wrote this from life, after awakening from a pleasant nap.

---

1. pg.435: Nail-dyed Peaks A *ku* from a 1744 *haikai fest*: "*The mountain crest / dyed by a nail-dye-red / first sun*"(山のはを爪紅ひの初日かな 秀二 *yamanoha wa tsumakurenai no hatsuhi kana* shûji). This, according to Maruyama, is a haikufication of the opening lines of *The Pillow Book* of Sei Shonagon (10-11c), which says the mountains crest/s is/are dyed crimson by what is best in the Spring, the sunrise. The "nail-red/crimson" is also the name for a flower, the *touch-me-not*. I suspect a pun; either "the wife/ husband (*tsuma*) won't put out (*kure-nai*)" – for, on the first day, sex is taboo; or, "crest" (*ha*) being homophonic with teeth, teeth with nail-polish.

2. Sobaku's Ku. Had a large collection of Fujimori Sobaku's haiku not been published recently, I would not have found this extraordinary *ku*. Although Sobaku was one of the best known *haijin* of Issa's day – better known than Issa – Shiki's haiku-by-poet anthology (俳家別子規全集=アルス) includes only fifty or so of his *ku*. As will be explained in the Afterword to part II (下), most old *ku* are not yet available in print or on-line.

七草や似つかぬ草も打まじり 松藤夏山 講談社大
nanakusa ya nitsukanu kusa mo uchimajiri matsufuji kasan? 20c
(seven-herbs: resemble-not grass/es too cut/thrown-in-mixed)

the seven herbs   seven herb day
i even chop in a leaf   i chopped in some
resembling none   resembling none

some chopped in
that bear no resemblance
the seven herbs

Though my name does not translate as pine-wisteria summer-mountain, I identify with this poet. Whether by accident I can not avoid or by experiment, I can not resist, *perfection* – doing things just right – is beyond me. That is, of course, obvious in every page of this book. If I were driven to be correct and consistent Kasan's *ku* would not be in a book that is supposed to be a *saijiki* of *olde haiku*. Then again, the very phrase *olde haiku* is contradictory, for any *ku* that is indeed *olde* would not have been called a *haiku,* but a *hokku, jiku, tadaku,* etc..

☆

☆ Since chopping into small bits is called "beating," I did not take it literally. But, seeing the above, I wonder if some of the greens were literally beaten with sticks/clubs. Otherwise (if it is a sword or cleaver) it sure looks dangerous!

no afterword

元日や非を改むる非の始 紹簾 古選
ganjitsu ya hi o aratamuru hi no hajime   jôren   1763
(original day:/! wrong/neg.[+obj.] fix/restore wrong/negative's start)

    the first day   the negation
  we correct error   of negation begins
      to err anew   the first day

first day
we start erring
correcting our erring

    the first day   the first day
all wrong made right   a new beginning for
   by new wrongs   all our wrongs

new year's day
when naught begins
restoring naught

In Japanese literary tradition, a postscript is the proper place for an author to give the history of the book, confess his shortcomings and complain, knowing the readers will have grown fond enough of the book to indulge him. We who spend sixteen or eighteen hours a day writing rather than going out to play (or earning a living) have a right to indulge ourselves that much. Unfortunately, I have found that some readers who make the mistake of reading the Afterword *first*, naturally enough, found it fulsome. So, if you have not read this book, please *stop!* (If you *must* start at the end, see the *Errata and Glosses* at the paraverse.org website!)

That is how I would have *begun* the postscript had this been a real postscript. But, because Book I and II of the Fifth Season is only the first-half of the New Year themes, or Upper Volume, 上, as Japanese put it, I am afraid that this exercise will be truncated and held in abeyance for the next, Lower 下 Volume. I will only repeat what I noted at the start, that Book III and IV, with *Gate Pines* and *First This & Thats* will be *at least* as entertaining as I hope Books I and II were, and add that they will [1] have a *real* Afterword explaining what brought me to appreciate Japanese, read haiku and so forth.

---

1. ***Will.*** Unfortunately, poverty does not permit me to be as sure about the next 下volume as my "will" suggests. I have no possessions whatsoever to borrow against and none of my books, despite good reviews, sell more than a copy or two a month. The last time I checked Amazon, all six written in English were being outsold by over a *million* other books (most so bad you couldn't pay me to read them). No university pays me a salary, no publisher (for I publish myself) an advance, and, unlike Blyth, I have no kind "Governor of the Bank of Japan" to thank for patronage. Besides help from my mother, I have received a gift of almost $3,000 from a Japanese on-line *haiyû* (haiku friend) that kept my fingers on the keyboard in the Fall of 2005. Until my books sell, or I receive substantial grants (or loans), I must give up the good *work of writing* books and waste time on the bad *business of selling* them.

◎ *Writing at the End of the World* ◎

While I may complain about the burden that poverty puts on a writer (especially one with a poor memory who does non-fiction), there is something worse, something beyond the personal handicap, beyond complaint. It is a cross born by *all* present-day writers, rich or poor, *whether they know it or not*. In a word, it is this: *How can I write when so much is wrong?* Is that not why there are so many excellent writers yet so few great books written nowadays? Granted, we have our short works of genius, the proverbial flight of fancy needs no runway, but the sustained effort necessary to produce masterpieces is hard to muster when the brightest people of our generation feel *guilty* for not spending their every waking moment trying to stave off the disaster happy idiots cannot see. ◎ Even if you did not have to witness the retreat of the beautiful reefs from the waters, the vanishing swamps and the paving over of paradise, even if you did not adore cool ceiling fans in the shade of giant trees and detest the air-conditioned nightmare, you might have known where we were heading by the late 60's and early 70's when books such as Ezra Mishan's *Cost of Economic Growth* and the Club of Romes' *Limits to Growth* clarified what had been obvious since the late 1950's. Indeed, surveys at the time, showed that many if not most of the educated classes in the so-called developed nations *claimed* they understood what the world faced and wanted to do something about it, even if it meant personal sacrifice; but that resolve evaporated by 1980. The citizens of my country, in particular, betrayed their ideals and sold out to mammon. Rather than living frugally to create a surplus with which to aid international development and slow or stop the growth of the global population, "we" turned physics into a Cargo Cult mediated by a God called The Free Market, and bet on harmless fusion energy, which never came, that was, with the aid of artificial intelligence, supposed to make great wealth for all, and not just force all who cannot afford secretaries to spend the time they do not have pushing buttons on phones to talk to fictive persons and "technicians," when they=we are not *on hold*. In the USSR, people used to waste their days standing in line, in the USA, people do the same sitting alone by the phone, looking at their computers. Private cars, which should have been rationed, have multiplied and grown obscenely wasteful, while so-called "flyer miles" reward people for wasting energy rather than for saving it by staying put. ◎ The problem is not just wealthy right-wing egoists who rationalize self-serving and cruel government as good for the world they know so little about, or even Christian fundamentalists delighted to help bring about the Apocalypse. The left travels and otherwise wastes resources as much as the right and I have yet to hear a single progressive say that had we only encouraged other countries to control their population as the Chinese have done, we might have *some* hope for a decent future. Of course, the Chinese population control program was not perfect, but it was far less cruel, less murderous than the Mad Max world we helped to create and are, even now creating. It disgusts me to hear complaint from the left about the growing Chinese consumption of fuel or pollution of the global environment. *What did we expect!* What *do* we expect! *We* are the ones who used up most of the easily obtained resources of the world and grew quickly at the expense of the environment. Not only have we no right to complain, but fairness would dictate that we repay the Chinese and others for the free ride we got in our salad days. ◎As a student, I wrote a long letter to President Nixon saying that even if Ho Chi Min was a scoundrel for betraying other nationalist leaders to the Japanese, we could not help in South Vietnam because too many of our soldiers were either immature if not juvenile or racist and the expense of the war was draining resources needed to create a more energy-efficient infrastructure *while we still had the surplus to do so*. Nixon did not start the Vietnam War. He got trapped in it. And, thirty years later, the Neo-cons, with their figure-head president and mercenary corporations *lied* us into the same fix. And now, even more of our country is laid out wrong – i.e., for cheap and abundant fuel – and our debt to credit card companies (which, with the complicity of a corrupt Congress, behave worse than crime syndicate loansharks), future generations and those we import the most from has grown to record heights. Decades of neglect of development and family-planning aid has helped triple the Muslim population, a large part of which are fundamentalists who care no more for this world, the only one we have, than their benighted Christian counterparts, while we have gone out of our way to breed terrorists by talking up freedom and rights while building permanent bases and acting like tyrants. ◎I tell myself that books such as mine help people realize what counts in life and give them the conviction and courage to *Just say No!* to a criminally wasteful yet conceited culture, and seriously question the assumption that ours is the only major civilization. Fundamentalism does indeed threaten our future, not because it tends to create terrorists – it could as easily create *peaceniks* – but because only rationalism, graced with a touch of mysticism, has any chance of conserving the world, which is to say our cultural and biological diversity, by convincing us that our happiness and our duty lies in changing in order to cope with and delay the otherwise cataclysmic change to come. As Joseph Needham has demonstrated, China (and, now the whole Sinosphere) has a tradition of rationalism as old as that of the Occidental Monotheists (note: Islam is part of that Occident) and, in some ways, broader). For a concrete example, it suffices to compare the game Japanese call *igo* and Chinese call *weichi* to the cruder board game we call chess. The thinking people of the West will need to join hands with their counterparts in the Far East to create responsible societies, practicing not only population but *consumption* control (only workable with limits on wealth) yet attractive enough to stop and even reverse the growth of know-nothing fundamentalism. ◎ It is decades too late to avoid the real horrors that could have been avoided had the idealism of the sixties and early seventies taken root for good, then. But, there is always room for *more* disaster, so we might as well keep *trying* to save the world. Perhaps I am deluded, but I cannot imagine any intelligent person can believe otherwise in his or her deepest heart, even if he or she calls upon the Invisible Hand to give its benediction to the sin of living "life as usual" when *nothing* is. *Amen*.

After that *sad* page about *Writing at the End of the World*, another page to help the good reader cheer up again –

Banana, Turnip Village and *One Tea* – or, the haiku *nom de plume*.

In 1585, Luis Frois S.J. contrasted European women named after saints with Japanese women named "kettle, crane, turtle, sandal, tea and bamboo." As Michael Cooper noted in *They Came to Japan* (1965), "he might also have included more pleasing names such as Spring, Plum, Bounty and Purity." In 1900, Lafcadio Hearn, whose last name was Sinofied as Eight-Clouds 八雲(ha-un), gave us a more balanced and charming 48-page sketch of "Japanese Female Names," broken down by type in *Shadowings*. Japanese of both sexes have far greater variety in first names than Occidentals. That may partly be due to the variety of ways that Chinese characters may be pronounced in Japanese, but also involves choice. If Japanese tended to have their personal bowls and chopsticks, they were, likewise, more individualistic than Occidentals when it came to names, though not so strict about it as the Balinese who, I have read, took care that no one born was given a name anyone else had. In the case of the *haigô* or *haimyô*, the *nom de plume* used by haikai, and later, haiku poets, however, the principle of having unique names was strictly observed, though mistakes were made due to ignorance of obscure predecessors or the secondary *noma de plume* of poets better known by other names. The names tend to come from favored moral qualities, the name or names given to the atelier (with the brush involved, the poet always has the air of an artist) – both of these common practice with Chinese poets – part of the name of beloved poets, living or long dead, themes of a *ku* by the poet that became well-known, and names that represented something about the poet's taste or attitude. Enough analysis. Doubtless, someone has done a thorough job of it already, and I have only to locate the work and translate it into English. So for now, let us just amuse ourselves with a rough sampling of five or ten score examples from the Poet Index in this book.

15c

One Break (rest)	ikkyû	一休
Worship Humbly	sôgi	宗祇

☆ Ikkyû, the famous Zen monk wrote many poems, many of which rhymed in Chinese, some of which were outrageous. Most 15c poets, i.e. the linked verse masters who started what came to be haiku, had boring names.

16c

Inherit Ha	jôha	紹巴
Bright Scold	shôshitsu	昌叱

☆ The few 16c names in this book include these two which are hard to translate. "Ha 巴" is a place name, a bug or an elephant-eating snake and only a scholar (not me) would know which. 昌 is "bold" and "open" as well as "bright."

16-17c

Purely Moral	teitoku also ↓	貞徳
SS Long Head	↑ also	長頭丸
Moral Foundation	tokugen	徳元

☆ Though I like more Teimon school *ku* than anyone I know, I find their pen names fulsome. At least, Teitoku had the sense to use another pen name ! The 丸 is "round" but also indicates the name of a ship.

17c

Banana	bashô	芭蕉
Dancing Stone	buseki	舞石
Bamboo Door	chikuko	竹戸
Mud Cow	deigyû	泥牛
Road Can	dôka	道可
Not Seek	fukyû	不求
No Profit	futoku	不得
One Leaf Child	ichiyôshi	一葉子
Turtle Hole	kidô	亀洞
Season Chant	kigin	季吟
This Horn/Gate/Corner	kikaku	其角
Happy Rule/Gov.	kôji	幸治
Light Is/Have	kôyû	光有
Leave Come	kyorai	去来
Break/Rest Sound	kyûon	休音
Storm Orchard	ranran	嵐蘭
Wave Blossoms	rôka	浪花
Right Head (boss)	seichô	正長
Quiet Longevity	seiju	静壽
SS Only / Just Round	shigan	只丸
Double Trust	shigeyori	重頼
Faith Tranquil	shinan	信安
Win Peace	shôan	勝安
Right Balance	shôhei	正平
Worship Cause	sôin	宗因
Swamp Quail	takuchi	澤雉
Set Time	teiji	定時
Friend Quiet	yûsei	友静
Is Color	zaishiki	在色

☆ Banana is Bashô, a name he took after students got him a place and planted them. 17c names tend toward Confucian (Teimon school moralizing) Taoist (natural-ism) and some natural motif. 長 denotes "long" but can mean "boss."

17-18c

Pasture-kid	bokudô	牧童
Road Easy/Fun	dôraku	道楽
Not Cornered	fukaku	不角(
Floating Stone	fuseki	浮石
Word Water	gonsui	言水
Word Hue	gonshiki	言色
One Look	◎ikken	一見
Like Wind	jofû	如風
Ten Sophies	◎juttetsu	十哲
Cannot	◎ kafu	可不
Can Bend	◎ kakyoku	可曲
Can Win	◎ kashô	可勝
Lucky White	◎kippaku	吉白
Turtle Wood	◎ kirin	亀林
Not Yet Heard	◎ mibun	未聞
Before Existence	◎mizon	未存
Gull Walk	◎ ôho	鴎歩
Demon Pierce	onitsura	鬼貫
Come Mountain	raizan	来山
Flow Hare	◎ ryûto	流兎
Sand Gate	◎ samon	沙門
Three Men	sanjin	三人
Cedar Wind	sanpû	杉風
Voice Doubt	◎seigi	声疑
Poem Fisher	◎ shichô	詩釣
Stop Moon	◎ shigetsu	止月
Support Thought	shikô	支考
Believe Snow	◎ shinseki	信雪
Pine Chant	◎ shôgin	松吟
Laugh Water	◎ shôsui	笑水
Grass Bug	◎sôchû	草虫
Park Woman	sonojo	園女
Cloud Dust	◎ unjin	雲塵

Evening Walk	◎	yûho 夕歩	Stone Tusk	sekiga 石牙	'Mum Male	kikuo 菊雄
Play Leaf	◎	yûyô 遊葉	Sage Fish	sengyo 仙魚	Capital Horse	kyôma 京馬
			Thousand Cogs/Cars	sensha 千車	Storm Without	rangai 嵐外
			Paper Chief	shichô 紙長	Cuckoo	shiki 子規
			White Male	shirao 白雄	Plain Water	sosui 素水

☆ The circles show *ku* and poet are from the collection Shiki's *Categorical* shorthanded as 大三物. The phrase is in many titles. One scholar wrote that she thought it a mid-18c work, but I bet on one published in 1697. Because the poet's name fits the content of the *ku* too often for chance and few of the poets are found in my *haiku name dict.* (俳句 人名辞典). I suspect most of the names were invented by the editor who may have written their *ku*, too (俳諧研究者諸君、頼むよ). If so, my hat is off to him, but I hope it does not retire the names forever!

Invite Waves	shôha 召波			
Smiling Child	shôshi 笑子	☆ Shiki 子規 is one of dozens of names for the cuckoo! The magazine he started, "Hototogisu," is another.		
Spring Thunder	shunrai 春雷			
Spring Come	shunrai 春来			
Plainly Outside	sogai 素外	**19-20c**		
Grass Saw	sôkyo 草鋸	Charcoal/ink-water	bokusui 墨水	
SS Plain, or Plain Round	somaru 素丸	Five Skies	gokû 五空	
Worship Spring	sôshun 宗春	Hundred Herbs	hyakusô 百艸	
Water Room	suishitsu 水室	Usually Can	jôka 常可	
Bold Modesty	taigi 太祇	Demon Castle	kijô 鬼城	
Many Era Woman	tayojo 多代女	Verse Buddha	kubutsu 句佛	
Peach Sage	tôsen 桃仙	Mirror Bloom	kyôka 鏡花	
Rain Voice	usei 雨声	'Mum Crazy	kikukyô 菊狂	
Rabbit Cloud	uun 卯雲	Empty Child	kyoshi 虚子	
Soft Corners	wakaku 和角	Humming Snow	meisetsu 鳴雪	
Field Slope	yaba 野坂	Snow Man	setsujin 雪人	

18c

Turnip Village	buson 蕪村
Chant Long/Chief	ginchô 吟長
Gem Wave	gyokuha 玉波
Sunrise Stage	gyôtai 暁台
Fat Sparrow	hajaku 巴雀
White Wings	hakuu 白羽
Hundred Men	hyakujin 百人
North Branch	hokushi 北枝
Move Bamboo	ichiku 移竹
One Bog	ittaku 一澤
Wet Child	junshi 潤子
Double Thick	jûkô 重厚
Complete Come	kanrai 完来
Crown Dew	kanro 冠露
This Road	kidô 其道
Harp Thoughts	kinkô 琴考
Old Mountain	kosan 古山
Old Friend Nun	koyû-ni 古友尼
Chestnut Pavillion	kyodô 栗堂
Mirror Tree	kyôju 鏡樹
Teach Nothing	kyômu 教無
Full Bright	manmei 満明
Small Woman	mine 小女
Sleepy Road	minji 眠路
Like Happiness	nyokô 如幸
SS Big Inlet	ôemaru 大江丸
Pleasant Dreams	rakumu 楽夢
Storm Shine	rankô 嵐光
Herons Ten	rojû 鷺十
Rush Boat	roshû 蘆舟
Good Rock	ryôseki 良石
Nettle Thick	ryôta 蓼太
Dragon Tail	ryûbi 龍尾
Tea Quiet	sasei 茶静
Blue Rock	seiseki 青石

☆ On the whole, nature has won out and we have fine names like Sleepy Road and Peach Sage.

18-19c

Plum-room	baishitsu 梅室
Horse-shine	bakô 馬光
Eyebrow-peak	bihô 眉峰
Letter-melon	bunka 文瓜
Bamboo Man	chikujin 竹人
Spider Willow	chiryû 蜘柳
Thousand Eras	chiyo 千代
Butterfly Dream	chômu 蝶夢
One Tea	issa 一茶
Fish Gulch	nabuchi 魚淵
Become Beauty	seibi 成美
Star Cloth Nun	seifu-ni 星布尼
Grass Shine	shikô 芝光
Plain Moon	sogetsu 素月
Sun/Day Man	watsujin 日人
Exists Doubt	zongi 存疑

☆ More of the same. The last name, Zongi, is also used to describe *ku* allegedly but possibly not Bashô's.

19c

Moon Guard	gesshu 月守
Flower Hat	hanakasa 花笠
Ice Urn	hyôko 氷壺
One Tool	ichigu 一具
Pensive Grass	isô 惟艸
Summer Wind	kafû 夏風
Draw-near Pillar	kijû 寄柱

☆ Kyoshi's name puns on an over-rated warrior or gentleman 虚士 and not long ago was adopted by Quantum physics for what Indo-European's call _____.

20c

Foam-path-woman	awajijo 淡路女
Butterfly Robe	chôi 蝶衣
Freed Bay	hôkô 放江
Baggage Wind	kafû 荷風
Lucky Boat	kishû 喜舟
Empty Pore	kyokô 虚吼
Mountain Head Fire	santôka 山頭火
Laughing Moon	shôgetsu 笑月
New Child	shinko 新子
Spring Elephant	shunshô 春象
Winter Leaves	tôyô 冬葉
Eight-fold Cherry	yaezakura 八重桜

<u>Contemporary</u>

Most people today use their own names but some make them up. My haiyû Tenki, got his *haigô*, literally "sky-mood" or "heaven-spirit," but *meaning* "weather," from his last name, Ueda, written "upper-field," but *sounding* like the Japanese pronunciation of the English word "weather!" My own *gô*, Keigu, 敬愚, literally,"respect/ful-fool/ish/ness" reflects my attitude and puns on a standard sign-off, 敬具, "respectful-tool."

Lost specs for Shifû 紙風 *Paper Wind!*

A selection of New Year's *ku* from *A Dictionary of Haiku Classified by Season Words with Traditional and Modern Methods* by Jane Reichhold (1992), ○ with a few minor changes by the author, with her permission.

the first gong
pushed out of the steeple
by the second one

mountain echo > older < when i hear it

bells
in the natal place
a womb opens

a new year
rising from wild seas
a few stars

champagne bubbles
fifty years
up my nose

a new year's dream
very close to shore
a whale blows

new year's day
a wind-blown twig
writing on snow

sky-clad
the new-born comes wrapped
in previous lives

a huge wave
thunders up the beach
my birthday

year of the snake
a banner waving ~
she's my friend

threading a needle on new year's day the spool unwinds

new year's breakfast
peeled cold eggs
snowflakes

birthday beach walk
wetted by the seventh wave
to be born again

moon mirror
reflecting a wrinkled face
born the same day

new year's day
meeting the neighbor's smile
with cold on my teeth

that too
a present of sour plums
on my birthday

new year's day
no resolutions for me
i've shoveled snow

Jane's birthday is in mid-January; but, regardless of the actual date of her birth, the unity of the Cosmic and the individual reflects the wisdom of the Sinosphere's concept of the New Year. The Year of the Snake *ku* is "- For Elaine Sherlund," why I did not ask; and the last, dedicated to the memory of Bruce Lamb, who had one too many . . . shovels.

Where and How This Book Began to be Sorted Out

Each strip of paper has a haiku, most of which are cut from copies of pages of books I could not afford to buy, some of which are hand-written, arranged alphabetically in piles, each a single seasonal theme, unless the theme was huge and the number of *ku* too large, in which case, several sub-theme piles were used. When piles got so high they tipped over they were transfered to envelopes. After months of this sorting, I arranged the piles into files. Since no files existed for strips of paper, I made them by weaving large strips of paper through slits cut into paper folded into folders as you can see in the second photograph. This work was done in a penthouse (sounds good until you know the AC units are on the roof right over your head) in Coconut Grove, Florida, where I house-sat (Thank you Hank and Lyle!). *And, special thanks to my mother for introducing me to creation myths and thereby turning me into a cosmopolitan when still a kid.*

Acknowledgment & Bibliographilia

Books in English (or particularly worth mentioning to those who cannot read Japanese)

I am in debt to the following:

◎The *OJD*. My shorthand for **The Only Japanese Dictionary**, in the original "Japanese National Language Large Dictionary," **Nihon Kokugo Daijiten**, a ten (small-print) or twenty (large-print) volume dictionary that includes many poems, from the classy *waka* to obscene *senryû*, as examples. In Japanese only. *It is more fun than Samuel Johnson.*

◎***Shiki's Categorical.*** My shorthand for the ***Bunrui-betsu Haiku Zenshû***, a 12-volume set of tens of thousands of *ku*, seasonally and phenomenologically arranged by Shiki, and published after his death in the early 20c. In an ideal world, it would be improved, enlarged and put up on the web, but the establishment in Japan, like that in the English-speaking world, either fails to see the importance of leveling the playing field for good scholarship, or prefers to keep their sources to themselves. The *Categorical*, which I am lucky to own, gives the sources of the *ku* but usually in an abbreviated form and if there is a separate bibliography with the full titles and date, I do not have it.

◎***Kato Ikuya's Droll Haiku.*** Luckily, most sources given in Shiki's Categorical can be found in a bibliography in Kato's *Kokkei Haiku Daizen,* for which I am grateful. ☆I could not verify the date of my single largest source of New Year's *ku* in the *Categorical,* the Big Three Thing, or *Dai-sanbutsu* (if that is how 大三物 is pronounced, here). My best guess is that it was 誹諧大三物, published in 1697, but it might be a whole series published from 1688 to 1703.

To a lesser degree, I am in debt to:

◎ **The annotators** of Japanese pocket book versions of the 8c collection of Japanese poetry ***Manyôshû,*** the early 10c ◎ ***Kokinshû*** anthology ◎ and the early haikai anthology ***Shoki-haikaishû*** (pub. Iwanami). Over 90% of the poetry came from books (in Japanese) that had no annotation, and where I have found anyone's comments, I give credit on the page where they appear. ◎ Yaba Katsuyuki's dictionary of Issa, ***Issa Dai-jiten,*** for its easy to reference chronology.

◎**R.H. Blyth:** *Haiku*, vol.2, *Spring* (Hokuseido Press. 1950/1981). Quoting myself (*Cherry Blossom Epiphany*) "I must confess I was half-sad to find he found so many of the best ku before me!" Luckily, he gives only 20 pages to the New Year, which leaves 99.9% of the body of New Year poetry, *i.e.*, the dregs, to me. I do not learn much about haiku in Blyth, but he is always fun. You can find something to agree with and disagree with on every lively page. Libraries, note: like Lafcadio Hearn, Blyth is one of few authors whose work is worth keeping.

◎**Steven D. Carter** *Traditional Japanese Poetry* (Stanford UP: 1991) The best anthology of Japanese poetry I have read. Carter not only gives the classics, but has a good nose for interesting metaphor. Though he doggedly clings to the English syllabet, he usually keeps the beat count low enough that it is not a problem.

◎ **Laurel Rasplica Rodd & Mary Catherine Henkenius:** *Kokinshû* Cheng & Tsui Company (1984/96). All 1,111 poems of this second of the major ancient anthologies. Some of the translations deserve praise for bold choices and the hard-found perfect word, but the enjambment after articles (imagine a line ending in "the!") and padding for syllables is misguided.

◎**Makoto Ueda:** *Bashô and His Interpreters* Stanford Univ. press 1992. Quoted only a few times, I mention it as it is the *only* book about Japanese haiku in English that I am completely satisfied with! Because the text is almost entirely translated selections of commentary/ interpretation of Bashô's *ku* – as opposed to the critical analysis or pre-digested pabulum which are the only templates recognized by "our" reviews of the scholarly and popular ilk, respectively – it has received far too little attention.

◎**Harold Stewart:** *A Chime of Windbells* (Tuttle:1969). Stewart's translation is fun both for being in rhymed couplet and for the padding, which is not just syllable-counting or beat-making, but reads between the words of the original *ku*. Perhaps because his 1960 *Net of Fireflies* neglected the New Year (including only a few *ku* within the Winter), *Chime* made up for it by putting the New Year Season up front and giving it pages of attention in the 90-pg postscript essay on traditional background. Readers who want more on the relationship of the New Year to Shintô, Taoism and Confucianism. Two sentences, in case you missed a couple more in this book: *". . . the extremely restricted outlook of modern science and philosophy at once stands revealed when it is seen that they recognize as real only the psychophysical modes of existence, ignoring all but the lowest of the "thirty-three" planes of the total Universe. For this mentality, the myth of Amaterasu's re-emergence becomes "nothing but" an infantile fantasy of the birth trauma, or a primitive attempt to account for an eclipse of the sun!"*

And, I cite my own books, mostly:

◎**Robin D. Gill:** *Topsy-turvy 1585* (Paraverse Press 2004). This 740 pg. translation+explication of the 611 ways Europeans and Japanese were contrary, according to Luis Frois SJ in 1585, covers so much ground I cannot help citing it whenever I think the reader might want to "see" this or that about Japanese culture. Note: you may search within the book *for free* at Amazon. A 500-page "short" version is also on sale for weak-armed readers.

◎◎**There are more books,** but I refrain from listing them, as I give enough information *when they are cited* – how I *despise* the practice of segregating notes from text and placing them at chapter/book's end! – and all may be found on the web. For more bibliographic information in English, please see *Rise, Ye Sea Slugs!*

◎◎◎Most help with interpreting *ku* came from Prof. Kikuchi a few years ago, from contributors to my more recent online *Haiku Mondôjô* set up by Tenki and from Masako – often called simply "my respondent," who deserves to be the *first* mentioned. She may well be the top translator in the world and I do not give her full name because she is already asked to do more translations than any one person can! I thank the handful of haiku poets who answered questions at my Haiku Q&A site (in Japanese only) and others for mental & monetary support.

I give more information on Japanese sources *in Japanese alone,* for it only matters to those who can read it.

Books in Japanese   歌・句の出典

◇歌　○『万葉集』は岩波の中西注。○『古今』は講談社学術文庫の久方注。○『新古今』も○『山家』も岩波の古い文庫で、注など皆無。高松注「新古今」あるが全歌もない、注が短い。○「後拾遺」他から幾つかの首がwebで。

◇句　○別な方で見つけた句も含めて、本書の句の大半までも掲載する子規の『分類別全俳句』（アルス）という古句中心の十二冊もある、最大の句集への借りが、最も大きいが、各句の出典の年付けが殆ど加藤郁乎『近世滑稽俳句大全』（読売新聞社1993）の引用書目のお陰でわかった。（安い分類別全12冊を見つけた鶴ケ谷さん、有難う。）○『一茶全集』（信濃毎日新聞＝全巻）では、一茶句だけではなく、△「素丸句集」なども掲載。改造社の『俳諧歳時記』（昭和8）の5冊における句の選択が素晴らしいが、多くが「分類別」に重複する。ただし、一茶、蕪村、千代、他なん人かの作品が何倍も多くなっているし、徳川末＋明治の句もある。○今井著『俳句大全』には、大正の句もあり、機知のある句も多い。○　アルス版の子規全集の11、12巻にある『俳家別全集』も大いに利用（変なことに講談社の子規全集にこの素晴らしい二冊が見当たらなかった）。『俳家別全集』を読むまで、大手　俳家に凝ったが、一度拝見すれば、様々の非人に惚れた。鶴ケ谷さん、有難う。○宗祇ら二万句も別『大発句帳』古典文庫版。「発句」の多くが只句と思うが！○岩波体系のDB捜索三回も断れた（涙）が「犬子」と「談林十百韻」などある『初期俳諧集』（岩波）が手元にあり、注に感謝。○集英社の「俳書体系」も数冊、十年前に読み、句をコピーしたりしたが、間違いないように確認することができない。○芭蕉は、岩波文庫の他、山本兼吉の解説本『芭蕉明句集』もある。山本兼吉のこの本こそが古句理解への大先生。やはり、多少実のある解説を読まなければ、古句の複層読みを想像すらできないものです。○『加賀の千代全集』1955 からの複写、尚美さん、有難う。○尾形他注『蕪村全集』（講談社 1992）○素檗の句が殆ど矢羽編『俳人藤森。。』から拾った。このような、一人の俳家の全集、なによりも欲しいものです。もっと買いたいが、お金がない。が、鈴木さん、有難う：『巴人の全句を読む』も役立ちました。当本頂いたら、その輪読大賛成で、夜半亭へ手紙だせば、『蕪村の『宇都宮歳旦長』がタダで。江連晴生さん、皆さん有難う。故丸山先生の素晴らしい姿勢が本書の注に書き止めた。○「柳多留」も初期川柳も岩波文庫（三万円の奴も欲しイ！）が中心が、「武玉川」の句と柳多留の年付がわが宝でもある、昭和2年の『川柳雑俳集』に借りある。○子規の句は何年か前全集を読んだときのノットから。岩波の子規句集の句数が少な過ぎるが全句も読んだ。虚子句は1902年まで全句読んだ。自分の手書き読まない、又子規と虚子の句の混同のため、度々虚子記念館の方の世話になりました。ただ、子規記念館も誰か作るべきと思う。◎子規の「類別」のほかに役立った歳時記は　改造社の『俳諧歳時記』（昭和八年）　◎現代句は原則として、除けたかったが、それでも載せたものの多くが、○　金子兜太ら編『子どもの俳句歳時記』（蝸牛社 1997）、○俳人協会編『季題別現代俳句遍集』（平成九 1997）。○その他に、『講談社大歳時記』。○そしてWebから。右脳俳句という、楽しい句の多いサイトからの句、幾つか入っているが、うまく連絡取れずお詫びします。○『類別』で句を再び見つけるのが大変で、単語などから捜索できる高沢良一の膨大な俳諧DBも大助になったが、著作権の問題のためか、只今NetからSiteのアクセスが難しくなった。いずれにして、高沢氏は句界の聖かと私はおもいます。○浮御堂、Satin Doll、水族館の俳友、感謝します。

☆　敬愚の句とは、拙句。『Rise, Ye Sea Slugs!』の場合と違って、初句索引などに入れなかった。

☆☆「再現」とは？ わがPCがまだ日本語できなかった頃、ローマ字で打ち込んだ句である。その原文、再び見つけなかった時、再現するしかなかった。同じ句の書き方が日本語の出典変れば、全然違うから、よくないと知りながらも、再現が現代読みよりも原文に近い場合もある。間違いも折々あるだろうが。

☆☆☆　総てにおいてのわが大師はOJDつまりOnly Japanese Dictionaryである。それが、小学館の『日本国語大辞典』。例句、歌などのみならず、無数の事を教えてくれる、毎日何十回も参考になる。そのおかげで、米国、しかもフロリダ州におりながら、このような本でも書ける。日本人はこの国宝をもっとつよく意識すべき、英国人がOEDを支持するように、この辞典をさらに立派なものに改造、拡大して、大いに利用してほしい（変な外人の意見）。

国研利用拒否、大学図書館DB不可用など、だけは。

Come to the *Haiku Q & A!*   俳句問答場へのご紹介

難句あるいは、私にとっての難句を解くための助言、常に求めております。句によっては、日本人で直感の効く者なら、誰でもいい場合もあれば、江戸歴史、あるいは生活様式の研究家、初期連歌以前の語彙＋文法に自信ある古語学者、特定の俳諧家の専門家でなければ、解決できない場合も少なくない。いわゆる bbs か blog でその難句解読を楽しく、しかも徹底てきに公の場で行いたい。そのために皆さんのご協力を頼みます。

The author needs assistance to read difficult *ku* and has a web-page for that purpose. It is only in Japanese, for discussions about difficult points in Japanese are sometimes only posible in Japanese and almost always easier.

Let's Do the *Errata* Together!   正誤表を御一緒にしたいが。。。

あらっ！と思えば、paraverse.org へ来て頂ければいい。直すべき誤訳その他の間違い。載せてもらいたいクレジット。ただ、こう加えないとなんとなく不足を感じたところ。教えてください！正誤表に御指摘を掲載します。お名前、又（あれば）短い宣伝も、その情報と一緒に載せても構いません。

Even if you do not read and write Japanese, should you find something wrong, or lacking, in this book, or any paraverse press books, please inform the author-publisher so it may be corrected or improved. You will be given as much credit as you want, on-line or in-print.

Gloss or *Marginalia:* Why Not?   欄外注を投稿して見ませんか

一人で本を書くのが淋しい。いつか、学生さんと、共著でも出したい。又、自分の言葉ばかりの本よりも、他人の文書も、そのまま（多少加減もあいうるが）入った、雑文が面白く読めるかと思います。自然あるいは不自然科学の専門家からの欄外注を、待っております。

To *gloss* something is to add your tongue, which is to say, words, to another's writing. Montaigne has harsh words for the practice as it was normally understood in the late-16c: *"Men do not know the natural infirmity of their mind: it does nothing but ferret and quest, and keeps incessantly whirling around, building up and becoming entangled in its own work, like our silkworms, and is suffocated in it."* (trans. DM Frame). I am not, however, limiting glosses to *criticism* or *interpretation*, though I enjoy and welcome both, but request your cooperation in *improving* my books – making them partly *yours* – with entertaining *marginalia*. Think about what *you* might add to educate nd entertain the readers of this book, or any paraverse press book. Natural or unnatural history is equally welcome, as are literary finds (as much as possible in the words of the original), so long as the information provided is sufficiently dense or delightfully surprising.

ロビン・D・ギル著の英訳俳諧書の好評抜粋

Rise, Ye Sea Slugs! (海鼠千句) について。五大学 (Amherst, Smith 等) の Literary Translation 誌、Metamorphoses 2005 春号評者＝スミスカレッジ日本語学、日本文学教授トーマス・H・ローリック

（前略）ギルの手によるその翻訳は簡潔で的をえており、しばしば優雅な味わいがある。これほど翻訳を詳細に説明してある俳句の英訳書は、私の知る限り他に類を見ない。すでに熟練した翻訳家であり、俳人でもある（本書中百句以上が敬愚というペンネームをもつ著者の作である）著者は、芸術としての翻訳の強力な擁護者でもある。どの句にも彼の翻訳のあとに続いて、それぞれ微妙に異なる解釈のあいだを日本文学、歴史、現代の文化についての余談、さまざまな色合いの逸話、ときには暴言までが自由に往来する。（中略）文学についても日常生活についても必ず信頼でき、しばしば愉快でもある彼の日本文化観に私は舌を巻くほかなかった。なにしろ徹頭徹尾ナマコが句題の俳句を集めた本と聞けば当然期待される（事実そのとおりの）風変わりな点はともかく、著者はくろうとの俳人であり、文化と文化間の違いを機敏に理解しながらものを読むことのできる優れた才能に恵まれた魅力ある評論家である。興味津々の本書は、広く俳句愛好家、日本文学と海洋生物の研究者、プロ，アマをとわず翻訳家のすべてに喜ばれるにちがいない。

同著について。Modern Haiku 現代俳句（2004年冬春 35. 1 号）Haiku World:1996 の著者、ウィリアム J. ヒギンソン の５ページにわたる書評より

（前略）一人の翻訳者として、わたしはギルの俳句翻訳に対する姿勢は刺激的で挑戦的であると思う。彼は「翻訳者の原作に対する責任」（「対応する力」＝ ロバート ダンカン）という点で、果たすべき水準をきわめて高いところまで引き上げてきているのだ。（中略）この単一季語の大著は、日本の俳句文化の迷宮への、今までで一番優れた英語の窓口であろう。（中略）もし、ヤスダやブライスや、ヘンダーソンやウエダやシラネ＊［注：過去半世紀の俳句英訳名家］を読んだことがあるなら、ギルもお読みなさい。あなたの意識を深く広く拡大させてくれるから。そして、先の方々の著作を読んだことがないのなら、やっぱり先にギルをお読みなさい。彼のほうがずっとおもしろいから。

科学者の評 ＝「凄い！惚れてしまった。小柄な我が友を何年も研究してきたが、悪態をつかれるか、さもなければ忘れられた存在でしかない、と思っていた。ナマコ文学をめぐる日欧の差！悲しいかな、互いに隔てられた科学と文学には、理論においてはむろんのこと、用語上ですら、とてつもないギャップが隋所にみられる。両者を深いところで見事に融合した本で、科学者も納得させる。恐れ入りました。」Alexander Kerr 博士 ＝ Web of Life プロジェクトの海鼠科担当、独語の海鼠研究（古典）の英訳、環境進化論の研究に従事する気鋭の生物学者。James Cook 大学属。

Fly-ku! (蝿句) について。オンライン句誌『Simply Haiku』創立者かつ編集者ロバート・D・ウイルソンの書評より

（前略）それだけにアメリカの詩人で学者のロビン・D・ギルの著書に出くわしたときの私の驚きは大きかった。書きぶりはジャック・ケルアック流即興を思わせ、ものの考え方はヘルマン・ヘッセ、小林一茶、ルイス・キャロル、このすべてを丸めて一つにしたような本なのだ。。。

桜・花見三千古句の英訳ある新刊 ***Cherry Blossom Epiphany:*** The Poetry and Philosophy of a Flowering Tree の書評と上記書評の全文は、http://www.paraverse.org で、ご覧に。

Critical Acclaim of Previous Haiku-related books by robin d. gill

Re: **Rise, Ye Sea Slugs!** (Close to 1,000 *ku* about sea cucumbers translated from Japanese).

"I wondered, can one really devote 480 pages to haiku on sea slugs? The answer is emphatically 'yes.' Although difficult to read from beginning to end, this book contains great learning and insight, and deserves a wide reading among specialists and non-specialists alike."

"For many of the haiku, Gill gives multiple translations as a way of showing possible interpretations. I know of no other book of English translations of haiku that goes to such lengths to explain translations, which in Gill's hands are accurate, economical, and often elegant. In addition to being an accomplished translator and poet (over 100 of the poems are by the author, under the nom de plume keigu), Gill is an articulate defender of the art of translation."

"Gill is also a master of the discursive footnote, and at times I found myself reading along the bottoms of the pages, jumping among footnotes, and marveling at his often amusing and always reliable views of Japanese culture, both literary and everyday. For all the eccentricities one might expect (and does find) in a book devoted entirely to Japanese haiku on the sea slug, the author is an accomplished haiku writer, a very talented and engaging critic, capable of reading with an acute understanding of culture and cultural differences. Haiku enthusiasts, scholars of Japanese literature and marine biology, and professional and amateur translators alike will certainly welcome this interesting book."

–Thomas H. Rohlich, Professor of Japanese Language and Literature at Smith College, from *Metamorphoses*: the journal of the five college faculty seminar on literary translation (Spring 2005 (Vol. 13.1)).

"Some of the most engaging commentary on haiku (and *senryû* and the occasional *tanka* or *kyôka*) ever to see print. . . .

"Reading it, we see the deep affection of the Japanese for the phenomena of their own environment and culture. At the same time, we encounter one of the most original minds to take up the related subjects of haiku and cross-cultural communication. . . .

"This single-topic tome may be our best English-language window yet into the labyrinth of Japanese haikai culture. If you have read Yasuda, Blyth, Henderson, Ueda, and Shirane, then read Gill. He will expand your mind. If you have not read those guys yet, then read Gill first. He's more fun."

– William J. Higginson, author, in *Modern Haiku* (volume 35.1 winter-spring 2004). From a five-page review.

Re: **Fly-ku!** (Translations of fly & fly-swatting *ku*, with an in-depth study of Issa's famous fly-ku, *"Don't swat!"*)

"An American scholar and poet who writes in an extemporaneous style akin to that of Jack Kerouac; thinks like Herman Hesse, Koyabashi Issa, and Lewis Carroll, all rolled into one."

– Robert D. Wilson, publisher+editor of the on-line magazine *Simply Haiku* (2005-summer)

"For those with the patience, the unfolding of 600 variations on a theme, with elegant discourse, is a treat, and, at times, when the author delves into the lively back-and-forth on the internet, the past and present of haiku, or the root and uses of various Japanese words, it becomes quite jolly."

"Gill strikes us as no less than amazing. Why isn't he teaching at Yale, or the University of California, or Tokyo University? His references include no end of obscure Japanese lore, plus quotes and notes from such artists as Clare, Lovelace, Steinbeck, Dumont, Verdi, Satie, Blyth, Shakespeare, Emily Dickinson."

– Carlos Amantea, author of *The Blob That Ate Oaxaca* in R.A.L.P.H. (Review of Art, Literature, Philosophy & History)

☆ ☆ ☆ ☆ ☆

for more of these reviews, please visit the respective websites or http://www.paraverse.org

One of the Author's Bookcases in Japan at the Time He was Studying Olde Haiku.

Can you see the plum blossoms to the right, just to the left
of the vine twisting around the branch? Kozo-kotoshi.
The Old Year is in the books, piled double
and the New one in the flowers.
The photo was taken
from my futon
on the floor
in ikuta
japan
1998
rd
g

INDEXES   POET: 451-5, POEM: 456-60, PEOPLE: 461, ODDS & ENDS: 462-   451

POET index: With the exception of the contemporary poet, only the *nome de plume*, or *haigo* is given 号のある俳人を氏名から引く辞典、大嫌い。Because many poets used more than one *haigo*, and names in some books may have been *ad-hoc* (made to fit the content of the *ku*, as once was common in English, too), their number is overstated とりわけ『大三物』には、そういう疑い大にあり。A *hyphen + single date means year-of-death*, while a hyphen-less single date means the work in which the *ku* appears. ある句は、出典の年付のずっと前のものだと確認できる場合、教えて下さい。再版の祭、直します! It can be impossible to tell the intended pronunciation of a name. Lacking sufficient references, my respondents and I often had to settle on an educated guess. Please check the *Errata* at www.paraverse.org before quoting. *Waka* poet names sometimes are not given. Neither are *senryû* poets. The first is not the main concern of the book and the second often not given in the original. The names and dates of the anthologies *are*. 発音未定の場合、原則として音読みにするが、古き俳号には訓読みも多い。又紹巴はjôhaでありshôhaでない等常用外の場合、大体「俳句人名辞典」の参考によるものです。きっと間違いが多い。再版の前に専門家のご協力を乞う。 I apologize for inconsistency. Sometimes a source is given here and not within the text, and vice versa. And there are ugly abbreviations. Requirements of formal style, aesthetic presentation+economy – space and time, for the author has no help and every second spent on the index takes away from that available for more important editing – often clash, and this was the best he/I could do.   rdg

Aioigaki kajin 20c 相生垣瓜人 221
akamatsu kaoriko 赤松薫子 20c 講談 389
akiyama minoryû 秋山巳之流 角川現代 309
☆ **anon 156, 276,281,291,297,297** ○毛吹草 (1645) 84,84,334   ○犬子(1633) 88
aoki chiyoko 青木千代子 1997 季題 316
arakida hisaoyu -1804 荒木田久老 273
ariwara no motokata 47
awajijo 淡路女 1890-1955 河出新 426
awano seikei 20c 阿波野青畦 321
awano seihô 阿波野 青畝 20c 角川新 359
ayabe hitoyoshi 1997 綾部仁喜 同 308

Baigô 1759 梅郷 248
baikô 梅郊 1777 句鑑 211
☆**baiô** -1825 梅翁 153, **but see sôin**, for it was one of this famous poet's pen names. Most baiô *ku* are credited to him in lieu of advice to the contrary.   原則として、「梅翁」句を、その号もち宗因作のものとした。専門家のご異見求む。
BAISHITSU   1768-1852 梅室 115,182, 238,256,259,278,281,337,399,404,411 411, 436
bakô -1751 馬光 162
BASHÔ 1654-94 芭蕉 47,65,96,107,149, 155,165,192, 357,369,391,424 & one more,
☆dubious bashô 存擬芭蕉 181
beiô 1723-92 米翁 __ 明山荘 188
bihô 眉峰 1777 安永 6 250
☆ 望一 bô→môichi
bokudô-1715 牧童 120,434
bokuga ト峨 19c? 百家類題 125
bokuin 木因 1706 本朝文選 264,264
bokushi 牧之 1830 秋月庵発句集 310
bokusui 墨水-1914 改造社 367
bucchô -1715 仏頂和尚 152
bunga 文賀 1751 玉かつら 354
bunka 文瓜 1793 新類題発句集 332
bunkaku 聞角 1751 玉かづら 123
bunkei 文雞 1797 元除春遊 32
bunsen 文川 1761 玉暦十一 197
bunson-1713? 汶村 327,398,
BUSON 1715-83 蕪村 95, 105, 108, 121, 194, 280, 285

Chihara eiko 千原叡子 20c 角川現代 298
chiharu 千春 fl 1670 玉かつら 353
chikujin 竹人-1764 年間俳句集 191
chikuko 竹戸 1698 続猿蓑 188
chikutai 竹滞 19-20c?春夏秋冬 358
chiô 19-20c? 痴翁(maybe-1913? 痴遊) 432
chiryû 蜘柳 1777   57
chitatsu 1697 知辰 大三 167
☆ **CHIYO, CHIYO-JO** the same as, **CHIYO-NI** 千代 1701-75 (女・尼) 53,53,53,54,54,54,54,55,126,126,253,276, 304,320,332,373,396,398,401,402,402,402, 402,402,403,403,405,406,406,409,411,412
chôchôshi 蝶々子息? early-18c 二葉?あやにしき 262
chodô 1748-1814 樗堂 131

chôfukan early-20c 鳥不関 177
chôhô→shigekata
CHÔI 1886-1930 蝶衣 98,104,315,368, 373,380,413
chôjo 笘女 early-20c?花笠 109
chômu 1731-1795 蝶夢 192
chora -1780? 樗良 391
chôsho 重正 1697 大三 196
chôsui -1769? 鳥酔 104,129,146
chôsui 潮水 1860's 文久五百 63
chôsui 鳥睡 文永六 266
chôsui -1813 長翠 63
chôu-1741 蝶羽 201
chôwa 1637-1715 調和 144
☆長頭丸 **chôzûgan**?とは貞徳の号ぞ
chûshi/tadayuki 忠之 1697 大三 163

Daishi-oshô 18c?19c?大施和尚 264
dakotsu1886-1962 蛇笏 or 蛇笏? 320
danyû 團友 1712 千鳥掛 328
deigyû 泥牛 1697 大三 68
dôka 道可 1683 虚栗 352
dôraku 道楽 17-18c 談林 2 集英社 155
dôsetsu 道節 1592-1642 滑稽太平記 83
dôtaku 道宅 1645 毛吹草 81

Ekitei 易貞 18c? 同書入 249
endô goitsu 遠藤梧逸 285
enfû 圓風 1775 安永四 146
enshi 19c? 20c? 炎子+黄第一句集 168
enten1883-1963 炎天 373
ezure **seisei** .江連晴生 夜半亭の録 74,74

Fuchô 富長 1666 洗濯物 146
fûga 風峨 1793 親類題発句集 190
fujaku late-17c 芙雀 97
fujimoto hideo1997 富士本秀峰 172
fujiwara **shunzei** 1114-1204 藤原俊成 272,272
fûka 楓鹿 1697 大三 334
fukaku1651-1743 不角 101,186
fukuda ryôtei 福田蓼汀 20c kdsds 282
fûkoku 風国 c1700 古句を観る 127
fûkotsu?風凪（山の下に「豆」） 172
fukuzawa 富沢 1633 犬子 245
fukyû 不求 1680   江戸ヘンケイ 127
fumikuni 史邦 late-17c   小文庫 359
funasako taka1997 船迫たか 306
fura1883-1954 普羅 431
fusei?巾声 1697 大三物 135
fûsei 1885-1979 富安風生 381
fuseki 浮石 1697 大三 324
fushun 富春 1761 宝暦九 221
futoku 不得 1697 大三物 78
fuza 風山 n 1674 桜川 301

Gahô 我峰 1695 ありそ海 421
gain 雅因 -1818? 新選 92
gakô1777 雅郊 55
gazen -1911 瓦全 昭和一万句,年刊俳句集 298,372
genkô 元弘 1645 毛吹草 50
genkô 元工 1759 宝暦九 352
genshi 17-18c?玄仍 失出典 213
genshi 玄旨=細川幽斎 -1610 衆妙集 273
gensui 原水 1697 大三物 138

POET: 451-5, POEM: 456-60, PEOPLE: 461, ODDS & ENDS: 462-   INDEXES

gesshu 月守 1819 新五百題 139
getsuan 月庵 1930 最新俳句歳時記 58
getto 1868-1949 月斗 294,317
gidô 祇道 1765 歳旦帳 162
gikô 祇江　1765 明和二 134
ginchô 吟長　1765 明和二 199
ginka ＿＿ 吟霞 萬題 180
GINKÔ　1775/1776/1780 吟江 67, 100, 126, 156, 208, 248, 248, 251, 347
ginsei 吟静 1697 大三 331
giryô 1697 義量 大三物 38
gisan 祇山 1697 玉桂 100
gisen 祇川 1774 類題 350
gitoku 1765 祇徳 140
giyû 祇有 1765 明和二 69
gokû 五空 1874-1928 改造社 410
gomei 五明　-1803 大全 388
gonshiki 言色 1697 大三 339
GONSUI 1646-1719 言水　117,180,222, 276, 304,328,332,355,375,375,394
goshûi-shû 1086 後拾遺集 429?
gotô hinao 後藤比奈夫 20c 講談社大 294
gotô yowa 後藤夜半 contemp 276
gyokan 魚澗 1772? 文車(see nabuchi) 144
gyokuha 玉波 1751 鶉たち 396
gyokukô 玉江 四季 c1800 星布尼 336
GYÔTAI1731/2-92/3 kyôtai/gyôdai 暁台 389,390,390,391
gyûan ↓ 牛庵-1693? 238
gyûchô↑ 牛長俳諧人名録 238

Hagi-jo はぎ女 19-20c? 大全 295
hajaku 巴雀 1774 類題発句集 354
HAJIN 1672-1742 巴人 56 = sôa 宋阿, 90, 166, 257, 277, 325
hakon 19-20c 波岑 同 287
hakuei 白英 ~1720 1697 大三物 92
hakufû 泊楓 1728 桃の首途 248
hakutei 柏筵 1763 雑談 古選 129
hakuu 白羽 1744 宇都宮歳旦帖 280
hakuyû 白雄→ shirao
hamamo-jo/me? 19c?濱藻女 題業名所 167
hana はな 2001/1/1 右脳俳句 74
hanakasa 花笠 19c 明治俳句改造車 303
hanmin 1697 半眠 大三 186
hanzô 班象　1779 失出典 112
hara akiko 原晃子 中 1 (contemp.) 115
hara hatsuko1997 原はつ子 269
harigaya naoki 針ヶ谷直希 小五 219
hase hiroko1997 長谷弘子 172
hashimoto keiji 橋本鶏二 contemp 283
hatsuyû 鉢友 17-19c 失出典 435
hekigodô 碧梧桐-1937 同句集 379
hekisen 碧泉 early-20c?最新二万句 361
hino sojô 日野草城 20c 講談社大 282
hiramatsu asako1997 平松あさ子 308
hirose nakimaro1997 広瀬泣麻呂 314
hisajo 20c 久女 283
hitoyo 一夜　　右脳俳句 contemp 231
hogi 保義 mid-19c 文久 135
hôkaku 方角 花 (玉？1751?)かづら 325
hokko 1777 北国 112
hôkô -1930 放江 297
hôkoku 方谷 1761 宝暦十一 327
hokugen 北元 1775-1838 紙つひえ 145

hôkyû 法久　1697 大三物 73
honda shizue 本多静江 20c 講談大 338
honda yûka 20c 本多由加 172
hôsan　法三　1697 大三 210
hôshû 峰秀 mid-19c 文久五百 75
hôshû 芳洲 1856 新葉 238
hôtô 峯島 1775 安永四 141
hotta hisae1997 堀田ひさ江 174
hoyû 保友 1651/1656 夢見草 50
hyakujin 百人 1775 安永四 323
hyakujô 百丈 1775 安永四 339
hyakuo 百夫　1765 明和二 134
hyakusô　百艸 early 20c? 改造社 72
hyôko 氷壼 mid-19c　文久五百 143

Ichida? kazutada? 一只 1697 大三物 159
ichigi 一旦 19c 百家類題 135
ichigu-1853 一具 1855 断稿思藻 190
ichijû 一十 1775 安永四 239
ichiku 移竹　prob.1709-1760 (& somewhere)1764-1831??? 68
ichiryû 一流　大三 265
ichiyô 一蓉 1811 春山集 261
ichiyôshi 一葉子 1642 鷹づくば 88
ichû 1638 -1711 惟中 39
ikei 意計　　大三物 1697　68
ikken 一見 1697 大三 341
ikkô 一耕 1759 p48
ikkyû 1394-1481 一休 257
inahata teiko 稲畑汀子 35
ippyô -1840 一瓢 玉山人歌集 136
ISSA 1762-1827 一茶 43,49,52,52,65,66, 66,69, 89,96,98,98,98,102,105,105,106,111, 115,117,118,118,119,119,119,120,120, 127,128,128,140,140,147,156,157,157, 157,157,158,158,159,159,160,160,160,161, 161,161,165,178,178,182,184,186,187,215, 224,224,224,225,225,225,226,226,226,227, 227,227,227,228,228,228,229,229,229,229, 230,230,230,230,244,255,255,255,259,259, 260,261,263,275,278,278,278,283,283,292, 299,300, 306,309,324,325,326,336,336,342, 342,342,343,343,343,343,343,343,344,345, 345,345,345,349,351,356,356,362,362,369, 370,370,374,374,390,392,397,397,400, 400,400,405,405,407,407,408,410,419, 420,420,425,425,428,435
Issei 一清 c.1845 新草 252
isshi 一之 1697 大三 145
isso 一鼠 1772 其雪かけ 344
isô -1853 惟艸 251
isobe sekisui1997 磯部石水 303
ittaku 一澤 1706 心一つ 257
ittetsu 一鐵 (鉄= f.1675?) 262

Jichô 1783 治長　反故集 29
jiko 事紅＿＿堅並 103
jinbo kazunari 神保和成 98
jinbo namiko 神保奈美子　河出 384
jinbô tensetsu 神保愃 20c 角川 329
jinkô 尋香 百家類題 61
jitoku early-20c 自得ホトトギス 170
jiyû 二夕 1763 古選 260
jiyû 二遊 19-20c? 改造社 431
jofû 1661-1740 如風 1765 未来記 378
JÔHA1523-1602 紹巴 68, 101,122,412

jôka 常可 19-20c ?雑中 312
jôren 紹簾 1763 古選 374
jororo?如露露 改造社 年鑑俳句集 312
jôseki -1779 丈石 58
jôsô-1704 丈草,丈艸 406
jôsoku 1767 城仄 134
jotô 如稲 1697 大三 339
joun 如雲 18c?雑中 260
☆重は jû でなく shige になる事ある
jûhô 重方 19-20c 大三 123, 266
jûji 重次　1642 鷹つくば 81
jûkô 重厚 1786 30
junshi 潤子 1751 玉かづら 332
jushin 壽信 1666　洗濯物 351
juttetsu 十哲 1697 大三 358

Kadô 佳棠 1789 己酉初懐紙 310
kadokawa teruko 20c 角川照子　角川俳句 歳時記 第三版 185
kaen 佳園 1697 大三　199
kafu 可不 1697 大三物 95
kafû 荷風 1879-1959 永井荷風 285
kafû 可風 1775 安永四 161
kafû 夏風 late-19c 明治新俳句集 385
kagurai akio 20c 加倉井秋を 講談社大 293; kaidô 枴童 -1947 同 286
kakô カコウ　1777 安永六 127
kakô 可候 1777 安永六 267
kakyoku 可曲 1697 大三物 137
kanajo かな女 early-20c 大正新俳句 329
kanazaki masano1997 金崎雅野 同 269
kanetatsu ayako1997 金龍あや子 308
kanrai 完来 1747 五元？146
kanrô 19c? 20c? 寒樓　168, 303
kanro 冠露 1765 明和二 421
kansui 観水 1687 64
kanryû 澗龍 1761? 57
kasan late-19c 可山 明治一万句 181
kariki 何力　1765 明和二 207
kashô 可勝 1697 大三物 319
katei?鹿貞 1697 大三 133
katen?何云 nani iu?! 1697 大三 226
katori -1817 可都里　発句大業 97, 248
katsura かつら mid-19c 文久五百題 267
kawaguchi nobuko1997 川口登子 177
kawai jôko 川井城子 20c 角川三版 317
kawasuji keisui 1997 川筋渓水 175
kayo 華鴬 1777 新虚栗 356
keidô 景道 18?19?20c? つつきの原 421
keigu 敬愚 61 and a score more my alter wrote you will have to find in context.
keiseki 1774 溪石 141, 165
keisen 輕賎 1697 大三物 83
keisô 桂双　1807 類聚 99
keisui 渓水 late-19c 明治一万句 381
keiyû 慶友 1651/1633 いのこ 46, 243
kendô 絢堂 1799 元除春遊 32
kenmochi shiori 20c 劍持 志織 172
kenshi 見志 1697 大三物 62
kiboku 奇木 1700 東華集 265
kichichô(発音は岩波の犬子から)吉長　1697 大三 299
kidachi?kitatsu?紀 1712 正風彦根体 158
kidô fl 1690 亀洞 344
kien 奇淵 1765-1834 俳句大全 345

INDEXES   POET: 451-5, POEM: 456-60, PEOPLE: 461, ODDS & ENDS: 462-   453

kifû 枳風 1707 類柑子 104
kidô 其道 1761 宝暦十一 142
kigin 1624-1705 季吟 49, 257
kiin 希因 -1748,1763=古選 78
KIJÔ 1864-1938 鬼城 298,358,360
kijû 寄柱 mid-19c 文久五百題 95
KIKAKU-1707 其角 63,130,233,267,296, 333,348,349,368,373,378,392,406,414,422, 422,427
kikuo 菊雄 mid-19c 文久五百 147
kikukyô 菊狂 19-20c?古今類範 418
kinen lost ref.亀年 失出典 71
金月 1775 安永四 104
kinkô 琴考 1775 安永四 194
kinko c.1700 釣壺 201
kippaku 吉白 1697 大三物 222
kiren1775 鬼恋 154
kirin 吉林 1645 毛吹草 79
kirin 亀林 1697 大三物 106, 246
kiryû 其柳 1801 夢の猪名野 93
kiryû 其流 1683 虚栗 357
kisen 其川 18c 蕪村発句集九部 416, 430
kishû early-20c 喜舟 同 287
kisui 器水 1697 大三 181
kitamura kôichirô 1997 北村耕一路 307
kitanaga chieko 北永智恵子 小四 166
kiteki 帰的 1728 桃首途 116,120
kitô 1740-89 几董 426
kobune 小船 1697 大三 192
kochû 18c?19c? 壷中 263
kôetsushi 幸悦子 1697 大三 346
kogetsu 湖月 1775 安永四 124,337
kohaku 1867-1895 古白 303
kohô early-20c 孤峰 381
kôji 幸治 1633 えのこ 86
kojin 18-19-20c?鯨人 360
kojû 湖十-1738?46?80? 89? 1773=湖十 新選 136
kokaku 壺角 1772 其雪影 421
koken 1697 古軒 大三 71
kôken 幸賢 反故集(1810 if it's 反古供養 if not?)141
KOKINSHÛ (waka anthology) (905) 47, 48, 259, 393
kokoku 小蛄?最新二万句改造社 311
kômo 高茂 1697 大三 152
kondô keiko 1997 近籐けい子 174
korezô 是三 1656 夢見草 82
kosan 古山 1774 類題発句集 340
kôsui 好水 1697 大三 239
kôyô1866-1903 紅葉 255
koyô 菰葉 1765 明和二 331
kôyû 光有 1645 毛吹草 74, 87
koyû-ni 古友尼 late-18c 改造 335
kôzan 江山 1697 大三 149
kubota getsureishi 久保田月鈴子 20c 講談社大 293
kubutsu 1874-1943 句佛 167
kukinshi 九斤子 19-20c 改造社 383
kumanji 九萬字 20c 改造 285
kuson1881-1943 駒村 430
kutsuwada susumu 轡田進 20c 角川 383
kyodô 栗堂 1777 句鑑 104, 305
kyôju 鏡樹 1759 宝暦九 363
kyôka1873-1939 鏡花 397

kyokô 虚吼-1935 改造社 170
kyokusui 曲水 1697 大三 148
kyôkyoku 橘旭 1751 玉かづら 132
kyôma 京馬 1819 新選 267
kyômu 教無 1765 明和二 106,429
kyorai -1704 去来 194,362
kyorai 巨籟 early-20c ホトトギス 169
kyoroku or kyoriku -1715 許六 48, 222
kyôsen1765 擧扇 333,346
KYOSHI 1874-1959 虚子 60, 60, 164, 189, 195, 284, 294, 302, 350, 389
kyôtei 共貞 1697 大三 106
kyûho 休甫 1774 類題発句集 215
kyûhô 旭富 1819 文久五百 147
kyûkô 丘高 17?18?19c? 題業名所 142
kyûon 1633,1645 休音 212,352
kyûshitsu 旧室 (-1764) 142

Maeno seiko1997 前野聖子 385
manmaru1843 萬丸 260
manmei 満明 1765 明和二 332
manô 萬翁 1819 新選 160
manshi 1653-1719 萬子 393
mansuke 年付？満助 河越千句 71
mantarô 万太郎 1888-1963 講談社大 324
MANYÔSHÛ 8c 万葉集 387,393
maruyama kaido 丸山海道 20c kdsds 294
masaakira-1673 正章 87
masahide 1656-1723 正秀 305
masataka 正隆 失出典 9
matsuda chizu1997 松田知都 175
matsufuji kasan?20c 松籐夏山 kdsds 437
matsumiya mikiko1997 松宮美喜子 173
matsumoto takashi20c 松本たかし 287
matsumura miho 松村美穂 99
meian1892 明庵 205
meikakushi 鳴各子 20c 改造社 338
MEISETSU 1847-1926 鳴雪 109,151, 300, 419, 426, 431
miben 1697 未辨 大三 188
mibun 未聞 1697 大三 118
michihiko1755-1815 or -1819 道彦 43
michizane 845-903 道真 245
MIDORIJO 1885-1990 阿部みどり女 151, 288, 305, 413
mikan mitsuharu1997 美柑みつはる 333
mikyu 未及 1697 大三 218
minagawa hakuda 皆川白陀 20c 河出 384
minami daisuke 南大輔 子供俳句 172
minami kako 南佳子 98
minamoto nakamasa 源仲正 old 夫木集巻三十二雑部十四 364
minji 眠路 1765 明和二 116
misono eiko1997 御園英子 176
mitori みとり mid-19c 文久五百 263
mizon 未存 1697 大三 143, 178
mizuguchi yasuko 1997 水口泰子 175
mochiku 茂竹 19-20c?青嵐 418
môichi (-1643) 望一 50,244,335
momoi katsuo 桃井克夫 1997 季題別 317
monku 文句 1697 大三物 107
morikami ryô 森上 涼 1997 季題別 384
moritake -1549 守武 141, 245
motoori → norinaga
murin 無倫 1660-1723 其袋 430
murozumi sôshun 室積祖春 講談大 214

Musha no Kôji Saneatsu 武者小路実篤 260
MUTAMAGAWA senryû 武玉川 99,125, 164?, 356,398
muyô 夢幼 late-19c 明治新俳句集 382

Nabuchi 魚淵 1755-1834 or gyokan 魚淵 1772?文車 144
nagano taneko1997 長野多禰子 177
nagashima shûyûshi 1997 長島舟遊子 308
nakamura masaharu1997 中村将晴 307
nakano fumiko1997 中納フミ子 176
namoto kimi 1997 名本喜美 306
nanmei 南溟 俳諧名録 146
南天樓 nantenrô mod.現代俳句大観 169
ninzan 忍山 1697 大三 347
niyô 二葉 19c?百家類題 64
norinaga 1730-1801 宣長 273
nyokô 如幸 1775 歳旦集 121

ÔCHI 19-20c? 鴬池 286,315,394
oda akiko 小田晃子 98
ÔEMARU 大江丸 1719-1805 俳懺悔 90, 137, 137, 156, 208, 262, 262, 271, 292
ogawa sachiko1997 小川幸子 308
ôgyoku 18c?19c?20c? 鴎玉 242
ôho 鴎歩 1697 大三物 68
okuda tomoyasu 1997 奥田智静 174
ONITSURA 1660-1738 鬼貫 59, 61, 63, 91, 101, 217
ontei 1873-1926 温亭 401
ôreiko?王？五．？玲子?scribbled illeg., but found 2001/1/3 右脳俳句 377
ôsa? 鴬梭 1697 大三 127
ôsan 横山 1697 大三物 72
otokuni-1720 乙州 163
otsuji 乙二→ otsuni. The poet is as often or not called otsuji, but that led to confusion with another otsuji, so . . .
otsuji 乙字 1881-1920 改造社 307
otsushi? 乙子（加生妻）1697 大三 183
OTSUNI -1823 乙二 165,302, 378,423
OTSUYÛ 1670-1739 乙由 51,126,335
ozaki akiko 尾崎亜紀子 contemp. 231

Raifu 来布 early-20c?最新二万句 171
RAIZAN -1716 来山 133, 179, 180, 251, 395
rakumu 楽夢 1765 明和二 286
rakusui 楽水 19c?百家類題 164
rangai -1845 嵐外 146
RANKÔ 1726-99 蘭更 94,132,139,168
rankô 嵐光 1775 安永四 154
ranran -1689 嵐蘭 416
RANSETSU -1707 嵐雪 93, 190, 346, 391, 394
reichhold, jane contemp. 79,304, 413
reisen 冷泉 19-20c?最新二万句 279
reitoku 令徳 1674? 再現 261
reiu 零雨 20c?愛吟集 296
reppo 列甫 顕本 KK 新帖 301
rijû 理重 1642 鷹筑波 80
rikô 里耕 四季 in c.1800 星布尼 336
rinjo 1673-1757 りん女 126
rinjô? 1759 麟上 427
rinya 林也 1697 うらわかは 422
risan 里山 1765 明和二 86

POET: 451-5, POEM: 456-60, PEOPLE: 461, ODDS & ENDS: 462- INDEXES

risen1759 里川 156
risshô 立松 1697 大三 220
ritsuda kiyoko 律田清子 20c 角川 322
ritsumei 栗銘 1812　元除遍覧 332
riyû 鯉遊 1751 玉かづら 338
riyû 李由-1705　風俗文選 267
rodô 魯堂 c1860 文久五百 63
roen 露艶 1697 第三物 94
ROGETSU 1873-1927 露月 292,310,385
rojû 1765 鷺十 185
rôka 弄香　1694 蘆分船 256
RÔKA 1669-1703 浪花 423
rokishi　櫻磯子 19-20c? 日本俳句鈔 333, 346
rokushô 六松 19c? 閑古鳥 改造社 419
rokyû 路及 1725 三千花 247
roshû 蘆舟 1751 玉かづら 123
rotsû -1738 路通 411
ryôho 了輔　1829 霞袋 59
ryôjo? 蓼リ 杖 early-20c 大正新俳句 217
ryôkei 良継　1642 鷹筑波? 88
ryôko c.1800 良湖 347
　良石 1795 ryôseki 248
ryôshun 良春 1633 狗 238
RYÔTA 1707-87 蓼太 46, 124, 144, 277, 295, 295, 335, 338, 394, 429
ryôtô 涼兎　1699 皮こすり 189, 252
ryôtoku 良徳 1633 犬 84
ryûbi 龍尾 1751 玉かつら 191
ryûjo 柳絮 1775 安永四 323
ryûki 柳几=鹿嶋=1819 新五百題 137
ryûkyô 柳興 1683 虚栗 369
ryûto 流兎 1697 大三物 163
ryûu 1934 龍雨 372

Sadakiyo fl 1670 定清　86
saiba 1803-1858 西馬 151
saigin 西吟 1763 古選 95
SAIGYÔ 1118-90 西行 71, 207, 210
saika 1784-1840 榎柯 99
saimu 1605-78 西武 263
saishi 西斯 18-19c? 雑中 329
saitô sanki 西東三鬼 1899-1962　角川 359
sanbon 山本 1856 新葉 149
samon 沙門 1697 大三物 96
sanga 山河 -1958? 19c? 百家類題 67
sanhô 山蜂（峰）1698 続猿蓑 321
sanjin 三人 1761 宝暦十一 322
sanka 傘下 1697 大三物 108
sankei 三徑 1728 桃首途 396
SANPÛ 杉風 1646-1732 卯辰 144,341,399
sansen 山川　1683 虚栗 417
santen 山店 1687 続虚栗 186
SANTÔKA 1882-1940 山頭火 128, 156, 435
saren 左簾(-1779) 句鑑 132
sasaki hisayo 佐々木久代 1997 季題 311
sasaki yûfû -1959 佐々木 有風 角川 357
sasei 茶静　1730 三日月集 95
satei 沙汀 20-c 現代俳句大観 170
satô kôroku 佐藤紅緑　講談社大 314
satô yôjin? 佐藤漾人 20c 講談社大 296
satôjo 佐登女 early-20c 同人俳句集 372
SEIBI 1748-1816 成美 45, 51, 72, 112,

139, 241
seichô 正長　1666 古今夷曲 215
seichô? 清重　1697 大三 196
seichû 清忠 1697 大三 266
seifû 晴風 1697 大三/1795 百漂 248
seifû 青楓 late-19c 明治一万句 315
seifu-ni 1732-1814 星布尼 268
seiga 清峨＝五車か 春来＝新選 324
seigi 声疑 1697 大三 214
seiha 青巴 1751 玉かつら 246
seijô 正常 1697 大三 127
seijû 正重 1633 犬 86
seiju 静壽 1642 鷹つくは 259
seikan 静澗 1860's 文久五百 61
seiken 政顕 1697 大三 326
seikô 政公 1645 毛吹草 214
seikô 政幸　1697 大三物 107
seira -1791 青蘿 427
seisa 1751 静茶 玉かづら 170
SEISEI -1937 青々184,310,418?,422,423,
seiseiko 青々子 右 2001/1/#3 脳俳句 114
seiseki 青石 1775 安永四 198
seishô 政昌 1633 狗 85
seishun 清春 1697 大三 197
seishô→masaakira
seizan 青山 18c?末若葉 291
sekiga -1797 石牙 58
sencho 千蝶 1751 玉桂 140
sencho 千頂 1751 玉かつら 353
senga1776 沾峨 340
sengyo 仙魚 1745-53 役者の俳句 369
senhyo 1751 千兵　玉かづら 302
seni 千慰 1751 玉かづら 254
senka 千河 -1706 玉かづら 84
senkei 千慶 1751 玉かつら 191
senna 1651-1723 千那 190, 202
senpû 沾仙 fl.1800 丁巳元除遊 214
senryo 千驢 1751 pg125
SENRYÛ (not specifically Yanagidaru or Mutamagawa) 138,
sensan? 千珊 1751 玉かつら 155
sensha 千車 1751 玉桂 275
senshifû? 扇子風 19c?20c? 雑中 109
sentoku -1726 沾徳　199, 392
sentoku 千得 1751 玉かづら 319
setsujin1918 雪人 372
shichô 1764 紙長　160
shichô 詩釣 1697 大三 349
shifû 紙風　失出典、年付? 46
shigan 只丸 1639-1712 俳諧漢和 422
shige = 重 = see jû for 18c & later
shigeharu 重治 1642　鷹筑波 365
shigekata 重方 1645 毛吹草 50, 213
shigetsu 止月 1697 大三 354
SHIGEYORI1601-1680 重頼 48, 85, 401, 418, 425, (&many anon. (崑山集 1651) may be his,
shiji 18c?19c? 襄埔 247
shijû 氏重 (1633) 85
SHIKI　1867-1902　子規　61,62,62,73,102, 105,111,112,113,116,139,139,143,179,180, 182,183,183,183,187,188,189,193,193, 196,224,239,268,271,277,279,282,284,285, 289,296,311,316,325,327,355,380,383,429
shikin -1735 此筋 93
SHIKÔ1664-1731 支考 216,395,431

shikô 芝光 18c?19c? 花笠 265
shikôko 志毅子 1799　元除春遊 200
shimada chizuru 島田千鶴 季題別 322
shimizu katsuko 1997 清水佳津子 173
shinan 信安 1642　鷹筑波 81, 89
shichiku 師竹 late-19c? 382
shingi fl 1760 心祇 54
shinchô 親重 1633 狗 221
shinho 新甫 mid-19c 文久五百 136
shinhô 真宝 1697 大三 225
shinkei 深鏡 1765 明和二 124
SHINKOKINSHÛ (waka anthol 1205) 52,77,77,78,108,215
shinpo -1747 進歩 55-14
shinrô 蜃楼　1884-1946 改造社 197, 295
shinsei 心成　1697　大三物 30, 353
shinseki 信雪 1697 大三 347
　紫之 18c?19c?宝普斉引付 264
shinshô 信勝 1697 大三 209
SHIRAO 1735-1792　通称白雄　31, 328, 398, 407, 418
SHIRÔ 1742-1813 士朗　36, 70, 102, 248, 408, 408, 415, 417
shisui 禾水 19-20c? 大全 413
shiu 示右(　　)匿袋 108
shizan 1700 禾束山　暁山集　100
shô? 1775 唱 249
shôan 勝安　1660 境海草 58
shôbi (-) 松尾 66
shôdô 松洞 1697 大三(?) 326
shôfû-ni 1668-1758 梢風尼 216
shôga LS 失出典省我　131
shôgetsu 笑月 late19c 明治一万句 383
shôgin 松吟 1697 大三 328
SHÔHA -1771　召波　63, 223, 224, 281, 293, 363, 399,
△紹巴see jôha!
SHÔHAKU 肖柏(-1527) 260
shôhei 正平 1642 鷹筑波 84
Shôhei 正平　瑕 2001 右脳俳句 120
shôi 昌意 akinori? 1645 毛吹草 288
SHÔKÔ 1412-1494 正広　100, 202, 273, 273, 273
shôkoku 嘯谷 18-19c 俳諧五百題 251
shôryû 焦笠 1697 大三 186
shôsan 勝山 1697 大三物 266
shôsatsu 1734 昌察 1481 老葉? 255, 256
shôshi 1775 笑子 181
shoshi 初子 1697　大三 355
SHÔSHITSU-1603　昌叱　32,112,113,212, 217,344
shôshû19-20c? 鱗洲 330
shôsui 笑水 1697 大三 153
SHÔTETSU 1381-1459 正徹 272,272,272
shôu 1859-1943 松宇 309,429, or he is ↓
shôu 松宇- 1827 改造社 414, or he is ↑
shôzan 嘯山 1717-1801 葎亭集 138, 220
shûchô 秀重 1645 毛吹草 81
shuen 種圓 1697 大三 194
shugetsu (early-18c) 収月　万句合 8
shûgyô 20c 鷹羽狩行 103
shûigusô anthol? 1216 拾遺愚草 257,429
shûji 1744 秀二 in 宇都宮歳旦帖 436
shunka 春可　1633 ゐのこ集 211, 418
shunkô 春郊　1777 句鑑 336
shunpa 春波　1749-1810 類題発句集 320

INDEXES   POET: 451-5, POEM: 456-60, PEOPLE: 461, ODDS & ENDS: 462-

shunrai 春雷 1773 新選 140
shunrai 春来 (1763?) 51, 324?
shunsei 春盛 1633 狗 121
shunzei → fujiwara
shusetsu 朱拙 1655-1733 アルス 420
shunshô 春象 mid-20c 昭和一万句 361
shushô 酒笑 1775 安永四 250
shûshu 秋守 1829 霞袋 254
shunya 俊屋 or shunoku 1642 鷹筑波 221
shunzei → fujiwara
shusuirô 守水老 19-20c? 改造社 382
shusuirô 1835-1907 守水牢 428 ↑ must be the same! A mistake somewhere...
shuteki? -1706 朱迪 (=迪?) 56
shûzan 秀山 1744 宇都宮歳旦帖 280
skks → shinkokinshû
soa 宋阿 → hajin
SOBAKU -1821 素麥 66, 68,191,199, 200, 200, 265, 270, 300, 301, 302, 327, 388, 436
sôboku -1545 宗牧 218
sôbô 宗房 49 (俳諧人名辞典は、これを若き芭蕉の号とするが嵐山集＝1651に出ると。）
sôchû 草虫 1697 大三 338
sodô 1641-1716 素堂 93, 425
sôfu 窓布 1799 己未元除春遊 198
SOGAI-1809 素外 100, 239, 415
sogan 素丸 → somaru そまる
sogetsu 素月 c1800 星布尼の四季発句集 331
SÔGI 1420-1502 宗祇 43, 149, 209, 209,
SÔIN 1604-82 宗因 55, 133, 150, 153, 162, 193, 209, 210, 242, 252, 262, 267, 355, 363, 364
sôji 宗治 1645 毛吹草 261
soka 疎香 20c 昭和一万句 379
SÔKAN 1465-1553 宗鑑 300,433,433?,
sokô 1777 素候 33
sokushô 即章 1697 大三 254
sokyô (18-19c?) 祖卿 百家類題 67
sôkyo 草鋸 1747 五元 147
SÔKYÛ 1760-1842 蒼虬 161,184,253,283
sôma senko 相馬遷子 講談社大 316
SOMARU 1712-95 素丸 110, 123, 124, 263, 401, 404, 404, 406, 425, 432
soô 祖翁 1645   毛吹草 80
soô 素翁 1697 大三 340
sôrô 1760,1761 滄浪 133, 349
sôsei 1697 宗清 大三 83
SÔSEKI 1474-1533 宗碩 247,347,413
巣枝 sôshi 19c? 俳諧五百 91
SÔSHUN 宗春 1734 三籟 73, 142, 150, 246
sosui 1813-1897 素水 417
sôtô 素十 1751 玉かづら 92
sôun 挿雲 1889-1961 昭和一万句 171
SÔ
soyû 旦猷 1829   霞袋 102
sozan 素山 1818-92 文久五百 72
sôzei 宗砌 (-1455) 68,247
sugioka senjô 1997 杉岡せん城 337
suimeikei 水明溪 19-20c? 改造社 286
suishitsu 1765 水室 279
suizan 翠山 1765 明和二 140

Tadachi 忠知 1674 俳諧桜川 313-314

tadanori? 忠のり？1651 嵐山集 214
tadashi 正 1775 安永四 69
TAIGI 1709-72 太祇 94, 223, 223, 258, 279, 295, 412, 423, 424, 426
tainen 岱年 19c 百家類題 246
taisui early-20c 台水 89
takahashi mutsurô 高橋睦郎 contemp. 114
take-no-kado 1895-1966 竹の門 432
takashi 孝 287
takuchi -1693 澤雉 309
tamajo たま女 early-20c 年間俳句集 428
tanchô 丹頂 1775 安永四 148
tantan 1673-1761 淡々 51, 69
TAYOJO 1775-1865 多代女 64, 135, 143, 258, 399
teigo 庭後 18-19c? 江戸発句集 393
teigu (teitoku+keigu) 貞愚 78
teiji 定時 1642 鷹つくば 80, 84
TEIKEI 貞継 or sadatsugu 1645 毛吹草 120, 137, 265
teikichi 貞吉 1697 大三物 70
teimin 丁眠 1697 大三 339
teishitsu 1609-73 貞室 213
TEITOKU 1570-1653 貞徳 53, 77, 80, 87, 214, 214, 245, 432, 432, 433?
tekkan 1731   鐵冠 51
tenga 沾峨   1776 吐屑庵 292
tochimenbô 橡面坊 深山榮 127, 297
tôichi .桐一 ホトトギス mod. 292
tokizane shinko 時実新子 20c 有夫恋 270
tokô 都貢 18c?19c?たてなみ 94, 239
tokugen1558-1647 徳元 245, 352
tokushi 得之 1829 霞ふくろ 70
tome とめ 1697 大三物 182
tôri 桃里 1751 玉かづら 131
tôrin 桃隣 (-1719, or -1806) 55
tôrin 桃林 1751 玉かづら 124
tôsen 桃仙 1728 桃の首途 410
tôshô 冬松 1689 あら野 148
tôsui 桃水 ~1720   大三物 91
tôyô 冬葉 1892-1956 改造社 360
toyotake haruno 1997 豊竹春野 176
tsuhô 津富 1770 句鑑 132
tsujita katsumi 辻田 克巳 20c 角川 322
tsukazuki bonta 塚月凡太 季題別 384
tsuna hiromi 宏美 contemp.小一 299
tsurayuki → kokinshû

Udô 烏堂_ 続春夏秋冬 or18c?卯堂 323
kotatsu deru tabi no shirosa ya kisohajime
ufu? 右茶   1697 大三 147
unjin 1697 雲塵 大三 166
unokichi 卯の吉 early20c ホトトギス 358
uryû 雨柳 1699 皮こすり 168
usei 雨声 1751 玉かづら 249
utei 雨丁 20c 漁火 298
uun 卯雲 1773   新選 132
uyama karitake 1997 宇山雁茸 174

Wakaku 和角 1751 玉かづら 106
wasei 和城 1777 安永六 132
watanabeshi 渡邊氏   1697 大三
wright, richard 109, 380

Yaba 野坡 ~1740 類題発句集 341,423
YAEZAKURA 1879-1945 八重桜 78, 286, 353, 368, 419

yamada mizue 山田みづえ 20c 角川 309
yamaguchi seishi 20c 山口誓子 321
YANAGIDARU (senryû) 68, 86, 158, 163, 190, 317, 320, 371
yasegiku 瘦菊 1819 新五百集 145
yaseki early-20c 他石 現代俳句大観 171
yasuda haruyo 保田治代 1997 季題 308
yasui 野水 1657-1743 講談社大 407
yatô 夜濤 1880-1953 改造社 284
yau 屋烏 1819 新五百集 249
YAYÛ 1701-83 也有 29, 122, 183, 392, 396, 409, 413, 434
四方赤良 yomonoakara ___ 164
yôseki 佯石 19-20c? 青嵐 329
yoshimoto noboru 1997 吉本昇 306
yû 游 contemp. 右脳俳句 318
yûgo ___雄樹 紅___集 181
yûhei -1704 由平 258
yûho 夕浦 1761 寶曆十一 108
yûkichi 友吉 1697 大三 340
yûho 夕歩 1697 大三 93
yûkei 浮輕 1697 大三 140
yûryaku (emperor mid-5c) 雄略天皇 387
yûsei 由誓 1788-1859 百家類題 133
yûsei 友静 late-17c 元禄 198
yûtei 由廷 1645 毛吹草 88, 243
yûto 由ト 1697 大三物 117
yûwa 友和 1697 大三 154
yûyô 遊葉 1697   大三物 108, 147
yûzan 幽山 1680 江戸ベンケイ 46

Zaishiki 在色 1675 談林十百韻 117
zokuseki 続石 19c?20c? 落椿 316
zongi 1701-82 存疑 162

~~~~~~~~~~~~~~~~~

of *ku* per POET = TOP 26

152   ISSA 1762-1827 一茶
45   SHIKI 1867-1902 子規
32   CHIYO 1701-75 千代女
17   KIKAKU-1707 其角
15   SÔIN 1604-82 宗因
14   SOBAKU 1758-1821 素麥
13   BAISHITSU 1768-1852 梅室
12   BASHÔ 1654-94 芭蕉
11   GONSUI 1646-1719 言水
10   KYOSHI 1874-1959 虚子
10   RYÔTA 1707-87 蓼太
10   SOMARU 1712-95 素丸
10   TAIGI 1709-72 太祇
10   TEITOKU 1570-1653 貞徳
9   GINKÔ fl.1770 吟江
9   ÔEMARU 1719-1805 大江丸
8   SHIRÔ 1742-1813 士朗
8   YAYÛ 1701-83 也有
7   BUSON 1715-83 蕪村
7   CHÔI 1886-1930 蝶衣
7   SHÔHA -1771 召波
6   HAJIN 1672-1742 巴人
6   MEISETSU 1847-1926 鳴雪
6   ONITSURA 1660-1738 鬼貫
6   SEIBI 1748-1816 成美
6   SHÔSHITSU-1603 昌叱

POET: 451-5, POEM: 456-60, PEOPLE: 461, ODDS & ENDS: 462-   INDEXES

POEM index: In Japanese, like German, it is often hard to say just where a word starts and ends. So, this alphabetization is absolute: spaces are ignored.

A

abaraya no 66   ○ achira muku 254
aimiru ni 138   ○ aisatsu no 154
akabeni ya 217   ○ akatoki no 418
akazume ya 435
akebono no haru 324; ~ hoshi 248
akebono ya murasakizome 326
    ~ nazuna 427
akenikeri 273 ○ akenoharu 301
akete haru taigyo 104; ~ taigyo 305
akeyuku ya 280 ○ akuru yoru 378
ama kuraku 431
amanohara fuji 215. ~ kawa 346.
~ mito 142. ~ to mo 142. ~ o 100, & 273
amari yoki 309
ametsuchi-jibo 249. ~ ni ayamari 92
~ no hajime 32, 212. ~ idemono 277.
~ yawaragu 239. ~ yurumu 414
ana ureshi 323. ○anagura wa 83
andon no 380. ○anraku ya 328
aoao to 123. ○ aokabi no 357
aoshi aoshi 395. ○ aozora ni 120
araoke wa 336, 345.
arasowanu kuni 277
aratama ni 46. ~ no harugi 324
~ no toshi tachikaeru 120
~ wa mina 138
~ ya fukuro 116,
    ~ kururi 120. ~ kuwa 109
arata nari yorozu 162
ariyô wa inochi 133
aru hanashi 363. ~ mono o 389
asaboroke 72. ~ kayu 432
~ no ma ni 407. ~ gasumi 117
~ hi 285. ~ ne shite 315
~ oki no toku 92
ashi ni 396
asobu hi 57. ~ mi mo 267
asu wa asu 263. ~ ganjitsu 435
atataka ni 107. ○atatamete 329
aware ika ni 292

B

babazure 159. ○baka neko 227
bakumakura issui 313
~ ko no 313. ~ yume ni 314
banchô ya 225. ○biidoro ni 396
binbôsô 278. ○binchû ni 382
byôshitsu 286

C

chi o kaete 133. ○chiru koto o 374
chito no ma 147. ○chiyochiyo 390
chiyo made 364. ○chôbako 275
chônin ni tanjô 265

D

daibutsu no kokoro 145
daidai no 116. ~ o kuwanu 186
~ ya hôrai 186. ~ ya kumihôrai 186
~ ya senki 267
daimyô no 255. ○dakiyosete 329
damatte 128. ○ dappi seru 269
dare ga tame 388. ~ hitori 124
dôjô ya 361. ○dote no uma 414
dotto kite 173

E

edo gomi 405. ~ shû ya 226
eiya'tto 50. ○ e-mehru 74

F

fudan 410. ○
fuji miyo to 300. ~ san o hôrai 181
fuki-kiyasu 64. ○fuku kaze 74
fukubiki no makeppara 427
fukujusô heikin 282
~ hirakite 283. ~ issun 276
~ kage 284. ~ katana 276
~ kazoku 282. ~ kusa to 281
~ mite 286. ~ toso 287. ~ yori 276
~ binbôgusa 289
fukunokami o 84
fukuwara ni tagoto 126
~ ni ushi 127. ~ ni wara 127
~ no chiri 320. ~ ya atatakasô 127
~ ya chiri 126. ~ ya gosho 126
~ ya omoeba 127
fumi-wakete 180. ○fumoto ni 344
fundoshi o 327
furuki-mono 259. ~ yo no 146
furusato wa 161. ~ ya uma 140
furutoshi 208. ~ zukin 324
fusoku- 354. ○futa moto 281
futatsu mitsu 163
futon kite netaru sugata 93
~ neteiru ue 93
futsuka ni 96 ○fuyu no inoko 89
fuyu to haru 53. ~ no haru 45
fuyuzora ni 120

G

gajô kaite 170. ○gakuryô ya 363
ganchô ni haku 127. ~ ya iwau 101
~ ya kamiyo 141. ~ ya kome 139
~ ya nezumi 426. ~ no miru- 300
ganjitsu mo futsuka 96
~ onna 138. ~ tachi 65

ganjitsu ni ebi 102
~ tagoto 107. ~ towaba 260
ganjitsu no asahi 112. ~ fuji 302
~ guchi 156. ~ hanashi 143
~ hinataboko 66. ~ hito ya 137
~ hokori 125. ~ hôkyaku 132
~ ichinichi 147. ~ igokoro 258
~ iriai 112. ~ kokoro 270
ganjitsu no miru- 300. ~ yûhi 112
ganjitsu o tenchi-wagô 143
ganjitsu to omoi no 94
ganjitsu wa amari 302. ~ ban 163
~ dare 94. ~ hôshi 141.~ ichi- 132
~ kokoro 136. ~ mada 68. ~ nan- 146
~ okisô 158. ~ tofuya 94. ~ ze 139
ganjitsu ya buppô 144. ~ chikau 148
chiyo 250. ~ daiju 31. ~ daiku 279.
~ dare mo 86. ~ furuki 67, 251
~ garan 102. ~ hamaguri 266
~ hazukashisô 164.
~ hito no tsuma 256.~ hito no yo 212
~ hito to umarete 142. ~ hogo 66
~ hokori 125. ~ hôraisan 181
~ ichi no 264. ~ ikikô 140.
~ ikkei 300. ~ kamiji 141
~ kesa wa 139. ~ kimi 286
~ kinô ni 68. ~ kino no 165
~ **kono** akebono 129. ~ kokoro 132
~ kono toki 262. ~ kotoshi mo 89
~ kozuchi 121. ~ ku no 146
~ kurai 52. ~ kusa no naka 277
~ kusa no to-goshi 63. ~ ma ichi- 99
~ mada 264. ~ majiwaru 124.
~ mazu 250. ~ mimi 337.
~ miyako 248. ~ nan to naku 134
~ nani 140. ~ nikai 252.
~ okidokoro 188. ~ omoeba 149
~ onaji 139. ~ osanaki 136
~ sareba 251. ~ saru 155. ~ sora 124.
~ suzuri 170. ~ tama ni 238
~ tatami 235. ~ toshi no 257
~ toshiyori 260. ~ totemo 111
~ tsuki minu 63. ~ tsukuzuku 144
~ ushibeya 127, 267. ~ ware mo 238.
~ yo no 123. ~ yuki o 122
ge ni mo haru 94
gejo made 266. ~ no na 50
gusoku-biraki/hiraku a-un 360
~ hiraku tajikara 360

H

hadaka ni 327. ○hae warae 244
hagoita 167   ○hahakata/ue no 321
hakuhatsu no 159. ○hakushu ni 100.
hamaguri no 239   ○ hanaiki ni 296
hana made 402. ~ noharu hito 38.
~ noharu shin 48. ~ noharu to iu 145.
hanatare 350 ○hana yori mo 276
harugi no ko 322

INDEXES   POET: 451-5,   POEM: 456-60,   PEOPLE: 461,   ODDS & ENDS: 462-

haruka-naru 321. ○ harukaze 64
haru kinu 247. ~ kureba sode 52
~ kuredo 259. ~ meganu 54
~ mo haya 43. ~ mo yaya 51
~ ni akete 218. ~ ni tsure 209
~ no kuru 213. ~ no mochi 357
~ no rei 163. ~ no yo no 313-314
~ shôgatsu 69
~ tateba (tachite wa?) yuki 247
haru tatsu ya asa 239. ~ dare 91
~ gu 263. ~ neraruru 91
~ sasuga 120. ~ shijûsannen 260
~ shôji 131. ~ ten 248.
~ tsurara 78. ~ uite 125
haru to ieba 68. ~ to shi 71
~ wa ake- 92. ~ wa kozo 101
~ wa tatsu 137. ~ ya kesa 117
~ ya koshi 47. ~ zo kesa 249
hatake kara zukin 392
hata no kado 405. ~ o meguri 167
hatsubare o miagete 114
hatsufuji no 302. ~ ya sôan 302
hatsugasumi hori 217. ~ itsu 118
hatsugeshiki totonou 114
hatsuharu ni yogore 131
~ no hatsuhi 273. ~ ya kesa 131
~ ya otoko 139
hatsuhinode kotoshi 98
~ mi ni 115. ~ minna 99
~ ogamitai 98
hatsu-ichi ya 416. ~ kei 86
~ nagi ya 151. ~ nazuna katsuo 425
hatsurei no koe154. ~ya meoto 166
hatsuzora ni 61.~ wa yokunaki 123
hatsuyume mo goza 309
hatsuyume ni furusato 306
~ neko 300. ~ ôinaru 305
~ ôinaru umi 303~ ôki na mon 306
hatsuyume no asaki 309
~ bôbaku 317. ~ fuji 299.
~ kichi 310. ~ kirin 307.
~ kojin 308. ~ konton 306.
~ mamemameshisa 308
~ mukashi no mama 308
~ mukashi no shigoto 308
~ nani 316. ~ nanyara 316
~ oboe no 317. ~ oboyuru 312
~ pari 307. ~ samete 303
~ shisha 308. ~ towazu 318
~ uso 310
hatsuyume o koshiraete 292
~ mi wa 315. ~ miteite 309
hatsuyume to omoiki 316
hatsuyume ya ano 308
~ baku 312. ~ e ni 310. ~ fuji ni 310
~ fuji tobi 303. ~ himete 309
~ hitai 296. ~ itaru 311. ~ niwa 299
~ rengakusari 311
~ samete 304. ~ tadashiku 304

~ ume 305. ~ ura-ura 317
hatsuzora ni haya 119
~ ni muita 65. ~ ni naran119
~ no kokoro 126. ~ no moyô 119
~ o ima 118. ~ o koshiraete 117
~ o yogi 119. ~ wa yama 214
hatsuzora ya habakari 118
~ iruka 104. ~ mono 132
~ nemaki 93. ~ tabako 117
~ yorokobu 129
hayaku 81. ○haya-uma no 84
hazukashiki 426. ○hedate 307
heta heta to 421. ○hi mo hito 239
hi no ataru 285. ~ hajime 78
~ hikari 108. ~ kao 85. ~ shôji 287
hi o hito 95. ○hi zo samuki 71
higashi yori 88. ○hingashi 146
hinoharu o 130
hinomoto no hikari 273
~ wa sakayaki 137. ~ ya kane 268
hito-ashi ni sagi 406
~ bito no 151. ~ goto ni 138
~ hachi no 284. ~ mishiri 384
~ moto wa 281. ~ no-hi to 113
~ no ki kara nioi 106, 246
~ no tsura 140. ~ oke o 345
~ oto o tsuru 406
hitori okite-iru 384
hito-shizuku 283
hitotose mo 90
~ ni 391. ~ no 430
hitotsu hitotsu 171. ~ zutsu 253
hito wa sumika 190
hitoyo akete 43. ○hiwarekeri 358.
hiza ni 321. ○hokku 170
honokuraki 379. ○ hôô mo 87
hôrai ariya 202. ~ mo kazaru 199
~ ni binbô 183.
hôrai ni itô 196. ~ jôfuku 195.
~ kakete 194. ~ kikabaya 192.
~ kiriri 185. ~ ko wa 186.
~ kuubeki 193. ~ ma-hitotsu 194
~ matsu 192. ~ miru 183.
~ na[n]mu 182
~ nezumi nakunari 188
~ nezumi no emimiru 188
~ nezumi no ukara 187
~ tokoro 197. ~ toshi 193
~ waga-mi 179. ~ yoru 180
hôrai no atama 186. ~ chiisaki 193
~ daidai 184. ~ ebi 192
fumoto e kayou 187
~ ni netaru 189
hôrai no sata 199. ~ shio 191
~ taki 196. ~ tegiwa 198
~ tsurajiro 187. ~ yakume 200
~ yama matsuri 194. ~ yama wa 194
hôrai o hiki 187. ~ wa fuji 181
hôrai ya aruji 189. ~ fuji 181

~ hi no 201. ~ hitai 182. ~ kami 197
~ kazaru 198. ~ koko 205.
~ kozue 196. ~ masu 179
~ namsan 182. ~ nietatsu 180
~ tada 184. ~ waga 199.
~ zukuri 199
horikawa 413. ○ hori no kôri 164
hoshi hitotsu 332
~ sukuu 332. ~ hoshi-iwashi 109
hôshoku ni haiku 2. ~ no kage 188
hotoke yori kami . . kesanoharu 182
           ~ . . yadonoharu 183
hotsuhotsu 190. ○hyaku made 262

I

ichi-ban no toshidama 229
~ mura o 359. ~ nen no 248
~ nichi no 301. ~ nin no 294
ido kuraku 338. ○ie ni aru 199
iebie ni tsumitemo 412
ii mono 69. ○ika ni 58
ikijini no mukashi 348
ikite iru 287. ○ ikkenya 321
iku mawari 230. ○ ima ikiru 74
inishie 388. ○inu no ko ni 86
io no i 336. ○io-nushi no 298
irig/kawaru secchin 158
irogawari 278. ○isasaka 320
ise e okuri 171
ise ebi ya hôrai-san 192
           ~ yaso 261
ishi ni 363. ○ isohata 413
issetsu 238. ○ isshô 350
itaike ni 295. ○itsu ni naku 172
itsumademo 152. ○iwagane 283
iwa hitotsu 335
izaya nen 105. ○izuru hi 102

J

jiji baba ga 200. ○ jiji-ga-yo 259
jû-no-mono 53. ○ jûshoku 100

K

ka wa yomo 245. ○kabitan mo 165
kado kado 157 ○kadomatsu 257
kadonoharu 160
kadorei ya katagawa 157
~ neko ni 225
kagai noren 293
kagami mochi benten 359
~ iwaishi 356. ~ hachiman 358
~ kasanete 353. ~ kuraki 359
kageboshi 160, 178n. ○ kago no 58
kairei ya shi 168. ~ toguchi 168
kakedai 266. ○ kakureya 225
kamakeru 369 ○kame no se 101
kamiguni ya kusa 278
kamishimo de geta 157.

~ de miru 207. ~ no oto 319
~ o kiru 320
kan-no-uchi wa 71 ○kanai ni 251
kankotori 90 ○kao no shiwa 339
kara[tô] no mono 144
kareshi no ya 413
kashikoku 239 ○kashikomaru 181
kasumi maku 209
kasumi no ne 218 ○~ sae 80
kasumu hi mo 96
~ hodo 407. ~ nari 272
katakana no 170
katsuji 174 ○ katsushika 159
katta hodo 411 ○kazedoshi 358
keisei ni 388 ○ kenkô ga 385
kesa haru 162 ○kesa kamiyo 211
kesanoharu ariakezuki 62
~ chie 263. ~ mizu 339
~ nan 133. ~ ogan 352
~ ri po 144. ~ sabishi- 148
~ sono 156. ~ wa ômu- 87
~ ya mazu 72
kesa samete 298
kesa taruru tsurara ya dare no 78
~ ya yodare 77
kesa ya nao 106 ○ kichimomo 185
kiegataki 260 ○ kigen 271
kimi ga tame 393. ~ yo no 429
~ -yowai 261. ~ yo ya tatami 267
kimi hi 393
ki ni mochi no hana 370
~ naru 371
ki no haha 243 ○ kimi no haru 266
kinô made 400. ~ to wa 69
kinuginu ya oki/oko saretsu 419/426
kisohajime harukaze 323
~ kôbi 322. ~ kôkotsu 330
~ yama 325
kiyogoshita 53 ○kiyomuru 336
ko o futatsu 383 ○ko wa oya 352
kochi fukaba 245
koetori no 222 ○ko-hasami 436
koi wa tôshi 176 ○kojiki ni 389
koka ni iwaku 355, 364
kokora ka 402
kokoro iyo-iyo 430.~ kara 106
~ made 136. ~ ni mo 248
~ yo 106, 429..
komo yo 387
konata ni 349. ○konna mi 261
kono en wa 154. ~ kado o 390
~ kuni ni 272. ~ nanuka 409
~ okina 385
koriyo soke 227. ○koronde 397
koshigawari 328
~ terasu 109
koshôin 279
kotatsu deru 323. ~ kara 392

kôtei ni 404 ○ kotonoha 163
kotoshi mo mata 137
~ to mo 46. ~ wa to 268
ko-warawa 399 ○ koyoi mata 383
kozo kara 246. ~ no hito 73
~ no hoshi 62. ~ no ko no 220
~ no koto 68. ~ saite 243
~ to ieba kinô 68
~ to ieba tôki hedate 68; ~ yô 68
kozo-kotoshi dandan 74
~ kata-ashi 73. ~ tsuranuku 60
~ waga 72. ~ yuki 63
kozuchi 162 ○ kubi agete 102
kuchi akete 84 ○kui ni kishi 314
kuitsumi e sasoi 188
~ ni isshoku 191. ~ ya ha 190
~ ya iwau 191. ~ ya mina 190
~ ya suzume 191
kumi kumite 339
kumo wa nemaki 325
kuni no haru 97. ~ wa oroka 86
○kuokukô 152
kurisumasu ni 183
kuru haru no 221
~ wa kami 272. ~ wa kozo 48
~ wa toshi 50. ~ ya yomo 212
kuru hito no 162
kuru toshi no mono- 8
~ no muma- 84
kurumaza de 79 ○kusa mo ki 238
kusamakura 417 ○kuute nete 29
kyô miru ya 112. ~ no ashi 107
~ saku wa toshizuyo 244
~ saku wa 288. ~ tatsu ya 87
~ to ieba morokoshi 272
~ kyô to ieba tôdo 108
~ yori wa hana- 80. ~ yori ya 242
kyôshi tarishi 174.
kyûsei o 177

Ls lost source

M

ma byôshi 280. ○madoromeru 288
makura 313. ○mama naraba 147
mama soro yo 257
manaita ni 431. ~ no nazuna 422
manryô no 279. ○marukereba 355
masayume 307. ○matagura de 356
matsu wa haya 413. ○~ kazari 197
matsukage 391. ○matsukaze 98
mayudama no koban 372
~ no utsuru 372. ~ o kau 372
~ ya koban 372
mazu haru 431. ~ hiraku 248
~ iwae 331. ~ kesa wa 332
~ sora ni 251. ~ wa sayu 110
mazushisa ni 184

me ni 267. ○medetasa 255
megurikuru 85. ○mezamashi 343
mi no toshi 83. ○michi shirite 84
michibata 128. ○michigusa mo 409
midasabaya 54. ○midori go/ko 404
miira to mo 111. ○mikazuki o 378
minahito no yawaragu 140
~ egao 353.
mine 247
minokasa ni 295. ~ o 183
minomushi no 306
miyako 30 ○miyo ni furu 259
mizuhiki ni 177. ~ kagami 269
~ kuroi 324
mochi no deru 351. ~ no kona 382
~ no sei 358
mochibana ni haru 368
~ no kokage 367. ~ no oku 369
~ no potari- 374. ~ no sakari 374
~ no tomoshibi 368. ~ o sakasete 370
~ o teinei 371. ~ ya haha 375
mochibana ya hibachi 367
~ itsu 374. ~ kabe 373
~ kazashi 369. ~ miyako 375
~ nezumi 368. ~ tomoshibi 373
mochi kagami 353. ~ kake 356.
~ ni tsukuru 352
modori ni 411 ○ mô fuchô 177
mo hitotsu 161. ○mono to ware 64
mononoke 378 ○ moratte mo 399
moromoro 124. ○mottomo zo 81
mukashi 394 ○mukou naka 260
muku-oki no shoben 158
~ ya futon 93
murasaki o 216
musashino 301 ○mutsumutsu 265
myôdai no suzume /karasu 343/342

N

na no takaki 166. ○nadete oku 67
nadokoro 327. ○nagaki o o 379
nagane-shi ni 92. ○nakagaki 61
naki-hito no 176. ○nama-ei no 164
nana ana 100
nanakusa mo 412. ~ ni nezumi 426
~ ni niawanu 405. ~ ni tengoku 425
~ no furuki 428. ~ no oto 428
nanakusa o tatakinaosu 425
~ uchi-osame- 416, 430
~ uchite inetaru 418
~ uchite sore 419. ~ uchi-uchi 425
nanakusa wa tôdo 425
nanakusa ya abura 393
~ amaredo 412. ~ ato ni 406, 427
~ hi 417. ~ kayu 432. ~ kazu 399
~ kehai 423. ~ kyôdai 423
~ manoita 423. ~ me ni 410
~ nitsukanu 437. ~ tonari 420

INDEXES   POET: 451-5,   POEM: 456-60,   PEOPLE: 461, ODDS & ENDS: 462-   459

~ uchi yori 410. ~ yaoya 398
~ yogi 420. ~ yoku 401
~ yoso 424. ~ yuki 402
nanatsu na no 418
nanigoto mo kokoro 133
~ mo nakute haru 36
~ mo nakute nana- 418
~ to nakute 134
nani mo naki toko 284
~ o taru 256
nan to naku 140
narabe-oki 421
nazuna utsu tô 419
~ utsu[chi?] naka 421
~ yu ya 435
negawakuba 132 ○negokoro 95
neko no hana 110
~ iru 285. ~ kao 116
nekorondeiruru 95
nengajô chiisai 172. ~ ichiban 172
~ kaku ni 169. ~ kotoshi 172
~ shinsetsu 169
nenrei ya getamichi 157
nete toshi o 99. ○neteiyo ga 95
nichi getsu 248. ○nichi-nichi 112
nido tatsu 213 ○nigashi na 349
nigiyaka ni 148. ○~ ya 373
nihonki ya 142
ni-kamiko 326. ○nikki mada 285
nikkori to 100. ○ ningen mo 29
ningyô no 329. ○niwatori 390
nodoka[e]sa ya minna 150, 267
~ ya tsunoburi 80. ~ yo tada 150
nokoru yuki 88 ○nori kowaki 319
norizome 84. ○noshi nagara 225
nugikanuru 349. ○nukarumi 105
nuketederu 241. ○nyôshû ni 408

O
ôi-naru hôrai miyuru 183
ochitsuite 99 ○ôgon no kesa 275
ôhan de ii 292 ○ ôhara ya 405
oi ga tsumu 408. ~ no ato 252.
~ no kage 354. ~ no koshi 434
~ no kure 264. ~ no nochi 252
~ nureba 296
oite kesa 265. ○ ô-iwashi 108
ôkami mo 89 ○okanu mono 402
ôkata wa 422 ○okora ko ni 167
okosarete 72 ○okumen mo 384
okushû 104. ○omedetô 173
omisoka 156 ○omoi-idatsu 355
omoikane hashigo 406
omokage 354. ○omomuro 231
omoshirosa 317 ○omoshiro ya 62
onadomo ga 313
onaji kao 155. ○onensho o 161
oningyo to 299. ○ onjaku 392

onna koyo 311. ○onna ni mo 155
oroka iu kuniguni 108, 147
ôta ko 400. ○oto mo naku 217
otoshidama chiisai 231.
~ poketto 219
oya ni nita 147. ~ no toshi 242
~ to ko 423. ~zato no 161
ôyuki ni akete 419 ~ no ashita 398
~ o kabutte 283. ~ wa tada 335
ôzora o 210

R
rakujin 381. ○reimu kara 328
rengashi no 48. ○ rinjin to 338
risshun no 49
rôbe ni oite 285
rô-go to ya 293. ○~ -riki 361
○ryôhô ni 158

S
saijiki o yo 32 ○saitan ya 59
sake are 432. ~ no ka ni 286
~ shizuku 356. ~ sukoshi 172
samurai ya 160 ○san chô no 353
san mon ga kasumi 215
~ no[ga] wakamizu 345
san sai no 322
sanbô ni 189. ○sannin ni 315
sao-hime mo ko 214
~ mo haru 51. ~ no ne- 214
~ no ni 51. ~ no otoko- 51
~ no tegai 80. ~ no ubugi 214
~ wa chichitaru 214. ~ wa osana 214
saru no kao 175. ○sashi izuru 273
satogaeri 166. ○sawagani 429
sawarabi 422. ○ sazukaru 292
secchin ni 264. ○ sei dashite 407
shikai mina 146 ○ shikaku ni 164
shikoku 86. ○ shima tsunagu 149
shimenawa ni 336 ○ya haru 88
shimo wa 394. ○ shin seiki 377
shinnen no hitsugi 73
shinshun no gyokei 153
shinu made wa ikiru 262
~ sadamete 262
shirakawa 347 ○shirami 327
shirimochi 397 ○ shirotabi 51
shiwasu 68 ○shizu ga ko 399
shôben mo 115 ○shôben no 362
shôgatsu kotoba 143, 178
shôgatsu no geko 165
~ keshiki 69. ~ kodomo 137
~ kokoro 265. ~ sakana 108
shôgatsu o dashite 362
~ netemiru 98. ~ neteshimai 98
~ shôgatsu o 362
shôgatsu wa bunbetsu 265
~ kirei 71. ~ minna 43

~ shôgatsu 143
shôgatsu ya gorori 98
~ jitsu 141. ~ kokoro 135
~ mazu 56. ~ mikka 168
~ tsuji 127. ~ uchikina 149
shôjiki ni 250 ○shûnen ya 126
sode baka ya 292
sono mama 63 ○soragoto to 314
sore mo ô 252. ~ rashiki 316
~ so[zo?] to mo 415
~ tomo ni 422
sorihiki ya 326
suetearu 67 ○ sumôtori no 360
sunakane ni 347 ○ surikogi no 259

T
ta no naka 82. ○tabako 215
tabi no to 369
tachikaeru nami 61
~ toshi mo 32. ~ toshi-no-ya 60
tachikawaru haru o 208
tachimachi 103 ○ tachinikeri 39
tachiyasushi 262
takarabune akemutsu 297
~ arashi 295. ~ ashita[tan] 297
~ kokoro 295. ~ medetaki 294
~ ô-hinomaru 294. ~ shiite 296
~ shikine 298. ~ shiwa 298
~ wake 295. ~ ware ni 298
takasuna ya 59
takekago ni 407 ○takusan na 418
tama mo tama 230 ○tamago 46
tami no to 113 ○tanomoshiya 121
ta o megurite 167
tatsu toshi mo 209. ~ no 213
tazune miyo 202 ○tekkotsu 377
ten amatsuyu 331
tenchi → ametsuchi
tenchi-jibo 249 ○te no ato 403
tenokubo 200 ○tenouchi 334
tobashiri/ru 422
tobimume ya toshi 245
tobiume ya karo- 245
tomogaki 171 ○tonari tonari 418
torase tabi 258 ○tori mushi 325
tori naite **hôshoku no yama** 180
tori wa haya 88
toshidama-cha 230
~ ni mise 230. ~ ni nezumi 190
~ ni ume 222. ~ no saisoku 229
~ no ue 226
toshidama o atama 229
~ futarimae 228. ~ inu 227
~ kubaru 224. ~ mago 221
~ mina 221. ~ morai 224
~ narabete 224. ~ oku 227
~ tsukandekuru ya 221
toshidama ya daki 223

~ futokoro 229. ~ katari 228
~ neko 228. ~ rusu 226
~ shakushi 223. ~ wabine 224
~ warabe- 220
toshidoshi [ganjitsu]ya saru 155
toshi-goto 70. ~ toshi koete 50
~ kurau 208. ~ kurenu haru 210
~ kureshi namida 78 ~ mo hitsuji 85
~ mo kesa kosu 211. ~ mo kyô 121
~ -nami o 81. ~ -no-ga ya 153
~ -no-hana 247. ~ no ni 70
~ no o o 365. ~ no tama hirou 222
toshinouchi e fumikomu 49
~ e oshiiri 49. ~ ni haru ichi 55
~ ni haru kite moru 58
~ ni haru o haru 56
~ ni haru o nozoku 57
~ ni haru wa kinikeri ame 55
~ ni haru wa kinikeri aomushiro 56
~ ni haru wa kinikeri hitotose 47
~ ni haru wa kinikeri iranu sewa 49
~ ni haru wa kinikeri neko 52
~ ni haru wa kirisuto 58
~ ni sorori 46
~ **no haru ya** shirazu 53.
~ tashika 54. ~ yoichi 55
toshinouchi wa kataashi 74
toshi o motte 60. ~ tatsu ya 233
toshi tsuki 280. ~ tsumoru 257
~ wa mi 83. ~ yoranu 214
~ yoru wa 258
toto haha 391 ○tsubomi 282
tsuchibeta 404 ○tsuchi no tomi 123
tsuki ni hi 352. ~ no aki 149
~ no yo 249. ~ yuki ni 248
~ yuki wa hito 249
tsukuzuku to 294 ○tsumabeni 397
tsuma e kishi 172
tsumarete 433 ○tsumatori 389
tsumi ni deta 399. ~ sutete 411
~ tamuru 429. ~ tataki 432
~ tsumite 394
tsumu ato 411. ~ hito 401
~ onago 433

U

uchi ni nete 93 ○uchi-tatsuru 106
uchûyuei shite 303 ○uekiya no 281
uguisu mo gyokei 160
~ mo naku 428. ~ ya mochi 357
~ ya ura 160
ukihashi 291 ○umarego no 291
umarenagara 145 ○umashi tote 422
ume bakari 55
ume-ga-ka ni chikara 246
~ ya oroshya 165. ~ ya tori 73
ume ni mazu 246
~ sasu ya 345. ~ yori mo 161

umi chikashi 104, 146
~ no aru 104. ~ bara e 103
unaiko ga 322 ○uragaesu 325
urayamashi 388 ○ureshigaru 113
urusai na 98 ○ushi uma 140
uso tsukanu kao 263, 401
utsu tama ni 226 ○utsukushiki 329
utsuwa utsuwa 124
wabi-sumi?[juu?zumai?] ya 255
~ tsukushi 70
wadatsu umi no nami … 273
waga haru o 398. ~ haru ya 255
~ in ni 216. ~ io ya kesa 224
~ kado wa 105. ~ kao ni 422
~ ko yori 174. ~ koto to 406
~ kuni no hanabashira 301
~ kuni no mono 151
~ niwa ni 413. ~ suki na 282
~ suso no 320. ~ tame ni 398
~ toshi no 257. ~ mono ni 108
wakadono 434 ○wakakusa 415
wakamizu ni chie 346
~ hakuga 342. ~ katsuo 333
~ kokoro 346. ~ maegami 341
~ nozoku 338. ~ shiwakage 341
~ tsuru 338
wakamizu no ha 344
~ kagami 340. ~ soko 333
~ taru 334. ~ yoshinaki 342
wakamizu o ikutabi 341
~ kumu 337. ~ uchikakete 344
wakamizu wa momo 339
wakamizu ya agaru 337
~ chôzu 335. ~ dobin 343
~ fuyu 341
~ ginka to … odoru 333
~ ginka to … nigoru 346
~ hokuto 347. ~ ido 335
~ ironaki 333. ~ kingyô 332
~ kinô 336. ~ kore 340
~ kumaruru 332. ~ masu 338
~ mita 343. ~ nagare 347
~ nagaruru 332. ~ narabu 343
~ oi hiki 340. ~ sôto 345
~ utsuru 334
wakamizu yo 340 ○wakamochi 380
wakana no ya 400
~ tsumeba (tsumi-wa?) 408
~ tsumu hito 390. ~ tsumu te 395
wakanatsumi hôchô 420
~ kyô 396. ~ no 391
wakaunaru waga 355
wakayu chôzu 347 ○waraware 421
ware nagara ganjitsu 135
~ nagara kokoro 135
~ oroka 91. ~ tomeri 65
wasureme ya 132 ○watadono 198

Y

yabunami 278. ○yado no neko 78
yagotonaki 293
yama ni [「「蝦宝山」に入テ」にルビない。果報喰いのごろ合わせかも知れないが、「やま」だけでも六音字で「やま」にした]。あるいは間がなかったが蝦宝が前置きか？ 168
yama-no-ha 436. ○yama no ki 210
yamato mochi 351
yamazato wa kasumi 207
~ wa ume 156. ~ ya hatsubi 105
yami ni dete 385. ○yamu tomo 175
yane no mado 147.
yaso no saka 268. ○yaso tose 261
yasurakeku 286
yasu yasu 254 ○ yogosuna 54
yohaku- 176. ○yoi nazuna 429
yoki hachi 279 ○ yoki koto 253
yokudoshiku 342
yomegakimi deban 384
~ dete 381. ~ fuji 377
~ kojin 381. ~ kono 383
~ no tôiji 383. ~ tegata 382
yomo ni utsu 424
yo no asane 95. ○ yo no hito 256
yononaka o iwanu 156
~ o yurinaosuran 138
~ wa kokoro 133. ~ wa kuute 30
yoru no ame 81. ○ yoshino yori 174
yoshiwara no 297, ○yoshi ya 260
yosonami 255. ○yo to tomo 328
yotta te de 393. ○ yo wasure 417
yuagari no 135. ○ yukaba 402
yuki kasumi 209. ~ ni sode 344
~ no iro 122. ~ no mi 261
~ no shita 401. ~ no to ya 394
~ take no 323. ~tsubute 403
~ yo yuki 63
yume mo naki 315. ~ no ato 297
yuruyakasa 134. ○yutakasa ya 254
zabuzabu to doro-waranji de 128,
~ no 156
zen ni tsuite 283. ○zeppitsu to 175
zoku na na 277. ○zôrimichi 396
zôsui no na 431

INDEXES　　POET: 451-5,　POEM: 456-60,　PEOPLE: 461,　ODDS & ENDS: 462-

PEOPLE index: Because poets have their own index, I only note where particularly interesting comments are made. The index was finished under duress (pc broke) and may be improved for future editions.

A Hopi Girl 115
Addiss & Yamamoto 14
After My Computer Died 466-71
∀Q 53

Bacon, Alice Mabel 221
Barnstone & Ping 23
Barthes, Roland 7
Bashô 15, 16, 17, 391, 403
Ben Trovado 28
Bird, Isabella 412
Blyth, R.H. 11, 22, 23, 28, 37, 68, 75, 103, 109, 139, 141, 184, 252, 300, 309, 343, 382
Brower transl., cited by McCullough 47
Brown, Charlie 74 & Lucy 107
Bulwer 157, 412

Carter Gill (just to see if my nephew ever reads this (PYG, don't tell him!))
Carter, Steven 358
Chesterton, G.K. 1, 12, 355
Chiyo 15, 16, 52, 401, 403
Coles, Robert 115

Dalby, Liza 352
Darwin, Erasmus 336
Dickinson, Emily 230
Diogenes 263
Donegan & Ishibashi 304, 305

Emerson 133

Fitzgerald 96
Frazer I should have mentioned his *Golden Bough* in my Bibliography, though I have not visited it in 30 years. For people with their own minds, no "critical analysis" is half so important as primary sources in cultural anthropology.
Frois S.J., Luis 166, 394-5, 412,
Frost, Robert 17

Gandhi 274

Geert 11
Ginzberg 25
Go toba (Emperor) 39-40
Golownin, Capt. 165
Greve, Gabi 18

Hamada Chinseki 264
Hass 255
Headland, I.T. 380, 382
Hearn, Lafcadio 7, 18
Hein, Piet 263
Heywood, Thomas 257
Higginson, William J. 12, 18, 26, 27, 41
Homer 25
Hoshino (CZ) 380
Hurtzel Rackety Masquerado Gill (gotta hunt for her, the pg# is lost)

Iida Ryûta 飯田龍太
Inahata Teiko 42
Issa 15, 51, 52, 160, 255-256

Jofuku 195
Joyce 13

Kai Michiko 42
Kawabata Yasunari 59
Kenkô 385
Kinky Friedman 52
Kitahara Hakushû 274
Kurogane Hiroshi 305
Kyoshi 16, 42, 47, 60-1,

Lady Daibu 154
Lamb, the essayist, 317
Lanoue, David G.
Lao Tse/Tsu 81
Lee, Joseph J. 144
Li Po 144
Lowell, Percival 7, 241, 243
Lu Ji 23
Lumbago 267-8

Maruyama *et al* 56-7, 257-8, 280, 436
Michizane 245
Mickey Mouse 79
Mitani, Kazuma 8
Montaigne (Cited or not, he is everywhere but in Bill Gate's Microsoft Word, which proves beyonf doubt that the richest man in the world is a cultural illiterate).
Morris, Ivan 393
Morse, Edward S. 301, 382
Muir, John 138

Murasaki 385
Norinaga 273

Orca/Oruka 134, 259, 416
Origuchi 134

Prishvin, Mikhail 129

Reichhold, Jane 19, 79, 304
Rudloe, Jack 305
Rudofsky, Bernard 142
Ruskin 122-3

Santôka 128
Sei Shonagon 393
Shiki 1, 22, 47, 188, 380
Shirakawa Shizuka 154
Sobaku 436
Sôgi 18, 19
Stewart, Harold 25, 65, 102, 103, 130, 301
Sato, Hiroaki 202
Starfield (Hoshino, *aka* Charlie Zhang) 380

Takiguchi, Susumu 60
Tanabe Seiko 157
Teitoku 77
Tenki (俳友) 60
Thoreau 20, 57, 96
Tsunoda et al. 146
Tsurayuki 47, 48
Twain 74, 391

Uematsu Akinari
Ueda Makoto 13, 28, 155

Valignano 121

Watts, Alan 81, 355
White, Gilbert 55
Whitney, Adeline Dutton Train 70, 155
Wilde 263
Williams, Hank 130
Wright, Richard 7, 109, 343, 380

Xu Fu 203-5

Yamamoto Kenkichi, 19, 59, 60,155
Yasuda Kenneth 16, 25, 433, 434
Yasumiko 254

Zhuangze (the spell check suggests "humanize"!) 137

ODD & ENDS: Chapter headings, indexes of poems, poets, and other people, not to mention the original Japanese of the poems, with Romanization, and direct transliteration, *in situ,* etc. should be more than enough service for a book of translated poetry, but I thought an odd selection of subjects **to indicate at a glance the fun within the book** might be useful for 1) enjoying the book while answering the call of nature, 2) quickly refinding favorite items or, 3) showing the pleasures of creative nonfiction to friends or family who slavishly follow one fashionable novelist (or NYT/LAT/PBS/etc.-covered historian, political critic or journalist) after another, obli-vious to the greater world of letters (as are the book reviews they view, read and listen to).

Apologia: I confess to doing a more inspired job of distilling the odd in a book that, boasting a thousand holothurian haiku, was, itself, odd: *Rise, Ye Sea Slugs!* There, I did it with headers: *"more 'ugh' in the slug and alternative japanese names for the sea cucumber"* (p.18); *"sôseki and tristam shandy, or writing like a sea slug with neither head nor tail"* (p.51); *"sequential chimerism, i.e., the stages of life, or why all sea slugs have more lives than a cat."* (p.78); *"lao-tse and the namako discuss 'nothing' in the head of a famous japanese physicist"* (p.89); *"mother nature, how could you? your child blown up, forgotten, left behind, thrown out"* (p.122); *"a unique observation: round anger ~ or, does the sea slug make a fist?"* (p.137); *"private parts on the sea bed and a shrinking pestle in the kitchen"* (p.167); *"why oysters are jealous of sea slugs and what*

makes them more "serious" than jellyfish." Imagine. Almost 500 headers (different for every page of the text), the likes of which are unparalleled in the history of literature (unless Borges did it) and not one reviewer had a word for them! Must I gather my headers into a book for them to get the attention they deserve? At any rate, that sad experience is why, this time, I made an Odd *Index* instead. The argument for "usefulness" came later.

A Call to Collect Olde Haiku especially by lousy poets 219
A Day Without Entropy 124
A Hole in its (and his?) yard 195
A Tiny Sneeze at first-sky 114
AAB & ABA in Haiku 25
"About Average" to "Pretty Wretched," Issa's New Year 255
Advantage of Plucking Drunk 393
Age of the Gods 141
Aging → Mixed Emotions
Alchemy and the Milky Way 347
An Amorous Man 314
And the Night Soil Man 222-223
Animal Dreams Below Our Feet 377;
Animals Aware of the Holiday 140
Anime Roots 122n
Ânno Japani or, the rarely encountered long-count of Japanese History 271
Another Stringless Zither 137
Anthropomorphism, 382
Anthropometamorphosis 157
Artificial Blossom Shadow-viewing 373; Waiting for Them to Fall 374
Automobiles: What They *Really* Do 1
Autumnizing the New Year 126, 149, 154
Argonaut 202
Artlessness 371
"Average" New Year → About
Awareness of the Arbitrary 40-41
Bad Boy 228
Bamboo Wives, a minor subject 19 (for 9 ku, see end-note for "Homes & Gardens" in *Topsy-Turvy 1585*)
Barefoot in the Sand, a hypothesis 107
Bashful Hills and Amish Language 214-215; ~ Princess-bride (mice) 384

Bashôism, or *More Bashô Than Thou* 15
Be Happy, Haiku! 287
Before Mind Precipitates 133
Best Gift *ku* by a Grown-up 231
Best Excuse for Sleeping-in 114
Betrayed by the Sun 113
Beyond Relativity 91
Big Balls for a Gold-digger? 305
Big Mountains for Little People 183, and Two for a Poor Man 184
Big Tree Shôgun 32
Bigarade as Queen of the West 186
Birds Watching People 390
Birthday of a Nation 271
Birthdays: How Everyone is Born (and Reborn) on the Same Day 241, And Questions about it 272
Blank Page 234
Blue Sun Mother 214
Born Again (part of the Sinosphere's birthday spirit) 250
Both the First Day of Creation *and* the Seventh 135
Bringing Spring to China: Ethnocentric and Nationalistic New Year's Poems 272-273
Breath, the Dreaminess of It 123
Buddhism On the First Day 144, 182
Buddy-buddy with the Sun 108
Buenos Aires, vowel capital of the world 27
Camelopard steals a hat 307
Cards From the Dead 175-176
Cats Get Their New Year's Gifts, *Plunk!* 225, 228, ~ Fixated on Snapper 266
Celebrating with Sand 30-31
Charming Straw 126-128
Checking Synchronicity 90
Chi (Chinese) or Ki (Japanese) Exampled 134
Children Applauding Children 167; ~ or Adults: Who Deserves Presents Most? 223
Children's Haiku, or Why Anyone Can Compose a Masterpiece 219; & What It Can Teach Us about the Nature of Haiku 299
Chinese Dreaming 312; ~ Ponce de Leon and Hôrai Computer-translated from Mandarin 203-205; ~ Things, No use for ~ 144
Clam Vendors and Maids with Red Aprons 266
Clapping for the Gods: There is a word for it! 100
Clean and Dirty Stars 333

INDEXES   POET: 451-5, POEM: 456-60, PEOPLE: 461, ODDS & ENDS: 462-   463

Clouds o' Joy 129; & Decoration 247
Cocoons and Safes 372
Cold Beauty 71
Collecting Years Like Shells on the Beach 222
Coming Of Age in Japan 269
Commutative Law, Math versus Translation 410
Comparison Is Odorous? 256
Complex Reading of Haiku 257-258
Cosmopolitans versus (Proud) Edoites 146. More Cosmopolitan Thought 197
Cosmic Production 277
Cosmos Flowers, the Problem with Little-known Subjects 21
Courtesan Names and the Freedom of Japanese Women 166
Crude as Beautiful 121; see Occidental and Straw
Dawn as a Blank 69
Dead protagonists 308
Deathdays 39, 242
Deconstruction, a Strategy for Eternal Youth, or the Ise Shrine 142
Decorating Hôrai and X-mas Trees: Tradition or Taste? 199
Definition of a Great Man 265; Entrepreneur 86;
Desire and Number: Japanese Equate it, English-speakers Don't 283
Different Roads for Different Shoes 157
Dirt: When it is Rare and Beautiful 128-129; ~ Washing it from your Nails with Young Green Water 435-436
Dogs and Doves and Foxes Get Gifts 226-227
Does It Matter? 355
Doggerel → Slobberel 77,
Do-nothing Bird, the Legendary 90
Doors Frame Rivers Well 64
Dream of the Flying Banana Leaf – Postscript for Book I 232-233
Dreams and the Nature of Japanese Linked Verse 311, ~ Appearing from the Nose 296, ~ That are Most Desirable 297; ~ of Space-walking 303, ~ Frog and Plumtree 305, Bagworm turning into Angel 306, . . . Drunk and All Over the Road 164
Drunken Turtles 305
Dust-pinching 125
Earthquake-lovers 138
Easter Sunrise Service on Key Biscayne When the Grackle Came 428, 429

Edo, or New Year's in the World's Biggest City 147-148
Eggs, Spying within them 45-6; ~ that Stand Up for Spring 46
Elementary Experience of New Year's Dawn 98-99
Elysian Well 336
Equality, or The Poor Man's Birthday 265-266
Explaining Poetry 13
Eternal Feminine vs. Mother Earth 7
Even Leibniz might have thrown in the towel 23
Faces In the Clouds 314
Fairyland Haiku 367
Fans as Dildos 297
Felicitations for the Fox 161
Female Poet Who Was Perfectly Honest and Lived to be Ninety 258 ~ Loved Premature Spring 52-55
Feng-lai Is Hôrai 179; ~ Fuji 181
"Fictitious Birthday of the Community" 241
Fifth: Is it First or Last? 36
Firmament of Sweet-rice? 352
First Heart/Mind 132. ~ of All Our Feelings Fill the Sky 251;
Flower as a Modifier for the New Year 30
Flowers Have Birthdays, too 243
Flying Tree and Preening Tree 245
From Fish Head to Dewey Garbage Can to Shiny Hips and a Resting Hoe 108-9
Forever: Do you or don't you want it? 152
Forming and Reforming the Sky 118-119
Four Ways to Write Mount Fuji 181
Frog-viewing 332
Fuji and First-Dreams 299-301, ~ : It Must Be ~ 310, Though Only a Painting 310; ~ As National Nose and Lodestone 301.
Fuji is Feng Lai is Hôrai 181
Fukujusô, Barely a Flower 276; ~ Vulgar Through and Through 277; ~ A Plant With Rhythm 280; Plant as Shadow Puppet 281; ~ Cause of Longevity or Effect? 282; ~ as Guardian Angel
Funbetsu – or, Discrimination is a Handhold in the Crapper and a Bald Pate 263-264
Gained In Translation, or the paradox of bad poetry 17
Gem/ball/precious/beautiful/perfect all rolled into one 116
Gift Circuit (Without Fruit Cake?)

230
Giving and Receiving, Even the Former a Desire 258
Grassless Lawns 394-395
Gratitude For A Young Wife (though 28 was old, then) 261
Green-beating Song With Chinese Birds 424-425; ~ Awakens Lovers 427; ~ As Revenge for Losing at the Lottery 427, ~ Drives Birds Batty 427-428; ~ Enjoyed by Marsh-Crabs 429; ~ as Maid Beating 432-434; Green Seller Plucks for Herself 398
Green Soup or Gruel or What? 431; ~ or, Okayu, as a Family 431-432
Greens with Seven in Their Name (Nazuna), also Shepherd's Purse and Mother's Heart 399
Greeting One's Plants 161
Growing Mountains: Why the *Masu* is Metaphysically Appropriate. 179
Grumbling on the First Day? 156
Haiku for Health 287; ~ What Counts Most In It 299
Head-bobbing Aunties a Paean to the Tokugawa 159
Heaven's Window on Your Head 159
Hôrai is Feng-lai 179; ~ and First-Dream 303
How the Gregorian Calendar Cost Japanese Government Workers Two Months Salary! 42
How to Pass Through Willows 165
Humans: A World of ~ Born Among ~ 212
Icicle Teardrops 78
If Beauty is in the Heart and the New Year is All Heart . . . 138-139
If You Will Turn Crossroad's Forty 270, Silly Sixty 263, Lucky Seventy 253-4, Infinite Eighty 261, 268; Even a Hundred 262; Twenty Thousand *ditto*
"I'm Xu Fu!" or Kyoshi's Most Amusing *Ku* 195
Imperialism, or *Hey, Riff-raff, Adore the August Faces of the Gods* . . 273
Inoculation Against Haiku 85
Ise *Uber Alles* 142
Japanese as Groundhogs 147
Joyce → Thuarpeatrick
Kami: Are they God/s? 29
Kikaku vs. Bashô 368 - 369
Kimono inside-out 316, 325
King of the Shrimp, a Florida Crawfish (spiny lobster) 101
Kokoro, a Popular Character 29
Kokoro as a Pillow-word 136
Kyoshi's Pole 60-61

POET: 451-5, POEM: 456-60, PEOPLE: 461, ODDS & ENDS: 462- INDEXES

Kyôto as the Center of the World: Believer or Cynic? 272
Lady Who Flew Every Night 309
Leisurely Plucks 407, 409
Little Things 276, 284
Lumbago Turns Tail and Other Toasts to Happy Times 267-268
Luna's New Year 43
Magic Mallet Pounds Out Wealth 121
Making-up for Modesty (cosmetics turned on its head) 382
Making Water Carefully 115; and just making it 158
Manger 267
Mermaids and Mermen with a change of tail? 328; ~ Fins in New Year's Soup 329
Merhu, Another Mountain of Eternal Life, Connecting to the Yellow Spring 197n
Metaphors of Time 61
Metaphysics of Clear and Cloudy Wine 212
Mice on Magic Mountain 181; ~, Tit-mice and Diligent Wooers of Women 188; ~, How Finely Wrought They Are 369; ~ Always Getting into Trouble 380, in Nursery Rhymes 380n; ~, Cats, Gecko and Miyamoto Musashi 381; ~ More Trainable than Cats 385; See *Princess-Bride*
Minds, How They Work When They Don't 135
Mirror, Star, Cross and Sword 123
Mist Like Ribbons and Chinese Goddesses Dancing 209
Mist-Riders of the Sky 208n
Mixed Emotions About the New Year 257
Mo The Neglected Riddle of the ~ 33, The ~ of it 427
Model Mountains 179-181
Mom's Rule (and mine) 16
Money and/for Children 268
Monkey Mask Mystery 155
Mount Fuji as a Flower Bud 247
Mount Hôrai Walking Down the Hall 198
Mountain ~, no *Fountain* of Youth for the Elderly 193-194
Mountains Breath and the Mist Proves It 210
Mountains Dripping Brine 191
Mud *vs* Snow 69
Mummy: *I would become one!* says Issa. 111
Murmuring Sand 151
Naïveté: Good in Japanese, Bad in English 132
Names, or Why a *Fukujusô* by Any Other Name is not a *Fukujusô* 276
Nationalism in Our Lord's Spring 167
Native Sun (from the Land of the Rising ~) 151
New Clothing, Made of Mist 212
New Sandals Every Day 128
New Year As a Flower 248
New Year as Sleight of Hand 37
New Year's Day In Bed 95-6; ~ Water, or, a Younger Me Looks Back 339
Night-mare-Gobbling Tapirs 312; ~ - Owls 93 (+see *Topsy-turvy 1585*)
Nineteen Weis? See My *Thirty Six Ways!* 97
No Afterword 439; ~ Mythology of Naked Beginnings in Japan 211; ~ One a Stepchild on N Y's 249
Nom de Plume: For the most common first character, see pg. 57, ~ of many poets Englished!
Nose-wind-powered Treasure-ship 296
Nothing But Blue Sky . . . and Smoke-rings 117
"Nothing" is *Fine,* or, *Nichyevo* and the Japanese New Year 37
Numbers in the Sun 106
NY in the WC 264-265
Occidental Aesthetics, "spoiled child of the human body and precious metals and rare minerals" 128 (& see "Crude")
Ocean Elders = Shrimp & turtle 101
Oddity, an affirmation of 12
Old Age as a Guilt-trip 260; ~ Folk Pluck Too 408, 434; ~ Men, Rotten and Flowering 259; ~ Water Turns Into Young 332, Or, Just the Pail Does 336;
One Charm of Having Little 65; ~ -string Harp and Haiku 23
Ontogeny Recapits Phylogeny 306
Ordinary as Extraordinary 2
Paper Ships and Tatami Oceans 295
Paraversing and *Ku* Clusters, or Composite Translation 25
Pathetic Fallacy as Less Common than Robbing Animals of Their Emotions 382
Pathos in Scrap-paper 66
Peach Chopstick Bamboo 185
Pebbles: In Japan, They Can Grow Up 197
People Roasted as They Toast Mother's Heart 422
Phoenix in China are Different 87
Picture of Bale of Rice in the air 236; ~ Greens Which Doesn't Show Much 414; ~ of Green Chopping that Looks Like Beating! 437; **And more: You better mark the book!**
Pigeon Toes and Tiger Paws 80
Pinching and Beating Maids for the Sake of a Pun 432-434
Pipeline from the *Godera* 33
Pissing on Frogs & Toads 341, 362
Plant Birthdays 243
Plucking Greens in an Ancient Sea 389; ~ as Knightly Battle 390; ~ in Your Own Garden 392; ~ while Carrying a Heater 392; ~ Beneath the Snow 393 - 395; ~ Taking Tumbles & Leaving Butt Prints 397; With the Help of Little Children 399-400; ~ a Paradox 400; ~ Like Gold-mining? Easter-egg Hunt? Or, Fishing? 401 ~ and No Time for Snowball War ~ and Leaving Handprints as Voucher, and a dozen more by Chiyo! ~ 402-403;
Plum (Flowering Apricot) Blossoms *As* Spring 246
Pocket Gallantry 412
Polite Boy 229
Ponce de Leon of the East became a Mouse, then? 195
Poverty, the God 307; ~ the Plant 278, 289
Pretty Spring as a Trophy Wife 254
Princess Bride Scuttles Home at the Dawn of the Millennium 377; ~, a Ghost Among Dolls 378; ~ a Literal Cinderella 382; Oh, Hell, There's a Whole Chapter of Her! (But, also, see *Mice*)
Princess Sao, Nubile Woman, Mother or Baby? 214
Proxies, Representatives and Delegates 343
Pure Expression of Honest Emotions Not Limited to Deathbed 230
Purple Haze 216
Questionable Practices by the Author-translator 26
Quilts With Sleeves 93
Quote Me With License 6. Even reorder my words! 27
Raccoon Teeth and Child Tears 187
Raifu, or Why All Japanese Have More "Lives" than a Cat 39
Rape, a Problem for Translators 395
"Rationality is Not Allowed Within these Premises" 264
Rats, Mice and Prosperity 189-190n

INDEXES   POET: 451-5,   POEM: 456-60,   PEOPLE: 461,   ODDS & ENDS: 462-   465

Reading Between the Words 13
Recreating Mountains as Home 180
Red & Green 395n (If you understand this, invest in the right products and make millions, please remember me!)
Religious *vs* Sacred (and you could substitute "sense of *Cosmos*" for "~ Sacred") 41.
Resolutions 268
Reverse Mona Lisa 309
Rice Cake as Biosphere 357
Rice Cake Petrifaction 356
Rice Cakes as Heart-strings 365
Rice Cakes as Time Machines 355-6
Riddle of the Morning Glory 92
Rouge-stained Snow 397
Rye Whiskey Humor in Haiku? 262
Samurai and Square Behavior 160
Sao-hime, Goddess of Spring, is Man-hungry and Hangs a Split? 50-51 See 'Princess."
Save-the-world-itis 39-40, 440
Sea: Something that binds 149 (See Nitobe in *Orientalism & Occidentalism* for more)
Second Day, When You Swallow the First 270
Self-depricatory Old Tatami 259
Scent of Mother's Heart 375; ~ Plum (apricot flowers) & Glow 156
Senryû in Haiku 371
Seri with the Pretty White Roots 404; And a Ladder 406
Sexless Stars in a Bucket 333
Shallow Words 143 (three translations), 178 (ten more showing why shallow can be deep)
Shinkokinshû: A "Really Disgustingly Insipid Poem" that I like! 47
Shit, Take One & it's New Year's 30
Shrimp → King
Silence is Golden? (a debate in socio-linguistics) 318
Silent Night is Tranquil Dawn 150
Sky-art/vandalism 120 n2
Sleeves as Bags 391-392
Slobberel → Doggerel 77
Slugs: Why they can be Cucumbers and *vice-versa* 14
Slush, Putting a Good Face on it 126
Smiling Underwater, a Figure of Speech? 333-334
Smith, Mr. = Ordinary as Extraord. 1
Snail Horns 277
Snakes, Stripteasers, Holes and Wealth 83
Snow & Mist Fight for the Year 209
Space-walking 303

Specificity of English Hurts Poetry: "Spring Blossoms *With/As/In/Through/By* the Plum" 246
Splendid Synchronicity and Haiku's Jung at Heart 79, 109 n2
Spring in 1 Flower in 1 Vase 255
Spring Go Home! 49, 52
Spying into Hearts and Seasons 57
Standard Greeting, but no standard translation 154
Stars in the Sky as Left-overs 233; ~ in Pails of Young Water 332, 333
Stereo Script in the Manyôshû 388
Straw Is Beautiful, an Alternative Aesthetic of Beauty 266 (and see *Crude* and *Occidental*)
Stick that was a Dragon, the 82
Strip-mining a Foodpile 190, 193
Subjectivity, or the Place of the Self in Haiku 256
Sumo With Your Food 361
Superfluity and the Paradox of Plenty 411-412
Sweetheart called Baby or My Papoose 388
Syllabet: Spread the Word! 7, 49
Taipu of Haiku (beyond good and bad) 17
***Tao Te Ching* and the Way of English (scores of weis) 97**
Tasting Mountains 186
Ten Ways Years Come and Go 48
The Cold God 72; ~ Moon Out of Place 56; ~ New Year as a Question 40; ~ Supernatural Season 41
Thirteen Etymologies for People (*hito*)? 113
Three Billion New Year's Cards! 169-177
Thuarpeatrick, or Why Joyce Should have Written Haiku 13
Tidings from Ise? Ise Shrimp = Spiny Lobster Squeaks Up 192
Tobacco Mist + Tobacco Rings 215
Tokonoma, Japan's Gift to the World, a Household Shrine for Beauty 196n
Tortoise Walking on Water 2
Tooth-hardening 312
Translating "Life" 39
Treasure Ship, Made for Your Dreams with Palindrome included 291, The Original Cargo Cult 295 (more in *Topsy-turvy 1585*)
Turtles and Whales and a Woman's Heart 304
Unpainted and Unglazed, a Religion of the Origin 121

Voluptuosity Without Things 154
Wakasa, an overlooked Pun 202
Water Sounds: Dripping, Pulleys, Neighbors . . . 338
Warmth derived from Splitting Hairs 47
Way of Waka, or Poetry Will Keep You Young 202
We Should All Have One Well of Our Own 335
Well-flower water 335
What separates the years 68
When Even the Old Are Young 260; ~ Everything Matters 115; ~ Common is Exotic 251; ~ *Tofu* Is Hay 94; ~ Winter Was Split in Two 35
White-caps Turning into Lice, or Issa's All-time Worst *ku* 120
White Hair – a Mine of Metaphor 259-260
Why New Year's Day Can Not Exist 74; ~ 1x1=3 353; ~ We Live in the Twenty-first rather than Twentieth Century 244n; ~ Does a Bonito Dance at this Time? 333
Why Work, Why Worry? 369
Willows: The Most Liberal of Trees 265; The Tree Where You Supply the Scent 246;
Women, Treatment in Japan 155
Words Have a New Year, too 162-3
Words As Flowers 247
World War II 274
Writing at the End of the World 440
Xanadu and the Visitor 316
Xmas and Early Spring 58
Yasumi-ko="Child-easy-on-the-eyes" – the Winning Suitor's Boast, Easily the Worst Poem Ever Written 254
Year-eating Demons, Invented or Kosher? 208
Years: Do They Begin at Conception, Quickening or Birth? 46
Zen: The Original Non-discrimination, or New Year's Day as ~ 263-264

☆ Please tell me what *you* want in the Index for the next Edition!

— rdg

◎ これだけは、是非、再版の「索引」に加えたいと思う事柄を、教えてください。

— 敬愚

Unexpected Postscript

"Repose after agitation is like the pool under a waterfall, which the waterfall has made." – Coleridge

Between Solstice and Christmas, as I was preparing to put this book to bed in plenty of time for the Chinese New Year (2/18 in 2007), my IBM Thinkpad blew its brains out and almost took your author with it. If you relish the ugly details of my torture by computer (or, rather, hard and software corporations and techies), a long version of this postscript is up at paraverse.org.. Were this book not about a *happy* season, believe me, I would repeat the entire litany of curses Skelton (-1529) gave to the cat who murdered his mistress's beloved *Philip Sparrow*. Here, I will only share the good things which bear upon this book, discovered as I lay reading, unable to work on my computer or sleep. The first was a selection of Coleridge's *Anima Poetae* in a book of nature writing bought at a garage sale:

> In natural objects we feel ourselves or think of ourselves, only by *likenesses*; among men, too often, by *differences*. Hence the soothing, love-kindling effect of rural nature – the bad passions of human societies.

Rightly understood, our differences only go to prove our similarity at heart but, unfortunately, such comprehension is not intuitive. This may bear upon the paucity of human-centered haiku in translation, because they require explanation, while most people interested in poetry (who have not read my books) are not aware any is needed, much less compatible with good taste.

にごるべきいは井の水にあらねどもくまばやどれる月やさわがん
nigoru beki iwa-i no mizu ni aranedomo kumaba yadoreru tsuki ya sawagan

Though this stone-bound spring is unlikely to cloud –
Not I to draw its water and disturb the resting moon!

After Coleridge, I read a translation of Saigyô's *Sankashû* (c1190) by a Japanese man who knew more English than he could command, and was delighted to find something I overlooked reading the book in Japanese, standing in a train, a decade ago: *0947 "Clear is the rock-bound spring. / 'Tis never soiled with mud, / but I draw not its water, / fearing to disturb the moon reflected."* Does this *waka* not provide fine supporting evidence for my defense of Chiyo's maligned morning glory *ku*, in the interest of keeping haiku open and friendly, in the IPOOH *Series Preface* beginning this book? My point, if you recall, was that neither Issa, Kyoshi, nor, for that matter any detractor of Chiyo I know of, ever had a bad word to say for Saigyô, yet *his* poem is far more *precious* – it might have been fun to disturb the water mirror and see how long it took to repair itself – in the negative sense of the word than hers. And, he has two more like it, one where he hesitated to walk on colored leaves and "stain the brocade" (1129), and another expressing anxiety lest he knock off dew from clover (265). To me, Chiyo's giving in to the morning-glory vine on her well pail is far more understandable, that is, natural. Why dwell on this? Because the righteousness with which content infractions (?) are decried in haiku sometimes seems religious if not fundamentalist! If I come down hard on young Issa and old Kyoshi, it is partly because I do not want beginners to be afraid to take risks, which mostly means *reveal their feelings*. I am delighted to have found an ally in Saigyô, whose poetry probably had a bigger influence on the Japanese aesthetic than that of any single Japanese poet.

The author, working like a beav.,
His readers' pleasure could redoub.
Did he but now and then abbrev.
The work he gives his pub.

Even in *italics*, doggerel howls. My excuse for printing the four lines from Harry Graham's "Poetical Economy," found in *The Comic Muse* (early-20c, long before an English philosopher suggested we pay to develop the atomic bomb by simplified spelling), also read while the computer was down, is that I forget if I explained that my way of writing *centuries* (11c, 20c, etc.) was copied from a famous French historian whose name I forget, and done not only to save paper *but to give readers a taste of the way Japanese read Chinese characters*. For that matter, I may also have forgotten to explain **an inconsistency in my dating of poets**. Or, at least, I *hope* I did not explain, for I wanted *you* to guess what I was up to. But, now, it is time to explain. To save those reading this part of the book *first* from losing the opportunity to wonder for themselves, the explanation is at the bottom of the page.

◎大覚寺の、金岡がたてたる石をみて◎
庭の岩にめたつる人もなからましかどあるさまにたてしおかねば
niwa no iwa ni metatsuru hito mo nakaramashi kado aru sama ni tateshi okaneba

Seeing the Stones Set by Kanaoka at the Daikakuji Temple

Who would come to behold the boulders in this garden,
Were they not placed as placed by genius?

This, too, I found in H.H. Honda's translation of Saigyô, which, I am afraid, included a misreading (*kado aru* became "in a peculiar way"). Barely a poem, it still set me to thinking. How many 5- or 7-syllabet-long *ku* (here, meaning the *parts*, or, in English, *lines* of a haiku) are impressive, by themselves, in the manner of "a good line" from a longer poem? *Very few*. Like boulders in a rock garden, most are nothing much individually but, masterfully arranged, please in concert. It also provides a good visual metaphor to explain why it is often necessary to shift the position of the parts of the *ku* in translation. With our languages' lack of equivalent grammar and vocabulary, the various silhouettes of the stones – Saigyô's poem uses a phrase for "genius" punning on "angle" (*kado* 才・角 *aru*) – can be so different that a radically different arrangement must be made. But, who can say whether different rocks arranged in different ways can do justice to the genius behind the original, much less re-create the "same" rock-garden! We can only know that if the translator is inspired by the original, at any rate, by his or her understanding/ misunderstanding of the original, then the result may be called "a translation/mistranslation," though the reader may, by now, have come to realize that a translation from Japanese to English (or *vice versa*) is never *just* a translation.

> *"The child,"* says Wordsworth, *"is father of the man;"* writes Thomas De Quincey (*Autobiography of ~*), *". . . Yes, all that is now broadly emblazoned in the man, once was latent – seen or not seen – as a vernal bud in the child. But not, therefore, is it true inversely – that all which pre-exists in the child finds its development in the man."*

De Quincey's *"mighty silence which infancy is thus privileged by nature"* is like the *"first-heart of childhood"* (初心 pg.132), cherished by all Japanese, and associated with the *Original Day*, New Year's.

◎**And, *now*, the unexplained inconsistency.** Did you notice most poets with both a birth-date and a death-date were long-lived? Since longevity is feted on the New Year, I could not resist favoring it. I also must admit to feeling that *haikai* poets were, on average, long-lived – due to the contentment found composing *ku* and chuckling over them (誰か調査を!). I also thought that if 40-60 years was the average lifespan, it made sense to note exceptions (I noted some short ones, too). Other causes of inconsistency in dating include the nearness of other *ku* giving the same information and the space, *i.e.*, design restrictions. As a rule, *I favor inconsistency over ugliness,* and for that I do *not* apologize.

www.ingramcontent.com/pod-product-compliance
Lightning Source LLC
Chambersburg PA
CBHW080538230426
43663CB00015B/2635